INDIAN OCEAN

Serpent I.
(Île aux Serpents)

Round I.
(Île Ronde)

Flat I.
(Île Plate)
Gabriel I.
(Îlot Gabriel)

Coin de Mire
(Gunner's Quoin)

Pte l'Hortal
Péreybère
Pointe aux Canonniers
Cap Malheureux
Grand Gaube
Grand Baie
Petit Raffray
Île d'Ambre
Trou aux Biches
The Vale
Fond du Sac
Goodlands
Triolet
Plaine
des Papayes
Poudre d'Or
Morcellement
St-André
Baie aux
Tortues

THE NORTH

Pte Lascars

Baie du Tombeau
Pamplemousses
Pte de Roche Noire
▲ Mt Piton
267
Rivière du Rempart
Grande Rosalie

PORT LOUIS

Pte Radeau
Taillache
colaire
Pointe aux Sables
Abercrombie
Bon Acceuil
Poste de Flacq
Port Louis
Salazie
Le Pouce
811▲
Centre de Flacq
Belle Mare
Pte Petite Rivière
Moka
Malinga
St-Julien
Albion
Roselyn Cottage
Beau Bassin
Côte d'Or
Quartier
Militaire
Pte Moyenne
Rose Hill
Providence
Mare Jacot
Bel Air
(Rivière Sèche)
Trou d'Eau
Douce
Bambous
Coignard
Deux Frères
Flic en Flac

**WEST COAST AND
PLATEAU**

Blanche Mtn.
Montagne
Blanche
Kawal Nagar
Pte Sud Flic en Flac
Vacoas
Pointe
du Diable
Tamarin
Mt du Rempart
545
CUREPIPE
Curepipe
Midlands
THE EAST
Pte du Tamarin
Ste-Madeleine
Ferney
Pte Bambou
Providence
Grand Rivière Noire
Tamarin
Curepipe Point
686 ▲
Grande R. Noire
Mare aux
Vacoas
Nouvelle
France
Riche en Eau
Petite Case Noyale
Black River Gorges
National Park
Grand Bois
Pte de la Colonie
Île aux Bénitiers
Piton de la
Petite Rivière Noire
Mt Cocotte
771
Mahébourg
Île aux Aigrettes
Pte Pecheurs
Chamarel
Nouvelle
New Grove
Pointe D'Esny
Le Morne Brabant
556
Coteau Raffin
Rivière Dragon
Pte Corps de Garde
Blue Bay
Pte Sud-Ouest
L'Embrasure
SOUTH COAST
L'Escalier
Le Bouchon
Chemin Grenier
Savannah
Pte Chaour
Baie du Cap
Rivière des Anguilles
Bel Ombre
Surinam
Souillac
Le Gris Gris

INDIAN OCEAN

D0317838

N

Mauritius

0   5 km

0   5 miles

FREQUENTLY UPDATED LISTINGS

Restaurants, bars and hotels change all the time. To ensure you get the most out of your guide, the app features all of our favourites, as well as the latest openings, and is updated regularly. Simply update your app when you receive a notification to access the most current listings available.

Shopping in Oman still revolves around the traditional souks that can be found in every town in the country – most famously at Mutrah in Muscat, Salalah and Nizwa, which serve as showcases of traditional Omani craftsmanship and produce ranging from antique khanjars and Bedu jewellery to halwa, rose-water and frankincense. Muscat also boasts a number of modern malls, although these are rare elsewhere in the country.

TRAVEL TIPS & DESTINATION OVERVIEWS

The app also includes a complete A to Z of handy travel tips on everything from visa regulations to local etiquette. Plus, you'll find destination overviews on shopping, sport, the arts, local events, health, activities and more.

HOW TO DOWNLOAD THE WALKING EYE

Available on purchase of this guide only.

1. Visit our website: www.insightguides.com/walkingeye
2. Download the Walking Eye container app to your smartphone (this will give you access to both the destination app and the eBook)
3. Select the scanning module in the Walking Eye container app
4. Scan the QR code on this page – you will be asked to enter a verification word from the book as proof of purchase
5. Download your free destination app* and eBook for travel information on the go

* Other destination apps and eBooks are available for purchase separately or are free with the purchase of the Insight Guide book

Contents

THE BEST OF MAURITIUS, RÉUNION & SEYCHELLES: TOP ATTRACTIONS

From beautiful beaches to breathtaking landscapes, and rare wildlife to adventure activities, here is a rundown of the most spectacular attractions in Mauritius, Réunion and Seychelles.

△ **Grand Baie, Mauritius**. A vast, horseshoe-shaped turquoise bay dubbed the Creole Côte d'Azur is the island's tourism hub, with plenty of beaches and excursions to choose from and après-sol entertainment. See page 111.

△ **Piton de la Fournaise, Réunion**. One of the most active volcanoes on the planet, producing blood-red fire fountains and rivers of lava. Hike through lunar landscapes to reach the summit. See page 184.

▽ **Vallée de Mai, Praslin, Seychelles**. Mistaken for the Garden of Eden by British general Charles Gordon in 1881, this is the primeval forest that time forgot, dense with coco de mer palms and their suggestive fruit. See page 313.

△ **The Cirques, Réunion**. Three huge caldera-like valleys, the remains of an extinct volcano, form a landscape of lush gorges, waterfalls and jagged peaks – all the more stunning when seen from a helicopter. See page 221.

△ **The Outer Islands, Seychelles**. A plethora of remote beaches, each one as stunning as the last.

Most islands are uninhabited and remain largely unexplored; wildlife experiences are superb, from Aldabra giant tortoises to whale sharks. See page 337.

△ **Le Morne Brabant, Mauritius**. Former hideout of runaway slaves, the forbidding bulk of Unesco-listed Le Morne mountain rises from a peninsula fringed with fine sands and luxury resorts. See page 145.

▷ **Adrenalin-pumping adventure, Réunion**. The dramatic terrain of Réunion was made for all manner of activities, from white-water rafting to horse trekking and scuba diving. See page 179.

◁ **Black River Gorges National Park, Mauritius**. Hiking in the forested interior, criss-crossed with walking trails, is a must for nature lovers, with waterfalls and rare endemic plants and birds. See page 142.

▽ **Anse Lazio, Praslin, Seychelles**. Consistently tops the polls as the best beach in the world for its butter-soft sands and sculptural boulders. See page 312.

△ **A trip to Rodrigues, Mauritius**. This rustic island, just a 90-minute flight hop, is Mauritius' best-kept secret. Go for hiking, *table d'hotes*, tranquillity and laid-back Creole charm. See page 153.

THE BEST OF MAURITIUS, RÉUNION & SEYCHELLES: EDITOR'S CHOICE

Sandy shores, spectacular marine life, French colonial mansions, botanic gardens and scenic hiking trails are all waiting to be explored in Mauritius, Réunion and Seychelles. Here, at a glance, are the editor's top tips for making the most of your visit.

The pristine sands of Anse Soleil.

SPORTING ACTIVITIES

Diving. The coral reefs of the Indian Ocean support hundreds of species of fish. See pages 87 and 263.

Big game fishing. Spending a day on the waves doing battle with a marlin is big business in Mauritius. See page 268.

Casela World of Adventures, Mauritius. The island's premier eco-adventure park and bird sanctuary offers activities from ziplining and quad-biking to walks with lions and cheetahs. See page 140.

Kitesurfing, Le Morne, Mauritius. 'One Eye' at Le Morne is one of the world's best spots for kitesurfing. See page 145.

Hiking, Réunion. More than 1,000km (620 miles) of trails, the Grandes Randonnées, criss-cross Réunion, a walker's paradise. See page 182.

A sweetlips swimming over coral, Seychelles.

BEST BEACHES

Île aux Cerfs, Mauritius. Limpid waters, lovely beaches and water-sports galore make this east-coast island a favourite with day-trippers. See page 121.

Northern Islands, Mauritius. The pristine sandy beaches and coral gardens of Îlot Gabriel (Gabriel Island) and larger Île Plate (Flat Island) are far from the madding crowd. See page 113.

Trou d'Argent, Rodrigues. This pirate haunt, accessible only by foot, is among the best preserved beaches on the planet. See page 159.

L'Hermitage, Réunion. This long, white-sand beach is lined with casuarina trees and protected by a coral reef. See page 210.

Beau Vallon, Mahé, Seychelles. Busiest beach in the Seychelles and lined with hotels but still pristine and excellent for bathing. Clear water and good reefs make it a popular diving and snorkelling spot. See page 291.

Anse Soleil, Mahé, Seychelles. Small and perfectly formed, this picturesque cove on Mahé's west coast is overlooked by the luxurious Anse Soleil Beachcomber Resort. See page 288.

Anse Source d'Argent, La Digue, Seychelles. Dazzling white sand and swaying palms; the calm sea – thanks to a protective reef – makes this an ideal beach for snorkellers. See page 328.

CULTURE AND HERITAGE

Vieux Grand Port and Mahébourg, Mauritius. The Dutch landed at Vieux Grand Port in 1598, where the remains of Fort Frederick Henry and 18th-century cannons can still be seen. At Mahébourg's National History Museum, eclectic exhibits tell the tale of the colonial periods under the Dutch, French and British. See page 122.

Grand Bassin, Mauritius. Dominated by a sculpture of the Hindu god Shri Mangal Mahadev, this volcanic crater, known as the Lake of the Ganges, is a sacred place of pilgrimage. See page 145.

Plantation houses and cases créoles. Before the concrete tide takes over these lovely wooden homes, with their airy verandas and delicate 'lacework', visit St Aubin and Eureka (Mauritius) or Villa Carrère and Villa Folio (Réunion). See pages 132, 149, 202 and 224.

Musée de Villèle, Réunion. Once home to notorious coffee and sugar producer Madame Desbassyns, this colonial mansion houses memorabilia and fine French East India furniture. See page 210.

Dauban Mausoleum, Silhouette, Seychelles. Modelled on the Madeleine in Paris, the imposing six-columned mausoleum set amid coconut palms pays homage to the Dauban family, owners of the island for more than 100 years. See page 304.

Giant roots in Pamplemousses Botanical Gardens.

WILDLIFE WATCHING

Île aux Aigrettes, Mauritius. Look out for the bands of pink pigeons, immortalised by the late naturalist Gerald Durrell. See page 125.

Whale-watching, Réunion. Snorkel with humpback whales between June and September, or admire them from a boat as they breach. See page 181.

Ste Anne Marine National Park, Seychelles. Established in the 1970s, it was the first such park in the Indian Ocean, with prolific marine life. Day trips by glass-bottom boat or subsea viewer depart from Victoria. See page 295.

Aride Island Nature Reserve, Seychelles. Home to more breeding sea birds and more sea bird species than Seychelles' other granitic islands put together, there are also jaw-dropping views at the pinnacle. See page 321.

Bird Island, Seychelles. The sooty tern colony here has more than 750,000 breeding pairs, but guests are encouraged to help with the island's hawksbill turtle conservation project too. See page 333.

PARKS AND GARDENS

Pamplemousses Botanical Gardens, Mauritius. A maze of shady palm-lined avenues lead to beautiful sights such as the Lily Pond, concealed under the floating leaves of the giant Amazon water lily. See page 115.

La Vallée de Ferney, Mauritius. Nature trails run through forests with more than 100 native plants and daily appearances from the endangered Mauritian kestrel. See page 124.

Jardin de l'État, Réunion. A botanical collection born from the European trees brought to the island by botanist Nicolas Bréon in 1817. The centrepiece is a natural history museum. See page 194.

Conservatoire Botanique de Mascarin, Réunion. A magnificent botanical garden landscaped into themed areas, with a restored 19th-century villa, hunting lodge and old family kitchen. See page 209.

Jardin du Roi, Mahé, Seychelles. Originally laid out in 1771 for the cultivation of spice plants, the present garden is reminiscent of 18th- and 19th-century farms. See page 287.

Whales and dolphins, Réunion.

Looking down over Bird Island in the Seychelles.

The Trou de Fer waterfall in
Belouve forest on Réunion.

Children play by fishing boats at sunset on Mahe.

A reclining palm on the beach at Praslin.

INDIAN OCEAN ISLANDS

The main draw may be white beaches and crystal waters, but beyond these are exotic cultures and breathtaking landscapes to explore.

Restaurant in Sennevile, Mauritius.

Visitors who have already been to both Mauritius and Seychelles always have a firm favourite: 'The beaches are better on the Seychelles'; 'But the people are so wonderful in Mauritius… and I've never seen such hotels…'; 'But what about the diving?'.

And what about Réunion? Until recently this corner of France in the Indian Ocean, with its breathtaking volcanic landscapes and opportunities for outdoor adventure, was France's best-kept secret. But in the last few years the island has promoted its attractions further afield and it is now appearing in an increasing number of brochures, mainly as a twin-centre holiday with Mauritius.

Réunion, with Mauritius, forms part of the Mascarenes, along with Rodrigues, Mauritius' isolated, serene sister island, with its unspoilt beaches, chilled Creole culture and ecotourism.

All these Western Indian Ocean islands share the same history to a certain point: all were colonised and cultivated with sugar, tea or vanilla plantations, and their populations are the descendants of explorers and colonists, slaves and indentured labourers. Kreol in one form or another is spoken in all of them, and some of their songs and dances share similar roots, as do their cuisines. But there is also great diversity, both culturally and in the tourist experience.

A small boat off Mauritius.

The cultural diversity of these islands, whose roots spread across three continents, is more visible in the Mascarenes than in Seychelles. The culture of Mauritius, from its politics to its cuisine, is heavily influenced by Asian customs and beliefs, while Rodrigues aligns itself more to the people and character of Africa. In Réunion, where culture is rooted in Gallic tradition, *boulangeries* sell baguettes and croissants alongside Creole specialities.

Seychelles, an archipelago of 115 mainly uninhabited islands, boasts chart-topping beaches, world-class diving and birdlife to make ornithologists weep. With the first settlers arriving little more than 200 years ago – a mix of French colonists, African slaves and Indian workers – Seychelles has a relatively new culture. Thankfully the government's commitment to conservation has resulted in more than half the landmass being given over to nature reserves and national parks.

This guide aims to bring out the truth behind the clichés so often attached to these tropical islands, and also to introduce the lesser-known islands and features of the region.

Children playing on tree swing of aerial roots in Pamplemousse Botanical Gardens.

PEOPLE OF THE INDIAN OCEAN

Indian Ocean islanders are all descendants of immigrants – pioneers or pirates, settlers or slaves – and at least three continents are represented among them.

The only thing that distinguishes a Mauritian or Seychellois away from home is the French lilt of their English. Otherwise you could be forgiven for believing that you are meeting a person of European, Asian or East African origin. And, leaping across a few generations, you would be right. The diversity, intermingling and surviving distinctions of the ethnic groups, who have arrived over the past 400 years, create the intriguing hotchpotch of cultures and physiognomies that characterise the Western Indian Ocean peoples today.

Ethnic diversity

Travellers to the islands of the southwest Indian Ocean often remarked on the ethnic diversity of the inhabitants. Charles Darwin, visiting Mauritius in 1836 on the *Beagle*, noted that 'the various races of men walking in the streets afford the most interesting spectacle'. He would have seen Arab and Persian traders dressed in long, flowing robes, Malagasy with elaborate hairstyles, turban- and langouti-clad Indians, and Chinese shopkeepers with long plaits.

The piecemeal settlement of the islands helps to explain the diversity of the inhabitants. In the 17th and 18th centuries, small groups of French prisoners and pioneers, along with a few Malagasy, Indians and Malays, set up bases, initially in the Mascarenes, and later in Seychelles and Rodrigues. With the importation of women from these same regions, the foundations of 'white' and 'coloured' communities were laid. Free immigrants were offered grants of land and encouraged to produce cash crops such as cotton, coffee or spices for export to Europe, or to cultivate foodstuffs and raise livestock which could be used to provision the

A warm welcome at Mahe International Airport.

ARTISTS' IMPRESSIONS

In the days before photography, artists travelled from place to place, capturing and publishing famous moments – such as the conquest of an island (for example, R. Temple's drawings of the British conquest of Mauritius in 1810), or sketching and labelling 'types' of exotic peoples for a curious European audience. L.A. Roussin and A. D'Hastrel published *Albums of Réunion* in 1863 and 1847 respectively, while Alfred Richard illustrated individuals as diverse as the 'Persian Groom', the 'Indian Labourer' and the 'Muslim Barber' for his *Types de l'Île Maurice* published in 1850.

Some French Mauritian families are genuine descendants of aristocrats who fled the French Revolution, while more outlandish claims of noble descent from Arab princesses and heroic corsairs can be heard in rum shops across the islands.

ships calling at the islands on their way to or from the Indies.

Merchants, adventurers, pirates and refugees from many nations were soon attracted to

passing ships to the labour-hungry colonists. From the mid-18th century, however, organised slaving voyages brought large numbers of Mozambicans and Malagasy to the islands, so they became the dominant ethnic groups, swallowing up the diverse pre-19th-century minorities into a Creole population that increasingly reflected this East African cultural heritage.

Asian immigration

The conversion of Mauritius and Réunion into plantation societies in the late 18th and

Buying fresh fruits in Réunion.

these new centres of trade and maritime construction, and the demand for skilled labour spiralled. Asians were cheaper to employ than Europeans, and agreements signed with Indian artisans led to the establishment of a wealthy free 'Malbar' class in the islands by the late 18th century. The crews of sailing ships were also frequently sourced from Asia, and were known as 'Lascars'. Many were Muslims. To this day the term 'Malbar' is local slang for people of Indian origin in both Mauritius and Réunion, but visitors should avoid using it, as it can also be considered an insult.

Slaves and convicts from countries as diverse as Guinea, the Canary Islands, Bengal, Java and Timor were also off-loaded from

early 19th centuries led to the large-scale introduction of estate workers, chiefly from India. Mauritius recruited indentured labour from several states: Biharis and Tamils were the most numerous; Marathis and Telegus arrived in smaller numbers. Réunion recruited mostly Tamils. Principally Hindus, some Muslim and Christian Indians were also indentured. Smaller numbers of African and Chinese labourers arrived over the same period. In the 1860s and 1870s several thousand 'Liberated Africans' were brought to Seychelles and Mauritius. They are thought to have mostly come from Malawi.

Merchants and other service migrants followed these population flows: Gujarati merchants and Chinese traders (chiefly Hakka and Cantonese speaking) established themselves in wholesale and retail, first on Mauritius and then across the region. Chinese women did not immigrate in large numbers until the turn of the 20th century, and the earlier relationships established by Chinese men produced a substantial Creole-Chinese population on the islands.

Seychelles and Rodrigues, less well suited by size and terrain to sugar cane cultivation, received fewer Asian immigrants and have remained principally Creole societies.

complained of as having favoured status. Integrationist French policy in Réunion, which ensured that generations of Tamils have taken Christian first names, has been relaxed recently, leading to a rediscovery of separate Hindu and Creole identities.

The ethnic compartmentalisation of present-day Mauritian society is more apparent. Here, a white settler class has survived and maintains its ethnic exclusiveness by marrying within its ranks and with acceptable outsiders – typically white Europeans and, increasingly, white South Africans, who have a shared experience of

Woman harvesting tea at Bois Chéri Tea Factory, Mauritius.

Old inequalities, new attitudes

The Mascarene and Seychelles island groups are all ex-slave societies in which the three tiers of the population – whites, 'coloureds' and slaves – were clearly demarcated and discouraged from intermarrying. Distinctions, grounded in membership of these 'colour-coded' groups remain, in varying degrees, on all the islands.

Vestiges of this old hierarchical society seem to have little relevance in modern Réunion and Seychelles, where intermarriage is now the norm, with equality of opportunity an official policy. A light-skinned elite nevertheless remains influential in Seychelles politics and society, while in Réunion, a new class of *z'oreilles* (white metropolitan French) is

CREOLE OR KREOL

In its historical sense, the term 'Creole' meant someone born on an island and was applied to all island inhabitants, regardless of their ethnicity. Thus Napoleon's consort, Josephine de Beauharnais, was a French Creole of Martinique. This is still the case on Réunion today. In more racially segmented Mauritius, the term 'Creole' applies only to islanders of African origin. A colonial language often became the basis of a new lingua franca, also called 'Creole'. To avoid confusion, the language is often spelt 'Kreol', as it is throughout this book.

enclave status in a multicultural environment. The old three-tier society has been replaced by one of five or more subgroups which each claim specific caste, religious and regional distinctions, maintained through intermarriage. Most Mauritian communities view marriage with a foreigner as a preferable option to an alliance with a Mauritian of another ethnic group. Intermarriage is not unusual, but it is not yet the norm. Politically, ethnic divisions are reinforced by a constitution that provides electoral safeguards for minorities and by a tradition dating from Independence of select-

Celebrating Dipvali on Réunion.

ing candidates and even ministers according to their community. Every prime minister apart from Paul Bérenger has come from the Vaish subcaste of the North Indian Hindu community, numerically the most powerful ethnic group in Mauritius.

Distinctive traditions

Despite a shared history, and collective musical, linguistic and other traditions, each of the Indian Ocean islands has evolved a unique brand of Kreol and a distinctive set of social customs and religious practices. The African cultural heritage is strongest in Seychelles and Rodrigues, where the proportion of Afro-Creoles is highest. Réunion is greatly influenced

by France and the Francophone world – the zouk rhythms of Martinique are as popular as Paris fashions. In Mauritius, the preponderance of people of Indian origin means that cinemas here are as likely to show Hindi as French films, the sari and the *shalwar kamiz* (trousers and tunic) are common forms of dress, and bhojpuri bands compete with sega and European music for the hearts and minds of the island's youth. The ubiquitous red flags or *jhandi* which can be seen in front of houses throughout the island signify that the occupants are Sanatanist or orthodox Hindus – an eloquent symbol of the cultural dominance of this community in modern Mauritius.

While there are latent tensions between ethnic groups, the Indian Ocean islands are characterised more by syncretism, and participation in each other's celebrations, than by communal conflict. Many non-Tamils make vows to participate in the Cavadee fire-walking ceremonies (see page 74) and people of all religions light candles at the Catholic shrines.

Superstition and sorcery cut across ethnic divides: individuals perceived to possess the requisite skills – from traditional practitioners of alternative medicine to specialists in the art of black magic – attract followers from every community, and may be called in to administer remedies, settle quarrels and banish evil spirits.

The food of the islands is perhaps the best expression of a shared ethnic heritage: Creole cuisine incorporates European, Asian and African influences and offers dishes to suit every palate, from creamy gratins to Indian-style curries and Chinese-style fried noodles.

BRAIN-TEASERS

Kreol *sirandanes* or riddles are a legacy of the African storytelling traditions that are now disappearing in the Indian Ocean islands. When someone had a few riddles to tell they would shout 'Sirandane!', their audience would reply 'Sampek!' and the brain-teasing session would begin. Here are some typical examples:
Dileau dibout? Canne. Standing water? Sugar cane.
Dileau pendant? Coco. Hanging water? A coconut.
Menace dimoun, napas koze? Ledoigt. I threaten but I do not speak? A finger.
Ki lalangue ki zames ti menti? Lalangue zanimaux. Whose tongue never lies? An animal's.

Lingua Franca

The peoples of the Seychelles and Mascarene Islands are united by forms of a shared spoken language, which exists today as a sign of their shared identity.

As a legacy of their shared history of settlement during periods of French rule, the mother tongue of the inhabitants of the Seychelles and Mascarene Islands is Kreol. The various forms of Kreol spoken have evolved from adaptations of French to which a sprinkling of words and speech patterns from the other languages of immigrants has been added.

The formative period of Indian Ocean Kreol in the late 17th and 18th centuries has left its mark on the language. The Breton origins of many early French settlers means that traces of their regional language survive in modern Kreol, while the influence of Malagasy immigrants is reflected in local words such as *fangourin* or cane sugar juice, which derives from the Malagasy term *fangorinana*. South Indians who arrived on the islands in the 18th century as slaves and artisans have left their mark in culinary terms. The herb known as *kaloupile* in Réunion, *karipoule* in Mauritius and *karipile* in Seychelles is derived from the Tamil word *kariveppilai* or curry leaf.

Kreol is often referred to in the singular as if it is one language, when in fact Réunion (Réyoné) Kreol, Mauritian (Morisyen) Kreol and Seychelles (Sesel) Kreol are three separate languages that are not necessarily mutually intelligible. A native speaker of Réunion Kreol will not understand all Mauritian Kreol, and will understand little Seychelles Kreol.

Over time, different islands have developed particular speech patterns. Seychelles Kreol is said to be more sing-song in style, while Réunion Kreol has been exposed to greater influence from the Francophone world, particularly the French Caribbean. Mauritian Kreol uses many words deriving from its large population of North Indian origin. Other expressions derive from the Bhojpuri dialect spoken widely in rural Indian villages on the island.

The politics of language

The emphasis given to Kreol in the various islands is strongly linked to political factors. Because Réunion is a *département* of France, the French language is given priority, and is used in all official communications and the written media. In Mauritius and Seychelles, where French rule was succeeded

by British government, English is the official language. In Seychelles, however, Kreol also has this status and is treated equally in the media and government institutions. In Mauritius, as in Réunion, Kreol is spoken but rarely written. However, the language has gained greater respect in recent years, with the publication of a French-Kreol dictionary.

For all the islands, these varying political solutions to the language question pose further problems. Middle-class Seychellois complain that the prominence given to Kreol restricts the opportunities for their children to become proficient in French. Réunion suffers from being a Francophone island in

Shopping in Port Louis.

a largely Anglophone Indian Ocean. Mauritius, with its multiplicity of competing Asian ancestral languages and chiefly French media, struggles with internal dissent. The island is becoming increasingly Francophone, while the education system is slanted towards the use of English and Oriental languages, although Kreol is an optional language in schools.

As a rule, English is widely understood in Seychelles and Mauritius, but not in Réunion. French is the preferred language in Mauritius and Réunion, but will not be appreciated by all Seychellois. Switching from English to French and back will not daunt a Mauritian who can usually reply in kind. A few words of basic Kreol should provide a channel of easy communication on all islands. A pronunciation guide and glossary of basic phrases are on page 368.

Dinarobin Hotel Golf & Spa is one of several luxurious resorts in the region.

THE IMPACT OF TOURISM

Seychelles and Mauritius continue to lure celebrities,
Réunion is no longer such a well-kept secret, and
Rodrigues is yet to be 'discovered'.

The development of tourism is relatively recent in the Western Indian Ocean and its growth and quality have been carefully monitored. Planners, all too aware that the islands' natural assets are what attract visitors, have kept conservation very much at the forefront of their development schemes. There are no sprawling miles of concrete coastal resorts here, and the isolated location of the islands, together with high standards of service and beautiful natural beaches, mean that the tropical island paradise experience as presented in the brochures and glossy magazines actually lives up to expectations.

Tourism development

Trendiness has been a key factor in determining the way tourism has evolved both in Mauritius and Seychelles, which are at different stages of development. Seychelles was the first island group to be popular with European visitors, and by 1979 tourism was the chief earner. Sporadic political conflict, however, as in Madagascar and the Comoros, slowed economic growth in Seychelles while Mauritius remained stable. Despite the coup d'état and succeeding radical governments, Seychelles still attracts a steady stream of holiday-makers. The beaches are as stunning as ever and are often rated among the world's best in travellers' surveys (see page 31). Nevertheless, this has not been enough to stop Seychelles from being overtaken by Mauritius, which has been riding the crest of a popularity wave for some years now. The 'Vanilla Islands' alliance has been set up to encourage tourism between Seychelles, Mauritius, Réunion, Madagascar and the Comoros, promoting twin-centre holidays that combine the beaches of Mauritius, for example, with adventure in Réunion or Madagascar.

Infinity pool at Maradiva Villas Resort & Spa.

The Mauritian tourist industry has concentrated all its energies on developing the luxury end of the market, building splendid hotels and gaining a reputation for excellent service. Since 1993, the island has outstripped Seychelles in tourist numbers and currently welcomes just over one million tourists a year (visitors to Seychelles numbered around 230,000 in 2014). Indications are that this figure will reach 2 million by 2020, probably exceeding Mauritius' own population.

State vs the private sector

Politics has also affected the development of tourism in the region. The state has a deeper level of involvement in tourism on 'socialist'

Seychelles than on 'capitalist' Mauritius. While it was the government that initiated tourist development in Seychelles, the role of the private sector in the building of exclusive resorts in Mauritius was significant. Seychelles' population of 91,000 is low compared to Mauritius, which has 1.3 million inhabitants, so labour and production costs are less advantageous. In addition to this, the wages of workers in the Seychelles hotel sector are regulated, as are the number of privately owned guesthouses and the prices they can charge. All of these factors contribute to a higher cost of living than on Mauritius.

Celebrities and royalty in search of an exclusive destination the paparazzi can't get to opt for Seychelles, where whole islands can be hired out – Frégate, Félicité and D'Arros, all privately owned, are perfect hideaways for those who can afford to pay for the privilege of having a tropical island to themselves. The Seychelles' most famous guests were the Duke and Duchess of Cambridge, Prince William and Catherine, who honeymooned on North Island in 2011. The Miss World competition has been staged here on more than one occasion; its co-ordinators exploited the paradise cliché to the full, billing the event as a unique

Shangri-La's Le Touessrok Resort & Spa.

Seychelles recognised the fact that to maintain its appeal and the high quality that people have come to expect, it needed to reinvest. The result is some of the best private island resorts in the world, such as luxury eco retreat North Island and celebrity favourite Frégate. High-end hotel chains have also set their sights on the prime stretches of sand, so in recent years Constance Lemuria Seychelles and Raffles Resort have sprung up on Praslin, and the Four Seasons, Banyan Tree and Maia opened on Mahé.

Celebrity spotting

Whatever the economic and political ups and downs, both Mauritius and Seychelles are still hot favourites among the rich and famous.

opportunity to see 'the most beautiful girls on earth in the most beautiful place on earth.'

With its larger tourist industry, Mauritius has more five-star hotels than Seychelles. Seychelles had no five-star facilities until the late 1990s, but this has since changed dramatically and new hotels have capitalised on the twin advantages of more private islands and better beaches than Mauritius. Both countries have hotels in the 'leading hotels in the world' category. They cater to every whim of their celebrity guests, providing security, a high standard of service and world-class chefs. Supermodels, footballers, pop stars and film stars regularly appear in glossy magazines, captured languishing in their designer swimwear by the poolside cafés and seaside

> *It used to be said that Mauritius is a three-star destination with five-star hotels while Seychelles is a five-star destination with three-star hotels, but Seychelles facilities are rapidly catching up.*

bars of Mauritius' most fashionable hotels. Old favourites Shangri-La Le Touessrok Resort & Spa (photogenic and popular as a Bollywood location), One&Only Le Saint Géran and the Royal Palm Hotel, popular with visiting heads of state,

compete with newer glitzy resorts such as Constance Le Prince Maurice, The St Regis Resort Mauritius and The Westin Turtle Bay Resort & Spa. Lesser mortals cannot expect automatic access to these hotels. If you want to have lunch or dinner it's best to make a reservation first.

Affordable luxury

In principle, these islands are luxury destinations. A two-week holiday at a good hotel on Seychelles or Mauritius can cost several thousand pounds per person. That said, you don't have to be a celebrity or tycoon to enjoy the

Le Canonnier Hotel.

COASTAL FORTS AND QUARANTINE SITES

The Indian Ocean islanders feared two things above all else – enemy attack, which their small populations could not easily fend off, and the introduction of contagious disease, which drastically reduced their numbers. The dangers came from visiting ships, and elaborate measures were taken to protect their coastlines. Defence and quarantine buildings were erected on shores and islets – precisely those areas that are most in vogue today as tourist sites. Flat Island off the north coast of Mauritius was a quarantine station, while Seychelles' Île Curieuse was once a leper colony. Some hotels have incorporated these ruins into their grounds. Le Canonnier hotel in

Mauritius is built on the site of an important fortress and a quarantine station. The old defence walls are now an integral part of the hotel and the mounted cannon still point out to sea. Maritim Resort Spa, further along the coast, offers guests and non-residents the opportunity to walk around 18th-century ruins of a French arsenal. Mauritius also has some of the best preserved Martello towers in the world (see page 141). On your travels, you may come across the ruins of old lime kilns. The French spent a great deal of time and manpower in the manufacture of lime, which they used for the building of roads and in construction work.

best that the region has to offer. There are so many small islands in the Seychelles group that anyone can find their own 'private' cove complete with swaying palms, fine white sand and turquoise lagoon. Cruising the granitics sounds like an expensive luxury but there are a range of options available for those with a more limited budget. Honeymooners and others looking to splash out on an exceptional holiday can spend their fortnight on islands such as La Digue, where cars are rarely seen, or enjoy the utter isolation of Denis or Frégate, where your very own island wedding can be arranged. Cousine

The palm-fringed pool at Le Prince Maurice.

is also an exclusive hideaway, with four to eight rooms that can be reached by helicopter.

The tourist industry on Mauritius targets the well-heeled lover of luxury and exclusivity – charter flights are limited here. This is the destination of choice for those who want to exploit the service and amenities of a five-star hotel and the tropical beach on its doorstep to the full. However, such luxury can be surprisingly affordable, with competitive packages, including all-inclusive deals, offered by some 120 luxury hotels and an increasing number of accommodation options, from 'glamping' to self-catering. The key to a successful holiday on Mauritius lies in choosing the right accommodation to suit you, both in terms of style and location. The latest trend is to stay in more than one hotel or resort for contrasting experiences, and self-catering options are increasing, with the addition of luxurious properties in recent years.

Natural assets

While both Mauritius and Seychelles have been effectively marketed as idyllic beach holiday destinations, their other natural assets have been widely exploited to draw in people looking for more than just a 'sun, sea and sand' experience. The Seychelles government is anxious to attract the 'discerning and environmentally aware' tourist and promotes the archipelago as the Galapagos of the Indian Ocean. Top of its list of highlights are two Unesco World Heritage sites – the Vallée de Mai on Praslin (home to the rare and indigenous coco de mer nut) and far flung Aldabra Atoll. Other designated bird sanctuaries and tropical forests attract twitchers and trekkers,

---

THE WORLD'S BEST HOTELS

The hotels of Seychelles and Mauritius are the Indian Ocean's best assets, and continue to win awards on the world stage. Mauritius boasts five members of The Leading Hotels of the World (Shanti Maurice, Shangri-La Le Touessrok Resort & Spa, Constance Le Prince Maurice, Maradiva Villas Resort & Spa and Royal Palm), and Seychelles boasts two (Maia Luxury Resort & Spa and Constance Lemuria). In 2014, Seychelles was named as one of the Huffington Post's '12 most scenic islands in the world'. At the World Travel Awards 2014 – the Oscars of the travel industry – Mauritius was crowned the 'world's leading honeymoon destination', Maradiva Villas Resort & Spa in Mauritius was voted the 'world's leading luxury island resort', and Seychelles' Raffles Praslin was voted the 'world's leading luxury villa resort'. North Island, Frégate Island, Banyan Tree and Four Seasons scored in the Condé Nast Readers' Travel Awards for the Middle East, Africa and Indian Ocean region, alongside the Oberoi Mauritius and One&Only Le Saint Géran in Mauritius. To restore a sustainable balance between supply and demand, in 2014 Mauritius announced a two-year moratorium on new hotels, aside from the 130 new rooms in the pipeline.

Fans of Hindi cinema have a good chance of glimpsing their screen idols in Mauritius, where Bollywood films are almost constantly in production.

while live-aboard cruises around the Outer Islands are becoming increasingly popular.

In Mauritius although water sports, including kitesurfing, diving and big game fishing – the annual World Marlin Fishing competition is a major event on the fishing calendar – remain big business for those who can afford it, ecotourism ventures inland are being promoted as an alternative activity, with some success.

The flora and fauna of Seychelles and the Mascarenes is in many respects unique and, like all small island ecologies, endangered. Coral reefs are notoriously fragile and prone to destruction by over zealous exploitation. Seychelles has a long tradition of ecotourism, with several islands declared nature reserves and access to them limited to the daytime. Mauritius is belatedly recognising the advantages of exploiting the few remaining areas on which unique species have survived. Thankfully, it's now following the example set by the Seychelles government in requiring permits for visits to some of its islets and in opening them up to responsible, supervised nature tours. Île aux Aigrettes, off the southeast coast, is home to the only remaining example of coastal savannah, which the dodo and other local birds found a natural habitat, and tours have been set up by the Mauritius Wildlife Foundation (see page 125).

Holidaying on a budget

Backpackers are not encouraged, but there are ways of staying more cheaply on the islands. The resorts of Grand Baie/Pereybère and Flic-en-Flac in Mauritius offer numerous flats and guesthouses where a studio can be rented for around £25 (US$37) a day. Once you have paid for your flight, this is the one island in the region where you can live more cheaply than at home, and some seasonal workers from European coastal resorts choose to spend the winter here, staying for the three to six months that is allowed them on a tourist visa. Prices of imported goods are higher than in Europe, but essential foodstuffs are subsidised, and if you bring your own luxury items, you can live very cheaply.

Seychelles also has a number of small guesthouses; though not particularly cheap compared to other countries, they are less expensive than hotels, the service is much more personal and standards are generally high. Self-catering establishments are also good quality, and shopping for yourself brings down costs: shop prices for drinks are half those charged by hotels, while local produce, including fish, is inexpensive.

Adventure playground

Réunion is the most expensive of the Indian Ocean islands because its economy is artifi-

Hiking in the Forêt Plaine des Tamarins, Réunion.

cially boosted with regular injections of French capital. Prices are somewhat higher here than in mainland France. It has long been popular with French visitors – as an overseas *département* there are no customs or immigration checks for arrivals from the métropole (mainland France) – but its lack of coral-fringed beaches and its monolingualism have lessened the island's appeal to non-French tourists. The Réunionnais themselves often take their annual holidays on Mauritius where, beyond the big hotels, the cost of living is much lower.

As its coastline doesn't fit the tropical island profile, Réunion has escaped invasion from international tourists. Most of us still need persuading that hiking – even to an active volcano – is more fun than lounging by a palm-fringed lagoon, and until recently the island's breathtaking landscape remained a well-kept secret from all but the French and the ardent adventure traveller. However, Réunion is now being featured by more UK tour operators as part of a 'beach and adventure' twin-centre holiday with Mauritius.

The tourist authorities were quick to recognise and exploit its potential as a paradise for backpackers and thrill seekers, and over the years they have built up an efficient infrastructure. The trail network is well-mapped and maintained, as are the purpose-built mountain lodges or *gîtes*. The

Anse Ally Beach on Rodrigues.

adventure sport potential has been developed to the full. Other than trekking, organisations and facilities for mountain biking, climbing, horse riding, canyoning, canoeing, caving, even bungee-jumping can be found all over the island

Réunion has also countered its shortcomings with the marketing of its colonial heritage, which it seems to have preserved far better than its neighbours. Plantations and colonial houses have been faithfully restored and opened to the public. In contrast, despite the opportunities for cultural heritage tourism that the rich history and diverse population of Mauritius offer, museum development and tours of cultural and historic sites remain unsophisticated. The marketing of the island's cultural heritage,

particularly around gastronomy, will be a strong focus for the Mauritius Tourism Promotion Authority in the coming years.

The forgotten island

Rodrigues, granted regional autonomy in 2002, is the minuscule and often forgotten partner in the twin-island Republic of Mauritius. Until not so long ago, the island could be reached only by a cargo vessel which docked at Port Mathurin just once a month and only the most determined travellers reached its rugged shores. Nowadays, the *Mauritius Trochetia* makes the crossing two or three times a month, bringing in islanders and the odd tourist on short breaks.

Tour operators are beginning to turn their attentions to Rodrigues, but tourism is still very much in its infancy here and further development seems to be hampered by the difficulties of air access, water shortages and concern about its infrastructure. Light aircraft make regular flights to and from Mauritius and visitors from Réunion have to fly via Mauritius before continuing to Rodrigues.

The Association of Rodrigues Tourism Operators is a body of guesthouse and hotel managers, tour operators, car hire companies and shopkeepers who, in conjunction with the Mauritius Tourism Promotion Authority, are promoting cultural and niche tourism, with some success. Their organised activities include staying in islanders' homes, going to folklore shows, walking, fishing and diving. The gigantic lagoon for which Rodrigues is famous is an unspoilt haven for divers, and is currently the subject of detailed research by scientists studying the Indian Ocean's unique coral islands.

Rodrigues remains uncrowded and unspoiled. There are no high-rise hotels or malls, and chickens still roam the capital's streets. Interestingly, the island is visited mostly by Mauritians looking for a relaxing weekend break and small numbers of European and South African tourists travelling from Mauritius who are keen to discover another facet of life in the Mascarenes.

It was hoped an extended airport runway, built in 2002 with European funding, would attract more flights, increasing Rodrigues' popularity as another Indian Ocean destination, but little has changed. Developers will one day home in on its beaches, but hopefully with the sensitivity to the natural environment that is essential to the survival of such a small island.

Seychelles' top ten

With its soft crescents of white sand lined with palms and backed by dramatic granite boulders, it's little wonder Seychelles regularly appears on lists of the world's best beaches.

In 1987, the film *Castaway* – nothing to do with the later Tom Hanks-vehicle, *Cast Away* – was released. It was based on the true story of two Londoners who dreamed of living for a year on a tropical island, but the beaches on the real island, which lies between Papua New Guinea and Australia, weren't photogenic enough. The director, Nicolas Roeg, looked around the world for the perfect tropical paradise. He settled on the perfect arc of white sand at Anse Kerlan on Praslin, lapped by crystal-clear blue waters and surrounded by lush tropical vegetation. The film starred Oliver Reed and Amanda Donahue, but according to one review: 'The real star was the beach.'

Award-winning beaches

The beaches of Seychelles are legendary. The German travel magazine *Reise & Preise* conducted a survey to rate the world's most fabulous beaches. Thousands of its readers responded to the 'Beach Test', rating sand, surf, sunbathing, accessibility, water quality and so on. Many beaches and many countries were listed, but Seychelles emerged the clear winner, with six of the top 12 beaches in the world. In a supplementary list of insider tips for those beaches rarely mentioned in the guidebooks (this one excepted), Seychelles again dominated with two of the world's top five. No other country had more than one slot in the same category. 'There is no doubt,' concluded the magazine, 'that the best beaches in the world can be found in Seychelles.'

Top of the league table is **Anse Lazio**, followed at number two by its close neighbour **Anse Georgette**, both on Praslin. La Digue also had two entries, **Anse Source d'Argent** at number five and **Grande Anse** at 12. Frégate Island's **Anse Victorin** was rated at number seven and Mahé's **Anse Intendance** at nine. In the supplementary rankings, **Anse Soleil** on Mahé and **Anse Cocos** on La Digue completed the roll of honour. Seychelles is never absent from similar polls. Anse Source d'Argent was voted the best beach in the world by the UK's *Independent* newspaper, Condé Nast's *Traveller* magazine and the American cable TV station the Travel Channel.

The stark white sands, swaying palms and emerald seas of these and other idyllic coastal stretches are the answer to many a film-maker's, not to mention advertiser's, dream. Roman Polanski chose to shoot scenes for his swashbuckling adventure film *Pirates* on Frégate, while Sylvie Kristel stuck with Anse Source d'Argent for the erotic romance *Emmanuelle in Paradise*. Take a closer look at the classic paradise backdrop to any fashion shoot, TV or glossy magazine ad, and there's a good chance you'll recognise a Seychelles hotspot.

The truth is, when beaches are this good it is difficult to choose. There are beaches for every mood.

Anse Lazio's acolade-winning beach.

Romantic beaches to wander along, surf-lashed beaches to frolic on, fish-rich waters to snorkel in, child-friendly beaches on the edge of sleepy lagoons, lively beaches with water sports and restaurants, and beaches where you'll not see a soul all day except perhaps for a fisherman. Mahé's **Beau Vallon**, though the most developed beach in Seychelles, retains a majestic beauty. It remains uncrowded and unspoilt relative to most destinations. At the other extreme of sophistication are the remote **Outer Islands**. These little-visited islands all have stunning beaches awaiting discovery. Small resorts and live-aboard cruising are slowly opening up this corner of Eden so that next time a poll is conducted, there will be even more Seychelles contenders to add to the list.

A dream setting for a tropical wedding at Sugar Beach resort, Flic-en-Flac.

THE WEDDING INDUSTRY

**Weddings and honeymoons in the Indian Ocean
are increasingly popular, and affordable.
Forward planning is the key to their success.**

The lure of Mauritius and Seychelles comes in many guises for brides and grooms to be. (As Réunion operates under French rule, European visitors are forbidden by its residency laws to marry here.) More often than not, it's the desire to escape all the hassle and cost of a formal white wedding at home that tempts couples overseas. Apart from an idyllic setting and perfect climate, these islands offer the freedom to kick off your shoes and tie the knot barefoot in the sand if the mood takes you.

Mauritius and Seychelles have so far managed to avoid the tackiness to which other destinations have succumbed. Unlike many Caribbean resorts, where newlyweds often bump into each other, most hotels here prefer to limit ceremonies to one a day. Mauritius was tour operator Kuoni's top wedding destination worldwide in 2015, and Seychelles was at number 10.

Honeymooners on Denis Private Island.

Tying the knot

Weddings are generally civil, the ceremony held either under a gazebo beside the beach or in a hotel garden. Church weddings are possible, but they involve a little more organisation and often an extra cost for hiring the church. However, provided the hotel or tour operator is willing to make the arrangements, there's nothing to stop more adventurous couples getting married anywhere they choose. In Mauritius, couples can helicopter into the highlands for a ceremony at the Varangue Sur Morne near the Black River Gorges with awesome views of the dramatic landscape and turquoise ocean. Or they can board a catamaran decked out in bougainvillaea for a wedding on the water, or get married on a submarine under water. In Seychelles, at resorts such as Denis or Frégate, you can have your own private island wedding, providing your budget stretches that far.

The key to a successful Indian Ocean wedding is finding the right tour operator to handle your needs (see Travel Tips, Transport, for a list of reputable organisations) and making sure you have complied with all the legal requirements (see Travel Tips, A–Z). Then there is little or nothing to organise except the provision of the necessary documents, and the arrangement of a few details like hair appointments, flowers, wedding cake and choosing between, say, a sunset cruise or a romantic dinner.

Mauritius has a sophisticated wedding scene, with its four- and five-star international resorts well equipped to organise ceremonies, many with dedicated wedding co-ordinators who guide couples through all their arrangements. Seychelles may not be as slick as Mauritius when it comes to organising weddings, but in many ways this adds to its charm. With its pristine beaches, dramatic peaks and rainforest, not to mention the notorious coco de mer 'love nut', Seychelles is just as seductive.

Trends show that weddings abroad are on the increase and more and more couples are accom-

Top Mauritian wedding venues

Foreigners marrying in Mauritius can incorporate elements of traditional weddings into their ceremonies if they wish, but must advise the hotel as to what they want.

Six hotel groups – Beachcomber, Sun Resorts, LUX* Resorts, Veranda Resorts, Heritage Resorts and Attitude Hotels – dominate the island. All are geared up for weddings and take care to make couples feel special. Most of the other upmarket hotels on the island, such as La Résidence, The St Regis Mauritius, Shangri-La Le Touessrok Resort & Spa

A wedding at Lemuria Luxury Hotel on Praslin.

panied by friends and family. The beauty of the Indian Ocean is that once the wedding is over, guests can stay on for a holiday while newlyweds can honeymoon on another island, take an island-hopping cruise, go on safari in Africa (not a long plane journey away) or go for a spell on Réunion – a great contrast to Mauritius or Seychelles, with its dramatic volcanic scenery and intensely French culture.

The average two-week wedding and honeymoon in the Indian Ocean costs in the region of £4,000 (US$6,000) per couple. If the wedding party is big enough, some of the larger hotels may waive the cost of the wedding package (usually £350–£600/US$525–$900) – but you'll need to book well in advance.

WEDDING ADVICE

Do book well in advance and plan your wedding date at least three days after your arrival so you can acclimatise and get all the details and legal paperwork completed (check the latest regulations for how many days before the wedding you need to be on the island). Hang your wedding dress or suit in a steamy bathroom on arrival to remove creases. Check exactly what's included in your wedding package, in case you want any extras such as live music. Take out wedding and travel insurance. Don't wear new or tight shoes, as your feet will expand in the heat. And remember – formalities often proceed at a slower pace in a hot climate.

Couples wanting to marry in Mauritius and Seychelles send their requests as much as 18 months in advance. November and December are particularly popular months, so book early to avoid disappointment.

and Constance Le Prince Maurice resorts, also cater for weddings. LUX* Resorts even offers the possibility of getting hitched on its Robinson-Crusoe-style private island, Île des Deux Cocos.

can also marry in church, but this comes at an extra charge.

Most hotels in Seychelles welcome weddings. As they tend to be smaller than in other destinations, they lend themselves to intimate gatherings. Coco de Mer on Praslin decorates its wooden pier with local flowers and banana leaves to create a wedding venue over the water. A ceremony just before sunset allows the photographer to capture some stunning shots. Some of the best-known hotels for weddings on Mahé are the Four Seasons, the Berjaya hotels, Coral Strand and Banyan

The perfect place for a classic honeymoon – Sainte Anne Island Beachcomber.

Seychelles weddings

In Seychelles there are registrars on the main islands of Mahé, Praslin and La Digue. However, resorts on the other islands can also assist with wedding arrangements, including photography if required.

Foreign couples can marry anywhere they want to, although strictly speaking they are not supposed to marry on the distinctive white sand beaches. However, hotels such as Four Seasons have pavilions or gazebos erected beside the beach. A favourite beach wedding setting is Anse Source d'Argent on La Digue. Anse Lazio on Praslin, proclaimed the best beach in the world by many glossy travel magazines, is equally idyllic. Foreigners

Tree. Over on Praslin favourites include Coco de Mer Hotel and the Black Parrot Suites, Le Domaine de La Réserve, Raffles Resort and the Constance Lemuria Resort. On La Digue couples can arrive by ox cart for their wedding at La Digue Island Lodge. As there are so many islands to choose from, it's worth considering marrying on one island, such as Mahé or Praslin, and honeymooning on another, or even island-hopping by air or sea.

Those who really want to get away from it all can make arrangements on several of the small outer islands: Denis has its own tiny wedding chapel; Desroches, Alphonse, Cousine and Frégate Island Private all fit the tropical paradise bill.

Myriad small fish surround a red sea fan on a Seychelles coral reef.

MARINE LIFE

Not far beneath the surface of the Indian Ocean lies a fascinating world, teeming with life and easy to explore.

For many people the 'Underwater World' is a strange and inaccessible place, full of mystery and danger. While it is true that most of the submarine environment will remain an area that few have the opportunity to experience, the temperature and generally favourable conditions here make the shallow waters easy to explore. The most popular holiday destinations in the Indian Ocean are on the coast and have easy access to the sea. Mauritius is encircled by an almost continuous reef barrier, interrupted only to the south between Le Souffleur and Souillac; many of the Seychelles islands support fringing coral reefs, while some experts maintain that Rodrigues' corals are even better than those of the Seychelles.

School of Moorish idols.

Tidal zone

The first type of terrain you are likely to come across is the tidal zone. Here at sea level, rock pools host a number of small fish species adapted to the inter-tidal way of life. Prominent

Many parrotfish sleep in a mucus 'bubble', which they blow around themselves as an early warning system of approaching danger.

among these are the rock skippers, small brown blennies and gobies which have modified fins that act as suckers, allowing them to cling to the rocks as the surf sweeps back and forth.

Many species of crustaceans are found only in these refuges. Most striking of the rock pool treasures are the crabs that scurry nimbly from rock to rock, such as the aptly named Sally Lightfoot. Barnacles spend their life attached to rocks. From their cone-shaped structure, they extend hairy paddle-like legs that beat to create a current, bringing nutrient-rich water to their mouths.

Sandy areas

As you wade into the sea and peer through the water, the sand beneath the surface looks like a submarine desert when compared to the busy reefs beyond. But look a little closer and you'll spot some interesting sea creatures. Often the most obvious are the slow-moving crawlers such as crabs, sea urchins and sea cucumbers, the long sausage-like objects littered around many sandy bottom areas. These creatures are the caretakers of the sea bed and feed on detritus and algae in the sand's surface layer. The small submarine 'volcanoes' characteristic of some areas are built by marine worms, generally hidden from view.

Flat-fish species, such as the peacock flounder, are difficult to see. Generally well camouflaged, they only give themselves away when they glide off in search of another resting spot. Various types of ray also inhabit sandy bottom areas, especially in the shallow lagoons. They can be quite large, measuring up to 2 metres (6.5ft) across their wide wing-like disc. You have to look quite hard to spot a resting ray as they often cover themselves with a coating of sand, but their whip-like tails, which tend to stick out

Arc eye hawkfish in shallow waters, resting on coral heads.

of the sand like flagpoles, often give them away. While the sting ray is indeed well equipped with a sting mechanism in his barbed tail, it is used purely for defence and divers and snorkellers should have no fear of attack unless they provoke the animal or tread on it. A few minutes spent watching a sting ray hunting through the sand for molluscs and crabs can be very rewarding. Manta rays are among the biggest Indian Ocean fish and feed on plankton and small fish. They are quite harmless and a joy to watch as they sail gracefully through the water.

A number of the unique animals inhabiting the sandy sea bed are often mistaken for plants; sea pens, for example, have a feather or plume-like structure on a fleshy stalk that protrudes

Cone shells, with their beautiful intricate designs, are among the most attractive shells in the world. But beware! Never pick one up by the thin end, for its poison is deadly.

from the sand. The 'plume' is in fact an intricate structure of arms that is rotated to face into any water currents and strain out plankton and other particles of food.

Look out for areas of algae or sea-grass which provide food and shelter for a number of animals. Wrasse are often found feeding here and you may even come across a charismatic little seahorse clinging to the grass with his tail.

Sea-grass beds are also visited by larger algal browsers, notably the green turtle, the larger of the two turtle species found in this region. Watching the turtles feeding is one of the rare opportunities you will have of observing them at close quarters. The other prime time for a good sighting is when the female turtles come up the beach to lay their eggs.

Rock reefs

Rock reefs are another easily accessible and productive zone in the Indian Ocean and provide the habitat for a profusion of marine life. The rocks themselves are often covered in a variety of marine plants and creatures ranging from subtly coloured encrusting hard corals, barnacles and limpets to brightly coloured sponges and soft corals, so much so that little of the actual rock surface may be visible. Each of these encrusting structures is itself host to a number of other creatures and provides a micro-ecosystem on the reef. In soft coral formations look out for small fish such as gobies and blennies that often mimic the colour of the coral for protection. They actually nest on the corals and feed on zooplankton. The hard coral formations are home to a number of brightly coloured fish species including hawkfish, damselfish and small scorpion or rockfishes, all benefiting from the protection that the branching structures provide. Various crabs also use the branching corals for shelter, such as the red-spotted crab and hermit crab, which hides in its borrowed shell for protection.

Many fish species hide in the gaps and crevasses between the rocks of the reef for protection from predators and can be found feeding above the reef during the day. Along the reef you are sure to see brightly coloured surgeon-fish that graze algae off the rocks, often just below the wave zone. Their name derives from the sharp spines found at the base of their tail, which is why fishermen are extra careful when handling them.

Coral reefs

Coral reefs are the submarine equivalent of the rainforest and have the greatest diversity of marine life. They are formed by tiny animals, coral polyps, which secrete a hard external cas-

Others produce a horny resilient material called gorgonin and develop into long spiral whip cor-als or intricate fans. These grow at right angles to the current and act as living sieves, filtering out food particles as the water flows through.

All corals are really predatory animals and their polyps have tentacles that are armed with stinging cells that stun microscopic prey. Most of these stings are harmless to humans, but the one coral to learn to recognise and avoid is the so-called fire coral. If you brush against one, the potent sting it inflicts on your skin feels like the burn from a stinging nettle.

Snorkelling in clear water above coral, Seychelles.

ing of calcium. Successive generations build on top of each other to form the limestone of the reef with just the outer surface covered with the living corals.

There are a vast number of hard coral for-mations. The real reef builders are known as 'massive' corals. They form enormous rounded coral heads which coalesce to form reefs. Other hard corals are highly branched, with delicately ornate structures, giving rise to such evocative names as staghorn and elkhorn.

While the stony corals secrete a calcium cas-ing, many of the soft coral species grow on even more complex structures. Some – the colourful tree corals, for example – support their bod-ies with a latticework of tiny calcium needles.

CORAL BLEACHING

During 1997–8, a rise in sea temperatures in the western Indian Ocean (attributed to climate change and the El Niño effect) killed many corals, bleaching them white. In areas of good environ-mental conditions a natural cycle of colonisation by algae was triggered, allowing re-colonisation by coral larvae. In Seychelles, the reef life was further protected by the underlying granitic structure that gave shelter to displaced species. Long-term pros-pects for Mauritius' reefs, which endured another bleaching in 2009, are good. Meanwhile a 2011 Wildlife Conservation Society (WCS) study praised Réunion for its reef protection programme.

Sea anemones

Related to the corals are the sea anemones – a bit like giant coral polyps without the external shell. These creatures are generally hidden within cracks and ledges of the reef but a few species are conspicuously stuck to the surface of the rocks. They are mostly host anemones and are almost always associated with the anemone fish, also known as the clown fish. Theirs is a classic symbiotic relationship: the anemone fish gains shelter and protection from the anemone, and in return the anemone gets scraps of food from the resi-

Butterfly fish swim over a Seychelles reef.

dent fish. Although the anemone fish is able to develop a protection against the anemone's stings, they are still a powerful deterrent to a would-be predator. The exact mechanism of the anemone fish's immunity is not clearly understood but it is thought that the mucus coating covering the scales of the fish, which it wears like a coat, absorbs small amounts of the anemone's sting; the anemone begins to accept this coated fish as being itself and thus no longer tries to sting it.

Colourful tropical fish

For many snorkellers, and even divers, it is the brightly coloured and most visible fish which gather in the shallower waters around and

above the reef that leave the strongest impression. Many of these fish are in fact deep water species which come into the shallows to feed. Colourful schools of fusiliers, known locally as mackerel, have the characteristic 'fishy' shape of a torpedo-like body with small fins, and feed on phyto-plankton above the reefs. Most of the common species have bright blue body colourings with a mixture of stripes and flashes ranging from yellow through to pink, which shimmer in a vivid colour display as the school moves.

On the reef itself the two most colourful species are the angelfish and butterfly fish, both of which have bodies which are flattened from side to side when viewed from ahead and are almost circular when viewed in profile. Butterfly fish are generally small, around 8–15 cm (3–6ins) across the disc and are predominantly algal and coral grazers; most have body colours that are yellow, black or white. Angelfish species are larger in size, up to 25cm (10ins), and display a wide range of markings. They also have different patterns in juvenile forms compared to the final adult phases and so add enormously to the colour of the living reef.

A larger visitor to the coral reef is the hawksbill turtle; this is probably the most

> *Many molluscs secrete chemical substances which, without being poisonous, are distasteful enough to put off a would-be predator.*

commonly found marine turtle species in this region and takes its name from its hooked, hawk-like beak which it uses to carve chunks off sponges and soft coral formations. In some areas of Seychelles these turtles may be found nesting on the beaches in daylight – a very unusual sight.

Just like a rock reef, the coral reef offers shelter and protection to a vast number of species as well as being a food source for some of its residents. Some fish are especially adapted to feeding on coral polyps, such as certain butterfly fish and filefish; others feed on small shrimp and other invertebrates that shelter between the branches, such as the razor or shrimpfish.

Molluscs are frequent residents; the most obvious of these are the brightly coloured nudibranchs, or sea slugs. Despite their small size they are the most apparent because of their bright coloration that warns would-be predators that they do not taste good and might be poisonous. A number of shelled molluscs can be found during the day as well but many have highly camouflaged shells to conceal them so they can be difficult to spot.

Other animals actually live within the limestone of the coral colony; these include the tube or 'feather-duster' worms that are evident from their coloured fans which extend above the surface of the coral colony to trap particles. Some are spectacularly formed into twin spiral cones, as in the Christmas-tree worm, and these pretty structures are often brightly coloured. All fan worms are sensitive to changes in light and therefore will disappear into their tubes on the sudden appearance of a snorkeller or diver.

Deep waters

The open ocean is a very different and much more inaccessible environment. The deep waters and their currents support marine life from microscopic plankton to some of the largest creatures on the planet but often the concentration of individuals is very low. Due to the constraints of deep water activities, most people will only get the chance to see these creatures when they come to the surface. Luckily, some places seem to have special properties that encourage deep water species to aggregate at the surface; in these areas it is possible to find whales and dolphins at specific times of the year.

Dolphins are one group that visitors are likely to come across on boat journeys around the islands, although in-water encounters are unfortunately a rare occurrence. There are a number of species in this area and the larger bottlenose and common dolphins are most often seen. In more remote areas there are local populations of the smaller species, notably spinner dolphins, which are readily recognisable by the habit of the youngsters to leap out of the air performing aerial twists and acrobatics. In some instances these places are special feeding or breeding areas and although the animals may appear to be easily approachable in organised encounter programmes, there are strict codes of conduct to ensure the safety of visitors and the protection of the animals concerned.

Within the last decade Réunion has seen increasing numbers of migrating humpback whales visit its waters. These marine mammals make the long journey up from Antarctica between June and September to mate, give birth and nurse their young in the warmer waters around the island. Scientists can identify each whale from its tailfin, the colour and shape of which is unique to each creature. They breach frequently and spectacularly, allowing visitors a chance to admire them.

Some deep water species are generally only seen when landed by fishing boats; these big

Leaping humpback whale at St Paul's Bay Cap la Houssaye.

game species such as sailfish, marlin, wahoo and dorado are relatively abundant but are seldom seen in their natural environment. Other deep water creatures are sometimes washed ashore by the ocean currents. These include several varieties of medusa or jellyfish; characteristically these have a clear gelatinous bell-shaped body and like their coral cousins they have a ring of stinging tentacles. While some jellyfish are harmless, others can deliver a powerful and possibly lethal sting and so contact should be avoided.

The Indian Ocean offers a huge diversity of life. Whether you choose to scuba dive, snorkel or take a glass-bottom boat trip, a glimpse into this magical underwater world will most certainly be a highlight of your trip.

TROPICAL ISLAND BLOOMS

From delicate orchids and hibiscus to vibrant bougainvillaea and flaming red flamboyants, the richness and variety of plant life are astounding.

When the first explorers set eyes on the Indian Ocean islands, it was the luxuriant forests and sweet-smelling colourful plants that led them to believe they had found Eden. In Mauritius, four centuries of human habitation have brought plantations, roads and logging, and destroyed many of the island's plants. In Seychelles, the shorter human history, absence of plantations and mountainous islands have helped preserve the environment. Réunion, too, was fortunate: its rocky and mountainous landscape is more inaccessible, so swathes of natural forest remain untouched.

Although many species are still endangered, the islands' flora remains rich: Mauritius has 670 native species, of which 315 are endemic; Réunion has over 700 indigenous species, of which 161 are endemic; in Seychelles, too, around 1,500 species, over 400 are native, with 75 endemic and a further 43 found only in the Aldabra group.

Botanical gardens

All the islands have botanical gardens where visitors can admire the abundant plant life. Mauritius has the Pamplemousses Botanical Gardens near Port Louis, the Curepipe Botanical Gardens and Le Pétrin Native Garden in the Black River Gorges area; Réunion has the Conservatoire Botanique National in St-Leu and the Jardin de l'Etat; and in Seychelles there's the Botanical Gardens and the Jardin du Roi spice gardens.

With its dense canopy of bright red flowers, the flamboyant tree in bloom is an impressive sight. It flowers between November and January.

Tropical Réunion orchids are often epiphytic, meaning they tend to grow on other plants such as trees. They often bloom in the wet season.

Frangipani (plumeria) flowers in Mauritius.

Dried vanilla pods, Réunion.

LA VANILLE BOURBON

Vanilla was introduced to Réunion from Central America in 1819, but attempts at natural pollination failed. Then, in 1841, a 12-year-old orphaned slave called Edmund Albius discovered that its flowers could be pollinated by grafting. (Edmund had been raised like a son by botanist Ferreol Beaumont Bellier, who was cultivating vanilla in his garden.) By the end of the 19th century Réunion was churning out 100 tons a year, using the techniques of drying and fermentation of vanilla beans practised by the Aztecs. In its heyday in the 1930s, Réunion accounted for three-quarters of the world's vanilla production.

Annual production has dropped significantly since then, but the island remains one of the world's leading producers. Cultivation is concentrated on the lush eastern side of the island where the warm, wet conditions are ideal. The pods are harvested between June and September, about eight months after pollination. Still green, they are scalded in boiling water, fermented, then laid out in the sun to dry. Now brown, the pods are then left in airtight containers for two to three months, during which time they develop their strong aroma.

...tus blossom, one of around 500 plant species you can see in ...auritius' famous Pample-mousses Gardens, not far from the ...pital, Port-Louis.

...xuriant passion ...it vines grow all ...er Seychelles. The ...it is used for ...ices.

The delicate hibiscus flower comes in myriad colours, but the bloom only lasts for one day.

Hikers in Belouve forest on Réunion.

Paddling on Blue Bay beach at
Mahebourg, Mauritius.

THE MASCARENES

The Mascarene Islands may form a whole,
but each offers very different landscapes
and completely different experiences.

A local Creole cook.

Named after the Portuguese admiral Pedro Mascarenhas, whose fleet anchored by these uninhabited islands more than 500 years ago, the Mascarenes had lain undisturbed since they rose from the sea in a series of volcanic eruptions millions of years earlier. Even so, their discovery hardly led to a mad rush to colonise. And as far as tourism is concerned, they were a dot on the map until a trickle of visitors arrived in the 1970s.

For most people, Mauritius is the best known island, a favourite with both honeymooners and families, but the French have been holidaying in Réunion for years. If you're in Mauritius, the 35-minute hop to Réunion's capital St-Denis is easy and you can see some of the best of the island in just two or three days if time is limited. For Mauritius regulars, the short hop to Rodrigues is becoming an increasingly attractive proposition, and shouldn't be missed if you've got a few days to spare.

Mauritius is, in many ways, the archetypal romantic idyll, with gorgeous fine-sanded beaches lined with exclusive luxury hotels – sporting world-class golf courses, top-notch spas and gourmet restaurants – whose high standards of service attract the rich and famous.

Get ready to water ski.

Rodrigues, an autonomous part of Mauritius, lies 560km (350 miles) east and is markedly different from the motherland in character and culture. This is the place to come for a taste of authentic, remote island life: just rugged beauty, a warm and welcoming people and serenity.

Just 160km (100 miles) southwest of Mauritius is Réunion Island, where the first thing that strikes you is the awesome nature of the landscape, whose volcano and massive cirques force most islanders to live along the coast – and gives visitors the urge to pull on their hiking boots. Wherever you go you will be beguiled by the mixture of classic Frenchness and local Creole culture.

Few people discover all the islands of the Mascarenes in one trip, but whichever you choose, you're unlikely to be disappointed.

DECISIVE DATES

Early discoverers

10th–12th centuries
Arabs sight the Mascarenes.

15th century
Arab names Dina Arobi, Dina Margabim and Dina Moraze for Mauritius, Réunion and Rodrigues appear on early world maps.

Declaration of the abolition of slavery on Réunion, 1848.

1505–7
Portuguese navigator Diogo Fernandes Pereira names Mauritius the Ilha do Cirne, probably after one of his ships.

1513
The islands are named after Portuguese admiral Pedro Mascarenhas.

1528
A Portuguese seaman Diogo Rodrigues visits Rodrigues and gives the island his name.

The Dutch years

1598
First Dutch landing on Ilha do Cirne. The island is annexed to Holland and renamed Mauritius after Prince Maurice of Nassau, son of William of Orange.

1601
First Dutch landing in Rodrigues.

1638–1710
Dutch settle at Port South East, Mauritius, but abandon it after several attempts to colonise. The first slaves are imported from Madagascar. Sugar cane, deer and pigs from Java are introduced.

1642
The French take possession of Rodrigues and Réunion, which they name Mascareigne and later Bourbon.

1646
First French settlers occupy Bourbon.

1688
Last recorded sighting of dodo on Mauritius.

1691–3
François Leguat and crew become Rodrigues' first settlers.

The French period

1715
France annexes Mauritius, naming it Île de France; it is controlled by the French East India Company.

1721–1810
French occupation of Île de France. Slaves from Madagascar, Africa and Asia are imported to work on sugar cane plantations.

1735
Labourdonnais becomes governor of the Mascarene Islands, based on Île de France. He expands Port Louis.

1756–63
The Seven Years' War so seriously affects French interests in the Indian Ocean that by 1764 the French East India Company is forced to officially hand Île de France to the French crown.

1790
News of the French Revolution reaches the Mascarenes and provokes a rebellion.

1793–1805
Indian Ocean privateering reaches its peak. The French Revolution leads to the creation of colonial assemblies in all the islands. Fear of losing their slaves provokes local resistance to French political emissaries. Bourbon is renamed Réunion.

1799
General Decaen restores order to Île de France in the name of Napoleon after islanders had enjoyed years of autonomy. Slavery continues.

The British period

1810
Weakened by Napoleonic wars, Île de France and Réunion capitulate to British naval forces. Île de France reverts to its former name Mauritius.

1814
The Treaty of Paris places Mauritius, Rodrigues and

Statue of Sir Seewoosagur Ramgoolam.

Seychelles under British ownership, while Réunion reverts to France.

1835
The British abolish slavery in Mauritius and introduce Indian indentured labourers, or 'coolies'.

1848
Slavery is abolished in Réunion.

1885
Mauritians William Newton and Virgile Naz found the Reform Movement, leading to the introduction of the country's own constitution.

The modern age

1909
Indian immigration ceases and political and social reform begins in the Mascarenes.

1936
The Labour Party is formed in Mauritius.

1946
Réunion becomes an overseas French *département*.

1968
Mauritius achieves independence, with Sir Seewoosagur Ramgoolam elected its first prime minister. Rodrigues becomes a dependency of Mauritius.

1982
Sir Seewoosagur Ramgoolam is defeated by a political alliance. Anerood Jugnauth becomes prime minister.

1992
The Republic of Mauritius is declared, with Cassam Uteem as its first president. Rodrigues becomes part of Mauritius.

1995
The Labour Party wins elections in Mauritius under Navin Ramgoolam.

2002
Rodrigues is granted regional autonomy.

2003
Paul Bérenger becomes Mauritius' first non-Indian prime minister.

2005
Navin Ramgoolam returns as prime minister and leader of the Social Alliance Party.

2008
Le Morne Brabant becomes a Unesco World Heritage Site.

2008–10
Construction of Sino-Mauritian Economic and Trade Cooperation Zones at Riche Terre.

2010
The Pitons, Cirques and Remparts of Réunion, covering 40 percent of the island's interior, become a Unesco World Heritage Site. Navin Ramgoolam is re-elected prime minister of Mauritius.

2014
A surprise shake-up at the Mauritius elections sees Anerood Jugnauth return as prime minister.

2015
Debris from the Malaysia Airlines flight MH370 washes up on the shores of Réunion, a year after going missing.

Debris discovered on Reunion belonged to missing flight MH370.

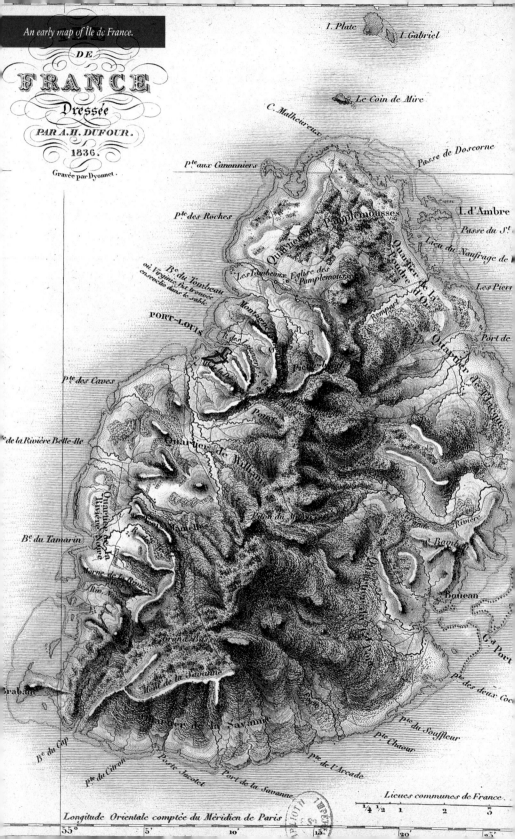

An early map of Île de France.

SAILORS AND EXPLORERS: DISCOVERERS OF THE MASCARENES

From Arabs to Europeans, the history and culture of the Mascarenes has been determined by traders, explorers, colonisers and corsairs.

The Mascarenes were all uninhabited until the arrival of European colonisers in the 16th century. Ever since, these islands have been subjected to the whims of European taste and ambitions which have determined their population, their pursuits and, to a large extent, their politics.

The Mascarenes are oceanic islands – they did not break away from continental land masses but developed independently as a result of volcanic action. Mauritius is the oldest at about 8 million years, Réunion and Rodrigues are around 3 and 2 million years old respectively. The islands are affected by volatile weather conditions; and the vagaries of trade winds and cyclones, which blew countless sailing ships off course or onto reefs, meant that it was as likely accident and misfortune as intrepid exploration that provoked the first sightings of these small land masses in the southwestern Indian Ocean.

The earliest recorded proof of the identification and location of the islands is from Arab documents and maps. Writings dating back to the 12th century include descriptions of islands which may be the Mascarenes. In 1498, Vasco da Gama saw maps by Ibn Majid in which three islands southeast of Madagascar are named Dina Moraze, Dina Margabim and Dina Arobi, which roughly translate as 'eastern', 'western' and 'deserted' islands.

It was not until the early 16th century that Portuguese explorers became the first recorded European visitors to the Mascarenes. They named Mauritius 'Cirne', probably after one of their ships, Réunion 'Santa Apolina' after the date of its discovery and Rodrigues after the navigator Diogo Rodrigues, the only one of the islands to retain its Portuguese

A scene from the 18th-century novel 'Paul et Virginie'.

name. The Portuguese only occasionally used the Mascarenes route on their way to the Indies but it was a welcome place of respite for damaged ships and weary crews which found themselves blown towards these archetypal desert islands.

Nature's bounty

Still uninhabited in the early 17th century, the fertility and unspoilt nature of the Mascarene Islands were extolled by Dutch, French and English visitors. Samuel Castleton, who first set eyes on Réunion in 1613, described thick forest, cascading waterfalls, fat eels in the rivers and plentiful turtles and birds. In homage to its natural beauty, he named the island 'England's Forest'. The Dutchman, Mandelslo, wrote that Mauritius teemed with figs, pomegranates, partridges and pigeons. There were no cats, pigs, goats, dogs or even rats – at least not until some escaped from ships wrecked near Mascarene shores.

These early visitors brought back drawings of a strange flightless bird, indigenous to Mauritius and Réunion. It was described as fat, clumsy and bigger than a turkey. In 1628, Emmanuel Altham sent a live specimen of this 'strange fowle' home to his brother in Essex. This was the dodo (see page 61) whose relative, the solitaire,

> *The Mascarene Island group is named after the Portuguese navigator Pedro Mascarenhas. Like Columbus, he has probably been given more credit than his due, as he did not discover any of them.*

convicts and slaves from Southeast Asia and Madagascar to help them with wood-cutting and crop cultivation. Runaways from these groups combined with soldiers and sailors who deserted from the garrison and visiting ships'

The Dutch settlement at Vieux Grand Port.

was found on Réunion and Rodrigues.

The ebony forests on Mauritius, and its two natural harbours, made it a colonial prize for European traders and explorers. Annexed for the Netherlands in 1598, the Dutch felled much of the valuable black wood on the island, until a glut in the European market slowed the destruction.

Colonisation begins

The Dutch occupied Mauritius twice, between 1638 and 1658, and again from 1664 to 1710. Their first settlement was around the southeast harbour (where present-day Mahébourg is now situated). The garrison and commander, along with a small group of free farmers, brought

crews to form a counter-settlement in the forested interior. They launched frequent raids and arson attacks on the fort and farmers. The difficult conditions of the earlier settlers were made worse by seasonal cyclones, which ripped through their fragile wooden homesteads, and by the depredations of rats who ate the crops and stores. The ruins of the Dutch fort at Vieux Grand Port can be seen to this day, having only been excavated by archaeologists in 1977.

While the Dutch were establishing settlement on Mauritius, the French had annexed the other Mascarene islands. Both nations supplemented piecemeal colonisation by sending unruly settlers from their bases at the Cape, Batavia and Madagascar into exile on the Mascarenes.

Bourbon, later renamed Réunion, was given its royal name by the French governor at Madagascar after hearing from a group of returned exiles of its beauty, abundance and healthiness. In 1654, the French attempted a permanent settlement of the island with a mixed group of French and Malagasy. They left four years later and Bourbon remained unoccupied until 1663.

The next group of settlers included three women, but disputes over them led to the creation of rival camps of French and Malagasy men. Attempts to send volunteers from France met with mixed results – many died en route.

Two events then proved a turning point for Bourbon: firstly the French were massacred on Madagascar, forcing the abandonment of that base, and secondly war with Holland closed off the Cape to French ships. Bourbon now became an important post for them on the Indies route. A governor was appointed from France, and, in a series of efforts to boost the size of the population, Indian convicts were imported, Indo-Portuguese women were induced to settle, and pirates, tired of a life of plunder, were invited to marry into the growing Bourbon community.

Ecological destruction

The glowing description of Bourbon made by its first forced inhabitants had also inspired a group of Protestants, persecuted in France, to set up their Eden on the last remaining desert island of the Mascarenes. François Leguat was one of eight males who settled on Rodrigues until the effects of solitude and the lack of women led them to escape in a small boat to Mauritius.

The reality of life on a tropical desert island was far removed from the visions of recuperating sailors and persecuted Protestants. The small settlements, peopled with prisoners and pirates, neglected by the trading companies, presided over by frustrated commanders and weakly defended, found survival a struggle. Geographical constraints – isolation and unreliable weather – had been revealed to be major determinants of Mascarenes history.

The impact of these visitors from across the seas was immense. The fragile island ecologies were irreparably damaged by human settlement and by the animals they imported that upset the natural balance. The coastal palms and the ebony forests were depleted. Eventually 30 species of birds, including the dodo and solitaire,

and some of the large tortoises and turtles with whom they cohabited, would become extinct – casualties of the fragility of unique small island populations.

The Mascarene Islands have become the archetypal example of the destruction of ecological systems by outsiders. Once this process began, it took only a few decades for these small island 'Edens' to change irrevocably.

The French century

Between 1710, when the Dutch left, and 1810 when the British took control, the French had

Maurice of Nassau.

> The Mascarenes were legendary refuges. Mandelslo's description of a man marooned on Mauritius in 1601 is one of many such tales said to have provided Daniel Defoe with inspiration for his tale of Robinson Crusoe.

a century of uninterrupted supremacy in the Mascarenes. Over this period the islands served several purposes: as a rest and refuelling point for European ships on the Indies route, where goods could be traded and ships repaired; as cultivating grounds for spices and coffee; and as good vantage points for the study of astronomic phenomena.

Already established on Bourbon, in 1721 the French sent a party of colonists from there to settle on Mauritius, renamed Île de France. A governor and several hundred soldiers and colonists were also sent from France, arriving the following year with 30 Malagasy slaves they had acquired en route. They settled in the southeast of the island, building on top of the Dutch ruins. Administered from Bourbon, both islands struggled to master their environment. One visitor to Île de France at this time sarcastically renamed it 'Kingdom of the Rats', describing the discomfort of nights spent trying

visiting ships was regularly supplemented by the organisation of slave trading voyages to East Africa and Madagascar, and the importation of skilled workers from India and France. With serious food shortages threatening the increased population, Labourdonnais introduced manioc to the Mascarenes, which became a staple food of slaves, and began the systematic plunder of tortoises from Rodrigues. This marked the beginning of the irreversible decline of its endemic land and marine fauna, a process accelerated by the periodic presence of naval squadrons.

> The French author of Paul et Virginie, Bernardin de Saint Pierre, observed: 'I do not know whether coffee and sugar are necessary to the happiness of Europe, but they have certainly made much of the world miserable.'

The Mahé de La Bourdonnais statue in Port Louis.

to ignore them crawling over his body.

A decisive change occurred in the administration of the French Mascarenes in 1735, with the arrival of Mahé de Labourdonnais, and the decision to transfer the seat of government to Île de France. For the rest of the 18th century, Bourbon was relegated to what its colonists believed to be the inferior position of 'granary', supplying food for its sister island, and watching as the latter developed into a substantial trading and naval repair post.

Labourdonnais aimed to transform Île de France into a flourishing colony, but his ambitious plans could not be achieved without labour, and from this period, the trickle of West Africans and Asians arriving with

By 1764 the French East India Company, suffering severe financial losses occasioned by years of warfare, gave up control of the Mascarenes to the French king. Port Louis was able to expand its trading activities, which had been limited by the company's monopolistic practices, and developed an air of prosperity and style which led to its designation as the 'Paris of the Indian Ocean'.

But this facade of culture, elegance and profit concealed an economy based on speculation and a society in which the presence of celebrated intellectuals and naturalists could not prevent the continuing destruction of nature and the differentiation of men by colour and chains.

The French had hoped to use the Mascarenes to further their interest in the spice trade and to cultivate tropical produce. Colonists were encouraged to grow coffee, cotton, indigo, sugar cane, cinnamon, tea and pepper. Cloves and nutmegs were introduced. Many crops failed – eaten by birds, rats and monkeys or destroyed by adverse weather conditions. Coffee and spices grown on Bourbon nevertheless became the principal exports of the Mascarenes, while sugar cane was found to resist the onslaught of the elements best on Île de France. Its cultivation, expanding towards the end of the 18th century, was to become the defining feature of the Mascarenes in the 19th century.

Revolution and rebellion

French rule in the Mascarenes had instituted a kind of social apartheid which subjected slaves to the provisions of the Code Noir – a famous law the French applied to their colonies which prevented the free coloured population from marrying white colonists. After 1789, the revolutionary fervour emanating from France swept away such laws and unleashed a chain of events in the French colonies that culminated in the breakaway of Haiti and provoked a rebellion in the Mascarenes.

News of the French Revolution did not reach

representatives to the Mascarenes to put this into effect – they were thrown out within three days. For a while the islands ruled themselves but not without serious disagreements which almost led to Réunion separating from its sister island.

The arrival of Napoleon on the political scene led to the re-establishment of slavery and in 1803 he sent General Charles Decaen to rule, granting him absolute power over the Mascarenes. Réunion was briefly named Bonaparte Island but, once again, did not flourish in the shadow of Île de France. The rigid social

Slaves carrying a palanquin, Ile de France, Mauritius, 1817–1820.

the Indian Ocean islands until the following year, but once ships bearing the tricolour arrived, Colonial Assemblies were set up on the islands and the royal name of Bourbon was changed to Réunion. The revolution was not very bloody in the Mascarenes, although one notable victim was MacNamara, a royalist naval officer who was hacked to death by a mob in Port Louis. Restrictions on mixed marriages between white and coloured colonists were lifted and the gulf between social groups was briefly narrowed.

In 1796, however, the Revolutionary government in France took matters too far for the liking of the colonists. Having proclaimed the abolition of slavery, France sent two

MAHÉ DE LABOURDONNAIS

Mahé de Labourdonnais is fêted in Mauritius and his statue stands in the centre of Port Louis, its capital, because in a few short years he transformed this natural harbour into the beginnings of a flourishing port.

Some of the works he undertook are still in evidence today, including the renovated mill and granary on Port Louis waterfront. Labourdonnais also built a hospital, established a road network and imported the first primitive sugar processing equipment to be used in Mauritius, now seen in the grounds of Pamplemousses Botanical Gardens, formerly the site of his estates.

and fiscal legislation introduced by Decaen was designed for, and discriminated in favour of, the latter.

Pirates, traitors and spies

For Portuguese and particularly British ships plying the route to the Indies, the French Mascarenes were by now chiefly known for being a 'nest of pirates'. Between 1793 and 1802 more than a hundred captured ships were brought into Port Louis, where the booty on offer attracted neutral peoples like the Danes and Americans. The port was also popular with

Robert Surcouf captures the British vessel, Kent, in 1800.

FRIENDLY ENEMIES

Despite the relentless conflict between the two nations during the Napoleonic wars, Anglo–French relations remained chivalrous. When the wife of the English officer commanding the squadron blockading the islands between 1803 and 1810 gave birth to a child on board ship, the French Governor, Decaen, sent her a boatload of fresh produce.

After the battle of Grand Port in 1810 – the only Napoleonic victory over the British that is inscribed on the Arc de Triomphe – the wounded leaders of both forces were treated side by side in what is now the National History Museum of Mahébourg.

---

sailors: the increasing cultivation of sugar cane meant that one of its by-products, rum, was widely available, and it was one of the few places on the Indies route, outside the Cape, where men did not heavily outnumber women.

This privateering (led by the king of the corsairs, Robert Surcouf) was one of the reasons why the British decided to target the Mascarenes. In 1806 they blockaded Île de France, where the celebrated British explorer and naturalist Matthew Flinders was then imprisoned. The British sent an armada from Bombay and the Cape, which regrouped at Rodrigues and took Réunion in July 1810 without much struggle.

Île de France was not so easy a conquest. In August, the British were defeated after a three-day naval battle in Mahébourg bay, known as the battle of Grand Port. In November 1810 they returned to attack with 70 ships and 10,000 troops, landing on the north coast and marching to the capital. Both sides recognised the numerical superiority of the British and General Charles Decaen therefore negotiated an honourable capitulation.

After the conquest, Île de France reverted to its former name, Mauritius. The British retained control of Réunion until 1814, when the Treaty of Paris returned the island to French rule. Louis XVIII is supposed to have commented to the British minister who negotiated the deal: 'You are leaving us the volcano and you are keeping the port.'

Abolition of slavery

The British conquest of Mauritius and Rodrigues, undertaken for strategic motives, did not lead to a large influx of British settlers, and the Francophone character of the Mascarenes has consequently never been lost.

Early British colonial officials not only had to deal with a largely French settler class, but had to implement unpopular slave amelioration laws. The abolitionist movement, which had a massive following in Britain at this time, turned its attention to Mauritius at the worst possible moment for that colony. The island was in the process of converting itself into a plantation society and needed extra labour to clear land and plant canes. When John Jeremie, a known abolitionist, was sent to the island in 1832 to take up an important legal post, the colonists gave him a 'welcome'

In 1811 a slave revolt on Réunion led to the execution of 30 ringleaders. A later uprising in Mauritius was also snuffed out. But for as long as slavery was in force, the Mascarene mountains remained a refuge for runaways.

akin to that received by the delegates from France during the Revolution. A general strike was organised which paralysed the capital and the fearful British governor ordered Jeremie

the first opportunity to import Indian workers under the indenture system. Almost half a million indentured workers were introduced in the 19th century, making Mauritius the largest recipient of Indian labour in the empire and helping the island to achieve the position of Britain's premier sugar colony within a decade.

Both Réunion and Mauritius had turned increasingly to sugar production as falling supplies from the British and French West Indies encouraged the newer colonies to fill the gap. Réunion was given the go-ahead to import Brit-

Indian labourers.

to re-embark almost immediately. In response, the British built the Citadel (Fort Adelaide) on a hill overlooking the capital – a striking symbol of colonial power designed to quell its unruly inhabitants. The colonists were appeased by a £2 million compensation package given to slave owners (including those whose slaves had been illegally introduced) and the day of emancipation passed without incident in 1835.

Immigrant labour

From 1835 the British decided to make Mauritius the site of a 'great experiment' to see whether free labour could produce sugar as cheaply as slaves, by allowing the colony

ish Indian labour from 1860, and both islands continued to recruit smaller numbers of Chinese, Malagasy, Comorian and Mozambican workers. Africans rescued from slave ships by British naval cruisers were also offloaded at Mauritius and the Seychelles from the mid-19th century and 'liberated' into lengthy apprenticeships with local employers.

Réunion adapted to socio-economic change at a more gentle rate than Mauritius. It was slower to abolish slavery (abolition was declared in 1848, 13 years after Mauritius), and slower to develop into a monoculture economy. Both islands, nevertheless, underwent a revolution of sorts, as mechanisation and centralisation of estates transformed them into plantation societies where plantocracies confronted increasing ranks of immigrant labour. Only Rodrigues remained primarily an agricultural colony and did not experience the vast influx of Indian labour which had transformed the demographic characteristics of its neighbours. Administered from Mauritius, Rodrigues was only rarely visited by British governors.

Indentured labourers were contracted to work at a fixed wage for a number of years. Breaches of contract or an inability or unwillingness to work were punishable by impris-

> Mark Twain, who visited Mauritius in 1896, noted a local saying about new settlers: 'The first year they gather shells; the second year they gather shells and drink; the third year they do not gather shells.'

A labourer working in the cane fields in 1956.

onment, and the physical chastisement and limited mobility of Indian workers made their treatment akin to that of slaves. In 1872 and 1877 Commissions of Enquiry were sent to Mauritius and Réunion to compile reports on the conditions of these workers, and they found much evidence of malpractice.

Disease and disaster

When sugar prices began to fall in the last quarter of the 19th century, the distress of the enormously enlarged populations of the islands increased their vulnerability to outbreaks of such deadly diseases as smallpox, cholera and malaria. In 1892, a fierce cyclone hit Mauritius, killing 1,260 people, and making 50,000

homeless, while Réunion experienced periodic eruptions of its active volcano. But the sequence of disasters did not end there – rats once again wreaked devastation on the Mascarenes as bubonic plague struck, and in 1902 a fly-borne parasite necessitated the slaughter of thousands of horses, mules and cattle in Mauritius. The islands were at their lowest ebb and were a far cry from the idyllic Edens encountered barely 200 years before.

With the sugar economy still in a state of depression, the flow of labour immigration had all but ended, but traders, principally Chinese and Gujarati, continued to settle in the Mascarenes, and gradually took over the retail and wholesale sectors. On the other hand, emigration began to take place from Réunion to Madagascar and from Mauritius to South Africa as colonists sought opportunities elsewhere.

Politically, progress was swift in Réunion, which moved from a system of absolute government to one of universal suffrage, and was given the right to be represented in the French Parliament from 1870. Mauritius, by contrast, did not have an elected legislative council and a constitution until 1885. In both islands, however, a few wealthy planter families continued to wield disproportionate influence.

Post-war Mascarenes

World War I brought an increase in sugar prices and a degree of prosperity was restored to the Mascarenes, but by the 1930s the disaffection among labourers had transformed into widely orchestrated strikes on both Mauritius and Réunion.

World War II affected the islands much more directly. The British hurriedly set up naval and air bases on Mauritius, while the Vichy regime, installed on Réunion, isolated the island and brought it to the verge of famine. Following the war, both islands were supplied with a regular air service, becoming increasingly accessible to visitors.

Réunion was given the status of a département or district of France in 1946 (along with Martinique, Guadeloupe and French Guyana). The flow of capital from France produced a socio-economic power shift from the planter class towards the growing public and commercial sectors of the economy.

Departmentalisation entailed a process of assimilation, which Réunion, little touched by the 'negritude' movement of the French Caribbean to assert 'black power', seemed initially disinclined to resist. However, since 1959 when the Communist Party was set up, there

Mauritius against the competing claims of ethnic identity – goes on.

Mauritian independence

Independence was something of a brokered affair in Mauritius, with Britain willingly divesting itself of the island in 1968 in return for the British Indian Ocean Territory created from a group of smaller, dependent islands. The Americans were promptly leased one of these – Diego Garcia – for use as a military base, which has become of increasing importance to them in Indian Ocean geopolitics.

An Indian merchant's shop at Port Louis in 1955.

has always been a movement on the island fighting for the recognition of a distinctively Réunionese identity. This was partly achieved in 1981 when the acknowledgement of a 'right to difference' produced a kind of cultural revolution to accompany the political departmentalisation revolution.

The 1980s was a period of political radicalism in Mauritius also, with the rise of the left-wing Mouvement Militant Mauricien, the MMM, which gained a huge following under the banner of 'One nation, one people'. Both of these movements have ultimately been limited in their effects, and the struggle to create a sense of national identity – Réunion against the linguistic and cultural hegemony of France, and

The cutting of the Suez Canal robbed the Mascarenes of strategic significance. Ironically, the wife of De Lesseps, the man responsible for building the canal, was Mauritian and many of her compatriots worked on the construction.

The growing recognition that independence would lead to rule by the Indian majority led to fears of Hinduisation policies, and the 1968 celebrations were marred by ethnic violence and the emigration of disaffected minorities. Between 1968 and 1982 the ruling Labour Party did indeed become increasingly identified with its Hindu power base, but it was the combination of corruption scandals, overpopulation and high unemployment which swept the opposition MMM into office in the early 1980s. The shift to radicalism was short-lived. Since then, Mauritius has been governed by a series of coalitions of four principal parties – Labour, the MMM, the PMSD and the PSM – all of which have a pro-capitalist stance. The 2014 elections brought back former prime minister Aneerood Jugnauth, indicating that Mauritians were not quite ready for a change.

Aneerood Jugnauth.

In 1992, Mauritius became a Republic, and the Queen was replaced as head of state by a locally nominated president.

Rodrigues, formerly a dependency of Mauritius, is politically integrated with its sister island. In 2002 the island was granted regional autonomy.

Economically the islands remain fragile, although Mauritius has gone furthest down the road towards diversification with manufacturing and textile production. Until 2003 Mauritius earned more money exporting manufactured goods than from sugar exports. But changes to international sugar pricing agreements hit the sugar industry hard, and textile factory closures caused by cheap competition from India and China have increased unemployment.

Sugar barons are now turning their lands over to tourism and real estate development. Tourism brings more than a million visitors annually, while it is hoped that financial services and communications technology – the latest additions to the economy – will provide new jobs to replace those lost in other sectors.

Some Rodriguans have sought a share in the development of their country's infrastructure by migrating to work on Mauritius, as their own island lags behind in resource-allocation – its economy remains largely agricultural and youth unemployment is high. The economic prosperity which has kept ethnic frustrations at bay in this two-island Republic has been unfairly redistributed, with the Afro-Creole populations on both islands feeling increasingly aggrieved. In 1999 widespread rioting on Mauritius constituted a clear signal that socio-economic disparities were a source of tension. It remains to be seen whether the Mauritian political elite will respond effectively. As yet, little has changed.

Réunion inhabits a position midway between the developed and developing nations. Its health and education infrastructure are akin to those of 'first world' states, while its economy lags far behind. Unlike Mauritius, Réunion has not been able to develop a significant Export Processing Zone because wages are too high. The island has its own appeal for tourists, but lacks the plentiful beaches that have made the Seychelles and Mauritius internationally known as holiday destinations. The Chaudron riots of February 1991 underscored the problems of social inequalities and high unemployment that persist in Réunion. Ironically, these disturbances occurred at a time when the French government had at last begun to address the demands of the overseas *départements* for social and economic parity. Réunion has also been active in forging a regional identity: taking part in projects of regional cooperation with its Indian Ocean neighbours.

The Mascarenes constitute one of the few regions where Francophony continues to make advances against the worldwide dominance of the English language. The French have clearly returned to their 18th-century bastion in the Indian Ocean, ready to stand their ground in the 21st century, less in military than in political and cultural terms.

Death of the dodo

The most famous of Mauritius' unique wildlife might be the dodo. The island's national emblem, it continues to fascinate the world 400 years after its destruction.

This giant, flightless bird, which developed from the pigeon family and was killed off in the 17th century, has become a byword for stupidity and a symbol of man's destructiveness, throughout the world.

The dodo was first seen in Asia and Europe in the 17th century when Dutch sailors brought live specimens from Mauritius to the world's attention. Their name for the bird is thought to derive from Dutch words meaning 'round arse'. The Dutch described the bird as fearless of man, ungainly, so fat that it could not run, and so foolish that it did not recognise danger. In pre-Darwinian days, the dodo was seen as an example of a mistake made by God, and later as an evolutionary failure. In Grant's *History of Mauritius* published in England in 1801 it is described as a 'feathered tortoise', an easy target for hunters.

For many years, contemporary paintings and written descriptions of the birds were practically all that were known of them – only a disputed claw and other remnants having survived from the birds brought to Europe. Naturalists began to argue that the dodo was a figment of sailors' rum-fuelled imagination. In the mid-19th century, however, dodo bones were dug up at Mare aux Songes and models of the bird were constructed and placed in museums throughout the world. Lewis Carroll saw one such model at the University Museum in Oxford, which evidently sparked his imagination – the flightless bird was immortalised in *Alice in Wonderland*.

The real dodo

With the reality of the dodo's existence, and its fame now firmly established, naturalists began to turn their attention to the bird itself. Travellers' accounts and cultural artefacts were re-examined along with the skeletal evidence unearthed in the 20th century. Bones excavated in Rodrigues were found to belong to a similar bird with longer legs, named the solitaire. These findings vindicated the account of French Huguenot, François Leguat, two centuries before.

The overweight, ungainly dodo was rehabilitated when it was discovered that the bird ate seasonally and was both fast and trim at other times of the year.

The new slimline model of the dodo is now on display in several museums. Naturalists also absolved the Dutch from the ignominy of killing the last dodo. While men were the catalyst of its destruction, it was the pigs, rats and monkeys they introduced to Mauritius which ate the eggs and chicks.

Some facts about the dodo remain to be elucidated. Travellers' accounts speak of a grey dodo in Mauritius and a white dodo in Réunion. Others assert that the dodo in Réunion was more like a solitaire. It is clear that a similar large bird to the dodo and solitaire was found on Réunion but no bone discoveries have been made. Scientists in the UK are now

An artist's impression of the dodo, which was extinct by 1661.

attempting to use new genetic techniques to re-create the dodo, so we may one day see the bird back in what remains of its natural habitat. Until then, the dodo remains the world's most famous example of extinction, food for thought when we visit today's examples of rare species in Mauritius.

Île aux Aigrettes, just off the southeast coast of Mauritius, is thought to be the site of the dodo's extinction. Since 1987, the MWF (Mauritius Wildlife Foundation) has been working on restoring the island's original ecosystem. Obviously it's too late for the dodo, but the pink pigeon has been saved from the same fate and can be seen flying free here. Most hotels organise day trips to the island and a percentage of the cost goes towards wildlife conservation.

Graviers beach on Rodrigues.

Livestock for sale at Port Louis's Central Market.

MAURITIUS

Mauritius, as its people will tell you, is a tropical paradise, but there's more to the island than beaches and hotels.

Windsurfer at the Paradis Hotel and Golf Club.

Bounded by a coastline littered with glittering beaches, protected by a virtually unbroken coral reef, Mauritius fulfils fantasies of a tropical island paradise. Furthermore, its excellent hotels offer everything most visitors could possibly want, from plentiful water sports to gourmet restaurants, top-notch golf courses to world-class spas. The quality of the service you will receive is not due simply to good training, but also to the genuine good nature of the people of Mauritius. And, with ice-cold drinks served to your sun lounger, it can be hard to drag yourself away to explore inland.

Mauritius has its fair share of traditional tourist attractions, notably Pamplemousses Botanical Gardens, some wonderful old plantation houses, and museums – not forgetting the eco-adventure tours, animal parks and colourful local markets. It is an island ripe for exploring: take a scenic drive among coastal fishing communities or discover the verdant plateau at the heart of the island, once the floor of a gigantic volcano which blew its top and left behind the jagged peaks and rock formations that now characterise Mauritius' scenery. Rainfall on the plateau feeds many rivers and streams, providing abundant irrigation for the sugar cane fields that cover most of the island's arable land, as well as waterfalls to visit.

Sega dancer.

Mauritius is a multicultural society, with a diversity of races and cultures living side by side. Brightly coloured Hindu temples and shrines glisten in the sun, and some Mauritians of Indian descent wear the traditional clothes of their forbears, while Creole fishermen still set sail in traditional wooden pirogues. Hardly a week goes by without some celebration or religious ritual taking place, from Tamil fire-walking and Hindu body-piercing ceremonies to Catholic pilgrimages and Chinese dragon dances.

But, in reality, although you'll be pleasantly surprised by the attractions of this island and its people, you will always be drawn back to the sea. Whether you end up lazing by a lagoon or diving over the coral reef, it is probably the delectable coast that will remain imprinted on your mind long after returning home.

Locals shopping in Port Louis.

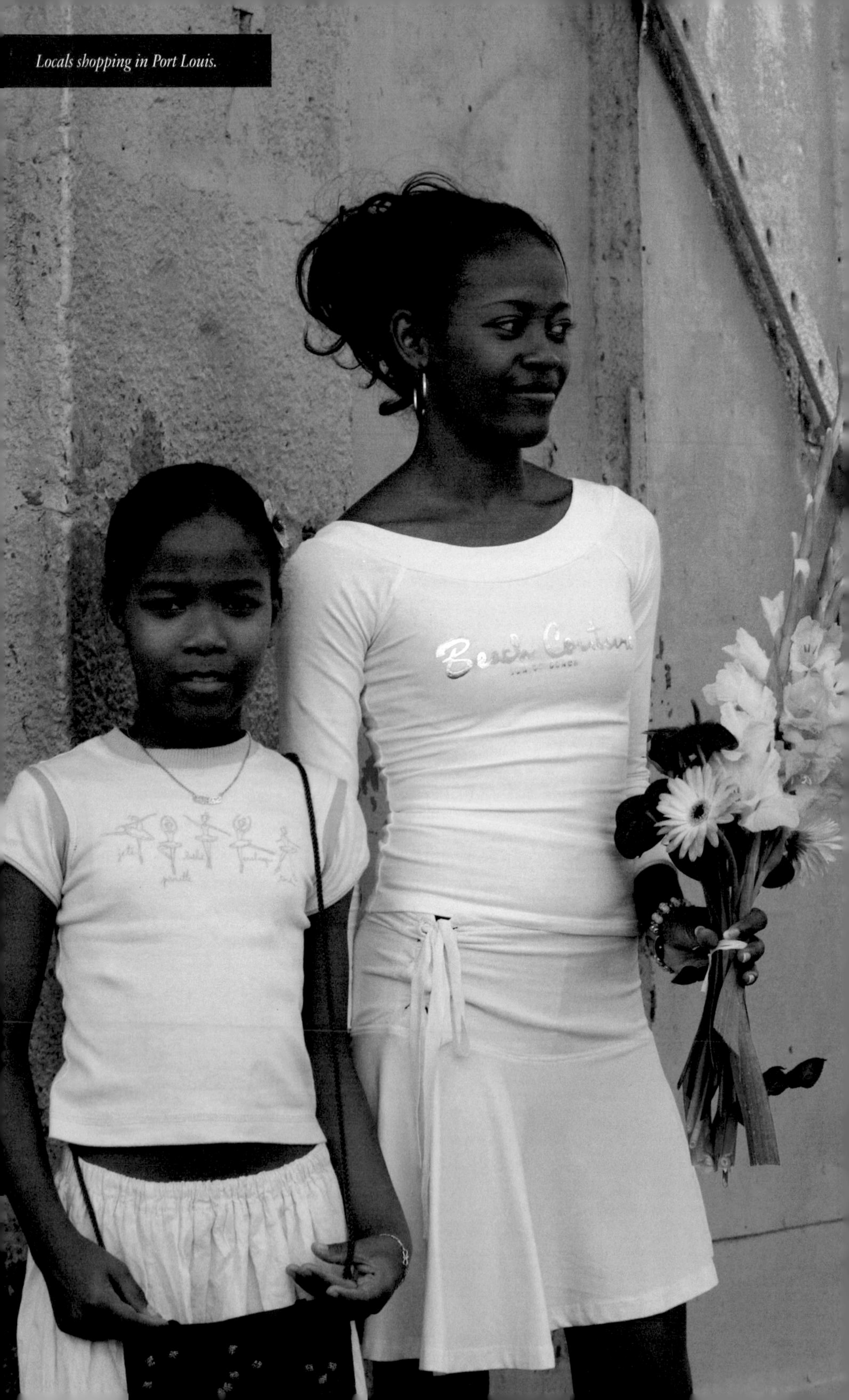

THE MAURITIANS

The complexity of ethnic groups in Mauritius is bewildering, but Mauritians are happy to explain the intricacies of their nation.

I t is said that Mauritians only consider themselves such when abroad – at home they are first and foremost members of a community. Descended from immigrants from Europe, Asia and Africa, the ethnic mix of the island population is both fascinating and incredibly complex. Racism does not exist in Mauritius – or so its political leaders claim – but colour, creed and language continue to divide its people.

Origins, religions and cultures

The French colonial period, which lasted just under a century, until 1810, has left an enduring legacy in Mauritius. The Franco-Mauritians are a distinctive community who trace their ancestry to the early white settlers and, while numerically very small, remain important in economic terms. Slaves and free labourers from Africa and Asia who also arrived in the 18th century are now mostly subsumed into the Creole population. Within this group, characterised not by ethnic homogeneity but by a shared religion – Catholicism – an old hierarchy that favoured those of mixed origin and lighter skin still persists.

In the 19th century, during British rule, large-scale Indian immigration transformed the island's demography. Two-thirds of the population is now of Indian origin. These Indo-Mauritians are not a homogeneous group, but are divided on regional, caste and religious lines. About 15 percent of the population are Muslims, mostly from Bihar – known, confusingly, as Calcuttyas, to distinguish them from the smaller, endogamous groups of mainly Gujarati Muslims. The Hindus, who constitute around 50 percent, also differentiate themselves along regional lines with a larger Bihari Hindu component and smaller Tamil, Telegu and Marathi

Clothing stall proprietress, Port Louis Central Market.

minorities. The Bihari Hindus play a key role in politics – every prime minister since Independence, apart from Paul Bérenger, has been a member of this community.

Other small minorities include the 3,000 or so Chinese, who mostly came during the mid-19th century to engage in commerce, and still run many of the shops, while now also important in the professions and other sectors of the economy. The Chinese have embraced Catholicism, but many continue to practise Buddhist traditions in the home. Even today, most Mauritians marry within their community, and although mixed weddings are becoming more common, shared religious belief remains a strong element in the choice of a life partner.

Despite Mauritius being a British colony between 1810 and 1968, the English did not settle in large numbers, and those who have remained have generally intermarried, mainly into the Franco or Creole communities. The most visible legacy of British rule is on the roads, where the British system of driving and signage is used.

A multilingual society

The mother tongue of most Mauritians is Kreol. The language of education and government is English, and that of the media overwhelmingly French. To add to this linguistic complexity, Official forms at customs/immigration or at police stations are in English. Indo-Mauritians generally have at least a basic knowledge of Hindi, and if you attempt a few words in the island's lingua franca, Kreol, you will be sure to raise a smile (for a short list of Kreol words and phrases, see page 368).

Religious life

Religion is a way of life in Mauritius, and mosques, churches and temples have full and thriving congregations. The islanders put as much effort into the preparations for Hindu,

Hindu ladies preparing to make temple offerings.

French. To add to this linguistic complexity, some Indo-Mauritians can only converse in Bhojpuri, a regional dialect based on Hindi, while the older generation of Chinese are more proficient in Cantonese or Hakka than their adoptive tongues. The so-called 'ancestral languages' of Mauritians of Asian origin are actively promoted by members of these communities, and state controlled television and radio are obliged to broadcast in all the community languages. The island's cinemas show either Hollywood films dubbed in French, or Bollywood productions in Hindi.

Visitors to Mauritius will find that most islanders are reasonably proficient in English, though they are more at ease with French.

FORMS OF ADDRESS

Human interaction in Mauritius is a compelling mix of the formal and the endearing. Old habits of deference linger in the custom of politely addressing even the children of influential people as *Mamzelle* and *Misié (Monsieur)*. A middle aged person might be hailed as *tonton/tantine* (uncle/auntie). Once on friendly terms, you might be jokingly referred to as a *cousin* or *cousine*. Indo-Mauritians have specific terms for relatives on the paternal or maternal side, some in common use. For example, the first prime minister of Mauritius, Sir Seewoosagur Ramgoolam, is affectionately termed *chacha*, or uncle.

Muslim or Catholic festivals as other societies do for their annual carnivals. The biggest crowd-puller in Mauritius is still a pilgrimage and all the major religions organise such events. The island's public holidays take account of the different communities, so at least one festival of every ethnic group is celebrated. Non-participating Mauritians may organise a family picnic at the beach on such occasions.

Weddings are another common weekend activity on the island. Hindu nuptials take place over several days, and innumerable sittings are organised in marquees for guests, who

Folklore and superstition

Diverse beliefs and practices, some originating in the popular customs which African and Asian immigrants brought to the island, have persisted into modern-day Mauritius. There are all kinds of quirky customs and taboos, ranging from cutting your toenails only at certain times of day to leaving out food to pacify malevolent spirits. Chinese Mauritians are partial to the number nine, as their car numberplates testify.

Local sorcerers, known as *longanistes* or *traiteurs*, have followers from diverse backgrounds, and are called in to settle quarrels, exact revenge,

Young boys on the dock.

are served vegetarian curries on a banana leaf. The bride will wear a traditional red or cream sari, and her groom – probably for the only time in his life – will don an ornate turban, and slippers. Muslim weddings are characterised in Mauritius by the serving of a biryani meal, accompanied by a soft drink, generally Pepsi. The ceremony, or *nikah*, is shorter than that of Hindus, and at some gatherings male and female guests are accommodated in separate areas. Weddings of Catholics, be they Chinese, Creole or Franco-Mauritian, generally involve a ceremony at the local church, followed by a reception. Sooner or later, at most functions, the sega will be played and guests of all ages will join the dancing (see page 73).

reverse bad luck and administer love potions. When one's spouse or lover loses interest, a rival may well be suspected of having used the services of a sorcerer. Cemeteries are powerful sites for such practitioners of magic, and they can often be seen at midday, sacrificing a small chicken, breaking coconuts, and lighting candles on the graves, surrounded by a small knot of followers.

The phenomenon of the loup garou, or werewolf, is a good example of how a popular belief can become a serious issue in Mauritius given propitious circumstances. In 1994 a serious cyclone, Hollanda, brought down most of the island's electricity pylons, leaving many areas without power for several weeks. During this time, the notion that a loup garou was on the loose took hold of the popular imagination. Women claimed to have been raped by the creature, and there were daily sightings. The loup garou became front page news for several weeks, and hysteria mounted daily, with women and children barricading themselves indoors. The police issued a communiqué, assuring people that it was tackling the problem, and only when the issue took on a communal dimension, with Muslims asserting that the werewolf was hiding in a Catholic shrine, and inter-religious tensions increased, did the president intervene, disputing the existence of such a creature.

Herbal teas for sale at the Central Market in Port Louis.

KAYA

Joseph Reginald Topize was born in Roche Bois in 1960 and began his singing career in the early 1980s. He called himself 'Kaya' after one of Bob Marley's albums and his 'seggae' (a fusion of reggae and sega), dreadlocks and pot-smoking gained him a following among young islanders. In 1999, Kaya's death in police custody sparked off communal riots on a scale not seen since Independence. He has become a symbol of discrimination against Afro-Creoles. The president, sensing that things could turn ugly, pleaded with the nation to form a human chain around the island to symbolise solidarity among Mauritian ethnic groups.

Community, class and generation

It is one of the peculiarities of Mauritian society that any seemingly insignificant object can become an ethnic signifier. Here, the company you work for, the kind of car you drive, even the type of soft drink you buy, is often a decision governed by communal factors. The reason may simply be that the importer of a certain make of vehicle or product is a member of your community, influencing your decision. There is a popular saying in Mauritian Kreol, '*sak zako bizin protez so montan*' (each monkey must protect his mountain), which refers to the tendency to put members of one's own ethnic group before others.

That tensions sparked by the prevalence of favouritism and nepotism do not erupt into more serious violence can be attributed to the pragmatism of most Mauritians and to the elaborate balancing act performed by all governments. In fact, ministerial posts are assigned in cabinet so that members of competing caste and ethnic groups each have at least one representative. Alongside relatively recent strategies of ethnic lobbying, the old demon of racial discrimination still exists, however. Widespread rioting in 1999, following the suspicious deaths of a number of Afro-Creoles in police custody, highlighted the frustrations of this group, who are most affected by the persistence of racial stereotyping.

The generational differences in Mauritius are also marked, but may ultimately be an antidote to the long-standing divisions based on community and colour. School is a bastion of cultural mixing in a society with a large youth population, and increasing exposure of teenagers to Western media is impacting on old preconceptions. While most Mauritian girls still do not have the freedom of their Western counterparts, or even of their male peers, dance clubs provide a means of socialising that was not available to their mothers.

Mauritius today is a fascinating blend of the spiritual and the material. A place where the accountant working in the booming offshore sector will take a day off to participate in a religious pilgrimage, maybe buying a herbal infusion from a stallholder at the Port Louis bazaar – who claims to know the remedies for all the world's ailments – which he will sip as he logs on to the internet, effortlessly combining 'olde worlde' beliefs with an enthusiasm for all that modern technology has to offer.

Sega

The sensual dance unique to the Mascarenes and Seychelles may have its roots in Africa, but it is performed by all island communities at celebrations today.

Sega goes back at least to the early 18th century, when it evolved as the soul dance of the African slaves as a form of escapism from the harsh reality of their daily lives. After a long week toiling in the cane fields, they would gather around a fire drinking alembic (home-brewed rum) and singing and dancing what became known as the sega.

Sega has been described as 'an erotic dance that leaves little to the imagination', as 'provocative in the extreme' or even as 'a simulated sexual act'. The movements are sensuous and the flirtation real, but however tempestuous it becomes, the sensuality is controlled and it is never obscene.

The original sega instruments were made from anything the slaves could lay their hands on. The ravan (a goatskin tambour), maravan (a hollowed out tube filled with dried seeds) and triang (a triangular-shaped piece of old iron) were played, along with anything else that could produce a sound – pots and pans, empty bottles and spoons. The ravan, maravan and triang are still played, but modern *ségatiers* also use guitars and keyboards.

The accompanying songs, often scattered with double entendres and sexual overtones, are today an added amusement. In the past, these songs were also a way for the slaves to express their pent up feelings and vent their anger on their masters, whom they ridiculed in the lyrics.

Sega today

Although its roots are in Africa, sega in its present form is found only in Mauritius, Rodrigues, Seychelles and Réunion, and each place has its own particular version (see page 253). In classical Mauritian sega, or *sega typic*, the women begin the dancing. They hold out their bright, long skirts in both hands and sway to the rhythmic music, swinging their hips to reveal a glimpse of leg, enticing the men to join them. As more and more dancers join in, shuffling their feet and swaying to the powerful beat of the drums, the dance develops into a sort of courtship drama. Both men and women try to attract a partner of their choice. The women are teasing and provocative,

changing partners, until they single out their man. The men stretch out their arms as if to catch a dancer they admire or to prevent their chosen partner from escaping. When at last a pair form, the woman leans backwards while the man extends his body over hers, at which point the singers may encourage the dancers by shouting *'enba! enba!'*, literally 'get down!' Then they swap positions and the woman dances above the man while he lies on the floor inviting her to come lower and lower. The drumbeats become more frenzied as the dancers move closer to each other – they never touch. Onlookers may be forgiven for thinking that anything could happen next. But the

A traditional sega dance.

crescendo of the drum reaches a dramatic climax and, on a last exciting beat, ceases.

Nowadays, classical sega in Mauritius is mostly associated with the Rivière Noire area on the west coast. Public holidays are the best time to try to catch authentic performances; you may be lucky enough to see locals gathered around a fire on the beach, drinking rum and spontaneously breaking into dance.

'Sega hotel'

However, if the only sega performance you get to see is at your hotel, you may well wonder what the fuss is all about. 'Sega hotel', as the locals call it, is a refined, formalised version of the dance. It makes a pretty sight but is often nothing to get excited about – though you may be asked to join in.

CEREMONIES & CELEBRATIONS

This multicultural society's festival calendar is full all year, but the colourful Hindu and Tamil celebrations draw the biggest crowds.

So many festivals are celebrated in Mauritius that visitors are bound to see one or more in any month of the year. The majority emanate from the Indian communities and they are great and colourful occasions of religious celebration.

Cavadee (Thai Poosam) is a Tamil festival which is celebrated in January or February. It is an amazing if blood-curdling sight. Tamil devotees pierce their bodies with needles; some also partake in fire-walking ceremonies. The Cavadee – a wooden arch decorated with flowers with a brass pot of milk attached to each end – is carried in a procession to the temple, where it is placed before the Tamil deity, Muruga.

Holi is a raucous two-day festival held in February or March. It begins with a bonfire on which an effigy of the evil demon Holika is burnt. Men, women and children then all join in squirting coloured water and smearing red and purple powders on each other's faces and hair.

Divali is the Hindu's happiest festival. Celebrated in October or November, at the darkest period of the autumn months, it marks the victory of Rama (an incarnation of Vishnu) over the demon Ravana and also commemorates Krishna's destruction of the demon Narakasuran. Candles and simple earthen lamps are lit around houses, gardens and even at business premises to brighten the moonless night.

Women making offerings during a Hindu ceremony at Beau Champ on Mauritius's east coast.

The festival of Holi is characterised by red, the colour of joy f Hindus. Be careful not to get caught in the line of fire during the water and powder battles – unless, of course, you want to join in the fun.

On the day of Thai Poosam several processions are held in the major towns. They usually start from a river and end at the temple.

Devotees immerse a huge statue of the Hindu elephant god Ganesh in the sea at Belle Mare, eastern Mauritius.

PILGRIMAGE TO GRAND BASSIN

In 1972 sacred water from the Ganges was poured into Grand Bassin lake, which is some 550 metres (1,800ft) above sea level, after which it became known to the Hindus as Ganga Talao – the Lake of the Ganges. It is the most sacred spot on the island for Mauritian Hindus, presided over by a statue of Shri Mangal Mahadev. Candy-coloured temples are scattered around, along with altars where islanders come at weekends to lay fruit and flowers as offerings, burn incense and pray. One of the most important festivals for the Mauritian Hindu community is Maha Shivaratree (February/March) which is celebrated in honour of Lord Shiva, also known as the upholder of the sacred Ganges. Following an all-night vigil, Hindu pilgrims, dressed in white, make their way to the lake carrying bamboo structures decorated with flowers and multicoloured bells. At the lake, devotees offer prayers to Lord Shiva and other deities. Some bathe and many take the sacred water home. The whole colourful scene is reminiscent of the great rituals on the banks of India's holy Ganges.

an act of penance, some Tamil devotees pierce their faces d bodies with skewers and needles during Cavadee; some er the whole torso, front and back.

ebrating Divali.

Praying at a statue of Shiva at holy lake Grand Bassin, for the Hindu festival of Maha Shivaratree.

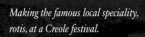
Making the famous local speciality, rotis, at a Creole festival.

CUISINE OF THE MASCARENES

Local cuisine is an inspiring combination of
Indian, Creole, French and Chinese influences,
using local produce with great flair.

The people of the Mascarene Islands, whose ancestors came from Europe, Africa, India and China, are dab hands at throwing together a bit of this and a bit of that and turning out a cuisine as richly diverse as its people. Ever since Mauritius was discovered in the 16th century, colonial powers popped in and out, each leaving their own gastronomic legacy. The Portuguese brought pigs and monkeys, the Dutch introduced deer and sugar, the French brought fruit trees and spices. Indian and Chinese incomers brought rice, while African slaves utilised the lands' natural bounty of fruit, greens and wild animals. Out of this cultural melting pot came a unique cuisine.

Key ingredients

Rice is at the heart of both Mauritian and Réunionnais cuisine. Whether you dine in upmarket restaurants or gather round *en famille* you'll find mountains of it – plain boiled, fried or steeped in saffron. Noodles are a popular alternative and come in all shapes and sizes, from the vermicelli-like *meefoon*, ideal for a light bite, to the gut-busting fried version, *mine frite*. As versatile as a plain pizza base, you can ring the changes with chicken, meat or seafood (the '*mine frite* special' comes with a bit of each).

Seafood here is as good as you would expect on a tropical island. It is prepared in a mouth-watering range of ways – fat shrimps and octopus, firm and flaky *cordonnier* (surgeon fish), *cateaux* (parrotfish) and the close-textured *licorne* come stewed, curried and fricasseed. *Carangue* (trevally fish), *bourgeois* (red snapper) and *vieille rouge* (grouper) are marinated in lemon juice, oil and spices and simply grilled. *Capitaine* (white snapper) is good in a bouillabaisse or oven-baked.

Creative seafood with a view at Shanti Maurice Hotel.

Meat appears in similar guises. Beef, chicken and even the humble sausage are thrown into casseroles and curries. Venison, usually curried or served in a thick sauce, and *cochon marron* (wild boar), traditionally served with sweet potato, are seasonal foods, reserved for special occasions.

Eating out

There are scores of restaurants, bars, cafés and fast food outlets to choose from. Restaurants usually close by 11pm and booking is rarely necessary. Generally, the atmosphere is relaxed, the service good and, compared to hotel dining, prices are very reasonable.

Nearly every restaurant menu lists Indian, Creole, Chinese and European dishes. Standard fare includes the spicy Indian *vindaye* curry and *bri-ani*, a typical Muslim dish made with beef, venison or meaty fish; *bol renversée*, literally 'upturned bowl', a quirky Creole rice dish with slivers of pork, spicy sausage and chunks of chicken; *fooy-ang*, a Mauritianised Chinese omelette, filled with lobster, crab or prawn; *rougaille*, a Mediterranean type of stew made with any meat or fish cooked in a mixture of fried tomatoes, onions, garlic, herbs and ginger; and *daube*, a smoother version of *rougaille*. Among the many exotic vegetables you'll come across are heart of palm (*coeur de palmiste*) or 'millionaire's salad', *gros pois*

Barbequeuing fish on a hot grill in Port Louis.

MONKEY BUSINESS

The monkeys that inhabit the forests of Mauritius are not protected, and are seen as a pest. They are still hunted for their meat, though the practice is becoming rare and the meat isn't for sale anywhere. However, some enterprising hunters are well paid for their troubles by licensed exporters and 6,000 live monkeys a year are shipped to overseas labs. Other local delicacies you won't find on the average tourist menu include curried tenrec, or hedgehog, curried chauve-souris or fruit bat, and mouches jaunes… crispy fried wasp larvae! However unappealing this may sound, people risk life and limb to shake them from their nests.

(fat butter beans), *brèdes* (fresh greens), *lalo* (lady's fingers) and a variety of pumpkin and marrow.

Mauritians often pick up their lunch from street vendors who serve spicy snacks such as *gâteaux piments* (fried lentil and chilli balls), curry-filled *samousas* and *dal puris* (lentil-based pancakes filled with vegetables and sauces), along with a variety of soups and noodle dishes, all eaten piping hot. Take a couple of days to acclimatise before sampling any roadside snacks, which can cause tummy upsets.

Home cooking

If you are lucky enough to be invited to someone's home, go with an open mind and an empty stomach. You could be offered anything from smoked marlin or a spice-packed meat *massala* to Indian-style pancakes (known as *puri*, *roti*, *chapati* and *farata*, depending on how they're cooked). Few islanders serve Creole food without rice. The Japanese 'rice cooker' is as common in the Mauritian kitchen as the microwave is in Western homes. Another key utensil is the wok, into which just about anything edible is thrown and stir-fried to perfection. Less common in an age of ready-made spices is the curry stone, the Indian equivalent of a pestle and mortar, which is used to make *massala*, a curry paste made of ground turmeric, coriander, black pepper, nutmeg, ginger, garlic and as many chillies as the cook or guests can stand. Chillies turn up everywhere, either in a dish or as an accompaniment. Strengths vary, so be warned.

Mauritians buy their bread fresh every day. In addition to crusty French-style loaves, most bakeries offer a choice of croissants, choux buns and sweet or savoury puff pastries, but other than the rich milk-based Indian sweetmeats, you won't find a great variety of cakes and puddings, which are reserved for special occasions. Fruit is the most common dessert and home cooks are experts at throwing together fruity creations from their own back gardens: pawpaws, mangos and lychees parade alongside sweet pineapples, tiny gingli bananas, watermelons and guavas.

Drinks

Some very palatable white and rosé wines are made in Mauritius from imported grape concentrate and labels to look for are Chateau Bel Ombre, Eureka and Saint Nicholas. The purist can buy imported South African and Australian wines. French wine does not always travel well and is more expensive. The best beer brands to go for are the locally brewed Phoenix and Stella, and the slightly stronger Blue Marlin. Better still are craft beers produced by The Flying Dodo, the island's own microbrewery. Mauritian men drink imported or local whisky, and neat rum. Rum cocktails and punches are popular with women who drink. The best local rum brand is Green Island, although it's the island's artisanal rums, from St Aubin and Chateau Labourdonnais, that are making waves on the world stage.

Of the usual range of fizzy drinks on offer, Pepsi reigns supreme. Fresh fruit juices are pop-

cephalopod turns up fried, grilled or curried on most of Port Mathurin's restaurant menus. The lagoon is nature's larder, from which lobster and crab are simply steamed, or prawns are smothered in chilli-rich tomato sauce. *Cono-cono*, similar to the whelk, makes a light lunch when mixed with salad, while freshly caught fish, cooked Chinese-style in ginger and garlic, wakens the taste buds. But for a typical Rodriguan meal, try *carri de poulet aux grains*, chicken curry with red beans and mashed maize served on fluffy white rice.

There is no such thing as genetically modified vegetables in Rodrigues and the meat, poultry

Piles of red and green chillis for sale.

ular and Indian *lassi* is a refreshing yoghurt and water drink. For something more Mauritian, try *alooda*, a Persian import comprising of coconut milk, basil seeds, rosewater and gelatine.

Tea comes in a variety of vanilla-flavoured strengths, with the Bois Cheri brand a favourite. If you prefer vanilla-free tea, a choice of local brands is available. Most hotels and restaurants offer filter and espresso coffees. The locally produced Chamarel coffee is palatable, but pricey because it is produced in small quantities.

Rodriguan specialities

Rodrigues is famous in Mauritius for its food. Octopus fishing is one of Rodrigues' greatest industries so it's hardly surprising that this

and fish are additive-free. Onions, limes, lemons and chillis form the basis of the famous mind-blowing *chatinis* (chutney) and *achards* (sun-dried pickles). Some of the hottest chillies on earth are grown in the back gardens of Rodrigues; crammed into bottles and preserved for posterity, the tiny green ones are so ragingly hot that Mauritians and Réunionnais make special trips to bring them home.

The little luxuries of life may be absent in Rodrigues, decent coffee being one of them, but there's no lack of sticky puddings. Many of these are creolised versions of old-fashioned stodgy puddings, such as *pain frit* (fried bread sprinkled with sugar), *gâteau patate* (sweet potato cake) and *gâteau manioc* (manioc pudding).

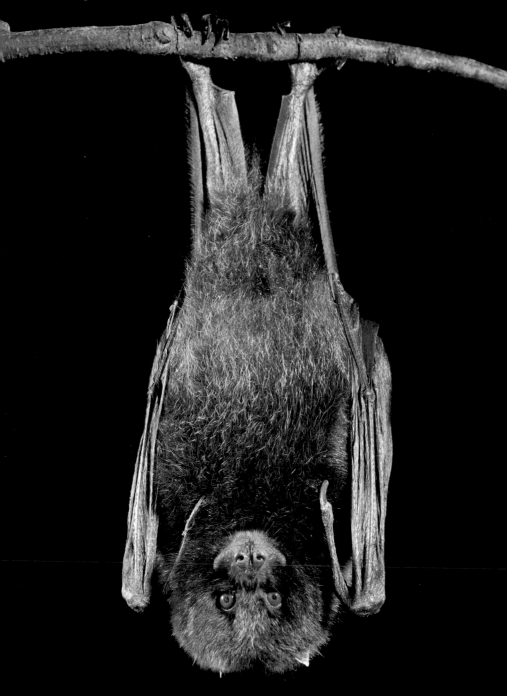

A Rodrigues flying fox, native to the island, roosting.

BATS, BIRDS AND BANYAN TREES

With the help of conservationists, the native
wildlife is starting to flourish in the protected
parks and reserves of Mauritius and Rodrigues.

For the naturalist, tropical oceanic islands
are akin to a Pandora's box of the unique
and strange. Once upon a time, Mauritius
and Rodrigues were home to flightless birds,
giant tortoises and dwarf lizards, but today there
are other species, equally remarkable in their
own way, that still live on these islands and surrounding islets isolated in the Indian Ocean.

Originally, wildlife had to get here by flying,
swimming or hitching a ride and many species are now endemic. But since the nearest
land mass is Madagascar, 855km (550 miles)
away, the only mammals that made it over on
their own were bats and sea mammals. Due
to the lack of land predators, reptiles evolved
from the latter and birds had no problem
establishing themselves here, bringing seeds
from other lands which grew up into hardwood forests. In the 17th century, humans
arrived, triggering the demise of many species
of flora and fauna.

A Mauritius lowland forest day gecko.

Conservation efforts

During the past 50 years, conservationists have
been hard at work, and their endeavours can
now be witnessed in small protected areas, such
as the Black River Gorges and Île aux Aigrettes,
supporting the remaining original forests that
are home to the island's wildlife.

Giant fruit bats are still going strong and the
Mauritian fruit bat is a truly stunning animal
with a wingspan of about a metre (nearly 4ft)
and a furred body that varies from dark brown
to a gorgeous golden orange. Around 20,000 of
these bats range over the island at night and
feed on fruits in gardens and forests. By day they
sleep in gorges or on mountain sides hanging
on trees in huge colonies of up to a thousand. A
roost can be seen beneath the Black River Peak

WILDLIFE WATCH

Forests in the Black River Gorges National Park
shelter a large proportion of Mauritian endemic
wildlife. Well mapped out trails allow visitors to
see these endangered animals and plants, now
part of a major conservation programme. Go to
the Black River Visitor Centre, or the Pétrin
Information Centre (near Grand Bassin) for details
of walks and sites to explore. The Île aux Aigrettes
nature reserve off Mahébourg is gradually being
restored to its pristine state. The island is covered
with coastal forest and is home to a population of
pink pigeons that are easily spotted. Visits can be
arranged through your hotel.

Viewpoint, or spot them at La Vanille Réserve des Mascareignes. The Rodrigues golden fruit bat can be seen flying overhead in many parts of Rodrigues at dusk.

Mammals and vermin

Most of the mammals on Mauritius have been introduced. The Javan deer and the black feral pigs are common in the forest and are hunted for food. Both are also farmed, as the meat is very popular. One of the most interesting of the introduced mammals is the tenrec, a nocturnal insectivore similar to a hedgehog, from

appetite for birds.

The lesser Indian mongoose, most common in the dry lowlands, was introduced in 1900 to control the rats. The founding population of 16 males and three females quickly multiplied and soon wiped out several populations of game birds. Their diet is eclectic, including insects, lizards, rats and birds but a favoured food is the toad, which most animals find poisonous. The discovery of a young endangered Mauritius kestrel in the stomach of a mongoose also revealed that they played a large part in the falcon's struggle for survival.

A cheeky monkey hitches a ride on the back of a deer in Gazela Park.

Madagascar, although it is rarely seen. Monkeys, long-tailed macaques from Java, abound in the forests and woods. About 60,000 in all, they are a terrible pest, damaging native plants and destroying bird nests. Nevertheless they are very interesting and intelligent animals and a good place to see them up close is next to the sacred lake of Grand Bassin where they are fed by visitors, and sometimes at Black River Peak Viewpoint.

The black rat, feral cat and mongoose have contributed the most to the demise of the endemic wildlife. The rats climb the trees and raid birds' nests and damage the fruit on native trees. Similar to the African wildcat, the spotted tabby cat with russet orange ears has an

Roaming reptiles

Since pristine Mauritius had no land mammals, many of the reptiles evolved to fill their niche. Two species of giant tortoise have gone but have been replaced by the Aldabra giant tortoise (see page 257), which roam in the parks. Queen Victoria had them brought to Mauritius after Charles Darwin advised that the last population on Aldabra should be protected in captive herds. Some may even be original immigrants.

Out of the island's many native and endemic geckos and skinks (a smooth, shiny lizard), the nocturnal house gecko is the most common and the Phelsuma day gecko the most spectacular. A group of bright green and red lizards, the latter lives on coconut palms and banana plants, avoiding the greedy eye of mynah birds.

The house gecko can also be seen in gardens, along with the common Agama lizard, known erroneously as a chameleon. There are some real chameleons in Mauritius, but not many.

> *The Rodrigues fruit bat, known as the blonde bat due to a pale tuft of fur on its head, was saved from extinction in the 1970s by the late naturalist Gerald Durrell.*

Contrary to popular belief, snakes do live on the main island of Mauritius, although none of them are poisonous. There are two species of blind, worm-like, burrowing snakes and a larger wolf snake, which bites if handled but as it rarely reaches half a metre (2ft) in length it does little harm.

Free from rats, Round Island is home to a whole community of native reptiles, including three species of skinks and two Phelsuma geckos, one of which is a Durrell's night gecko, named after the late naturalist Gerald Durrell, who made Round Island famous in his book *Golden Bats and Pink Pigeons*. Two rare types of endemic boa live here as well, but one of these, the burrowing boa, has not been seen since 1975. This island is so important that visits can only be made with special permission. However, a population of the Round Island or Telfair's skink has now been introduced on Île aux Aigrettes.

Surviving birds

There are 11 surviving species of land birds endemic to the islands of the southwest Indian Ocean, and seven of them are endemic to Mauritius. The best known are the Mauritius kestrel, pink pigeon and echo parakeet, for these have been the subjects of a conservation programme since the mid-1970s (see page 85). The remaining survivors are the Mascarene cave swiftlet, Mascarene swallow, Mauritius cuckoo shrike, Mauritius black bulbul, Mauritius fody, paradise flycatcher and two types of white-eyes. The swiftlet breeds in lava tunnels but has been in decline for many years on Mauritius as its nest is considered a delicacy for bird's nest soup. There are 2,000–3,000 birds

today, which can be seen flying in flocks over the island. The heavily built swallow keeps to the dry southwest of Mauritius and is most active in the late afternoon when it feeds on flying insects. The only other endemic bird that you are likely to see around and about is the grey white-eye, a tiny grey bird with a white rump that travels in small flocks and is known as a *pic-pic*. You would be lucky to see any of the other birds, which are all perching songbirds (passerines), unless you specifically go to look for them in the forests of the Black River Gorges and Bassin Blanc.

Echo parakeet.

WILDLIFE FOUNDATION

Formed in 1984 by Gerald Durrell and other naturalists, the Mauritius Wildlife Foundation (MWF) is a charity dedicated to the conservation of the native wildlife of Mauritius, Rodrigues and their islands. It is best known for its work on the Mauritius kestrel, pink pigeon and echo parakeet, but is also protecting endemic passerines and the endangered reptiles of Round Island, and Rodrigues' golden fruit bat. Several small islands have been restored by the foundation. Île aux Aigrettes, for example, has been cleared of rats and many weeds and is being repopulated with endemic fauna and flora.

The woods along Cascade Pigeons River and at Solitude on Rodrigues are home to two of the world's rarest birds: the endemic warbler, which only has about 25 pairs left, and the striking yellow and orange fody, with about 200 pairs.

The colourful birds commonly seen around the hotels and houses have mostly been introduced to Mauritius. Many of these may seem very familiar since they are common cage birds that long ago escaped from captivity and established themselves in the wild. The most prolific are the mynah bird, the elegant,

Spinner dolphins.

crested red-whiskered bulbul, the bright red Madagascar fody and the yellow village weaver.

Coastal creatures

Nesting on the small islands around Mauritius, and most easily seen on Île aux Cocos on Rodrigues, are boobies, sooty terns and noddies, as well as several species of petrel. A wonderful sight to see is the elegant, rare red-tailed tropicbird which nests in cliffs on Gunner's Quoin, Flat Island and Round Island. But its more common smaller cousin, the white-tailed tropicbird *(paille-en-queue)* can be watched from the Black River Peak Viewpoint.

Fourteen species of whales and dolphins have been recorded around the Mascarene coasts. Spinner and bottle-nose dolphins can often be seen from the shore and in Tamarin Bay, beyond the reef. The chances of seeing dolphins on a boat trip are high and you may also see sperm whales off the west coast. A school of humpbacked whales returns to the waters between the mainland and Round Island during July and August most years, probably to breed.

At one time dugongs, or sea cows, lived in the lagoons around Mauritius and Rodrigues feed-

> The beautiful boucle d'oreille (Trochetia boutoniana), meaning earring, is the national flower of Mauritius. However, it can only be seen in cultivated sites or on the slopes of Le Morne Brabant.

ing on sea-grass. These sea beauties are believed to have been the creatures sea-weary sailors mistook for mermaids, but it didn't stop them from being hunted. Luckily, some still survive off Madagascar in the Mozambique Channel.

Fascinating flora

The native hardwood forests of Mauritius are now largely limited to the mountain tops and deep in gorges, where they could not be exploited for their timber. Only 5 percent of the island is forested, and only small areas of that are in good condition. Nevertheless, Mauritius has 685 species of native plants of which 311 are endemic and most are endangered.

It is a sobering thought that Mauritius has some of the rarest plants in the world. The palm *Hyophorbe amauricaulis* is down to its last plant, surviving in the Curepipe Botanical Garden. Rodrigues is hanging on to its last specimen of café marron *(Ramosmania heterophylla)* but we are too late for the *Pyramid pandanus*, which succumbed to Cyclone Hollanda in 1994.

Many of those that haven't survived have been supplanted by alien plants, such as the Chinese guava and *Lantana camara* that have run riot, suffocating seedlings. The familiar casuarina tree seen lining the beaches was brought from Malaysia as a windbreak and the mighty banyan tree with dangling roots, so typical of tropical forests, comes from India.

Mauritius' endangered birds

Mauritius' most celebrated bird may be dead, but the island is still home to some of the rarest birds on earth, including the famous pink pigeon.

The dodo is the best known of Mauritius' extinct birds, but there are many others that have vanished, including a large black flightless parrot, the largest parrot ever known, a blue pigeon, some ducks, owls, more parrots and others. Indeed scientists still argue about the numbers of species that have disappeared.

However, since the mid-1970s three birds – the Mauritius kestrel, the pink pigeon and the echo parakeet – have been rescued from the edge of extinction by a group of conservationists, led by the ornithologist Carl Jones along with Gerald Durrell's Jersey Wildlife Preservation Trust (JWPT).

Conservation successes

The Mauritius kestrel *(Falco punctatus)* is a small falcon which lives in the forested gorges and mountains, feeds on bright green day geckos and nests in cliff holes. In 1974 there were only four wild birds, and only one pair were breeding. The rescue operation was started by breeding birds in captivity. Over several years, eggs were harvested from the last pair – every time a clutch of eggs was taken from the wild kestrels, they would lay again, increasing their productivity. Many of the young reared from harvested eggs were released back into the wild together with birds that were bred in captivity. These were fed and provided with nest boxes and protected from predators such as the mongoose and feral cats. The released kestrels began to breed well and between 1984 and 1994, 331 birds were put back into the Black River Gorges and tracts of forest that had not had kestrels for decades, including La Vallée de Ferney. Today it is believed there are between 500 and 800 birds.

Almost as rare as the kestrel, the pink pigeon *(Nesoenas mayeri)* was believed by some to be extinct. But in the 1970s a population was found in an isolated pocket of woodland near Bassin Blanc. These birds were slowly declining because rats and monkeys were stealing their eggs or they were being caught by feral cats. By 1990 there were only 10 birds left in the wild but a small population had been established in captivity; since then, the captive-bred birds have been

released into the wild, boosting the numbers. A programme controlling the introduced predators has also been put in force. The pigeons have responded dramatically to these initiatives and the population has increased to more than 470 birds, but the pink pigeon still has a way to go before it is safe.

The echo parakeet

The work with the kestrel and pigeon may have been tough but the problems were minor compared to those encountered rescuing the echo parakeet *(Psittacula echo)*. This emerald green parrot – distinguishable from the introduced ring-necked parakeet

Pink pigeons.

by its shorter tail, more rounded wing and darker green – had the distinction of being the world's rarest parrot, until recently. In 1987 there were thought to be only eight left, with only two females. The problem was their low breeding rate. Working under the auspices of the MWF (see page 83), conservationists tried rearing the young and eggs taken from nests that seemed doomed to failure. Many died until it was learned how to nurture them with a good diet, filtered water and scrupulous hygiene. The wild parakeets were provided with extra food and their nest sites in hollow trees were improved, with nesting birds guarded against predators. The population increased and now the future looks good, with around 550 echo parakeets flying free along the Macchabee Ridge in the Black River Gorges National Park.

Divers explore a coral reef.

INTO THE BLUE

The sea is never far away in the Mascarenes, with
plenty of activities on offer on, in or beside it.

The Réunionnais surf on it, the Rodriguans fish in it and the Mauritians love to sit, eat and chat beside the sea, which is central to leisure time in the Mascarenes. At weekends huge parties of Mauritians head for the beach armed with picnic hampers, curry pots and all the necessary accoutrements for a day or two's relaxation beside the lagoon.

Tourism has brought new and exciting activities to these translucent Indian Ocean waters. Most hotels offer free windsurfing, water-skiing and boating, although scuba diving, big game fishing and parasailing come at a price. If you don't want to go as far as learning to dive, the tranquil lagoons are perfect for snorkelling. Otherwise there are plenty of kayaks, canoes and pedalos to keep you amused and rides in glass-bottom boats for views of life in the lagoon without getting your feet wet.

Beyond the reef is the game fisherman's sporting ground, where wahoo, shark, marlin,

Windsurfing fun.

The best time for catching marlin is from October to April, although big game fisherwoman Birgit Rudolph says 'You never know when a big one is coming.'

tuna and other big fish prowl the depths of their deep blue domain. They have few enemies, but even the great speed and strength of a blue marlin requires some cunning to outwit that most determined of ocean predators – the deep sea fisherman. The business of sport fishing is bigger, bolder and more macho in Mauritius and Rodrigues than in Réunion or Seychelles (see page 91).

The best dive sites

The waters around Mauritius offer some exciting diving experiences. There are dozens of sites to choose from where shoals of small reef fish, such as blackspotted sweetlip, humpbacked snapper and squirrel fish, play hide and seek; or you could venture further out for sightings of hammerhead shark, ray and barracuda.

The best dive sites, no more than an hour's boat ride away, are found off the west coast near Flic en Flac (see page 139) and include some wonderful wrecks. Well worth exploring are *Kei Sei 113* and *Tug 11*, sunk in the late 1980s to form artificial reefs and now inhabited by giant moray eels and a vast community of colourful reef fish.

On the east coast, organised diving is rather more limited due to prevailing winds and exposed seas and nearly all diving takes place in or around passes through the reef. However, the region has excellent facilities at the major hotels, many of which have PADI dive centres.

When weather conditions become too unpleasant for diving in this area, clients are transported to Grand Baie in the north, where nearly a dozen sites – including the wreck *The Silver Star*, sunk in 1992 to form an artificial reef – can easily be reached by boat.

See shoals of fish just below the water's surface.

Diving conditions in the south of the island are best in the sheltered lagoon at Blue Bay where you can dive all year round in complete safety for sightings of weirdly shaped corals and dancing reef fish. Experienced divers can choose from several sites beyond the reef where caves and tunnels attract shoals of kingfish, crayfish and black-tip sharks.

Snorkelling

While authorities argue that safeguards and restrictions are in place to protect the lagoons, such as a ban on dynamite fishing, collecting shells and corals from the seabed and spear fishing, many islanders complain of increased pollution and impaired visibility. However, there is still an amazing marine world to be discovered just below the surface. Snorkelling is just as popular as diving. Hours of pleasure can be had gliding silently over shallow reefs to observe the many creatures which live there. Hotel boathouses provide free snorkelling trips to the nearest best spot and equipment for their guests, though this is not always in tip-top condition. If you've been bitten by the snorkelling bug, you might want to invest in your own equipment. Good quality masks, fins and goggles are on sale everywhere. The best destination for snorkelling on the island is down south, at Blue Bay Marine Park.

A walk on the wet side

An alternative way of discovering the seabed is to take an undersea walk or 'helmet dive'. Undersea walking began in the Bahamas in 1948, but the idea was patented and brought to Mauritius

TAKE THE PLUNGE

Mauritius' warm waters and rich marine life make it the perfect place to learn to dive. Dive centres attached to hotels are affiliated to CMAS (World Underwater Federation), PADI (Professional Association of Diving Instructors), NAUI (National Association of Underwater Instructors) and BSAC (British Sub-Aqua Club) and operate under strict safety rules, providing all the equipment you need and multilingual instructors.

Most dive centres offer a brief resort course designed to test your affinity with the sport. For more in-depth training, you can enrol on an intensive five-day course leading to a PADI Open Water One certificate, followed by a number of qualifying dives. Children are specially catered for, with themed dives introducing them to the wonders of the ocean.

Experienced divers can expect to pay up to R1,400 for a day dive and R2,000 for a night dive, although packages of six and 10 dives are better value. (See Travel Tips, Activities, for a list of recommended dive centres.)

Diving accidents are rare but if you get into trouble, arrangements are quickly made to convey you to the island's recompression chamber at the paramilitary Special Mobile Force (SMF) Headquarters at Vacoas (tel: 686 1040), about an hour's drive from the coast.

in 1990. Following the success of the first company, Solar Undersea Walk (which started as Captain Nemo's Undersea Walk) in Grand Baie, others followed, including Aquaventure in Belle Mare (see Travel Tips, Activities).

Undersea walking attracts people of every age and ability, including non-swimmers and children over seven. A boat ferries you to a floating dive platform inside the reef where a glass fronted steel helmet is placed over your head and rests loosely on your shoulders. Initially it feels heavy but once you are under water it becomes relatively weightless. Compressed air is then pumped into the helmet and filtered out through valves ensuring a fresh air supply and preventing the water from seeping up to your face. You can even chat to your fellow undersea walkers, and wearers of contact-lenses or glasses need not worry. Experienced guides stroll with you through a garden of spectacular coral inhabited by giant clam and flowering anemones, and let you hand-feed the shoals of zebra fish. A version of this, for children over eight and the less mobile, is a 30-minute ride on an enclosed motorised aqua scooter. This cross between a scuba bike and a mini submarine chugs along at around 3 knots, some 3 metres below the surface in Trou aux Biches (see Travel Tips, Activities).

Submarine safari

To observe the colourful corals teeming with fish, and stay dry, join an hour-long submarine safari from Grand Baie with Blue Safari Submarine (see Travel Tips, Activities). You can also hire the submarine for a private party, a night dive, or even as the venue for an underwater wedding.

Unmissable for families with young children is a trip in *Nessee*. This semi-submersible boat can be booked through hotels and tour operators and guarantees viewings of marine life gliding through a riot of ornamental vegetation, in the comfort and safety of an air-conditioned compartment attached to the hull.

Sailing

Most hotels offer free use of Hobie cats, windsurfing boards and kayaks for pottering about inside the lagoon. But to experience the real McCoy, you could spend a day sailing along the coast with an experienced crew in a luxury catamaran or yacht. Join in pulling a few ropes

or just relax on deck and watch the shapes and shadows of miniature mountains unfold. Full-day tours cost around R2,500 per person including lunch and soft drinks (see Travel Tips, Activities). Mauritius is a favourite with kitesurfers, with 'One Eye' at Le Morne, in the southwest, cited as the world's third best kitesurfing spot. Le Morne Bay is one of the safest spots for beginners and improvers to learn, and kitesurfing is also found at nearby Bel Ombre, and around Île aux Benitiers, offshore from La Gaulette, which offers the cheapest places to stay. Professional operators certified by the

A Blue Safari submarine.

LETHAL WEAPON

The stone fish *(Synancea verucosa)*, known locally as the laff, lurks like a barnacle of basalt in mud and rock, clamping its upturned mouth on whatever takes its fancy. Hollow dorsal spines emit a highly toxic poison causing excruciating pain and swelling, and days of incapacity to anyone unfortunate enough to step on one. In some cases the injury can even prove fatal. Wearing plastic water shoes when wading through mud and rocks is essential to protect your feet from the laff's noxious spines (and to avoid cutting yourself on rocks and corals). If you fall victim to the laff, clean the wound and seek medical help immediately.

IKO (International Kiteboarding Organisation) include Club Mistral (www.club-mistral.com).

Motorised water sports

Sea-karting is the latest craze, from Fun Adventure (www.fun-adventure.mu), based in Black River. A cross between a jet-ski and a speedboat, and with room for four people, sea karts can reach 100kmh (62mph). You can take to the helm with an hour's tuition (over 16s only) or ride as a passenger (minimum age of 8 years) to Flic en Flac, with a barbecue lunch on Île aux Beniticrs and views of Le Morne.

Kite-surfing.

THE SHOALS OF CAPRICORN

Initiated by the Royal Geographical Society (www. rgs.org), the Shoals of Capricorn marine science research programme ran from 1998 to 2001 and studied the marine environment of the Mascarenes plateau, comprising Seychelles, Mauritius and Rodrigues. Larger than the Great Barrier Reef, longer than the Red Sea and covering around 115,000 sq km (44,000 sq miles), it is one of earth's few submerged features clearly visible from space. Findings included the expansion of the species list in the Rodrigues lagoon from 45 to 1,000 – with more than 100 species new to science – and new coral growth on Seychelles' reefs.

Unspoilt Rodrigues

When it comes to corals, many experienced divers maintain that Rodrigues wins over Seychelles. In *Islands in a Forgotten Sea*, author T.V. Bulpin refers to the scenery outside the lagoon as 'dreamlike jungles of coral reefs', while Jacques Degremont, instructor at Jacky Diving, Tekoma Hotel, believes the island's waters are far superior to anything he has seen in Mauritius, especially since 1998, when many Indian Ocean corals died because of the rise in water temperature caused by El Niño. Because of its southerly location, Rodrigues escaped the worst of the El Niño effect. (The 2004 tsunami had little or no impact on the waters around Mauritius bar flooding in Port Mathurin, but an early warning tsunami system for the Indian Ocean is now in place.) Today pristine sites in crystal-clear waters can be enjoyed for most months of the year outside the cyclone season.

One of the best sites for both divers and snorkellers is The Aquarium, inside the lagoon near Cotton Bay Hotel, where you need only slip over the side of the boat to see beautiful coral outcrops infested with brightly coloured reef fish. Just beyond the reef, at Aquarium Passe, lie canyons inhabited by shoals of king and unicorn fish. You may even spot some turtles.

Two hotel dive centres at Cotton Bay Hotel and Les Cocotiers Hotel provide equipment and instruction with qualified PADI instructors (see Travel Tips, Activities). Both are affiliated to international dive associations. Rates here are slightly higher than in Mauritius, but groups tend to be smaller and more intimate. As the island does not have a recompression chamber, dives deeper than 30 metres (100ft) are never undertaken and precautionary decompression stops are compulsory for dives deeper than 12 metres (40ft).

The range of other water sports on offer in Rodrigues is similar to Mauritius, though there is no parasailing or water-skiing because the lagoon is too shallow. Kitesurfing is excellent here, and centred on Marouk in the southeast. Big game fishing was only introduced to Rodrigues in 1997, and is still in its infancy, but the unpolluted waters attract yellow fin tuna, dog tooth tuna, skipjack, dolphin fish, blue, black and striped marlins and sizable sailfish. With just five big game fishing boats to choose from and an entire ocean to play in, your chances of hooking 'The Big One' are high.

The big ones

World record-breaking Blue Marlin put Mauritius firmly on the game fishing map, and it's still there for the taking for those who like a challenge.

Big game fishing is big business in Mauritius all year round. It's no secret that the numbers of fish in Mauritian waters have dropped in recent years. Nevertheless, the seas are still rich in game and some of the top big fishing grounds in the world are around here.

The best season for black and blue marlin is usually from October to the end of March or April, although the World Cup Blue Marlin Championship is held in Black River each July. For 16 years, Mauritius held the world record for blue marlin at 648kg (1,430 lb). Yellow fin tuna traditionally migrate in massive shoals to Mauritian waters between March and April. They can weigh anything between 63 and 90kg (140–200 lb). Then in September the ocean sees prolific runs of wahoo (reputed to be the fastest moving fish in the sea), sailfish (averaging around 45kg/100 lb), which literally fly through the air when hooked and furiously fight for their freedom, not to mention bonito, better known to the supermarket shopper as skipjack tuna. Then, of course, there are the different species of shark, from blue, hammerhead, mako and tiger to black fin and white fin.

Reeling in the catch

Most of the big hotels have their own boats and there are a number of boat clubs that operate fishing excursions for tourists. The largest fleets are based at the Corsaire Club at Trou aux Biches and JP Henry Charters at Black River, which is the centre of the deep-sea fishing scene. If you're staying at Paradis Hotel & Golf Club at Le Morne in the southwest, you can get to the fishing grounds from the fishing centre at the hotel jetty, just a 20-minute ride away. Luxury craft are all equipped with ship-to-shore radio, trolling equipment for live and artificial lures, life-saving rafts and jackets and everything you would expect from an experienced skipper and deck hand.

If you're up to flexing your muscles with a marlin, just sit back in a fighting chair, strap on your harness and wait for the big moment. There really is nothing quite like the thrill of the chase to get the adrenalin levels pumping when a marlin strikes. These majestic, hugely powerful fish don't give themselves up easily and if they are hooked and landed, the winners pose for pictures alongside their catch.

You may prefer just to sit back and scan the ocean for signs of marlin or shark fins while the professionals prepare themselves for a fight. If you're just going along for the ride, the sun deck of any big game fishing boat is designed for a long sultry day at sea. You need do nothing more strenuous than cover yourself with high factor suncream and equip yourself with a cool drink.

Tamarin fishermen carrying a yellow-fin tuna

Eat or release?

As for the catch, professional operators encourage tag and release, especially for marlin. Smoke houses in the Black River area process and package marlin, which is similar in taste and texture to smoked salmon and is perfect served with a twist of lemon and black pepper. If you want to taste your own catch then smaller fish, such as bonito, can be cooked to order by the chef at your hotel.

If your luck is out and you're keen to get a glimpse of a marlin, there's a fine specimen hanging from the rafters of the Blue Marlin Restaurant at Paradis Hotel & Golf Club.

Most boats take up to six passengers and a half day's hire is from R14,000.

For good operators, see Travel Tips, Activities.

Sailing from Coconut Island in Blue Bay, Mahebourg.

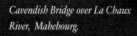

MAURITIUS: PLACES

A detailed guide to Mauritius and
Rodrigues, with principal sites clearly
cross-referenced by number to the maps.

*Canyoning on the Black
River Gorge.*

Although just a speck on Indian Ocean maps, Mauritius is a large island, so it is important to think carefully about where to base yourself. The most established tourism centre is on the northwest coast – in particular Grand Baie, the island's only conventional resort, with a wide choice of hotels and excursions, and evening entertainment. Nearby Trou-aux-Biches and Mont Choisy are quieter, with beautiful beaches, and further down is the exclusive enclave of Baie aux Tortues (Turtle Bay).

The sheltered west coast resorts, Flic en Flac and Wolmar, renowned for year-round fine weather and magical sunsets, offer some of the finest beaches, best diving and water sports, and are well located if you are keen to explore. Within easy reach is the forested Black River Gorges National Park, a perfect place for walking, with the chance to glimpse Mauritius' endangered birds. The rugged south coast is the site of the newest development, with leading hotels, a golf course and tourist trails. It's best to hire a car to travel the quiet roads past isolated fishing communities, lonely beaches and a windswept coast. At Mauritius' tip, Le Morne Peninsula, known as the 'five star strip', is the island's most exclusive address.

Le Touessrok Resort & Spa.

For some, the east coast may feel too isolated. People come here to enjoy the established top-class hotels, the superb Belle Mare beach and the picture-postcard islands off Trou d'Eau Douce.

Smaller hotels and guesthouses at Pointe D'Esny, Blue Bay and the former capital Mahébourg, in the historic southeast, are handy for the airport, and for exploring the quiet south and east coasts.

It's possible to go to Mauritius and not even visit the capital, Port Louis, especially as the airport is on the opposite side of the island – but you'd miss out on the real Mauritius.

Likewise, few people make it across the water to Rodrigues. Yet what this island lacks in sophistication is compensated for by the warmth of its residents; and it offers a simple, no-frills insight into remote island life.

In Central Market.

PORT LOUIS

The capital of Mauritius may lack obvious appeal, but the busy streets, the jumble of new and old buildings, and the market are worth exploring.

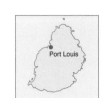

Not so long ago, when office workers chorused 'pens down at 4pm' and left the stifling heat of the capital for the cooler uplands, Port Louis simply shut up shop and went to bed. The city was as dead as a dodo and, save for late-night gambling with Sino-Mauritians and newly arrived sailors in the casino, there was nothing else to do. Since then, Port Louis has undergone something of a transformation or, as the locals would say, a 'lifting', a hand-me-down expression acquired from the British, meaning a face-lift. This is thanks largely to the development of the Caudan Waterfront, which, with its trendy designer shops, alfresco cafés, cinemas, museums and 24-hour casino, has become the focal point of the city – and is generally considered the main attraction for tourists.

But anyone not interested in shopping is likely to find more of interest in the rest of the city, with its jumble of new and decrepit old buildings, mosques, churches and temples, Chinese and Muslim quarters, racecourse and, above all, the lively, attractive market. There is enough to keep you busy for half a day at least. Remember, though, that between November and April the city can be uncomfortably hot.

History of Port Louis

Port Louis started out in 1722, when the infant French East India Company transferred its headquarters from the old Dutch settlement at Warwyck Bay (now Mahébourg) to what was then North West Harbour. It was renamed Port Louis after Louis XV of France. From its early days, fortune seekers descended on the city, prompting an 18th-century traveller to note that it contained 'a sort of scum of bankrupts, ruined adventurers, swindlers and rascals of all kinds.' Those characters have long gone, but, for all the modernity of air-conditioned shopping malls and fast

Main Attractions
The Waterfront
Blue Penny Museum
Natural History Museum
Central Market
Aapravasi Ghat
Chinese Quarter
The Citadel

Port Louis's city skyline.

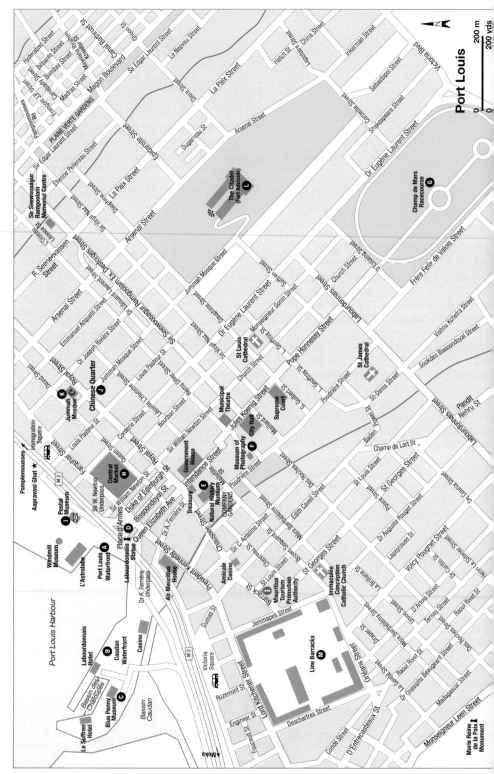

Port Louis

N

200 m
200 yds

Port Louis Harbour

ood outlets, the past has not been completely erased.

Under the British, Port Louis developed into a major port for sailing hips, but by the late 1800s, with the ntroduction of the steamer and the opening of the Suez Canal, the city had lost much of its appeal, while outbreaks of disease, cyclones and fire caused many of its folk to flee to the healthier climate of the uplands.

A look across the Caudan Basin oday, with its cargo and freighter hips, reminds you that Port Louis is till very much a working port and commercial centre. Many thousands pour into the city each day to work, congesting the roads with traffic and adding to the resident population of 150,000 – all packed into 10 sq km (4 q miles). It is no surprise that Port Louis, like most modern capitals, s crowded, dirty and noisy. But the Moka Mountains behind, and the sea n front, provide a resplendent setting.

The Waterfront

The waterfront development is offi-ially divided into two sections – the large, privately run Caudan Water-front and the smaller, government-run Port Louis Waterfront. A good place to start a walking tour of the city is from the **Port Louis Waterfront** Ⓐ, where you'll find several cafés and L'Astrolabe shopping mall.

The most curious sight in this area is the **Windmill Museum** (tel: 211 7465; Mon–Fri 10am–noon and 1–3pm; free). A windmill was first built on this spot by the French in the 18th century, and it was France that donated the mechanism inside the modern reconstruction and which also supplies the grain used in occasional demonstrations. The collection of old photographs and the video focus on the transformation of the waterfront.

Over on the **Caudan Waterfront** Ⓑ, beyond the complex of shops and restaurants, rises the vast **Labourdon-nais Hotel**. Patronised mainly by international businessmen, the hotel is not a bad pit stop in the evening – particularly if you're flush with rupees from the nearby casino.

Kwan Tee Pagoda, on the rounda-bout south of the Caudan Waterfront,

The city's waterfront promenade is lined with bars and restaurants.

is the oldest Chinese temple in town and is dedicated to the Chinese warrior god who fought for justice.

One of the best views of the city is from the sea, and you can take a **harbour cruise** from just outside the Labourdonnais. The pleasure boat chugs past a panoramic view of a delectable landfall of peaks and knolls. Looking inland, from right to left, the bulk of Signal Mountain dominates the city. Next, Le Pouce (The Thumb) rises from the south wing of the Moka Range in a 'thumbs up' sign. The most distinctive peak of all, whose pinnacle looks like the cloak-shrouded shoulders of a man, comes in the form of **Pieter Both**, named after the Dutch Admiral who drowned off the coast. Closer to the city to the north is a knoll known as La Citadelle, named after the ruin of a fortress at its crest.

A museum well worth calling into is the **Blue Penny Museum ⊙** (tel: 210 9024; www.bluepennymuseum.com; Mon–Sat 10am–5pm). Home to a rich collection of national treasures, it exhibits fine art, old maps and sections on philately and postal history, coins,

Looking out over the racecourse.

paper money, postcards and photography. Many items were formerly in the possession of private collectors.

Place S Bissoondoyal

If you cross by the subway beside the waterfront you reach the **Place S. Bissoondoyal ⊙** (often still referred to by its previous name, **Place d'Armes** where you'll be greeted by the most famous landmark of the city, the bronze statue of Bertrand François Mahé de Labourdonnais. He arrived in 1735 as the newly appointed French governor-general of the Mascarene Islands and went about transforming shambolic Port Louis into a thriving sea port and commercial centre.

Some local people seem to enjoy having a chat beneath the royal palms that line the square, but the constant buzz of cars around the edge does not make the Place S Bissoondoyal a peaceful place. At the top stands **Government House**, the official centre of government. It started life as a ramshackle wooden hut, was enlarged by Labourdonnais in 1738 and later embellished by the British. In the

ourtyard, secured by wrought-iron gates, is a rather severe marble statue of Queen Victoria, shaded in summer by brilliant red flamboyant trees. Beyond it stands a statue of Sir William Stevenson, British governor from 1857 to 1863. To the right, on the corner of Chaussée, the old Treasury Buildings (1883), refurbished in 2004 as the prime minister's office, provide good cover if you get caught in a downpour.

Along La Chaussée is the Mauritius Institute, home of the **Natural History Museum** Ⓔ (tel: 212 0639; www.mauritiusmuseums.com; Mon, Tue, Fri 9am–4pm, Sat 9am–noon). This museum used to be an apology for what was once a priceless collection of flora and fauna, but that was before a successful redesign in 2009, complete with a new dodo gallery. It's the only place on the island where you can see a skeleton of Mauritius' iconic bird. The **Company Gardens** next door is busy at lunch time, when city workers take a break beneath giant banyans and bottle palms, to eat a *dal puri*. On Chaussée Street is **l'Amicale Casino** (tel: 210 9713; daily 10am–2am), built

to replace the original, which rioters reduced to a heap of ruins in an arson attack in 1999 during which seven people lost their lives. Today's smoke-filled, seedy den is open to tourists but is mainly patronised by male hopefuls huddled around blackjack and roulette tables or trying their luck on the gaming machines. Further down the road, turn right for the **Mauritius Tourism Promotional Authority (MTPA) office** (tel: 210 1545; www.tourism mauritius.mu; Mon–Fri 9am–4pm, Sat 9am–noon), on the fifth floor of Victoria House, St Louis Street.

From Intendance Street to the racecourse

A quick stroll south from Place S. Bissoondoyal along Intendance Street takes you past the city's other main historic buildings. First is the **Municipal Theatre**, which was built in 1822 and is the oldest theatre in the Indian Ocean. If it is open during the day, ask the caretaker to show you the beautiful painted dome and crystal chandeliers. During the 1930s, the citizens of Port Louis were entertained by old favourites like

A DAY AT THE RACES

In Mauritius, it is said that there are three seasons – summer, winter and the racing season. The Mauritius Turf Club, the second oldest in the southern hemisphere, was founded by Colonel Draper in 1812. He had friends in high places on both sides of the divide and, being a passionate punter, thought it only gentlemanly to bring the French and English together in an atmosphere of leisure.

Today, most horses come from South Africa and Australia and are trained in one of the island's eight stables. Race meetings are held every Saturday afternoon from the first week in May to the end of November. Spirits run high, with screams of *'Allez, allez!'* following the horses as they gallop round the course. Music is played between races as punters press round bookies to place their bets or collect their winnings, and food sellers do a roaring trade.

Many Mauritians are well versed in the international race scene. They follow the progress of individual horses closely and the use of starting stalls, photo-finish systems and adherence to Newmarket disciplines attracts jockeys from all over the world. There are even professional gamblers who try to make a living from picking a winner; most of them will have a 'hot tip', but remember, despite what some may tell you, there is no such thing as a 'dead cert'.

Shopping for fresh produce at the market.

Madame Butterfly brought to them by visiting troupes from France. The theatre had virtually shut down by the 1950s but re-opened in 1994 after a massive face-lift. Seats now sell fast for modern jazz gigs, sega, operas and plays, but it's also the hotspot for weddings and prestigious functions, when big shots get invited by moneyed Mauritians.

Opposite the theatre, cobbled Rue du Vieux Conseil (Old Council Street) leads to the **Museum of Photography** **F** (tel: 211 1705; www.musee-photo.voyaz. com; opening hours vary), where you'll find one of the island's oldest displays of cameras and prints, which includes daguerreotypes as well as photographs of colonial Mauritius. All these have been collected by photographer Tristan de Breville, who fights a constant financial battle to keep his museum open.

Heading east, you reach the austere **St Louis Cathedral**. The original French church was reduced to rubble by cyclones in the 1800s. It was rebuilt twice before the present version was consecrated in 1932. To the left is the **Episcopal Palace**, a fine 19th-century colonnaded mansion. The other

important church in the city is **St James Cathedral**, nearby in Poudrière Street which looms over gardens shaded by palm trees and tumbling bougainvi laea. It was once a gunpowder store an prison under the French, before the British turned it into a church, and also saw service as a refuge centre when Port Louisiens would abandon their wooden houses on the approach of a cyclone for the security of its 3-metre (10ft) walls.

From these two places of worship it is only a short diversion to **Champ de Mars Racecourse** **G** (also known as the Hippodrome; tel: 210 2212 www.mauritiusturfclub.com; May–Nov cradled by the Moka Mountains at the eastern edge of the city. Once the training ground for French soldiers, today it is often used for Independence Day celebrations on 12 March – and the nation's most popular sport: horse racing. An invitation to the members enclosure on classic race days, like the Gold Cup or the Maiden Cup, should not be refused; you get a bird's-eye view of the paddock, free rein of all facilities, which include bars and comfortable terraces, and an unmissable opportunity to rub shoulders with those in the know. On non-race days joggers replace the horses.

The Central Market

If there is one place no one should miss in Port Louis, it is the covered **Central Market** **H** (daily 6am–6pm) known as the Bazar Central in Kreol two blocks north of Place S. Bissoondoyal. Built in 2004 to replace its old tumbledown predecessor, where traders from all continents had converged for more than 150 years, this attractive building accommodates over 300 stalls in rather more hygienic and pleasant conditions, yet manages to retain its traditional charm and atmosphere.

On the ground floor you can follow the locals picking out the best from the mounds of tropical fruit and vegetables, or picking up herbal remedies claiming to cure everything from diarrhoea to diabetes. Upstairs, Indian

Creole and Chinese traders sell T-shirts, basketware, spices and cheap clothing, and there are good views from the gallery of the bustle below. You can pick up spicy pancakes *(dal puris)*, curry-filled *samousas* and other popular Mauritian snacks for just a few rupees, perfect for a mid-morning snack or light lunch. Those with a more sensitive constitution may want to steer clear of *bombli*, the dried salt fish with a stench that defies description.

Postal Museum and Aapravasi Ghat

After the bustle of the market, you can find solace in the calm of the **Postal Museum** ❶ (www.mauritiuspost.mu/postal-museum; Mon–Fri 9am–4.30pm, Sat 10am–4pm), which lies across the busy road from the market in the former General Post Office. This well laid-out museum contains 19th-century postal equipment such as telegraph and stamp-vending machines and a fine collection of stamps, postal stationery, original artwork and printing plates. For serious collectors there are stock books, stamp albums, mounts, magnifying glasses and tweezers, and first-day covers and commemorative sets of stamps, such as the 400th anniversary of the Dutch landing that was issued in 1999.

A short walk north alongside the busy road takes you to the gardens of the **Aapravasi Ghat** (tel: 241 0386; www.aapravasighat.org; Mon–Sat 9am–4pm; free), a Unesco World Heritage Site. Once known as the Immigration Depot or Coolie Ghat, it housed the first Indian immigrants who were brought here before being farmed out to the sugar estates. Look for the 11 bronze murals showing scenes of immigrant life, including one depicting a pair of hands breaking free from chains. A poem dedicated to the Unknown Immigrant recalls how 'He… turned stone into green fields of gold', a reference to sugar cane.

The Chinese Quarter

The **Chinese Quarter** ❷, encompassed in several streets to the east of the market, is the most colourful part of the city with its specialist food and spice shops and herbal remedy stores. There are plenty of eating houses too, where

FACT

The Twopenny Blue stamp was issued in Mauritius in the mid-19th century when the island was one of the first colonies to have its own post office. It has become one of the rarest stamps in the world.

The Chinese Quarter is a bustling part of the city.

fast cheap meals, such as the ubiquitous noodles *(mines)*, can be slurped from bowls. A variety of snacks, such as *gâteaux piments*, crispy *samousas* or the more unusual combination of fresh pineapples with hot red chilli sauce, are also sold from mobile food wagons on street corners.

The **Jummah Mosque** Ⓚ in Royal Street is open to tourists only at certain times, but one of its most striking features is the beautifully carved teak doors and the ornate decorations of the outer walls. Built in around 1853 for the growing Muslim community and subsequently enlarged, it is the island's most impressive mosque. Plaine Verte, the Muslim Quarter to the north of Port Louis, is home to the annual Ghoon festival, but other than its small teahouses and tumbledown textile shops, it has little to interest the visitor.

The Citadel and Line Barracks

The only reason for going to **The Citadel** Ⓛ (La Citadelle; Mon–Sat 8am–8pm), also known as Fort Adelaide, is the panoramic views of the city's amphitheatre of mountains, the Champ de Mars racecourse and the harbour. The basalt fort was named after Queen Adelaide, wife of William IV, and must rank as Port Louis' greatest white elephant. Apart from the occasional concert and a few small shops selling local arts and crafts, it never seems to wake from its apathy, even when the silence is broken by the babble of tourists.

For some Mauritian quirkiness wander down to **Line Barracks** Ⓜ *(caserne)*, home of the Mauritian Police Force, which contains fine examples of 18th-century colonial architecture. Inside, look out for learner drivers taking their tests. See the prison dubbed 'Alcatraz' and the Golden Gates at the main entrance, which caused a stir because they cost a fortune. Nearby is an incongruous blue-tiled archway marked 'Gateway of Discipline' which leads to the old drill square.

Attractions around Port Louis

The Church and Shrine of Père Laval at Sainte-Croix in the foothills of Long Mountain to the northeast is only a

Port Louis street life.

10-minute drive from the city centre. Père Laval, known as the black apostle, arrived as a missionary in 1841 and was soon revered for his work with the poor. When he died in 1864 his body was buried at Sainte-Croix and became the object of pilgrimage. The church was renovated in 2014 to mark the 150th anniversary of his death. Many Mauritians still believe in his special healing powers and every day hundreds of people of all faiths file past the stone sarcophagus that contains his remains, topped by an effigy framed with flowers, and pray for the sick. He was beatified by the Catholic Church in 1979 and is one step away from being canonised, so it won't be long before Mauritius has its very own patron saint. An annual pilgrimage to the church takes place during the nights of 7 and 8 September. The curate's residence nearby is a superb example of colonial architecture.

About 10 minutes' drive south of the city centre, and well signposted off the motorway, is **Domaine les Pailles** (tel: 286 4225; www.domainelespailles.net; daily 10am–4.30pm). With two restaurants, a casino, the futuristic Swami Vivekananda Conference Centre where cultural shows and trade fairs are held, and 1,200 hectares (3,000 acres) of grounds, the estate attracts both tourists and business people seeking an escape from the brouhaha of the capital. A short guided tour (by mini-train or horse-drawn carriage) aims to inform visitors about the production of sugar, rum and other local products, and is popular with children. The tour takes in an early sugar factory and rum distillery (no longer in use), as well as a spice garden, and ends at one of the restaurants.

Breathtaking views of Port Louis can be enjoyed from the peaceful setting of the Marie Reine de la Paix monument on the flanks of Signal Mountain, southwest of the city. In 1989 this place of pilgrimage swelled as thousands of islanders gathered for Mass held by Pope John Paul II. In the foothills of Signal Mountain, on the southeast edge of town, is **Thien Thane**, Port Louis' best Chinese temple for its pagoda architecture and serene location.

Thien Thane temple.

Fun in the sun at Pereybère.

THE NORTH

The beach-lined north coast is the most popular on Mauritius, and has the island's only proper resort town, Grand Baie. The Pamplemousses Botanical Gardens lure people away from the sea.

Port Louis

Most visitors to Mauritius head for the hotels north of **Port Louis ❶**. Tourism is well established between the resorts of Balaclava and Grand Baie, which act as bookends to one of the loveliest stretches of beach on the island, with an unbroken chain of powder-white beaches and gentle, crystal lagoons. Hotels, guesthouses and private villas and bungalows are plentiful in this area, and more hotels are also sprouting up in the less accessible areas between Balaclava and Port Louis. The coast's best-kept beaches are attached to hotels with beach loungers reserved for residents' use, but if you want to mix with the locals the public beaches at Balaclava, Mont Choisy and Pereybère are lively, particularly at weekends.

Away from the coast, the sugar-swathed plains of the north are not as scenic as the mountainous interior of the south, but the flat terrain, broken up by the gentlest of hills, is ideal for cycling, and there's something exciting about getting lost in the maze of sugar cane fields and asking for directions – only to get the reply back in Kreol, French, English or a combination of all three.

Bay of Tombs

The fastest route to the northern beaches is to take the motorway – either straight to Grand Baie or Trou aux Biches, or to the turn-off for the

resorts further south – but if you are in no hurry, you could opt for the longer coastal route. The Terre Rouge–Verdun Link Road, which bypasses the capital, opened in 2013 and has cut travel times from the south to the north.

Just beyond Port Louis' suburbs is **Roche Bois ❷**, where the mass of headstones in the Chinese Cemetery are bright red, the colour of good luck, and bear witness to the island's Sino-Mauritian population. But Roche Bois is also a poor Creole suburb and a byword for poverty on the island. In

Main Attractions

Maheswarnath Temple, Triolet
Grand Baie and Pereybère
Cap Malheureux
Northern Islands
Goodlands
Pamplemousses Botanical Gardens

Le Canonnier Hotel.

The North

0   2 km
0   2 miles

INDIAN OCEAN

INDIAN OCEAN

Coin de Mire
(Gunner's Quoin) **12**

Flat Island **13** Gabriel Island

Pte I'Hortal

Pte d'Azur

Pte Église

Pte Butte aux Sables

Anse la Raie

Pte Madras

Grand' Baie

Pereybère

Pavillon

Royal Palm Hotel

Cap Malheureux **11**

Butte à l'Herbe

Pte aux Roches

Bernachois

Zilwa Attitude Hotel

LUX* Grand Gaube

Paul & Virginie Hotel

Petit Paquet

St-François

Grand Gaube

Kalodyne

Pte Bernard

Petite Pointe

île d'Ambre **16**

Grande Pointe

Pte Orientale

Anse Bonserjent

Pte Bernache

Madame Azor

Réunion Maurel

Roche Terre

Germain

Manzelle Jeanne

Goodlands **14**

St-Antoine

Bassin Goémons

Bassin Humbert

Pte d'Azur

10

Le Canonnier Hotel

Pointe aux Canonniers

9

20° Sud Hotel

Mont Choisy

Grand' Baie

8

Grand-Baie

The Vale

Petit Raffray

Forbach Hill
101

Forbach

Esperance Trébuchet

Poudre d'Or Hamlet

Poudre d'Or

15

Pte Lascars

Baie la Rivière

Pte de la Rivière

Pointe des Lascars

Roches Noires

Pte de l'Embarcadère

Rivière du Rempart

Sugar Factory

Pte de Roche Noire

Poste Lafayette

Pte Lafayette

Poste d'Esny

Pte de Mer

Bras de Mer
Belcourt

Poste de Flacq

The One & Only

Le Saint Géran Hotel

Constance Belle Mare Plage Hotel

Pte Radeau

Roches Noire

Constance Le Prince Maurice Hotel

Poste de Flacq

Camp Poorun

Pte de Flacq

Centre de Flacq

Pte de Puits

Françoise

Pont Blanc

Bois d'Oiseaux

Grand Bois/Fond

Constance

Flacq

Plaines des Roches

Plaine des Roches

Laventure

Grand Retraite

Mare d'Australia

Bon Accueil

Belvédère

A 2

19

Moka

Nicolière Mts

Salazie

Matenga

632

Les Mariannes

Congomah

Brisée Verdière

Pont Praslin

Ville Bague

Petite Julie

Grande Rosalie

Petite Rosalie

A 6

The Mount
162

Mt Piton
267

A 2

A 6

Piton

Beau Séjour

Esperance

Mapou

Labourdonnais

18

Château Labourdonnais

Bois Marque

Belle Vue Harel

Fond du Sac

M 2

A 5

Pte Église

Maheswarnath Temple

7

Mt Virer
70

Plaine des Papayes

Morcellement St-André

Solitude

Triolet

Camp Bestel

5

The Oberoi Hotel

Maritim Resort & SPA

Westin Turtle Bay Resort & SPA

Balichava

Citrons

Trou aux Biches

Pointe aux Piments

Le Meridien Hotel

Le Victoria Hotel

4

Intercontinental Hotel

Baie aux Tortues ou de l'Arsenal
(Turtle Bay)

Baie du Tombeau
(Bay of Tombs)

3

Petit Gamin

Arsenal

**Aventure du Sucre
(Sugar Museum)**

Pamplemousses Botanical Gardens

Pamplemousses

17

Calebasses

Camp de Embrevades

L'Espoir

D'Epinay

Mon Goût

Mon Loisir

Belle Vue Maurel

Amaury

Antoinette

Antoinette

Barlow

Amitié

Gokoola

La Clémencie

R. du Rempart

Brémen

Mon Songe

Bois Jacot

Piyolyar Nagar

Grande Rosalie

Camp Créole

Belvédère

Balliacha

Walton

Notre Dame

Bois Pignolet

Khoyratty

Bois Marchand

Beau Plan

Madame Cayeux

The Mount

Roche Bois

La Cocoterie

Pte Roche Noires

Baie du Tombeau

A 4

Pterre Rouge

R. du Tombeau

Le Hochet

Ste-Croix

Terre Rouge

Abercrombie

Priest's Peak

Robinson

Caroline

Pieter Both

632

Long Mtn

Ruisseau Rose

Les Mariannes

Calebasses

A 2

Pont Praslin

Port Louis

1

2

M 1

M 2

M 3

Signal Mtn.

Curepipe

Grand River Bay

Grand River

Black River

Pte aux Sables

Pointe aux Sables

Petit Vergel

Port Louis

N

1999, one of its sons, a Creole singer called Kaya, was arrested for smoking cannabis at a pro-pot public demonstration and next day died in a police cell (see page 72).

In 1615, four Dutch East India Company ships were swept on to the reef during a cyclone and sunk at nearby **Baie du Tombeau ❸** (**Bay of Tombs**). Everyone died, including the Dutch Admiral Pieter Both who was on his way to Holland after a spell as the governor of the company. The sleepy village of Baie du Tombeau lies on the bay's southern flank, apparently turning its back on the world, and blocking its lovely, deserted beach from view. Access to the beach is not easy – to find it look out for the ruin of an old French fort partially hidden in shrubbery nearby.

You link up again with the Grand Baie road at the crossroads near **Arsenal** (named after a French ammunition store nearby), where you can also turn inland towards the Pamplemousses Botanical Gardens (see page 115).

Turtle Bay and Pointe aux Piments

Beyond residential **Balaclava**, reached through sugar fields on the B41, is an area that is fast being developed – though passers-by will see nothing but the entrances to private drives leading to hotels such as The Westin Turtle Bay Resort & Spa, The Oberoi and Maritim Resort & Spa. These neighbouring hotels flank the banks of the River Citrons, which enters the estuary forming the **Baie aux Tortues ❹** (**Turtle Bay**), also known as Baie de l'Arsenal, where great armies of turtles once swam. The Maritim Resort & Spa occupies grounds that formed part of a French arsenal at nearby **Moulin à Poudre**, where ammunition for ships was supplied for expeditions to India.

A cluster of high-class hotels surrounds the bay and they are doing their best to restore the health of the coral with replanting schemes. The bay once contained 90 percent live coral, but sadly the current figure is just 20 to 25 percent.

The road finally hits the coast at **Pointe aux Piments**, where filao trees rustle in gentle breezes and life chugs on slow and unhurried on the beaches. If you can leave the pristine paradise fronting Le Victoria, Le Meridien and Recif Attitude hotels, then take a stroll outside and surrender to the magic of a Mauritius sunset and watch wellie-booted fishermen wading in a shallow lagoon. Alternatively, visit the Aquarium Mauritius (tel: 261 4561; www.mauritiusaquarium.com; Mon–Sat 9.30am–5pm, Sun 10am–4pm) on the Coastal Road.

Trou aux Biches

The small resort of **Trou aux Biches ❺**, with its gently shelving sands and deep blue lagoon, is a mecca for beach-lovers. It is much more sedate than its northern neighbour, Grand Baie, particularly midweek when you can glimpse snapshots of how life used to be, and still is in parts of this former fishing village. At the start of the 3km (2-mile) beach, beside the fish landing

Sailboats lined up on Trou aux Biches's beach.

FACT

A 10-minute drive from Grand Baie to the deep cove of Anse la Raie, on the northeast coast, leads to a little bridge crossing an inlet over Bain Boeuf, just after Paradise Cove Boutique Hotel. On holy days such as Ganga Asnan, Hindu women swathed in deep pink saris carry food on banana leaves to a colourful shrine right on the water's edge.

The private beach at the Royal Palm.

station, fishermen huddle beneath casuarina trees talking in Kreol. Here you'll find a couple of restaurants and Chez Popo's supermarket, where you can hire bikes and, if self-catering, buy a wide range of essentials.

The hotels all have facilities for water-skiing, windsurfing, diving and snorkelling, and will also arrange sailing and glass-bottom boat trips. At weekends the tranquillity of the lagoon is broken by the roar of an increasing number of speedboats, but the beach remains a retreat for relaxation and beach games. Old boys on bicycles sell freshly caught fish and touts sell seashells, pareos and trinkets, keeping you amused with gentle banter. There's no shortage of fruit sellers wandering along the beach and to watch them peel pineapples with their machetes is quite a spectacle.

Triolet and Mont Choisy

Triolet ❻ can claim to be the largest and longest (and perhaps plainest) village on the island. It has played a lively part in Mauritian political life since Independence, and is the constituency of Mauritius' first prime minister. The village also has the highest population of Indo-Mauritians, and is home to the biggest Hindu temple in Mauritius (just inland from Trou aux Biches police station). Built in 1857, the Maheswarnath Temple complex (daily 6am–5pm) is a kaleidoscope of colour. It stands beside an enormous banyan where a placard welcomes all pilgrims.

At weekends and holidays it seems that everyone from the area toddles off to **Mont Choisy** ❼ beach, where turquoise seas meet a long strip of sugar-soft sand backed by a forest of casuarina trees. Matronly Indo-Mauritian mums make for the shade and unpack pots of rice and curry from great baskets (*tentes*) around which families gather to eat. Children play on a former landing strip, now a grassy football pitch, where a monument celebrates the first ever flight made by French pilots from Mauritius to Réunion in 1933. Midweek, Mont Choisy is a perfect spot for a quiet dip in the warm lagoon or a trip in a glass-bottom boat and has recently become a favourite for water-skiing.

Grand Baie

Grand Baie ❽ is the island's hub of tourism, where not only hotels and restaurants but also bars, clubs and designer shops are strung around a huge horseshoe-shaped bay. Dubbed the 'Creole Côte d'Azur' and, by Mauritian standards, brash, busy and boisterous, Grand Baie's development from a tiny fishing village to a large holiday resort seems to have dealt a fatal blow to the village atmosphere. Many shops have become supermarkets, property development is haphazard and islanders often complain of the lack of pavements, congested coast road and a rise in petty crime. Yet it remains popular with local residents, many of whom have second homes here, as well as with tourists who can find plenty of places to eat and drink. From here you can book island tours, including to Rodrigues, find self-catering accommodation and hire a car through tour operators, such as Mauritours, and many other smaller travel agents.

Much of the activity centres around **Sunset Boulevard** (www.sunsetboulevard.mu), a modern waterside shopping mall (closed Sun) opposite a cluster of supermarkets, restaurants and fast food stalls. You'll find a centre for big game fishing on the waterfront and facilities to book undersea walks, undersea safaris and parasailing trips over the lagoon. The bay, which at times is crowded with small pleasure craft and catamarans, has no decent bathing beach; for peace and relaxation take a short stroll to the soft wide sands of La Cuvette public beach to the north of the bay, which has modern facilities including showers, toilets and changing cubicles. Just beyond the black basalt rocks to the right of the beach is the luxurious **Royal Palm Hotel**, but be aware that casual beach strollers are not welcome unless they have a reservation for lunch or dinner. A good place to shop is at Super U complex, a short stroll inland from Sunset Boulevard. Here, a large supermarket provides everyday items, and you'll find good-value restaurants, such as Happy Rajah.

Grand Baie has more nightclubs (*boîtes de nuit*) than any other resort on the island (which draws quite a few local prostitutes to the area). For

a spot of balmy nightlife try Banana Beach Club for drinks and live music or let your hair down at the Buddha Bar & Club, which attracts a trendy, young crowd.

Pointe aux Canonniers

Enormous flamboyant trees, emblazoned with deep red flowers in summer, flank the road leading to **Pointe aux Canonniers** , a beach-belted headland at the northern end of Grand Baie which was once used as a garrison by the French and later turned into a quarantine station by the British. Eighteenth-century cannons and a ruined 19th-century lighthouse watch over the reefs (which have caused the doom of dozens of ships) from the gardens of **Le Canonnier Hotel**.

Hotels and shady villas house tourists and locals attracted by the tranquillity of the area. At the opposite tip of the headland from Le Canonnier is the **20° Sud Hotel**, a colonial-style boutique hotel, complete with planters' chairs and faded pictures, overlooking a swimming pool and a private sandy cove.

Temple detail in Pereybere.

Pereybère

Just 2km (1 mile) to the north, **Pereybère** ⑩ seems to be merging with Grand Baie. But the pace of life i much slower, providing a foil to the sometimes brash atmosphere of its sister resort as well as cheaper day-to-day living. Traditionally a holiday retrea for the Chinese community, Pereybère is changing rapidly to accommodate increasing numbers of foreign self caterers, as well as holidaymakers from Grand Baie who come for a change of scene, and to stretch out on the lovely casuarina-fringed beach or snorkel in the lagoon.

A smaller version of Mont Choisy (see page 110), Pereybère is swamped at weekends by islanders, who come to picnic, chat under the trees, swim, go for glass-bottom boat trips, and maybe even round off the day with an impromptu sega party. Food stalls sell hot snacks drinks and fresh fruit (conveniently cut up into small pieces and sold in bags) and, if you're lucky, there'll be an ice cream van, too. Away from the beach, small shops provide basics and simple restaurants serve slap-up meals at

COLONIAL MANSIONS

For a touch of bygone French glamour, wander around the island's colonial plantation homes and gardens, stopping for an elegant lunch on the veranda. Most of the colonial mansions on Mauritius were created during the French colonial period and date back to the 18th and 19th centuries. With a building style adapted to the tropics, they were usually constructed from wood, with lime-washed walls and rain-resistant *armagasse* roof tiles. A wide, long *verangue* (veranda) helped keep the house cool and dry, doors replaced windows for ventilation and lacy wooden or metal fringes, or *lambrequins*, decorated the roof. The kitchen and bathrooms were typically in an outside building.

Some of these elegant plantation homes are living museums, open to the public, with decent restaurants for a lunchtime stop. Three lie in the island's north: Eureka at Moka, perhaps the best example of colonial architecture on the island, with turreted windows, a wrap-around veranda and 109 doors; Château Labourdonnais at Mapou, whose famous orchard once supplied the island's fruit and now produces artisanal gourmet rum; and Demeure de Saint Antoine near Goodlands, with paintings from celebrated Mauritian artist Malcolm de Chazal. Other colonial houses worth visiting are Domaine les Aubineaux, in Curepipe, on the central plateau, with pretty turquoise shutters, and Saint Aubin, near Rivière des Anguilles, as part of The Tea Route.

nockdown prices. And if you're after a areo, the tree-lined catwalks along the main road offer plenty of choice; prices re lower than those offered by both hops and beach hawkers.

Cap Malheureux and Grand Gaube

Taking on the appearance of a country lane lined with casuarinas shading hallow bays and rocky coves, the coast road swings east to **Cap Malheureux** ❶, 6km (4 miles) beyond Pereybère. This, the island's most northerly point, probably got its name – Cape of Misfortune – from the number of ships that foundered here. It offers a stunning view of the Northern Islands. Nothing much goes on in this tranquil beauty spot, though if you get there around 4pm you will see the village wake up momentarily when fishermen bring in their catch to sell to islanders congregating beside the striking red-roofed church of **Notre Dame Auxilatrice** (daily 6.30am–5.30pm; free). There is a small beach where local kids play, just one restaurant, a general store and petrol station.

A 5km (3-mile) drive east through sugar cane emerges at the sparkling white beaches of the fishing village **Grand Gaube**, where the luxurious LUX* Grand Gaube overlooks the curvaceous bay. Or you could enjoy tasty snacks and drinks at the Caribbean-style restaurant and bar Di Sab on the main road, or become 'an islander' at Zilwa Attitude in Kalodyne, the newest, funkiest hotel on the block, whose bar overlooks the Northern Islands.

The Northern Islands

Gunners Quoin (Coin de Mire), Flat Island (Île Plate) and Gabriel Island (Îlot Gabriel) all make good day trips. Depending on weather conditions, you can have a fun day out sailing around the islands, being pampered by experienced crew. Full-day tours from Croisières Australes with lunch in the luxury catamaran cruiser *Le Pacha*, accommodating 20 to 30 passengers, leave from Sunset Boulevard in Grand Baie. It drops anchor in sheltered bays with plenty of opportunity for snorkelling and swimming or

Notre Dame Auxillatrice.

sunbathing on deck. Other operators in Grand Baie lay on similar tours.

Coin de Mire , the closest island to the shore, is composed of layers of crumbling volcanic sandstone, making landing difficult. Getting on to **Flat Island**  is worth the effort just to pad along the lovely beaches ringed by coral reef. The same coral reef encircles neighbouring **Gabriel Island**. These last two islands once served as quarantine stations for immigrants during the cholera epidemic of 1856, which nearly wiped out the population of Port Louis. Picnic parties to Flat Island are popular and you can spend the whole day exploring the little pathways that meander round its lighthouse and cemetery.

You need permission to land on Round and Serpent islands, 24km (15 miles) north of Mauritius, which are both designated nature reserves; but they are difficult to land on anyway because of their sheer cliffs. **Round Island** (Île Ronde) is home to many endangered species, including the rare Telfair skink, two species of snake and the *paille-en-queue* – the tropicbird that graces the tail fins of Air Mauritius

planes. Serpent Island (Île aux Serpent is a bird sanctuary, but there are n snakes. And in case you were wondering, **Pigeon House Rock** (**Le Pigeor nier**), north of Flat Island, doesn't hav any pigeons either.

Goodlands and Amber Island

From Grand Gaube the road finall draws you away from the coast an swings south to **Goodlands** . Th streets in this densely populated tow are usually heaving with people, wh frequent the high street shops and th daily **market**. Goodlands is also hom to the largest model sailing ship fa tory in Mauritius, **Historic Marin** (tel: 283 9304; Mon–Fri 9am–5pn Sat–Sun 9am–noon; guided tours There is a large showroom downstai (with many wooden objects othe than ships), while upstairs you ca watch the craftsmen patiently workin on these mini masterpieces (weekda only). Colonial mansion **La Demeur de Saint Antoine** (tel: 282 1823; www lademeuresaintantoine.com; Tue–Sa lunch, afternoon tea and dinner b

At Historic Marine.

eservation only; guided tours), tucked behind a high wall on the outskirts of own, was built by a relative of painter nd poet Malcolm de Chazal, and has room scattered with his paintings.

The road southeast of Goodlands its the coast at **Poudre d'Or** ⑮ (Golden Powder), an appealing village where you can linger on the headland opposite the reef where, in 1744, the *aint Geran* foundered in a storm, a ragic incident that inspired French novelist Bernardin de Saint Pierre to en his famous love story *Paul and Virinie*. Some objects rescued from the wreck are on display in the National History Museum in Mahébourg (see page 123). **Île d'Ambre** ⑯ (Amber Island), an uninhabited island, is just 0 minutes' boat ride from here, and if you ask around, you should find a local fisherman to take you from the jetty at Poudre d'Or; arrange for him to pick you up later so that you can enjoy the excellent swimming and snorkelling. Or take a guided kayak excursion from Goodlands with Yemaya Adventures o learn about the island's history and ecology. A picnic lunch is included.

The headland marking the boundary between the north and east coasts is dominated by the wild and windy beaches of Roches Noires and Poste Lafayette, studded with black volcanic rocks. They are often deserted but for men fishing in the shallows or landing their catch from boats. Be careful if you want to swim as the seas can be rough.

Pamplemousses Botanical Gardens

From Poudre d'Or the road heads inland to the **Botanical Gardens** ⑰ at Pamplemousses (http://ssrbg.govmu. org; daily 8.30am–5.30pm), a 30-minute drive from Port Louis or Grand Baie. They are well worth a visit, the best time being between December and April.

The 25-hectare (62-acre) gardens were renamed the Sir Seewoosagur Ramgoolam Botanical Gardens in 1988 in honour of the late prime minister, but they are still known by everyone as Pamplemousses (French for grapefruit). The village was named after a variety of citrus plant, imported from Java by the Dutch in the 17th century and which once grew in the area.

TIP

Those interested in learning more about sugar cultivation and its history should visit L'Aventure du Sucre Museum on the Beau Plan Sugar Estate near Pamplemousses (tel: 243 7900; www.aventure dusucre.com; daily 9am–5pm).

Poudre d'Or.

You should allow a couple of hours to explore the maze of palm-lined avenues. Tour operators often combine a visit with a shopping spree to Port Louis and tend to lead groups on lightning-quick tours. The official guides will also whisk you around rather quickly for a fixed fee of R100, but they do point out the main attractions and provide interesting nuggets of information about some of the more unusual species; try to collar one of the older guides, who are likely to have worked in the gardens for years and are usually more informative. If you want to explore independently, it's a good idea to buy the guidebook (available at the main entrance), which contains a map as well as an authoritative explanation of the plant species – only some are labelled – and other attractions. There are no refreshment facilities inside the gardens, so stock up on water from the food stalls by the car park (near the motorway turn-off).

Wrought-iron gates (exhibited at the 1851 Great Exhibition at London's Crystal Palace) mark the original entrance to the gardens but the main entrance is now by the big car par on the other side. From here, guide will lead you along shaded avenue named after botanists and benefactor and show you trees such as the bastar mahogany (Andira inermis), marma lade box (Genipa americana), chewin gum (Manilkara achras) and sausag tree (Kigelia pinnata).

In all, there are about 500 plant spe cies out of which 80 are palms and 40 such as ebony, mahogany and pandanu are indigenous to the Mascarene Island Among the most impressive sights ar the **Lotus Pond**, filled with yellow an white flowers, and the huge **Lily Pon** Half concealed by the floating leaves c the giant Amazon water lily (*Victori amazonica*), this is everyone's favourit photo opportunity. The flowers of th lily open white, fade to a dusky pink b the end of the second day and then di the unmistakable flat leaves can reach a much as 1.5 metres (4.5ft) in diamete The talipot palm is another remarkab species. It waits 40 to 60 years to flowe then promptly dies. Ginger, cloves an cinnamon are among the many spice you can sniff out.

The Lily Pond at Pamplemousses Botanical Gardens.

The gardens' origins go back to 735, when Mahé de Labourdonnais bought a house in the grounds, which he called Chateau Mon Plaisir. In 1768 it became the residence of the French horticulturist Pierre Poivre, who planted the seeds for the specimens seen today (see page 242). The present **Chateau Mon Plaisir**, a 19th-century British legacy, is now used as an administration office, although it is crying out to be transformed into a museum and restaurant.

Château de Labourdonnais

An impressive tree-lined driveway leads to the colonnaded **Château de Labourdonnais** ⑱ in Mapou (tel: 266 7172; www.unchateaudanslanature.com; daily 9am–5pm). Modelled on Versailles, this colonial mansion was built in 1859 and opened to the public in 2010. Its orchard once supplied fruit to the island and the château is now known in international circles for its gourmet artisanal rum – visits include a rum tasting. Informal restaurant Le Table de Château, with home-made condiments, is really rather good.

Scenic route to Pieter Both

For a scenic drive – where a foreground of sugar cane is framed by the quirky peaks of the Moka Mountains – take the A2 from Pamplemousses towards Centre de Flacq and the east coast. En route you pass **Grand Rosalie**, where the first sugar estate was established in 1743. The plantation house is closed to the public, but you can get an idea of the lay of the land from **La Nicolière Reservoir** ⑲. The road winds uphill, giving bird's-eye views of the luscious landscape, and descends through woods and sleepy villages. If the light is right, stop at the welcoming hamlet of **Malenga**, the nearest you'll get to **Pieter Both**, whose pinnacle resembles a man's head perched precariously on cloaked shoulders. They say that the day the head comes off a great catastrophe will destroy the island, but even the worst cyclones of 1892 and 1960 have failed to shift it. From Malenga you can watch the mountain as sun and clouds cast shadows across its face. From here, the B34 joins the motorway at Terre Rouge. The more direct route to Malenga is along the Verdun to Terre Rouge bypass.

Château de Labourdonnais.

An inviting hammock at the Shangri-La Le Touessrok Resort & Spa.

THE EAST

The east – with its glorious beaches, secluded hotels and sleepy villages – is tranquil and uncrowded, despite the presence of the airport.

Port Louis

Tourism development has been slow in the east compared to the north and west coasts, though hotel developments are starting to monopolise the white beaches to the north and south of Belle Mare. Some of the island's best hotels are already well established here, including the world-famous Constance Le Prince Maurice, the One&Only Le Saint Géran and the Shangri-La Le Touessrok Resort & Spa. There are few local excursions to tempt you away from the beach, and due to the relatively poor road links, access to the north and west coast isn't particularly speedy. If you are eager to do a lot of exploring, it's best not to base yourself on the east coast for your entire stay.

Flat Flacq

The northern area of the east coast lies in the district of Flacq, which derives from Groote Vlakte (Great Plain), the name given to the area by the Dutch when they arrived in the 17th century. The flat terrain is perfect for the cultivation of sugar, and much of the land is owned by sugar estates, including FUEL (Flacq United Estate Limited), the largest in Mauritius. This is the most rural area in the country, and the vast sugar cane fields are interspersed with

crops of onions, tomatoes, chillies, peanuts and aubergines, grown for local consumption.

When the French arrived they called the main town **Centre de Flacq**, now dominated by a 19th-century British-built District Court House. Apart from a small lively Sunday market (*foire*) and stacks of shops there are few other attractions, but if you want to get around independently, you'll find plenty of buses and taxis to take you to Port Louis, Mahébourg and the east coast villages.

Main Attractions
Île aux Cerfs
Fort Frederick Hendrik Museum, Vieux Grand Port
Mahébourg and its National History Museum
Blue Bay
La Vallée de Ferney
Île aux Aigrettes

A sugar cane plantation located at the foot of craggy mountains.

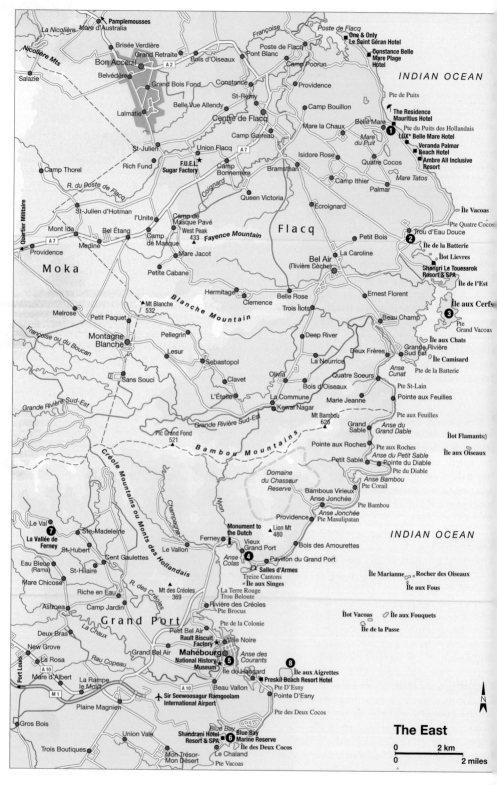

The East

0   2 km

0   2 miles

Belle Mare Plage

The main concentration of beaches and hotels is around **Belle Mare ❶**, about 10 minutes' drive from Centre de Flacq. There is a better-than-average public beach, backed by casuarina forests where old kilns remain as monuments to the once thriving coral burning industry; from the top of them you get lovely views of coast and cane fields. The public beach is a mere extension of the more pristine, regularly swept ones fronting the nearby **Constance Belle Mare Plage**, newly refurbished **LUX* Belle Mare** and chic **Long Beach** resorts.

As you head south, keep an eye out for brightly painted statues of Hindu gods, peeking out of the thick vegetation. The string of hotels continues with **The Residence Mauritius**, an imposing, plantation-style place, and **Veranda Palmar Beach**, with its distinctive thatched roofs, and several newer four-star contenders, including the all-inclusive resort **Ambre**.

Trou d'Eau Douce

Arriving in the village of **Trou d'Eau Douce ❷** (Hole of Sweet Water) after the string of hotels further north, you may feel jolted back to reality. The village underwent a renaissance with the opening of an MTPA information office (tel: 480 0925; www.tourism-mauritius. mu), a small car park and a refurbished waterfront where enthusiastic operators are happy to ferry you to Île aux Cerfs. Many tourists stop at the handful of souvenir shops and simple restaurants, which make a welcome change, especially if you've been holed up in a resort for a few days. Beyond the village the pace of life has barely changed despite the proliferation of visitors to the area.

Island-hopping in the east

The **Île aux Cerfs ❸** is a long-time favourite with Mauritians and foreign visitors. It is managed by Shangri-La Le Touessrok Resort & Spa, just south of Trou d'Eau Douce, but is open to the public (unlike Îlot Mangenie, which is restricted to hotel residents only). Bear in mind, however, that the free car park inside the grounds of Shangri-La Le Touessrok Resort & Spa is reserved for golfers with a reservation at the golf course on the island. If you don't have your own transport you could join one of the full-day excursions (including by catamaran) offered by tour operators in tourist centres around the island. A couple of companies in Trou d'Eau Douce run a regular ferry service from the waterfront.

The island is covered by 285 hectares (700 acres) of woodland and has a golf course, lovely beaches and limpid, blue waters. You can swim and snorkel from the shore. A boathouse near the jetty provides equipment for water-skiing, windsurfing and boating, and scattered among the trees (and even in the trees) nearby are open-air shops and restaurants. The atmosphere is relaxed, but it can get very crowded. If you want solitude, there are quieter beaches close by, and enjoyable walks can be made round the island along marked paths. In the trees beyond the jetty is a small Turtle Park.

Shangri-La Le Touessrok Resort & Spa's spectacular location.

TIP

To see how essential oils are made from the fragrant yellow ylang ylang flowers, visit Ylang Ylang L'Huiles Essentielles (Royal Road, Anse Jonchée; tel: 634 5557; Mon–Sat 7am–6pm), in the foothills near Vieux Grand Port.

Fishermen sailing in the bay by the islet of Mouchoir Rouge.

A possible trip from Île aux Cerfs is to the deep estuary of Grande Rivière Sud-Est, the longest river in Mauritius, where at a small but pretty waterfall you can often see bold young islanders diving into the water from the basalt cliffs, hoping to be rewarded with a few tourist rupees.

The Old Dutch Coast Road

The drive from Trou d'Eau Douce south along the B28 or Old Coast Road to Mahébourg is one of the loveliest on the island. Head inland to Bel Air where the road veers towards the coast, hitting the sea at the gorge of **Grande** Rivière **Sud-Est**. From here, it barely manages to keep a toehold on land as it contrives to avoid the steep foothills of the Bambou Mountains. Fishing hamlets and picturesque villages are scattered along the route.

The **Grand Port** district in the southeastern corner of Mauritius is full of historical connections since this is where the French and Dutch began their colonisation of the island. There are many ruins in the area, some dating from the 17th century, but most are in a

poor state of repair. Lying in the shadow of Lion Mountain, **Vieux Grand Port** ❹ is of particular historical interest as it was the first base established by the Dutch, in the 17th century. The original Dutch fort disappeared beneath defences built by the French in the 18th century. Now all that remains are a few blackened and disintegrating walls, but in 1997 archaeologists unearthed beakers, pottery, glass and Chinese porcelain from the 17th century. These and other finds are displayed in the adjacent **Fort Frederick Hendrik Museum** (tel: 634 4319; Mon, Tue, Thu–Sat 9am–4pm, Sun 9am–noon; free), along with a model of the fort, while audiovisual displays explain the history of the Dutch East India Company and its role in Mauritius.

Along the water's edge are the caves of **Salles d'Armes**, where French gentlemen once fought duels. They are best approached by sea with a local fisherman, but you can make your own way by zigzagging through the cane fields at the northern end of Vieux Grand Port village. Further north, the **Bois des Amourettes** was a favourite haunt of

rench soldiers and their sweethearts. During World War II the British built a naval lookout post but all that remains are some old concrete bunkers poking through the sugar cane on the shore.

Between Vieux Grand Port and Mahébourg, you pass two memorials: one commemorating the first Dutch landing in 1598 and another marking their introduction of sugar in 1639. These memorials sat unnoticed for years, but were spruced up for the royal Dutch visit in 1998, when Mauritius celebrated the 400th anniversary of the Dutch arrival.

Mahébourg

Named after the first French governor of the Mascarenes, Mahé de Labourdonnais, **Mahébourg** ❺ (pronounced Ma-y-bourg) lies on the southern shores of the immense Vieux Grand Port Bay. Under the French, Mahébourg was a busy, thriving port, which the British later linked by rail (now abandoned) to Port Louis. The names of the neatly laid out grid-style streets reflect the influence of European settlers, and there is a historical feel here that is absent in many Mauritian towns.

These days Mahébourg is a dusty, rather run-down place, crammed with grocers' and fabric stores. Yet it has an appealing, laid-back bustle. The seafront Rue des Hollandais is done no favours by the sprawling presence of the bus station, but the area benefited from a face-lift in 2003. The waterfront, with its memorial to the Battle of Grand Port, makes for a pleasant stroll. Multicoloured pirogues bob around the islet of Mouchoir Rouge (Red Hanky island), while, in the backstreets, life trundles slowly by; women still scrub clothes on the stone sinks at Le Lavoir, the outdoor wash-house off Rue des Hollandais. There is a lively daily market, best on Mondays, worth visiting for its exotic fruit, vegetables, herbs and spices.

National History Museum

Mahébourg's **National History Museum** (tel: 631 9329; Mon, Wed–Sat 9am–4pm, Sun and public holidays 9am–noon), on the southern outskirts of the town, is housed in an 18th-century building. Its original owner, Jean de Robillard, turned the house

An old colonial building in use as a hardware shop in Mahébourg.

BATTLE OF GRAND PORT

In August 1810, British ships arrived in the Bay of Grand Port to capture Île de France (present-day Mauritius) from the French. The superior British navy expected an easy victory as they waited on Île de la Passe for French ships returning from a voyage. They intended to trick them by flying the French flag, before opening fire. But then gunpowder exploded on the island, causing injury and confusion, and two British ships ran aground on the reef, allowing the French to regroup and defend their territory. This historic three-day Battle of Grand Port, which ended in a British surrender, is the only naval battle the French won against the British in the Napoleonic era, and is commemorated on the Arc de Triomphe in Paris.

into a hospital where the commanders of the French and British forces who had fought in the Battle of Grand Port convalesced side by side. The museum contains an eclectic display of exhibits from the Dutch, French and British periods. Portraits line the walls, among them Prince Maurice of Nassau, Pieter Both, botanist Pierre Poivre and 'king of the corsairs', Robert Surcouf, who donated the dagger he seized in 1800 from Captain Rivington of the English ship *Kent* following an attack in the Bay of Bengal. One of the most famous relics is the ship's bell from the ill-fated *St Géran*, which sank off the northeast coast in 1744. A newspaper cutting recalls the fate of the British steamer *Trevessa*, which sank hundreds of miles from Mauritius in 1923. The survivors landed at Bel Ombre on the south coast after 25 days in a lifeboat with nothing to eat but ship's biscuits. You can see the remains of the biscuits and the cigarette tin they used to measure water rations. Other exhibits include Mahé de Labourdonnais' four-poster bed and two wooden palanquins in which slaves would carry their masters.

Taking a boat trip around the picturesque aera of Blue Bay, near Mahebourg.

Around Mahébourg

The approach to **Blue Bay** ❻, south of Mahébourg, isn't promising as you drive past some very poor housing, but Pointe d'Esny is considered a desirable place to live, and high-walled private bungalows dot the coast. En route you pass **Le Preskil Beach Resort** hotel, a nice enough spot, on its own small peninsula with views of the mountains, but unless you want easy access to the airport, it's rather an isolated place to stay. The public beach at Blue Bay, however, is worth an excursion. You can hire a glass-bottom boat here to view wonderful corals in the Blue Bay Marine Park and sail past the islet of **Île de Deux Cocos** (tel: 698 9800; www.iledes deuxcocos.com; daily 10.30am–3.30pm), an exclusive luxury retreat that can be visited for the day and hired for weddings and private functions. On the other side of the bay, the **Shandrani Resort & Spa** is the height of luxury. It stands on its own peninsula in 30 hectares (74 acres) of gardens, just 6km (4 miles) from the airport. To the west of Shandrani Resort & Spa, at Mare aux Songes, an almost intact set of dodo bones was discovered in 1865 and the skeleton is on display in London's British Museum. In 2006 Dutch scientists unearthed more dodo bones, which will enable them to understand more about this extinct bird.

From **Ville Noire**, north across La Chaux River from Mahébourg, signs point the way to the **Rault Biscuit Factory** (tel: 631 9559; www.biscuitmanioc. com; Mon–Fri 9–11am and 1–3pm) where you can take a guided tour to see women baking *biscuits manioc* made from the cassava that grows in the nearby valley.

The B7 from Ville Noire runs through cane fields to the village of **Riche en Eau**. The area, literally 'rich in water', was home to small family-owned sugar estates, where isolated chimneys, now listed as national monuments, mark the sites of early factories. Signs in the area lead to **La Vallée de Ferney** ❼ (tel: 624 0440; www.valleedeferney.com; daily

0am–6pm), where the former Ferney ugar factory has been converted into a visitors' centre. Wall maps and information boards highlight conservation ssues, and guided walks through the 00-hectare (494-acre) valley reveal rare irds – including the Mauritius kestrel, vith guaranteed sightings at feeding ime – and indigenous plants thriving amid mountain-backed landscapes and ubbling streams. A simple restaurant erving traditional Mauritian specialiies in the forest is an atmospheric place or lunch.

le aux Aigrettes

Ecotourism is developing at Île aux Aigrettes ❽ (tel: 631 2396; www. mauritian-wildlife.org; Mon–Sat 9am– 2.30pm, Sun 9.30–10.30am), a nature reserve that opened to the public in 1998. It's a 20-minute ferry trip from Pointe Jerome near the Preskil Beach Resort Hotel. A guide from the Mauritius Wildlife Foundation (MWF) leads no more than 20 visitors at a time along marked paths. Look out for bands of pink pigeons (see page 85) breeding among flora found nowhere

else in the world. The MWF has been active in regenerating the island, its main aim being to re-create a microcosm of the original coastal habitat. It has introduced Aldabra tortoises, seen lumbering under the canopy, Telfair's skink and the Mauritian fody. During World War II, much of the native forest was cleared to make room for British troops, who installed guns (still in place) as defences against a Japanese invasion. Old hands remember waiting for the enemy which never came. The old generator room has been converted into a museum and if you climb to the rooftop viewing platform panoramic views unfold across the sweeping bay and **Île de la Passe** beyond.

Among the historic ruins on this islet off Vieux Grand Port are the remains of French defences, an old reservoir and a beautifully preserved 18th-century powder magazine, complete with a harp etched into its wall. This was probably engraved by a homesick soldier of the 87th Royal Irish Fusiliers, stationed here in the 1830s. Both islets make a wonderful half-day excursion.

A distinctive pink pigeon on Ile aux Aigrettes.

Rochester Falls.

THE SOUTH COAST

The rugged south coast is the island's wilder side, far from well-trodden shores, and is easily explored in a day's drive.

The south coast from Bel Ombre to Riambel is currently undergoing major development to increase tourism and revive the economy of this forgotten region. The lack of tourist amenities is offset by gorgeous scenery and the sense that you are witnessing Mauritius as it used to be. Great stretches of rugged basalt cliffs assaulted by strong southeasterly winds lie against a backdrop of hills and undulating sugar fields that are part of century-old plantations. The old estates, built to withstand the southern winds, have survived better here than elsewhere. Apart from a scattering of luxurious hotels dominating sandy beaches in the west, there is scant evidence of the 20th century, let alone the 21st. Yet although still a far cry from the north, changes are afoot in the south, heralded by the 2004 Heritage Resorts development at Bel Ombre in the southwest, and the strip of hotels which followed nearby. Among them are Shanti Maurice, with its spacious beach-side accommodation at St Felix, midway along the south coast, and more recently, the redevelopment of the Movenpick Hotel into Outrigger Mauritius Beach Resort. Le Morne, on the southwestern tip, is the recipient of the latest development, with 500 beds added in 2015, courtesy of Rui hotels.

Rivers flowing from the central uplands to the ocean have, in many places, prevented coral reefs from gaining a foothold, depriving the area of the gentle lagoons reminiscent of the north, and swimming, except from designated beaches, can be dangerous. In the west, the Savanne Mountains (which give the district its name) rise steeply from deep coves, relegating the coast road to a narrow strip west of Souillac. The east is flatter. Here, the roads run through cane fields and over bridges spanning rivers and streams, linking shanty villages. Not a lot of tourists pass this way.

Main Attractions

Robert Edward Hart Museum
Rochester Falls
Le Gris Gris
Saint Aubin a Le Bois Cheri Tea Factory
La Vanille Réserve des Mascareignes

Walking through sugar cane near Rochester Falls.

TIP

In Frederica Nature Reserve look out for the relics of an old mill standing on the site of a former sugar factory, indigenous plants and trees, plantations of edible palms and herds of deer. Book through Terrocean (tel: 5729 4498; www.adventure.frederica.mu).

If you're driving, the south coast can easily be explored in one leisurely day – less if you're based at one of the hotels on the west coast or on the southeast coast near Mahébourg. If you have a full day to spare, you might even consider making a circular drive by taking in the route through the Black River Gorges National Park (described in The West chapter, see page 137). Most hotels offer full-day tours of the south coast, which usually include lunch in an old sugar estate house.

Around Bel Ombre

Our tour begins at the western end, just east of Le Morne. Here you'll find a quiet rock-strewn beach, where fishermen sit mending their nets and children play among the trees. The first significant hamlet is **Baie du Cap** ❶, typical of many villages along the south coast: there are just a few Chinese-run *boutiks* (and a police station built by a local sugar magnate from a ship that sank offshore in the 19th century).

A short distance beyond is **Bel Ombre** ❷, where at certain times of the year lorries laden with sheaves of sugar cane are seen, bound for St Aubin and Savannah factories further east. Bel Ombre has long been the heartland of the south coast's sugar industry. Back in 1816, philanthropic businessman Charles Telfair, after whom the hotel nearby is named, bought the factory. Newly arrived from England, he immediately set about turning Bel Ombre into a model sugar estate, only to incur the wrath of local slave owners who did not agree with his idea of providing proper food and shelter for slaves.

Adjoining the colonial-style Heritage Le Telfair Golf & Spa Resort is the 18-hole Heritage golf course; all that is left of the factory is the chimney. Guided nature tours, 4x4 excursions and quad-biking trails into **Frederica Nature Reserve**, coupled with elegant haute cuisine in the evening at the splendid 19th-century Château de Bel Ombre, attract golfers, 'green' tourists and gourmets. Other contenders offering grand-scale sanctuary, serenity and space are the Heritage Awali, with its enormous African-village style spa and Heritage Villas, nestled on the hillside with spectacular views across the estate. A nudge east along the coast is the sumptuous Outrigger Mauritius Beach Resort and the red-roofed Tamassa Hotel.

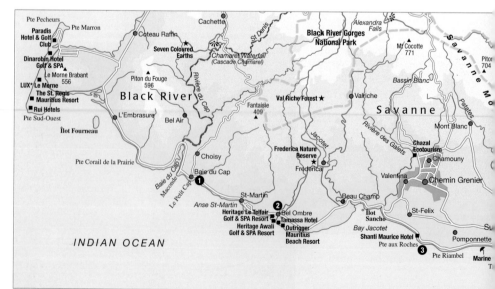

Beau Champ to Riambel

the 'unspoilt' southwest, where the lush foothills of the Black River Gorges National Park merge with the forests of Bel Ombre, is a natural place for ecotourism. Driving east through swaying fields of sugar cane, a mile or so east of Beau Champ, the B10 branches inland to **Chemin Grenier**, where a minor road runs north to the water-filled crater of **Bassin Blanc**. Here, with a little patience, you may be able to spot the brilliant green echo parakeet and Mauritius kestrel.

The B9 coast road to the west of **Pointe aux Roches** ❸ fringes a public beach; the area to the east is dominated by the Shanti Maurice Hotel. If you would like to combine beach activity with 'green tourism', Chazal Ecotourism at the 2,400-hectare (6,000-acre) St Felix Sugar Estate offers speed zip wire rides and river trekking on the Rivière des Galets. More sedate activities on offer include archery and guided nature tours through the estate, and camping.

Meanwhile, the coast remains beautifully rugged, although it is not without its dangers due to an absence of coral reef. Further east, **Pomponette** is known for its treacherous currents, and most locals head for the safer **SSR**

Public Beach just before the peaceful hamlet of **Riambel** (from the Malagasy word meaning 'beaches of sunshine'), where the well-established Green Palm restaurant provides delicious south Indian meals.

Souillac

The largest settlement on the south coast is **Souillac** ❹, which lies on an inlet where the rivers Savanne and Patates form an estuary (about 30 minutes' drive from Le Morne on the west coast). At the height of sugar production in the 19th century, steam ships loaded cane from nearby estates and shunted along the coast to Port Louis, but the port fell into decline when road and rail replaced the steamers. In the 1990s, substantial improvements were made to the old port area, prompting the town's designation as a 'tourist village'. While such a billing owes more to optimism than reality, it is worth stopping off to explore the handful of sights that are scattered around the bay.

On the western side a road turns off to Souillac's **Marine Cemetery**, one of the most beautiful in Mauritius. Who knows what graves were washed out to sea over the years, but in 1957

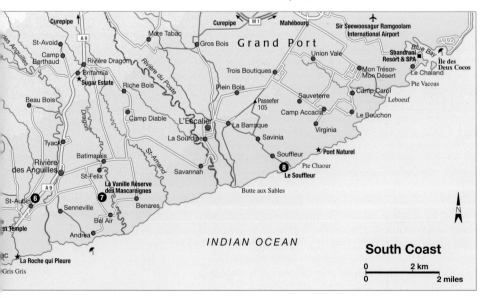

people reported seeing hundreds of skulls and human bones littering the cemetery as a result of a tidal wave. Meanwhile, constant erosion of the sea wall threatens even more damage to graves, many of which date back to the early 19th century. One of the oldest tombs is that of Thomas Etienne Bolgerd (1748–1818), a Souillac bigwig and owner of 500 slaves who was captured by the British in 1809 and released in exchange for some goats. The most famous member of the d'Unienville family, Baron Marie Claude Antoine Marrier d'Unienville (1766–1831), is also buried here, as is Robert Edward Hart (1891–1954), the country's most celebrated poet and writer.

Next stop is the old **port** area, where the most evident improvement is the restoration of a 200-year-old sugar warehouse, part of which is now occupied by **Le Batelage** restaurant, where tourists on organised trips are often fed and watered. The shady terrace on the quay at the front provides good views over the river, now so tranquil after years of inactivity.

The **Telfair Gardens** are just across the road from the bus station. Shaded by gigantic Indian almond trees and banyans, the gardens are a favourite spot among the locals who come here to pass the time of day while kids quite oblivious to the skull-and-cross-bones signs, swim off the rocky coast. The cemetery is visible across the bay.

From here it is a 10-minute stroll to the **Robert Edward Hart Museum** (tel: 625 6101; Mon, Wed–Fri 9am–4pm, Sat–Sun 9am–noon), the former home of Souillac's most famous son. The half-Irish, half-French poet and writer lived alone in a charming little coral-built bungalow, known as La Nef (The Nave), which contains manuscripts, books and personal belongings. Hart churned out work in English and French and his efforts were recognised in both English and French literary circles, with an OBE and a gold medal from the Académie Française. He was obviously inspired by the beauty of his surroundings and you can understand why when you see the golden beach pounded by ferocious seas at the rear of the house.

AIN'T NO MOUNTAIN HIGH ENOUGH

Mauritius' 28 quirky-shaped mountains, reminders of its volcanic past, may be miniature compared to those in Réunion, but the climbing is easier and you are rewarded with spectacular views. Follow in the footsteps of Charles Darwin on a three-hour return climb up Le Pouce (812 metres/2,663ft), 'The thumb', protruding from the Moka mountain range, for views of Port Louis. Hike up independently along a well-marked trail from Le Dauget village, or take a guided climb with Yemaya Adventures (tel: 5752 0046; www.yemayaadventures.com). For the highest views on the island, take a straightforward three-hour hike along a forested path in the Black River Gorges National Park to Mauritius' highest mountain, Piton de la Petite Rivière/Black River Peak (828 metres/2,716ft). The two-hour return climb up Lion Mountain (480 metres/1,574ft) with Vertical World (tel: 5251 1107; www.verticalworldltd.com) is brought alive with stories of myths and legends, and affords sweeping views over the historic southeast. A dramatic climb, for those of moderate fitness, is up the iconic monolith Le Morne Brabant (556 metres/1,824ft) with Trekking Île Maurice (tel: 5785 61177; www.trekkingilemaurice.com), with inspiring views of forested estates and coral gardens in a translucent lagoon. Its poignant slave past earned this mountain Unesco World Heritage status in 2008, and it's the only place to find the large, red *Trochetia boutoniana*, the island's national flower.

Rochester Falls

Not far from Souillac's seafront, a road runs 5km (3 miles) inland through cane fields to the **Rochester Falls**, which tumble from the Savanne River from a height of 10 metres (33ft). Constant erosion has fashioned the basalt rock into upright columns, and young boys enjoy scaling the jagged cliffs before diving into the cold fresh water. It's also a great place for a swim. Taxi drivers will take you there (and wait to take you back), but you can also hoof it. The track weaves uphill for about 15 minutes before descending to the falls. However, it is an isolated spot and at the time of writing there have been reports of intimidating behaviour from locals, so visiting it alone is discouraged.

On the way, you pass **Terracine**, one of the island's earliest factories, dating back to 1820. It closed down in 1947 but the chimney, a national monument, stands as a reminder of its sugar-producing days. Right next to it, the colourful Mariamen Temple, which remains quiet for most of the year, bursts into life in December and January when it is taken over by Tamil fire-walking and body-piercing Cavadee ceremonies (see page 74).

The wild south

If you continue along the road from La Nef you reach **Le Gris Gris ❺**, the most southerly point of Mauritius, more like the windswept coast of Scotland than the gentle shores of a tropical island. Some say it is called Gris Gris because black magic (*gris gris* in Kreol) used to be performed here. If you walk along the yawning sandy beach and allow your imagination to run riot, you can pick out the figure of a sorcerer scored out of the rock, who appears to be holding a cauldron. Up on the headland, where weather-beaten casuarinas attest to the ferocity of the winds, a 15-minute walk along a small path leads to a rocky outcrop called **La Roche qui Pleure** (The Crying Rock), so named because the sea which cascades around it gives the impression that it is weeping. (A monochrome photograph in La Nef illustrates the uncanny similarity between the silhouette of this rock and the profile of Robert Edward Hart.)

Wild terrain at Le Gris Gris.

EAT

The Hungry Crocodile restaurant in La Vanille Réserve des Mascareignes has an interesting menu. If you're not tempted by the idea of crocodile croquettes, you can always opt for a croc-free *croque monsieur*.

Saint Aubin.

The Tea Route

One of the highlights of a south coast tour is a visit to the area's colonial homes. Many are off-limits to the public but local tour operators offer The Tea Route, a full-day guided tour that starts at Domaine les Aubineaux, a former tea planter's residence in Cure-pipe, with tea tasting in the attractive tearoom, and finishes with lunch at the residence of **Saint Aubin** ❻ (tel: 626 1819; www.saintaubin.mu/laroutedute; Mon–Sat 8.30am–4.30pm), built in 1870, on the A9 5km (3 miles) north-east of Souillac. The visit provides a leisurely glimpse of colonial life, with relaxation on the broad verandas, a tour of the vanilla and anthurium planta-tions, rum tasting at the distillery and a stroll through spacious grounds.

It also includes the **Bois Cheri tea factory**, 10km (6 miles) inland. Although tea is no longer produced in large quantities, the factory is worth visiting to see how it is processed and packaged. You will also be driven to a hilltop tea pavilion overlooking a lake surrounded by neat tea fields. Here, you can sample plain, vanilla or even passion fruit flavoured tea, and go fo a stroll on the hillside, with magnifi cent views of the coast.

Off the beaten track

Worth considering for the contrast i scenery are visits to **Andrea** and **L'Exil** former seaside and hunting lodge respectively of Franco-Mauritian suga barons. You can enjoy a traditiona lunch at Andrea, in an exceptiona location on a grassy-sloped clifftop where surf beats on the boulder-strewi mouth of Rivière des Anguilles. Privat trekking and quad-biking excursion are offered to L'Exil, which overlook the Rivière Savanne and has pano ramic views of the nature reserve o Combo, where a guide will point ou endangered plant and animal species.

Book a guided day tour of th area with local operators or direct a Andrea (tel: 5471 0555; www.relaisde lodges.mu); it includes lunch at Andre and transport.

If you head north along the A9, yo pass the manicured lawns and pineap ple plantations of the **Britannia Suga Estate**, the south's last significan

sugar plantation. It is still very active, with a pristine estate village of stone-built homes and a school.

The Crocodile Park

You don't need to be on an organised tour to visit **La Vanille Réserve des Mascareignes** ❼, still known locally as The Crocodile Park (tel: 626 2503; www.lavanille-reserve.com; daily 9.30am–5pm), signposted right off the road running through the large village of **Rivière des Anguilles** (on the banks of the river of the same name). The park occupies a valley that features about the closest thing you'll get to tropical rainforest, which is why Owen Griffiths, an Australian zoologist, chose the area to farm Nile crocodiles. The stud of the estate and four females were brought from Madagascar in 1985, and the mating process produced little critters that grew into man-eating monsters. They are kept in secure enclosures, waking only at feeding time to snap mighty jaws with a sickening thud on freshly killed chicken.

A nature trail meanders through the forest, past squads of giant Aldabra tortoises at all stages of development, wide-eyed Mauritian fruit bats, wild boars, macaque monkeys, an insectarium and a host of luminous green geckos and chameleons. (Be sure to douse yourself with plenty of insect repellent before you visit.)

Le Souffleur

If you are heading towards Mahébourg, you can follow the little-used B8, which branches east from Rivière des Anguilles. About midway, at **L'Escalier**, a road runs south to **Le Souffleur** ❽, a blowhole fashioned in a dramatic outcrop of rock (due to erosion it is now more a cloud of spray than the fierce jet of water that shot skywards until the 1970s). If you walk along the coast you'll get a clear view of the break in the coral reef that allows the sea to rush up against the cliffs. There's also a striking *pont naturel* (natural bridge), which formed when the roof of a sea cave collapsed. Le Souffleur is accessed via the grounds of the Savinia sugar estate (turn right at the L'Escalier police station).

Some of the residents of the Crocodile Park.

SUGAR PRODUCTION

Despite rapid developments in the tourism and textile industries, the giant sugar estates are still the country's third biggest employer.

Until recently, over 90 percent of arable land in Mauritius was given over to the cultivation of sugar. With the diversification of agriculture and expansion of the tourism and textile sectors, sugar production is no longer the country's number one earner. Many sugar workers have opted for more comfortable employment in offices, factories and hotels. Nevertheless, mechanisation has ensured that sugar production continues to play a major role in the economy and there are perks for those who have remained in the industry. Sugar estates provide housing, hospitals and free medical facilities, free school transport and leisure and sporting activities. Many have scholarship schemes and sponsor the training of workers and their families in technical schools.

Mauritius produces the best unrefined sugar in the world and most of it is exported to the European Union. One important by-product is *bagasse* or cane fibre, which is used to fire boilers in the factory and any excess burned to generate additional electricity for sale to the national grid. Another is molasses, used in the production of vinegar, drugs and perfumes, while cane spirit is used to make rum. Nothing goes to waste; even the scum from the purification process contains essential nutrients which are fed back into the soil, and the long green leaves of the cane are used for animal feed.

Between June and December the air is thick with the sweet scent of molasses as cane is cut and loaded into lorries.

Although much of the work traditionally undertaken by labourers is now being done by machine, teams of cane workers toiling in the fields are still part and parcel of the Mauritian landscape.

Just over half of Mauritius is owned by several giant sugar estates; the rest is shared among 30,000 individual farmers or "planters".

Mechanic equipment is now increasingly being used for the sugar cane harvest.

CRUMBLING GIANTS

The island's sugar industry has had an impact on everything from the landscape to the economy, politics and population. Sugar cane was introduced to Mauritius by the Dutch, who brought it over from Jakarta in 1639, and the French expanded the plantations. By the time the British came in 1810 thousands of acres had been planted with sugar cane. For generations sugar was the lifeblood of Mauritius. People got rich on it, fought over it and died for it. It wasn't until the 1980s, with the progressive centralisation of the sugar industry, that the number of sugar estates began to dwindle. Of the hundreds of factories that once thrived across the island, only a few are left. But the ruins of the old sites remain, and the chimneys – which have been designated national monuments – are dotted all over the countryside.

To see how the brown sludge from the crushed canes was transformed into sugar crystals, before mechanisation took over, visit the early sugar mill reconstructions at l'Aventure du Sucre or at Domaine les Pailles, a 10-minute drive south of the capital.

...sing sugar cane for the distillation of rum at Domaine de ...t Aubin.

... rum distillery at Chamarel makes a refined rum from the ...rcane fields surrounding, where sugarcane is not burnt, ... ensuring the purest of juice extracts for distillation.

An ancient chimney pipe in an old sugar cane factory.

The beach at Dinarobin Resort, Mourne Brabant.

THE WEST

The west's draw is beautiful beaches –
and for nature lovers the Black River
Gorges National Park is on the doorstep.

Port Louis

Soon after leaving the uninspiring suburbs and industrial installations of Port Louis, the quirky angles of the Corps de Garde, Rempart and Trois Mamelles mountains and, in the distance, the solid hammer head of Le Morne Brabant peninsula stay with you as you travel southwards, offering a range of rewarding views unmatched in other parts of the islands. The A3, which runs the length of the 50km (30-mile) coast, meanders inland south of the capital, with side roads periodically offering access to the sea, but from Tamarin the road hugs the coast. The glistening beaches of Flic en Flac, Wolmar and Le Morne and their turquoise lagoons remain tantalisingly hidden from view.

Port Louis suburbs and beyond

It is all too easy to speed through the suburbs of Port Louis as you make a beeline for the obvious attractions of the coast, reachable in about 30 minutes, but there are a few places that might attract your attention along the way.

Heading out of Port Louis along the A1, before the A3 branches off to Flic en Flac, you pass through **Grande Rivière Nord-Ouest**, notable for the iron bridges that span the river of the same name, and for the ruin of an 18th-century hospital. There are splendid

views over the river at the point where the B31 leads coastwards to **Pointe aux Sables ❶**. The beach here is mediocre by Mauritius' standards, but attracts a crowd due to its proximity to the capital. Note that the resort has a seedy reputation due to its popularity with local prostitutes; the beach and overall scene is more pleasant at the point than in the village itself.

The B31 links up with the B78 (just before it rejoins the A3), which veers west to **Pointe aux Caves ❷**. A climb to the top of the early 20th-century

Main Attractions
Casela World of Adventures
Tamarin Bay
Tamarin Falls
Black River Gorges National Park
Seven Coloured Earths, Chamarel
Grand Bassin
Le Morne Brabant

Chamarel Waterfall.

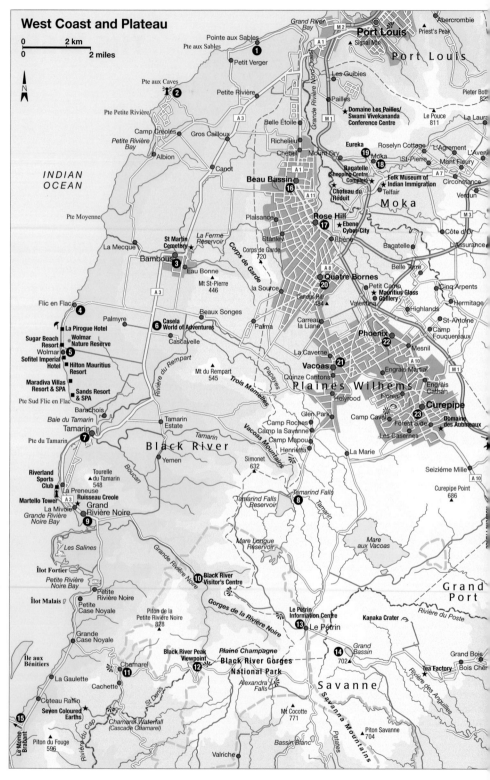

West Coast and Plateau

0   2 km
0   2 miles

N

Pointe aux Sables
Pte aux Sables
1
Petit Verger

Pte aux Caves
2
Petite Rivière

Pte Petite Rivière
Camp Créoles
Petite Rivière Bay
Albion
Gros Cailloux
Canot

INDIAN OCEAN

Pte Moyenne

La Mecque

Bambous
3
St Martin Cemetery
La Ferme Reservoir
Eau Bonne
Mt St-Pierre 446

Flic en Flac
4
Palmyre
La Pirogue Hotel
Wolmar Nature Reserve
6 Casela World of Adventures
Beaux Songes
Cascavelle

Sugar Beach Resort
Wolmar
5
Sofitel Imperial Hotel
Hilton Mauritius Resort
Maradiva Villas Resort & SPA
Sands Resort & SPA
Pte Sud Flic en Flac
Barachois
Baie du Tamarin
Tamarin
7
Pte du Tamarin

Riverland Sports Club
Tourelle du Tamarin 548
La Preneuse
Martello Tower
Ruisseau Creole
La Mivoie
Grand Rivière Noire
9
Grande Rivière Noire Bay

Les Salines

Îlot Fortier
Petite Rivière Noire Bay
Îlot Malais
Petite Case Noyale
Grande Case Noyale
Piton de la Petite Rivière Noire 828

Black River Visitor's Centre
10

Île aux Bénitiers
Chamarel
11
La Gaulette
Cachette
St Denis
Coteau Raffin
Seven Coloured Earths
15
Piton du Fouge 596
Chamarel Waterfall (Cascade Chamarel)

Black River Peak Viewpoint
12
Plaine Champagne
Black River Gorges National Park
Alexandra Falls

Grand River Bay
2
Port Louis
Abercrombie
Priest's Peak
Signal Mtn

Les Guibies
Pailles
Pieter Both 823
Le Pouce 811
La Laura

Domaine Les Pailles/ Swami Vivekananda Conference Centre

Belle Étoile
Chebel
Richelieu
Mount Ory
Eureka
19
18
Roselyn Cottage
L'Agrement
L'Aveni
Moka
St-Pierre
Mont Fleury

Bagatelle Shopping Centre Complex
Folk Museum of Indian Immigration
Telfair
Circonstance
Verdun

Beau Bassin
16
Chateau du Réduit

Plasance
Stanley
Corps de Garde 720

Rose Hill
17
Ebene Cyber-City
Ebène
Bagatelle
Belle Terre
Côte d'Or
L'Assurance

La source
Candos Hill 484
Palma

Quatre Bornes
20
Petit Camp
Mauritius Glass Gallery
Valentina
Highlands
St-Antoine
Camp Fouquereaux
Hermitage
Cinq Arpents

Carreau la Liane
La Caverne
Vacoas
21
Phoenix
22
Mesnil
Camp Martial
A 10

La Ferme
Rivière du Rempart
Trois Mamelles
Pacapes
Quinze Cantons
Plaines Wilhems
Engrais Cathan
Engrais
Curepipe
23
Forest Side
Domaine des Aubineaux

Mt du Rempart 545

Tamarin Estate
Tamarin
Yemen
Boucan

Vacoas Mountains
Camp Roches
Camp la Savanne
Camp Mapou
Henrietta
Simonet 632
Glen Park
Holyrood
Floreal
Camp Caval
Les Casernes
La Marie
Seiziéme Mille

Tamarind Falls Reservoir
Tamarind Falls
8
Tamarin

Mare Longue Reservoir
Mare aux Vacoas

Curepipe Point 686

Gorges de la Rivière Noire
Grande Rivière Noire

Le Pétrin Information Centre
13
Le Pétrin
Kanaka Crater
Rivière du Poste

Grand Port

14
Grand Bassin 702
Tea Factory
Grand Bois
Bois Chér

Savanne
Savanna Mountains
Mt Cocotte 771
Piton Savanne 704
Rivière des Anguilles

Le Morne Brabant
Piton du Fouge 596
Valriche
Bassin Blanc
Petates

ghthouse here provides good views f the mountains and coast.

Back on the A3, the road continues southwards bisecting a wide and ertile plain and separating the plateau towns from a picturesque coast f low cliffs. At the busy village of **ambous ❸**, with flamboyant tree-haded avenues and pretty dwellings, sk for directions to **St Martin Cemtery**, nestling in cane fields north of he village. Here, 127 identical tomb-ones are the final reminder of 1,580 ewish wartime refugees from Eastern urope. Having been refused entry o Palestine by the British in 1940 ecause they were considered 'illegal nmigrants', they were transported to Mauritius. They were well received, ut conditions in their refugee camp, here they were kept until the end f the war, were poor. After the war, hany started new lives abroad but heir families still return to Mauri-us to pay their respects to those who ever made it back home. There are so some beautiful Tamil tombs in he cemetery.

lic en Flac

he name of the village **Flic en Flac ❹** is Dutch in origin and is thought o derive from 'Fried Landt Flaak', heaning 'Free and Flat Land'; later, nder the influence of the French, this volved into Flic en Flac. Most visitors on't waste too much time wondering bout etymology but head straight for he beach.

If Grand Baie is the Creole Côte 'Azur then Flic en Flac is the Creole Costa del Sol, with a concentra-on of small seafront hotels, shops, estaurants and bars backed by conete apartment complexes spreading hland to replace the sugar plantations f yesteryear. But it's a popular choice or self-caterers, independent travel-rs and islanders themselves (many f whom have weekend homes here), ared by the nightlife, a superb beach hd public transport giving easy access o Port Louis, the Plateau Towns – just

a 45-minute bus ride away – and the Black River Mountains.

At the entrance to Flic en Flac is a small clutch of bars and cafés, together with the resort's main hotel, **Villas Caroline**, which overlooks the northern reaches of the enormous beach. Soft, powdery sands shelve into the lagoon, where people windsurf and swim. Further along the main road ubiquitous casuarina trees back the beach, where the sand is packed hard enough for cars to drive on. Sunsets here are often a hypnotic vision of feathered clouds flecked with silvery-peach hues. On weekdays it is quiet, with just a couple of food stalls. But on weekends, the resort springs to life as locals descend from all around, and at the end of the day, great groups of islanders wait in orderly queues for the homebound bus.

Flic en Flac is a haven for divers, windsurfers and snorkellers. Unlike Grand Baie, no speedboats disturb the waters with wash thrown up from their bows, and the best dive sites in Mauritius lie off this part of the coast (see page 87). One of the best places

Flic en Flac hosts a range of water sports and activities.

in Mauritius to learn is **Sun Divers**, based at La Pirogue, while more experienced divers will find interesting opportunities at Villas Caroline (see Travel Tips).

Less than 2km (1 mile) south, **Wolmar ❺** is really an extension of Flic en Flac. The original hamlet has now been completely swamped by a handful of very smart hotels, which include the Sugar Beach Resort, La Pirogue (complete with casino), the Sofitel Imperial, the Hilton Mauritius Resort, the most luxurious on the west coast, Maradiva Villas Resort & Spa and Sands Resort & Spa. These hotels certainly have better facilities than anything you'll find in Flic en Flac.

South to Tamarin

Casela World of Adventures ❻ (tel: 452 2828; www.caselapark.com; daily 9am–5pm) focuses on fun and 'green tourism'. Sitting on the flanks of Rempart Mountain on the A3 just south of Flic en Flac, the extensive grounds include walkways over delightful ponds, a petting farm, dozens of aviaries containing 142 species of birds from all over the world including the rare pink pigeon an Mauritius kestrel – fishing and a re taurant overlooking the west coast rolling, cane-clothed countrysid Guided tours include photo safar for sightings of antelope, ostric deer, zebra, wild boar and giraff exciting nature escapes by qua bike, buggy and Segway, and roc climbing, ziplining and a canyo swing. Unmissable for a humblin and exciting experience is the pop lar attraction of walking in the wil with Casela's lions and cheetah accompanied by expert guides.

Pressing southwards, the massiv mound of Le Morne Brabant appea to rise over Tamarin Mountain, whi inland the horizon is dominated b the bulk of Rempart and the Blac River mountains. Some 6km (4 mile south of Casela you hit the coast an **Tamarin ❼**. The village, overlookin a tranquil bay, is showing encoura ing signs of development as a quiet alternative to Flic en Flac and its *pe sions* provide a good base for explorin the southwest.

Braving a Vertical World trip.

The Tamarin Hotel right on the beach has jazz nights on Thursday and a number of other nightspots have opened here in the last five or so years. The Riverland Sports Club (tel: 483 4956; www.riverland.mu), with its large pool, tennis courts, golf course, gym and pleasant restaurant, welcomes day visitors. The area is also the focus of Mauritius' first Integrated Resort Scheme (IRS) and an example of how sugar barons are turning their lands over to real estate development. Under the scheme foreigners can buy property – albeit in designated areas and for a minimum investment of US$500,000 – making it a popular place for South African expats to live. In 2007, luxurious villas and an 18-hole golf course were completed at Tamarina Golf Estate, making Tamarin a fashionable resort.

There is a good unspoilt beach but the coral reef is subdued by fresh water that flows from the central highlands via the Rempart and Tamarin rivers. The waters are famous for the black and long-beaked dolphins, and local people run dolphin-spotting tours from the bay. Between June and August waves can reach over 2 metres (6ft) and the bay is also popular with surfers.

The area around Tamarin is one of the west coast's most scenic. In summer the River Tamarin is lined with scarlet-blossomed trees, and at any time of year, especially in the late afternoon, there's definitely a romantic feel about the place. If you're a photographer this is the best time to capture the reflections of Tamarin Mountain on the river and watch the pencil-thin surf rolling in.

The River Tamarin starts at the Tamarind Falls ❽, where a reservoir near the small village of Henrietta on the central plateau (see page 151) supplies water for irrigation and to a hydroelectric power station some 250 metres (820ft) below. Also known as The Seven Cascades, the main falls tumble over seven stepped cliffs through a deep narrow gorge and are the tallest falls in Mauritius. The best way of getting there, particularly if you're an adrenalin junkie, is with Vertical World (tel: 5251 1107; www.verticalworldltd.com), who offer trekking and canyoning trips, where they provide ropes and harnesses to abseil your way down. Beginners are first given lessons on how to abseil on dry cliffs before taking the plunge. Intermediate and hard-core enthusiasts can try their skills negotiating 45-metre (145ft) drops into ponds and smaller waterfalls followed by a strenuous hike back to the top.

Other ways of getting to Tamarind Falls are from a rough track from Henrietta or hiking from Le Pétrin in the Black River Gorges National Park (see page 142), but neither option is recommended unless you go with a qualified guide.

Black River area

Vast rectangular pans, where salt is extracted from sea water by solar evaporation, lie alongside the A3 south of Tamarin en route to **Grande Rivière**

MARTELLO TOWERS

Overlooking the public beach of La Preneuse, 2km (1 mile) or so south of Tamarin, is the best-preserved Martello Tower in Mauritius. The tower is one of five such fortifications that were constructed on the coast of Mauritius by British soldiers in the 19th century; three remain, all on the west coast: one in Pointe aux Sables (see page 137), another at La Harmonie and one at Les Salines just south of Grande Rivière Noire. The tower at La Preneuse is open as a museum (tel: 493 6648; Tue–Sat 9.30am–5pm) and is worth visiting for the guided tour and rooftop cannon.

The towers were built to withstand gunfire and have walls that are an impressive 3 metres (11ft) thick on the seaward side. They included a powder magazine and store, living quarters for 20 men, and revolving cannons on the roof. They were veritable fortresses, entrance to which could be made only by a ladder that was let down from high up the building so that attackers would find it almost impossible to enter.

The name comes from Mortella Point in Corsica, where British soldiers first came across such a tower during the French Revolution. Between 1796 and 1815 the British went on to build around 200 Martello Towers in Britain and throughout the Empire – in places as far flung as Bermuda, Ireland and the Ascension Islands.

Noire , at the estuary of the eponymous river that tumbles through some of the most rugged areas of Mauritius. The Rivière Noire (Black River) area is sparsely populated, with no proper towns, only small villages and hamlets. Once regarded as the poorest region in Mauritius, with a predominantly Afro-Creole population, the area now has an influx of cash-rich expatriates building luxurious homes there.

Contrasting sharply with the laid-back lifestyle of Grande Rivière Noire village and its traditional eateries and stores, which are strung out along the A3, is the gleaming Ruisseau Creole complex and the newer La Place, Cap Tamarin, with their designer shops and restaurants. Just a stone's throw from the main road of Grande Rivière Noire village is the west coast's centre for big game fishing, where trips can be arranged through **JP Henry Charters** (tel: 483 5060; www.jph.mu). If staying elsewhere, your hotel should also be able to arrange a trip for you. Between September and March, marlin, sailfish, yahoo, yellow fin tuna and various species of shark

The picturesque falls at Chamarel.

migrate to the warm waters around Mauritius (see page 91) and feed just beyond the reef where the sea bed falls abruptly to a depth of 60 metres (1,970ft).

Black River Gorges National Park

Much of the beauty of the west lies inland, and nowhere more so than in the southwest corner of Mauritius, where the rugged mountains once provided a hideaway for maroons (runaway slaves), who lived in isolation, safe in the knowledge that their masters would never find them. The good news for visitors is that these mountains are now easily accessible via the **Black River Gorges National Park**, which was officially opened in 1997 in an attempt to preserve what is left of the island's disappearing native forests. The 6,575-hectare (16,250-acre) park offers something for everyone, from dedicated walkers to those who just fancy a scenic drive and a break from the beaches. This green heart of Mauritius is not a place to spot wildlife on a grand scale, but you could spend days tracking down the 150 endemic species of plants and nine endemic species of birds, including pink pigeons and Mauritius kestrels. While you may be lucky enough to spot these two endangered species, you are more likely to see the graceful white tropicbird, cuckoo shrike and Mauritius blackbird.

From the west coast you can access the northern area of the park by taking the new road which leaves the A3 just south of Grande Rivière Noire village. This leads through sugar fields to a picnic and parking area just 5km (3 miles) inland, where the **Black River Visitor Centre** ⑩ (tel: 258 0057; Mon–Fri 9am–3.25pm, Sat–Sun 9am–4pm) provides walking maps and information on the condition of the trails. From here you can explore the lower slopes of the park or follow the boulder-strewn Grande Rivière Noire or a strenuous 16km (10-mile) uphill ek on the 'Parakeet' and 'Macchabee' rails, which link the Gorges area with he Plaine Champagne.

The other way to get to the Black iver Gorges is to drive south from lack River village to Grande Case oyale, and then turn inland and pwards to the forested plateau of **laine Champagne**, named after the reamy white flowers of the privet that all to mind the white froth of champagne. This route leads to Le Pétrin, he park's other visitor centre (see page 44), but is also better suited to those nterested merely in a scenic drive.

he Highlands

rom Grande Case Noyale the road vinds steeply through the forested oothills to the village of **Chamarel** ❶, offering glorious views down to he coast; if you are heading downhill, e sure to test your brakes first. The Chamarel area is known for its cof-ee, but the reason most people come ere is the waterfall and the curious eological phenomenon the village is amous for.

Chamarel Waterfall (Cascade Chamarel) tumbles from the St Denis River into a large crater, and at 83 metres (272ft) it is the most accessible high waterfall in Mauritius. About 1km (half a mile) further on are the Seven **Coloured Earths** (tel: 622 6177; daily 7am–5pm). Geologists are fasci-nated by this unique rolling landscape of multicoloured terrain, thought to have been caused by the uneven cooling of lava, now fenced off and beautifully landscaped with viewing platforms and timber walkways. Inter-estingly, the colours never fade in spite of torrential downpours.

Just opposite the entrance is the **Curious Corner of Chamarel** (tel 733 3963; www.curiouscornerofchamarel. com; daily 9.30am–5.30pm). Although it has little to do with Mauritius, this house of illusions – with stairs made of piano keys, an upside-down kitchen and a mirror maze in the basement – is well run and entertaining.

East of Chamarel village, nestling in a verdant valley, is **La Rhumerie de Chamarel** (tel: 483 4980; www. rhumeriedechamarel.com; Mon–Sat

The Seven Coloured Earths.

Grand Bassin is a Hindu pilgrimage site.

9.30am–5.30pm). Bundles of cane are cut daily and brought to this state-of-the-art distillery where *fangourin*, a sweet non-alcoholic juice, is extracted, fermented and turned into high-quality Chamarel rum. Guided tours include rum tasting and the shop sells unusual Mauritian-made handicrafts and gifts, such as candles, honey, salt from Tamarin and a range of designer clothing and accessories.

From the waterfalls, you can continue southwards through sugar cane via a tortuous road to the south coast emerging at Baie du Cap (see page 128), or backtrack to Chamarel village and push eastwards.

Black River Gorges views and walks

The road east of Chamarel running high up across the Plaine Champagne is narrow and lined with scrubby vegetation, offering fleeting chances to admire the scenery. It has no verge and only the occasional stopping place, though there are a couple of designated viewpoints. Most people stop at the **Black River Peak Viewpoint ⑫**,

where there's usually a snack van and man selling freshly cut fruit in the car park – the only source of refreshment for miles. A few miles east, a track runs a short way to the **Alexandra Falls** with less extensive views down to the south coast, and you can hear the fall more than you can see them.

Just east of the Alexandra Falls the road veers suddenly north taking you to **Le Pétrin Information Centre ⑬** (tel: 471 1128; Mon–Fri 9am–3pm, Sat–Sun 9am–4pm), the first port of call for those approaching the Black River Gorges area from the plateau towns and the best access point to all areas of the park. Next to the Information Centre is the **Pétrin Native Garden**, a mini showcase of native species including many medicinal plants. Among the plants are the national flower, the *boucle d'oreille* (earring), the quirkily named *patte poule piquant* (prickly chicken legs), used for stomach upsets and liver problems, the *pot de chambre du singe* (monkey chamber pots) and the umbrella-shaped *bois de natte* tree, often draped with tree ferns, wild orchids and lichens.

Grand Bassin

Located 2km (1 mile) east of Le Pétrin and surrounded by forests infested with monkeys, the water-filled crater of **Grand Bassin** attracts crowds not so much for its natural beauty but for its religious significance. The volcanic crater is known among Hindus as Ganga Talao, and is dominated by Mauritius' tallest sculpture, of the Hindu god Shri Mangal Mahadev, which stands 32 metres (108ft) high. Legend has it that the lake contains nocturnal fairies, but it was after a Hindu priest dreamed that it was linked to the sacred River Ganges that Grand Bassin became a place of pilgrimage for the annual Maha Shivaratree festival. In February/March, thousands of Hindus dressed in white walk from all parts of the island and converge on the lakeside to make offerings at the colourful shrines as a sign of devotion to Shiva. Bus lanes and vast car parks designed to cope with the crowds are empty the rest of the year.

To see a classic example of a volcanic cone, head 5km (3 miles) further east through tea fields to **Kanaka Crater**. Only the determined should make the challenging trek to the 180-metre (590ft) high rim for views into the choked up crater.

Le Morne Brabant

The peninsula of **Le Morne Brabant** is the most westerly point of Mauritius. It is named after the 555-metre (1,820ft) mountain that rises from its centre. Runaway slaves used Le Morne as a hiding place. In 1835, soldiers were sent here to announce the abolition of slavery, but the slaves, thinking this was just another attempt to hunt them down, are said to have flung themselves to a watery grave.

The isolated spot, which was added to the Unesco World Heritage list in 2008, is now an upmarket tourist area with just seven hotels – Paradis Hotel and Golf Club, Dinarobin Hotel Golf and Spa, LUX* Le Morne,

St Regis Mauritius Resort and three Rui hotels – overlooking the idyllic beach. The silence is broken only by the arrival of helicopters whizzing tourists to and from the airport and motorised caddies speeding across the golf course. Lagoons fronting the luxury hotels lure water lovers to try scuba diving, snorkelling, windsurfing, water-skiing and boat trips to the uninhabited Benitiers Island nearby. It is also the island's kitesurfing centre, with beginners' lessons offered in the protected Le Morne Bay and experienced kiters aiming for 'One Eye', with some of the best wave conditions in the world. The main lure of this romantic spot is the 5km (3 miles) of powdery beach – undoubtedly the best on the island.

You can also enjoy some fine hiking on this private mountain reserve with an experienced guide from Yanature (tel: 5785 6177; www.trekkingilemaurice.com), and the island's best horse riding, either on the mountain's lower slopes or into the surf, with Haras du Morne (tel: 5705 1644; www.harasdumorne.com).

Paradis Hotel & Golf Club.

Curepipe as viewed from Trou aux Cerfs crater.

PLATEAU TOWNS

The heavily populated towns in central Mauritius aren't attractive, but they offer shopping bargains and an insight into ordinary Mauritian life.

Port Louis

Main Attractions
Eureka
Mauritius Glass Gallery
Shopping bargains in Curepipe and Floreal
Trou aux Cerfs
Domaine des Aubineaux

n the early days of settlement, you had to be mad, bad or indifferent to live in the interior. The area was unexplored and full of runaway slaves who booby-trapped the unwary, but over the years one or two adventurers, such as German wanderer Wilhem Lechenig, settled in the uplands. When the French replaced the vacuum left by the Dutch in 1721 they found Lechenig leading a reclusive life and named the district of Plaines Wilhems after him.

Today, **Plaines Wilhems** contains all the island's significant towns other than Port Louis – that is, Beau Bassin-Rose Hill, Quatre Bornes, Vacoas-Phoenix and Curepipe. With about 40 percent of the population, it is the most densely populated district of Mauritius. The towns grew as a result of several migrations from Port Louis after fire, disease and cyclones sent people scurrying to the healthier uplands. For Mauritian professionals, they are desirable places to live, offering better facilities and housing and more shops.

While for Mauritians the plateau towns have a distinct identity, for visitors passing through they tend to merge into one and, in truth, have no immediately obvious appeal. Indeed, most tourists come here only to shop (all tour operators arrange shopping trips). However, anyone interested in discovering the 'other' Mauritius should come here. There are pockets of architectural interest and a few minor attractions to seek out, while the cooler climate makes a change from the sultry temperatures of the coast. Getting to (or away from) the plateau towns is easy, either by taking the motorway or the Royal Road (A1), but avoid rush hours if possible. The map of the key towns supplied by Mauritius Tourism Promotion Authority (MTPA) offices is a great help if you want to explore.

Church of St Jean, near Quatre Bornes.

*An interior at
Eureka Villa.*

Beau Bassin-Rose Hill

Like Vacoas-Phoenix further south,
Beau Bassin and Rose Hill are not so
much sister towns as joined towns.
Beau Bassin , the less frenetic of
the two, has one or two sights worth
visiting. The backstreets contain
some beautifully preserved colonial houses. One such is **Le Thabor** (entrance on Swami Sivananda
Street), in an area that once attracted
the English aristocracy and diplomats, whose love for gracious living,
horse riding and gardening earned
it the name of the 'English Quarter.'
Le Thabor, now a pastoral centre for
the Catholic Church, has seen some
famous faces in its time. During a
visit here in 1836, Charles Darwin
noted 'How pleasant it would be to
pass one's life in such quiet abodes.'
Pope John Paul II dropped in on an
official visit in 1989.

In the same street are the **Balfour
Gardens** (Thu–Tue 6am–6pm), giving
wonderful views of the Moka Mountains across a ravine and to a waterfall
that tumbles into the Grande Rivière
Nord-Ouest.

You may be lucky enough to catc
one of the rosy sunsets (after whic
Rose Hill ⓱ got its name) over Corp
de Garde Mountain, which serve
as a lookout post for runaway slave.
Concrete, rain-stained office build
ings juxtaposed with brightly painte
tin-roofed shops and eateries contras
with a modern infrastructure of road
leading east to Ebène, home to th
Cyber City complex, a gleaming 21st
century symbol reflecting the island'
desire to become a leader in informa
tion technology in the Indian Ocean
For a local shopping experience cros
the road from the Victorian pos
office to **Arab Town**, named after th
original Muslim traders who gathere
here, where Mauritian housewive
barter for household goods. Bacl
on the Royal Road, you can pass th
time browsing through the jumbl
of wares, from statues of Hindu god
and Virgin Marys tucked betwee
bottles of shampoo and underwear, to
swathes of sari fabric.

The **Plaza Theatre**, housed i
Rose Hill's Town Hall (on the righ
hand side of the Royal Road as yo

pproach from Port Louis, and before he town centre), rarely stages plays hese days but is worth noting for its Creole architecture.

Diversion to Moka

ust north of the A7, less than 4km (2 miles) east of Rose Hill, is the university town of **Moka** ⑱. The Mahatma Gandhi Institute here is home to the Folk Museum of Indian Immigration (tel: 403 2000; Mon–Fri 9am–.30pm, Sat 9am–noon), which traces he life and times of the Indian cane workers brought to the island in the mid-19th century. It is popular with locals wanting to trace their ancestors, but attracts few tourists.

The president's official residence s in Moka. The magnificent **Le Chateau du Réduit** was built in 1748 as a country residence and retreat for wives and children of the French East India Company in the event of an invasion. Situated on a peninsula isolated by wo ravines, the chateau overlooks lawns and is surrounded by exotic rees and shady pathways. The house s open to the public only twice a year, on specially allocated days in March and October.

Just north of Moka is the splendid Creole house of **Eureka** ⑲ (tel: 433 3477; www.maisoneureka.com; Mon–Sat 9am–5pm, Sun 9am–3pm). It was built in 1856 by an Englishman and bought a few years later by the wealthy Franco-Mauritian Leclézio family. Apparently, Henri Leclézio, who devoted his life to restoring the mansion, cried 'Eureka' when his bid was accepted at auction. The house and birthplace of many more Leclézios has been known as Eureka ever since. The property comprises wo houses and three pavilions. The main house, built of wood, is filled with colonial-style furniture. In the external stone-built kitchen, crammed with original Creole cookware, a traditional Mauritian lunch is prepared, which you can enjoy on the veranda. A path through the gardens deposits

you unexpectedly by a deep ravine, and there is usually a guide waiting by the small waterfall – a lovely picnic and swimming spot – if you want to explore further down the ravine.

Moka is also home to the island's most popular shopping mall, **Bagatelle** (tel: 468 8555; www.mallof mauritius.com; Mon–Thu 9.30am–8.30pm, Fri, Sat 9.30am–10pm, Sun 9am–3pm), set against the backdrop of the Moka Mountains. With 130 shops, a food court, bars and restaurants, locals flock here at weekends.

Quatre Bornes

On leaving Rose Hill you enter **Quatre Bornes** ⑳, named after four sugar estates which marked the original boundaries (*bornes*). To the west rises the Corps de Garde mountain, to the south Candos Hill, a firing range for SMF officers but also a venue for fêtes, cross-country running and other sporting events. In February, the Indian temples on the flanks of Corps de Garde come alive when Tamils undergo a remarkable ritual of body piercing at the most dramatic

Busy stalls at Curepipe's bus station.

FACT

Curepipe's origins go back to the 18th century. The popular theory is that it was the halfway point where soldiers and travellers crossing the island would stop to rest and clean or 'cure', in French, their pipes.

of festivals, Cavadee (see page 74). Little exists here to lure tourists from the beach. There's nothing grand about the Grande Route Saint Jean, which slices through town, but wander into the streets behind and you'll find a maze of bamboo-clad avenues with some lovely old villas set in large gardens. Elsewhere, numerous little restaurants and snack bars provide a taste of local life. On Thursdays and Sundays traders converge for the market or *foire*, where they sell just about everything beneath multicoloured canopies.

Vacoas-Phoenix

Vacoas and Phoenix, traditionally occupied by expats, diplomats and Franco-Mauritians because of the cooler temperatures, are essentially one big urban sprawl. Other than an animated bus station and market, there seems to be no heart to **Vacoas** ㉑. The old HMS building, once occupied by the British, now houses the Special Mobile Force headquarters. It's a fine example of colonial architecture: formerly a Scottish Presbyterian church

and then a rum store in Port Louis it was dismantled stone by stone and rebuilt in its current spot.

Phoenix ㉒ is an industrial area famous for its glassworks, the **Mauritius Glass Gallery** (tel: 696 3360 email: mgg@pbg.mu; Mon–Fri 9am–5pm, Sat 9am–noon; free). See artisans hand-blowing products out of recycled glass in the workshop, from ashtrays to swans, which can be purchased in the adjoining shop. The town is also home to food and drink processing companies, including **Phoenix Beverages** (formerly Mauritius Breweries), which produces the local Phoenix Beer.

Curepipe

Curepipe ㉓ is the highest plateau town at 550 metres (1,840ft), and is traditionally the stronghold of the white Franco-Mauritian community who live in grand houses hidden behind high hedges in nameless streets around the centre and in the suburbs of **Floreal** and **Forest Side**. Curepipe has the dubious distinction of having the highest rainfall on the island, and

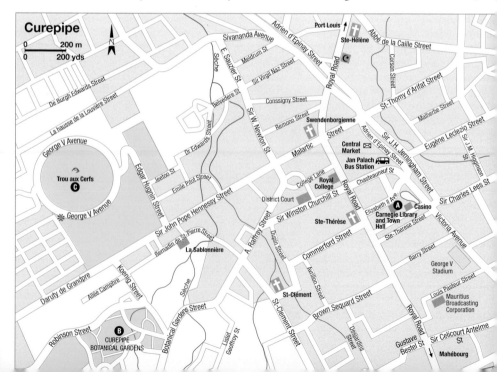

n rainy days, which is most of the me, the buildings look depressingly rey. The town's most attractive public buildings are clustered in a compound on Elizabeth Avenue near the market. Of most interest are the 1920s Carnegie Library Ⓐ and the impressive Creole-style **Town Hall**, which overlooks a statue of *Paul et Virginie*, central characters of the 18th-century romance inspired by a shipwreck off the Île d'Ambre.

Most people come to Curepipe to shop. **Currimjee Arcades** (on the corner of Royal Road and Chasteauneuf Street) is not particularly large, but has a few good clothes shops downstairs. **La Sablonnière**, in Pope Hennessy Street, is a classic example of colonial architecture, complete with miniature Eiffel Tower, and has been turned into a shopping emporium with 'duty free' Oriental carpets, objets d'art and furnishings. For serious shopping, you'd do better to go to Floreal shopping complex, where you can purchase quality garments made from raw imported materials, such as cashmere, cotton and silk.

Curepipe Botanic Gardens Ⓑ, in the west of town, are not as big or as impressive as the Botanic Gardens at Pamplemousses, but are perfect for a quiet stroll (daily, Oct–Apr 7am–7pm, May–Sept 8.30am–5pm).

The most famous local attraction is **Trou aux Cerfs** Ⓒ, a 300-metre (980ft) diameter crater. Formed as a result of volcanic activity millions of years ago, it is now choked with silt, water and dense vegetation. The crater is a 15-minute walk or a short taxi ride from the centre of town. The view stretches beyond the blanket of buildings to the spectacular mountains, which so far have remained untouched by developers.

To the southeast of Curepipe, along the A10 at Forest Side, **Domaine des Aubineaux** (tel: 676 3089; www.saint aubin.mu; daily 9am–5pm), the turquoise-shuttered 19th-century family home of tea plantation owners which

opened as a museum in 2000, is one of the prettiest, and least visited, colonial mansions on the island. Rooms are filled with furniture imported from around the world, old photographs and antique paintings, and visitors can enjoy a stroll through its camphor-scented gardens and a traditional lunch on the terrace.

Heading south

The plateau towns are a good starting point for a drive south through the Black River Gorges National Park. Either take the B3 from Quatre Bornes south through Glen Park and La Marie to Le Pétrin, or the B70 from Curepipe to La Marie, where you turn left for Le Pétrin. If you're short of time, you can get a taste of the area by driving just past the village of Henrietta, where touts will show you a viewpoint overlooking Tamarind Falls (see page 141), a 15-minute hike along a rough downhill path. It's better to go with a specialist operator, such as Yemaya Adventures (tel: 5752 0046; www.yemayaadventures.com) to see the falls up close.

Curepipe's Town Hall is housed in an Old French-style chateau.

A tropical idyll at Île aux Cocos's beach lagoon.

RODRIGUES

This island is remote, laid-back and rugged. Its charm
lies in its simplicity and eco-friendly credentials –
and its marine environment is hard to beat.

Mauritius   Rodrigues

Hidden in a lagoon almost twice
its size, Rodrigues is the smallest of the Mascarene trio. Lying
60km (350 miles) east of Mauritius
nd shaped like a plump fish, the
sland is just 18km (11 miles) long and
km (5 miles) wide. A hilly ridge runs
long its length, from which a series of
teep valleys extend to narrow coastal
latlands. The appeal of Rodrigues,
s discovered by Prince William and
riends during a holiday in 2004, lies in
ts rugged and simple beauty. There are
tunning coves and deserted beaches.
You can fish in shallow lagoons, dive
nd snorkel the reefs and enjoy magnificent walks through casuarina for-
sts. The Creole people are warm and
velcoming, in spite of being cut off
rom the rest of the world.

Rodrigues welcomes visitors who
re unbothered about swift service and
ive-star trappings. The island has just a
andful of hotels and a growing number of guesthouses. Tourists from Réun-
on and Mauritius often come here on
hree- or five-day packages that include
he flight and half-board accommoda-
ion. Those who have more time can
ake a cabin on the *Mauritius Trochetia*,
vhich makes regular crossings to Rod-
igues (see Travel Tips).

A pint-sized capital

Rodrigues was occupied in 1726 by
he French who established a tiny

settlement at **Port Mathurin ❶**. They
imported slaves from Mozambique
and Madagascar and settlers from
French-occupied Mauritius, increasing the population to just over 100 in
1804. The town, laid out in grid style in
1864 by the British, had many streets
named after local administrators.
After the island became autonomous
in 2002, they were officially renamed,
but people still use the old names.

At last count, Port Mathurin numbered around 6,000 inhabitants. The
capital may be bereft of monuments,

Main Attractions
Port Mathurin
Caverne Patate
François Leguat Giant
  Tortoise and Cave Reserve
Île aux Cocos

Port Mathurin.

but a wander round will give you a taste of Mascarene Island life at its most leisurely. A good place to start is the jetty where a memorial stands to Rodriguan volunteers who fought in both World Wars. It's worth hauling yourself out of bed early for the **Saturday market** in Wolphart Harmensen Street (formerly Fishermen Lane). Many of the islanders set off from their villages in the hills at midnight to set up stalls (trading starts at around 6am) or to be the first to bargain for the best fruit and vegetables. By 10am most people have packed up and gone home. Parts of the market are given over to touristy knick-knacks, but bottles of home-grown chilli and chutneys and fruit and vegetables sell like hot cakes.

There is no tourist strip as such and most shops, no more than corrugated iron shacks with handwritten nameplates nailed to the door, are concentrated in the block bounded by Rue François Leguat, Rue de la Solidarité and Rue Hajee Bhay Fateh Mamode. A few shops in Rue Max Lucchesi sell more unusual gifts and lethal home-bottled chillies, but for great range of island handicrafts ca at the **Careco Workshop** (tel: 83 1766; email: careco@intnet.mu; Mon–Fr 8am–4pm, Sat 8am–noon, shop only at Camp du Roi at the back of town Careco employs 30 people with dis abilities, who make and sell origina souvenirs. An apiary also produces th clear and distinctly flavoured Rodri guan honey. The workshop is a tour ist attraction in its own right and tou operators feature it on every itinerar of Port Mathurin.

The main artery of the town i Rue de la Solidarité (formerly Jen ner Street), one block back from the waterfront, that starts from th island's only petrol station to th west and continues over a footbridge built to replace the Winston Church ill Bridge which collapsed in 2006, t the bus terminus in the east. At th western end of Rue de la Solidarité tucked between shops, is the tiny six minareted **Noor-ud-Deen Mosque** built for the few descendants of th first Muslims who arrived in 1907 a textile merchants. In the same street i

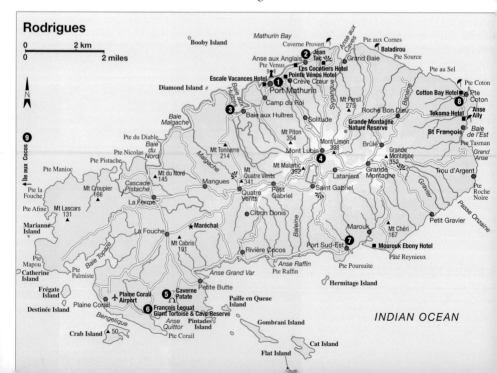

a Résidence, the former Island Secretary's house, with the original wide veranda shaded by a gnarled Indian almond tree. It is opposite the Rodrigues Tourism Office (tel: 832 0866; www.tourism-rodrigues.mu).

A short stroll east leads to the Anglican **St Barnabas Church**, surrounded by gardens and trees. Most Rodriguans are Catholics and the little **St Cœur de Marie Church** in Rue Mamzelle Julia sees a regular congregation. Crossing the footbridge over the River Cascade you stumble across the spot where Rodrigues' first settlers, led by François Leguat, set up camp in 1691.

Further up river towards Fond La Digue, the latanier huts of the 1940s once occupied by 'women of easy virtue' have been replaced by Port Mathurin's only hotel, the simple, Creole-style **Escale Vacances**, set in a deep-wooded valley overlooking the river. There are some lovely walks from here (some uphill) along jungly boulder-strewn tracks – sturdy shoes are advisable.

Around Port Mathurin

In 1761 a British fleet arrived and camped on a strip of beach at **Anse aux Anglais** ❷ (English Bay) east of Port Mathurin and, meeting with little opposition from the handful of French inhabitants, stayed for six months. The Englishness of Rodrigues was compounded in 1901 when cablemen from the Eastern Telegraph Company (later Cable & Wireless) laid a submarine telegraph cable linking the island with Mauritius, thus completing the line of communication between Australia and Europe. There are good views across Port Mathurin from the headland where French and British astronomers recorded the Transit of Venus in 1761 and 1874.

A cluster of small guesthouses overlooks the beach at Anse aux Anglais and at low tide the lagoon is a favourite haunt of groups of fisherwomen, known as *piqueuses ourites*, who make a living spearing octopus, which they

hang out to dry in the sun. A stiff uphill climb from Anse aux Anglais, via the tranquil beach-side bungalows of well-to-do Rodriguans and Mauritians at Caverne Provert, leads to a fairly flat area where acacia trees border the road. From the headland are resplendent views over **Grand Baie**. You can follow the road up from Grand Baie beach until it peters out to a narrow uphill track towards the sweeping deserted beach at **Baladirou**. A less strenuous way of getting there is to take a 40-minute boat ride along the coast from Port Mathurin.

Just 2km (1 mile) west of Port Mathurin is **Baie aux Huîtres** ❸ (Oyster Bay), an enormous bay surrounded by hills and thick casuarina forest. For the best views, drive up to **Allée Tamarin**, a hamlet at the back of the bay.

Inland from Port Mathurin

Port Mathurin's bus station and taxi stand are a boon for independent travellers and a handy location to start a journey inland, around fearsome hairpin bends, to the spine of the island

A vegetable seller at Port-Mathurin's market.

where little villages overlook the north and south lagoons.

You can jump on a bus, thumb a lift or drive yourself to the Meteorological Station on the windswept **Pointe Canon** for panoramic views over Port Mathurin and the lagoon. Here a cannon, erected by British troops during World War II, points out to sea and is oddly juxtaposed beside a white statue of the Virgin Mary, La Reine de Rodrigues. If you're around on 15 August, the approach road and hills are a riot of colour with islanders trekking towards the statue to celebrate the Feast of the Assumption.

The forest at **Solitude** is 2km (1 mile) south of Port Mathurin on the Mont Lubin road. Bounded by deep valleys and thick with eucalyptus trees, the forest also has small copses of jamrosa and mango trees, which provide food for the Rodriguan fruit bats that swoop down to feed on them at dusk.

Mont Lubin ❹, a busy little village of tumbledown shops, gives the impression of being at the top of the island, but the highest point is actually nearby Mont Limon at 398 metres

The view from Mont Limon.

(1,289ft). Most visitors drop in at th **Women's Handicraft Centre** to watc women weaving baskets from vacoa leaves and perhaps buy one of the fir ished articles on display, before mal ing their way to Pointe Coton and th beautifully isolated beaches of the eas

Heading westwards on the Mor Lubin road, it's worth making detour to Rodrigues' biggest churc at **St Gabriel**. The church was bui by locals in 1939 under difficult co^ ditions. Specially trained donkeys ca ried most of the sand from the coa: to the heights of St Gabriel and vo untary helpers, including women an children, brought cement, lime, block of coral, corrugated iron and timbe up narrow mountain paths. It can b visited any time, but for a splash c colour, music and singing, get there i time for 9am Mass on Sunday.

The 5km (3-mile) stretch of twis ing road between the hamlets of Pet Gabriel, Quatre Vents and Mangues peppered with glimpses of translucer blue lagoons and scenes of rural life.

The next main settlement after Mar gues is the large and noisy village c

VOYAGES AND ADVENTURES

The first settlers on Rodrigues were a band of Huguenots (all men) led by François Leguat. Fleeing religious persecution in France, they set sail from Holland in search of their own island paradise. Travellers' tales drew them to the Mascarene archipelago and, in 1691, they landed on the uninhabited island of Rodrigues. They lived for the next two years on 'very wholesome and luxurious foods which never caused the least sickness'.

During his stay, François Leguat wrote the island's first guidebook, *Voyages and Adventures*, a classic tome documenting the island's unique flora and fauna. In it he describes how the beaches were covered with tortoises weighing over 136kg (300 lb) so that he literally used their shells as stepping stones to reach the sea. Leguat's name would have sunk into oblivion were it not for the opening in 2007 of an amazing reserve named after him, the **François Leguat Giant Tortoise and Cave Reserve** at Plaine Caverne. Conservation programmes to restore Rodrigues' native habitat are paying off here with the planting of thousands of endemic plants plus a colony of more than 1,500 giant Aldabra tortoises shipped over from Mauritius. Explore caves with qualified guides and visit the only museum devoted to Rodrigues' history, fauna and flora.

a Ferme, which has a small stadium where Pope John Paul II held mass during his visit to Rodrigues in 1989. You need to pass through La Ferme to reach **Cascade Pistache** (2km/1 mile west of the village), an enormous crater hewn out of granite surrounded by grassy hills. The waterfall that tumbles into Rivière Pistache is particularly beautiful after heavy rains. Alternatively, take the road northwards from La Ferme to Baie du Nord for a scenic 9km (5-mile) coastal drive back to Port Mathurin, passing isolated homesteads swathed in poinsettias, hibiscus and marigolds, and causeways filled with mangroves at Baie Malgache.

In search of the solitaire

For an invigorating walk (not for the faint-hearted or claustrophobic) through dark passages studded with stalagmites and stalactites, head for the coral caves in the southwest corner of the island at **Caverne Patate 5** (tel: 832 1062; daily 9–11am and 1–3pm). The caves, some 18 metres (60ft) below ground, have fascinated naturalists ever since the first official exploration in 1786 when bones, believed to be those of the dodo, were found by a French captain. Later searches by British naturalists in 1894 led to more bone discoveries and comparisons with earlier findings proved that they belonged to the solitaire, described by François Leguat back in 1691. According to early accounts the caves contain 'superb petrifications of an infinite variety of shapes all different from each other', but modern visitors can, depending on their imagination, discern carved rock lookalikes of Winston Churchill and the Great Wall of China. The tour takes around one hour, with professional guides who issue visitors with hard hats and torches. Do come with sturdy shoes. You complete the 500-metre (550-yd) circuit and emerge at the exit where locals stand waiting to sell coral-carved solitaires and souvenirs.

Better caves containing impressive formations of stalactites and stalagmites, some sprinkled with a yet to be identified quartz-like substance, can be explored with guides at the nearby **François Leguat Giant Tortoise and**

A vacoa basketwork weaver on Rodrigues.

Cave Reserve ❻ (tel: 832 8141; www. tortoisecavereserve-rodrigues.com; daily 9am–5pm). Well-lit timber walkways and handrails make this a safer, easier option for most people, especially children. Visitors also get the chance to stroke a giant tortoise.

For the active, the **Tyrodrig Zipline Adventure** on Montagne Malgache (tel: 499 6970; email: worldcanopy@ yahoo.fr; daily 9am–5pm) is a 30-minute ride across deep ravines stuffed with thirsty plants – the highest is 100 metres/328ft above the ground.

The south

The 6km (4-mile) journey from Mont Lubin to Port Sud-Est must rank as the most beautiful in the entire island. The road snakes its way down hillsides, twisting and turning along a series of hairpin bends, each giving way to vistas of the lagoons around Port Sud-Est, dotted with small coral atolls. Your journey's end is the **Mourouk Ebony Hotel** (see Travel Tips, Activities), sitting atop a gentle cliff and as isolated as Rodrigues itself. It has good diving facilities and

Sundown over Cascade Pistache.

is a centre for wind- and kitesurfing. The nearest shop, a crimson-red shack, sells basics such as bread, water, sweets and cigarettes; the nearest village is at Songes, where cyclone-proof houses are scattered on the hillside like dominoes.

Were it not for fishing, life around **Port Sud-Est** ❼ would grind to a halt. As it is, it's pretty inert except in the mornings, when fishermen wade out to the lagoon to retrieve cages they've left out for a couple of days, which they hope have trapped lobster, prawn and crab. Now and again they venture out in pirogues and an opportunity to go with them (for a small fee) should not be missed.

Hikers might enjoy the walking trails, native plants and views of the south coast, including the pretty beach of Petit Gravier, in the **Grande Montagne Nature Reserve**. The Information Centre (tel: 832 5737; www. mauritianwildlife.org; Mon–Fri 8am–3pm, Sat 8am–10.45am) at Grande Montagne provides maps and there is a museum displaying solitaire and giant tortoise bones.

Pointe Coton and the east

Cotton Bay Hotel ❽ overlooks the island's best swimming beach and is flanked by low coral cliffs. The hotel, popular with holiday-makers and honeymooners, makes a comfortable base for walks to **Roche Bon Dieu**, a sandstone outcrop said to have fallen from heaven. For more superb beaches you could pant your way south along cliff-top pathways to **Anse Ally**, **Saint François** and **Baie de l'Est**. The walk veers inland from here into the protected forest of **Tasman**. The area is fenced off to prevent grazing cattle from eating young shoots, but the watchman will let you in. The pathway, bounded by great forests of casuarina trees and acacias, runs parallel to the coast, crossing a plateau of dead coral where massive white rollers pound the reef. From here the paths rise and dip into the lovely coves and bays of **Grand Anse**, **Trou d'Argent** and **Anse Bouteille** before linking up to Port Sud-Est. Looking out to sea from this, the most easterly point of Rodrigues, the nearest landfall is the western coast of Australia 5,500km (3,400 miles) away.

Sleepy lagoon islands

Île aux Cocos ❾ (11 km/7 miles from Port Mathurin) is the last refuge of the fody and brush warbler, which have virtually disappeared from Rodrigues. This idyllic island, one of 18 floating inside the lagoon, promises an all too short experience of desert island living. Soft-spoken fishermen ferry you to sugary white beaches where the only resident, a government watchman, leads a Robinson Crusoe existence in a large bungalow. You can camp out for the day beneath the trees. To visit the island you need a permit from Discovery Rodrigues (tel: 832 1062; email: discoveryrodrigues@intnet.mu) in Port Mathurin, which most tour operators will arrange for you (see Travel Tips, A–Z).

Fishermen from Port Sud-Est make trips to equally beautiful **Cat Island**, ideal for swimming and snorkelling, and **Hermitage Island**, one of the most picturesque of all Rodrigues' satellite islands.

A coconut grove under a stormy sky at Port Sud Est.

St-Denis from La Montaign.

A waterfall and peaks along the Mat River.

RÉUNION

This may be a Gallic outpost, but you won't find
scenery or a local culture like this in France.

Local gecko.

Réunion, born three million years ago as a result of an undersea volcanic eruption, consists of two great volcanic mountain masses. The oldest, in the north-west, covers two-thirds of the total area of the island and rises to form the Piton des Neiges, which, at 3,070 metres (10,072ft), is the highest peak in the whole southwest Indian Ocean. Over time, the Piton des Neiges, an extinct volcano, collapsed and eroded to form three caldera-like valleys, or cirques. Piton de la Fournaise (2,632 metres/8,635ft), one of the most active volcanoes in the world (but well-monitored), formed the more recent mountain mass, in the southeast around 530,000 years ago. Almost half the island has been desig-nated a Unesco Natural World Heritage site.

Réunion has its share of popular beaches, but the big-gest thrill for tourists is taking in the beauty of the verdant cirques and the eerie landscape of the volcano. The island cannot compete with Mauritius in terms of beaches and luxury hotels, but it has many more conventional sightsee-ing opportunities in the shape of museums, sugar factories and well-preserved colonial and Creole architecture. Many people come just for the adventure sports, which are the big thing here – from trekking, mountain biking and horse riding, to kayaking, canyoning and paragliding.

Chillis at Marché de Saint Paul.

Eighty percent of Réunion's visitors are French. They see the island as an extension of the motherland and feel comfortable with the left-hand drive Renaults and Peugeots, the smooth roads, the out-of-town hypermarkets, and the bistros and boulevards. They feel at home in the Novotels and mountain gîtes and can even bring their dogs with them, and of course everyone speaks French.

The tropical warmth and breathtaking scenery are intoxicating and the Réunionnais are an attractive, gentle people. Ethnically a fascinat-ing mélange of Malagasy, European, Chinese and Indian, they are tak-ing inspiration from their counterparts in Mauritius and rediscovering their heritage.

Réunion remains little-known in the English-speaking world and, for the discerning traveller, in many ways it is the most fascinating of the Mascarene trio.

An old Creole gentleman.

THE RÉUNIONNAIS

The melting-pot phenomenon is seen more clearly in Réunion than anywhere else in the Western Indian Ocean.

The culture and people of Réunion can be defined in two words – 'melting pot'. The overriding importance of the French language and culture throughout most of the island's history has meant that religious and ethnic differences were always subordinate to the notion of integration with the mother country. The assimilationist tendency that characterised the period from 1946 to 1981 hindered the emergence of a separate Réunionnais identity, but today the inhabitants happily juggle several identities and recent years have seen a cultural and religious resurgence among Réunionnais of Tamil, Muslim and other non-Christian minorities.

The foundations of society

The first inhabitants of Réunion were a few exiled Frenchmen and a handful of Malagasy. The birth of their Franco-Malagasy children heralded the beginning of a process of *métissage* (ethnic mixing) that has always characterised Réunionnais society.

In the 17th century, more settlers arrived in dribs and drabs from Europe and Asia, and pirates relocated to what was then called Bourbon from their old haunts in Madagascar. With the development of coffee cultivation, and the importation of slaves from East Africa and Madagascar, 18th-century Bourbon became a society where blacks outnumbered whites. During this period the Kreol language was in its formative stage. Some whites, however, became pauperised as the subdivision of landholdings between siblings forced the less fortunate to the higher regions, to farm the inhospitable terrain of Les Hauts. In 1830 land concessions were made for Salazie, and in 1840 for Cilaos, but Mafate, the largest of the cirques, was still too difficult to access.

Divali in St Andre.

The 19th century saw the arrival of sugar cane culture in Réunion – Charles Desbassyns introduced the first steam-powered machinery – and other *grands blancs*, or powerful white families, joined him to form the island's plantocracy. By mid-century cane had become the island's principal crop. On 20 December 1848 slavery was abolished, and many of the new free men established themselves in Les Hauts as blacksmiths and charcoal makers. Among the indentured workers subsequently imported to Réunion were Malagasy, Indians and Chinese. A few Comorians and Yemenis were also brought.

Towards the end of the 19th century, free immigrants began to arrive from

Cantonese- and Hakka-speaking regions of China. They gravitated into hawking and shopkeeping in the north and south of the island respectively, establishing community networks for themselves and schools for their children. Traders arrived from Gujarat and Bombay over the same period. This last wave of chiefly commercial immigrants adopted a dualistic pattern of socialisation: absorbing one culture while retaining another. To this day, these communities are perhaps the most self-enclosed and distinctive within a largely integrationist culture.

Réunion's demographics reflect its varied background.

Social realities

Today, roughly three-quarters of Réunion society is composed of *métis* – persons of mixed origins. There are few signs of racial antagonism, although a few white families still wield an economic influence disproportionate to their numbers. They are the remnants of the large landowning class, some of whom have moved into banking and import/export businesses. Professionals and senior civil servants, including many recent arrivals from France, have swelled their numbers. Their luxury homes are in the best quarters of St-Denis and St-Pierre, and they keep holiday villas in cool Cilaos or Hell-Bourg for the summer and often have a beach house at St-Gilles that they use in winter.

The less well-off whites, or *petits blancs*, who have been living in Les Hauts for generations, have evolved into a tight-knit but distinctive community, attached to the traditional agricultural and handicraft occupations of their forebears.

The Réunionnais today are differentiated less by colour than by creed. The descendants of Indian traders, most of whom are Muslims, are known as *Zarabs*. Almost a quarter of all Réunionnais are of South Indian descent; their forebears were mostly Tamil-speaking Hindus. Freed from the enforced Catholicism of the colonial period, many Tamils are rediscovering

> The term *zorèys* ('ears'), used for the French living on Réunion, is said to originate from the habit new arrivals had of cupping their hand behind their ear as they attempted to understand the Kreol language.

their religious roots. This group are also called *Malbars*. The largely Catholic Chinese of Réunion are increasingly intermarrying, and may not be a distinctive community for much longer.

The newest constituent of society are the *zorèys* from mainland France, who help to run the modern state as civil servants, teachers and the like. The status of Réunion as a *département* of France means that any EU national can apply to work and live on the island, just as the Réunionnais have the right to travel to, work and stay in France. The plum posts occupied by *zorèys* sometimes provoke resentment among the Réunionnais, just as the mainland French occasionally give vent to less than charitable assessments of the laid-back approach of the islanders.

Despite the preponderance in Réunion of individuals of mixed ethnicity, the African origins of a significant proportion of the population are clearly evident. Descendants of these Afro-Creoles are sometimes known as *kafs* (from the Arab *kafir* or heathen); a woman is a *kafrine*.

Society as a whole is characterised by dependence: the population (totalling 840,000 in 2013) is young – about 40 percent is below the age of 25 – and unemployment in Réunion currently stands at 29 percent. A significant proportion of the population relies on social security payments. The evident disparities between the haves and have-nots have created latent tensions that occasionally erupt: in February 1991 riots in Chaudron, a disadvantaged suburb of the capital, brought these social problems into sharp relief.

Many of these problems are structural – the high living standards that the French have fostered in Réunion mean that entrepreneurship of the kind that has given neighbouring Mauritius a dynamic economy is untenable in a society where wage rates price the islanders out of the market. The political relationship with France is not often questioned and is presumably sufficiently important to the French to make the prospect of jettisoning what must be a financial burden unthinkable. But as long as this is the case, Réunion has little prospect of becoming an economically viable entity.

Culturally, Réunion benefits greatly from membership of the Francophone world. Sophisticated media links bring French television into every home and reinforce the commonality of the French–Creole diaspora through the diffusion of French Caribbean rhythms and style.

Culture and religion

Hindu beliefs and practices on Réunion date from the settlement of plantation labourers of Indian origin who built small temples near the sugar estates, some of which can still be seen. The goddesses Draupadi, Mariammen and Kalimai are celebrated in annual festivals, and several Hindu temples in Réunion regroup all three. The monkey-god Hanuman used to be celebrated with an annual dance through the streets led by a devotee painted in bright colours, known as the *jacot* (monkey). Traditional funeral rites, or *samblani*, continue to be performed by Tamils.

The older generation of Chinese in Réunion still celebrate their own rites of passage, and they have built a number of pagodas on the island. Ancestor worship is practised on small altars in the home, and the pagoda at St-Pierre is used by Hakkas for honouring the souls of the dead in an annual ceremony. Distinctive Chinese tombs can be found in several of the island's cemeteries.

There are 38 mosques and prayer rooms on the island, the oldest of which dates from 1905. Most Muslims here regularly attend Friday prayers and practise fasting during the month

of Ramadan. Many also pay *zakat* (tithes) to the mosque. Most women of Islamic faith in Réunion wear Western dress, although a minority have adopted a head-covering or the veil.

The African and Malagasy cultural heritage is omnipresent – in the faces, music, language and place names of the island. The *maloya* is a former dance of slaves, and many Kreol words derive from Bantu and other languages associated with East Africa. Malagasy place names in Réunion are particularly evocative. Cilaos is said to mean 'the place where cowards do not go' and Cimendef, at Mafate, is so named after

Local entertainment.

DANCING THE MALOYA

Maloya and sega music are the two major traditional music genres that evolved among slaves and developed into contemporary forms in Réunion. While Réunion's sega resembles the sega typical of Mauritius and the *moutya* of Seychelles, *maloya* retains a unique Réunionnais sound, and was inscribed on the Unesco list of Intangible Cultural Heritage of Humanity in 2009. The word 'maloya' is said to come from a Malagasy expression meaning 'fed up', and employs instruments that reflect its African roots: the large *roulèr* barrel drum, flat *kayamb* rattle and *piker* bamboo percussion. French Caribbean *zouk* can also be heard on the radio.

a Malagasy who escaped – it means 'he who cannot be a slave'. A few families of Malagasy origin continue to practise traditional funeral rites, known as *velasa*, and ancestor worship.

A multitude of faiths

For many years, the practice of non-Christian religions was frowned on in Réunion and, partly as a result of this, some Hindu traditions have been absorbed into Christian celebrations. The cult of Mariammen, for example, is often assimilated with worship of the Virgin Mary, while Krishna's birthday is

Chinese New Year in St Denis.

associated with that of Jesus Christ. The veneration of St-Expédit (nominally Catholic, but not recognised by the Vatican) is symbolic of the confluence of religious practices found in Réunion, for the saint is also identified as a manifestation of Kali.

Catholicism itself has developed a particular style in Réunion where Christians visit shrines such as that of the Black Virgin at Notre Dame de la Salette to honour a promise made in exchange for a request exacted, in a striking resemblance to Hindu practices. This is just one of hundreds of shrines to the Virgin scattered around the island, always bedecked in flowers and ceramic *remerciements* (thank you notes).

Chinese Catholics continue to adhere to Buddhist rituals in the home, and to venerate their ancestors in the colourful pagodas dotted around the island.

Many folk practices and superstitions brought by immigrants have survived the centuries of French acculturation. Hindus believe that prayers made to specific gods and goddesses can cure certain diseases, while Muslims trace some forms of illness to possession by evil spirits, or *djinns*. The word for an Indian sorcerer is *pusari* in Réunion, and given that Tamil priests are known as *pujaris*, this suggests a crossover of religious and magical practices. A sorcerer of Malagasy origin is called an *ombiasy*.

Formulas for casting black magic spells have circulated in Réunion for many years. *Petit Albert*, the collection of magic spells imported to the region from Europe, and the brand of African black magic known as *gris gris* in the islands, still have many practitioners.

The belief in wandering, troubled souls is also very common in Réunion and may originate in the Malagasy concept of the *matoatoa*. People who have died of the plague or of other epidemic diseases are believed to be possessed of special powers and cemeteries in St-Denis and at Le Port, where such graves are found, are frequented by believers at auspicious times.

Public holidays and festivals

The first Hindu festival of the year, Pandyale, takes place in early January when fire-walking ceremonies are held. Cavadee, the spectacular body-piercing festival, takes place in January/February, when fire-walking is also part of the proceedings. Hindus honour Mariammen, a goddess associated with Tamils, in May each year. Kali's festival in August is marked by the sacrifice of cockerels and goats. Chinese New Year is also celebrated in Réunion, in February/March, and in September the mid-autumn festival provides an opportunity to taste moon cake. The Muslim trader families, or *zarabs*, celebrate Eid ul Fitr and Eid ul Kebir, when animal sacrifices are made. Some rituals are grounded in very real, local fears: on 15 August each year pilgrims go to the shrine of the Madonna with a Parasol, Ste-Rose, to pray that there will be no volcanic eruption. The abolition of slavery in 1848 is commemorated annually by a public holiday on 20 December.

Cases Créoles

Réunion, Mauritius and Seychelles are home to a number of diverse colonial-era buildings, all of which reflect the islands' histories and ways of life.

The architectural heritage of the Indian Ocean islands is fast disappearing, as the once ubiquitous delightful wooden homes, with their long verandas, are being replaced by modern concrete buildings that have little of their predecessors' appeal. Do take the opportunity on your visit to appreciate the charm and ingenuity of the remaining colonial homes, from the humble *case créole* to the grandiose plantation house.

The design of the typical *case créole* dates from the 18th century when settlers employed marine carpenters to build their houses from local wood. The *bardeaux*, or shingle roof, still a feature of many Creole houses, and the plank-lined outer walls were clearly inspired by boats. Local weather conditions also played an important role in the development of building styles. The triangular and porch roofs were designed to protect houses from heavy tropical rains, while the *varangue*, or veranda, was spacious and airy to combat the humidity and heat of the tropics and formed an extension of the main living quarters. The inhabitants added their own decorative touches, which over time have given the Creole house its distinctive style. The designs of the *lambrequins*, mantle decorations that help to shield the house from the elements, often have a unique motif which was the owner's cultural trademark. One of the finest examples of a typical *case créole*, complete with a type of garden extension known as a *guetali*, can be seen at Villa Folio, in Hell-Bourg (see page 224).

Colonial legacy

In the 18th century wealthy merchants built more grandiose versions of the *case créole* close to centres of commerce, and enclosed them within ornate railings. Some of these stylish and historic houses can still be seen in the backstreets of Port Louis and in Rue de Paris in St-Denis. As the middle classes moved to new residential areas, Creole architecture became more refined and was complemented by elegant lawns and gardens. The towns of the Mauritian central plateau, from Rose Hill to Curepipe, are still dotted with the well-maintained former residences of prosperous 19th-century colonists.

The most impressive of the island residences are the grand homes built by the sugar barons and planters of valued export crops such as vanilla and spices. The plantation houses, with their turrets, columns and balustrades, manage to harmonise the classic features of Creole design with the evident pretensions of their owners. The verandas are enclosed by colonnades and extend around the house, on two or three sides. Most are still privately owned, but visitors to Mauritius can take a guided tour of the Maison Eureka in Moka, to see how the plantocracy really lived, or dine at stately St Aubin in the south. Holiday-makers in Mahé, Seychelles, can stay at La Residence

A Creole house in the village of Cilaos.

Bougainville, which has been converted into a guest-house with a sea view, or at the Château St Cloud on La Digue, a vanilla plantation house dating from the Napoleonic period.

The seats of government of the French administrators, much enlarged and restored over succeeding years, particularly Le Reduit (the Mauritian president's official residence), retain the simple beauty of colonial architecture, while providing an appropriately stately venue for visiting dignitaries. At the other end of the scale, look out for the quaint stone post offices that the British built in Mauritius and Seychelles. One enduring and endearing feature of the insular landscape is the Creole corner shop, with its gaily coloured walls, hand-painted hoardings and corrugated roof.

RÉUNION CUISINE

French cuisine is the norm at most hotels and restaurants, and Chinese, Indian and Italian food is on offer in the bigger centres, but traditional home cooking is Creole.

The food may appear to have a strongly French influence – *café au lait* and croissants for breakfast, *croque monsieur* (toasted cheese and ham sandwich) for lunch and *civet* (a type of stew) for supper are all standard fare. Nevertheless, even in Réunion Creole cuisine holds sway. Its absence from some of the bars and bistros of St-Denis or St-Gilles-les-Bains may send you searching, but head for the cirques and you'll find local people living on *carris* (mild curries), as well as white rice or yellow rice (cooked with turmeric), pulses (red or white haricot beans, lentils or peas) accompanied by a variety of *rougails* (the hot and spicy chutney known as *chatini* in Mauritius) and *achards* (pickled spiced vegetables).

Meat curries are usually made with chicken, beef or pork, but one of the tastiest curries you'll find on a menu is *cabri masalé* (goat masala). The meat is cooked slowly in a rich flavoursome sauce and melts in the mouth. Fish and seafood are also curried, *zourit* (octopus) and prawn are favourites.

Measuring vanilla.

Versatile vegetables

Vegetarians are well catered for in the markets, which are stocked with an enormous variety of fresh fruit and vegetables. However, ordering a vegetarian meal in a Creole restaurant is a little more tricky. Meat or fish is central to many mains, but a number of starters and accompaniments are vegetable based. Vegetable or lentil *carris* can be made if requested and *salade de palmiste* (heart of palm) appears on some menus, but check before ordering any other salads, as they may contain meat or fish. *Tarte brèdes chou chou*, a creamy pie made from spinach-like greens on a pastry base, is a filling alternative.

Chou chou (also known as christophine) is a very versatile vegetable, which tastes like watery courgette. It is added to cakes, jams and curries, served *au gratin*, as *brèdes chou chou*, or just boiled. The plant stems can be split and dried and used to make woven handicrafts.

Vanilla

Réunion is one of the world's leading producers of vanilla and it plays an important role in the island's cuisine. You'll find vanilla in sweet and savoury sauces, rum-based liqueurs such as Pause Café and sometimes tea and coffee. If you're interested to see how it is grown and processed, visit the Vanilla Cooperative in Bras-Panon (see page 203).

Home cooking

For a taste of real Réunionnais cuisine, track down a *ferme auberge* (farmhouse inn) where you could try traditional offerings cooked by enthusiastic home chefs. A typical tourist menu (around €15) might consist of a set number of courses such as *gratin chou chou* for starters, followed by a sumptuous fish curry or duck in vanilla sauce and finished off with *fondant au chocolat* – also with vanilla sauce. One of the most popular *ferme auberges* is in Bras-Panon at Chemin Rivière du Mat (tel: 0262 51 53 76); booking is essential.

Snacks and sweets

There's no shortage of mobile food stalls along the popular west coast beaches selling filled

Grapes have long been grown in Cilaos and the region is the only wine-producing area in Réunion; you'll find some decent table wines there made from the Cot, Pinot Noir and Chenin grapes. In 1991 a small group of vine growers formed Le Chai de Cilaos Cooperative, which markets and exports the wines to France, but if you're in Cilaos then drop in for a winetasting session. The dry white wine goes well with grilled fish and cheese, the smooth sweet white is an excellent dessert wine and the fullbodied red from the Cot grape makes an excellent accompaniment to red meat.

Rhum arrangé.

baguettes and sweet and savoury Breton-style *crêpes* (pancakes). Look out for *pâtisseries*, *croissanteries* and 'sandwicheries' at out-of-town hypermarkets such as Jumbo or Super U, where you pick from mouth-watering displays of savoury Creole snacks: *bonbons piment* (spicy chickpea cakes), vegetable or meat *samousas* and *brinjals* (aubergine fritters) piled high and sold cheap.

Rum punch or wine

Rhum arrangé, literally, 'arranged rum', is a mind-blowing concoction of rum and fruit that is left for months to macerate and mature in a mixture of spices. Marginally easier on the brain cells is *punch créole*, usually rum based, made from a range of fruits and berries, cane syrup and juice.

SWEET TREATS

Lots of interesting goodies exist to satisfy the sweet-toothed in Réunion. At St-Gilles-les-Bains there are several places just right for that sugary bite: two to look out for are Chez Loulou (86 rue Général de Gaulle) and Au Vieux Quimper (Place Paul Julius Benard). Try *macatias*, a local version of a butter-free brioche that can come plain or jazzed up with chocolate chips, coconut or both. Other sweet treats include *tartes*, made with pawpaw or mango, honey biscuit rings called *bonbons au miel,* Indian-style *goolab* glistening with sugary syrup and flour-based cakes called *napolitains*.

Waterfall at Anse Des Cascades,
south of Piton Ste Rose.

VOLCANIC HABITATS

With large swathes of virgin rainforests still remaining, Réunion's dramatic volcanic terrain provides refuge for a wide variety of wildlife.

The high rugged mountains and deeply chasmed gorges of Réunion have ensured that, unlike on the other Mascarenes, much of the island's original forests still exist and are in good condition. Nevertheless, this hasn't stopped the demise of some spectacular wildlife, namely, as with Mauritius and Rodrigues, the giant tortoise, flightless birds and gaudy parrots.

Réunion once had a bird that was thought to be a white dodo or solitaire but recent discoveries have revealed that this creature, which was about the size of a turkey, was a flightless ibis. In the 17th century, before the advent of travel guides and bird books, the names of birds were not fixed and were sometimes used to indicate a complete species, hence the term dodo came to be used for any flightless bird.

Other birds lost to Réunion have been the crested starling, called the *huppe*, which was last seen in the middle of the 19th century, and a beautiful russet brown parrot with a lilac head that died out in the late 18th century. It is believed that these creatures' habitats had mainly been in the lowland rainforests, which had fallen under the settlers' axes for coffee, cotton and spice plantations.

In the cooking pot

Considering the amount of high altitude rainforest Réunion has, it has long puzzled naturalists why the island should have lost its equivalent to the pink pigeon, kestrel, echo parakeet (see page 85), forest fody and fruit bat, the latter of which can be found in great numbers on the other Mascarenes. It has been suggested that extinction rates are higher on French-owned islands because much of the wildlife is heavily hunted for the cooking pot! Today, the best place to see specimens and models of

A yellow-streaked tenrec.

Réunion's extinct wildlife is in the Natural History Museum at St-Denis (see page 194).

Newcomers to Réunion

Many species of mammal were brought to the island by settlers mainly for food, including wild boar, lemurs, squirrels and hares, but most have died out, although not the boar. The Javan deer that arrived in 1761 had already been hunted to extinction by 1793. Regrettably, they were reintroduced in the 1980s to Plaine des Chicots and Bébour. They feed on the saplings of native trees, preventing natural regeneration of the forest.

One of the most interesting of the introduced mammals is the tenrec (*Tenrec ecaudatus*), a hedgehog-like insectivore which comes from Madagascar and is known locally as *tang*. Brought over for the dinner table, it is still on the menu in some rural areas, although many meet their end flattened on the road. The female produces huge litters, the record being 34 young in one litter. Apparently only one egg has to be fertilised, which then divides repeatedly so all the young are the same sex and genetically identical.

The *musaraigne* or Indian house shrew, an omnivorous mammal that can also be found on Mauritius and Rodrigues, is common over much of the island and preys on reptiles and invertebrates. Apart from the rats and feral cats, similar

Manapany day gecko.

to the spotted tabby African wildcat, there are few mammals on Réunion and none that are indigenous.

Island birds

Despite the rats that steal birds' eggs and the cats that have catching birds down to a fine art, there are large numbers of native birds that should be easy to spot, especially in Roche Écrite or the Forêt de Bébour. The stonechat, or *tec-tec* (the exact sound of its call) is the most common, appearing everywhere except the low coastal areas of the north and west. You are more likely to see a paradise flycatcher – known locally as the *vierge* because it has a bluish-purple head and is believed to have seen the Virgin Mary – in

Réunion than in Mauritius. The same goes for the island's black bulbul *(merle pays)* and two species of white-eye.

The Mascarene cave swiftlet lives here too and can often be seen feasting on clouds of flying insects. However, swallows are quite rare, keeping to the lowland east of the island and Cilaos. The bird you are least likely to see is the rare Réunion cuckoo-shrike *(tuit-tuit)*, which hides in the forest of Plaine des Chicots above St-Denis.

Soaring or gliding over forests and in the cirques, the Réunion harrier or *papang* is the largest and most spectacular bird on the island. A bird of prey with a wingspan of more than a metre (3ft), the adult male is stunning in its grey, white and black plumage; the females are brown. They have a varying diet of tenrecs, rats, birds and invertebrates.

Escaped cage birds

Many of the pretty perching birds you will see around the gardens are descendants of common cage birds that have escaped from captivity and are relative newcomers. These include yellow village weaver birds, waxbills, spice finches, the beautiful (more yellow than green) green singing finch and the not-so-pretty mynah bird.

The gentle cooing sounds are provided by the small grey barred ground dove and the Madagascar turtle dove, which was thought to have come from Madagascar but sub-fossil bones have since been found, proving that it is native. The bright red Madagascar fody can be seen everywhere.

Fortunately for the game birds, the mongoose has never been introduced to the island, so three species of quail, two of partridge, wild chickens

---

RARE PETRELS

Réunion is most famous for two threatened species of endemic petrels, the Barau's petrel (Pterodroma baraui) and the Mascarene black petrel (Pterodroma aterrima). The former was only discovered in 1963 and its nest sites found a few years ago in the high cliffs of Piton des Neiges. The nesting sites of the black petrel are in the region of Grand Bassin and Le Dimitile. The Barau's petrel can be seen over the beach at St-Gilles in the late afternoon and in the cirques and mountains as they fly in to roost. They are a wonderful sight to watch wheeling around the cliffs of Cilaos in the evening.

and a button quail, thought to be a native, all live in relative peace.

Important seabirds

As well as the endangered Barau's petrel and Mascarene black petrel, Réunion is home to Audubon's shearwater, a small black and white seabird that nests in the cliffs and feeds on fish and squid; and several small colonies of wedge-tailed shearwater. Keep an eye open in the cirques, gorges and around cliffs for the spectacular white-tailed tropicbird *(paille-en-queue)*, which has a long, streaming tail and is the island's national bird. Petite

up coconut palms and the pandanus, or screw pine. The Réunion day gecko, however, is a much more difficult species to find as it only lives high up in the forests of the northeast and east. A blue-green colour with red stripes down each side, its distribution has been split by lava flows from the volcano, creating different races of the same species. You can sometimes spot them lurking around the tourist kiosks up there.

The beautiful green, blue and red panther chameleon from Madagascar is the only introduced species that is protected; it can be found all over the island.

Tree ferns in the Bebour Forest.

Île, just off the south coast and Réunion's only satellite island, has a breeding population of at least 300 pairs of common noddies and up to 300 non-breeding lesser noddies, who have recently been joined by a fairy tern.

Colourful geckos

Apart from the many nocturnal house geckos that you see darting about the gardens and houses, the island has two brightly coloured endemic day geckos that are worth looking out for. As the name implies, the only place you will see the stunning green, red and white Manapany day gecko is on a walk through Manapany on the south coast. There you will see them all over the place, basking on banana leaves, scuttling

Tamarinds and orchids

Cultivated land bearing sugar cane reaches as high as 800 metres (2,600ft) above sea level, then gives way to verdant mixed forest which becomes a dwarf heath as you move up to the higher elevations. There are more than 60,000 hectares (148,000 acres) of natural forest on the island, and the endemic tamarind of the acacia family, alongside an island bamboo called the *calumet*, is quite a common sight. A wide variety of orchids (seven of which are unique to Réunion), and ferns grow in abundance on trees.

Some of the introduced plants are a menace, such as the *goyavier* from Brazil, which runs rampant in the forest undergrowth. But its small guava-like red berries are rich in vitamin C.

Taking in Réunion's landscape on horseback.

ISLAND OF ADVENTURES

The spectacular landscape of Réunion is punctuated by trails, craters, peaks, rivers, forests and waterfalls, tailor-made for a vast array of outdoor pursuits.

Experiencing the great spectacle of the interior uplands of Réunion can take as little or as much effort as you choose. Whether you take it easy and fly across the island in a helicopter or take a stroll along a nature trail, or prefer the challenge of hiking along a Grande Randonnée (see page 182), testing your nerve abseiling down a waterfall, or paragliding off a mountain ridge, you will discover mystery in its isolation, magic in its inaccessibility and power in its grandeur.

The cirques, mountains and plains providing the magnificent terrain for such activities were formed at different stages of the island's volcanic development over many thousands of years. Originally the Piton des Neiges (3,070 metres/10, 072 ft) was the summit of a massive volcanic dome that collapsed around it and then was eroded to form the three great amphitheatres of gorges, waterfalls and ridges known as the cirques – perfect for canyoning, white-water rafting, rock climbing, paragliding and tree-top adventures.

A helicopter ride in Iron Hole canyon.

The High Plains (Les Hautes-Plaines), comprising La Plaine-des-Palmistes and the Plaine-des-Cafres, form an open landscape of forests and pastureland between the extinct volcanic landscape and the active Piton de la Fournaise. They are criss-crossed with mountain-bike tracks, hiking paths and horse-riding trails. The higher Plaine-des-Cafres is the gateway to the volcano summit (see page 213), while Le Grand Brûlé on the southeast coast offers the possibility of visiting some of the world's most recent lava tubes, dating from a 2004 eruption.

Be prepared

The best time to take on any arduous, lengthy activity, such as hiking, horse trekking or mountain biking, is during the cooler and drier months of May to November when mountain temperatures hover between 12°C (54°F) and 18°C (64°F) during the day but can drop to near zero at night. Weather conditions can change very rapidly so check online or, if you understand French, you can phone the meteorological office (see Travel Tips, Activities).

It's important that you are aware of your own level of fitness and stamina before starting any activity and stick to rules of basic safety. Helicopters frequently survey the cirques and should you be injured or in trouble you can send a distress signal by raising both arms in a V shape. Every year, scores of people, mostly suffering from broken bones or twisted ankles, are rescued in the cirques.

For overnight stays en route, there are several types of accommodation, ranging from *gîtes de montagne* (mountain huts or lodges), to *chambres d'hôtes* (B&Bs) and youth hostels. Campsites are infrequent, but there are a few *abris* (shelters) on trekking routes. The shelters consist of only a roof so you need your own tent and sleeping bag.

Many places provide meals and at several of the *chambres d'hôtes*, a *table d'hôte* is offered when all the guests sit down to a meal together with the host. Reservations must be made in advance for all accommodation through Réunion's tourist board. There is usually a grocer's shop *(épicerie)* in the villages *(îlets)* scattered around the interior, selling a basic range of foods, but not in all of them.

Up, up and away

The cirques and mountains are an awesome sight, especially from the top, and you can experience the sensation of flying between the peaks in a helicopter (see page 216) or smaller still, in a microlight. One or two people can fly

Gorge walking.

HEADING INTO THE MOUNTAINS

Whether you spend a day or a week in the cirques and mountains, Réunion's tourist board (tel: 0810 160 000; www.reunion.fr) can assist you with whatever you would like to do. Knowledgeable, English-speaking staff will advise on hiking routes, can arrange mountain accommodation and provide guides if necessary. They can also organise horse-trekking trips, canyoning, mountain biking, hang-gliding and many other mountain sports.

To ensure safety in the mountains, it is important to take some common-sense precautions. Never venture out alone, and if you don't know the mountains, take a guide. You must be fit to take full advantage of

the mountains – plan an itinerary on a par with your physical capacity. For peace of mind, book a room and board in advance. Good shoes, and warm and waterproof clothing ensure comfort. Take enough water with you; do not drink water from rivers or pools. Do not light fires and always keep the mountains litter free.

To avoid accidents never take closed or unmarked paths; check the state of paths before setting out on a hike and always follow trail blazes. If you do get lost, stay calm and remember the distress signal – arms held up in a V. Never leave a wounded person alone. Wait for help.

> *The mountainous cirques of Salazie and Cilaos are sensational for hiking, rock climbing and canyoning. For rafting and kayaking, head to the south or east coast.*

in a microlight round a choice of the lagoon, the cirques, Piton des Neiges or near the volcano. Alternatively you can skydive from a plane (south coast) or a helicopter (west coast), although once you've jumped you might not have much time to admire the scenery.

To fly like a bird with only the rush of wind in your ears has to be one of the greatest thrills, especially over, within and around such dramatic scenery as Réunion's. The most popular paragliding spot is from Colimaçons, above St-Leu, but hang-gliding and paragliding are also possible from Piton Maïdo on the edge of the wild and secluded Cirque de Mafate, from the top of Piton des Neiges and the Hauts de St-Paul, where protected from the strong winds, the conditions are perfect for beginners, too.

Rivers wild

Streams cascading over ridges and waterfalls powering off the mountains provide ideal conditions for the hair-raising sports of canyoning and gorge walking (*randonnée aquatique*). For daredevils only, in a well-padded wetsuit, canyoning means abseiling down waterfalls and torrents in the heights of the cirques, while gorge walking is slightly less physical. Try Rivière Langevin at St-Joseph, Îlet Fleurs Jaunes and Îlets du Bois Rouge in La Cirque de Cilaos, or Trois Cascades in La Cirque de Salazie. As the slopes become less steep, rivers, such as the Rivière des Roches, provide exciting conditions for kayaking; and there are plenty of rapids, such as those of the Rivière des Marsouins, for white-water rafting. Companies specialising in river sports often organise mountain climbing expeditions as well.

At sea

Sea-based activities are clustered around – but not limited to – St-Gilles-les-Bains. Scuba diving is the second most popular activity in Réunion after trekking, and there's something for everyone, whether you'd like a beginner's dive or are already certified. You don't need to dive to see the humpback whales who, every June, travel up

from the Antarctic to reproduce and give birth in Réunion's sheltered waters, staying until September. Snorkelling, kitesurfing, big-game fishing, stand-up paddle and sailing are available too.

Mountain bike challenges

Seven large areas of the island's magnificent interior have been devoted to mountain biking (VTT), and marked tracks, approved by the French Cycling Federation, total nearly 700km (435 miles). These areas, each with their own steep challenges and beautiful views, include Maïdo, Entre-Deux, Cilaos, two at Hautes-

A bird's-eye view via paramotoring.

Plaines, St-Philippe and Ste-Rose. Suitable bikes can be hired locally.

Trekking on horseback

Viewing the beauty of Réunion at your own pace from the back of a horse has to be an enriching experience – for an hour, a day or for several days, with tent and meals included in the price. Possibilities include a sunset ride at Cap La Houssaye, a three-day circuit through the Forêt de Bébour-Bélouve or a two-day ride to the volcano. The horses in Réunion are the gentle Mérens breed brought over from the Pyrénées in France, on which even a beginner will feel at ease. (For more details on adventure sports, see Travel Tips, Activities.)

Hiking along the Grandes Randonnées

Mysterious valleys, magnificent forests and soaring peaks are just some of the spectacular delights that await those who step onto Réunion's network of hiking paths.

Hikers trek the Rivière des Remparts.

Réunion is a walker's paradise, in spite of what novelist Walter Besant had to say about it when he walked to the Piton des Neiges in 1863. His tramp in the tropics may have been 'a time of bruisings, and barkings of the skin, of tearings and scratchings, of dirt, discomfort and disaster', but today there are more than 1,000km (620 miles) of well-marked trails across the island, mostly maintained by the Office National des Forêts (ONF) and ranging from accessible adventures such as an hour's easy walk to a challenging week-long hike.

There are several organisations that will help you plan your route, book accommodation in advance and provide guides, the main one being Réunion's tourist office (www.reunion.fr). If you are not familiar with the island, hiring a local *guide-pei* (native guide) through the tourist office can be a good idea. Not only will you be in safe hands but they enjoy sharing their in-depth knowledge of their native land.

Grande Randonnée trails

The opening of GR R1 in 1979 made trekking less hazardous than in Besant's days. The 60km (37-mile) trail encircles Piton des Neiges through the three cirques of Salazie, Cilaos and Mafate. No visit would be complete without spending at least one night in the cirques, if only to wake at sunrise and gaze upon verdant valleys clothed in thick forests. The air is clear and sharp and rouses even the weariest walker to experience a world of lofty peaks.

The 135km (84-mile) GR R2 crosses the island from the north to southeast, cutting through diverse landscapes of rugged mountains, fertile plains, volcano and humid forest to St-Philippe. The GR R3 was opened in 2005 and covers 47.5km (30 miles) in the remote Cirque de Mafate. The following are some ideas for hikes that take in the Grandes Randonnées and last from half a day to as long as you would like.

La Roche Écrite

One of the most popular walks, starting from St-Denis, takes you south to La Roche Écrite (2,277 metres/7,470ft). The trail passes through humid lowlands and tamarind forests with an abundance of rich flora to the almost denuded summit of La Roche Écrite itself.

If you're on limited time, the return trip can be done in one full day, but overnighting at the *gîte* at Plaine-des-Chicots will enable you to wake early to complete the final ascent to the ramparts of La Roche Écrite, where you can experience the best views of Réunion's two highest mountains, Piton des Neiges (3,070 metres/10,072ft) and Le Gros Morne (3,019 metres/9,905ft) and the cirques of Mafate and Salazie to the right and left. The trail is clearly signposted from Le Brûlé in the highlands above St-Denis, rising gently through forests of cryptomeria and eucalyptus and lush areas of wild flowers and fruits and endemic bamboo *(Nastus borbonicas)*.

Continue southwards, crossing two ravines surrounded by forests of mixed evergreens or *bois de couleurs* and tamarinds to reach the *gîte* at Plaine-des-Chicots, where you can stop for the night. From here it is another 1.5-hour trek southwards to La

Roche Écrite through landscape that changes to a plateau of lichen and moss.

You'll pass two intersections on the way but you should ignore both and keep to the marked path; the first on the right after about 45 minutes leads to La Mare aux Cerfs, a small watering hole noted for dawn sightings of Réunion's deer, which you could visit on the way back. The second leads to Caverne Soldats. Continue on for another 25 minutes to La Roche Écrite.

Mafate

The most isolated of the cirques, Mafate is wild and peaceful, only disturbed by the sound of the odd helicopter coming in for a closer look. It has plenty of trails, offering walkers anything from a simple but not so interesting three-hour walk along the Rivière des Galets to more difficult day- or week-long hikes. Alternatively, you can stay in Mafate trekking from *îlet* to *îlet* and overnighting in mountain *gîtes*, where breakfast and an evening meal are provided (booking ahead is essential).

The *îlet* of Dos d'Ane on the D1 is a handy starting point for a couple of days of trekking along the GR R2. This trail descends steeply for two hours, taking you down to the Rivière des Galets, which flows from the slopes of Le Gros Morne through a huge valley of *bois de couleurs* and meets the ocean at Le Port on the northwest coast. The trail crosses the river several times before it forks off to the left, leading to the *îlet* of Aurère, a good two-hour climb.

The next day you can do a four-hour hike to Le Bélier on the edge of the Cirque de Salazie, along either the Sentier Scout path or the shorter, but more dramatic, direct path. This descends to the bottom of a ravine before climbing up to the top of the Grand Rein ridge, then down again and along the Route Forestière for the last leg.

Grand Place, past the turn-off to Aurère, is a good central *îlet* to utilise as a base for a few nights if you would like to spend several days exploring Mafate, as many of the trails pass through here.

Salazie

Hell-Bourg (see page 224), at the end of the D48, has plenty of places to stay and is where you can start a hike to the Piton des Neiges, lasting about 5.5 hours. The Gîte de la Caverne Dufour offers basic but hospitable dormitory-style accommodation at the foot of the mountain. From there it is a

1.5-hour climb to the top, best started before dawn before the clouds descend.

Cilaos

The GR R1 winds and climbs its way west from Cilaos to Marla in the Cirque de Mafate. The six-hour hike goes via the Cascade de Bois Rouge and Col du Taïbit (2,142 metres/7,028ft). If you want to try to do it in a day, start from the trailhead on the Îlet à Cordes road, 6km (4 miles) west of, and accessible by bus from, Cilaos.

Alternatively, you can opt to hike up to Piton des Neiges (see page 225), or do a round walk to the

You will need the correct footwear and kit for a volcano trek.

Cascade de Bois Rouge waterfall, which will take you around two hours.

The volcano

Starting at Pas de Bellecombe or from the RF5, an alternative to climbing the Piton de la Fournaise (for more details on this, see page 184) is to follow the GR R2 along the southern ridge (l'Enclos) of the volcano to the Nez Coupé du Tremblet.

This five-hour hike, which passes through the lunar landscape of Plaine des Sables (see page 215), has been graded as not too difficult, but if you're not sure about your fitness or inclination to tackle it, you could just go halfway by returning at Foc-Foc, where the trail forks.

PITON DE LA FOURNAISE

In 1801, explorer Bory de St Vincent described the volcano as 'immense, tumultuous, bloody and majestic'. He was inspired by it, but many feared it.

Piton de la Fournaise ('Peak of the Furnace') is a 'Hawaiian-type' shield volcano and is one of the most active on earth. Since Réunion was first inhabited in 1640, it has erupted on average once every eight months. In 1778, it added notably to the size of the island by pouring millions of tonnes of lava into the sea; in 1786 the explosion was so loud that it was heard in Mauritius.

Piton de la Fournaise (2,632 metres/8,635ft) has two main craters. The highest, Bory, has been inactive since 1791, while the active Dolomieu manages, most of the time, to confine its eruptions to within the enclosure. On 8 April 1977 islanders witnessed the sheer power of their volcano when lava rolled down the mountainside destroying houses and a petrol station at Ste-Rose on the east coast, only to stop just before the doorstep of a church, since renamed Notre Dame des Laves (Our Lady of the Lava).

On 20 March 1986 an eruption extended the island's land mass by several hectares. On 9 March 1998 another spectacular eruption, this time lasting for 196 days – the longest in the 20th century – caused panic and excitement as blood-red fire fountains turned into rivers of lava.

April 2007 saw a major eruption that led to the spectacular collapse of the crater floor of Dolomieu, leaving it 300 metres (985ft) lower.

Any volcanologist will tell you that all live volcanoes, no matter how predictable, should be treated with caution and respect.

Just south of L'Étang-Salé lesBains, the RN1 cuts through a jagged expanse of black lava rock with views of crashing w◄ and water jets, known as souffleurs.

The incredible sight of bright plants blooming out of cooled lava.

A helicopter tour reveals a clear view of a river of fire.

FOUNTAINS AND RIVERS OF FIRE

Like the volcanoes of Hawaii, Piton de la Fournaise is a shield volcano. It produces spectacular fire fountains and churns out rivers of basalt lava, which flow over great distances. Because the lava is so fluid it trickles easily downhill without piling up, which explains why shield volcanoes are not steep. During the 1986 eruption the lava flowed at a rate of 100,000 cubic metres (353,100 cubic ft) per hour, reaching temperatures of up to 1,160°C (2,120°F). Around the Piton de la Fournaise you'll find two types of solidified lava flow which have been given Hawaiian names: *pahoehoe* (pronounced pa-hoy-hoy) and *aa* (ah-ah). *Pahoehoe*, which looks like coils of rope, is smooth and easy to walk on. This type of lava cools slowly and remains viscous for a while, allowing the gases to ooze through a steadily solidifying 'plastic' skin. In contrast, *aa* flows quickly and solidifies into sharp chunks of lava called scoria, which make hiking slow and can ruin your shoes. Low-viscosity lava flows have led to the creation of lava tubes, which can be visited (see page 378).

...kers hiking on Formica Leo.

...aerial view shows how new land forms around the volcano.

A glowing rush of lava from the volcano's eruption in May 2015.

Vineyard by the roadside on Îlet à Cordes.

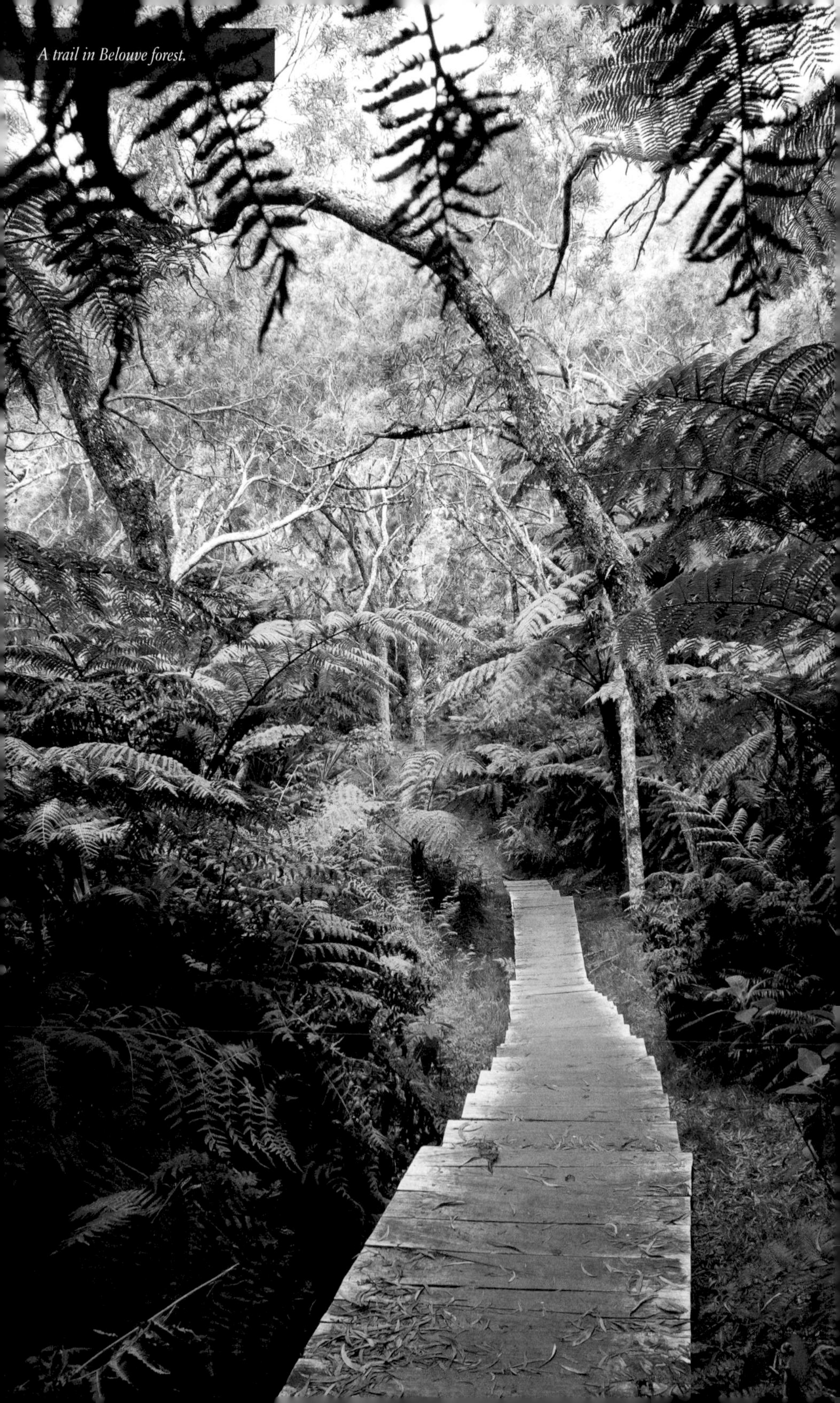

A trail in Belouve forest.

RÉUNION: PLACES

A detailed guide to Réunion, with principal sites
clearly cross-referenced by number to the maps.

Volcanic eruption.

I f you've just flown in from Mauritius, the contrast
in landscapes will come as a shock as you'll discover
awesome volcanic craters, rugged coastlines and lush
gorges. Most people head straight for the west coast, but
no trip to Réunion is complete without a visit to the
volcano and at least one of the cirques. There's no doubt
that the island's greatest assets lie inland, and getting
around is easy thanks to the good roads. At the heart of
the island you'll find mysterious mountains, jagged peaks and gorges,
rivers and waterfalls, extinct craters, isolated villages and a tempera-
mental volcano.

It's possible, though not necessarily advisable, to get
round the island in a day, which you can do either in a
hire car or on the comfortable public buses. The capital,
St-Denis, has some attractively restored buildings and
a couple of interesting art collections, but there is not
much to see or do here.

Most beaches can be found in the west, between
St-Paul and St-Pierre. A good place to base yourself if
you want to be by the sea might be St-Gilles-les-Bains,
a lively resort with plenty of bars and restaurants and
all the facilities you need for water sports, but it can get
crowded. At the far end of the island's western beach
stretch is the pleasant town of St-Pierre, another good
base, being within easy reach of the southeast coast and
about an hour from Piton de la Fournaise.

Natural arch on Piton Sainte Rose.

The east coast areas around the town of St-André and the sleepy
corner of St-Philippe are often neglected, but deserve more than a
brief stop to explore the inland forests, volcanic wastelands, rugged
seascapes and walking trails.

For an altogether different experience, Hell-Bourg, in the Cirque de
Salazie, is a popular base for trekkers and adventurers. From there you
can climb the Piton des Neiges and admire some of the best-preserved
Creole architecture on the island.

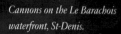
*Cannons on the Le Barachois
waterfront, St-Denis.*

ST-DENIS

Sometimes called 'Paris of the Indian Ocean', St-Denis is more like a provincial capital, but it's worth pausing to look at the lovely Creole architecture.

When French governor Regnault founded St-Denis in 1669, he chose a sheltered pot on the uninhabited north coast. Life for the first 77 inhabitants was dull and, save for the odd pirate or two who dropped by, fairly uneventful. Even when the headquarters of the French East India Company was transferred from the old capital, St-Paul, in 1738, the town still had little going for it, in spite of a hundredfold increase in population. Successive governors tried to turn the new capital into a maritime and military base, but it ended up as neither, and by the late 1950s the infrastructure was so poor that even tourists had a job finding a place to stay.

All that's changed, and St-Denis has transformed itself into a reasonably sophisticated capital of 200,000 people, and these days offers much that you'd expect from any major town in mainland France. The difference, of course, is the tropical setting. Splendid renovated Creole homes, often with grand wrought-iron gates and lush gardens, are one of the chief attractions for casual visitors. And while the restaurants may look typically French, you'll find *carri* (curry) and unfamiliar vegetables such as *chou chou* on the menu; as well as dozens of small Creole eateries offering all the local delicacies, such as *samousas* and *bonbons piments*.

Traffic on Avenue de la Victoire.

Spending a day in St-Denis will give you plenty of time to stroll the streets, visit the major sights, and book accommodation in the interior if you need to. But two words of warning: St-Denis is not a cheap city, and there are better things to do and see elsewhere. If you want to base yourself on the coast, you would do better to opt for St-Gilles, Boucan-Canot or St-Pierre.

The waterfront

Your first glimpse of St-Denis will most likely be from the air. The plane

Main Attractions
Barachois
Villa Carrère
Musée Leon Dierx
Jardin de l'État
Musée d'Histoire Naturelle

DRINK

To order a bottle of the local Bourbon beer, ask the barman for 'une dodo'.

descends into Roland Garros airport, 11km (7 miles) east of the city, sweeping past dark mountains that must have struck awe into the hearts of the early settlers. Hemmed between the Rivière des Pluies and the Rivière St-Denis, the city spreads upwards onto the hill slopes, where modern apartment blocks and luxurious houses have replaced the shanty towns of the 1950s.

A good place to start is at the shaded waterfront promenade known as **Le Barachois A**. The area, once an inlet for unloading ships, had an adjustable jetty affixed to the shore by a set of iron chains, which was raised or lowered above the sea to allow passengers to disembark; according to the writer T.V. Bulpin, they 'had to leap upon it with some display of acrobatics, with

the thought of sharks if they slippe The contraption was rendered usele during cyclones, and the iron pier th later replaced it was equally ineffe tual, so the inlet was eventually fille in and planted with palm trees. Nir cannons face out to sea, placed the to symbolise St-Denis' supposed da as a military base. They are amor Réunion's many coastal cannons th were either salvaged from shipwrec or bought for decorative purposes b various governors.

Le Barachois is as chic as St-Den gets, overlooked from across the bus Boulevard Gabriel Macé by Hôtel S Denis and a handful of cafés and re taurants. Several former French Ea India Company warehouses surviv here, in Place Sarda Garriga, with the

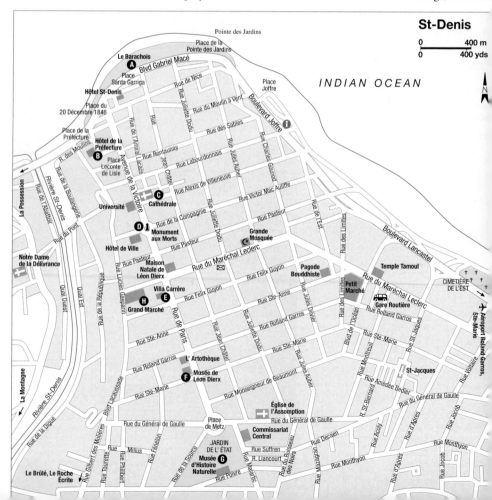

cades still intact. One houses the own's oldest restaurant, the **Roland arros** (see Travel Tips, Restaurants), amed after the famous aviator who as born in the capital.

n architectural tour

walk inland, south along Avenue de la ictoire, leads to some of the city's fin-t buildings. First is **Hôtel de la Préfec-ıre B**, an attractive colonial mansion verlooking pretty gardens. It began as humble coffee warehouse, grew into ıe headquarters of the French East ıdia Company and later became the fficial governor's residence. In 1942 was occupied by Free French Forces, ho arrived to rid the island of its ichy sympathisers. Later visitors have ıcluded General de Gaulle, Giscard 'Estaing and Jacques Chirac. The Pré-cture is closed to the public.

In the adjacent square, now used as car park, a **statue of Mahé de Lab-ırdonnais** stares solemnly out to sea. was here that important announce-ıents from the motherland were made, ıcluding the abolition of slavery in 848 by Sarda-Garriga. Labourdonnais

is best remembered in Réunion for treating the island as a rather forgotten satellite when he was governor of the Mascarene Islands.

Three blocks beyond, past an unchar-acteristically unobtrusive branch of McDonald's in a converted warehouse, is the 19th-century **Cathédrale C**. It has some interesting bas-reliefs of St-Denis, but is not a beautiful build-ing. The square at the front, with vast, twisted trees and a 19th-century iron fountain, is more attractive.

As you head south, on the right in quick succession are several more notable colonial buildings, including the **Université**, built in 1759, but the best old buildings are still to come. The towering **Monument aux Morts D**, which commemorates the death of over 1,000 Réunionnais who fought in World War I, marks the start of **Rue de Paris**, lined with some of the capital's grandest Creole homes.

Villa Carrère E (14 Rue de Paris; tel: 0262 41 83 00; Mon–Sat 9am–6pm) is a typical 19th-century Creole house (the only one open to the pub-lic in St-Denis) and is also home to the

FACT

In 1913 Roland Garros (1888–1918) became the first pilot to fly across the Mediterranean. Taken prisoner during World War I, he escaped only to die in action a month before it ended. His statue stands outside the Hôtel St-Denis in Place Sarda Garriga.

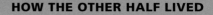

Monument aux Morts by the town hall.

HOW THE OTHER HALF LIVED

Engineers of the French East India Company designed St-Denis' draughtboard layout in 1720. At the time, the town was divided into sections – business, residential and defence. These areas blended over time but their organisational structure didn't change. Mansions were located in an upper middle class district in which only the richest could live.

All the houses on Rue de Paris shared the same layout as Villa Carrère. The front part of the house, which includes the *baro* (gate) and garden, was spotlessly maintained, while the rear part consisted of scruffier outbuildings and a backyard. The *varangue* (veranda), at the front of the house, was open to all visitors, but not every room would have been open to guests – in fact, the further you entered a house, the more intimate the rooms became.

Importing elements of the house – such as the gate at Villa Carrère – was common practice for Reunion's upper middle class families, as it indicated their wealth. Another sign of opulence would have been a pond; some gardens would have had three!

Whether a *varangue* was closed depended on the prevailing wind. If it faced east it would have been enclosed to protect against the wind, but if it faced west it was open. In either case, families gath-ered there daily to play, knit, read and gossip.

TIP

You may be lucky enough to find a parking space in Place Sarda Garriga or by the Jardin de l'État. Otherwise there's a car park in Rue Felix Guyon (between Rue de Paris and Rue Jean Chatel), and two near the Grand Marché on Rue du Maréchal Leclerc and on Rue Lucien Gasparin.

tourist office, which is on the veranda. Built in 1820, the house had fallen into disrepair until it was renovated in the early years of the 21st century. Only a few rooms have been restored, based on pictures, sketches, historical information and original elements. They're not exact replicas, but offer an approximate idea of the furnishings and style of the past. At the tourist office you can ask for advice, plan walking itineraries, book gîtes and so on.

Poet and landscape artist Leon Dierx (1841–1912) was born in one of the houses on Rue de Paris, and the **Musée Leon Dierx** ⓕ (tel: 0262 20 24 82; Tue–Sun 9.30am–5.30pm), in a fine colonnaded mansion, displays his work alongside original sculptures and engravings of rather more famous artists such as Cézanne, Gauguin, Renoir and Picasso, as well as work by other Réunionnais artists. Unfortunately, the museum earns money by lending its best works to foreign museums, but there is normally at least one Gauguin or Picasso piece on show. Next door, in another superbly restored 19th-century villa, regular exhibitions of modern art

Enjoying a horse-drawn carriage ride.

are held in the former Maison Ma now **L'Artothèque** (Tue–Sun).

Jardin de l'État

Rue de Paris ends at Place de Me and the **Jardin de l'État** ⓖ. A golde age blossomed under botanist Nicol Bréon, who came to Réunion in 181 with a collection of European tree From his continued expeditions to fa flung places, he brought back the see with which to produce one of the mo interesting botanical collections i the Indian Ocean. Two busts of gree fingered giants attest to the garden importance: Pierre Poivre, who founde the Pamplemousses Botanical Garden in Mauritius (see page 115), and Réu ion-born botanist Joseph Hubert, wh brought back some useful spices fro his travels. Labels cater to those inte ested in plants, while shady benches, th café and space for *boules* are the ma attraction for most locals.

The centrepiece of the gardens is th **Musée d'Histoire Naturelle** (Nat ral History Museum; tel: 0262 20 0 19; Tue–Sun 9.30am–5.30pm), in th former Palais Législatif. The theme

...ctions inside show how fauna survived before the arrival of humans, how ...suffered under them and the meas...res that can be taken to protect already ...reatened species. Upstairs, a separate ...oom devoted to Madagascar includes ...isplays of stuffed lemurs. Centre stage ...s a moulded replica of a stuffed coe-...canth, a prehistoric fish known only ...n fossil form until 1938, when a living ...ecimen was caught off the Comoro ...lands. Other exhibits include stuffed ...ecimens of the island's fauna, and ...econstructed skeletons of extinct Mas-...arene birds, notably the solitaires of ...éunion and Rodrigues, and the dodo.

...long Rue du ...aréchal Leclerc

...ue du Maréchal Leclerc is the centre of ...e shopping scene in St-Denis – though ...is isn't saying much. Most popular ...mong visitors is the **Grand Marché** (...pen daily) at the street's western end, ...n the corner of Rue Lucien-Gasparin. ...his craft market caters mainly to tour-...ts and lacks the buzz of most tropical ...arkets, including the Petit Marché ...rther east. But don't let this stop you

trying to bargain with the traders, many of whose prices deserve to be reduced. You can't miss the tablecloths which are draped above many stalls, while down below you'll find *tentes* – shopping bags made from the dried leaves of the vacoas tree – T-shirts and crafts, mostly from Madagascar.

East of Rue de Paris, the Rue du Maréchal Leclerc is partially pedestrianised and lined with shops catering to the everyday needs of the local people. Nestled among the shops, near the corner of Rue Jules Auber, is the **Grande Mosquée** (daily 9am–noon, 2–4pm); the minaret is easier to locate than the entrance. For fruit and vegetables, people head east to the **Petit Marché**, at the end of Rue Ste-Anne. Just opposite the market is the **Chinese pagoda** (Pagode Bouddhiste) and on the other side of the market is the Tamil **Kalikambal Temple** (Temple Tamoul), a madly colourful confection with lovely bas-reliefs of deities. To complete the religious medley, visit the 19thcentury Gothic **Church of St Jacques**, in the street of the same name nearby, just off Rue du Maréchal Leclerc.

The Three Graces in Jardin de l'Etat.

TIP

Golfers can enjoy the mountain views and a challenging enough course at the Colorado leisure park. For information and reservations, tel: 0262 23 79 50.

Heading back to the waterfront from Rue du Maréchal Leclerc, you'll see some delightful Creole homes along **Rue Juliette Dodu** and nearby streets. There are several shops, restaurants and hotels in this area.

Cimetière de l'Est

You could take a detour to the seafront **Cimetière de l'Est** (Eastern Cemetery), about 3km (2 miles) east of the Barachois, with early tombs and the communal graves of the thousands who died during the Spanish flu epidemic of 1919. In a separate section are the unmarked graves of sentenced men, including one containing the head of Mr Zett, who was decapitated in Salazie in the early 1900s for taking part in an orgy of rape and pillage. Right-thinking citizens of the day, afraid that his soul would rise again to terrorise the population, ensured it wouldn't by sending his head to St-Denis.

Into the hills

If you have time for just one short excursion from St-Denis, take a drive along the **Route de La** Montagne, a well-signposted road southwest of th capital on the D41. With enough switc backs to make you dizzy, this scen route gives a small taster of Réunion winding roads, as well as panoram views of the city: at night you'll see th light flashes of Bel Air lighthouse i Ste-Suzanne (see page 202).

About 15 minutes along the route the **Jardin de Cendrillon** (48 Route d Palmiers, La Montagne; tel: 0692 86 3 88), a garden with over 300 varieties orchid, a profusion of variously coloure anthuriums and a collection of medic nal plants and spices. Don't worry abou the large but harmless armour-plate spiders *(nephila inorata)*, known local as the 'bib', spinning fine silky webs i the greenhouses. If they get too close fo comfort, you can always sit outside, su rounded by bird-of-paradise flowers, an admire the views over St-Denis. The ga den is in private hands and to access i it is necessary to book a tour (minimu of four people) at the tourist office in S Denis. The 1.5-hour tours are in Frenc but an English interpreter can normall be arranged.

Of more popular appeal is the eno mous outdoor leisure park at **Col rado**, just beyond La Montagne an about 30 minutes by car from St-Deni The park gets busy with local picnic ers at weekends, but also offers a rang of activities, from walking, mountai biking and horse riding to tennis an even golf (9-hole).

For a wilder experience, you shoul head south along the D42 up to th highland village of **Le Brûlé**, fro where you can explore the surroundin cryptomeria forests. A well-marked tra runs 4km (2.5 miles) – it takes abou 30 minutes – southwest to the love waterfalls of **Cascade Maniquet**.

A more challenging 18km (11-mil trek leads southwards from Le Brû to the 2,277-metre (7,468ft) peak of **L Roche Écrite** for spectacular views the Cirque de Mafate (see page 221 Allow a full day for this excursio starting from the car park at Cam Mamode.

Route de La Montagne at dawn.

St-Denis
Pointe du Gouffre
Les Brises
Ruisseau Blanc
La Montagne
Le Chaudron
La Grande Chaloupe
Colorado ★
Bellepierre
Pointe de la
Ravine à Malheur
N 1
St-Bernard
St-François
La Bretagne
Pointe des Galets
Le Camp Magloire
Le Dix-Septième
Le Brûlé
Piton
Patates
La Ravine à Malheur
Morne de
St-François
Belle Vue
Le Port
950
L'Esp
Ste-Thérèse
Cascade
Maniquet
Cascade
du Chaudron
La Possession
Pointe de la
Rivière des Galets
N 4
La Mare
Ilet Lautret
Piton
la Rivière
des Galets
St - Denis
Baie de St-Paul
N 1
La Plaine
Dos-d'Âne
Plaine des
Le Bout de l'Étang
Savannah
Mon Repos
Ilet Nourry
Chicots
St-Paul
24
Le Bois de Nèfles
Les Deux Bras
La Roche Écrite
2277
Cimetière Marin
Le Ruisseau
Aurère
Cap la Houssaye
Grande Fontaine
Ilet Fougères
CIRQU
Mare
à Martin
Cap Boucan Canot
N 1a
Bois-Rouge
Ilet à Malheur
Grand Îlot
Boucan
Canot
Grotte des
Premiers Français
Cayenne
CIRQU
Pointe des Aigrettes
22
L'Éperon
Le Guillaume
Ilet des Orangers
Le Bélier
DE
Piton d
St-Gilles-les-Bains
21
Le Bernica
Grand Place
Ilet à Bourse
DE
Cap des Chameaux
Musée
de Villèle
23
St-Gilles-
les-Hauts
Les Palmistes
Roche Plate
Ilet Cimendal
SALAZ
Villa Bourbon
Villèle
Piton Maïdo
2203
La Nouvelle
Jardin d'Eden
Tan Rouge
MAFATE
Le Gros Morne
2991
Piton de
3069
Hermitage-les-Bains
L'Ermitage
La Saline
Marla
Le Grand Bénard
La Saline les Bains
La Saline-les-Hauts
2896
Ilets de
Bois Rouge
Le Barrage
Forêt des Bénares
Ilet Fleurs Jaunes
CIRQUE
Pointe des Trois Bassins
Les Trois Bassins
St - Paul
Le Bois de Nèfles
Le Petit
Mata
N 1a
N 1
Cilaos
DE
Conservatoire Botanique
Jardin de Mascarin
Le Piton Rouge
2401
Mare Sèche
Les Colimaçons
La Chaloupe St-Leu
1130
Ilet à Cordes
CILAOS
Pointe des Châteaux
Bras Mouton
Ferme Corail
Élevage de Tortues
St-Christophe or
Etang-les-Hauts
Ilets du Bras
de St-Paul
Ilet à Cordes
Palmiste
Rouge
La Fontaine
Peter Both
St-Leu
20
Le Cap Camélias
1837
Le Cap Lelièvre
L'Étang St-Leu
La Fenêtre
Le Pavillon
Grand Fond
les Hauts
1190
Ilet A
Stella Matutina
Le Plate
1392
Le Petit Serree
Pointe au Sel ou
Pointe de Bretagne
Stella
Les Makes
18
Le Gouffre
Le Piton St-Leu
Le Tan Rouge)
Le Grand Serré
Le Portail
Souffleur
Pointe du Portail
N 1a
N 1
Les Bananes
Les Canaux
Les Avirons
Le Piton Rouge
Le Maniron
Entre-Deux
16
Bois Blanc
Les Canots
Bellevue
Le Gol les Hauts
Le Qua
Pointe des Avirons
L'Étang-Salé-
les-Hauts
La Rivière
La Mare
Les Troisiè
19
L'Étang-Salé-les-Bains
Roche Maigre
Le Ouaki
Pointe de l'Étang Salé
Croc Nature
Park
Le Camp du Gol
La Plaine
des Cabris
Cor
Le Gouffre
St-Louis
17
Les Cocos
Exotica
La Vallée
Pierrefonds
Mon Caprice
N 1
Caserne
Basse Terre
les Hauts
Aérodrome
de Pierrefonds
Les Casernes
La Ravine Blanche
St-Pierre
Pointe de la Ravine Blanche
15
Terre Sainte
Pointe du Parc

INDIAN OCEAN

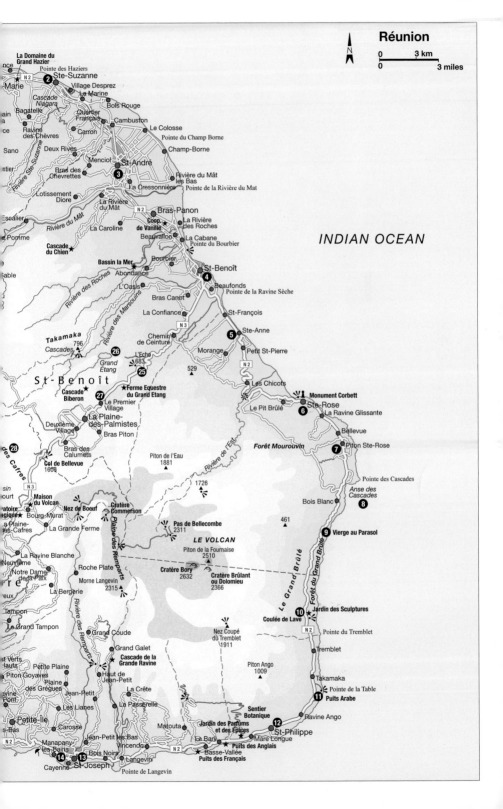

Réunion

0   3 km
0   3 miles

INDIAN OCEAN

La Domaine du
Grand Hazier
Pointe des Haziers
N 2
Ste-Suzanne
2
Marie
Village Desprez
La Marine
Cascade
Niagara
Bois Rouge
Bagatelle
Quartier
Français
Cambuston
Ravine
des Chèvres
Carron
Le Colosse
Pointe du Champ Borne
Deux Rives
Champ-Borne
Sano
Menciol
St-André
Bras des
Chevrettes
3
Rivière du Mât
les Bas
La Cressonnière
Pointe de la Rivière du Mat
Lotissement
Diore
La Rivière
du Mât
Bras-Panon
N 2
Coop.
de Vanille
La Rivière
des Roches
La Caroline
Beauvallon
La Cabane
Pointe du Bourbier
Cascade
du Chien
Bourbier
Bassin la Mer
Abondance
St-Benoît
4
L'Oasis
Beaufonds
Pointe de la Ravine Sèche
Bras Canot
La Confiance
St-François
Chemin
de Ceinture
N 3
Ste-Anne
Takamaka
796
26
L'Echo
5
Morange
Petit St-Pierre
Cascades
Grand
Etang
683
529
N 2
25
Les Chicots
St-Benoît
Ferme Equestre
du Grand Etang
Monument Corbett
Cascade
Biberon
27
Le Premier
Village
Le Pit Brûlé
Ste-Rose
6
La Ravine Glissante
Deuxième
Village
La Plaine-
des-Palmistes
Bras Piton
Bellevue
Bras des
Calumets
Piton de l'Eau
1881
Forêt Mourouvin
7
Piton Ste-Rose
28
des Cafres
Col de Bellevue
1608
Pointe des Cascades
1726
Anse des
Cascades
Maison
du Volcan
Bois Blanc
8
N 3
atoire
gique
Bourg-Murat
Nez de Boeuf
Cratère
Commerson
461
a Plaine-
es-Cafres
La Grande Ferme
Pas de Bellecombe
2311
Vierge au Parasol
9
La Ravine Blanche
Roche Plate
LE VOLCAN
Neuvième
Notre Dame
de la Paix
Morne Langevin
2315
Piton de la Fournaise
2510
Cratère Bory
2632
Cratère Brûlant
ou Dolomieu
2366
Jardin des Sculptures
10
La Bergerie
Coulée de Lave
Tampon
Le Grand Tampon
Grand Coude
Nez Coupé
du Tremblet
1911
N 2
Pointe du Tremblet
Grand Galet
Tremblet
t verts
auts
Petite Plaine
Cascade de la
Grande Ravine
Piton Ango
1009
Takamaka
Piton Goyaves
Plaine
des Grègues
Haut de
Jean-Petit
La Crête
Pointe de la Table
Puits Arabe
11
Jean-Petit
Les Lianes
La Passerelle
Sentier
Botanique
Ravine Ango
Petite-Île
s-Bas
Carosse
Matouta
Jardin des Parfums
et des Epices
12
St-Philippe
N 2
Manapany
les-Bains
Jean-Petit les-Bas
Vincendo
La Bani
Mare Longue
Puits des Anglais
14
13
Bois Noirs
Basse-Vallée
Puits des Français
Cayenne
St-Joseph
Langevin
N 2
Pointe de Langevin

An aerial view of Cap de la Houssaye.

THE COAST

Discover the extremes of Réunion's coast on the Route Nationale, from sugar fields and volcanic wastes in the east to coral-fringed beaches in the west.

There's little doubt that Réunion's main attractions lie inland: compared to the lush interior, the coastal area is dry and scrubby, particularly in the west and south. But it does have a handful of interesting towns and a few stretches of sandy beach. You can drive around Réunion's 207km (128 miles) of coast in a day thanks to one well-asphalted road, the Route Nationale (RN1), though it is worth spending at least two or three days exploring. Most of the towns have recent accommodation and tourist offices, and several are natural gateways to the cirques and other inland excursions.

The most popular coastal stretch is on the west coast between St-Paul and St-Pierre, where all the beaches are; but don't neglect the area around the eastern town of St-André and the southeast corner around the sleepy hideout of St-Philippe, whose inland forest, volcanic wastelands, rugged seascapes and walking trails deserve more than a brief stop.

Driving along the Route Nationale is reasonably straightforward, though it's perfectly possible to tour the coast on one of Réunion's comfortable public buses (see Travel Tips, Transport). There are stretches of dual carriageway, but this often reduces to single lane traffic through towns, when impatient local drivers tend to hang onto your

Boucan Canot.

tail, desperate to pass. If you are planning to drive through St-Denis, try to avoid travelling at rush hour (7–9am and 4–6pm), when the road into and out of the capital is clogged up with commuter traffic.

On the sugar and spice trail

The gently sloping plains east of St-Denis ❶ were transformed into vast sugar plantations during the colonial era, and cane still smothers the area today. The other legacy of those

Main Attractions
La Vanilleraie
Le Grand Brûlé
Saga du Rhum
Kelonia
Jardin d'Eden
St-Paul seafront market

TIP

About 2km (1 mile) south of Ste-Suzanne is the 30-metre (98ft) Cascade Niagara, a mini version of the Niagara Falls and a good place for a dip. Go midweek unless you are happy to share the pool with plenty of locals, for whom this is a popular picnic place.

early entrepreneurs are the grand houses that they built for themselves. One such abode is **Le Domaine du Grand Hazier** (tel: 0262 52 32 81; email: info@domainedugrandhazier.re; pre-booked guided tours only), just 3km (2 miles) west of **Ste-Suzanne ❷**, which opened to the public in 1998. Concealed at the end of a palm-lined road, the 18th-century mansion contains original furniture and paintings and is surrounded by lush vegetable gardens and orchards. In the grounds is **La Vanilleraie** (tel: 0262 23 07 26; www.li-sandbox.com; Mon–Sat 8.30am– noon and 1.30–5pm), where you can follow the stages of production of the precious vanilla pod; the plantation produces pods in sufficient quantities not only to stock its own shop but also to export. The tours (9am, 10am, 11am, 2pm, 3pm and 4pm) are informative, and the shop sells vanilla-flavoured everything.

Sugar production boomed in Réunion between 1815 and 1832, but when slavery was abolished in 1848 plantation owners had to source labour from India. Waves of immigrants arrived as contract workers, and today many of their descendants still live in the area between Ste-Suzanne and St-André. Some of these work at the sugar factory and distillery at **Bois Rouge** (tel: 0262 58 59 74; www.distilleriesavann com; Mon–Sat 9am–6pm, guided tour only). Several temples nearby catered to the spiritual needs of the India sugar workers, including an impressive **Tamil temple** tucked away in the fields beside the Rivière St-Jean, just west of Bois Rouge, and three other nearby at **Le Colosse** on the coast.

Quartier Français, just south of Bois Rouge, was home to some of Réunion's first settlers back in 1647 and to one of the oldest sugar factories, which once formed part of the vast Kerveguen sugar empire. The factory, in Avenue Raymond-Verge closed in 1981 but is worth visiting for the finely preserved chimney.

St-André ❸, 10km (6 miles) from Ste-Suzanne and about 30 minutes drive from St-Denis, is the gateway to the Cirque de Salazie (see page 223). It is a pleasant enough town, with a buzzing main street but few interesting

Tamil Divali in Saint-André.

BEACON OF LIGHT

Bel Air lighthouse was built at Ste-Suzanne in 1845 and was the island's first lighthouse – it is the only one still standing. Constructed to prevent shipwrecks off this dangerous stretch of coast, it has long served as a landmark for sailors. With its base 40 metres (130ft) above sea level, it stands 20.25 metres (66.5ft) tall and was staffed until 1985 with keepers who had to wind the clockwork mechanism every four hours. It was automated in 1989 and fully restored in 1996. Come nightfall, three white flashes are emitted every 15 seconds, which are visible for 23 nautical miles. Now a listed building, Bel Air can be visited on the last Tuesday and second Saturday of every month. For more information contact the Ste-Suzanne tourist office, right next to the lighthouse.

ghts. Like Ste-Suzanne's La Vanill-
raie, the **Vanilla Cooperative** (tel:
262 51 61 74; http://vanillebourbon.e-
onsite.com; Mon–Sat 8.30am–noon
nd 2–5pm, guided tours only) in
earby Bras-Panon also offers tours of
s factory and grounds.

On the ocean side of the Route
ationale, you can take Chemin Lag-
urgue to the coast. At the seafront turn
ght for **Champ-Borne**, where you
n see the remains of a 19th-century
hurch, seriously damaged by Cyclone
nny in 1962 when huge waves swept
land and partially destroyed the
emetery.

t-Benoît to Ste-Rose

he next bead in the necklace of coastal
wns, **St-Benoît ❹** is of scant interest
nless you like ghost stories. The ghost
f local mayor Louis Brunet (1847–
905), whose mausoleum is behind the
wn's 19th-century church, is said to
ander through the town. For many
eople, St-Benoît simply marks the
oute Nationale's junction with the
13, which heads up to the high plains
nd volcano (see page 213). If all you
ant is a taste of the interior, you could
ke the D53, which runs 15km (9
iles) along the course of the **Rivière
es Marsouins** to Takamaka and the
ovely **Cascade de l'Arc-en-Ciel** (and
ydroelectric complex).

Ste-Anne ❺, 5km (3 miles)
eyond St-Benoît, would seem an
nlikely place to feature in a film if
: weren't for its church, whose intri-
ate, Baroque-style stonework must
ave appealed to François Truffaut:
e used it in *La Sirène du Mississippi*
1969), starring Catherine Deneuve
nd Jean-Paul Belmondo. The church
ates from the 19th century, but the
xtraordinary carving was done in
ne first half of the 20th century by a
roup of Tamil craftsmen.

From Ste-Anne the road winds
nland to the foothills of the volcano,
rosses a suspension bridge over the
ivière de l'Est, and then descends to
ne small fishing town of **Ste-Rose ❻**.

In 1809, British men o'war tested the
town's defences just before they took
the island from the French; on the
waterfront there is a monument to
Commodore Corbett, second-in-com-
mand of the British fleet, who died in
one of the skirmishes. Ste-Rose is constantly under threat from the volcano
which, in April 1977, twice disgorged
its molten lava into the next village of
Piton Ste-Rose ❼, destroying some
20 houses. People watched entranced
as the lava flowed around the church,
now known as **Notre Dame des Laves**,
without destroying it, and instead hardened to form a thick black girdle – still
visible today – around the building.
Newspaper cuttings inside the church
reveal that some villagers saw their
lucky escape as 'God's miracle'. Local
artist Guy Lefèvre made the stained-
glass windows.

For the calm and quiet of a spectacular seascape, follow the signs south
from Piton Ste-Rose for 3km (2 miles)
to the turn-off for **Anse des Cascades
❽**. Here, waterfalls tumble from towering cliffs into a shaded bay where
fishermen sell their catch on the jetty.

Notre Dame des Laves.

The secluded restaurant makes a perfect lunch stop and at weekends the cool forests of coconut trees are popular with picnickers.

Volcanic wasteland towards Puits Arabe

Some of the most dramatic coastal scenery of Réunion can be seen along the next stretch of road to St-Philippe as the RN2 negotiates the southeast corner of the island, skirting an immense volcanic caldera known as **Le Grand Brûlé**, formed by the lava flow from Piton de la Fournaise and *Les Grandes Pentes* (The Steep Slopes). Every now and then, barren wastes of solidified lava indicate the progress of previous eruptions. Just inside the ravine, soon after **Bois Blanc**, pilgrims often lay flowers at the **Vierge au Parasol ❾**. The shrine was erected by a 19th-century landowner who believed it would protect his vanilla plantation from the fury of the volcano.

There are several red shrines to St-Expédit in the area, one of which lies right beside a **lava flow ❿** (*coulée de lave*) which cut off the RN2 in 1998.

Vierge au Parasol.

If you stay on the coast road you'll be treated to more moonscapes of hardened black lava at **Puits Arabe ⓫**, where information boards describe the sequence of events which resulted in the evacuation of 500 people as lava flowed in four stages between 19 and 30 March 1986, coating the slopes of **Takamaka** above the village before stabilising itself just 300 metres (980ft) from the road. You can scramble for 200 metres (650ft) over the solidified lava to **Pointe de la Table** where another lava flow from the same eruption extended the island by 25 hectares (62 acres) into the sea; or opt for a lengthier 5km (3-mile) trek northwards towards **Tremblet**, crossing cliffs where an 18th-century lava flow is a good example of the structures of cooling.

St-Philippe to St-Joseph

Rugged, ragged and fierce best describes the south coast, where screw pines torn by warm winds watch over wild seas beating against black basalt cliffs. The sleepy little town of **St-Philippe ⓬** is a good place to

eak your journey through the volcanic wastelands of the east coast and ock up on supplies if you need to. has some interesting examples of reole architecture and, in addition o a helpful tourist office, there are oadside eateries that provide ready-acked baguettes and other snacks – erfect fodder to take on a walk up ito the hills.

West of town, tracks head inland om Mare Longue, Le Baril, Basse-allée and Langevin, some of them inning all the way up the flanks of ie volcano. If you aren't keen on the lea of a major hike, the forest inland om **Mare Longue**, just west of St-hilippe, is easy to explore. Here, the orest spreads over 70 hectares (173 cres) and includes pandanus and asuarina trees entwined with vanilla reepers, mixed evergreens (*bois de puleurs*) and tall edible palms. Rare lants can be seen along the Sentier otanique, but if you have more time, sk the St-Philippe tourist office (Rue econte-Delisle; tel: 0262 97 75 84; mail: officedutourismesaintphilippe@ ahoo.fr; Mon–Fri 9am–noon, 1–5pm,

Sat 10am–noon, 1–5pm) to organise a visit to the **Jardin des Parfums et des Epices**, where orchids, moss and ferns grow wild among aromatic plants.

At **Basse-Vallée** tiny Creole houses in flower-filled gardens cram the roadside like cardboard cut-outs from a children's story book. A couple of kilometres east along the Route Nationale is **Hôtel Le Baril**, one of the few places to stay along this remote coast. It is flanked by two lava wells, Puits des Anglais and Puits des Français. The story goes that one of them contains a treasure chest watched over by the spirit of a dead slave, but which one may be a matter for Anglo–French debate. Try asking the boss at the hotel, who claims to know the answer.

There's not much to see at the next town of **St-Joseph** ⑬, but it is the starting point for a challenging trek up the gorgeous valley of the **Rivière des Remparts** – the river that flows through the town and whose source is 30km (19 miles) north at **Nez de Boeuf** (see page 215). Experienced hikers only should try this two-day

In the Jardin des Parfums et des Epices.

TIP

Between May and December you can see (and smell) the vetiver plant, which grows around St-Joseph. The essential oil of the vetiver is used in the perfumery industry, and the leaves can also be dried to make thatched roofs. You can buy bundles of vetiver in some markets. Place among your clothes for a pleasant aroma.

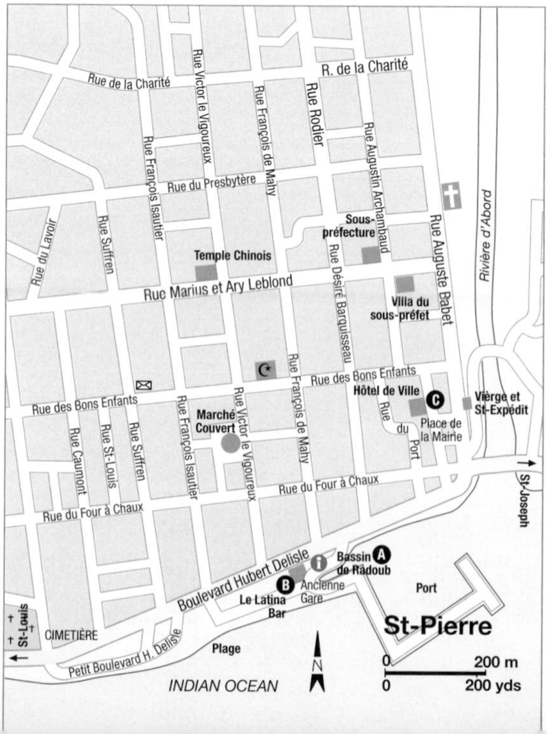

Hôtel de Ville, St Pierre.

uphill trek along the Rivière des Remparts. The path from St-Joseph traverses some of Réunion's original lowland forest before the final, tough climb up to the Nez de Boeuf. A *table d'hôte* option in the isolated hamlet of **Roche Plate**, 19km (12 miles) along the way, provides meals and overnight accommodation (book ahead: tel: 0262 59 13 94).

If you want views without the effort, a road runs halfway up the valley, on the eastern side, to **Grand Coude**.

The pebble beach at **Manapany-les-Bains** ⓮, 3km (2 miles) west of St-Joseph, and the sandy beach at Grande Anse, beyond, are often dangerous due to the fierce currents, but there are natural pools among the rocks where it is safe to swim. If you want to treat yourself to some fine Creole and seafood dishes, try **L'Etoile de Mer** at Basse-Vallée. Although pricey, this is one of the best restaurants on the island, and also offers spectacular sea views. You'll get more great views as you head west over the impressive Manapany ravine en route to St-Pierre.

Forgotten St-Pierre

St-Pierre ⓯, which lies on a wid coastal plain at the mouth of the Ri ière d'Abord, is the largest settlemen in the south, with 80,000 inhabitant It is one of Réunion's most pleasan towns and makes a good base, bein well placed for reaching the southea coast – as well as being just 45 min utes' drive from St-Gilles-les-Bair on the west coast, and about an hou from Piton de la Fournaise.

The town sometimes receives th full fury of cyclones raging in from th Indian Ocean. In 1990, Cyclone Fi inga left it nearly in ruins, but a fac lift ensued: a new marina was bui and an airport at Pierrefonds opene nearby, bringing in a fresh wave of tou ists, mainly from Mauritius. St-Pierre waterfront restaurants, late-night ba and clubs, choice of hotels and adequat (but windy) beach attract islander from as far away as St-Denis. The port packed with fishing boats and pleasur craft and is fun to stroll around; on on side is the pretty **Bassin de Radoub** Ⓐ a small creek where boats were careene in the 19th century, now a histori onument. Just behind it is the **Anci-nne Gare** (old railway station) **B**, hich houses a number of cafés spilling ut onto a sea-facing terrace. There are everal restaurants on the other side of he seafront Boulevard Hubert Delisle, where you'll also find the tourist office email: saintpierre.tourisme@gmail.com; Mon–Sat 8am–6pm, Sun 8am–noon), irectly opposite the port.

It is worth having a quick stroll round the town. The restored **Hôtel e Ville C**, a former East India Com-any building, is a fine example of olonial architecture, and further west n Rue Victor le Vigoureux you'll find very attractive market – an unusual ircular structure. The Marine Cem-tery, at the western end of Boulevard lubert Delisle, is a lovely flower-filled emetery that contains the grave of itarane, one of Réunion's most noto-ous bandits, said to have drunk the lood of his murdered victims. Each ight, offerings of cigarettes and head-ess black cocks or fruits and flowers re left as an inducement to Sitarane o bring mishap, misfortune or even worse to enemies. Nocturnal visits are nly for the courageous.

A few kilometres from the town entre is **La Saga du Rhum** (tel: 0262 5 81 90; www.sagadurhum.fr; daily 0am–6pm), in one of the island's ldest rum distilleries. This interest-ng and informative museum tells he story of Réunion's sugar and rum ndustry (in English and French).

Around 11km (7 miles) west of St-ierre, inland along the D26 towards ntre-Deux, are the quirky gardens of xotica (tel: 0262 35 65 45; Tue–Sun am–5pm), which children at least hould enjoy.

Nestled between two rivers, the ptly named village of **Entre-Deux** ❾ makes a pleasant side trip from the oast. Many of its picturesque Creole ouses are decorated with *lambrequins* filigree woodwork) – see how many ifferent patterns you can spot.

St-Louis ⓱, the next town along he coast from St-Pierre, is home to the

MADOI (Indian Ocean Decorative Arts Museum; 17A Chemin Maison Rouge; tel: 0262 91 24 30; http://madoi. re; Mon 10.30am–6pm, Tue–Sun 9am–6pm). The museum is in the renovated stables of the Domaine de Maison Rouge, a former coffee estate. You can wander around the grounds for free, and interesting bilingual information panels tell you about the history of the house and Réunion's ill-fated cof-fee industry.

At St-Louis you'll drive past one of the island's two sugar factories, Le Gol, and the town is also the starting point of the winding RN5 to the Cirque de Cilaos (see page 226). However, for a glimpse of the cirque without the long drive, you could take the D20, which runs 12km (7.5 miles) inland from St-Louis to **Les Makes** ⓲. This tiny vil-lage, situated at 1,000 metres (3,280ft), is home to **L'Observatoire** (18 Rue Georges Bizet; tel: 0262 37 86 83; www.ilereunion.com/observatoire-makes; Mon–Fri 9am–noon and 2–4.30pm, Sat 9–11am), where you can study the stars on a guided tour or attend a special night show. Ten kilometres (6

TIP

In St-Pierre there is plenty of room to park under the trees right next to the old railway station.

St-Pierre's coastline.

miles) beyond Les Makes, along the wildly twisting RF14, you'll come to **La Fenêtre**, a natural window on to Cilaos cirque. If you arrive before the mid-morning mists you should get glorious views.

L'Etang-Salé-les-Bains to St-Leu

If you've experienced the white beaches and lagoons of Mauritius you may find Réunion's coast disappointing. The beaches are clean but small and get crowded at weekends. Midweek, however, they are a delight, and at any time of the week there are several tourist attractions inland that are well worth a visit.

L'Etang-Salé-les-Bains ⑲ marks the beginning of the west coast beach stretch, but it is very quiet, with just a couple of hotels and restaurants, and the 5km (3-mile) black sand beach is not particularly picturesque. If you have children, you could take them 2km (1 mile) up the hill to the **Croc Nature Park** (tel: 0262 91 40 41; www.crocparc.re; daily 10am–5.30pm) in L'Etang-Salé-les-Hauts. In addition

to the 150 Nile crocodiles (brough from Madagascar and fed on Wedne days and Sundays at 4pm), there a farm animals and peacocks, as we as a model Réunion village. A tour the park takes about an hour; there a snack bar and a shop.

The 2km (1-mile) trip south alon the coast road from L'Etang-Salé-le Bains to **Le Gouffre** is likely to b of more universal appeal. Here, yo can witness the ferocity of the India Ocean as the waves crash against th basalt cliffs.

The RN1 slices through jagge black lava rock close to the shore f the next 22km (13.5 miles) to St-Le You'll pass a couple of laybys on th way where you can stop for spectacu lar views of *souffleurs* (blowholes): the sea is rough enough, tall jets water spurt through these rocky cre ices. For a different perspective, co sider taking the high road (the D1 between L'Etang-Salé and St-Leu vi **Les Avirons**. Known as the Allée d Flamboyants, this is a delightful rout and also offers lovely views of the coas Keep your eyes on the road, howeve as it twists and turns and local drive like to move at speed. Just before yo rejoin the RN1, you'll pass the Stel Matutina museum (see page 209).

Around St-Leu

The town of **St-Leu** ⑳ witnessed slave revolt in 1811, survived a choler epidemic in 1859, and has been hit b several devastating cyclones, but othe wise life here is reasonably uneventf and easy-going. The large, black-san beach accommodates the weeken crowds reasonably well. When th conditions are right, experienced sur ers flock here to ride what are repute to be some of the best waves in th Indian Ocean (although at the time writing, surfing has been temporari banned due to a rise in shark attack see Travel Tips, Activities, page 380 The best spot is near the mouth of th **Ravine des Colimaçons**, north of th town centre. In addition to the beac

On the "Sud Sauvage".

ere are several attractions in the cinity of St-Leu, so it's worth devoting at least half a day to the town.

The church of **Notre Dame de la alette** was built in the town in honour of the Madonna who the Réunnais believe saved the lives of the eople of St-Leu when the 1859 cholera epidemic swept the island. Every eptember there is a festival in her onour, which culminates in a pilimage to the church.

About 4km (2.5 miles) south of St-u along the Avirons road is the **Stella atutina** (tel: 0262 34 16 24; Tue–Sun 30am–5.30pm), a former sugar facry and now a fascinating museum evoted to the history of sugar producon and agriculture on the island.

Kelonia (tel: 0262 34 81 10; www. lonia.org; daily 9am–6pm), 2km (1 ile) north of St-Leu on the RN1, is research and educational centre for e study of hawksbill and green turs. Visits include turtle spotting in rge tanks, but the centre itself is of storic significance since it is home to vo of the oldest lime kilns in Réun-n. Be aware that although commer-al breeding of turtles was banned in 998, you may still find turtle products n sale, which manufacturers claim ere produced before the ban.

Virtually opposite Kelonia, the D12 ns uphill to Les Colimaçons and the **onservatoire Botanique de Masca-n** (tel: 0262 24 92 27; www.cbnm.org; e–Sun 9am–5pm). This magnificent otanic garden, which contains 4,000 otanical species, offers an insight to Réunion's remarkable flora and landscaped into themed gardens of re indigenous and endemic plants, ants introduced by early settlers, a ollection of palm trees, an orchard local fruits and an eye-popping closure of cacti. But the pièce de sistance is the 19th-century villa, lly restored and filled with colo-al furniture. You can also visit the ables, hunting lodge and the old mily kitchen, which now serves as a feteria. Next door to the gardens is

the church of Les Colimaçons, which offers splendid views over the reef-fringed coastline.

To reach St-Gilles-les-Bains, you can choose between the winding inland route via St-Gilles-les-Hauts (and the fascinating Musée de Villèle: see page 210), the coastal route or the faster Route des Tamarins.

St-Gilles-les-Bains

Dubbed the 'St-Tropez of the Indian Ocean', **St-Gilles-les-Bains** ㉑ is the hub of Réunion's holiday scene, attracting local and French holiday-makers. This is the best place on the island in which to soak up the sun, enjoy all the pleasure of the sea, or just lie back and recover from a hard mountain trek. If that's all too sedate, then plenty of canyoning and para-gliding operators are on hand to book the jump of a lifetime down Réun-ion's ravines and gorges. At night, the restaurants, bars and clubs that line – and spill on to – Rue Général de Gaulle come alive. The cast of char-acters, from old-fashioned hippies to trendy young locals, is attracted by the

Zattes – a type of custard apple – for sale at Saint-Leu.

blend of Gallic chic and Creole insouciance that oozes from the restaurants and bars.

One reason St-Gilles' broad, sloping beach is so popular is that it has white, albeit rather coarse, sand. The focus of activity is north of the Ravine St-Gilles: it is here that most people gather to watch the sunset, something of a local tradition. South of the ravine, the more peaceful beach known as **L'Hermitage** is backed by holiday homes and *pensions* rather than loud bars and restaurants. The port in the mouth of the ravine is packed with boats belonging to game fishing and scubadiving operators. Half a dozen game fishing boats depart on day trips to hook blue marlin, sailfish, tuna and sea bream; October to April is the best time. If you're a first-time diver, enquire at Bleu Marine Réunion (tel: 0262 24 22 00), which also offers special packages for children.

If you have a car, park first and then walk to the beach, which is hidden from view by the shops and restaurants along Rue Général de Gaulle. Parking is not always easy, though;

On the beach at Boucan Canot.

there are a couple of small car par on Rue Général de Gaulle, but th are often full. A good place is t patch of ground just before the brid that crosses the ravine.

Just five minutes' drive north of Gilles-les-Bains, **Boucan Canot** 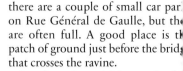 a smarter, smaller and more laid-ba resort than its neighbour. Unlike Gilles, most of Boucan Canot's caf and restaurants are by the beach, so i easier to potter off for a drink or sna in between stints on the sand. T sandy beach is clean but small, ar can get crowded at weekends. Dri ers should note that the main drag pedestrianised, and that the only pla to park is either at the north or sou end of the seafront.

On the RN1 at Hermitage-les-Bair just south of St-Gilles-les-Bains, t **Jardin d'Eden** (tel: 0262 33 83 1 www.jardindeden.re; daily 10am–6pr is a beautiful oasis of calm away fro the beach. Here, you can wand through lovely orchards of fruit tre and spices, learn how to cure a hang ver with medicinal plants, or settle f some mysticism in the mini rice fie surrounding the Zen garden.

St-Gilles-les-Hauts

The **Musée de Villèle**  (tel: 026 55 64 10; email: musee.villele@cg97 fr; Tue–Sun 9.30am–12.30pm, 1.3(5.30pm, guided tours only), in S Gilles-les-Hauts, is the former fami seat of the Desbassyns dynasty. Bui in 1787, the house's most famous res dent was Madame Desbassyns, a cc fee and sugar producer and notorio matriarch, who is said to have inflicte horrific punishments on her slave The local legendary figure Gran mère Kal – a fiendish old woma who scares children – is said to b based on her. The colonial mansio now houses memorabilia and fami portraits, maps of slave ship rout and fine French East India furnitu The slave hospital in the ground was established not out of altruis but to conform to the law. Madan

Desbassyns, who died in 1846, is buried in Chapelle Pointue, next to the ruins of the estate's sugar mill.

St-Paul: the old capital

St-Paul ㉔ is a pleasant town less than 30 minutes' drive from St-Denis and well worth visiting. It is the island's original capital, and many historical buildings survive, such as the Hôtel de Lassays, now a fire station, and Grand Cour, the abandoned home of the Desbassyns dynasty on the Route Royale. There are vestiges of the old French East India Company, too, including the town hall, built in 1767. But most holiday-makers come to St-Paul not for a historical tour, nor to lie on its long, black-sand beach, but to visit the **seafront market** held on Friday afternoon and Saturday morning. The crowd that flocks here is a lively mix of tourists searching for crafts, spices, baskets and other souvenirs and locals buying fruit and veg, fish and other fresh produce. Numerous stalls and vans sell tasty snacks. Towards the end of the day, bands start playing, and people gather in the beach-side bars to watch the sun disappear into the sea.

Don't miss the **Cimetière Marin**, in a stunning position right by the beach just south of the centre. Here is said to be the body of one of the Mascarenes' most notorious pirates, Olivier Le Vasseur, alias La Buse (The Buzzard), who was hung in St-Paul in 1730 (see page 240). His grave, right opposite the entrance, is marked by a simple skull and crossbones crudely etched on a basalt cross, and is still visited by followers. Presumably, they would not like the theory that La Buse's body isn't actually buried here – based on the fact that the cemetery did not exist in 1730.

La Corniche

Driving north from St-Paul the RN1 crosses the enormous estuary of the Rivière des Galets, bypasses **Le Port** and emerges at **La Possession**, where Governor Pronis took possession of Réunion in 1642, before continuing to St-Denis. The 14km (9-mile) stretch of the Route Nationale from La Possession to St-Denis is, along with the Route des Tamarins, one of the busiest stretches of road in the Mascarenes. Known as **La Corniche,** or the Route du Littoral, it's a dramatic ride as you whizz beneath cliffs and through a tunnel only metres from the sea. However it can be subject to rock falls, and a major new highway is being built just offshore (partly on stilts and partly on an embankment). The current road runs alongside the old railway line and the one place you can stop is at **La Grande Chaloupe**, site of one of Réunion's original railway stations. The rail service stopped in 1963, but a Scafader 030T is preserved in the small **museum** (daily 9am–5pm) to remind you of the heavy locomotives that plied the route from St-Denis to St-Pierre. You can also visit the nearby **Lazaret** (tel: 0692 97 40 40; www.cg974.fr/culture/lazaret; see website for opening hours), a restored 19th-century quarantine building for indentured workers arriving from India.

TIP

The Corniche, while generally well maintained, is susceptible to damage by rock fall and flooding. An alternative route back to St-Denis is the D41, La Montagne road from La Possession.

Chopped coconut at St-Paul's market.

A scientist examining lava at Piton de la Fournaise.

VOLCANO AND HIGH PLAINS

When Piton de la Fournaise trembles, fear and
excitement lure many to witness the great
natural phenomenon. Most of the time, however,
the volcano is an awesome but peaceful sight.

Main Attractions
Piton de la Fournaise
Cité du Volcan
Forêt de Bébour

The **Piton de la Fournaise** is one
of the most active volcanoes on
the planet; it has erupted at least
53 times since 1690 (the last eruption
was in 2015), and the lava flows have
left trails of destruction. For modern
visitors, however, getting a close-up
view of the smouldering volcano is
reasonably safe and easy to do, provided, of course, that you stick to the
marked route.

Born on the flanks of the extinct volcano called Piton des Neiges, between
500,000 and 600,000 years ago, Piton
de la Fournaise, a twin shield volcano
known to volcanologists as a Hawaiian
type, rises to 2,632 metres (8,635ft). It
is surrounded by a horseshoe-shaped
lava cliff enclosure, called Enclos Fouqué, which is 10km (6 miles) in diameter and has two craters; the higher
one, Bory, has been inactive since 1791,
while the active Dolomieu manages,
for most of the time, to confine its
eruption within the enclosure.

Reaching for the top

Each year some 200,000 visitors make
the journey up above the clouds to the
top of the volcano. Most people drive
to **Pas de Bellecombe** . Perched on
the edge of the canyon-like Enclos
Fouqué, it is a natural platform for
spectacular views of Piton de la Fournaise across a wild and barren moon-
scape. Irrespective of whether you join

an organised tour or make your own
way, you should aim to reach the caldera before 10am, when cloud often
descends to mask the volcano's wild
beauty. But don't despair if you can't
see a thing on the way up – or even
when you reach the top. The area is
subject to sudden climate changes,
which can go from swirling cloud and
mist and sharp drops in temperature,
to clear vistas across crisp blue skies.
For this reason, you should also go
equipped for all weathers. Good walking shoes are essential, and it can be

Taking a helicopter to the volcano's crater.

chilly, so wear long trousers, take a jumper and don't leave your hotel without a waterproof.

Bourg-Murat

The gateway to Piton de la Fournaise is **Bourg-Murat B**, on the RN3, the only cross-island route, which links St-Pierre in the south and St-Benoît in the north. The journey there from the two coasts takes about 40 minutes and an hour respectively. More a large village than a town, Bourg-Murat is home to the **Observatoire Volcanologique**, set up in 1979 after the 1977 eruption (see page 184), from where eruptions can be monitored in complete safety. High-tech equipment records seismic activity so that these days the islanders have plenty of notice of an eruption. Bear in mind, however, that there was only a 45-minute warning of an eruption – albeit small – inside the Enclos Fouqué on 19 July 1999. If you're in Réunion to witness such a spectacle, expect to find the Enclos Fouqué closed and droves of enthusiasts and experts jostling with cameramen and reporters for the best positions.

Bourg-Murat's other main attraction is the futuristic building of the **Cité du Volcan** (tel: 0262 59 00 26; www.maisonduvolcan.fr; daily 9.30am–5.30pm). Originally opened in 199 and refurbished in 2014 with state of-the-art technology, this fascinating museum owes much of its collection to French husband and wife volcanologists Maurice and Katia Krafft. Bilingual information panels, 'augmented reality' and interactive quizzes will teach you everything you ever wanted to know about volcanoes. There are also holographic projections, an art gallery and even a 4D cinema (French only). The shop sells all sorts of volcanic knick-knacks, from lumps of lava to posters, books and T-shirts commemorating particular eruptions. For a bite to eat try the nearby **Ti'Resto Lontan**, which serves tasty Creole curries.

Volcanic views on the Route du Volcan

Most people are too eager to get to the top to even pause in Bourg-Murat on the way up. From here, it's 23km

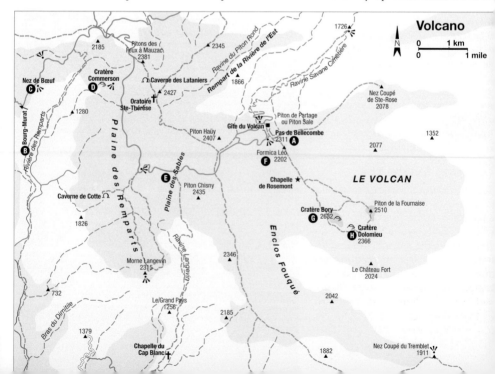

4 miles) and about 40 minutes' rive up to Pas de Bellecombe, but hat an interesting route. The RF5 – r 'Route du Volcan' – which heads ast from Bourg-Murat, becomes radually more winding as you leave he town behind and head ever pwards, sweeping through pine oods, dairy farms, small villages and pine meadows. The road is not in int condition but is paved as far as laine des Sables.

As you get higher, you will enjoy ew, and often astonishing, views at very turn. Some of the best of these re at established viewpoints. (However keen you are to reach the top, if he sky is clear on the way up, don't esist the temptation to stop, as you ever know when the clouds are going o roll in.) The first of these viewoints, 7km (4 miles) from Pas de Belecombe, is at **Nez de Boeuf C** (2,070 etres/6,973ft), from where there are bsolutely staggering views of the uge ravine of **Rivière des Remparts**. rom these heights, the river appears s a thin pencil line flowing southards to St-Joseph. A challenging rande Randonnée (GR) trail runs long the banks of the river from the oast and links up with the RF5 just eyond the Nez de Boeuf viewpoint; he 30km (18-mile) trek is rather easier orth to south than vice versa.

Next stop is **Cratère Commerson D**, here an observation platform perches ver a 120-metre (380ft) deep crater, a ew paces from the road. The extinct rater, named after French botanist Phibert Commerson, who discovered it y accident in 1771, is a dramatic sight. ost breathtaking of all, however, are he views across the crater's 200-metre 650ft) diameter towards the jagged idge of Cilaos cirque.

However, the view that is likely to emain etched on your memory for ongest is the one from the top of the empart des Sables ridge where the oad begins its dramatic descent into he **Plaine des Sables E**. An information board describes the landscape

that spreads below you – an utter wilderness of raw beauty and incredible wide-angle views of corroded lava, ground by the elements into fine black gravel and restrained by massive mountain ramparts and distant peaks. As the road descends across the eerie reddish-brown landscape, pockmarked with bizarre rock formations, the only signs of life are sparse bushes of gorse, heather and lichen and a trail of moving cars, before it climbs briefly to end at the parking area at Pas de Bellecombe. The track across the Plaine des Sables is unpaved and may be full of potholes if there's been recent heavy rain: drive slowly to avoid skidding, and be particularly careful in wet conditions.

A walk around earth's fire

Pas de Bellecombe is also the starting point of several walking routes to and around Piton de la Fournaise. In a shelter by the car park some displays provide information on the geology and fauna and flora of the area. Most useful, however, is the relief model of the volcano, which

On the way to Piton de la Fournaise.

shows the routes (and distances) of the various walking trails. You don't really need a map for the more well-trodden circuits, such as Pas de Belle-combe to Cratère Dolomieu, but for more involved trekking you should invest in the IGN 1:25,000 series map 4406RT Piton de la Fournaise. You can buy this in most bookshops or tourist shops, or pick it up at the Cité du Volcan in Bourg-Murat.

There is also a list of rules for walkers. The most important ones to heed are a) don't go alone, b) tell someone where you have gone, and c) take water and food. Light refreshments and toilets are available in the shelter. You can also walk to **Gîte du Volcan**, about 10 minutes away along a path from the car park. If you're driving, the track to the *gîte* branches left off the main track just before you reach the car park.

For the full experience you should consider doing the 13km (8-mile) circuit, a 'medium' classified trek, which takes about five hours. (Alternatively, you could choose to do just part of the route; for example, the return

A view of the volcano's dolomieu crater.

walk to Formica Léo takes about 4[?] minutes.) Make sure you pack som[e] energy-giving snacks and plenty [of] water. Provided you don't wander o[ff] the marked paths, and you heed th[e] danger warning signs and wear th[e] right clothes, you can't go wrong.

A stepped pathway winds its wa[y] down the 200-metre (650ft) cliff t[o] the bottom. On the way down take [a] good look at the plants that grow o[n] the cliff face – beyond there is noth[-] ing but layers of lava from across th[e] ages decorated with splodges of whi[te] paint that mark the entire route. Th[e] first landmark on the volcanic floo[r] is the rather undramatic scoria con[e] of **Formica Léo** . From here th[e] path continues about 2km (1 mile[)] to **Chapelle de Rosemont**, a hollo[w] volcanic mound which looks like [a] small cathedral complete with a doo[r] and window – hence the name. This i[s] a good place to rest and decide whic[h] of the two available paths you wan[t] to take. For the more strenuous rout[e] take the right-hand fork, which wi[ll] lead you directly up a steep slope t[o] the extinct 2,621-metre (8,599ft) hig[h]

A BIRD'S-EYE VIEW

Réunion's scenery is awe-inspiring whatever angle you look at it from, but the aerial views you get from a helicopter of Piton de la Fournaise, and the Cirque de Salazie and Cirque de Mafate (see the following chapter), are hard to beat. These tours may be expensive, but they are worth every euro. Pilots fly in and out of deep ravines and hover precariously over isolated hamlets and the cirques, allowing plenty of time for photographs, before heading east to the volcano.

Depending on weather conditions, helicopters, seating up to six or eight passengers, take off between 7 and 11am for flights lasting between 15 and 55 minutes. The price includes transfer from your hotel, individual headphones and commentary (in French unless all passengers are English speakers). Prices range from €95 to €320 per person, and you should try to book at least 72 hours in advance since these flights are extremely popular. Hélilagon (tel: 0262 55 55 55; www. helilagon.com) flies from Roland Garros Airport or from l'Eperon heliport near St-Paul. Corail Helicopters (tel: 0262 22 22 66; www.corail-helicopteres.com) operates from St-Gilles or Pierrefonds Airport. Starting at only €40, microlight flights organised through Felix ULM (Base ULM de Cambaie, St-Paul; tel: 0262 43 02 59; www.felixulm.com) are a somewhat cheaper option. Tours, in specially equipped two-seater microlights, cover the cirques, volcano massif, and/or the lagoon.

Cratère Bory ⑥. Caution should be taken on the potentially unstable paths. The left-hand fork leads you to an easier route that snakes gently northwards along the contours of the volcano to **La Soufrière** (2,530 metres/8,300ft), the northern wall of the active **Cratère Dolomieu** ⑪; you can sometimes smell sulphur emissions here. There is another choice of routes here: one carries on along the rim of both Dolomieu and Bory before heading back to Pas de Bellecombe; the other, shorter route cuts straight across to Cratère Bory.

There is a whole series of other walks to do. One of the easiest is the 9km (5.5-mile) walk north along the rim from Pas de Bellecombe to **Nez Coupé de Ste-Rose** and back. Another is the 8km (5-mile) circular route from the Rempart des Sables to **Morne Langevin** – you should allow about three hours for this relatively easy but scenic route.

Among the other much longer routes you could opt for are treks along sections of the Grande Randonnée R2, which crosses the island (IGN 1:25,000 series map 4406RT Piton de la Fournaise). One of these follows the southern edge of the volcano to **Nez Coupé du Tremblet** before descending to Pointe du Tremblet on the east coast. Another heads south from Pas de Bellecombe on the GR2, across the so-called Plateau de Foc Foc to link up with the **Vallée Heureuse** and the Gîte de Basse Vallée, before continuing all the way to the town of Basse Vallée on the coast.

The High Plains

The High Plains (*Hautes Plaines*) that separate Piton de la Fournaise and the three cirques may lack volcano-style drama but are still well worth exploring. Centred around La Plaine-des-Palmistes (named after the variety of palm trees that no longer grow there) and La Plaine-des-Cafres in the west, these upland areas reveal magnificent mist-enshrouded forests, waterfalls, lakes and mountains: in short, perfect terrain for tranquil walks, scenic drives and more active pursuits such as horse riding and mountain biking. The route described below runs in a north–south direction from the coast. A number of villages on the way, such as Le Vingt-Troisième (23rd) and Le Dix-Neuvième (19th), have been named unimaginatively after their distance in kilometres by road from the sea, but at least they're handy landmarks.

From St-Benoît, the RN3 meanders through sugar cane fields before hitting a series of switchbacks that lead to a viewpoint at **L'Echo** ㉕, which offers fine views north towards the coast and the ocean. Before the road winds up to L'Echo, about 12km (8 miles) from St-Benoît a track runs 6km (4 miles) west to **Grand-Etang** ㉖, a lake in a most stunning spot at the foot of an awesome ridge. To prolong the pleasure, you can follow the path right around the shores of the lake; there's a waterfall just off the path near the southern shore.

The road around Piton de la Fournaise.

TIP

Tourist offices in the Hautes Plaines area are located at: Maison du Parc National, (258 Rue de la République, Plaine-des-Palmistes; tel: 0262 41 17 70; Mon–Sat 8.30am–12.30pm, 1–5pm) or Bourg Murat. (160 rue Maurice et Katia Krafft, Plaines-des-Cafres; tel: 0262 27 40 00; www.tampontourisme.re; daily 9am–5pm).

Beyond L'Echo, 20km (12 miles) from St-Benoît, you hit **Le Premier Village** ㉗, the first part of **La Plaine-des-Palmistes**, a popular holiday retreat, particularly in January and February. Even so, the area remains a comparatively untouched agricultural heartland where the red-berried goyavier fruit has become so important that every June there is a festival in its honour. Attractive wooden houses are very characteristic of this area; you'll see them featured on postcards and posters. La Plaine-des-Palmistes is a centre of operations and you may want to stop here to make use of the tourist office, which can supply details of accommodation and walks, ranging from gentle to strenuous, in and around the Forêt de Bébour, or for some souvenir shopping at the adjacent Domaine des Tourelles (tel: 0262 51 47 59; www.tourelles.com).

Horse riding and forest walking

To the northeast of Le Premier Village, a dozen gentle Merens horses wait at the **Ferme Equestre du Grand Etang**

Grang Etang riders.

(RN3 Pont-Payet; tel: 0262 50 90 03 to take even the most inexperience rider for a pleasant half-day's trek. A morning with Rico Nourro, a forme farmer who turned his love of the ou doors into a going concern, shoul not be missed. His enthusiasm is infe tious as he leads groups of riders alon rocky narrow pathways to the stur ning lake of Grand-Etang where th horses take a break and splash abou in the cool water. The trek takes yo along a nature trail, passing through garden of traditional medicinal herb and citrus orchards where you ca help yourself to fruit without gettin out of the saddle. Rico believes in giv ing all his clients a hands-on exper ence, so you'll be expected to prepar the horses before the ride and hos them down afterwards. Four-day ride to the volcano can also be arranged.

For a gentle 2km (1-mile) walk, tak the marked path from Le Premie Village, which passes through boul der-filled streams, leading to the 240 metre (787ft) high **Biberon** waterfal There are a number of longer hike through the **Forêt de Bébour**, note

r the endemic tree, *tamarin des hauts* *cacia heterophylla)*, which contrasts height and huge girth with the digenous *bois de couleurs*, or mixed ergreens, and imported crypto- erias. For an in-depth look at this rest, which merges with the silvery marind forests of **Bélouve** and the in-soaked gorge of Takamaka to e north, you'll need to spend a full ay exploring the numerous trails d spend the night at the Gîte de élouve, about a two-hour trek uphill om Hell-Bourg in Salazie cirque (be re to book well in advance at www. union.fr). Serious trekkers should quip themselves with the IGN 25000, 4405RT map.

aine-des-Cafres

see La-Plaine-des-Palmiste's luxu- ant vegetation head southwards ong the RN3, stopping after a km (4-mile) upward sinuous drive a parking-cum-picnic viewpoint lled **Col de Bellevue**. Continuing uthwards along the RN3, the road raightens across **Plaine-des-Cafres** , once the hideout of runaway aves, where the pasturelands, dairy rms and cattle give it an alpine feel. lthough the area has less charm an La Plaine-des-Palmistes, there e some memorable walks and a nge of *chambres d'hôtes* and restau- nts dotted along the RN3 to neigh- ouring Le Tampon. As you enter La aine-des-Cafres from Col de Belle- ue, look out for the pretty flower- edecked shrine to St-Expédit, which ems strangely isolated as it stares cross countryside towards Piton des eiges. It's one of many dedicated to e Roman soldier (see page 204) who ied for his beliefs, but this one is dis- nctly religious, unlike the dozens of ther red-daubed shrines, which are ften linked to black magic.

There's a lovely 5km (3-mile) walk at goes from the village church of a Plaine-des-Cafres (also known as e Vingt-Troisième, or 23rd) north Bois Court and the waterfalls of

Grand Bassin. They tumble into a deep gorge where three rivers – the Bras Sec, Bras de Suzanne and Bras des Roches Noires – meet along the southeastern foothills of the Cilaos cirque. Another possibility is to take a pleasant 9km (5.5-mile) drive along the D36 from Le Vingt-Quatrième (24th) through Notre Dame de la Paix to the picnic area, where you can explore the surrounding forests and botanical paths overlooking the Riv- ière des Remparts.

The tortuous RN3 then descends to Le Tampon (which possibly takes its name from the Malagasy word *tam- pony*, meaning 'peak') to St-Pierre on the coast. Since 1830, when the land was bought by Gabriel de Kerveguen and developed into a sugar-growing area, Le Tampon has remained pri- marily agricultural. It also used to be the centre of a thriving geranium- growing area, but in spite of Réunion essential oil being the best in the world for the perfume industry, pro- duction has fallen to 10 tonnes per year compared with 165 tonnes back in 1962.

The Cascades de Takamaka.

Cirque de Mafate from Piton Maido.

THE CIRQUES

Only one road penetrates the cirques of Salazie and Cilaos, and you need a helicopter for Mafate, but this dramatic landscape is a paradise for walkers.

The spectacular natural showpieces of Mafate, Salazie and Cilaos are huge caldera-like valleys that radiate north, east and southwest in a clover leaf pattern, with the extinct volcano of Piton des Neiges at its centre. The three cirques became the home of runaway slaves *(marrons)* in the mid-18th century and later of impoverished white settlers *(petit blancs)*, who came up from the coast a century later. Here, they discovered awesome landscapes of jagged peaks, verdant gorges, rivers and waterfalls. As you take in the almost Dante-esque panorama, it is hard not to wonder how those first slaves and settlers ever survived in such an environment.

By far the easiest of the cirques to get to, if you're on limited time, is the waterfall-strewn Cirque de Salazie. Rains brought in by the southeast trade winds ensure that the area is lush and green all year round, unlike Mafate, which is much drier. Unsurprisingly, Salazie is the most visited of the cirques and in the tourist season can get relatively busy. If you're staying on the west coast, Cilaos appears deceptively close, but the drive from St-Louis is slow-going, and you should allow up to one and a half hours to negotiate the narrow and tortuous RN5. Whichever cirque you choose, weather conditions are very changeable, so go prepared for both sun

and rain. Finally, make sure you take enough euros with you as there are no banks in the cirques, although most restaurants and hotels in Cilaos and Salazie accept major credit cards.

The lost world of Mafate

With no cars, no roads and no large shops, the **Cirque de Mafate** is a happy escape from the maelstrom of the outside world. Runaway slaves knew that their masters would have a very hard job getting there, and even today tourists face similar difficulties.

Main Attractions
Mafate's îlets (villages)
Maïdo viewpoint
Villa Folio
Cilaos

Trekking in Cirque de Mafate.

The cirque's few hundred inhabitants live in a dozen scattered hamlets (*îlets*) linked by paths and tracks, and everyone, including the postman, walks.

Mafate is the least populated and least accessible of all the cirques, unless you take one of the dozens of hiking trails of the Grand Randonnée (see page 182). If you're on limited time, you can take a helicopter ride over hamlets and dizzying ravines before landing for an alfresco *carri* (curry) at La Nouvelle. Flights with Hélilagon (see page 216) leave every day from the heliport at L'Eperon, near St-Paul.

La Nouvelle ❶ is the most populated hamlet, with 130 inhabitants and three grocery stores, and has become the self-styled 'capital' of Mafate, relying on tourism, small-scale cattle farming on Plaine des Tamarins, an geranium oil production, though th number of distilleries has dwindle over the years. It is well worth th effort to trek as far as **Marla**, Mafate highest hamlet, if only to overnight a *gîte* and wake early to catch the spe tacular cloudless views. An alternativ – and comparatively easy – route fo trekkers is from Grand-Îlet in Salaz cirque (see page 223).

If you're not a trekker, you can sti admire Mafate from its western rim **Piton Maido ❷**, sometimes know simply as Le Maido. It is worth ma ing an early start in order to arriv before clouds descend between 10 an 11am. From St-Paul or St-Gilles, yo should allow up to two hours to driv the winding 25km (16-mile) road t

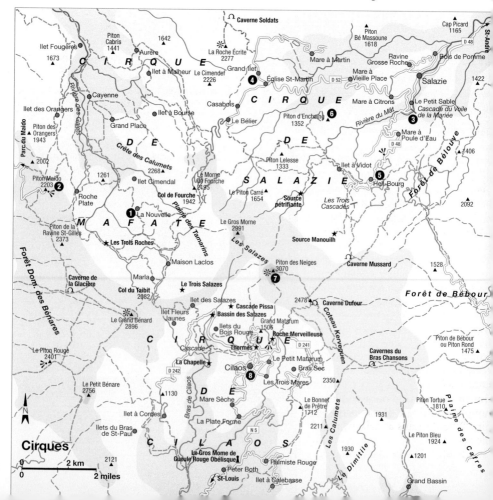

e top. The route takes you through
le geranium-growing area of **Petite
rance**, and past numerous essential
il stills and picnic places. A stunning
anorama spreads before you at the
laido viewpoint, at 2,203 metres
⁷,222ft). Looking from left to right
ou can see the peaks of La Roche
crite (2,277 metres/7,469ft), Le
Cimendef (2,226 metres/7,301ft) and
e Morne de Fourche (2,195 metres/
,200ft), which separate the Salazie
nd Mafate cirques. The peaks of Le
Gros Morne (3,019 metres/9,905ft)
nd the Piton des Neiges (3,070
letres/10,070ft) rise from the Sala-
ie range of mountains marking the
entre of the three cirques. To the
outh, Col du Taïbit (2,082 metres/
,832ft) and the peak of Le Grand
énare (2,896 metres/9,499ft) divide
Mafate and Cilaos cirques, providing
nother stunning spectacle. You can
ike along the rim of the cirque to Le
Grand Bénare, but it's tough going,
nd you'll need to allow six or seven
ours to do the return trip.

For gentler walking, or a place to
eep the kids happy, stop at **Parc du
Maido** (tel: 0262 32 52 52; www.luge
eunion.fr; daily 9am–5pm), a recrea-
onal centre about 15 minutes down-
ill from the viewpoint. You can go
obogganing, mountain biking or pony
rekking through the tamarind forests,
vhich are dotted with picnic sites, or
tay put and try your hand at archery.

Easy-going Salazie

The name Salazie comes from the
Malagasy word *salazane*, which means
'stake' or 'post', and probably stems
rom the three peaks of Le Gros
Morne, which stand like sentries at
he far southwestern corner of the
irque. Salazie's first European settler,
certain Monsieur Cazeau, lived in a
ome-made hut and made a name for
imself by surviving on nothing but
oumpkins during a 43-day period of
ain. 'When it rains at Salazie,' noted
 one visitor in 1863, 'it does rain…in
steady, business-like European way.'

It still rains in Salazie, making it
the most verdant of the cirques. These
days the 25 villages carry on the farming traditions introduced in the 1840s,
growing watercress, peaches, citrus
fruit and an abundance of *chou chou*.
The lime green, pear-shaped vegetable
(see page 172) is fêted each May in a
three-day carnival that attracts many
visitors to the colourful stalls groaning
with local produce. It's a jolly affair
with local music groups and a Miss
Chou Chou contest.

It does not take long, having left St-
André behind on the coast, to get a
taste of Salazie as you enter the luxuriant, tree-clad gorge of Rivière du
Mât, where soaring peaks and dozens
of pencil-thin waterfalls fill the space
above you. Some of the latter are
mere trickles of water – but not the
Voile de la Mariée ❸ or 'Bride's Veil',
which positively cascades into the
Rivière du Mât just beyond the village of Salazie. If you're driving take
advantage of the handful of stopping
places along the route to admire the
scenery safely. The road is winding
but mostly flat as far as Salazie; after

FACT

Geraniums were first
brought from South
Africa in around 1870
and became an
economic lifesaver for
the *petits blancs*, who
made a living cultivating
them for essential oil.

*Cascade Blanche in
the cirque of Salazie.*

that the climb is virtually continuous. There isn't much to Salazie, though it has a few shops and places to eat. For breakfast or lunch on the hoof, you can pick up freshly baked brioches, croissants and pastries at the *boulangerie* on the D48.

Close to the Voile de la Mariée, the D52 branches off west and snakes for 34km (21 miles) through the heart of the cirque to **Grand-Îlet** ④, a hamlet overshadowed by the peak of La Roche Écrite. This is a base for treks into Mafate cirque, and has a handful of cheap *chambres d'hôtes*. Most walks kick off from **Le Bélier**, a hamlet 3km (2 miles) south of Grand-Îlet (accessible by road), and follow the GR1 and GR2; one route penetrates south into Cilaos cirques (for details on long treks, see page 182). Alternatively, you can carry straight on to Hell-Bourg, a 30-minute winding drive above Salazie. There are two stunning viewpoints worth stopping at – one at **Mare à Poule d'Eau**, and the other at **Le Point du Jour**, just at the entrance of Hell-Bourg, at 892 metres (2,926ft). La Roche Écrite is right in front of you

and you can see Le Bélier up in th hills to the left.

Delightful Hell-Bourg

Hell-Bourg ⑤ – named after a ce tain Governor de Hell rather than th domain of sinners – is a slow-paced delightful village and a pleasant plac in which to spend a couple of day There are several things to see insid and just outside the town, and wal ers can join up with the GR1 here too. To cater for the steady flow c visitors, Hell-Bourg has a handful c small hotels, and there are a few sma food shops and restaurants on th main street, **Rue Général de Gaull** as well as a helpful tourist office (te 0262 47 89 89).

There are some lovely Creole house in Hell-Bourg, some of them bright painted and with luxuriant garden shaded by bamboo, orange trees an ferns like parasols. Note in particula the decorative little kiosks known a *guetalis*: strategically placed at the edg of gardens overlooking the street, the allowed the occupants to watch pa sers-by without being seen themselve The name comes from the French ver *guetter*, which means 'to watch out fo or 'look at.'

For a close look at a traditiona home, visit **Villa Folio** (tel: 0262 4 80 98; daily 9am–11.30am, 2–5pm fo guided tours), almost hidden amon its lush gardens opposite the churc in Rue Amiral Lacaze. Built in 187(the tiny villa is typical of the times an offers a rare insight into Creole lif when much of one's time was spen on the veranda. The two small pavi ions at the back used to be the kitche and servants' quarters and a receptio area for friends who'd drop by fo drinks made from the local rum an spices. The house contains origina furniture, including a 19th-centur English four-poster bed complete wit canopy – hijacked, so the story goe from an East India ship by privateers.

The discovery of medicinal spring near Hell-Bourg, in 1831, drew th

A traditional house at Hell-Bourg.

ck to its healing waters for over a
ntury. A landslide in 1948 reduced
em to ruins, which you can see
day by taking a pleasant 15-minute
alk west of the defunct Hôtel des
lazes (a former military hospital),
Chemin du Cimetière.

Some of the casualties of the land-
de were buried in the **Cemetery**, at
e north end of Chemin du Cime-
re. This is a very picturesque cem-
ery, framed by luxuriant bamboo
d verdant cliffs behind. Hidden
nong the graves of settlers, soldiers
d aristocrats is a grey mound of
ck with a simple iron cross, said to
ntain the headless corpse of a Mr
ett, a bandit and rapist, who terror-
ed the area in the early 1900s. To
sure he would not rise again he was
capitated and his head despatched
St-Denis (see page 196). Glasses
rum and cigarettes are sometimes
aced around the grave to appease
hat's left of him.

If you'd rather hook a trout than a
st soul, follow the signs to **Parc Pis-
cole d'Hell-Bourg** (tel: 0262 47 80
; www.truite.re; Sat–Sun 11am–5pm,

also public hols and local school hols),
near the Relais des Cimes Hotel. This
freshwater trout farm provides bait
and line, and you can have your catch
cooked to order in the restaurant.
For more active pursuits head for
the waterfalls at **Les Trois Cascades**,
about 1km (half a mile) south of Hell-
Bourg, which provide ideal conditions
for canyoning. And if hanging on a
rope in a wetsuit in the thundering
crash of a waterfall doesn't set your
pulse racing, have a go at white-water
rafting and career at breakneck speed
to a calm inlet.

For the best views of Salazie cirque,
head northwest out of town along
the D48 towards **Îlet à Vidot**. Rising
to 1,352 metres (4,436ft) from the
centre of the cirque is the flat-topped
Piton d'Enchaing ❻. You can follow
a very challenging section of the GR1
to the peak either from Hell-Bourg
or Îlet à Vidot, but take plenty of supplies. You'll need to allow at least five
hours to go there and back from Hell-
Bourg. A longer but more popular
trek is south to the top of **Piton des
Neiges** ❼. The best option is to stay

*Cirque of Mafate from
the Maido lookout.*

SECOND CHANCE

Every April new moon hundreds of
young Barau's petrels fly across
Cilaos to the sea for the first time.
Many of them won't make it. The
birds, whose breeding colonies are
high in the cliffs above the cirque, are
confused by the town lights below and
become stranded. Since 2009 Nights
Without Light have been implemented,
and during the critical period locals
ceaselessly walk Cilaos' streets to
recover the petrels. On a typical night
they might find 20 young birds. Many
others will collide with a cable, street-
light or vehicle – that's if they don't
meet a stray dog or cat – and will
never be found. After placing them in
a cardboard box, volunteers take the
birds to St-Pierre, where, together
with schoolchildren, they set them
free off the coast.

overnight at the Gîte de la Caverne Dufour, and then head on up to the summit first thing, before the clouds have descended (see page 183).

Cirque de Cilaos

Cilaos is named after a runaway slave called Tsilaos, from the Malagasy *tsy laosana*, meaning 'the place one never leaves' – and you probably won't want to after you've negotiated the 262 hairpin bends along the RN5, the only access road from St-Louis on the south coast. Following the course of the Rivière Bras de Cilaos, the RN5 climbs steadily to the entrance to the cirque at **Le Pavillon**. Early travellers were confined to sedan chairs as the only means of transport to continue their journey beyond Le Pavillon, along narrow roads which at each twist and turn open up new vistas of cloud-capped mountains and isolated villages dotted along the deep ravines.

The town of **Cilaos** ❽, at 1,220 metres (4,000ft), is similar in some respects to the French alpine resort of Chamonix, its twin town. It's an excellent starting point for hikes an walks, with a few things to enterta you in the town itself.

Cilaos' 6,000 inhabitants are main the descendants of 19th-century se tlers from Normandy and Brittan who dreamed up evocative nam for the peaks that surrounded the including Les Trois Salazes or Le Bon net de Prêtre (The Priest's Bonne These days, the local people make living through tourism and farmin though the area is also known for embroidery, wine and lentils.

In **Rue Père Boiteau** in the tow centre there are some beautiful restored bijou Creole houses: not ble examples include a pink an grey house called Soledad, across t road from the Stamm pharmacy; t 80-year-old restaurant called Ch Noé (which serves good goat masala and Cilaos' oldest house, painted blue and white.

Ever since **thermal springs** (*therme* were discovered in 1819 by a goa hunter, Cilaos has been a health reso attracting the sick and infirm, wh would make the long journey up fro the coast. In 1948, a cyclone destroye the springs but the **Établissemen Thermal d'Irenée-Accot** (Route Bras Sec; tel: 0262 31 72 27; Mon–F 9am–12.30pm, 1.30–5pm, Sat–Su 9am–5pm; closed Wed pm and June) is still active. Whether you' got digestive problems, rheumatis or arthritis, the waters from the san thermal springs can help put it rig If you're after sheer indulgence, or restorative after a long trek, treat you self to a sauna or massage, have a wor out in the gym and then flake out the Jacuzzi.

The best places to buy the loc wine are Cilaos and nearby Bras Se Locals sell cheap bottles of Cila wine along the roadside, but it is ofte of inferior quality. Export-quali wine produced and bottled und hygienic conditions can be boug at the **Chai de Cilaos** (34 Rue d Glycines; tel: 0262 31 79 69; Mon–S

Alpine Cilaos.

am–noon, 2–5.30pm) in Bras Sec, here you can also learn about local ine-making methods and enjoy a ine-tasting session. Modern meth-ls using stainless steel vats are used, .t the process of pressing, ferment-ig and bottling in makeshift cellars as not changed in years.

Many of the area's skilled embroi-erers work from home and are oncentrated in **Palmiste Rouge**, outh of Cilaos on the RD240, but handful come to work at the **Mai-on de la Broderie** (tel: 0262 31 77 8; Mon–Sat 9.30am–noon, 2–5pm, un 9.30am–noon) in Rue des Ecoles, hich was founded in 1953 by the sters of Notre-Dame-des-Neiges. A rge number of the designs origi-ated in Brittany, but today workers ruggle to keep up traditional pro-edures and patterns (see Travel Tips, ctivities).

tretching your legs

he tourist office (2 Rue Mac-Auliffe; mail: accueil.cilaos@otisud.re; Mon–Sat am–12.30pm, 1.30–5pm, Sun and ublic hols 9am–noon) is where even-g slide shows are held, followed by ine tasting. Here you'll find every ıap and walking plan imaginable and etails of accommodation and adven-ıre sports available in the cirques, as ell as a huge relief map of the whole land. And if you have ever wondered hat a sedan chair looks like, there's ı original one on display, dating om 1922.

For one of the most straightforward alks from Cilaos, requiring four ours for the return trip, turn left Route de Bras Sec and follow the gns north to **Roche Merveilleuse**. t is also possible to drive along the F11.) No real effort is needed to imb the rock and the views from e summit are great. From left to ght you will see the village of Bras ec, perched on a plateau overlook-g the cirque, followed by Palmiste ouge and Îlet à Cordes, where the est lentils are grown. Access to the

Roche Merveilleuse is through the **Forêt du Grand Matarum**, noted for the local *tamarins-des-hauts*, Japanese cryptomerias and Réunion's only oak trees. Marked paths weave through the forest.

For a more ambitious hike (three to four hours one way), head to the Col du Taïbit and then on to Marla in the cirque of Mafate (see page 221), which is more easily reached from Cilaos than anywhere else. Cilaos is also the start of the shortest but steep-est route to the Piton des Neiges. It takes around three hours to the Cav-erne Dufour *gîte* from the start of the path at Le Bloc (signposted on the road between Cilaos and Bras Sec). Other possible walks from the town are along the GR2 to Bras Sec and beyond to Palmiste Rouge.

The area around the hamlets of **Îlet Fleurs Jaunes** and **Îlets du Bois Rouge** is very popular for canyoning. The sport is enough to scare the pants off you as you abseil off cliffs into water-filled gorges, but at least a guide goes with you, and life-jackets, harnesses, helmets and jump suits are provided.

Canyoning at the Gobert Waterfall, Cilaos.

Anse Source d'Argent beach.

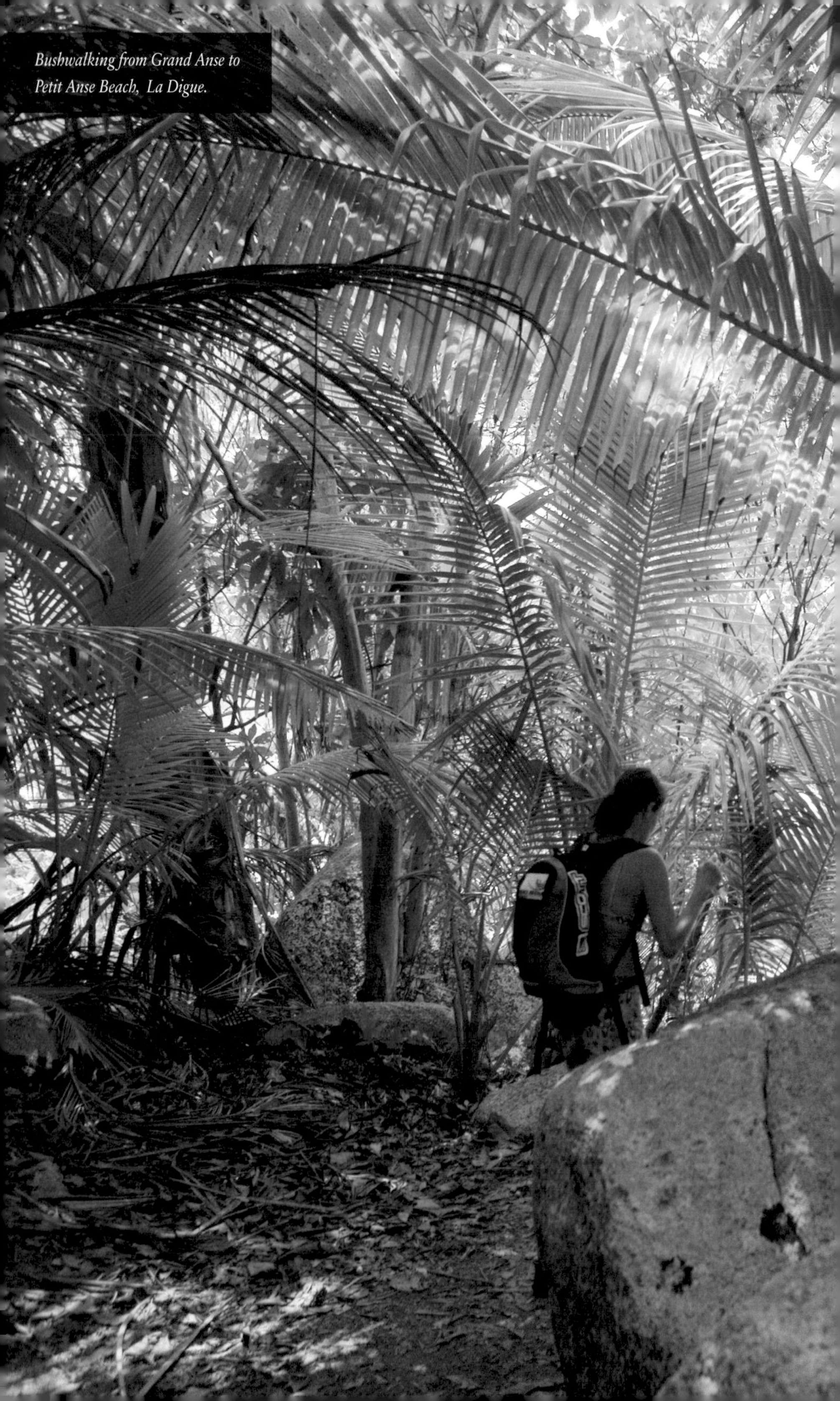

Bushwalking from Grand Anse to Petit Anse Beach, La Digue.

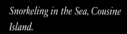

Snorkeling in the Sea, Cousine Island.

SEYCHELLES

The islands' reputation as a tropical paradise is well earned and preserving the environment continues to be a crucial concern.

A group of performers at the Carnaval International de Victoria.

The Seychelles are the oldest ocean islands on earth – once part of the ancient super-continent Pangaea, the archipelago became isolated some 65 million years ago, evolving its own flora and fauna, from which man, and indeed all land mammals, were absent. Seychelles' human history is much more recent, beginning just a few hundred years ago. In 1609 a small party of English sailors made the first recorded landing in Seychelles. They had left England in March the year before, and sailed past the Cape, through the Mozambique Channel, calling in at the Comoros and Pemba, north of Zanzibar. They stumbled upon Seychelles by accident, but were glad they did. The boatswain, one Mr Jones (see page 239), declared the islands 'an earthly Paradise.'

Seychellois are proud of their spectacular country, and happy to share it with visitors. They have a certain reserve on first acquaintance, but when relaxed are incredibly warm and generous. They love to talk, make music and create delicious Creole dishes, and throw open their homes and the bounty of their table to those they come to know.

Tropical birds of the Seychelles.

This is a young nation, dealing with the inevitable problems a small and isolated island population faces when struggling to keep up with the outside world. The characteristic 'mañana' syndrome is in some conflict with the need to modernise and perform to the standards of a faster, busier world beyond the coral beaches.

But it's precisely this relaxed attitude to life that appeals to visitors who come here in search of a stress-free environment and unrivalled natural beauty. If all you want out of your holiday is sun, sea and sand, there are other, cheaper tropical destinations. But if you are prepared to pay extra to enjoy unique flora and fauna, witness spectacular marine life and loll on some of the best beaches in the world, look no further. Many changes to the landscape have occurred since 1609, but there are so many beauty spots that still fit Bo's'n Jones' definition of 'an earthly Paradise.'

THE ORIGIN OF SEYCHELLES

An Indian Ocean Atlantis, the ancient Seychelles archipelago has the oldest and only granitic ocean islands in the world.

The Seychelles islands can be divided into five main groups: the granitic islands, the Amirantes, the Alphonse Group, the Farquhar Group and the Aldabra Group. The 40 islands that make up the granitic group are the world's only ocean islands built from the stuff of continents. All other isolated ocean islands are made up of coralline or volcanic rocks, both of which have grown out of the ocean. The main islands of Seychelles are different. Their rocks have never been completely submerged. They were formed from material ejected from deep within the fabric of the earth some 750 million years ago, perhaps in a frozen, lifeless wasteland close to the South Pole.

For millennia, the rocks of Seychelles were a part of Pangaea, the ancient super-continent that once encompassed all the world's land masses. Some 200 million years ago, the forces of continental drift tore Pangaea apart. It split into Laurasia (modern Europe, Asia and North America) to the north and Gondwanaland (South America, Africa, Antarctica, Australasia and the Indian subcontinent) to the south. Seychelles at this time lay near the point where Madagascar, India and Africa were linked.

As the process of continental drift continued, about 125 million years ago, Madagascar, Seychelles and India broke away as one land mass. Madagascar became an island around 90 million years ago, drifting away with its own unique assemblage of wildlife. Then 65 million years ago, Seychelles drifted from the western coast of India.

The death of the dinosaurs

It may not be pure coincidence that the birth of the world's only oceanic fragments of continental rock coincided with the death of the dinosaurs. There are many dinosaur extinction

Corals on Aldabra Atoll's beach.

theories. Many scientists believe that their disappearance was caused by the earth's collision with a comet that struck the Yucatan Peninsula in Mexico, sending shock waves through the globe and triggering volcanic activity at the opposite side of the earth. A second theory suggests that a vast comet broke up on entering the earth's atmosphere, major fragments of which hit the Yucatan, and 12 hours later, as the earth turned, struck the Indian Ocean. Other scientists believe that extinction was not instantaneous, but the result of an extensive period of volcanic activity in western India, close to the point where Seychelles was once attached to the subcontinent.

Isolated in mid-ocean, this new micro-continent was one land mass, covering an area of around 300,000 sq km (116,000 sq miles) – roughly the size of Britain and Ireland combined. Today, all that remains are the peaks of the highest mountains. The combined forces of erosion, sea level change and the sheer weight of coral growth (forming what geologists term a carbonate platform) have submerged all but 250 sq km (100 sq miles) of granite, less than one thousandth of its original extent, creating the archipelago we see today.

Though superficially similar to the other granitic islands, Silhouette and North Island are younger and made up largely of a type of volcanic rock called syenite. Silhouette was born rapidly and dramatically, the result of an eruption that probably occurred on land. Limited outcrops above the surface today make it difficult to determine with certainty, but it is probable that the volcano's crater lies southeast of La Passe, now almost entirely eroded away and submerged. This volcano erupted many times and Silhouette may have towered 3,000 metres (10,000ft) or more at one time. At Pointe Zeng Zeng, you can see the only volcanic ash above sea level in Seychelles, while fingers of basalt reach out from the island to Mahé and can be seen at Glacis and elsewhere.

Volcanic and younger islands

On the edge of the Seychelles Bank lie the much younger islands of Bird and Denis, thought to have emerged about 4,000 years ago when the sea level dropped as a result of a change in ocean currents. These currents stirred the waters, causing a shift in the average local sea levels. Mahé's sea level, for example, is now 5 metres (16ft) below the level in southern India. It is thought that the sea level change that revealed Bird and Denis exposed the Amirantes Group at the same time.

The Amirantes is a linear chain of coral islands and atolls that rises no more than 3 metres (10ft) above sea level. Volcanoes once rose out of the ocean, but as they died and were reclaimed by the sea, coral growth maintained contact with the surface. Farquhar Atoll, in the south of the Seychelles, must also have witnessed volcanic activity at one time. It is believed that while the granitic group was a micro-continent, Farquhar may have been a nano-continent (a tiny fragment of continent). Aldabra, Assumption, Cosmoledo and Astove in the southwestern corner of Seychelles are different again. These islands of the Aldabra Group are raised coral islands.

In fact Aldabra is the largest raised atoll in the world. Unlike the usual low-lying coral atolls, they rise to up to 8 metres (27ft) above sea level. This appears to go against the conventional wisdom that the volcanic basement of coral atolls is contracting and sinking.

The cycle continues today. The biggest fear is that global warming and the rise in sea levels may spell disaster for low-lying coral islands. Signs of beach erosion can be seen throughout Seychelles and nowhere more than in the coral islands, which could disappear if present trends continue.

L'Union Estate Monolith.

ON SOLID GROUND

Granite islands are what differentiate Seychelles from other tropical idylls and make them so instantly recognisable. The best example of ancient granite rock that can be seen today lies at L'Union Estate, covering half a hectare (an acre) of land at Anse L'Union on the west coast of the island of La Digue. This impressive monolith, which was formed during the Precambrian period (around 750 million years ago) by the slow cooling of molten rocks (magma) deep within the earth's crust, is a National Monument. The estate is also home to the cemetery of the original settlers of La Digue.

DECISIVE DATES

Africa and the Indian Ocean in 1663.

Early Discoverers

851
Arab traders probably visit Seychelles. An Arab manuscript of this date refers to the 'high island' beyond the Maldives.

961
Seychelles is referred to as Zarin (Sisters) on Arab charts.

1502
On its way to India via Mozambique, Vasco da Gama's expedition sights the outer islands, which later became known as the Amirantes.

1609
A ship from the English East India Company makes the first recorded landing on Mahé.

French Possession

1742
Lazare Picault leads an expedition to chart the islands, reporting to Mahé de Labourdonnais, the French governor of nearby Mauritius.

1756
Nicholas Morphey claims Mahé for France.

1778
A 15-man garrison is established at L'Etablissement du Roi (later Victoria).

1786
The colony now comprises 24 military personnel, five civilians and 122 slaves. Its income is derived from provisioning ships. A legal system is introduced.

1790
In the wake of the French Revolution, the Seychelles settlers create a Colonial Assembly to run the colony.

The War Years

1794
First capitulation to the British is signed by Quincy. It is renewed seven times.

1801
French political deportees arrive.

British Control

1815–1901
Britain assumes control of Seychelles.

1818
The population of 7,500 prospers from the cultivation of cotton.

1822
Price of cotton falls. Many planters return to Mauritius.

1835
Slavery is abolished.

1860s
Coconut oil is almost the sole export.

1861
Arrival of the first of around 2,400 liberated Africans.

1891
Vanilla becomes an important cash crop.

Independence

1903
Seychelles becomes a separate Crown Colony under its first governor, Sir Ernest Bickham Sweet-Escott.

1906
A fall in the price of vanilla rocks the economy.

1914–18
World War I causes hardship in Seychelles due to isolation from shipping. Seychelles Pioneer Corps serves in East Africa.

1921
The population reaches 24,500.

1926
Electricity and telephone services are installed.

1937
Creation of the League of Coloured Peoples to lobby for plantation workers.

1939–45
World War II. Seychelles is used as a refuelling base for flying boats and warships. Seychelles Pioneer Corps again serves with British forces.

1963
America begins the construction of a satellite tracking station on Mahé.

1964
Creation of two new political parties, the Seychelles People's United Party (led by Albert René, demanding independence) and the Seychelles Democratic Party (led by James Mancham, wanting closer links with Britain).

1965
Creation of a new British colony, called British Indian Ocean Territory, including several islands from the Seychelles group.

1967
Universal adult suffrage is introduced.

1970
First Constitutional Conference discusses the future of Seychelles. A legislative assembly is created.

1971
Completion of the International Airport. Tourism is now key to the economy.

The flag of the Seychelles.

The Modern Age

1976
Seychelles becomes an independent republic. A coalition government is formed, with James Mancham as president and Albert René as prime minister.

1977
Mancham is overthrown in a coup that establishes René as president of a socialist government.

1979
A new constitution makes Seychelles a single-party system, led by the Seychelles People's Progressive Front.

1981
A mercenary force led by Colonel 'Mad Mike' Hoare attempts to seize control of the country, and fails. The following year a mutiny in the Seychelles army is put down by Tanzanian troops.

1984–9
René is re-elected twice.

1992
Return to a multi-party system.

James Michel.

1993
A new constitution is adopted. René and his SPPF party are elected back into power.

1998
René is re-elected. Mancham's Democratic Party is forced into third place by the United Opposition (later renamed the Seychelles National Party or SNP).

2001
René wins snap presidential elections.

2003
René retires and James Michel succeeds him as president.

2006–2011
James Michel is re-elected twice as president.

2015
Seychelles reaches a landmark US$30 million debt buyback agreement, which will see the islands' debt transferred to a conservation trust and the creation of one of the Indian Ocean's largest marine reserves.

القرآن ثم ركبوا بعد اساطير بلادها وزخارف جلّاها وقال اركبوا فيها بسم الله مجراها

ومرساها ثم بنفس نفس المغرمين او عباد الله للمكرمين وقال لك اما ان

BIRTH OF AN ISLAND NATION

Quincy and René, the historic heavyweights of Seychelles, were key to its transformation from deserted paradise to modern independent state.

We can only speculate as to early human history in Seychelles. Polynesians, who eventually settled on Madagascar, may have lingered here around the 3rd and 2nd centuries BC. It is likely that Arab traders plying the Indian Ocean in around the 9th century knew of the islands' existence. A manuscript dated AD 851, written by an Arab merchant, refers to the Maldives and higher islands beyond them, possibly Seychelles. Evidence also suggests that long before European discovery of the islands, Arabs were trading the legendary coco de mer nuts, found only in Seychelles (see page 314). Because of the mystery surrounding their origin, the nuts were highly sought after. No shrewd trader would reveal the source of supply of such a rare and valuable commodity. To keep the myth alive the Arabs claimed they found them washed ashore in the Maldives, but as the nuts are not buoyant in saltwater, this is unlikely.

The first Europeans

The early history of Seychelles is a story of people passing through. In 1502, Vasco da Gama, on his way to India via East Africa, sighted the outer islands, which became known as the Amirantes, but the Portuguese made no attempt to colonise them. Later in the 16th century, the inner granitic islands began to appear on Portuguese charts as the 'Seven Sisters.'

The British were next on the scene. In 1609 the *Ascension*, one of the ships from a trading fleet of the English East India Company on its way to India, got lost in a storm. Its crew sighted 'high land' and headed for it, anchoring 'as in a pond.' They found plentiful fresh water, fish, coconuts, birds, turtles and giant tortoises

Vasco da Gama.

EARTHLY PARADISE

On 19 January 1609, the *Ascension*, a merchant vessel under the command of the English captain Alexander Sharpeigh, was separated from the fleet by a storm and anchored off Mahé. On board was one John Jourdain, an agent sent by the East India Company to trade and negotiate in India. He wrote an enthusiastic account of the 'earthly Paradise' they had happened upon. His is the first known written description of Seychelles: 'It is very good refreshing place for wood, water, coker nutts, fish and fowle, without any feare or danger, except the allagartes: for you cannot discerne that ever any people had bene there before us.'

with which to replenish their stores. The ship's captain reported the bounty they had found, but the British took no action and Seychelles was to remain unoccupied for more than a hundred years.

By the end of the 17th century, piracy in the Indian Ocean was rife. Pirates fleeing from the Caribbean, whose waters were by this time heavily policed, based themselves in Madagascar. From here they preyed upon vessels plying the Red Sea and the Gulf, probably using the islands as a hiding place and refreshment stop.

French occupation

It wasn't until 1710 that the French occupied Île de France (as Mauritius was then known), but the colony quickly grew in importance. In 1735 an energetic administrator, Bertrand François Mahé de Labourdonnais, was appointed. His brief was to protect the French sea route to India. Labourdonnais, himself a sailor, turned his attention to making a speedier passage from Île de France to India and in 1742 he commissioned Lazare Picault to lead an expedition to chart the islands northeast of Madagascar. On 21 November 1742 the *Elisabeth* and the *Charles*

'A Fleet of East Indiamen at Sea', by Nicholas Pocock (1741–1821).

LAYING THE HERCULEAN TRAIL

Olivier Le Vasseur, also known as La Buse (the Buzzard), was a notorious French pirate operating in the early 18th century. For a number of years, he teamed up with fellow brigands from Britain, Edward England and Charles Taylor. Together they cruised the Indian Ocean and terrorised European merchant ships. Their most lucrative haul came from a royal Portuguese ship, which they plundered as she lay helpless in the harbour of Réunion. The booty taken included the 'Fiery Cross of Goa'. Encrusted with diamonds, rubies and emeralds, it took three men to lift it. Le Vasseur kept this magnificent piece of treasure for himself. He was finally captured by the French authorities and on 7 July

1730 was taken to Réunion and hanged. The story goes that just before they put the noose around his neck, he threw a sheaf of documents into the crowd crying, 'Find my treasure, who can!' The search for this priceless cross has continued ever since.

Most famous of the treasure hunters was Reginald Cruise-Wilkins, who dedicated his life to the quest. He was convinced the treasure was buried on Mahé and that Le Vasseur had laid a series of traps and clues based on the labours of Hercules. He died in 1977 without finding the treasure, but his son has continued the diggings, some of which may still be seen by the shore at Bel Ombre.

anchored off Mahé at Anse Boileau (not Baie Lazare, later mistakenly named as Picault's landing place). They found a land of plenty. In fact, Picault's first name for the island was Île d'Abondonce.

Picault's mapping was poor, so in 1744 he was sent back on a second mission, this time anchoring off the northeast coast near present-day Victoria. He renamed the main island Mahé, and the archipelago the Îles de la Bourdonnais. He had high hopes for the islands, but his plans for settlement were thwarted. The colonial war between England and France had reached India. Labourdonnais was called away to fight a campaign and the islands were once more forgotten. It wasn't until 1756 that the authorities on Île de France decided to take possession of the islands before the British did. Two ships were sent to claim them, commanded by Corneille Nicholas Morphey.

After a thorough investigation of Mahé and the surrounding islands, Morphey raised the French flag and took possession for his king and the French East India Company on 1 November 1756, to hearty cries of 'long live the king' and nine shots from the ships' cannon. He renamed the largest island Île de Séchelles (the name later used for the island group, when the largest granitic island reverted to the name of Mahé).

The end of the Seven Years' War, France's loss of Canada and its reduced status in India accelerated the decline of the French East India Company. The settlements of Île de France and Seychelles, formerly controlled by the company, now came under direct royal authority and in 1768, during a commercial expedition for the collection of timber and tortoises, French sovereignty was extended to cover all the islands of the granitic group. But the French were in no hurry to settle Seychelles. A colony there could not pay for itself, and would be costly to maintain. Then, in 1769, the navigators Rochon and Grenier proved that a faster route to India could safely be taken via Seychelles and the importance of its strategic position began to be realised.

Frenchman Brayer du Barré (died 1777) was given royal permission to run a settlement in Seychelles at his own expense. He decided that the best place to begin a colony was the little island of Ste Anne, off the northeast coast of Mahé. On 12 August 1770, with 15 white colonists, seven slaves, five Indians and one African woman on board, Du Barré's ship, the *Télémaque*, set sail from Île de France and arrived on the island 14 days later.

Du Barré himself did not join the expedition, but stayed in Île de France seeking funds, though his appeals for help to Île de France and Versailles fell on deaf ears. In desperation, he went to Seychelles to try to rescue the situation, but to no avail. A ruined man, he left for India and died there shortly afterwards. By August 1772, Du Barré's people had abandoned Ste Anne and moved to Mahé or returned home.

Mahé de Labourdonnais.

IN THE NAME OF THE KING

On 1 November 1756, a Stone of Possession was laid on Mahé by Company Officer Corneille Nicholas Morphey, who claimed the islands for the French king Louis XV and christened them the Seychelles. It is generally thought that the islands were named after Louis XV's finance minister, the Viscount Jean Moreau de Séchelles. However, the name may also be a reference to the relationship through marriage of a female member of the Hérault de Séchelles family (themselves related to Moreau de Séchelles) and the man who sent Morphey on his voyage, Magon de la Villebague, governor of Île de France.

Cinnamon, nutmeg and cloves

The intendant of Île de France at this time was Pierre Poivre (1719–86), a man of ideas. Determined to break the Dutch monopoly of the lucrative spice trade, he thought Mahé would be perfect for spice cultivation. He had obtained seedlings of nutmeg and clove, and 10,000 nutmeg seeds, but his attempts to propagate them on Île de France and Bourbon (later Réunion) met with little success. So, in 1771, Poivre sent former soldier Antoine Gillot to Mahé to supervise the creation of a spice garden. Gillot chose Anse Royale, on the southeast coast, as the site, and set about establishing the 'Jardin du Roi', which was planted with nutmeg, clove, cinnamon and pepper.

When British ships were sighted around Seychelles, the French authorities were spurred into action and despatched a garrison from Île de France under the command of Lieutenant de Romainville. They built the Etablissement du Roi (Royal Settlement) on the site of modern Victoria. Gillot was nominally in charge of the civilian colonists, but had no real authority over them. So Île de France sent as replacement a man of stronger mettle, Jean Baptiste Philogène

'View of Mahe' by Sigismond Himely (1801-1872).

THE LOST KING OF FRANCE

An intriguing anecdote concerns the mysterious figure of Pierre Louis Poiret. Late in 1804, a boy of 19 years old came to Poivre Island, having been brought from France by a Monsieur Aimé, who treated him with great respect. Aimé continued to Mahé, where he presented secret letters to Quincy, the commandant. After working the cotton gin on Poivre, Poiret came to Mahé. He was given land at Cap Ternay and Grand Anse and slaves to help him farm it.

An aloof man, respected by his fellow planters, he led a largely unremarkable life. Then he suddenly declared he was actually Louis XVII, heir to the French throne. He said that, after the execution of his parents, he had been placed in the care of a cobbler, Simon Poiret. Later, Royalists smuggled him out of Paris in a box of hay, and brought him out to Seychelles. In his later years, he wrote repeatedly to Charles X of France, whom he said was his uncle. Interestingly, the names he gave all his four sons began with Louis, and the names of his five daughters with Marie.

Official history records that the crown prince Louis died of tuberculosis in 1795. His heart was removed and preserved in a crystal urn. This was opened in 1999, DNA extracted and compared to that of Marie-Antoinette and living relatives. Tests confirmed a relationship, though not necessarily that the heart was that of Louis.

de Malavois. He drew up 30 decrees which protected the timber and tortoises. In future, only sound farming techniques and careful husbanding of resources would be tolerated. He assumed command of the settlement in 1788.

In 1790, as a result of the French Revolution, the settlers declared independence from the other French colonies and formed a Colonial Assembly. They drew up their own constitution and decided that land in Seychelles should only go to the children of existing colonists, who should be able to dispose of the colony's produce as they chose, not as Île de France dictated. But independence did not last long. Enthusiasm for the Revolution began to wane, not least because revolutionary theory supported the abolition of slavery, which the colonists wholeheartedly opposed, believing that without slave labour, they could not survive. Eventually they agreed to hand over control to a commandant.

The war years

In 1794, Jean-Baptiste Queau de Quinssy (1748–1827), whose name was later anglicised to Quincy, took command of the colony. A wily man, he used skill and expediency to steer Seychelles through the years of war ahead.

Seychelles became a haven for French corsairs (pirates carrying *lettres de marque* from the French authorities entitling them to prey on British enemy ships). Quincy hoped this might go unnoticed, but in 1794 a squadron of three English ships arrived. They were well armed and in no mood for resistance. The British commodore, Henry Newcome, asked for help with his wounded, many of whom were French prisoners, but Quincy refused.

This resistance meant little in practical terms and was but a gesture. Quincy knew he was powerless and Newcome gave him an hour in which to surrender. There were only 20 colonists on the French side 'capable of carrying arms.' Newcome had almost 13,000 men. Quincy had eight cannons, Newcome had 166. In all, Quincy made seven capitulations to the English. While they were in port, he flew the English flag, but as soon as their ships were out of sight he raised the tricolour. The strategy worked. In effect, Seychelles remained neutral, supplying both British and French ships. The islanders avoided conflict and the colony flourished.

This was not an end to Quincy's problems, however. To his dismay, on 11 July 1801 the

French frigate *Chiffonne* arrived with a cargo of notorious French prisoners sent into exile by Napoleon and Quincy was warned that there were more on the way. Together, these deportees would outnumber the local population. Were this not enough, the British ship HMS *Sybille* arrived soon after. Quincy had no choice but to try to defend the *Chiffonne*, but after a brief battle, she was taken. Captain Adam of the *Sybille* demanded to know why Quincy had interfered, in contravention of his capitulation terms. With characteristic guile and charm, the commandant managed to talk his way out of the difficulty,

Pierre Poivre (Peter Pepper), brought spices to the Seychelles.

and even persuaded Adam to let Seychelles vessels fly a flag bearing the words "Seychelles Capitulation", allowing them to pass through the British blockade of Mauritius unmolested.

Although confrontation with the British may have been avoided, the problem of deportees, whom the Seychellois feared, still remained. As political prisoners they refused to work and talked of liberty and equality within hearing of the slaves. Quincy was afraid that the slaves and deportees might join forces and revolt. So he transported a number of them to the small island of Frégate and wrote to the Île de France authorities pleading for assistance with the rest. In the long run, however, his fears proved unfounded as very few of the deportees ended up staying: 33 were redeported to the Comoros, six stowed away aboard visiting ships, and a number of others were taken to Île de France. Only a few of the most peaceable settled down in Seychelles.

British control

The colony entered the 19th century with a population of 215 whites, 86 free blacks and 1,820 slaves. The war raged on, but the British were fast gaining the upper hand. They tightened the blockade on the French Indian Ocean colonies. Réunion surrendered, followed in December 1810 by Île de France, which they renamed Mauritius. In April 1811, Captain Beaver arrived in Seychelles on the *Nisus* to announce that while the preferential terms of Quincy's capitulation could stand, Seychelles must recognise the terms of the Mauritian surrender. Beaver left behind a royal marine, Lieutenant Sullivan, to monitor the Seychelles situation, but there was little Sullivan could do to stop the settlers continuing to provision French frigates and slavers. The British had outlawed the slave trade and Sullivan, later given the title of Civil Agent, played cat and mouse with the pro-slaver colonists. Once, acting on a tip-off, Sullivan was

Victoria clock tower in 1856.

A GILDED CAGE

The British saw Seychelles as a useful place to exile political prisoners. Over the years, it became home to prisoners from Zanzibar, Egypt, Cyprus and Palestine. The first was the Sultan of Perak, who arrived in 1875 after his implication in the murder of the British Resident there. Like many exiles who followed, he settled well into Seychelles life and became fond of the islands. Perhaps the most famous exile was Archbishop Makarios, who arrived in 1956. He too fell in love with his prison. 'When our ship leaves harbour,' he wrote, 'we shall take with us many good and kindly memories of the Seychelles… may God bless them all.'

rowed over to Praslin and confiscated a cargo of newly landed slaves. It was but a small triumph among many frustrations, and Sullivan, complaining that the Seychellois had 'no sense of honour, shame or honesty', resigned. In 1814, the first civilian administrator of the British regime, Edward Madge, arrived. Quincy was kept on as Justice of the Peace and remained a respected figure in the colony until his death in 1827.

The British allowed customary French practices to remain in place. The administrator may have been British, reporting to London, but he governed according to French rules.

The colonists had two main grievances with their new masters. One was their dependence on Mauritius. The other was the abolition of slavery

On 12 October 1862, Mahé was hit by a storm. Torrential rain and strong winds caused an avalanche of mud and rocks to fall on Victoria, killing more than 70 people and devastating the town.

in 1835. The plantations were already in decline, their soil exhausted by years of cultivation and a lack of investment. The plantocracy believed they could not farm without slave labour. Some planters took their slaves and left. The liberated slaves had no land, and most squatted on the estates they had tended in bondage, working sporadically to keep themselves from starvation. It was a poor sort of freedom, and the colony entered a period of stagnation. There were no exports, and no money to pay for new infrastructure. The situation was only improved when planters realised they could grow coconuts with less labour and more profit than the traditional crops of cotton, sugar, rice and maize.

The British took their anti-slavery stance seriously, and operated patrols along the East African coast, raiding Arab dhows transporting slaves to the Middle East. Slaves liberated south of the Equator were brought to Seychelles and apprenticed to plantation owners. It was these ex-slaves who saved the economy as they were a source of cheap labour. They worked the land in return for rations and low wages. Over a period of 13 years, from 1861, around 2,400 men, women and children were brought to Seychelles.

The main settlement on Mahé (named Victoria in 1841, to mark the marriage of Queen Victoria and Prince Albert) began to grow and prosper. Licences granted in 1879 give us some idea of the range of businesses in the town: there was a druggist, two auctioneers, five retailers, four liquor stores, a notary, an attorney, a jeweller and a watchmaker.

Crown colony

Seychelles yearned to be a colony in its own right, not an appendage of Mauritius, and the authorities in the mother colony supported this desire. Sir Arthur Gordon, the Mauritian governor, sent a petition on their behalf to London. Concessions were made, but Seychelles did not become a separate Crown Colony until 1903, when its first governor, Sir Ernest Bickham Sweet-Escott, took office. Befitting its new

status, the colony acquired botanical gardens, and a clock tower in the heart of Victoria.

World War I brought great hardship to the islands. Ships could not bring in essential goods, nor take away exports. Wages fell and prices soared. Many turned to crime and the prisons were bursting. Joining the Seychelles Labour Contingent formed during the war seemed to offer an escape, but it was no easy option. The 800-strong force was sent to East Africa. After just five months, so many had died from dysentery, malaria and beriberi that the depleted corps was sent home. In all, 335 men died.

A Seychelles Governor troops inspection in 1972.

By the end of World War I, the population of Seychelles, which was around 24,000, was feeling neglected by Whitehall. There was agitation from the newly formed Planters' Association for greater representation in the governance of Seychelles affairs. After 1929 a more liberal flow of funds was ensured by the Colonial Development Act, but it was a time of economic depression; the price of copra was falling and so were wages. Workers petitioned the government about their poor working conditions and the burden of tax they had to bear. Governor Sir Arthur Grimble instigated some reforms, exempting lower income groups from taxation. He was keen to create model housing and distribute smallholdings for the landless.

Sadly, many of his reforms were not approved before World War II had broken out, and everything was put on hold.

The Planters' Association lobbied for the rich white land owners, but those who worked for them had no voice. In 1937, the League of Coloured Peoples was formed to demand a minimum wage, a wage tribunal and free health care for all.

World War II caused more distress in the colony and led to political change. In 1939, the Seychelles' first political party, the Taxpayers' Association, was formed, but it was entirely

Britain was cool on the idea of integration, while opinion in Seychelles appeared to be split. In 1967, universal adult suffrage was introduced and at the first election each party gained three seats, with Mancham claiming victory through the support of an independent. Subsequent elections in 1970 and 1974 gave Mancham a small majority in votes, but a large one in seats, through the 'first past the post' voting system.

Meanwhile, Britain's lack of enthusiasm for integration convinced Mancham to join René in calling for independence. In 1975, a coalition was forged between the two rivals.

Fishermen landing their catch in the early 1970s.

concerned with protecting the interests of the plantocracy. A British governor described it as 'the embodiment of every reactionary force in Seychelles'. After the war, literate property owners were granted the vote; just 2,000 in a population of 36,000. At the first elections in 1948, most of those elected to the Legislative Council were predictably members of the Planters' and Taxpayers' associations.

It was not until 1964 that any new political movements were created. In that year, the socialist Seychelles People's United Party (SPUP) was formed. Led by Albert René, it campaigned for autonomy. By contrast, James Mancham's Seychelles Democratic Party (SDP), created the same year, wanted to retain its close links with Britain.

Independence

Independence was declared on 29 June 1976. James Mancham became the first president of the Republic of Seychelles and René his prime minister. Less than one year later, on 5 June 1977, while Mancham was in London to attend the Commonwealth Conference, René's supporters staged a coup. New elections were called in 1979 with René as the sole candidate. A one-party socialist state was established and the SPUP changed its name to the Seychelles People's Progressive Front (SPPF).

René used Seychelles' strategic importance to play America and Russia off against each other, while remaining non-aligned, obtaining substantial help from both superpowers without having to commit himself to either.

There were several attempts to oust René by force. The most dramatic of these took place in November 1981, when 50 mercenaries arrived on a Royal Air Swazi flight posing as a charitable organisation bringing toys for local orphaned children. Beneath the toys, however, hidden in secret compartments of their luggage, were guns and ammunition. The mercenaries were led by 'Mad Mike' Hoare, whose previous exploits had included installing Mobutu as president of Zaire. They passed undetected through customs, until an official discovered a bunch of bananas in the case of a French tourist, the only non-mercenary on the plane. The importation of fresh fruit into Seychelles is illegal and the customs officers decided to give the luggage of the last two passengers a more thorough check. On discovery of a gun, all hell broke out. The mercenaries took over the airport and after a shoot-out escaped to South Africa in a hijacked plane, where they were promptly arrested. Mancham maintained that the plot had nothing to do with him, and commented wryly that the coup 'had been foiled by a bunch of bananas'.

Mancham remained in exile in London for 15 years. In 1992, with the resumption of multi-party democracy, he returned and rivalry between the DP, as it was now known, and the SPPF, resumed. In 1993 the first multi-party presidential election since independence in 1976 was held. But it was René who triumphed with 59 percent of the votes cast.

Meanwhile, a third force was emerging. At the 1998 elections, the Seychelles National Party (SNP) gained more votes than the DP, but still fell short of the number of votes cast for the SPPF. Once again René was elected president of the Seychelles Republic. René managed to get re-elected for a third time at snap presidential elections held in August 2001. Mancham and his DP party declined to stand at this election but Wavel Ramkalawan of the SNP doubled his share of the vote. At the next National Assembly elections in December 2002, SPPF took 22 seats, while SNP took 11. Mancham's DP, however, received just 3 percent of the vote and was wiped out. In 2003, René announced his retirement and James Michel his successor as president of Seychelles.

Just as Quincy had done centuries earlier, Albert René used craft and guile to steer a course through the changes taking place in the world. Both have left their indelible marks as they led their small country through times of great change.

Seychelles today

Seychelles today has a focus. The tiny population of around 90,000 has largely rejected the traditional agricultural and fishing way of life, as a new generation embraces tourism, which now dominates the economy. It's a strategy

James Alix at the White House.

that's paying off. Despite the crippling effect of losing national airline Air Seychelles' direct service to Europe in 2012 (although as of July 2015, there are thrice-weekly direct flights to Paris once more) the World Economic Forum's 2015 Travel and Tourism report placed Seychelles in second position in the Eastern and Southern Africa category, chasing only South Africa and beating Mauritius and Kenya. Judged on categories such as price competitiveness, environmental sustainability, natural resources and tourist service infrastructure, it's a real coup for the archipelago. Best of all, its self promotion as one of the planet's last sanctuaries for unique nature is ensuring that Seychellois are preserving the environment for generations to come.

A young Creole man.

THE SEYCHELLOIS

Descended from African slaves, French settlers, British colonists and Asian immigrants, the Seychellois are an intriguing mix of people.

The Seychellois could be called a 'new' people. They have a short history, having existed as a separate entity only since 1903, fused more closely since independence in 1976, while facing the difficulties of a small island state embarking upon nationhood. They are heartening proof that people of differing ethnic backgrounds can live together in peace.

Origins

From the time the first settlers arrived in the 18th century, the Seychelles have been a melting pot. French colonists, who sought their fortunes in Mauritius and Réunion before arriving in Seychelles, brought with them slaves of both African and Indian origin and the process of racial intermingling began almost immediately. Pierre Hangard, probably the colony's first permanent settler, was an emigrant from Mauritius, who came to Seychelles with five slaves. He does not appear to have married, but did have a daughter by Annette, one of his slaves. He freed Annette and gave her a property at Bel Ombre. His daughter later married a Frenchman who owned one of the finest properties on Mahé. It was a scenario that was to be repeated again and again in the history of Seychelles; and there in a nutshell is the origin of the Seychellois. The colonial government census grouped people by ethnic origin until 1911, when it was decided that this was no longer possible. This bureaucratic decision can perhaps be seen as the date of birth of the Seychellois people.

Although slaves came, in the main, from eastern Africa, some were from Madagascar, but only a few came from India. The largest influx of Indians came much later, along with the Chinese. They arrived during the 19th century, working as road labourers or setting themselves up as traders. They brought with them their religions and

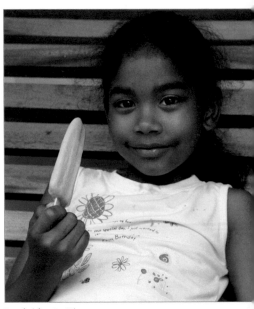

Local girl on La Digue.

customs, which they have retained. But the largest cultural influences are African and French. Despite the British takeover in the 19th century, few Britons settled in Seychelles, and the colonial government was slow to change French laws and institutions or the use of French in public life. Indeed, the British were reluctant rulers, initially attempting without success to persuade France to retain the islands in exchange for French possessions in India. French social customs were already well entrenched. Britain retained the same French governor and did very little to change the existing way of life. The British did contest the influence of the Roman Catholic Church as opposed to Anglicanism, but Catholicism was the faith that won the heart of the Seychellois.

Seychellois today

The modern Seychellois, particularly the young, look more to European culture than African or Asian: men are likely to follow the fortunes of a football team like Manchester United, girls to wear Western clothes. They dance to British pop music and aspire to Western values. This is not the third world, but a middle-income country where few go hungry. Prices in the shops may be high, but the ocean is full of fish and fruit is plentiful. There is no apparent tension between tourist and local. The Seychellois may display a certain reserve, which sometimes comes across as indifference, but when barriers are broken down, visitors soon learn that the Seychellois can be among the most kind and friendly people you could ever hope to meet. Top of the list given by many visitors of reasons to return to Seychelles, apart from the obvious natural beauty of the country, is the friendliness of its people.

Language

When the early French planters were trying to communicate with slaves, who often spoke only their own tribal languages, they used a

Beach football at Beau Vallon Beach.

A MULTILINGUAL SOCIETY

Seychelles has three official languages: Kreol, English and French. The Seychellois seem to have an innate ability to pick up languages quickly, not surprising perhaps in view of the nation's history. Most speak Kreol and English and happily drift from one to another when in conversation. These are the languages you are most likely to hear on the streets, though some of the longer-established families do make a point of speaking French in the home and among themselves.

Seychelles Kreol evolved from a mixture of influences. Though largely based on French, it has many African, Malagasy and Arab words, as well as an increasing number of English words. Terms used at football matches, a popular sport, are English, not French. A good goal kick, for example, becomes a *zoli goal kick*. The most noticeable features of Kreol are a very simple grammar, the extensive use of the letter 'z' (for example, *les oiseaux*, French for birds, becomes *zwazo*), and the use of 'k' instead of 'c'.

While English is spoken in hotels, shops and offices, a few words of Kreol are useful away from tourist sites and Victoria, particularly when talking to older Seychellois. If you can speak a bit of French, you should have no trouble understanding basic Kreol.

simplified form of French, interspersed with words they picked up from their slaves' conversations. In this way, Kreol evolved. Since it is based on a form of French spoken in the 18th century, it retains many archaic and dialect words rarely heard in modern French. Over time, Mauritius, Réunion and Seychelles developed their own accents and patterns of speech. Today, despite the inevitable local differences, all the islanders can generally understand each other's forms of Kreol. (For more information on language, see page 23. A list of useful Kreol words and phrases appears on page 368.)

in Seychelles. In Victoria, there is a Hindu temple and an Islamic mosque, while in recent years, the Bahá'í faith has become quite popular.

Family relationships

The Seychellois have a relaxed approach to marriage. Polygamy isn't practised, but it is common for couples to *kantmenm zot an menage*, in other words live together informally, often producing large families. It is not unusual for a man to drift away (a practice known as *marse marse*), set up a new relationship and father other children (although Seychelles' law

Palm Sunday Procession, Victoria.

Religion

Most Seychellois (around 82 percent) are Roman Catholics. Going to church is a social event, as well as a spiritual occasion, and an opportunity to get dressed up. Women compete in their colourful outfits, while older men wear long-sleeved white shirts as a mark of respect. You won't see anyone in shorts or skimpy beachwear, which are considered disrespectful. First holy communion is a major landmark in the life of a young Seychellois, and it is not unusual to see processions of little girls in frothy white lace dresses and formally attired little boys arriving at the cathedral in Victoria.

Anglicans, Seventh Day Adventists, Pentecostals and Jehovah's Witnesses are also represented

requires fathers to provide financial support for all their offspring). Sometimes, in later years, the wanderer returns to an earlier partner, to end his days in a more committed relationship. The reunited couple may even go so far as to have an elaborate and expensive wedding, with their children as pageboys and bridesmaids.

The family unit is female-dominated, with extended families often consisting of a mother and her children, some of whom will be adults with offspring of their own. Consequently children in such households tend to grow up with a great respect for their mothers, but less for their errant fathers, perhaps reflected in the traditional mourning period for parents: 18 to 24 months for a mother, nine to 12 months for a father.

Exorcising ghosts

Like the Malagasy people of Madagascar, the Seychellois have a healthy respect for ghosts and departed spirits, and death is treated very seriously. Modern Seychellois are perhaps no more superstitious than other peoples, but old traditions from Africa and Madagascar are still, to some extent, followed alongside Catholic rites. People still hold vigils at home for deceased loved ones, laying the body out in the best room of the house, with the head pointing towards the mountains and the feet towards the sea. In flickering candlelight, a solemn procession of visitors, family, acquaintances and the idly curious pass by the open coffin and sprinkle the body with holy water. The closest family and friends spend the whole night beside the body, but they certainly don't sit in silence. They play cards or dominoes, and make as much noise as possible to scare evil spirits away from their loved one and prevent them from stealing the body and turning it into a *dandosya* or zombie.

Funerals have always had a huge turnout, though sleek black hearses have now replaced the traditional handcarts that once conveyed the dead to church. A long trail of mourners follows the coffin and buses are often hired to bring the many guests to church.

Gris-gris

For generations, this blend of folklore, black magic and traditional medicine played an important part in people's day-to-day lives. Black magicians were once quite influential people and the power of gris-gris was greatly feared by the Roman Catholic Church and colonial administrators, who tried to stamp it out. It certainly still goes on, but like so many traditions, it is losing the hold on people's lives it once had.

The traditional theory is that *gris-gris* came with the slaves from Africa or Madagascar, but some experts claim that European beliefs in witchcraft also found their way into its practices. Two books on magic written in 1800 that came here from Europe were particularly influential. The spells and potions described in them became absorbed in local magic customs.

A *gris-gris* 'practitioner', known as a bonnonm or bonnfanm dibwa (man or woman of the woods), supposedly has the power to protect you from the evil eye, help you in your career or love life, or get revenge on your enemies. He or she might provide a love potion, a protective talisman or small package with bits of cooked food, iron, even urine and hair; or they might foretell your future using playing cards, tea leaves or by casting pebbles on a table.

A sound knowledge of herbal medicine is often combined with these more spurious talents, and the Seychelles flora is a veritable medicine chest. Seychellois were using the Madagascar periwinkle medicinally long before Western scientists used it in the treatment of childhood leukaemia, with spectacular results. Tea made from lemon grass to settle the stomach, *tokmarya* for sore throats, *montosyel* for hernias and bred mouroung

A Creole elder.

GHOSTS AND SUPERSTITIONS

The Seychellois revel in a good ghost story. Certain islands are said to be haunted: Ste Anne by a cruel French woman who had a slave girl beaten to death; Long Island by a Creole girl who drowned her child; Moyenne by an eccentric Englishwoman who lived there with her dogs. They are also renowned for their superstitions linked with good and bad luck, death and evil. It is said, for example, that bad luck will follow if you sweep the house after sunset; that a kestrel found roosting in the eaves of your house is a portent of death in the family; and that an unfamiliar voice in the dark should go unanswered – it could be a zombie.

leaves for liver complaints are just a few items from the herbalist's store cupboard.

Gris-gris is taken most seriously by older people, but younger people will certainly resort to a bonnonm, especially for the love potions. It is still a sensitive and secretive subject. Unless you were inquisitive and went out of your way to seek it out, it's unlikely that you would see any evidence of its existence.

Musical rhythms

Seychellois love to dance. Nowadays, it is most likely to be in a club to modern music, but traditional music is far from dead. The most commonly seen dance is the sega. In Seychelles, the sega is a flirtatious, light-hearted dance, less smoulderingly sexy than its Mauritian counterpart, the *sega typic* (see page 73). In fact, it is often performed by school children in dance competitions. It's not as easy as it looks. There is a definite knack to it and you need flexible hips. Men wear a long-sleeved white shirt, long black trousers and a colourful cummerbund, with perhaps a straw hat. Women dress in long, full, swirling skirts and bare feet are *de rigueur*. Although the movements are swaying and lascivious, dancers do not touch.

Heating Tanbour Moutya fire drums.

TRADITIONAL INSTRUMENTS

Sadly, the traditional instruments that once plucked out the rhythms and tunes for the sega and *moutya* dancers are no longer commonplace. These simply constructed instruments were introduced to Seychelles by the African and Malagasy slaves, who made them with whatever raw materials they could find. There are several stringed instruments, or zithers. The *zez* has one string and its sound box is a hollow dried out gourd. The string is plucked to produce music. The *bonm* is similar, but the string is attached to a wooden bow with a gourd on the end and played with a thin stick. The *mouloumpa* is a cross between a wind and a string instrument. It is made of a piece of bamboo with strings on the outside that the player plucks and blows down at the same time.

The most unusual of all these instruments is the *makalapo*. It is made of a string attached at one end to a sheet of tin half buried in the ground, and to a flexible stick a few feet away at the other. Notes are produced by plucking the string and their tone is varied by manipulating the stick to tighten or slacken the string. For percussion there are the skin drums, the *tam tam* and tambour, and the *kaskavel*, which is a small container filled with seeds or grit and shaken.

The *moutya* is more erotic and is unique to Seychelles. Invented by the slaves as a secret escape from the drudgery of plantation life, it was performed late at night in the forest. Colonial governors and bishops were outraged by its sexiness and tried to ban it (as they had tried to ban *gris-gris*). A description of a *moutya* from the 1930s reveals the attitude of the authorities: 'As soon as these drums are beaten with rhythmic measure the men and women dance back to back, occasionally turning round and facing each other while making suggestive signs. Compared to the *moutya*, the notorious *danse de ventre* [belly

set of dances modified from their formal origins in the courts of France: the *lavals* (waltz), *ekosez* (Scottish jig), *mazok* (mazurka), polka, *kontredans* (similar to a Scottish reel), *berlin* and *pas-dikat*. A *kanmtole* band must have at least a fiddle and a triangle, but can include banjos, accordions and a drum. The key band member is the *komandan*, who shouts instructions to the dancers in time with the music, in much the same way as a caller in a barn dance.

The dance shows laid on by the bigger hotels tend to revolve around sega. Only the more 'serious' cultural shows will include *moutya*, a more

Dancers at the Seychelles International Carnival of Victoria.

dance] is as innocent of offence as… a children's Christmas party.'

The dance begins with the men chanting, either a known song or an improvised one – usually a bawdy tale or a taunt aimed at a rival in love. In the old days, this would also have been an opportunity for slaves to vent their anger against the plantation owners. In due course, the drums begin the beat and the men approach the women of their choice, arms outstretched. The partners dance back-to-back with sensuous, shuffling movements, but again, never touch.

Both the sega and the *moutya* were of African origin, but from their European forebears, the Seychellois took the *kanmtole*, a dance tradition still very much alive. *Kanmtole* refers to a whole

sombre dance that doesn't lend itself so well to the glitz of a tourist spectacle. *Kanmtole* nights are often advertised. They are usually held at smaller hotels, local social centres or restaurants, and anyone going along would certainly be made welcome.

In recent years *Seggae*, a hybrid of sega and reggae, has caught on in Seychelles, and further afield in Europe. Groups such as Mersener and its lead singer Lyrical Sniper bring a whole new feel to sega with rap-like lyrics and electronic instruments. And listen out for the music of Seychelles' artist Sonny Morgan, who blends sega with different sounds such as pop and blues, and whose music is regularly played on the radio and in hotels.

An arts tour

Seychelles has an active arts scene, particularly nature-inspired batik, watercolours and craft, with numerous galleries and local artist studios to browse.

In the short time since the arrival of tourism, there has been an explosion in the arts and crafts output of Seychelles. Though the roots of the industry are not deep, they are uniquely Seychellois, drawing their inspiration from the dazzling colours and pristine nature of the environment. A tour of the numerous small art studios is a pleasant diversion from the beach and an opportunity to view paintings, prints, batiks and ornaments with little pressure to buy and, frequently, an opportunity to meet the artists themselves.

A good place to begin an arts tour of Mahé is the capital, Victoria, where there is no shortage of craft shops (see page 283). On the Bel Air road, north of Victoria, **Thoughts Stained Glass Studio** sells beautiful and colourful glass souvenirs of Seychelles.

Craft village

South of the capital on the east coast, the Craft Village is an essential port of call. At the entrance is **Maison Coco**, a shop dedicated to the coconut palm, housed in a building made of palm products. The range of goods includes leaves woven into bags and baskets, while the fibre that swathes the shoots, known as *tami*, is used to make various items including decorative stuffed fish, or wrappings for soaps perfumed with vanilla. The nut itself is used for napkin rings, candleholders, cups and trinket pots. Coconut oil is used to perfume soaps and bath oils. Inside the village, **The Natural Art Gallery** features works by local painters, including Barbara Jenson, Elizabeth Ragauin, Elizabeth Rouillon (who specialises in detailed watercolours of plants), etchings and vivid watercolours by George Camille, and prints by Christine Harter of local scenes. Nearby is the studio of **Colbert Nourrice**, one of the most innovative of Seychellois artists. His abstract works are a narrative on canvas, telling small anecdotes from his life and experiences almost in comic-strip form. One of his favourite themes is the local folklore character Soungoula, a tricky customer, always full of mischief.

Galleries and studios

Gerard Devoud has two art galleries, on the east coast at Les Mamelles and on the west opposite the entrance to Plantation Club. He uses light and colour broken into 'bits', creating mosaic-like landscapes and village scenes using watercolours.

The west coast of Mahé is the location for the studios of two of Seychelles' most famous creative geniuses, artist **Michael Adams** and sculptor **Tom Bowers** (see page 289). **Donald Adelaide** is another artist based on the west coast. He produces bright, piecemeal images of the island and island life, mostly in watercolour. He has a studio near Harvey's Café

One of George Camille's vivid creations.

where he sells prints and originals. Almost opposite Harvey's Café is the turning to Anse Gouvernement. It's worth a detour to see the distinctive wood sculptures on display at **Studio Antonio**, shortly before the beach on the right (see page 289).

On Praslin, there are many small galleries, including **Cap Samy Art Gallery** at Baie Ste Anne, and **George Camille Art Gallery** at Côte d'Or. On La Digue, the two most interesting art studios lie close to each other, near to L'Union Estate. **Green Gecko Art & Craft Shop** features a variety of local artists, while **Barbara Jenson**n's studio displays various works by just one artist, including original pieces in aluminium and acrylics. Silhouette Island is the home of **Ron Gerlach**, who produces authentic batiks celebrating the natural history of Seychelles.

Hawksbill turtles are an endangered species.

PRESERVING NATURE

The natural history of Seychelles echoes the ancient land link between Africa and Asia; much of the environment is still in relatively pristine condition.

Islands are laboratories of evolution. Nature's experiments have been going on for a longer period in Seychelles than in any other group of ocean islands, so it is no surprise that such a unique assemblage of flora and fauna should have evolved here. The roots of some species can be traced back to Africa, Madagascar, Asia and even to Australasia, originating from a time when all these land masses were linked in the supercontinent of Gondwanaland, before continental drift cast them apart.

Bats, tortoises and turtles

Seychelles was isolated in mid-ocean long before mammals appeared on earth. No mammals ever reached here by natural means except for those with the power of flight, namely the bat. Of the two endemic species, the sheath-tailed bat and the Seychelles fruit bat, the latter is by far the most common. It is one of the few creatures to have benefited from the arrival of humans and the consequent proliferation of fruit trees. Not so beneficial from the bats' point of view is the culinary speciality, curried fruit bat, a local favourite which often pops up on restaurant menus. Despite the Seychellois' taste for them, however, bats remain very common and their noisy squabbling in the trees at night is one of the islands' characteristic sounds.

With no mammals for competition, Seychelles became the last Kingdom of Reptiles. The estuarine crocodile was an early casualty of human settlement, but the giant tortoise still thrives. Aldabra has the world's largest population, with around 87,000 animals. Giant tortoises occupied islands across the Indo-Pacific for millions of years, safe from the mammals that came to dominate the continents. Their

A brown noddy on Bird Island.

PROTECTED AREAS

Literally 1,000 miles (1,600km) from anywhere – India to the north, Africa to the west, Sri Lanka to the east and Madagascar to the south – the Seychelles islands were uninhabited until the late 18th century. While the natural beauty of other Indian Ocean islands was gradually destroyed, that of the Seychelles has been carefully preserved. There are many protected areas where nature lovers can marvel at unspoilt flora, fauna and marine life: the Morne Seychellois National Park, Mahé; the Vallée de Mai, Praslin; the Veuve Reserve, La Digue; and special reserves on the islands of Cousin, Aride and Aldabra.

waterproof exoskeletons, ability to survive for weeks without food and the female's inbuilt mechanism for storing sperm made them ideal candidates for ocean transport. The luckier ones that had been swept away by the tide from the shores of the mainland were washed up on remote tropical islands. This happened rarely enough for unique island races to evolve. Sadly, most of these are now extinct, victims of human exploitation. It was thought the granitic island form had suffered the same fate until the discovery of some unusual tortoises. These were brought to Silhouette by the Nature Protec-

The tortoise would then be slaughtered at the wedding feast. This tradition has died out, though many Seychellois still keep a few lumbering giants as pets.

Likewise, the future of turtles is slowly brightening. In the past they were slaughtered mainly for their 'tortoiseshell', which was converted into jewellery and other trinkets for sale to tourists. Thankfully, the authorities recognised that live turtles have a higher value, enhancing the reputation of the country while encouraging ecotourism. The sale of all tortoiseshell products is now banned.

Mealtime for a giant tortoise on Corieuse Island.

tion Trust of Seychelles for captive breeding (see page 304). It is possible that they retain some characteristics of two granite island forms of tortoise, the Seychelles giant tortoise and Arnold's tortoise. However, most scientists believe there was only one species throughout Seychelles, the Aldabra Giant Tortoise, which survives in the granitics (Curieuse, Frégate, Cousin and Cousine) in several introduced wild populations. Many are also kept in pens in hotel gardens, at the Botanical Gardens and elsewhere, so there are plenty of opportunities to see this lovable Seychelles symbol.

Once it was traditional to present a baby tortoise to a newborn girl and raise the animal as a family pet until the girl grew up and married.

Two species breed here – the hawksbill turtle and the green turtle. Remarkably, the granitic islands are the only place in the world where hawksbill turtles come up to breed in the daytime. Green turtles occasionally nest in the granitic islands but their stronghold is Aldabra where around 4,000 females haul themselves ashore each year to breed. In the past, they were heavily exploited for their meat and, although poaching still poses a threat, they have escaped the near total extermination suffered elsewhere. Aldabra is one of the few places on earth where turtles, classed as among the most endangered of creatures under the Convention on International Trade in Endangered Species (CITES), are increasing in number.

The call of the male Aldabra tortoise is said to be the loudest noise in the reptile kingdom. It is, in fact, a seduction technique – the actual mating is a silent affair.

the higher hills. Another species, the croaking carrycot frog, has evolved the surprising habit of carrying its tadpoles on its back. Amazingly, the only other places frogs do this are New Zealand and tropical South America – opposite ends of the former super-continent.

Unique reptiles

For sheer quantity of reptiles, there is nowhere quite like the seabird islands of Seychelles, particularly Cousin, Cousine and Aride, which have a greater concentration of these beasts than anywhere else on earth. It

Land and sea birds

The lure of birdwatching in Seychelles is not the number of species. You may see more varieties in a single day in East Africa than in a lifetime in Seychelles. Also, island birds tend to be less colourful than their continental cousins.

A green gecko lizard on La Digue.

is partly thanks to the seabirds that the lizards survive in such large numbers. They feed on eggs or chicks left unguarded or a catch that has been dropped. Most reptiles found here are unique to Seychelles, including the Seychelles skink, Wright's skink and several species of green gecko.

One of the characteristics of ocean islands is the absence of amphibians. Once again, Seychelles is an exception to the rule. The islands support 13 amphibian species in all, 12 of which are unique to Seychelles; one of these was described for the first time in 2002. Among the frog species is the minuscule pygmy piping frog. Though difficult to spot, its high pitched squeak is often the only sound to be heard in

However, what they lack in variety and spectacular plumage they more than make up for in their rarity value.

Successful programmes have been implemented to restore the fortunes of two of the rarest birds in the world, the Seychelles warbler and Seychelles magpie-robin. Programmes are also underway to study, protect and reverse the historical decline of other species. This includes probably the most beautiful of the endemic birds of Seychelles, the Seychelles black paradise flycatcher. It is the symbol of La Digue, where a special nature reserve has been established for it. The male is staggeringly beautiful with its shiny black plumage and long tail feathers. Though less spectacular, the female is also an attractive bird, chestnut above, white below, with a black head.

The enigmatic Seychelles scops owl occurs only on Mahé, its population concentrated in the Morne Seychellois National Park, while the white eye survives on five islands. Both are among the rarest birds in the world. Praslin, too, has its own special bird, the Seychelles black parrot. Its piercing whistle is often the only sound echoing around the Vallée de Mai. One of the world's smallest birds of prey, and the only bird of prey in the granitics, is the Seychelles kestrel. It is found mainly on Mahé with smaller numbers on Praslin and elsewhere, often announcing its presence with its far-reaching 'ti-ti-ti-ti' cry (its name in Kreol is *katiti*). The Seychelles fody (*toktok* in Kreol) survives on five islands, including Aride and Cousin, the easiest places to spot it.

More common, but also unique to the granitic islands, are the Seychelles blue pigeon, Seychelles cave swiftlet, Seychelles bulbul and Seychelles sunbird. Even the laziest of bird-watchers can spot them, possibly in their hotel grounds, but certainly in Victoria's Botanical Gardens in the early morning or late afternoon.

Birds on the beach at Praslin.

SAVED FROM EXTINCTION

Conservation success stories are few and far between but Seychelles has more than its fair share. Take the humble Seychelles warbler. By 1960, it stood on the threshold of annihilation. An international appeal was launched and in 1968 Cousin was placed under the protection of the Royal Society for Nature Conservation and BirdLife International. The warblers thrived. By the 1980s numbers reached around 350. However, it was too early to take the species off the critical list so long as they remained confined to one island, where a local disaster might threaten their survival. In 1988, 29 birds were transferred to Aride. It was hoped they might settle to breed around the usual time in January. The birds had other ideas. With virtually unlimited space and food supply they bred year-round and by 1999 there were almost 2,000 birds. With smaller colonies also established on Cousine and Denis, the species is now one of the few to be taken off the Red Data list of endangered species.

The Seychelles magpie-robin is now receiving similar treatment. Once widespread in the granitic islands, its tame and trusting behaviour meant it fell victim to man and introduced predators. Down to fewer than 20 birds on Frégate, a BirdLife recovery programme was launched. Cousin, Aride, Cousine and Denis now host breeding populations and numbers have increased to almost 200 birds.

Aldabra Atoll is particularly rich in avifauna (see page 344). This World Heritage Site is home to the last surviving flightless bird of the Indian Ocean, the Aldabra rail. Aldabra is also famous for its seabird colonies, including the world's second largest colony of frigate birds. Closer to the main islands, there are more spectacular seabird colonies, notably Aride (10 breeding species), Cousin (seven breeding species) and Bird Island, named in honour of its million-plus sooty terns that return to breed annually between April and October. The attraction here is the sheer number of birds competing for every inch of space.

Yet the Seychelles species list contains far more visiting birds than breeding ones, most of which turn up between October and December.

Plant life

The large-scale deforestation that laid bare almost every tropical island during the age of exploration did not pass Seychelles by altogether but, unlike most islands, the scars have healed. Although virgin forest is now confined to the higher areas of Mahé and Silhouette, and the Vallée de Mai on Praslin, there are no large expanses of wasteland, no vast areas of cultivation or big sugar cane plantations. Seychelles is like one gigantic botanical garden. Today, there are well over 1,000 species of plants in the granitic Seychelles. About 250 occur naturally, of which around 75 are unique to the islands. Symbols of the tropics such as bougainvillaea, frangipani and hibiscus appear in almost every garden. The colourful flame tree and fruit trees such as breadfruit and jackfruit are common. Coconuts, once confined to the beach crest, have been planted in huge numbers further inland. In the coral islands, as with the birds, there is a much smaller variety of species, but again Aldabra is an exception. Here, a remarkably diverse flora includes about 40 endemics.

Some of the endemic plants of Seychelles are so rare they are only found in a few remote locations, such as the *bwa-d-fer* and *bwa-d-nat* trees, once prized for shipbuilding. The jellyfish tree has apparently always been rare, but still clings to survival on a few Mahé hilltops. The insect-eating Seychelles pitcher plant, though not so rare, can be elusive. Other unique plants are more common, including the beautiful wild vanilla, its leafless stems climbing over bushes.

No one can fail to notice the majestic palms of Seychelles. There are six species unique to the granitics, including the fabled coco de mer, confined

to Praslin and Curieuse. The female tree has the largest, heaviest seed in the world, a double nut with an uncanny resemblance to the female pelvic region. The enormous catkin of the male tree also has to be seen to be believed! Certainly, some male and female toilets in Seychelles bearing the nut and the catkin as symbols to tell them apart, leave no visitor in any doubt as to which is which.

For those able to drag themselves away from the beaches, there are several well-marked trails where many of the plants of Seychelles can be seen. More sedentary visitors may take a trip to Victoria's Botanical Gardens, while a visit to

Pitcher Plants at Mount Copolia in Mahe.

Vallée de Mai is virtually mandatory for any visitor to Praslin. However, such is the profusion of life in the hot and humid tropical climate of Seychelles, that even a stroll round a hotel garden can be very rewarding.

It is fortuitous that so many of the flora and fauna of Seychelles have survived to a more enlightened age in which their intrinsic value is appreciated. This is partly due to the fact that when compared to most other places in the world, Seychelles was settled comparatively recently. Thankfully, the government was quick to recognise how essential it was to protect its country's natural assets. Today, more than 40 percent of its land mass is given some form of legal protection.

Big eye and striped grunts.

UNDERWATER WORLD

Exploring the waters of the Indian Ocean,
where coral reefs support spectacular fish,
is like swimming in a giant aquarium.

The islands of the Seychelles provide visitors with access to some of the best protected ocean areas in the world, thanks to a long history of conservation which began with the establishment of the Ste Anne Marine National Park in the 1970s.

This enlightened and far-sighted approach has paid dividends in terms of the range and abundance of marine life found. Because spear-fishing and other destructive fishing techniques commonly used in other island states have long been banned, tourists are often impressed to find that fish species that are normally shy and elusive are easy to find and apparently visitor friendly.

Exploring the deep

Most hotels and resorts rent out snorkelling equipment (though the quality varies) or you can buy your own from one of the dive centres selling masks, snorkels and fins at very reasonable prices. A number of tour operators and some private companies offer snorkelling excursions by boat to favourite spots such as Ste Anne Marine National Park, Baie Ternay Marine Reserve and St Pierre in Curieuse Marine Park. These trips may be for a half or full day and many include lunch at one of the renowned Creole restaurants to be found on the smaller islands.

For scuba divers, Seychelles is a well-established world-class diving destination both in terms of diving conditions and professionally run diving operations. Most diving centres belong to the Association of Professional Divers, Seychelles (APDS), which sets additional standards for the operation and provision of diving services. Their members also support a number of marine-related environmental and conservation projects, such as the Whale Shark Monitoring Programme run locally by the Marine

Scissortail sergeant alongside diver, Ste Anne Marine Park.

GENTLE GIANTS

The largest fish in all the oceans is the whale shark, found around the coastal waters of Seychelles. This harmless plankton feeder can grow to a length of 18 metres (59 ft) and weigh over 25 tonnes. Until recently, these sharks were not regularly hunted; now, however, there is a big demand from the Far Eastern restaurant trade, particularly for their fins. Little is known of this impressive fish except that, like many sharks, it is slow growing. Several treaties recognise the need to protect sharks, but international cooperation is lacking. The whale shark has been listed on two treaties, the Convention of Migratory Species in 1999 and CITES in 2002.

Conservation Society of Seychelles, which tracks the numbers and migration of whale sharks. For those who have never tried diving, the shallow waters and rich coral reefs around Seychelles islands provide the perfect opportunity to learn, combining safe and enjoyable diving conditions with world-class diving instruction.

> *If you are unlucky enough to tread on a sea urchin, rub papaya onto the wound: the juice of the fruit contains an enzyme that helps dissolve the spines.*

Learners and pros

APDS centres offering the PADI programme introduce complete beginners to scuba diving, starting with a tutorial and confined water skill session prior to the first shallow open water

A scuba diver sees a school of fish.

dive. They all offer four-day courses culminating in the internationally recognised PADI Open Water Diver certificate. For already qualified divers they also offer a number of advanced and supervisory courses right through to those aspiring to become Dive Instructors. There are dive centres on Mahé, Praslin and La Digue, as well as on the outer island of Desroches.

Diving is possible all year round, with the calmest sea conditions and best visibility being in March, April and May and then in October and November. Visitors hoping for the thrill of diving with a whale shark should consider July and August or November and December. Either March/April or October/November is when the APDS hosts the annual SUBIOS Seychelles' Festival Of The Sea, where some of the world's top underwater photographers, film-makers and conservationists present a programme of films and lectures to visitors and residents.

Seychelles seascape

Whether you're an experienced or first-time diver, Seychelles has so much to offer. The unique granite rock formation of the northerly island group, known as the Inner Islands, creates underwater conditions that are much more varied than might be expected, supporting a prodigious variety of marine life. The diversity is further broadened

CLEANING SERVICES

Apart from moray eels and octopuses, the gaps and crevices in the granite rocks house creatures that would happily feature on the moray's diet sheet, especially crabs, shrimps and lobsters, but one group most closely associated with the moray is the brightly coloured cleaner shrimp. This little creature performs a valuable service not just for morays but for many fish species, cleaning parasites off skin, scales and even from between their teeth. The shrimp's bright red and white banding and long white antennae act as an advertisement for their cleaning services and seem to guarantee that they will not be eaten by their larger clients.

Another creature offering cleaning services to reef inhabitants is the little striped cleaner wrasse, whose vertical black and blue stripes are easily identified. Wrasse are very territorial and set up shop by particular rocks or coral heads where they bob and weave in a characteristic display to attract business. The careful observer will be able to see these little fish working away deep inside the mouths or gills of larger reef fish in apparent security.

Closer to the shore, meanwhile, the long sausage-shaped sea cucumbers scattered across the shallow sands keep the sea bed clean, as they feed on detritus and algae in the sand's surface layer.

by the coral atolls to the south, which include Aldabra, the world's largest raised coral atoll and a designated Unesco World Heritage Site.

The water temperature, which is somewhere between 26 and 30°C (79–86°F), traditionally promoted the prolific growth of sponges, corals and invertebrates, which painted the granite walls and canyons in a kaleidoscope of colours. Unfortunately huge chunks of reefs were decimated by coral bleaching in 1998, when El Niño caused sea temperatures to rise dramatically. It has taken years to recover, with some areas still affected. Groups such as Nature Seychelles are monitoring reefs and growing coral in underwater nurseries, which is then transplanted to degraded sites. The underwater terrain of the Inner Islands is a mirror image of the landscape above the surface, characterised by dramatic granite formations. The rocks and boulders form natural gullies and crevices that are prime real estate for many marine creatures. A common inhabitant of these nooks and crannies is the moray eel, a species with an undeserved notoriety. Its reputation stems mainly from the habit of greeting visitors with its toothy jaws gaping in an apparently threatening manner. But appearances are deceptive. These eels live quiet lives, bobbing about harmlessly in their crevices. There is little water flow and so they have to gulp water over their gills in order to breathe, hence the gaping jaws. Morays are successful hunters of fish, crabs and snails, but have little interest in bigger fare.

Another crevice inhabitant occasionally found around the reef during the day is the octopus. This, the most highly developed of all the molluscs, is an extremely active predator, feeding mainly at night on other molluscs, crabs and small fish, catching prey with the muscular suckers lined along its eight tentacles. The octopus is also a master of disguise, especially the marbled octopus commonly found on the granitic reefs. Its skin has special cells which allow it to change colour and alter its texture.

Distinctive fish

Visitors to Seychelles are always impressed by the sheer volume of fish encountered. The brightly coloured butterfly and angelfish are often the most apparent but with a little practice you can become familiar with the extreme body shapes of some species. The elongated cylindrical forms of the trumpet fish and flutemouths are an easy first step; however, discerning between the two

can take patience – the trumpet has a fan-like tail and is generally seen in several colour forms on the coral reef, while the flutemouth is normally seen just below the water's surface and has a whip-like tail.

Another easy to distinguish group are box fish and pufferfish, the former having angular cube-like bodies with apparently undersized fins while the puffers resemble deflated tropical fruit swimming over the reef – they only 'puff' up if harassed or cornered. Both these groups have teeth sharp enough to cut through coral and can deliver a deep and painful bite if tormented.

Yellowmouth sweetlips, Aldabra Atoll.

Lionfish and their cousins the scorpionfish are also fairly easy to identify; lionfish by their dramatic array of long feather- or whip-like spines on their back and side fins; scorpionfish by their camouflaged and bottom-dwelling habit. The problem with scorpionfish is actually finding them to begin with.

Once the odd-shaped fish species have been identified you're still left with a bewildering array of 'fish-shaped' fish. Of the reef dwellers, the majority belong to the parrotfish or wrasse families. Parrotfish come in a huge range of sizes and colours but all exhibit the characteristic horny coral-cutting beak, like that of a real parrot. Wrasse, an equally large group, have no such distinguishing characteristics. Keen divers and snorkellers should invest in a fish spotter's guide to identify fish beyond this level.

Outer island terrain

Visitors to the Outer Islands will notice a distinct difference in the underwater terrain to that of the Inner Islands. These islands and atolls are either large sandbanks, such as Bird Island and African Banks, or coral atolls such as Aldabra. The coralline islands often have dramatic walls, which plunge from the surface into deep water and thus have a very different range of inhabitants. The deeper sections of these walls are

Blacktip reef shark, Aldabra Atoll.

characterised by intricate gorgonian fan corals supported by a springy backbone of horn-like material. They grow at right angles to the current so that they can filter out food particles from the water as it runs along the reef's perimeter. Keen underwater photographers home in on these fans as they support their own array of co-inhabitants, ranging from small cowry shells and spider crabs to their own specialised, if somewhat small, predator. The long-nosed hawkfish uses the fan corals as a lookout point from which to capture the small crustaceans on which it feeds.

Big fish

The other attraction of these remote island spots is the chance to encounter larger fish and pelagic

Some fish have the ability to change sex: parrotfish, anthias and wrasse start as females and can become males as needed.

species such as barracuda and tuna. Diving and snorkelling along the vertical walls of some islands almost guarantees the sighting of the dog tooth tuna, a real warrior of the deep. These large powerful fish swim with a slightly open mouth proudly displaying a set of canine-like teeth; their large black eyes seem to follow your every move. Shark sightings are another highlight, most commonly blacktip reef sharks. Larger specics, such as bull and tiger sharks, patrol the Indian Ocean but snorkellers and divers rarely come into contact with them. Sadly, two fatal shark attacks did occur in Seychelles at Anse Lazio in the north of Praslin in 2011; however these were the first in 50 years and numerous measures have been taken since, including underwater nets, to ensure swimmers' safety. If in doubt, it's recommended to stick to water-based activities off beaches protected by a coral reef (Anse Lasio isn't).

As there is comparatively little fishing here, the marine ecosystems in the outer regions are under less pressure and should have more abundant marine life. The food chain supports a larger number of predators and on many reefs the various species of grouper, such as the rare potato cod, are typically abundant. These large fish can grow to well over 1 metre (3ft) in length and are characterised by large, black potato-like blotches on their grey bodies. The species has a reputation for being aggressive, which may or may not be deserved; however, any fish of this size should be treated with respect.

Turtle spotting

Turtles are another common sight on the Outer Islands. While hawksbill turtles are the predominant species of the Inner Islands, as you travel south the green turtle becomes more common. Green turtles are generally larger then their sharp-billed cousins and have a broader head and less pronounced bill. A third species, the loggerhead turtle, is rarely seen; while it seems to have a blend of characteristics from the other two species, it can normally be recognised by its massive head, large eyes and immensely thick and powerful beak, which is much more heavy-duty than that of either of the common species.

Top dive sites

Seychelles offers a wealth of world-class underwater experiences, from wreck and drift dives to encounters with reef sharks, stingrays and even whale sharks.

There are numerous world-class dive sites in Seychelles. The following are the top Inner Island sites as rated by resident divers. Apart from Ave Maria on Praslin, most of these are only suitable for experienced divers. However, the list is by no means comprehensive. The dive centres on Mahé, Praslin and La Digue include many other interesting sites in their programme, suitable for novices and experienced divers alike. For more information on diving and dive centres in the Inner Islands, see Travel Tips, Activities.

Shark Bank

A granite plateau with large boulders and a depth of between 20 and 35 metres (65–115ft), this outcrop between northwest Mahé and Silhouette island is a focal point for schooling fish and predators. The rocks are renowned for sightings of large marbled stingrays and whale sharks. A deep site which can have strong currents, it is suitable for experienced divers.

L'Îlot

This classic granite island lies off the northwestern tip of Mahé. Thanks to its position at the confluence of the east and west coast currents, its waters support a plethora of marine life. It is one of the few Inner Island sites with good soft coral formations and there's a chance of spotting schooling fish and whale sharks (October to December). Although the maximum depth is only 23 metres (75ft), currents and patchy visibility mean that in adverse conditions divers need to have suitable experience.

Brissare Rocks

A granite massif 5km (3 miles) off the northeast coast of Mahé, this site attracts many schools of fish including snappers and Napoleon wrasse, plus Hawksbill turtles, moray eels and reef sharks. With depths of down to 20 metres (65ft) this site is suitable for all but novice divers.

The Wreck of the Ennerdale

The remains of this stricken tanker lie 8km (5 miles) off the northeast coast of Mahé at a depth of 30 metres (98ft). Due to the distance from shore and its exposed position, the wreck is not often visited and so hosts good marine life. The structures are encrusted with corals and invertebrates but over the passage of time metal fatigue and corrosion have begun to compact some sections of the wreck. When conditions are good, this is an excellent dive for experienced divers, with schooling fish, shark and ray prospects.

Marianne

The southern tip of Marianne Island is a rarely visited site. The terrain of jagged granite rocks and giant boulders offers refuge for many large fish and it is the

There are some excellent sites to see schooling fish.

seasonal home for a group of grey reef sharks which, for some unknown reason, are all female. An exciting dive to 27 metres (88ft), for experienced divers.

Ave Maria

Praslin's version of L'Îlot; this granite group is renowned for a broad range of fish species as well as regular shark and stingray sightings. With a maximum depth of 26 metres (85ft), in good conditions this site is suitable for all divers.

The Outer Islands

The Desroches Drop is one of the best-known sites (see page 338), but anyone lucky enough to dive off Alphonse, Astove, Cosmoledo and Aldabra will find the richness of marine life incomparable.

FISHING

Fish and fishing are dear to the souls of
Seychellois, hardly surprising when they're
ringed by waters so rich with marine life.

Fish is the staple diet of all Seychellois and,
indeed, quite a few tourists. The bounty of
the Indian Ocean includes a tremendous
variety of fish, excellent for both sport fishing
and the dinner table. There are many game fishing boats to serve the tourist industry, equipped
with the finest fishing gear around. Fly-fishing
is a relatively new sport in Seychelles, following
the discovery of unexploited grounds, described
by specialists as among the best in the world.
Indeed, Seychelles holds world records for both
fly-fishing and game fishing.

Big game fishing

The majority of game fishing boats operate out
of Mahé. However, with the growth of tourism on Praslin and La Dîgue, these islands also
have a number of good boats available. Each of
the resorts on Silhouette, Frégate, Bird, Denis
(a popular venue for serious big game fishermen), Desroches and Alphonse also have boats.
Most charter boats fish exclusively by trolling
(drawing bait through the water with rod and
line), as this is the best way to catch the finest
game fish. Tag and release is favoured by some
operators and, if you believe in promoting this
technique, it is as well to discuss it in advance.

The quality of fishing will depend partly
on weather conditions, but the best fishing
grounds are at the drop-off at the edge of the
Seychelles Plateau (up to 32km/20 miles offshore), within easy reach of all the granitic
islands: bigeye tuna, dogfish tuna and yellow
fin tuna all inhabit the edge of the Seychelles
Bank; sailfish are commonly caught in waters
between Mahé and Silhouette; dorado can be
caught over the Bank in season; and barracuda,
jobfish (*zob*), even sharks are sometimes caught
on trolling lures.

*Big game fishing is a popular activity in the ocean around
the Seychelles.*

Though some fish – tuna and bonito, for
example – can be caught all year round, others come and go according to the season. The
best time of year for catching sailfish is during
the southeast monsoon, from June onwards.
Though dorado can be caught all year round,
it is most commonly seen between January and
September.

Kingfish, also known as wahoo, are most
plentiful from January to March, and trevally
(*karang*) from November to December. Huge
marlin weighing in at 150kg (330 lb) or more
can be caught year round, including blue,
striped and black marlin, but they are encountered far less frequently than sailfish.

Bear in mind that sea conditions can be rough during the southeast monsoon (June to September). Larger boats afford a more stable platform from which to fish but, unless you are sharing the cost with other people, this can be expensive, as the bigger the boat, the bigger the expense.

For the real enthusiast, live-aboard charters are available and may be customised to take into account the needs both of the fisherman and family members who may have other priorities, such as exploring the islands.

For details on live-aboard charters and game fishing specialists see Travel Tips, Activities.

Fly-fishing in St François

Seychelles offers world-class fly-fishing, primarily for bonefish and trevally. A few may be caught at Denis Island, but the best place by far is in the St François lagoon, which can be reached via the nearby Alphonse Island Resort (see page 341). St François is a natural reservoir that remains virtually unexploited. The resort is trying to keep it that way by restricting numbers to a maximum of 10 anglers per week. Hooks are barbless and all fish caught are released. Anglers are transported to the lagoon on two mother boats then transferred to flat boats (two fishermen per boat), which, depending on the state of tide, can travel throughout the lagoon, even in shallow water.

It is nothing remarkable for a reasonably good fly-fisherman to catch more than 50 fish in a day, while beginners can catch as many as 20. The average bonefish caught here weighs 2–3kg (5–7 lb) though they can weigh up to 7kg (15 lb). Not surprisingly, St François has claimed several world records.

Other fish caught here in the traditional way include small hammerhead shark, lemon shark, bigeye and barracuda. In 2002, fly-fishing operators at Alphonse became the first in the world to pioneer a technique for catching milkfish, a fearsome fighting fish despite its innocuous name.

Bottom fishing

Bottom fishing may lack the excitement of the chase involved in game and fly-fishing, but if it's dinner you're after, fishing with lines, lead weight and natural bait is a great way to get it. Local fishermen traditionally fish by this technique, baiting lines with crabs, shellfish, squid, mackerel or other fresh fish, and using two or three hooks.

The most sought-after of the 200 or so species of fish that can be caught on lines include red snapper (*bourzwa*) and grouper (*vye*). They feature on menus in most of the major hotels and restaurants, and are among the tastiest fish you can eat here.

Apart from in the Marine National Parks, where fishing is prohibited, you can fish almost anywhere. Enquire locally about renting a little boat and if you don't have your own equipment, you should be able to pick up what you need in Victoria. If in doubt, ask a local fisherman for advice.

A fly fisherman with bluefin trevally, off Alphonse Island.

LUCRATIVE WATERS

In 1977, the Seychelles Exclusive Economic Zone was established, giving the country control of 370km (200 nautical miles) of ocean around its shores. Commercial exploitation of these waters, which are rich in tuna fish, has proved lucrative, and Victoria port, which has its own tuna processing plants, throbs with activity. About 40,000 tonnes of fish make a huge contribution to the Seychelles economy each year. In November and December, huge schools of mackerel come close inshore at Beau Vallon on Mahé. They are harvested daily, but because they are so plentiful the market price drops dramatically at this time of year.

A Creole fish barbecue on the beach at sunset.

CREOLE CUISINE

Seychelles cuisine is rooted in its history and geography, from the riches of the sea to the tasty tropical spices.

With the exception of the family pig, a clutter of chickens kept behind the house and a few cattle, there has never been a tradition of rearing livestock in Seychelles because of the limited land available. Meat was only served on special occasions. The ocean has always been the main food supplier, and little has changed. Today, the Seychellois are among the biggest per capita consumers of fish in the world.

Roadside display of tropical fruit near Grand Anse.

Fish and shellfish

Seychellois love fish; but not just any old fish. They have such a bounty of marine life around their islands that they can afford to be choosy. For example, the meaty tuna known locally as bonito can make a delicious curry, but most Seychellois look down on it as inferior and feed it to their dogs. They love the firm, white, flaky flesh of the *bourzwa* or red snapper, which is left whole but scored with long slits on both sides that are stuffed with ginger, garlic, chilli, onions and other spices. It is then wrapped in banana leaf (for purists) or tin foil and cooked over charcoal. Many Seychellois consider the finest meat from a red snapper is to be found in the head, and make good use of it in fish soup. Mackerel is also grilled in a parcel over hot coals, or on bamboo skewers, and drizzled with freshly squeezed lime to keep the flesh moist. *Zob* (another type of snapper) and *karang* (trevally) are served as steaks.

Parrotfish is put into fish stews, or battered for a Seychelles slant on the British favourite, fish and chips. Steaks of tuna, kingfish and swordfish are marinated in oil and spices then grilled on the barbecue. Shark meat is grated with garlic, ginger, *bilimbi* (a sour fruit), lime, onions and turmeric, then stir fried until it looks like yellow desiccated coconut. This dish is known as shark chutney. Sailfish is cut wafer thin and smoked, to produce a delicacy every bit as good as smoked salmon, delicious on crusty bread with salad.

Shellfish are also popular in Seychellois cuisine. The favourites are tektek and palourd. Tekteks are winkle-like shells collected fresh from the sandy beaches and put into soup. It is not uncommon, even on busy Beau Vallon beach, to see a Seychellois woman, often assisted by a couple of her young children, stooped over the sand at the point where the waves lap the shore. As the water recedes it uncovers the tektek, which quickly burrow out of sight, pursued by a darting hand.

By contrast, *palourd* are found on muddy shores such as in the estuarine area north of Victoria's Inter-Island Quay. They are similar to cockles and delicious when cooked in herbs and garlic butter.

The superb local prawns offered in most restaurants are a relatively new addition to the local diet. Prawns do not occur naturally in sufficient numbers around Seychelles to be worth harvesting. However, there is now a farm on Coetivy Island producing both for the local and export markets. The prawns are excellent, particularly the large ones, grilled in garlic butter, in a traditional Seychellois curry or in sweet and sour sauce.

Hot and spicy

Indian and Chinese cuisines have not influenced Seychellois cooking as much as in the Mascarenes. Most restaurants specialise in Creole cooking and seafood. However, one Indian dish Seychelles has taken and made very much its own is curry. A Seychelles curry (usually fish, but also, commonly, chicken, pork, goat or beef) is simply crammed with flavours, and is hot! An exception to this rule is the *kari koko zourit*, a mild octopus curry with creamy coconut milk. How they get the octopus so tender is kept a closely guarded secret by some; others will happily confess the secret is to cook your octopus in a pressure cooker. Whatever the truth, when cooked properly, it comes out more tender than

Grilled goatfish at Lanbousir Restaurant.

CONSIGNED TO HISTORY

Seabird eggs were once of great importance to the Seychellois, simply because the annual bounty of eggs was a welcome variation in an otherwise monotonous diet. Egg exploitation is now controlled, in an attempt to ensure the survival of the sooty tern colonies, but a seabird egg omelette is still considered a delicacy. Turtles and tortoises were also eaten on special occasions. Traditionally, a baby tortoise was bought on the birth of a daughter and kept until the girl's wedding day, when it would be eaten at the wedding breakfast. This practice is now illegal. Both the giant tortoise and the turtle are protected species.

chicken, melting in the mouth.

Spicy local sausages figure in a local speciality, sausage and lentil stew. Although there are *tenrecs* on the islands (small mammals similar to hedgehogs in appearance), originally introduced from Madagascar as food, Seychellois no longer eat them. They occasionally eat fruit bat, caught by hanging nets close to the fruit trees where the animals feed.

As for accompaniments, be warned, Seychellois love their chillies hot. The tiny ones are the hottest. To the average Western palate a single seed can set the mouth on fire, yet Seychellois think nothing of eating them whole or ladling copious amounts of the minced chilli in vinegar that comes separately in a little dish onto their meal.

Vegetables and salads

Rice (plain, white, boiled) is the staple, but you will occasionally be offered breadfruit, a versatile potato-like 'fruit' served up as crispy chips, boiled and mashed, or stewed in coconut milk and sugar to make a gooey dessert. Best of all is baked breadfruit, the perfect complement to any beach barbecue. It is put whole among the burning coals until black on the outside and tender on the inside, then cut into piping hot slices and served with melted butter. Local legend has it that if you eat breadfruit, you'll be sure to return to Seychelles.

Preparing tropical fruit juice along La Retraite road.

CRACKING COCONUTS

Many a tourist works up a sweat trying to crack a coconut found at the roadside by hurling it against a rock or attacking it with a small penknife. It doesn't work. To remove the thick fibrous husk that protects the nut, most Seychellois have a sharpened spike stuck in the ground. The husk of the coconut is impaled on this and worked loose. It takes an islander a few seconds, but for the novice a little practice is required. On some excursions you may be offered *koko tann*, a green coconut with the top lopped off so you can drink the milk (refreshing, but an acquired taste). The thin jelly-like flesh of the unformed nut is delicious.

There is not a great deal of variety in the vegetable department. It is not easy to grow them in Seychelles due to the limited amount of flat land and the relatively poor soil. Exceptions include aubergines (usually served as deep-fried fritters), watercress and the tasty spinach-like *bred*. Avocados are abundant in season and salads are more than just the token lettuce leaf. Any true Creole spread will come with a range of so-called chutneys – finely grated pawpaw, mango or *fisiter* (golden apple) with onion, lime juice and pepper. They make a refreshing and cooling addition to a spicy meal.

Starters on a Creole menu usually include octopus salad, raw fish marinated in lime juice, and *palmis* salad. This became known as millionaire's salad because the whole tree had to be sacrificed to obtain the shoot. Conservation legislation now protects this unique majestic palm and today the salad is made with the living shoot of the coconut palm, which grows all over Seychelles, chopped into thin slices.

Banana feast

More often than not the dessert choice is limited to local ice creams or fruit salad. Occasionally the fruit salad will come with coconut nougat (caramelised coconut) or coconut milk. There are 25 species of banana in Seychelles, ranging from the foot-long *sen zak*, used to make crisps, to the stubby *mil*, which is extremely sweet and crops up in the fruit bowl, or comes flambéed or stewed in *ladob*.

Drinks

There are plenty of fruit juices, soft drinks, locally brewed beers and imported (expensive) wines available. At restaurants, it pays to ask if fresh juice is available. Try passion fruit juice or lime with a pinch of salt and sugar to taste. *Sitronel*, a kind of tea made from lemon grass, is also refreshing.

You are unlikely to be offered any of the local alcoholic brews with your meal but these are a part of local culture. *Kalou* (or toddy) is made from coconut sap, which ferments quickly and naturally, and makes the ideal lazy man's tipple. *Baka* is a rum-like drink made from fermented sugar cane juice (a far cry from Bacardi and incredibly strong). The most lethal of the local firewaters is *lapire*, made from almost anything that will ferment when mixed with sugar.

Villa on La Digue.

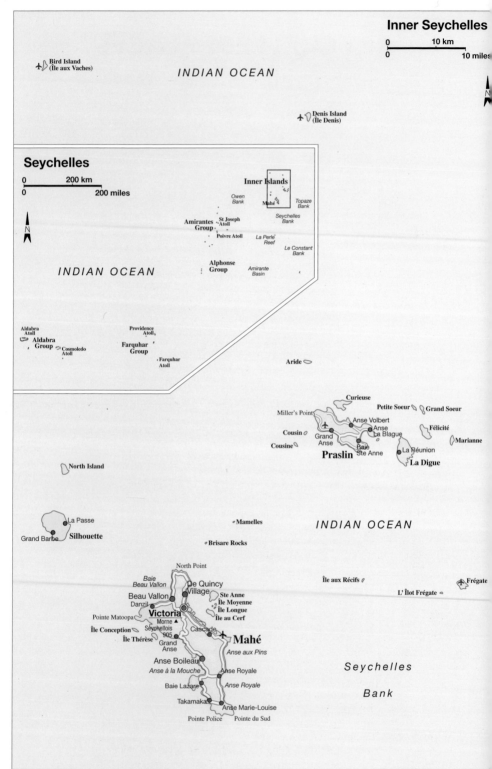

Inner Seychelles

0 — 10 km
0 — 10 miles

N

Bird Island
(Île aux Vaches)

INDIAN OCEAN

Denis Island
(Île Denis)

Seychelles

0 — 200 km
0 — 200 miles

N

INDIAN OCEAN

Inner Islands

Owen
Bank

Mahé

Topaze
Bank

St Joseph
Atoll

Seychelles
Bank

**Amirantes
Group**

Poivre Atoll

La Perle
Reef

Le Constant
Bank

**Alphonse
Group**

Amirante
Basin

Aldabra
Atoll

**Aldabra
Group**

Cosmoledo
Atoll

Providence
Atoll

**Farquhar
Group**

Farquhar
Atoll

Aride

Curieuse

Miller's Point

Petite Soeur

Grand Soeur

Anse Volbert

Félicité

Cousin

Grand
Anse

Anse
La Blague

Cousine

Baie
Ste Anne

Marianne

Praslin

La Réunion

La Digue

North Island

INDIAN OCEAN

La Passe

Mamelles

Grand Barbe

Silhouette

Brisare Rocks

Île aux Récifs

Frégate

L' Îlot Frégate

North Point

Baie
Beau Vallon

De Quincy
Village

Beau Vallon

Ste Anne

Danzil

Île Moyenne

Île Longue

Victoria

Île au Cerf

Pointe Matoopa

Morne
Seychellois

Cascade

Île Conception

905

Île Thérèse

Grand
Anse

Anse aux Pins

Mahé

Anse Boileau

Anse à la Mouche

Anse Royale

Baie Lazare

Anse Royale

Seychelles

Takamaka

Anse Marie-Louise

Bank

Pointe Police

Pointe du Sud

SEYCHELLES: PLACES

A detailed guide to Seychelles, with principal sites
clearly cross-referenced by number to the maps.

Coco de Mer Hotel.

To plan the perfect Seychelles holiday, you have to get three things right: the time of year (make sure you know beforehand when and where the monsoons hit); the quality of hotel (Seychelles is renowned for its five-star escapes but there are plenty of budget-friendly bed-and-breakfasts too); and, last but not least, the choice of island.

Each of the many Seychelles islands that now welcome overseas tourists has its own special attractions. Most tourists flying into Mahé head straight for their final destination, without taking time to explore the main island. It may be more commercial and developed than its fellow granitic islands, but beyond the tiny capital of Victoria, Mahé has some spectacular beaches and forests of its own to discover, with the added advantage of art and cultural attractions.

A boat on Praslin.

However, if you only have time to visit one island, Praslin is the one. Apart from its beaches, bordered with granite boulders, the other main attraction is the Vallée de Mai, a magnificent dense palm forest – home of the unique coco de mer, its notorious love nut – which could well have inspired the set designers of *Jurassic Park*. Praslin also makes a perfect island-hopping base: Cousin, Curieuse, St Pierre, La Digue and Aride are all just a short boat ride away.

Laid-back La Digue can be visited on a day trip from Praslin, but to take in the spectacular coastline – a favourite location for fashion shoots – and explore the inland trails by bike or on an ox-cart, a couple of days here would be well spent.

Even quieter than La Digue, Silhouette and North Island are the least known of the Inner Islands. Seemingly stuck in a time warp, Silhouette is a paradise for walkers. There are no roads but plenty of paths – not all well-trodden – that cut through the tangled and mountainous interior. North Island is home to a world-famous luxury eco-resort that draws environmentally conscious (and wealthy) tourists, such as the UK's Duke and Duchess of Cambridge, who spent their honeymoon on the island.

Frégate, another remote and exclusive granitic island, is privately owned. At five-star prices, for most of us it remains the stuff of dreams.

The coral islands of Bird, Denis, Desroches and Alphonse are perfect for getting away from it all. Each island has its own luxury resort, but has been developed to carefully preserve the environment. With facilities for sailing, diving, snorkelling, deep-sea fishing and birdwatching, there's plenty on offer for those who want to do more than just lounge by crystal waters.

Mahé

0 — 1 km
0 — 1 mile

N

INDIAN OCEAN

Frégate

0 — 500 m
0 — 500 yds

N

INDIAN OCEAN

Anse Bambous
Frégate Island "Private" Hotel
Anse Victorin 24
Glacis Carfouté
Plaine Magnan
Mont Signale
Bambous
Anse Parc
Au Salon
Pointe Sud
Settlement
Airstrip
Plantation House
Anse Coup de Poing
Signal Rock 125
Signal Rock 121
Pointe Fouqué
Frégate Island
Anse Victorin 23
Grand Anse
Petite Grand Anse
Anse Félix
Settlement 25

Praslin, La Digue

Albert Rock
Grand Anse
Anse Manon
Ile Seche
Anse Cimetière
Anse Cabot
Ste Anne 250
Ste-Anne Resort 19
Anse Mare Jupe
Jolly Roger Bar and Restaurant
Ile Moyenne
Ile Ronde
Ste Anne Marine National Park
Ile au Cerf 22
Ile Longue
Ile Cachée
Kapok-Tree Restaurant
Cerf Island 108 21
Grand Rocher
Ste Anne Channel
Cerf Passage

Eden Island
Seychelles International Airport

INDIAN OCEAN

Ile Anonyme
Ile aux Rats
Roche Tortue

Anse Nord d'Est
Krol Fleurage Estate
North East Point
North Point
North East Point
Carana Beach
Machabée
Mont du Nord
Mt Howard 458
St-Antoine Estate 119
La Retraite
Ile Aurore
Pointe Cèdre
Anse Étoile
Maldive Village
La Gogue Village
La Gogue Reservoir
De Quincy Village
Ile Preserverance

Victoria Lighthouse
Romainville
National Stadium

L'Islot
Vista Bay
Glacis
Mon Plaisir 18
Sunset Beach Hotel
Hilton Seychelles Northolme Resort
Mt Signal 417
Crève-Coeur
Mt Signal 388
St-Louis
Hangard 374
Conan
Pointe Conan
La Bastille
Seypot Factory
Mon Plaisir
Union-Vale
Mt Signal 374
Ile du Port
Victoria 1
Bel Air Cemetery
Pied du Morne
Mont Fleuri
Rochon Dam
Sans Souci
Chemin La Misère
La Misère
Le Rocher
Ma Josephine 335
La Misère
Petit Paris
Brillant
New Savy 587
Providence
Cascade

Baie Beau Vallon
Savoy Resort & SPA
Beau Vallon
Beraya Beau Vallon Bay Resort 232
Le Méridien Fisherman's Cove
Beau Vallon
Coral Strand Hotel
Anglaise
Maré
Mont Coton
Dans Cèdres
Le Niol
Pascal Village
Trois Frères Trail
Morne Seychellois 905
Mitson Historical Ruins
Chemin Sans Souci
Sans South 500
Val Riche
Audibert
Fairview
Grand Bois
Tea Factory 14
Rosebelle
Dans Létchis
Grand'Anse
La Bégoliare

Bel Ombre
Treasure Dig
Dan Zil
Beau Vallon
Mont du Nord
Poudaillet 206
Sixpenny Hill
Mt Le Niol 681
Mare aux Cochons
Morne Seychellois National Park 13
Mont Coton
Morne Blanc 667
Dugand
Congo Rouge
Mont d'Or
Constance Ephelia Resort
Tea Factory 14
L'Islette
Petite Île
Port Glaud

INDIAN OCEAN

Anse Major Trail
Anse Major (Anse Jasmin) 17
Anse Jasmin Estate
Mte Jasmin 643
Du Riz
Port Labuay
La Plaine
Constance Ephelia Resort
L'Islette
Port Launay
Port Launay National Park 12
Port Launay Marine National Park
Pointe L'Escalier
Anse Islette
Port Glaud

Cap Ternay
Baie Ternay
Baie Ternay National Park
Pointe Matoopa
Cap Matoopa
Le Passe Ternay
Île Conception

Ile aux Vaches
15
16
20

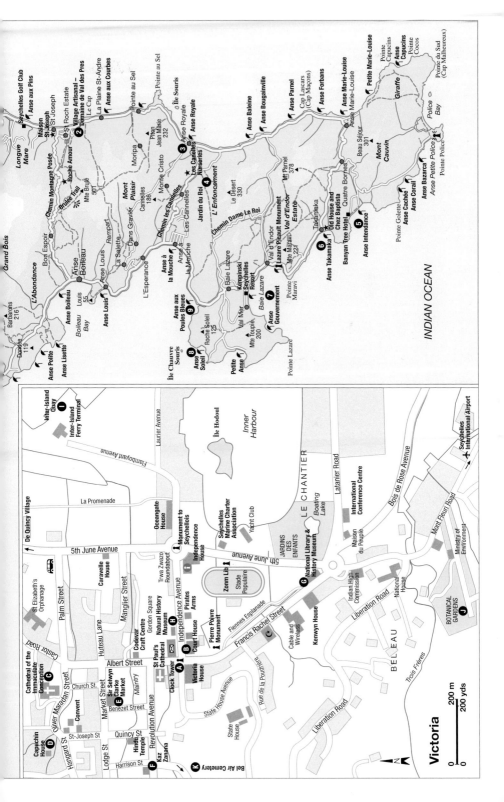

Victoria

0 — 200 m
0 — 200 yds

Longue Mare

Grand Bois

L'Abondance

Seychelles Golf Club
Anse aux Pins
Maison St-Joseph
St Roch Estate
Village Artisanal – Domaine de Val des Pres
Le Cap
La Plaine St-Andre
Anse aux Courbes
Pointe au Sel
Île Souris
Anse Royale
Anse Royale
Pointe au Sel
Piton Jean Marie 232
Moripa
Monte Cristo
Les Canelles Nurseries
Anse Baleine
Anse Bougainville
Cap Lascars (Cap Maçons)
Anse Parnel
Anse Forbans
Anse Marie-Louise
Anse Marie-Louise
Petite Marie-Louise
Pointe Capucins
Anse Capucins
Pointe Cocos
Pointe du Sud (Cap Malheureux)

Giraffe

Police Bay
Pointe Police
Anse Petite Police
Anse Bazarca
Anse Corail
Anse Cachée
Pointe Golette
Beau Séjour 301
Mont Cauvin
Mt Parnel 378

Chemin Montagne Posée
Roche Amour
Brûlée Trail
Mte Brûlé 501
Mont Plaisir
Cannelles 186
Chemin les Cannelles
Les Cannelles
Jardin du Roi
L'Enforcement
Le Désert 330
Chemin Dame Le Roi
Val d'Endor
Mte Maravi 221
Val d'Endor Estate
Takamaka
Old House and Chez Baptista
Banyan Tree Hotel
Quatre Bornes
Anse Intendance

Bot Espoir
Anse Boileau
Dans Gravier
Rempart
La Salette
Anse Louis
L'Esperance
Anse à la Mouche
Anse à la Mouche
Baie Lazare
Baie Lazare
Kempinski Seychelles Resort
Pointe Maravi
Anse Gouvernement
Anse Takamaka
Lazare Picault Monument

Barbarons 216
Dundie 119
Anse Polite
Anse Lisette
Boileau Bay
Anse Boileau
Anse Louis
Louis 55
Anse aux Poules Bleues
Île Chauve Souris
Anse Soleil
Roche Soleil 125
Val Mer
Mte Touple 200
Petite Anse
Pointe Lazart

INDIAN OCEAN

Inter-Island Quay
Inter-Island Ferry Terminal
De Quincy Village
La Promenade
Flamboyant Avenue
Laurier Avenue
Inner Harbour
Île Hodoul
Oceangate House
5th June Avenue
Caravelle House
Trwa Zwazo Roundabout
Seychelles Marine Charter Association
Yacht Club
Monument to Seychellois
Independence House
Zomm Lib
Stade Populaire
National Library & History Museum
LE CHANTIER
Boating Lake
JARDINS DES ENFANTS
Maison du Peuple
International Conference Centre
Indian High Commission
Bois de Rose Avenue
Seychelles International Airport
Mont Fleuri Road
Ministry of Environment
BELEAU
National House
Liberation Road
BOTANICAL GARDENS
Trois Frères
Liberation Road
Cable and Wireless
Kenwyn House
Francis Rachel Street
Fiennes Esplanade
Pierre Poivre Monument
Pirates Arms
Natural History Museum
Gordon Square
Codevar Craft Centre
Independence Avenue
St Paul's Cathedral
Court House
Victoria House
Clock Tower
Albert Street
Sir Selwyn Clarke Market
Market Street
Church St.
Benezet Street
Mantry
Convent
St-Joseph St
Castor Road
Cathedral of the Immaculate Conception
Capuchin House
Hangard St
Lodge St
Quincy St
Hindu Temple
Kaz Zanana
Bel Air Cemetery
Harrison St
Revolution Avenue
State House Avenue
Rue de la Poudrière
State House
Mangier Street
Huteau Lane
Palm Street
St Elizabeth's Orphanage
Silver Maradan Street

Waterfall near Port Glaud.

MAHÉ AND SATELLITES

Away from the spread of the capital, Victoria, there is breathtaking beauty around the scenic coast and rainforest-clad mountains.

Mahé is the largest and most densely populated island in Seychelles, home to 90 per-ent of Seychellois. The instinct of many visitors soon after touching down at the International Airport is to rush away to Praslin, La Digue or even further afield to discover the real Seychelles. This is a mistake.

Of course the capital, Victoria, has its fair share of traffic jams and build-ing works, but it's still the sort of place where everyone knows everyone else and where a game of dominoes out-side the local shop is a social highlight. Beyond the town, there are plenty of opportunities to leave the parapherna-lia of modern life behind, with escape routes down to the beach or up into the mountains.

Mahé covers an area of 158 sq km (61 sq miles) and rises to 905 metres (2,970ft) above sea level. It is 27km (17 miles) long and, at its widest, 8km (5 miles) across, so it can easily be covered by car in a day. There is a good network of roads, both coastal and inland, and a day spent driving round the island in an open jeep or Mini Moke is a great way to start your holiday.

Most of Seychelles' present popula-tion of 83,000 lives on Mahé, concen-trated on the north and east coasts. Land reclamation along the east coast created valuable stretches of flat new terrain for development, and allowed for the building of a straight route from the airport to Victoria, cutting out the many twists and turns of the old coast road. The creation of this 'new' land has meant that the vital development of the island's infra-structure has been largely concen-trated in the area around the capital, thus limiting its impact on the rest of the island.

Being the largest and highest island, there is an element of grandeur in Mahé's beauty the other islands don't have. The coastal scenery goes from

Main Attractions

Sir Selwyn Selwyn-Clarke Market, Victoria
Botanical Gardens, Victoria
Michael Adams' Studio, Mahé
Ste Anne Marine National Park
Île au Cerf
Île Moyenne

Market Street in Victoria.

TIP

Parking is restricted in Victoria and police are keen. If you have come to town by car, the best place to park is the Stadium Car Park on Francis Rachel Street, which is free. Otherwise, you have to buy parking coupons (available from many shops).

wild granite cliffs where waves crash against massive boulders tumbling into the ocean, to tranquil palm-fringed coves. If you feel jaded by turquoise waters and silver sands, you can escape into the high hills and experience the eerie silence of the remote rainforest. The atmosphere is unforgettable, and one which many tropical islands have long since lost.

Victoria

Victoria ❶ is still a tiny capital by modern standards. It lies on the east coast, 8km (5 miles) north of the airport, bounded by mountains on one side and sea on the other. The town grew up around the natural harbour formed by the sheltering satellite islands of Ste Anne, Moyenne, Ronde, Longue and Cerf. The original settlement was founded in 1778 by the French, who built a military base here. In the early days of colonisation the islands, considered remote by the colonial powers, remained sparsely populated and expansion of the settlement was slow. It was known quite simply as L'Etablissement (The

Settlement) until 1841, when it wa named after Queen Victoria. Toda Victoria is the commercial centre o Seychelles and during business hour the streets throng with people an traffic. 'Old' Victoria, the area that lie at the foot of the mountains, is buil around narrow streets with eccentri pavements that rise over great storr drains one minute, and drop into gutter the next. Elegant if dilapidate French colonial-style buildings ar huddled around them. The moder avenues of 'new' Victoria, laid out o the reclaimed land, are more statel their pavements broad and flat, an lined here and there with attractiv garden areas, bright with canna lilie and bougainvillaea.

If you're interested in Seychelles cu ture and the day-to-day life of its cap tal, it's worth spending a bit of tim here. However, if your top priority is t experience the forests and coasts, half day in Victoria should be enough.

The heart of town

The centre of Victoria is easy to explor and its hub, standing at a centra

The clock tower of Victoria is also known as Little Big Ben.

ossroads, is the **Clock Tower** Ⓐ. It as built in 1903 both as a memorial ⦁ Queen Victoria and to commemo- te the establishment of Seychelles as Crown Colony in its own right. Next ⦁ the Clock Tower stands the **Court louse** Ⓑ, a typical colonial-style uilding with a fancy ironwork balus- ade on the upper storey. The nearby ⦁untain is topped with the replica of a ⦁ry small bust of Queen Victoria. The ⦁riginal, now in the History Museum ee page 284), was unveiled in 1900 ⦁ mark Queen Victoria's 60th year on ⦁e throne.

On the corner of Albert Street and Levolution Avenue is the Anglican Cathedral of **St Paul**, Seychelles' old- st church, consecrated in 1859. A ew cathedral, preserving the original ⦁wer, was completed here in 2003.

he Cathedral of the mmaculate Conception nd Capuchin House

'he Roman Catholic **Cathedral of he Immaculate Conception** Ⓒ, uilt in the French colonial style, was nished in 1874, but has had many additions since. On weekdays the church is quiet, but on Sunday morn- ings the strains of the organ and choir ring out from the open doorways, and the congregation, dressed in their best, spill out onto the steps. Sunday Mass is as much a social occasion as a reli- gious one.

Just down the street from the cathe- dral is Victoria's most impressive building, **Capuchin House** Ⓓ. Built in 1933 with funds from the Swiss Capuchin order, and designed by one of the monks, it is used as a semi- nary for priests and brothers, some of whom still teach in the schools.

Morning market

Heading back south towards the town centre, you'll pass the pedestrianised Market Street and the **Sir Selwyn Selwyn-Clarke Market** Ⓔ, also known as Victoria Market. Saturday morning is the best time to visit. The fish stalls are the commercial heart of the market, piled with freshly caught barracuda, parrotfish, cordonnier, bonito and kingfish. Produce stalls are stacked with neat pyramids of exotic

An artist at Creole Craft Village, Anse aux Pins.

SOUVENIR SHOPPING

Codevar is an artisans' association set up by the government to promote local craftsmanship. One of the best places to pick up gifts and souvenirs is the **Codevar Craft Centre** at **Camion Hall** in Albert Street (named after the old open lorries, or *camyons*, used as buses, which used to set out on their routes from this spot). There is a shop on the street front selling pottery, wood- carvings, textiles and various objects made from coconuts and shells. In the arcade **Kreol Or** has a wide range of jewellery made out of green snail shell, tiger cowrie and coconut shell in combi- nation with gold, and crafts made from local woods, coconut shell, coconut wood and polished palm seeds. Immediately across the road, the **Sooty Tern** boutique specialises in stained-glass work. Round the corner in Revolution Avenue, **Memorabilia** sells a wide range of crafts and books. **Sunstroke Gallery** on Market Street has a range of locally made beachwear, jewellery, hand- printed tablecloths and bed linen. Upstairs there is a gallery of local artwork. **Antigone**, the town's best bookshop, is in Passage des Palmes. **Antik Colony**, in the Pirates Arms building, sells quality souvenirs on colonial themes. On either side of the entrance to the Stadium Car Park are craft kiosks that sell beach- wear, T-shirts, coconut crafts and spices.

fruits and seasonal vegetables. Others are laid out with trays of mixed spices, neatly rolled quills of fresh cinnamon bark, packets of turmeric and old jars crammed with small but deadly red and green chillies.

For a bird's-eye view of the goings-on, climb the stairs to the upper floor. There are a few craft shops open here, selling the more usual lines in souvenirs.

Cutting through the market, leaving by the side entrance, you come out into a little alley called Benezet Street. Turning left, past the bakery (which does excellent bread), you'll come back on to Revolution Avenue. If the heat and noise have made you weary, turn right and keep walking until you reach **Kaz Zanana** ❻ (Pineapple House), a quiet spot to pause for a bite to eat. The restaurant is on a terrace at the back, overlooking the garden. They serve light meals throughout the day and the best cappuccino and chocolate cake in Seychelles. The rest of the house is made up of small galleries which exhibit paintings and drawings by local artist George Camille.

Strolling south along Fiennes Esplanade

The shady **Fiennes Esplanade**, whic runs alongside Francis Rachel Stree was laid out by a British governo with the splendid name of Sir Eu tace Edward Twisleton-Wykehar Fiennes (1918–21), father of explore Sir Ranuph Fiennes. At the start c the esplanade is a **bust of Pierre Po vre**, the governor of Mauritius wh arranged for the first spice plants t be brought to Seychelles for propaga tion (see page 242).

Towards the end of the Esplanade a large modern building, the Nationa Library. The **History Museum** ❻ (Mon–Tue, Thu–Fri 8.30am–4.30pm Sat 9am–1pm) is housed on th ground floor. In the entrance is th Stone of Possession, a stone placed b the French in 1756 to claim the island Displays are fairly basic, but they giv an excellent introduction to the hi tory of the islands, from pirates an explorers through wars and colonia times to the modern day. The tranqui lity of the hall is a pleasant contrast t the hustle and bustle of Victoria, whi

Shopping for fresh seafood at Victoria Market.

e cool air-conditioned atmosphere is elcome after a hot walk.

There is a small commercial art llery on the opposite side of the useum car park to the library, Carfour des Arts (Mon–Fri 9am–5pm) ith original paintings on sale. Across e road is Kenwyn House (Mon–Fri m–4pm, Sat 9am–noon). Built in e 1860s and renovated in 2005, it is robably the best preserved 19th-cenry building in Victoria. It also conins an excellent art gallery featuring range of local artists.

ast to the quays

ist of the Clock Tower, on Indepenence Avenue, is the **Natural History Museum** ⊕ (Mon–Fri 8.30am–4.30pm, at 8.30am–noon), with displays of ndemic birds, reef life, tortoises, geolgy and the skulls of estuarine crocoiles that once lived in the mangrove vamps around Mahé's coast and terrised the colonists.

Opposite the museum is Victoria's est-known rendezvous, the **Pirates rms** (Mon–Sat 9am–11pm, Sun oon–11pm), a large, informal caféar popular with tourists and locals ike. There is a small arcade of shops eside it, several of which sell curios. little further down the street on ne same side is the **tourist office**, a ood place for advice and literature n accommodation, excursions and useum opening times. It also has eaflets on walks and trails in Mahé, raslin and La Digue.

Continuing straight on, past the rwa Zwazo (Three Birds) roundabout named after the sculpture erected in 978 to celebrate 200 years of human ccupation), the road swings left. his is Flamboyant Avenue, leading o **Inter-Island Quay** ❶, the deparure point for ferries and boats to the slands, and for fast catamarans to Prasin. The traditional island schooners lso ply between Mahé, Praslin and La Digue from this point, and the fleets f the largest charter boat operators re based here.

While waiting for your ferry, **Fish Tail** restaurant on the quayside offers a ringside seat to watch the comings and goings, or take a break in the Seychelles Port Authority's new passenger shelter, which has seating for 500 passengers, toilets, luggage storage and boat ticket and car hire booths. The charter boat marina is at the north end of the jetty, where catamarans and schooners line the pontoons. Just south of the Trwa Zwazo roundabout, on 5th June Avenue, is the **Marine Charter Association**, the departure point for glass-bottom boat and subsea viewer trips, and for some charter yachts.

The Botanical Gardens

The walk from the Clock Tower to the **Botanical Gardens** ❶ (daily 8am–5pm) at the foot of Mont Fleuri takes about 20 minutes. They were laid out in 1901 by a Frenchman, Rivaltz Dupont, who collected many of the plant specimens on his travels. The site he chose was not ideal – the soil was poor and the land scattered with huge boulders – but it was the only affordable piece of land near town. Wandering through this

Capuchin House.

green oasis today, it is hard to imagine the unprepossessing site Dupont was confronted with. The boulders are now an attractive feature, and the bubbling streams that run down either side of the park create a cool, soothing atmosphere.

At the top of the hill the gardens open out onto broad lawns dotted with specimen trees and shrubs. One of the most noticeable is the elephant apple, with fruits like huge, heavy apples that smell of rubber. There are attractive ponds with water lilies and darting dragonflies. The path leading from the ponds takes you past a mighty banyan tree and several drumstick trees that shed remarkable, long, thin fruits. One tree you can't miss, if it is in flower, is the cannonball tree, which sheds its leaves when flowering to reveal bizarre, fleshy coral pink flowers. A number of Aldabra giant tortoises are kept here in a large pen shaded by a coco de mer palm.

The gardens are shady enough to explore at any time of day, but it's best to avoid the heat of the midday sun. Ask at the entrance kiosk for the leaflet which maps out the garden and names all the plants. There are no refreshment facilities inside the gardens, so it's a good idea to pick up a drink on the way.

Bel Air Cemetery

On the outskirts of Victoria, at the beginning of the Sans Souci Road, **Bel Air Cemetery** Ⓚ, Seychelles' oldest cemetery. Tombstones lie strewn haphazardly, there are no signposts and no guide, but it is an atmospheric place, nonetheless. Settlers and their slaves were buried here from the earliest times. The more splendid tombs bear the names of illustrious Seychelles families. According to legend, a young giant was killed by local people and buried here in the 1870s. The grave of the French corsair Hodoul is also rumoured to be here.

The east coast

There are two roads leading out of Victoria that head south towards the airport. For speed and convenience, the new road (Bois de Rose Avenue) is the one to take. But if you're in no hurry, a journey along the narrow, winding, rather chaotic old Mont Fleuri Road (which becomes East Coast Road further along) will tell you far more about Mahé. The buildings that line it are a fascinating jumble of the modern (such as the Pentecostal Assembly on the junction of Mont Fleuri Road and Liberation Road) and the charmingly dilapidated. You can catch glimpses of elegant old planters' homes peeping over high stone walls, identifiable by their steep-pitched roofs, shuttered windows, wide verandas and high stone foundations.

The two coast roads recombine at Providence, leading to **Cascade**, a traditional fishing village now dominated not by the fishing industry, but the nearby airport built on reclaimed land. The blessing of the fishing boats here on the feast of St André (November) used to be an important celebration in Seychelles, attracting spectators

Victoria's streets back on to stunning scenery.

om all over Mahé. The number of
oats is far fewer nowadays, but about
alf a dozen pirogues, decorated with
ags and flowers, still gather here for
.e annual blessing.

raft Village

nother 6km (4 miles) down the coast
ad, past Anse aux Pins, on the site of a
rmer plantation, is the **Craft Village**
● (Le Village Artisanal), where you
n while away a bit of time looking at
.e workshops and shopping for souve-
rs (see Travel Tips, Activities). In the
iddle of the village the old planta-
on house, dating from 1870, has been
rnished in typical colonial style. The
ol, dark rooms smell of wax polish
id cinnamon, and conjure a picture
 the genteel existence once enjoyed
 the privileged few. It's easy to imag-
.e a candlelit social gathering, the
dies in their long dresses frantically
nning themselves and the gentlemen
 full evening dress savouring the fine
ines imported at great expense from
ance. **Vye Marmit Restaurant** is a
od place to sample local specialities
ich as fruit bat, octopus, crab and fish.

nse Royale

eyond the Pointe au Sel promontory,
nse Royale ❸ is the main east coast
each. The sheltered, sandy bay is scat-
red with giant boulders, dividing the
each into a series of mini-coves, pretty
uch deserted on most weekdays. The
orkelling is reasonably good around
e offshore islet of Île Souris. The cur-
nts between the mainland and the
land can be strong, but run parallel
 the beach, and it is fairly easy for a
nfident swimmer to cross them.

Kaz Kreol, at the southern end of
nse Royale, is an informal restaurant
ght on the sand, where you can turn
p in your swimming costume for
nch.

he King's Garden

ontinuing south, the next turning
f the main road is Les Cannelles.
weet Escott Road is a left turning off

this road. It was around here, in 1772,
that Antoine Gillot, under instruction
from the French government, planted
a Royal Spice Garden (see page 242),
but this is long since overgrown. In its
memory, the **Jardin du Roi** ❹ (King's
Garden; daily 10am–5.30pm) has
been established on the hillside above
Sweet Escott Road. This renovated
spice plantation, based on the former L'Enfoncement Estate, gives you
a chance to see many aromatic plants
growing (including nutmeg, pepper,
cinnamon, vanilla and cloves). There
is a walk laid out which you can follow using the printed guide. The small
museum in the plantation house has
some interesting exhibits, including
old prints, maps and photos of Seychelles, and information on growing
and using spices. On Sunday the restaurant serves a popular curry buffet
(see Travel Tips, Restaurants).

The west coast

The East Coast Road continues to Anse
Marie-Louise, where it turns sharply
inland and cuts across the southern
end of Mahé. At Quatre Bornes, a road

*Fishermen bringing in
the catch on Anse
Royale.*

leads down to a spectacular bay, **Anse Intendance ❺**, where there is a very exclusive hotel, **The Banyan Tree Resort**. The long, pristine beach is pounded by crashing breakers, exhilarating to watch as they sweep in with a tremendous roar and a haze of spray. A strong swimmer might enjoy body surfing in the waves, but it's easy to get caught in the rollers and dumped hard on the beach or rocks. As with many of Seychelles' beaches, conditions vary according to the monsoon season. Seas are at their roughest during the southeast monsoon (May to October) and there can be a strong undertow. During the northwest monsoon (October to April) the waves here are still big, but the water is calm enough to swim in. Intendance is a popular picnic spot for Seychellois at weekends and can get quite busy, but the beach is so long there is room for all.

Rejoining the main road at Quatre Bornes and heading west, you'll reach **Anse Takamaka ❻**, the first beach on the west coast road, whose large shady takamaka trees and golden sands entice many tourists and surfers.

The Banyan Tree Resort.

However, currents are strong arour here and swimming is dangerous.

Baie Lazare

The road swings northward, sta ing fairly close to the shore, offerir dramatic views at Pointe Maravi the rocks below before it descend again to **Baie Lazare ❼**. Here, besic the coast, there is a **monument** (a anchor on a stone pedestal) cor memorating the 250th anniversary the first recorded French landing c Mahé by Lazare Picault in 1742 (i fact, Picault landed at Anse Boileau Baie Lazare has a long expanse c beach, though swimming here durir the southeast monsoon is not recor mended. The best way to explore it to park near the monument and stro along the beach towards the luxuriou Kempinski Seychelles Resort.

Baie Lazare village, on the hi overlooking the beach, is a typic Seychelles hamlet, centred aroun the neo-Gothic church of St Franc of Assisi. This is the starting poir for the **Chemin Dame Le Roi** fore drive. The winding road leads uphi from Quatre Bornes takeaway, an passes through scattered houses, fore and plantations of pineapple, cassav and sugar cane (mostly grown to mal *baka*, a local spirit). This is old Mah still firmly fixed in another age, whe chickens peck around the washin laid out on the boulders to dry.

Attractive bays

Just north of Quatre Bornes takeawa a road leads on to a western promo tory which has three bays. The best c these is **Anse Soleil ❽**, an enchantir small sandy beach, rated the secon best 'hidden secret' in the world by th German magazine *Reise & Preise*, wit good swimming and excellent views. is rarely busy, except on Sundays, whe the simple but very good restaurar is popular with locals. Neighbou ing **Petite Anse** is another attracti sandy cove, about 10 minutes' wa along a shaded track. Reaching Ans ouvernement from here requires backtracking to the junction and following the signpost pointing to the right. The narrow concrete track leads downhill, passing on the right Studio Antonio – where unusual wooden sculptures are on display – before merging at the beach. This sandy bay, dotted with massive granite boulders, is wild and windswept during the southeast monsoon, so not good for swimming at this time of year. Weekends apart, it is very quiet and romantic.

rtists' studios

ontinuing northward on the coast road, the next place you come to is **nse aux Poules Bleues ❾** where ou'll find **Michael Adams' Studio** Mon–Fri 10am–4pm, Sat 10am–oon). The best-known artist in Seychelles, his jungle landscapes are a ot of leaves, stalks and stems, criss-rossing and clashing in every shade. le also takes a wry look at village life. xcellent prints of his work are on sale t the plantation-style studio, but they re expensive so the postcards and calndars may be more appealing.

The wide vistas of **Anse à la Mouche** open up as the road curves around the bay. The beach has the usual pristine white sand and plenty of shade, and the shallow waters are calm all year round, which makes it ideal for children. It's also a good place for beach parties, and groups of Seychellois often get together here at weekends, although on weekdays it is usually very quiet. The **Anchor Café** serves drinks, snacks and simple meals at reasonable prices.

Les Cannelles Road at the end of Anse à la Mouche leads inland to Santa Maria and **Tom Bowers' Studio** (Mon–Sat 9am–5.30pm), which is signposted on the right as you climb Les Cannelles from the coast. Like so many artists before him, the London-born sculptor visited Seychelles, fell in love with it and settled. He uses resin for his sculptures of local people, which are then cast in bronze.

Coastal views

Back on the west coast, the next right turn is Chemin Montagne Posée, not worth the diversion unless you intend to walk the mountain trail near the

Rock formations in the surf, Baie Lazare.

summit. For a less strenuous introduction to the lower slopes of Mahé there is an attractive palm forest at the Seychelles National Biodiversity Centre at Barbarons, including the rare coco de mer, and at the opposite end of the bay just after the hotel, an excellent well-marked walk, the **Sentier Vacoa Trail **. The shaded trail leads uphill alongside a clear stream bordered by endemic palms and trees.

The following turn-off, just after the unmistakable giant masts of the BBC World Service Relay Station, is La Misère Pass, which rejoins the east coast at Mont Fleuri close to Victoria. Cutting across the west side of the mountains, this pass is quiet, with few houses, and views over the coast. The road falls steeply from here and the views over the east coast and the Inner Islands are spectacular. There is an off-road **viewing point** about 2km (1 mile) after the summit.

The west coast road continues past Grand Anse Agricultural Station to the bay of **Grand Anse** ⓫. This is a majestic, tree-lined beach with fine white sand and granite rocks, but the

Explaining the view from Mission Lodge Lookout over the coastline and Mahe's rainforest.

treacherous offshore currents make unsuitable for swimming (a govern of Seychelles drowned here in 1962 Over the brow of the hill, the roa descends to tiny picturesque Petite Îl

The last 5km (3-mile) section of th west coast road is a narrow stretch th comes to a dead end just before **Bai Ternay**. There is no access beyon this point. The drive is spectacula passing over a causeway and throug a mangrove swamp and, as it climb giving marvellous views over the **Po Launay Marine National Park** ⓬ (formed in 1979 to protect the reef To reach the beaches of **Port Launa Bay**, pull over in a convenient spo and stroll down to the shore. The sno kelling here is good and reaching th reef is easy over calm waters.

Northern Mahé

If you only have a day on Mahé, th first place you should drive to is th Sans Souci Road, most of whic runs through the Morne Seychello National Park. The circuitous driv from coast to coast takes about a hour and is an ideal way to experienc

---

MISSION RUINS

The area known in colonial times as Venn's Town is now called Mission. The ruins, dating from 1875, are those of a school built by Anglican missionaries for the children of rescued slaves and were declared a National Monument in 1984. Following the abolition of slavery in the colonies, the British ran an anti-slavery patrol in the Indian Ocean. Their main purpose was to intercept Arab dhows transporting captive Africans to the Middle East. Those they managed to save from slavery were not taken back to Africa for fear they would be rounded up again, so they were brought to Seychelles and freed. Their children were given a basic education by the missionaries prior to being apprenticed or sent into service. Unesco speculates that this was probably the only place in the world at that time that educated freed slave children, and the school gave birth to formal education in Seychelles.

Marianne North, an intrepid Victorian traveller and botanical artist, made a trip to Venn's Town in 1883 by mule, and later commented in her diary 'The situation...is one of the most magnificent in the world, and the silence of the forest around was only broken by the children's happy voices.' Nowadays the only sound here is the rustling of the trees.

You can see this view for yourself. A short avenue leads to the viewing platform, called Mission Lodge, which was built for the visit of Queen Elizabeth II in 1972.

ie mood of the mountains; the eerie ilence is broken only by the distant roaking of frogs and the mighty trees ustling in the cool winds. Even on a lear day, clouds can suddenly settle n the heights or roll up from the sea nfolding you in a damp chill and a omplete silence. There are breathtak- ng views at almost every turn and nany places to pull over and enjoy hem. Some of the highest slopes are lanted with tea or mahogany trees, ut much of the vegetation is a wild angle of forest. On the Sans Souci Road, around 20 minutes from Vic- oria, you will pass **The Station Sey- helles**, a small hotel and wellness pa that has an excellent café, with ainforest and sea views. Stop off for reakfast before a day's sightseeing, r linger over the bargain 'meal of the ay' three-course lunch, made from resh, local dishes.

Mountain passes and nature trails

The **Morne Seychellois National Park** ⑬ was established as a pro- ected area in the 1970s. If you want to explore the area on foot, there are a number of well-marked nature trails and mountain walks varying in length and degree of difficulty (see page 292). Trail guide booklets are available from the Seychelles tourist office in Victoria.

Two places are worth a detour on this route. The **Tea Factory** ⑭ (Mon–Fri 7am–4pm, guided tours only) makes a pleasant refreshment stop. Locally grown tea is served here, but the coffee is imported and not of high quality. Just after the summit of Morne Blanc the **Mission Historical Ruins and Viewpoint** ⑮ offers one of the most stunning panoramas in Seychelles.

Beau Vallon and around

Mahé's main tourism centre is the bay of **Beau Vallon** ⑯. It might well be Seychelles' busiest beach, but most visitors would not call it crowded. The water is excellent for bathing, the sand is white and seaweed free, and there is plenty of shade. It is one of the best places in Seychelles for water sports, with facilities for windsurfing,

Port Launay village.

Nature walks

Discover unique indigenous plants, secluded beaches and vantage points with stunning ocean and island views during a hike on one of Mahé's many trails.

The best season for walking is during the cooler, less humid months from June to September. The worst time is at the height of the rains from mid-December to January, when paths are muddy and slippery. Avoid the middle of the day for your trek; early morning and late afternoon are best, remembering that it gets dark around 6.30pm. Do not attempt any walk (except Danzilles to Anse Major) after rain as the path will be dangerous. You will need a solid pair of shoes (trainers with a good grip are fine), a hat, sunglasses, a bottle of water and a snack to enjoy when you reach the top or the end.

Coastal walks

Danzilles–Anse Major Walk: An easy one-and-a-half hour walk (this one can be done in flip flops),

The trail to Mount Copolia.

most of which is within Morne Seychellois National Park. The peaceful walk follows the coast (one of the few coastal stretches in Mahé with no road access) and leads to a small, secluded beach. It starts at the end of the road from Beau Vallon to Bel Ombre, which turns into a well-marked path crossing the Danzilles River. Highlights include wonderful views of Beau Vallon and Silhouette Island, and spectacular areas of granitic rock slopes.

La Reserve and Brulée Walk: This is Mahé's answer to Praslin's Vallée de Mai; it's the island's best area of palm forest, with five of Seychelles' six unique palm species – only the coco de mer is missing. This walk should take about an hour and a half up and another hour back down. The trail begins by the Cable and Wireless station, with a steep climb under mahogany trees. It is signposted but there are a couple of points where you may go wrong, so go with the trail brochure, available at the tourist office, or, better still, take a guide. There are three main vantage points along the way, which offer fabulous views over the west coast and the islands of Île aux Vaches, Thérèse and Conception.

Mountain hikes

Tea Factory–Morne Blanc Walk: This is a short, sharp climb up to Morne Blanc in the Morne Seychellois National Park. The views from here are breathtaking and the rainforest very spooky. The walk starts at the Tea Company off the Sans Souci Road and should take about two hours altogether. The trail is marked with dabs of yellow paint on trees. Along the way you will see many of Seychelles' unique plants, but surprisingly few birds. Take care at the summit – the cliff you are standing on is almost vertical and it's a long way down. Return via the same route.

The Congo Rouge Trail: The best mist forest is on this trail, which circles the summit of Morne Seychellois. It's a Grade 3 walk, taking three to six hours, which should never be attempted without a guide as it is easy to get lost. You may get more enjoyment from your exploration of the mountains with a knowledgeable guide. Basil Beaudouin knows all the trails and can identify most of the 250 indigenous species of plants you may see. He leads walks of varying difficulty, lasting from as little as one to two hours to as much as six to eight hours. Excursions with him can be organised through your hotel or the tourist office (see Travel Tips, Activities).

living, sailing and water-skiing, even parascending and 'sausage' riding – where you, and whoever else is along for the ride, sit astride an inflatable tube towed through the water by a speedboat. The Coral Strand, Berjaya Beau Vallon Bay Resort, Le Meridien Fisherman's Cove and luxurious Savoy Seychelles are the main hotels on the bay, but there are plenty of guesthouses and apartments to rent too. The poolside bistros of the Berjaya and Coral Strand are accessible from the beach.

Beau Vallon by night

Beau Vallon is the only beach on Mahé that stays lively in the evenings. The stretch of pedestrianised road between the Coral Strand Hotel and the pizzeria is particularly busy. Apart from the hotels, there are three main eateries to choose from. During the day the **Boat House** runs game fishing trips to Silhouette Island. The day's catch is barbecued the same evening and served with a Creole buffet. It's a popular event and good value for money, so it's best to book and arrive about half an hour early so you can choose a good table and enjoy a drink before dinner. On the beach itself, tucked in the northern corner, is the ever-popular **Baobab Pizzeria**, which is simple, cheap and quick. **Perle Noire** restaurant, a short distance inland from Coral Strand, offers more substantial up-market fare.

On Wednesday evenings the road between Coral Strand Hotel and the Boat House is lined with craft stalls. Drinks are also offered at very reasonable prices.

There is no road around the northwest coast, but there is a beautiful and easy walk from Danzilles to **Anse Major** ⑰, a charming little beach; sheltered, secluded and good for bathing (see page 292).

To North East Point

North of Beau Vallon is Victoria's 'commuter belt', with occasional stunning views to the west of Silhouette and North islands. As the road climbs it passes several spectacular villas clinging to the granite cliffs. It also passes the **Hilton** Seychelles **Northolme**

Sunday Evening jam session, Beau Vallon.

Resort & Spa, where you could stop for lunch or afternoon tea. This was the site of Seychelles' oldest hotel, now completely rebuilt. In its heyday, it attracted several famous literary guests including Noel Coward, Somerset Maugham and Ian Fleming – you can stay in the Fleming Suite, the inspiration behind the author's book and Bond film *For Your Eyes Only*.

Just beyond the Hilton Hotel and Vacoa Village is **Glacis** ⓲, surrounded by some beautiful scenery. There are a number of hotels and guesthouses here, the most exclusive of which is the **Sunset Beach Hotel**, built on a promontory, whose beach is open to non-residents. The road carries on around the northern tip of the island, passing **Machabeé** and **Carana Beach**, a good spot for bathing, though there are no facilities.

The road between **North East Point** and **Pointe Cèdre** runs very close to the beach; sand and waves often blow onto the tarmac. It is a very attractive beach, but not ideal for swimming as it's rocky underfoot and a bit too close to the road for comfort. Just before the road curves around Pointe Cèdre to Anse Etoile, look out for **Kreol Fleurage** (daily 9am–5pm) across the road from the beach on North East Point. This perfumery, founded by a German microbiologist, manufactures a range of natural perfumes made from 10 local plants.

The Chemin la Gogue from Anse Etoile to Northolme is a pleasant two-hour walk (or a 20-minute drive) across the northernmost peninsula which takes you past **La Gogue Reservoir**, an attractive lake and ideal picnic spot.

Once around Pointe Cèdre, the hillsides to the right and cliffs to the left become more thickly dotted with houses as you approach Victoria's environs. The most notable building before you reach town is **La Bastille**, just after Pointe Conan. This sombre, impressive house was built in the 1930s as a family home. Today it is occupied by the National Heritage division of the Ministry of Arts, Culture and Information. The gardens are open to the public (Mon–Fri 8am–4pm). There is a collection of

The tombstone of famous pirate Olivier Le Vasseur (nicknamed 'La Buse', the buzzard) in Saint-Paul cemetery.

BEL OMBRE TREASURE DIG

In 1949, Reginald Cruise-Wilkins, a Grenadier Guard recuperating from malaria on Mahé, got hold of some documents that he believed belonged to the notorious pirate Olivier Le Vasseur (see page 240). He was convinced that Le Vasseur had laid a trail for would-be treasure seekers involving riddles and puzzles based on astrology, astronomy and mythology. He devoted his life to the quest for the fantastic treasure – gold coins, silver bars, diamonds, silks and the jewel-encrusted regalia of the archbishop of Goa, which included a huge cross studded with rubies, emeralds and diamonds – seized in 1721 from the Portuguese merchant ship *Virgen de Cabo*, en route from India.

Cruise-Wilkins concluded that the clues were based on the twelve labours of Hercules and he was spurred on by a series of proofs that he was on the right track – a pig's jawbone, bits of china, a bull's horn – but found no treasure. One unsolved riddle led him to Bel Ombre, where he believed the end of the trail lay in an underwater cavern. He brought in pumps, but to no avail. The treasure was undiscovered when he died in 1977. His son, Seychellois John Cruise-Wilkins, has since taken up the challenge and continues to explore caves and invest in expensive radar equipment and machines to find the elusive hoard.

raditional medicinal plants, a sugar
ane press and a dilapidated model of
traditional Creole house. Nothing is
abelled, but the staff are friendly and
villing to help.

he satellite islands

he Portuguese called Seychelles the
even Sisters on their charts because
Mahé stands like a grand elder sister
urrounded by her lesser siblings, of
which six lie just off the east coast,
ncircling Victoria's magnificent nat-
ral harbour. These islands lie within
he **Ste Anne Marine National Park**,
reated in 1973, the first such park in
he Indian Ocean. Unfortunately, the
oral has been harmed by siltation
rom land reclamation around Victo-
ia, the effects of the El Niño weather
ystem and perhaps global warming.
o protect this fragile environment,
notorised sports, fishing and the col-
ection of coral, shells and live shell-
ish are banned. The marine life is still
rolific (with more than 200 species
f fish) and the short journey to the
narine park, combined with lunch
n one of the charming and peaceful
slands that have restaurants, is still a
ery pleasant way to spend a day. Tour
perators offer full-day trips by glass-
ottom boat or subsea viewer starting
rom Marine Charter in Victoria (see
age 285). The subsea viewer gives
superior view, but is completely
nclosed and some people might feel
laustrophobic. Either way, you'll have
lenty of time to swim or snorkel.

Ste Anne ⓲ is the largest of the
slands off Victoria. The first Sey-
helles settlers lived here rather than
n Mahé, perhaps because of the
rocodiles then inhabiting Mahé's
xtensive coastal mangrove swamps.
)nce people began to settle on Mahé,
te Anne was largely left in peace as
coconut plantation, and since then
as been put to various uses. In 1832
whaling station was established here
nd in World War II the British had a
uel store here. In the 1980s, Ste Anne
vas briefly a centre for the National

Youth Service, a political experiment
that was eventually abandoned. Then
it became the headquarters of the
Marine Parks Authority (now moved
to Baie Ternay on Mahé). Today, it is
the site of a five-star hotel, the **Sainte
Anne Resort** (www.beachcomber-hotels.
com), which controls access to the
island and is part of the up-market
Beachcomber chain.

Île au Cerf ⓴ is a small, low-lying
island, mostly covered in coconut
palms and scrub, and it is easy to find
trails up the hill if you want to explore
inland. You can either come here as
part of an excursion organised by a
tour operator, or hire a boat from the
Marine Charter Association. Tourist
boats land on the sheltered northern
coast near **Kapok Tree Restaurant**,
where lunch is provided. After an
excellent Creole meal, you can take a
walk along the shore, past the homes
of some of the 80 or so residents, a
number of whom commute to Victoria by speedboat. One of Seychelles'
most famous residents, South African
writer Wilbur Smith, used to have a
house here.

*Île au Cerf and Île
Cachée.*

The best hotel is **Cerf Island Resort**, with 24 villas dotted among trees on a hillside and the excellent 1756 Restaurant, open for lunch and dinner. To stay on Cerf is a wonderful way to experience the tranquillity of life on an island with no roads or shops and just two small resorts, secure in the knowledge that all the conveniences of modern life are just a 10-minute boat ride away. The beach is always sheltered, good for swimming and snorkelling. Guests often hire pedalos to visit the beaches around Cerf, and even get as far as Moyenne, Ronde or Ste Anne.

Île Cachée is a tiny dot off the southeast coast of Cerf. It's possible to wade over to the islet at low tide.

Île Moyenne National Park ㉑ was declared a national park in 2008 (the smallest in the world) and is open to visitors daily (some hotels arrange excursions). It was previously owned by Englishman Brendon Grimshaw, a former newspaper editor who spent decades reintroducing native flora and fauna. He died in 2012. The island covers just 9 hectares (4 acres)

Snorkelling at Cerf Island Resort.

and is easy to explore. Around 16,00[] trees were planted here, including rar[] endemics such as coco de mer an[] Wright's gardenia, and there are gian[] tortoises and two supposed pirat[] graves (rumours abound that pirat[] treasure is buried on the island). A ci[]cular trail, which takes no more tha[] an hour at a leisurely pace, goes pas[] the house Miss Best built for her dog[] along the beach at Coral Cove an[] past the graveyard (where Grimshav[] is buried) and the chapel, throug[] Coco de Mer Vale, past the tiny, sham[]bolic museum and back to the forme[] Jolly Roger bar (no longer in opera[]tion). While the island's buildings ar[] sadly, looking run down, Moyenne [] still a magical place to visit. Snorke[]lers should head for the northwes[] coast and the waters between Moy[]enne and Ste Anne.

You can walk around the tiny **Î[]e Ronde** ㉒ (Round Island) in less tha[] 10 minutes. The island is now th[] exclusive domain of the residents c[] the small, up-market hotel Enchante[] Seychelles.

Île Ronde is best known for i[] excellent restaurant, **Chez Gab[]** housed in old buildings once part c[] an isolation camp for women suffe[]ing from leprosy. The menu feature[] Creole cuisine and its barbecued tun[] steak is a Seychelles legend. Afte[] lunch, most people are happy just t[] relax in the shade of the flame trees b[] the restaurant.

Île Longue (Long Island) was onc[] a prison and has been earmarked fo[] a five-star resort. Longue was a qua[] antine station in the days when th[] dreaded smallpox might arrive aboar[] a ship and spell disaster for the isc[]lated Seychelles' population.

Île Thérèse ㉓ on the west coast is[] beautiful island for a day trip. There [] no longer a regular boat service to th[] island but it's possible to paddleboar[] or kayak across the channel from th[] mainland. A beautiful beach face[] Mahé, and the shelter of the mainlan[] makes swimming here easy.

The pristine beach and crystal-clear waters at Cerf Island Resort.

Fregate Island, Anse Victorin.

FRÉGATE

Once home to pirates, Frégate is now an exclusive destination with seven beaches, 2,000 giant tortoises and one luxury resort.

The most isolated of the granitic islands, Frégate lies 55km (34 miles) east of Mahé. Covering sq km (1 sq mile) and surrounded y coral reefs, this privately owned land is the kind of place most of us n only dream of staying in. Frégate is ry exclusive; most of the guests (lim-ed to 40 at a time) are super rich and ome here to hide away in one of the esort's 16 luxury villas.

irates' lair

régate was christened by the French xplorer Lazare Picault during his 744 expedition. He probably named 'Île aux Frégates' after the frigate irds once present here. Among the ysterious ruins found on the island ere the walls of a large enclosure, nought to be the remains of a pirate ettlement, a lead-lined water conduit nd three tombs built of coral. Early esidents found a teak mast set in a tone platform at Anse Lesange and 1 1812 a gold cross-belt and shoulder trap were discovered. In 1838, a visitor rom Mauritius reported that golden panish coins were frequently found n the beaches. He also described the vreck of a large ship lying offshore. here is no direct evidence that these rtefacts were left by pirates; they ould just as easily be traces of an Arab rading post. Whatever their origin, hese various finds make Frégate one

of the few sites of archaeological inter-est in Seychelles.

In 1802 Frégate became a place of exile. A shipload of Jacobin terrorists, accused of having plotted to assassinate Napoleon, had been sent from France to Seychelles. Quincy, the commandant of Seychelles, suspected several of these deportees of joining forces with the slaves and inciting them to rebellion, and so he sent the ringleader, Louis Sepholet, together with three slaves, to Frégate. They were among the first inhabitants of the island, though they

Main Attractions
Plantation House restaurant
Wildlife walks to see the
    magpie-robin
Grand Anse

Guiding privileged guests on their way.

didn't stay long. Later the same year, Sepholet was transported to Anjouan in the Comoros with 35 of the other deportees. They all died there; it is said they were poisoned on the orders of the sultan.

Luxury resort

The only way you can stay on Frégate is as a guest of the hotel **Frégate Island 'Private'** 24. Opened in 1998, this resort is a celebrity haunt: Bill Gates, Pierce Brosnan and Brad Pitt and Angelina Jolie have all checked in. The design of the spacious villas, strung along the beautiful **Anse Bambous**, was influenced by the architecture of Bali and Thailand. Each one has a living room, large bedroom and two bathrooms with showers inside and out, all linked by a terrace, plus a private garden, secluded outdoor jacuzzi with amazing views, and a sundeck with a king-size sunbed. The resort is centred around Frégate House, where the main dining room, gymnasium and library are located, with a freshwater swimming pool and bar nearby. There's also a chapel, one of the island's oldest

Frégate Island 'Private'.

buildings, and the Rock Spa, where yo can enjoy anything from a yoga lesso to a hot stone massage while gazing the Indian Ocean. Facilities for eve water sport you can think of are ava able and the German multimillionai owner has also built a marina here f his own private yacht and other boa which can be chartered. In short, F gate is completely kitted out for t ultimate paradise island experience.

Plantation House

As a result of intense farming, most the island is now covered with intr duced vegetation. The higher hi are dominated by indigenous tree among which coffee, breadfruit, ba yan, cashew and ylang ylang all gro Plantations were laid out on the fl land and have been regenerated provide fresh food for the new reso including pawpaw, banana, cabbag lettuce and sweet potato. Cattle, pi and chickens are also reared to prov sion the hotel. The original **Plantatio House** 25, not far from the airstrip, ha been restored and houses a restaurar specialising in Creole cuisine, and

all museum with displays of antique furniture and information about the land's flora and fauna.

Wildlife walks

Apart from four other islands, Frégate is the only place where the Seychelles magpie-robin now survives. This pretty black and white bird had become extinct on the other granitic lands where it was once common. It was perilously close to disappearing from Frégate too but was rescued from extinction by the intervention of BirdLife International. It is now thriving again and new populations have been reintroduced to the other islands. Other birds that hotel guests can spot here include the Seychelles fody – a sparrow-like endemic species – and the Seychelles blue pigeon, which has striking red, white and blue plumage. There is a resident conservationist available for guided nature walks.

Gardiner's gecko, a species of green gecko, is also found only on Frégate.

Each guest is given the use of an electric golf cart to get around, but the best way to experience the diversity of Frégate's flora and fauna is to follow on foot one of the shady tracks that criss-cross the island. Apart from the path that runs around the main plantation, there are three trails worth exploring that radiate from the Plantation House. For the best snorkelling, take the path to the southeast of the island to **Anse Parc**. The walk takes only about 10 minutes. Close to the beach a sign points to the **Pirate's Wall**.

To reach the superb **Anse Victorin** ㉖, considered by some to be one of the finest beaches in the world, start from the Plantation House and take the path that runs inland at an angle from the airstrip. Cross the Bambous River and continue to the coast. At a leisurely pace, the walk takes about 30 minutes.

A third walk along a well-marked track heading inland from the plantation heads due west to **Grand Anse**, another beautiful beach. The hill to your left as you approach the bay is called Au Salon, where sangdragon trees flourish. To your right is **Signal Rock**, at 125 metres (410ft) the highest point on the island. The walk to Grand Anse takes about 20 minutes.

Anse Victorin, Fregate Island.

Sunset over Silhouette Island.

SILHOUETTE AND NORTH

Despite their close proximity to Mahé, Silhouette and North have a separate geology and an atmosphere akin to the Outer Islands.

Silhouette, the third largest island of the granitic group and the fifth largest in Seychelles, lies 20km (12.5 miles) northwest of Mahé. The island's topography and limited development mean an exceptional diversity of plants and animals has been preserved. Indeed, conservationists regard Silhouette as one of the most important biodiversity hotspots in the Indian Ocean. The highest of its three main peaks, Mont Dauban, rises to 740 metres (2,430ft) and is the second highest summit in Seychelles. Although it is bigger than La Digue, Silhouette is much quieter.

Silhouette has no roads, so its thick virgin forests remain largely untrodden. However, there is plenty to recommend it, not least the fact that it is one of the least known Inner Islands. The beaches on the east coast are sheltered by a coral reef and are perfect for swimming and snorkelling, and the forest trails, while not always easy going, take you through beautiful, dense vegetation. In 1987, the surrounding waters were declared a Marine National Park.

North Island is similar to Silhouette though less mountainous and it suffered more from forest clearance. However, the current owners developed the island with ecotourism in mind and reintroduced much of the endemic flora and fauna.

An aerial view of the coast.

The Dauban family island

The first recorded sighting of Silhouette was made in 1609 by the crew of the *Ascension*, an English East India Company vessel, yet the island was not settled by Europeans until the early 19th century. It was named after the French minister Etienne de Silhouette, Controller of Finances in 1759. It's a perfect name for the island, which appears as a mysterious shadow on the horizon when viewed from Beau Vallon on Mahé.

Main Attractions

Snorkelling, Silhouette
Aldabra tortoises, Silhouette
Dauban Mausoleum, Silhouette
Mont Pot à Eau hike, Silhouette

In the mid-19th century, Silhouette was gradually bought up by a French naval officer, Auguste Dauban, and it remained in the family for over a hundred years. They built a plantation house, cleared several paths across the island and introduced vanilla, cloves and other plants. Many coconuts were planted, often in seemingly inaccessible locations, because land had to be 'under coconuts' before it was deemed of any value. Today, most of these paths and crops lie abandoned and much of the forest has recovered. The Dauban era came to an end in the 1970s when the island was sold to a French hotel group that handed it over to the Seychelles government in 1983.

La Passe to Pointe Zeng Zeng

The majority of the island's 147 inhabitants live in and around the main settlement of **La Passe ❶**. Standing close to the harbour is **The Dauban Plantation House** (La Grande Case), the former Dauban family residence. Made up of four wooden buildings – the main house, toilets and bathroom,

The Dauban Mausoleum.

kitchen and dining room – the layout is typical of an island plantation house. The kitchen was usually built away from the house because of the risk of fire, with the dining room nearby so that the food could be served hot. In the days before air-conditioning was invented, the wide veranda provided the main living space. Today you can dine there on Creole dishes for lunch or dinner.

NPTS (The Nature Protection Trust of Seychelles) had it headquarters in La Passe for 14 years, but left in 2011 after its plans to reintroduce wild giant tortoises and terrapins were refused by the Islands Development Company and the Ministry of Environment on the grounds that similar tortoises were poached on Aldabra and Curieuse islands. Consequently 38 tortoises were transferred to North Island and 92 to Frégate.

A little south of La Grande Case, along the same track, is a gated enclosure containing the island's small population of captive Aldabra tortoises. Immediately behind the pens, the **Dauban Mausoleum ❷**, a grand

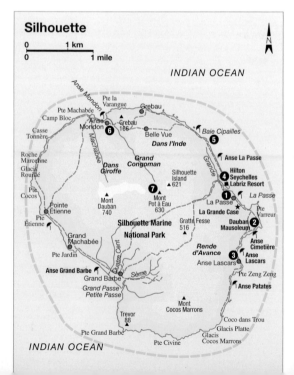

Silhouette map

ther incongruous construction surrounded by tall palms, modelled on the Madeleine in Paris. Adjacent to this is a marsh, where grey heron and black-crowned night heron (a recent coloniser) can be seen.

Continuing uphill from the mausoleum, the path leads to **Anse Lascars**. Legend has it that Arabs settled here prior to European settlement and for a long time it was thought that the graves found at Anse Lascars were those of Arab tradesmen who plied the Indian Ocean around the 9th century. However, bones from these graves have since been carbon-dated to around 1800 and are more likely to be the remains of the slaves who were the first occupants of Silhouette, having fled from Mahé in the late 18th century. From here, the path winds uphill to a viewing point at the headland of **Pointe Zeng Zeng**. It then descends to the secluded bay of **Anse Patates**, with its mature mangrove swamp and beach crest of windswept sea hibiscus. The walk to Pointe Zeng Zeng from La Passe takes about 20 minutes at a leisurely pace.

Best of the beaches

Hilton Seychelles Labriz Resort & Spa ❹ lies north of the La Passe jetty on **Anse La Passe**, a beautiful sandy beach that stretches northwest of the hotel. Beyond it lies an equally lovely, palm-fringed and deserted beach, **Baie Cipailles ❺**. The path running along the coast between the bays winds through an abandoned coconut plantation and a line of takamaka trees.

At the northern end of Baie Cipailles, there are two paths leading to **Anse Mondon ❻**, a one-house settlement that offers the best snorkelling on Silhouette. The lower path is overgrown and best avoided. The upper path, which runs over Belle Vue through thick forest, is easier and more scenic. Just before the descent back to the coast, the forest opens up to reveal a spectacular view of Anse Mondon. If landing at Anse Mondon, this walk may be done in reverse. Either way, it takes about two hours.

The old path from Anse Mondon to Grande Barbe has all but disappeared so this walk is no longer possible. However, the path connecting

FACT

Among the many pirate legends that echo across the Seychelles is the story of notorious French corsair Jean Hodoul. It is said he used Silhouette as his lair, hiding his treasure up in the hills.

Take a sunset cruise from the Hilton Seychelles Labriz Resort & Spa.

La Passe and **Grande Barbe** is well worn. It's about a three-and-a-half-hour walk from one side of the island to the other, but you can arrange for your boat to drop you at one side and collect at the other. Once home to many families, Grande Barbe is now a virtual ghost town. A short way inland from the beach, on the coastal plateau, is a marsh.

Mountain walk

The trek from La Passe to the summit of the magnificent **Mont Pot à Eau ❼** (630 metres/2,067ft) takes the best part of a day. It is not for the faint-hearted, and should not be attempted without a guide (obtainable from Silhouette Island Lodge): as it is infrequently used, the path is sometimes unclear and is often muddy and slippery due to high rainfall on the mountain side. However, if you enjoy a challenge, it's a wonderful walk that takes you through a fascinating mist forest, rich in exotic flora including the insectivorous pitcher plant that grows on its exposed summit.

North Island

North Island lies 7km (4.5 mile north of Silhouette and is conside ably smaller and less mountainou Most of the original forest was cu down, but a restoration programm has successfully reintroduced indi enous trees and a conservation tea has worked to save nesting sea tu tles, Aldabra giant tortoises (of whic there are now more than 100) an the Seychelles white-eye. The whit eye was once one of the world's rare birds, with just 25 left, but the 20 census revealed more than 100. The is a beautiful beach on each side the island, separated by a platea across the middle and rocky pror ontories either end. Day visits fro Mahé by helicopter (15 minutes) ca be arranged, and there is a five-st resort comprising 11 large villas, mac famous in 2011 as the honeymoo destination of the Duke and Duche of Cambridge. Their villa came with chef, butler, open-air bathroom wit sunken bath, four-poster bed made driftwood and a freshwater rock po in its private garden

Travel by helicopter to see North Island.

NATIONAL PARKS

In 1987 the waters surrounding Silhouette Island were declared a Marine National Park. Silhouette Island itself was declared a National Park in August 2010, with around 93 percent of the landmass included in the conservation area. The island is considered one of the most important biological spots in the Indian Ocean (most of the 75 endemic plant species of Seychelles are found on Silhouette) and the move to create a National Park has secured its virgin rainforest and helped to ensure the future of the critically endangered sheath-tailed bat, of which there was a population of less than 40. The creation of the park also means that Seychelles' largest area of freshwater marsh (Grande Barbe) is now protected.

Volcanic outcrops rise above the sandy beaches on Silhouette Island.

A particularly striking tree on Praslin.

PRASLIN

A slower pace of life, glorious beaches and the Vallée de Mai – a designated World Heritage Site – set Praslin apart.

Main Attractions
Anse Lazio
Black Pearl (Seychelles) tour
Vallée de Mai

Praslin is the second largest granitic island of Seychelles and lies 45km (28 miles) northeast of Mahé. It is much less mountainous, reaching a height of just 367 metres (1,204ft), and less populated, with about 5,500 inhabitants. The hills look rather threadbare after the green profusion of Mahé's mountains, but the sheltered valleys harbour primeval palm forest. Away from the shadows of the trees, there are many superb beaches and hotels. The island's popularity stems from these dreamy stretches of soft white sand and crystal waters, which have been declared the best in the world by many travel writers.

The pace of life is much more leisurely here than on Mahé. There are no towns and very little traffic. Taxis are available, but there is no taxi rank other than at the airport and Baie Ste Anne jetty. Buses are cheap, but it may involve a long wait at the roadside for one to appear and timetables are flexible. Ask any local when the next bus is due and they will tell you 'very soon'. This is more a hope than a statement of fact. The best way to explore the island is by car, though getting around by bicycle is a pleasant alternative and there are plenty of trails for those who prefer to explore on foot.

Praslin is connected with Mahé by air and by sea. The flight takes just 15 minutes and Air Seychelles operates services between the two islands throughout the day. Two fast catamaran ferries depart from the Inter-Island Quay, Victoria, and take one hour to reach Baie Ste Anne. They are popular with locals, making booking essential at weekends and advisable during the week. The same trip by schooner is cheaper, but takes three hours.

Baie Ste Anne to Anse La Blague

If you are arriving by boat, your first sight of the island will be the pretty

A smiling face at Praslin Airport.

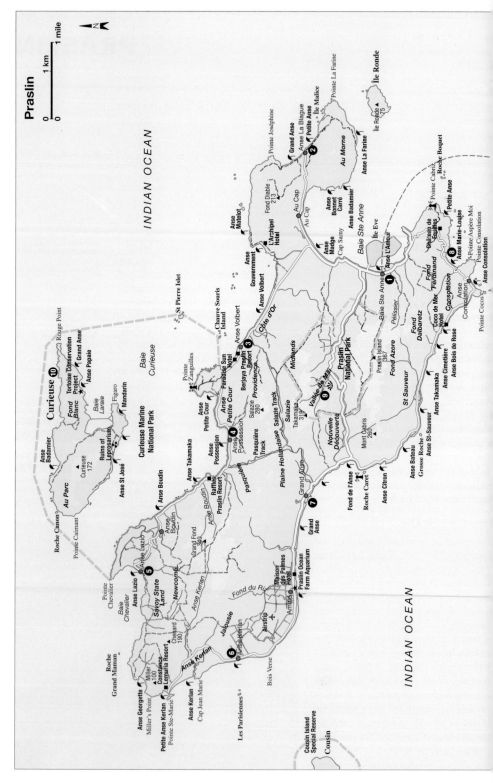

Praslin

INDIAN OCEAN

INDIAN OCEAN

aie Ste Anne ❶. It is one of the two apitals' of Praslin (the other being Grand Anse) and there is some rivalry etween them. The village has a coue of supermarkets, a hospital, church, ank and petrol station, but apart om a couple of self-catering estabshments, a boat rental company and handful of takeaways (Coco Rouge excellent), tourist facilities here are ninimal. Baie Ste Anne is a short drive om the Côte d'Or and the Vallée de Mai, and you can arrange a hire car as oon as you step off the ferry. If you are lying in, it would be best to collect our hire car at the airport.

The coast road running north from he pier forks at the northern end of he bay. The right-hand branch cuts cross the headland to the eastern hore at **Anse La Blague** ❷, a beauiful and secluded bay, which is great or snorkelling. There is a snack bar n the beach or for something more ubstantial dine at the boutique hotel 'illa Anse La Blague, on a terrace verlooking the sea. Diving, windsurfng and jet surfing can be arranged by 3leu Marine, based at the small hotel. A pleasant walk from the bay takes ou along the shore, past Petite Anse nd up a hill towards Anse La Farine. 'rom the top of the hill you can see Île Ronde and La Digue.

The Côte d'Or

The inland road that links Baie Ste Anne to Anse Volbert and the northeast oast passes through casuarina woodand. **Anse Volbert** ❸, also known as Côte d'Or, is the island's main tourism entre. Its long beach is sheltered by Curieuse Island so swimming is safe ll year and there are no large breakers, making it ideal for children. The beach helves very gradually so you need o walk out a long way to find water leep enough for swimming. The best norkelling is around the boulders at he northern end of the beach and out owards **Chauve Souris Island.**

While it is by no means overdeveloped, Anse Volbert is relatively crowded by Seychelles standards. Beside the beach there are several hotels, guesthouses, restaurants and souvenir shops, with more restaurants, boat operators and water-sports centres strung along the coast road. Several of these organise snorkelling trips to **St Pierre Islet**, as well as trips further afield to the islands of Curieuse, Cousin and Aride.

Next stop on the east coast road is **Anse Possession** ❹, a lovely bay with a view of Curieuse Island. It was around here, in 1768, that the first French explorers erected a plaque, claiming possession of the island. A cairn of stones and a flagstaff marked the spot. However, the location was lost. The French accused the English, who visited the island soon after, of deliberately obliterating the spot. The coast north of here, facing Curieuse island, is picturesque, quiet and good for swimming. The road runs through takamaka and casuarina groves and passes the pretty bays of **Anse Takamaka**, overlooked by five-star Raffles Praslin resort, and **Anse Boudin**. The short excursion from here to the top of Grand Fond (340 metres/1,115ft) is

Ferry docks at Praslin port.

worthwhile for the view across Praslin and the surrounding islands.

The best beach in the world

After Anse Boudin the road turns inland over the hill to **Anse Lazio ❺**, often hailed as 'the best beach in the world'. The sand here is as fine and soft as caster sugar and is scattered with granite boulders. The swimming is excellent except when the northwesterly winds are at their strongest, mainly around January and February. Snorkelling is best around the rocks and at the two small coves at the northeastern end of the bay. To enjoy the beach at its finest it is best to come early in the morning before the crowds. There are two restaurants, **Bon Bon Plume**, with thatched umbrellas dotted across a lawn by the sea; and at the opposite end of the beach, **Le Chevalier Restaurant**, set back from the shoreline. Both offer mainly seafood and Creole cuisine.

Exploring the west coast

If you are flying in, you will land on the west side of the island, 3km (nearly 2 miles) from Grand Anse – the other place to pick up a hire car (see Travel Tips, Transport). The coast road leading north of the airstrip from Amitié goes through a coconut plantation and farmland, past **Anse Kerlan ❻** to **Petite Anse Kerlan**, both beautiful sandy beaches framed by granite rocks. The sea can be wild in rough weather but on calmer days the area is excellent for swimming and snorkelling, though you should always beware of strong currents.

Petite Anse Kerlan is home to the **Constance Lemuria Resort**, an exclusive hotel complex in a spectacular location spread over 36 hectares (90 acres) with three beaches and Seychelles' only 18-hole golf course. Birdwatching in the grounds is excellent but it is necessary to call in advance to arrange access (see Travel Tips, Activities). Further north, lying within the grounds of the golf course, is **Anse Georgette**, a wild and remote beach worth exploring.

Back at Amitié, opposite the airstrip by the sea, is **Black Pearl (Seychelles) Ltd** (Mon–Fri 9am–4pm, Sat 9am–noon), where black pearls are cultured in the first and only pearl farm in the Indian Ocean region. A series of open concrete aquarium tanks have also been set up; here you can see giant clams and corals, reef fish and invertebrates. The guide is helpful and informative. Within the same complex is a jewellery boutique.

Around Grand Anse

The first settlement south of the airport is **Grand Anse ❼**. It's the largest village on Praslin, but it is far from commercialised and retains a sleepy character. The beach here is good, though often covered in seaweed. There are several small hotels, as well as shops, banks, takeaways and restaurants. The travel agents all have their Praslin offices here.

From Grand Anse the coast road continues southward past a series of picturesque bays. The 5km (3-mile) walk from Fond de l'Anse to Anse Marie Louise is pleasant and easy with beautiful views. There are a couple of hotels

Clear turquoise waters at Anse Lazio.

nd restaurants en route. This is the best stretch of coastline for deserted beaches, though not all are good for swimming as the water is shallow except at high tide. The first bay along this road is **Anse Citron**, followed by **Anse Bateau**, which has Les Rochers Restaurant, one of the best on Praslin, at its far end. **Anse Bois de Rose** is noteworthy for the Hibiscus Restaurant and **Coco de Mer Hotel and Black Parrot Suites**. Rounding Pointe Cocos, Anse Consolation is less ideal for swimming due to the beach rock barrier, but neighbouring **Anse Marie-Louise** ⑧ is the best bathing beach of all the above and a particularly quiet and picturesque spot. From this bay, the road winds steeply and passes the exclusive **Château de Feuilles Hotel and Restaurant** before descending to **Baie Ste Anne**.

A journey back in time at the Vallée de Mai

One of Seychelles' greatest natural treasures is the **Vallée de Mai** ⑨ (www.sif.sc; daily 8am–5.30pm; free for children under 12), a primeval forest claimed by General Gordon in 1881

to be the Garden of Eden. The valley, designated a Unesco World Heritage Site, occupies the heart of Praslin, midway between Grand Anse and Baie Ste Anne. Several well-marked nature trails run through it; the brochure maps these out quite clearly. It also lists the plants and wildlife you are likely to come across en route. You can choose between a short tour (about an hour) taking in most of the botanical sites, or a longer circular route, which includes a spectacular viewpoint (allow two to three hours). There are free guided tours by park staff at 9am and 2pm; tipping is discretionary. Or you can download the Vallée de Mai app for your smartphone before you visit, which is full of helpful information.

A visit to the Vallée de Mai is a journey back in time. Dinosaurs would have ambled through prehistoric valleys just like this. It is thought that the coco de mer palm evolved the world's longest leaf stems to keep its leaves out of the reach of herbivorous dinosaurs. Likewise, young palms probably developed spines to protect them from being eaten by the giant tortoises that

The Pagoda and beach at Coco de Mer Hotel.

Coco de Mer

The world's largest, heaviest seed is a much-prized symbol of the Seychelles and grows wild only on Praslin and Curieuse islands.

When he visited the Vallée de Mai in 1881, the British general Charles Gordon (of Khartoum fame) was so struck by its natural beauty that he truly believed he had discovered the original Garden of Eden. He concluded that the coco de mer tree (Lodoicea maldivica) must be the Tree of Knowledge and its nut the forbidden fruit.

His reasoning was that 'The heart is said by the scriptures to be the seat of desires and…the fruit [of the coco de mer] externally represents the heart, while the interior represents the thighs and belly…which I consider to be the true seat of carnal desires.' While some might disagree with his biblical conclusions, few people could argue that the coco de mer nut that grows on the female tree does resemble the thighs and belly of a woman, complete with a strategically placed tuft of hair. The

Some people believe the voluptuous coco de mer nut has aphrodisiac properties.

enormous catkin of the male tree is equally suggestive in form.

Height and weight

The average male coco de mer grows to 15 metres (50ft) and the average female to 9 metres (30ft). Each nut weighs somewhere between 18 and 22kg (40–49 lb), which makes it the heaviest seed in the world. The male tree, which can reach up to 32 metres (105ft), grows taller because it lives longer, but its height is also thought to facilitate wind pollination. The female tree, on the other hand, which can be heavily laden with more than a dozen nuts, is more susceptible to being felled by high winds. This may be nature's way of ensuring that the trees spread up the steep slopes as well as down the valley.

Spreading the seed

The pollination of the coco de mer is still a mystery. The wind probably acts as one agent, but the large white slugs often seen feeding on the male flowers and the green geckos common among the trees may also act as pollen carriers. Legend has it that on stormy nights the male trees uproot themselves and engage in passionate love-making with the female palms. Some say that witnesses to this orgy are certain to die. It is estimated that the coco de mer palm can live for between 200 and 400 years. Though now confined to Praslin and Curieuse, coco de mer trees may once have been much more common worldwide. During excavations for a new airport in Brussels in the 1980s, skeletons of large tortoises and fossils of nuts similar to the coco de mer were unearthed and dated to about 50 million years ago. 'Love nuts' have been highly prized since their discovery. They fetched such a high price in Europe that they became like gold dust.

Rich pickings

Today, they are carefully protected. Nuts gathered by the Ministry of Environment are hollowed out to reduce the weight and polished to be sold as souvenirs. Official collection is controlled (only four companies are registered to sell the nut) and each nut is numbered and stamped, and sold with a permit. The fact that they fetch a high price (a good one costs around 3,000 rupees, around €210) has encouraged poaching, which has had a detrimental effect on the rare palm forests. If you are offered a nut without a licence you can be sure it has been acquired illegally and is liable to be confiscated at the airport.

...ominated the ecosystem at one time. The enormous leaves of the coco de mer palms tower far above you like green vaulting and the dry leaf-litter that lies like a thick carpet on the forest floor rustles as geckos scuttle by. Streams can be heard tinkling and the giant leaves clatter in the breeze.

Primeval palms

About a quarter of the trees in the valley are coco de mer palms and almost half the remainder are endemic palms found only in Seychelles. These include the thief palm *(Latannyen fey)*, with its broad, undivided leaves, so called because the first specimen sent to Europe was stolen from Kew Gardens; the millipede palm *(Latannyen milpat)*, whose divided leaves are reminiscent of the legs of a millipede; and the Cinderella palm *(Latannyen oban)*, a comparatively short tree with a slender trunk. The palmiste *(palmis)* is a splendid, tall palm that was once the source of the main ingredient for millionaires' salad, so called because an entire tree had to be sacrificed to obtain the edible shoot near its tip. (The *palmiste* salad you now see on restaurant menus is made from the shoots of coconut trees, so you can tuck in with a clear conscience.)

Black parrots

You will see few birds inside the valley; they tend to stay above the tree tops. Only the piercing whistle of the black parrot reminds you that they are out there, somewhere. Of all the forest birds, the black parrot is the star attraction. It breeds only on Praslin, nesting in the hollows of rotten coco de mer palms and screwpines (artificial nest boxes have been erected in the valley). Because the vegetation is so dense, black parrots are, in fact, easier to spot outside the valley. In the early morning and late afternoon, they can be seen from the car park, flying in and out of the tall trees. They are also commonly seen at sea level where there are suitable feeding trees (such as at Villa Flamboyant and Britannia Restaurant at Grand Anse, and Coco de Mer Hotel at Anse Bois de Rose).

There is an Information Centre at the entrance which also sells souvenirs, snacks and drinks. It's a good idea to

Vallée de Mai.

arrive early to beat the crowds. Take drinks with you, but don't forget to dispose of the rubbish properly. Visitors are requested to stick to the paths, avoid the temptation of touching the plants, and smoking is strictly forbidden.

A short drive, or a 10-minute walk, from the entrance in the direction of Grand Anse will take you to a spectacular **waterfall**.

The Red Island

Just off the north coast of Praslin, **Curieuse Island** ❿ lies at the centre of a Marine National Park. From the sea, Curieuse is noticeably red, which explains why the island was first known as Île Rouge. The sparseness of the forest and redness of the soil is due to the many fires that have swept the island. The first recorded fire was in 1771, when the French suspected the English of arson. However, it seems more likely that fire is part of the natural cycle in the palm forest, helping new, vigorous plants to establish themselves and clearing out the old and dead vegetation.

A leper colony was established in 1833 at **Anse St José** on the south coast of the island. The old Creole style **Doctor's House** (daily 9am–5pm) has been renovated as a Visitor Centre and museum, though most of the leprosarium buildings lie in ruin. A footpath leads from here to **Baie Laraie**. (The causeway across the bay which used to enclose a pond where turtles were kept prior to export, was destroyed in the tsunami of December 2004 so it is no longer possible to take a shortcut across.)

A boardwalk follows the margin of the bay through mangroves where large *Cardisoma* crabs and colourful fiddler crabs are dominant. The path emerges at Baie Laraie, where there is a Tortoise Conservation Project. The young tortoises are kept in pens, while the adults over five years old are allowed to roam wild. These animals have been transferred from Aldabra, which has the world's largest giant tortoise population.

There aren't any hotels or villas on the island, but day trips can be arranged through most Praslin hotels and tour operators, and are often combined with a visit to Cousin Island nature reserve (see page 319).

Taking a snorkelling excursion to St Pierre.

SNORKELLING

The tiny uninhabited island of St Pierre, 15 minutes' boat ride from Curieuse, is a Robinson Crusoe-esque granite pile dotted with coconut palms. It has appeared in numerous adverts and glossy travel brochures and the sea surrounding it is a hotspot for snorkelling and diving. It's safe, the water is crystal-clear and an abundance of underwater boulders ensure an active marine world teeming with large bumphead parrotfish, Moorish idols, surgeonfish and emperor angelfish. If you wade ashore, there's the chance to see Wright's skinks and native sea birds. The coco de mer once grew on St Pierre, but can no longer be found there. The best way to visit is to book an island-hop day trip from Praslin to Curieuse, Cousin and St Pierre through a resort or local tour operator.

Walking through mangroves at Curieuse Marine National Park.

COUSIN, COUSINE AND ARIDE

A refuge for rare land birds and breeding
ground for thousands of sea birds, these islands
are key to conservation efforts in Seychelles.

These islands belong to the birds. Cousin and Cousine are the breeding ground for hundreds of thousands of sea birds; Aride is home to over a million. All three provide a habitat for rare land birds, most notably the Seychelles warbler and Seychelles magpie-robin. Thanks to the efforts of conservationists, particularly the Royal Society for Nature Conservation (RSNC), Government of Seychelles, and BirdLife International, both species have been saved from extinction.

Cousin

In the mid-1960s, **Cousin Island** ① came on the market. As a coconut plantation of insignificant proportions with no other source of income it was not deemed to be a particularly desirable investment. However, it emerged that Cousin was the final refuge of the Seychelles brush warbler, which was down to the last couple of dozen specimens. An international appeal was launched by conservationists and interest in the island grew, as did the owner's price. It was finally purchased by the RSNC on behalf of BirdLife International for £15,500 ($25,000), a small price for saving one of the rarest birds in the world. Today it is managed locally by Nature Seychelles.

Cousin is now a nature reserve for many other bird and animal species and attracts around 10,000 visitors a year. It is easily visited from Praslin, being just 2km (1.25 miles) from Amitié on the west coast, and is accessible all year round (Mon–Thu, mornings only), though landing is generally easier during the southeast monsoon (May to October), when Praslin provides shelter from the strong trade winds. This is also the best time to see the greatest numbers of nesting seabirds.

Most Praslin hotels and many independent boat owners arrange trips, which are often combined with afternoon visits to Curieuse and St Pierre

Pair of fairy terns on Cousin.

TIP

The landing on Cousin is a wet one, so put on beachwear or cotton shorts and a T-shirt – they'll soon dry off in the sun – and pack camera equipment in plastic splash-proof bags. A pair of solid walking shoes for the nature trail is also a good idea.

islands to make a full-day excursion. There is a resident Nature Seychelles warden and several knowledgeable rangers who provide guided tours that last about 75 minutes. Tours are given in French, English and Kreol. Visitors are not permitted to explore the island unaccompanied and there is no overnight accommodation available.

Birdlife

To minimise the risk of rats or other pests getting ashore no boats are allowed to land directly; instead, visitors transfer to the island's own boat to reach the sandy shore. As the noise of the engine is cut, the noise of the sea birds takes over. Seven species thrive on the island: four species of tern (lesser noddy, brown noddy, bridled tern and fairy tern), two shearwaters (Audubon's and wedge-tailed) and the white-tailed tropicbird.

However, it is the land birds for which Cousin is most famous, the Seychelles warbler in particular. The cessation of plantation activity and the regeneration of the native vegetation led to a rapid recovery in its numbers. The

future of this tiny wren-like bird has been deemed secure enough to remove it from the current world Red Data list of critically endangered species. It is a remarkable bird in that the sex of its offspring is determined by food availability. When food is plentiful, 80 percent of chicks are males, which leave soon after fledging to seek territories of their own. When food is scarce, nearly 90 percent will be female, which remain to help parents with future broods.

The Seychelles magpie-robin, a distinctive black and white bird, was once found on most of the granitic islands but was wiped out by a combination of direct persecution and introduced predators, which had confined the bird to Frégate island; there were only 23 left in 1990, making it one of the most critically endangered birds in the world. Attempts to establish a breeding population on Cousin, begun in 1994, then on Cousine the following year, met with success. Today, this charming, tame endemic is often spotted hopping along the tourist paths. Nevertheless, it remains one of the rarest birds on earth. A third rare endemic

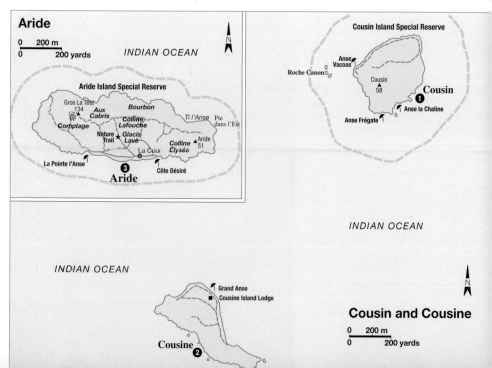

Aride

0   200 m
0   200 yards

INDIAN OCEAN

Aride Island Special Reserve

Gros La Tête 134
Aux Cabris
Bourbon
Colline Lafouche
Ti l'Anse   Pte dans l'Est
Complage
Nature Trail   Glacis Lavé
Colline   Aride 51
Elysée
La Cour
La Pointe l'Anse
Côte Désiré
③ Aride

Cousin Island Special Reserve

Anse Vacoas
Roche Canon
Cousin 58
Cousin ①
Anse la Chaline
Anse Frégate

INDIAN OCEAN

INDIAN OCEAN

Grand Anse
Cousine Island Lodge

Cousine ②

Cousin and Cousine

0   200 m
0   200 yards

e Seychelles fody, breeds here and on st five other islands (Cousine, Fréte, Aride, Denis and D'Arros).

ther fauna and flora

f the 11 reptile varieties on Cousin, inks are the most common. These onze-coloured lizards feed on dead icks and eggs. Hermit crabs are also mmon in the undergrowth and you'll obably spot one of the few giant tortises that roam the island. Cousin is so one of the few places where a visir stands a reasonable chance of seeing hawksbill turtle, as Seychelles is the ily place on earth where these animals me out by day.

The vegetation is dominated by indigous species. These include the *bwa rti* (tortoise tree), so called because fruits look like the carapace of a tortise. They are also eaten by Cousin's sident tortoises, not put off by their ipleasant smell. Also common here the remarkable pisonia that flowers coincide with the peaks of activity the lesser noddy nesting colony; its icky seeds attach themselves to the rds' feathers, the soft, malleable leaves make good nesting material and the horizontal branches are ideal nest sites.

Cousine

Cousin's sister island is a more exclusive destination. It is a privately owned nature reserve with four colonial-style luxury villas that can accommodate up to 10 guests at a time. It is a rare opportunity to experience living on an island teeming with wildlife. Attractions on **Cousine** ❷ include hawksbill turtles that come ashore to lay their eggs, mainly between September and January, along the sandy beach that fringes the eastern coast. Endemic birds include the Seychelles magpie-robin and Seychelles warbler, while many thousands of sea birds also breed here, including the largest population of wedge-tailed shearwaters in Seychelles. Day-trippers are allowed by special arrangement made in advance (tel: 4321107).

Aride

Lying about 10km (6 miles) north of Praslin, **Aride** ❸ is the most northerly of the granitic isles and arguably the most unspoilt island in the Indian

A scientist releasing hawksbill turtle hatchlings on Cousine.

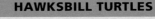

HAWKSBILL TURTLES

Though famous for birds, Cousin is also one of the most important breeding sites for hawksbill turtles, with possibly the longest-running monitoring programme (more than 40 years) anywhere in the world. Elsewhere, the hawksbill turtle population has been greatly reduced following years of exploitation – not for the flesh, which is sometimes poisonous, but for the shell which, until the early 1990s, was made into trinkets to be sold to tourists. It will take decades for populations to recover as hawksbills do not breed until 25 to 40 years of age.

In Seychelles, the turtles nest in daylight hours from September to March. A single female may emerge up to six times per season to lay her eggs at intervals of 14 days. Each nest may contain up to 180 eggs. Older turtles lay even more eggs, more frequently. They hatch after about 60 days. The young turtles that emerge scurry straight to the sea, but not all of them make it. On the way, some fall victim to crabs, others to sea birds. Those that reach the sea are still not safe, as many will be eaten by large fish. As a result, very few survive to adulthood. Recent research includes attaching transmitters to adult turtles linked to satellites in order to discover the mystery of where they spend their time outside the breeding season.

Cousine's shore.

Ocean. The name Aride (so called because there are no streams or other sources of fresh water) first appeared on French charts drawn up after exploratory voyages in 1770 and 1771, but the island had no settlers until 1861. Thereafter, it was run as a plantation until 1973, when it was purchased by Christopher Cadbury of chocolate fame (1908–95), a keen conservationist and at the forefront of campaigns to set up nature reserves on Cousin, La Digue and Aride. But it was his purchase of Aride island, which he gave to the Royal Society for Nature Conservation, and its establishment as a nature reserve in 1979 for which he is most remembered. An engraved granite plaque on La Pointe l'Anse is dedicated to his memory. Today, Aride is owned by Island Conservation Society.

The island is covered in a rich flora and fauna and all species can be seen from the set nature trail. This begins at the settlement of **La Cour**, crosses the flat coastal plateau and winds uphill to a **viewing point** at the peak of Gros La Tête, 134 metres (435ft), where the cliffs drop dramatically to the sea.

From here you can see hundreds of frigatebirds, noted for their huge wing span, which can stretch to 2 metres (6.5ft), soaring over the sea. On clear days, the coral island of Denis is just visible on the horizon, but where the waves crash against the foot of Aride's cliffs are the last granite rocks before India and Sri Lanka. Once on the hill visitors are not allowed to deviate from the path as the ground either side is riddled with the burrows of nesting shearwaters, which are easily inadvertently destroyed. You return to the Visitors' Shelter at the beach in time for lunch, with the afternoon free to swim, snorkel or explore the plateau.

The reserve is open Mon–Fri, and weekend visits are possible by prior arrangement with the island's manager (tel: 2719778); days and times can vary according to weather conditions. The island warden and local rangers, the only inhabitants, give guided tours lasting about two hours. Most of the large hotels organise day trips (the crossing from Praslin takes about 45 minutes) and lunch and the entrance fee to the reserve are included in the price.

A million sea birds

Like Cousin and Cousine, Aride is a rat free zone and so has remained a haven for vast numbers of sea birds. Eighteen species (including five found only in Seychelles) breed on Aride, more than the rest of the granitic islands combined. Chief among these is the sooty tern. Aride also has the world's largest colony of the lesser noddy, sheltering almost 200,000 pairs, as well as the largest surviving colony of the rare roseate tern in the Indian Ocean. The breeding season of terns and noddies coincides with the southeast monsoon, which lasts from May to October. All in all there are over a million breeding birds milling about the island, making Aride a noisy place at this time of year.

The elegant fairy tern, symbol of Air Seychelles, nests throughout the year as does the white-tailed tropicbird, one of the most beautiful of all sea birds.

ey can be seen all over the island but u need to walk to the top of the hill find the few pairs of red-tailed trop-birds breeding in the only site out-le the Aldabra group. Completing e sea bird scene are the wedge-tailed earwater and Audubon's shearwater. earwaters leave their burrows before wn, returning after nightfall and are ore likely to be encountered at sea en ute to Aride.

nder the canopy

digenous vegetation was reintroduced replace the monoculture of coconut lms. With the reappearance of a for-t canopy, two species of land bird, the ychelles sunbird and Seychelles blue geon – which disappeared when the digenous trees were removed – have w returned. The Seychelles warbler eded more of a helping hand. Since e transfer of 29 birds from Cousin in '88 numbers have rocketed to around 000 so that Aride now holds more an 80 percent of the world popula-n. In January 2002, two more rare demic birds, the Seychelles magpie-bin and the Seychelles fody, were transferred to Aride and, within a short time, both began to breed. This means Aride can now boast more breeding native species than any other island.

The prolific sea bird life supports one of the highest densities of lizards in the world, including three species of skink and three of gecko. The wolf snake can also be found. Large millipedes may also be seen on the hillside; do not touch as they emit an obnoxious spray.

Among the most beautiful of Sey-chelles' endemic plants is Wright's gar-denia, and Aride is the only place in the world where it occurs naturally. Its large white flowers, spotted with magenta, have a delicate fragrance and appear precisely 10 days after heavy rain.

Reef fish

The naturalist Sir Peter Scott, visiting Aride in 1986, recorded 88 species of reef fish in little more than 1.5 hours in the water. Since then, other visitors and successive wardens have added to the list, which now records over 450 species – more than on any other granite island. Dolphins, whale sharks and flying fish have also been seen around the island.

Frigate surveying the landscape

GIANTS OF THE SKY

After a long, hot walk to the viewing point near the summit at Grolatet, it is refreshing to emerge from the woodland onto the bare granite cliffs and feel the cooling breeze. Here, the enor-mous frigatebirds soar on outstretched wings, occasionally har-rying other sea birds as they return to feed their young, forcing them to relinquish their catches. Though notorious as pirates, frigatebirds are quite capable of catching their own fish. Using their long tails as rudders they steer with amazing agility. Yet they are primitive birds, unable to land on the surface of the sea as they lack webbed feet to swim. Their feathers also lack water-proofing and quickly become waterlogged. These sea birds spend much of their lives flying several thousand kilometres from breeding colonies across open ocean. They cannot even walk on their tiny stunted legs and once they land on a branch are rooted to the spot. Once aloft, they cruise with barely a flicker of their enormous 2-metre (6.5ft) wingspan. Their bones are incredibly light, only around 5 percent of their total weight, and they weigh little more than a kilogram (just over 2 lb), about the same as a small chicken. This gives them the lowest wing loading (weight per wing area) of any bird in the world.

The famous, beautiful beach of
Anse Source d'Argent.

LA DIGUE

Life proceeds at an agreeably slow pace on what is generally considered to be one of Seychelles' most beautiful islands.

n the early days of tourism in Seychelles, La Digue was billed as the island that time forgot, where fe went along at a pace little faster han that of its ox carts, then the only orm of public transport. Today, La Digue's ox carts are more of a tourist iversion than a necessity – bicycles nd pick-up trucks and one or two ars now share the tracks beneath he palms. Tourism rubs shoulders vith the traditional way of life and as combined with it to raise living tandards. Nevertheless, having no irstrip and a tiny population, the sland retains its 'out of the rat race' tmosphere and friendliness. The ourth largest island of the granitic roup, La Digue is generally considred to be one of the most beautiful f the Seychelles islands and should ot be missed. The spectacular coast, vith its huge boulders towering over erfect beaches, has been used as a ackdrop for many a film and fashon shoot. It is less than half the size f Praslin, just 4km (2.5 miles) to the vest, but rises almost as high, to 333 netres (1,093ft) at Nid d'Aigles. The sland population is also less than alf that of Praslin, with around ,000 inhabitants concentrated nainly on the west coast between La 'asse and La Réunion. Most tourist ccommodation is here too.

Exploring La Digue

There is no airstrip on the island, but it's no more than a 30-minute sail away from Praslin by schooner or 15 minutes by fast catamaran (see Travel Tips, Transport). A day trip is feasible, but to experience the island fully and soak up the atmosphere it is worth staying for at least two nights. Ferries from Baie Ste Anne arrive at the tranquil harbour of **La Passe** ❶, a haven for yachts and schooners that shelter close to the palm-fringed shore. There are a number of grand plantation-style

Main Attractions

Veuve Reserve
Belle Vue
L'Union Estate
Anse Source d'Argent
Snorkelling off Île Cocos

Tourists can enjoy rides in traditional ox carts.

TIP

When cycling round La Digue, take care on the mountain tracks, particularly after the rains, when they can become slippery with mud. Wind-blown sand on the east coast road can also be hazardous.

houses at La Passe, gracefully growing old and, on the whole, well maintained. The quiet fish market by the jetty turns into a hive of activity when the fishermen bring in their catches. Nearby is a small **café** next to a **Tourist Information Centre**.

You'll see very few cars here – there are only a handful of taxis and no hire cars – but La Digue is small enough (10 sq km/6 sq miles) to do without them. *Camions*, or open-sided lorries with fitted seats – four of them in all – pass for buses. There are no set timetables and they meander around the island according to the requirements of drivers and passengers. The flat coastal plateau and its beaches as far as L'Union Estate (see page 327) are easily explored on foot. Cycling is

quicker, of course, and will enable yo to travel further afield; south to Grar Anse or around the northern rim ar south again to Anse Fourmis. To ped at top speed from La Passe to L'Unio Estate takes less than 10 minutes, b the whole point of La Digue is that r one does anything at top speed. The are plenty of bikes for hire at the jet including children's models, but the are of varying quality and it's a goo idea to examine a few, the brakes particular, before settling on one.

Inland loop

Whether you're walking or cyclin the southbound road from La Passe a good place to begin your exploratic of the island (turn right on leaving t jetty). Looking out to sea as you hea

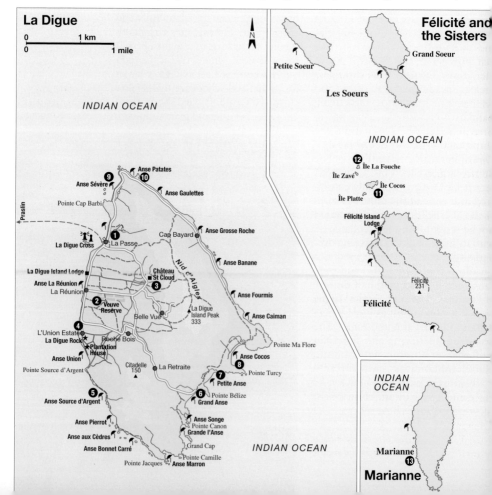

wards Réunion, the other main settlement, there is a view of **La Digue Cross**, a monument erected on top of granite rocks in the bay in memory of people who drowned while attempting to land on La Digue.

The road swings inland to round the chalets of **La Digue Island Lodge**, an up-market resort. It then runs parallel to the coast to a T-junction at Pont Bill. A left turning takes you to the **Veuve Reserve ❷**. Named after the beautiful Seychelles paradise flycatcher, the symbol of La Digue, the reserve was set up to preserve some of the last remaining takamaka and Indian almond *(badanmyen)* trees in which it feeds and nests. This habitat is under tremendous pressure from the island's growing population and boat-building industry. *Veuve (Vev* in Kreol) means 'widow', a reference to the magnificent, long black tail feathers of the male, reminiscent of a widow's black veil. The female, by contrast, lacks the elongated tail feathers and is chestnut and white with a black hood. Once widespread in the Praslin group, the paradise flycatcher has survived as a breeding bird on La Digue, where there are less than 300 birds, and on Denis Island, where there are around 50 after a successful translocation project from La Digue. A few sightings have also been reported on neighbouring Félicité. They can be seen almost anywhere on the coastal plateau in the early morning, but chances of a sighting in the reserve are more or less guaranteed in the early morning and late afternoon. A Visitors' Centre at the reserve entrance provides information on the birds and the warden gives useful pointers on where they can be spotted. Entry is free and the path that begins at the roadside Visitors' Centre is navigable both on foot and by bike.

Continuing inland from the reserve, the road bends northwards to run parallel with the coast road leading to **Château St Cloud ❸**, a grand and enchanting building that now houses a small hotel. It was built at the height

of the Napoleonic wars as the plantation house of a vanilla farm. Vanilla was introduced to La Digue in 1866 and quickly overtook coconuts as the most lucrative commodity. The further development of synthetic vanillin in the early 20th century caused the industry to crash, bringing hardship to the islanders. Ruins of the slaves' quarters and remnants of the vanilla factory can still be seen.

A road near the chateau heads up the steep hillside to **Belle Vue**, just below the summit of Nid d'Aigles. It is too steep to ride a bicycle and a tough walk, except in the cool of early morning or late afternoon. The easiest way to tackle this road is by taxi. It is worth the fare for the fabulous view over the coastal plateau and out towards Praslin.

South of the Flycatcher Reserve the road leads back to the coast and turns southward once more past two art galleries, and the pretty Catholic church of **Notre Dame de l'Assomption**. Beyond these, the track leads to **L'Union Estate ❹** (daily 7am–5pm), an old plantation. Here, there is a

La Digue Island Lodge's restaurant has a romantic location.

EAT

The restaurant at Grand Anse, Loutier Coco (daily 9am–5.30pm), serves Creole cuisine, sandwiches and omelettes at reasonable prices.

working *kalorifer* where copra (dried coconut) is heated and dried, and a coconut oil press pulled by an ox. Other features include **La Digue Rock**, a towering granite boulder appearing like a natural sculpture, giant tortoises, horse riding (strictly within the plantation grounds) and a picturesque **plantation house**, for which there are currently plans to create a museum. The old colonial **cemetery** nearby, where the early settlers are buried, is also worth a look.

Anse Source d'Argent

On the far side of the plantation reserve is one of Seychelles' most celebrated beaches, **Anse Source d'Argent** ❺ (Bay of the Silver Spring). It is reached by following the palm-shaded trail that runs past La Digue Rock and the plantation house. There are no facilities here at all, but that is part of its beauty. The silver white sands are framed by giant granite boulders and perfectly positioned palms – the ultimate in exotic backdrops and a popular spot for weddings and fashion shoots. Be warned, its reputation

means it attracts tourists, and low ti[d]e can prohibit swimming. A coast[al] path, easy to follow on foot, conti[n]ues southward past a series of equal[ly] beautiful coves.

East to Grand and Petite Anse

Near the entrance to L'Union Estat[e] the road turns inland and cu[ts] through an area of marshland know[n] as **La Mare Soupape** (*soupap* is th[e] Kreol name for the terrapins, or mu[d] turtles, that inhabit the area). Beyon[d] the marsh, the road climbs steeply an[d] it is quite an effort to cycle or walk [to] the crest of the hill. Perseverance [is] rewarded with stunning views as th[e] road descends through thick veget[a]tion to the velvety sands, granite ou[t]crops and turquoise waters of **Gran[d] Anse** ❻, the island's largest beac[h]. It's a perfect place to relax and picni[c], but the sea can be wild and dange[r]ous, particularly between June an[d] September, when the waves create [a] powerful undertow.

A footpath leads northeast of Gran[d] Anse towards two more magical bay[s]

Looking out over Anse Source D'Argent.

Often deserted, the white sands of Petite Anse **7** and **Anse Cocos 8** are also surrounded by spectacular rock formations. Like Grand Anse, however, currents are strong and swimming can be dangerous. Unless you are particularly adventurous it is not worth exploring further than Anse Cocos, where the track turns inland crossing **Pointe Ma Flore** – which offers a lovely view over Anse Cocos and the northeast coast – to Anse Caiman, then peters out before you reach the road at Anse Fourmis.

La Passe to Anse Fourmis

The easiest way to reach Anse Fourmis is by cycling the 4km (2.5 miles) around the northern coast from La Passe. Though walking is also easy, the route has not much in the way of shelter from the hot sun. The wild, unspoilt scenery is the main attraction. The beaches en route are all beautiful, though not all of them are good for swimming. The first of these is **Anse Sévère 9**, which lies beyond the promontory of Pointe Cap Barbi, followed a little further on by the rockier bay of **Anse Patates 10**. Both beaches are good for swimming and snorkelling (snorkelling can be difficult at low tide due to the swell over the shallow reef but is relatively easy a couple of hours either side of high tide). The corals are not fantastic but fish life is prolific, particularly around the rocks where the waters teem with butterflyfish, angelfish, parrotfish, squirrel fish, Moorish idols, batfish and hawkfish.

Continuing south, you'll pass a succession of small, rocky bays, washed by rougher seas – **Anse Gaulettes**, **Anse Grosse Roche** and **Anse Banane**. The road comes to a dead end at **Anse Fourmis**. Here, in calm weather, snorkelling is good around the rocks.

Islands north of La Digue

The waters around the neighbouring islands of Félicité, Marianne, Petite Soeur, Grande Soeur, Île Cocos, Île La Fouche and Île Zavé are rich in bird and marine life. All are within close proximity to La Digue and make ideal day-trip destinations, offering a choice of activities: swimming, diving, snorkelling, birdwatching, fishing, or just

Time for surfing at Anse Severe.

relaxing and eating. (All the islands, except Félicité, can also be reached by boat from Praslin.) Excursions to these largely uninhabited islands can be arranged through your hotel, the tourist information office at La Passe jetty or at one of the roadside stalls offering trips. Itineraries can be flexible if you discuss priorities in advance with the boat owner, and lunch and soft drinks are usually included. Most operators require a minimum of four people per trip.

For snorkelling, the best site is the tiny Île Cocos . Access to the waters of this Marine National Park was forbidden to visitors during the 1980s because of the damage to its coral reefs caused by tourists. The corals are now slowly recovering and it is still a beautiful site. Sea birds are the main attraction on Île La Fouche , a rocky islet off the north coast of Île Cocos, and Île Zavé; the latter, lying south of Île La Fouche, is little more than a jumble of rocks but holds five breeding species of sea bird: the wedge-tailed shearwater, bridled tern, lesser noddy, brown noddy and fairy tern. This

Spliting coconuts at Historical L'Union Estate Mill.

is also an excellent snorkelling site weather permitting. There are large numbers of parrotfish, sweetlips and groupers. Whale sharks are commonly seen around November.

Just north of Cocos, Marianne could have been Robinson Crusoe's very island. Uninhabited and blanketed with coconut palms, it has a single beach on the western coast where small boats can land. Grande Soeur and Petite Soeur (known collectively as The Sisters) are owned by the Praslin hotel Château de Feuilles, which reserves them exclusively for guests at weekends. During the week, other boat owners are allowed to offer trips.

It will soon be possible to stay on Félicité Island, 3km (1.5 miles) northeast of La Digue, following an announcement by Six Senses Hotels Resorts and Spas of plans to open its first Seychelles hotel there in 2016. The resort (Zil Pasyon – Isle of Passion) will occupy the north side of the island and take up one-third of the total landmass, with 28 one- and two-bedroom villas, two restaurants, a bar and a Six Senses Spa.

DEPORTED TO PARADISE

In 1798 there was a rebellion in the French colony of Réunion. The insurrection, led by a former sergeant, Etienne Belleville, and a priest, Jean Lafosse, marched on the capital, St-Denis, protesting against taxation levels and rumours that the island was to be given to the English. The revolt was easily quashed, and the decision taken to exile the dozen or so ringleaders to a suitable location somewhere on the coast of India. They were put aboard the *Laurette* under the command of Captain Loiseau, but were never to reach India. Loiseau later claimed that they had to seek shelter from bad weather at Mahé. Holding the crew at knifepoint, the deportees mutinied and forced them to sail the ship to La Digue, where they went ashore, letting the *Laurette* sail on to Praslin. This story is probably a cover-up. As the deportees told it, they thought La Digue made as good a place of exile as any, and Loiseau did little to dissuade them. In fact, more than half of the newcomers did settle peacefully on La Digue, with their families joining them later. Among those who stayed was Célestin Payet, and to this day the Payets are one of the leading families of the island. Belleville and Lafosse, the rebellion leaders, both returned to Réunion in the early 1800s.

Bikes are the main means of transport as there are few cars on the island.

Landing on Denis Island.

BIRD AND DENIS ISLANDS

Similar in appearance, these privately owned coral islands, each boasting a luxury island lodge, have developed in radically different ways.

Although very similar on first appearance, Bird and Denis islands have developed along different lines in recent times. Both have been in private ownership for many years, having once been plantations. Denis is now an island playground for tourists keen on water sports and game fishing. Bird, once a major source of sea birds' eggs for local cuisine, is now managed for ecotourism. Whichever approach you prefer, these dream islands are just a 30-minute flight from Mahé.

Bird Island

Bird Island is also known as Île aux Vaches (Island of Cows) after the dugongs or 'sea cows' that once thrived in its waters. Because it was an excellent source of oil, this marine mammal was soon exterminated. The island was named Bird Island by the British, after the millions of sea birds that flock here to breed. The secret of Bird Island is its simplicity. Lying 96km (60 miles) north of Mahé, it is relatively remote. There is only one flight a day, so the minimum stay is two nights here, though often visitors opt to spend longer than they originally planned. For many, it becomes addictive: 35 percent of guests are return visitors, who come back periodically to wash away the strains of modern life. The ethos of the island resort is firmly based on the

ideal that a balance is possible between man and nature. Visitors are free to wander wherever they wish, providing they do not harm or disturb the wildlife. Organised sports and activities are deliberately kept to a minimum. You can walk, go birdwatching, swim, snorkel, go game fishing, play table tennis or billiards, or just laze in the sun and do nothing. The more energetic might wish to go in search of Esmeralda, the famous giant tortoise. He (the name is deceptive) once held the record as the heaviest land tortoise in the world.

Main Attractions

Hawksbill turtle, Bird Island
Sooty tern, Bird Island
Tortoises, Denis Island
Diving, Denis Island

Conservationist working on Bird Island.

Turtles and terns

Guests are also encouraged to help with the island's turtle conservation projects. **Hawksbill turtles** come ashore to lay eggs between October and February (see page 321), and green turtles from April to October. There is a tagging programme, and 'turtle-spotting' (hawksbill turtles lay their eggs in daylight) or nest-watching gives an exciting dimension to an island walk. Since nests are closely monitored, some visitors are treated to the unforgettable sight of hatchlings struggling down to the sea.

Birds, appropriately, are the chief attraction and the best time to see them is in the breeding season between April and October. The island's most famous attraction is the enormous **sooty tern colony ❶**, which occupies one sixth of the island during these months. The colony was once harvested for sea bird eggs, considered a great delicacy by the Seychellois. In more recent years the birds have come to be appreciated more for the spectacle they provide than for their culinary value.

A sooty tern colony.

Bird Island is also a good place for birdwatchers outside the breeding season. Being on the edge of the Seychelles Bank, it is often a first landfall for migrants, and many rare species have been seen here. Regulars include turnstones, which are tame enough to peck about your feet, and there is a chance to glimpse rollers, bee-eaters, cuckoos and other species from far across the ocean.

Relaxing at the Lodge

The only place to stay here is **Bird Island Lodge ❷** (www.birdislandsey chelles.com), made up of 24 simple wooden chalets strung along the idyllic beach on the west side of the island. From here you can watch columns of spiralling birds in their thousands, circling over the colony. There are no televisions or in-room phones, so it's a great place for a break from modern life. There is a delightful bar at the main building of the Lodge in which to relax, and the cuisine, with strong Creole influences, is superb. Most of the dishes on the menu are prepared with produce of the island. Imagine

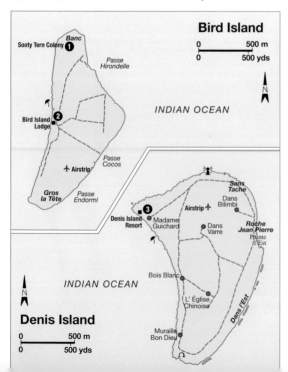

he delights of chicken soup with coconut milk, lemon grass and ginger, or fresh sailfish steaks grilled on a barbecue under the stars. The chef can cater to any special requirements and vegetarians claim Bird offers the best special dishes in Seychelles.

Denis Island

Similar in size to its sister island, Denis lies 80km (50 miles) north of Mahé. As with Bird Island, there is only one place to stay, but it's much more luxurious. **Denis Island Resort ❸** (http://denisisland.com) is one of the best places you can stay in Seychelles; the 25 villas have private pools or gardens, and the delicious cuisine is based around home-grown produce and fresh fish. Close to the hotel is a large enclosure sheltering **tortoises**. After just a few hours in this quiet and stunningly beautiful refuge, the world outside seems to lose all importance.

When early navigators wanted to take a claim to an island for their country, they could lay down a 'possession stone' if they had one handy; if not, they popped a deed of possession into a bottle and buried it. Somewhere on Denis Island such a bottle may still lie hidden, dating from 1773 and the visit of Denis de Trobriand, who claimed the island for France and blessed it with his name.

The lighthouse, dating from 1910, is still operational. It is open to the public and the view from the top is magnificent.

The local NGO Green Islands Foundation runs conservation programmes on Denis. Rats have been eradicated and three rare endemic birds introduced: the Seychelles warbler, Seychelles fody and Seychelles magpie-robin.

On and in the water

Situated on the edge of the Seychelles Bank, where the sea bottom plunges away to a depth of 2,000 metres (6,600ft), Denis Island has become a top game fishing destination: several records have been broken for dogtooth tuna and bonito. Other catches-of-the-day might include barracuda or sailfish. **Diving** has also become big here in recent years, and there are two resident divemasters.

Denis Island Resort's white sands.

THE OUTER ISLANDS

Remote and visited by just a handful of people each year, these island groups have an unsurpassed beauty and timelessness.

Even in our shrinking world, Seychelles' so-called 'Outer Islands' are, for the most part, remote, uninhabited and possessed of an unspoilt beauty which those fortunate enough to have experienced find compelling. There are few who come away unmoved by these serene, isolated worlds; their encircling pristine beaches, vivid blue lagoons, kaleidoscopic reef life and the stillness beneath the palms, which is only disturbed by the sigh of the waves.

The Outer Islands are divided into four main groups. From east to west they are the Amirantes Group, the Alphonse Group, the Farquhar Group and the Aldabra Group. In the early 20th century, these distant outposts were important elements in the economy of the Inner Islands. Schooners plied slowly from isle to isle collecting exotic produce for home consumption or export, returning with holds filled with coconuts, dried sea cucumber, green sea snail, guano and tortoiseshell. All that remains of the former trading posts and settlements are a few crumbling buildings and scattered ruins, which offer nothing more than a hint of what the way of life was like here. Today only a handful of the Outer Islands are inhabited, their tiny settlements peopled by hardy Seychellois *lois* (island workers) on contract, fishing or collecting and processing copra.

Although tourism is playing an increasingly important role, the Outer Islands remain largely unexplored. Shops and nightlife are non-existent, and the beaches and sea are consistently breathtaking and pristine. There is excellent game fishing, particularly around Poivre, and fly-fishing, especially in the St François lagoon. The diving is spectacular off Desroches and Alphonse, and around Assumption Island. Aldabra Atoll is a major wildlife attraction, being home to thousands of giant tortoises, while the whole area is rich in birdlife.

Main Attractions

Diving, Desroches and Alphonse
Sooty tern, Desnoeufs
Giant tortoises, Aldabra

At anchor in calm waters.

Sail away

There are two ways to visit the Outer Islands: either on a charter boat or by basing yourself at one of the hotels. Desroches and Alphonse are currently the only two islands with hotels. It is also possible to stay at the Research Station on Aldabra and, if money is no object, you can book the entire islands of D'Arros and St Joseph Atoll for yourself. There is an increasing number of habitable boats visiting the area and these have the flexibility to go to all but D'Arros and Rémire, which are private. All the islands are within a short distance of each other and, depending on how long you want to spend in each, they can be visited in a few days. Chartering is fairly expensive due to logistics and the small scale of things, but not over the top (see Travel Tips, Activities). Whether you plan to base yourself on land or charter a boat, you should plan your trip to the Outer Islands in advance of going to Seychelles. It is difficult, though not entirely impossible, to turn up and book an Outer Island excursion.

The Amirantes Group

Of all the island groups, this is the closest to Mahé, stretching from African Banks to the north, 235km (14 miles) from Mahé, down to Desnoeu Island, 325km (200 miles) southwe of Mahé. The islands were discovere during Vasco da Gama's second gre voyage in 1502, by which time he ha been promoted to admiral, hence th name Ilhas do Amirante (Islands of th Admiral). Now largely uninhabite the islands were once important com ponents in the economy of Seychelle producing copra, tortoiseshell, turtl meat, sea bird eggs and guano for loc use and export. Life on these remo scraps of land was tough and lonely. A world markets changed, their relative small harvests of goods became unec nomic to gather, and one by one the were abandoned to nature.

Desroches

The biggest island in the group Desroches, a long thin strip of lan with a fabulous sheltered lagoon an miles of sand, which make it the pe fect get-away-from-it-all island. Th

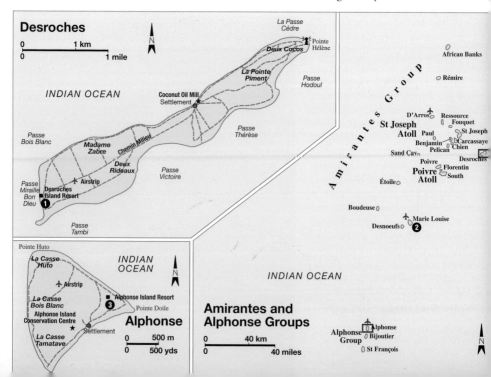

light from Mahé takes 40 minutes and lands at the grassy airstrip at the western end of the island by the **Desroches Island Resort** ❶ (www.desroches-island. om), the only hotel in the Amirantes. There could hardly be a greater contrast between the arduous life of an *lois* in the 19th century and the luxury of a holiday at this exclusive island lodge, nestling under the palms of an old coconut plantation. The 17 suites skirting the beach provide accommodation for no more than 40 guests.

Most of the 50 or so inhabitants of Desroches are contract workers, mainly from Mahé, engaged in agriculture. They live at **Settlement**, 2km (1 mile) northeast of the resort. Hotel guests and visitors on charter boats are free to visit this area, which is a good place to get a feel for island life in colonial times. Look out for the old copra drier and the circle where an oil press once stood. The little lock-up, with its barred doors, was the destination for anyone falling foul of island justice. Not surprisingly, the most common offence on these remote islands was drunkenness. The old hospital, if you can call it that, was little more than a room with a bed and a few basic medicines. In the early days, these would simply be medicinal plants that could be grown around the village, such as castor oil and datura.

Diving off Desroches is excellent, especially between November and April, and the island is famous among the diving fraternity for the amazing **Desroches Drop** – the edge of a coral plateau that forms the southern rim of the island, pitted with gulleys and deep caves (these can only be explored under the supervision of a qualified divemaster). The dive centre here runs courses for beginners and caters for other water sports (canoeing, windsurfing, sailing, snorkelling). A boat can also be chartered for game fishing trips or visits to nearby islands. The big game fishing is sensational, the waters rich in tuna, bonito, kingfish and sailfish. The hotel also has its own floodlit tennis court and hires out bicycles, perfect for exploring this flat island. A map with basically two routes – coastal and inland – is produced by the lodge.

FACT

Pierre Louis Poiret, the mystery man who claimed he was Louis XVII, the lost king of France (see page 242) came to Poivre in 1804 and was apprenticed at the cotton gin.

Palm trees stretch to the blue skies on Desroches.

FACT

Just south of St Joseph Atoll is a tiny deserted tuft of land called Sand Cay. It has no vegetation and is often submerged by high spring tides, but it is a popular destination for roosting terns. It is often seen covered with up to seven different species.

Southern islands and atolls

Only a day's sail from Desroches, **Poivre Atoll** is the largest atoll in the Amirantes group. It is made up of three islands – Poivre, South Island (joined together at low tide by a man-made causeway) and Florentin – all with first-class beaches. Although it was a coconut plantation before it was abandoned, in its early days its major production was cotton. Plans for the building of an island resort have been in the pipeline for years, but at present, there is nothing here except a small settlement on Poivre. One of the most beautiful of the Amirantes islands, Poivre is named after the former governor of Mauritius (1763–72), Pierre Poivre, who was responsible for introducing spices to Seychelles (see page 242). It is famous for its deep sea fishing and diving and, although it is privately owned, a limited number of visitors are allowed access, provided they have been given permission in advance: permission from IDC (Islands Development Company), New Port, Victoria; tel: 224640.

Étoile and **Boudeuse** are tiny uninhabited islands with nothing but breeding terns, notably the sooty tern and roseate tern, and Boudeuse has a huge colony of masked booby. The islands have the same uncanny beauty, enhanced by a sense of real isolation as African Banks. You can only visit by charter boat, and landing is only possible in very calm conditions.

Marie Louise ② is in some ways the prettiest of the Amirantes, a coral island version of the granitic islands of Aride and Cousin, with large populations of sea birds. It has an airstrip to serve the small settlement, but there are no regular flights and no facilities for visitors. It is simply a beautiful place to include on your charter itinerary.

The southernmost island of the Amirantes group is **Desnoeufs**, famous in Seychelles for the vast numbers of sooty terns that breed here, the eggs of which are considered a delicacy in the granitics. Egg-collecting is carried out between June and August by the few Islands Development Company (IDC) staff who manage the island. Outside the egg-collecting season, the island is largely deserted. Again, visiting is only possible on a charter boat; even then it's

The view from above of St Joseph Atoll and lagoon.

TWO ATOLLS

The tiny islands of D'Arros and St Joseph Atoll have an interesting past. Named after Baron d'Arros, a French marine commandant who was stationed in Mauritius in the late 18th century, D'Arros was privately owned from 1975 – by an Iranian Prince, then a French billionaire. The island was sold, for $60 million, and given over to the **Save Our Seas Foundation (SOSF)** in 2012. In 2015 it was announced that the whole of St Joseph Atoll and a large proportion of D'Arros would be made into a National Park, with a ten-year plan to reintroduce endemic species.

To this end, there is a shark nursery project based on D'Arros, where volunteers are able to give their time and help out; visit www.saveourseas.com for more information.

ifficult to get ashore. Landing should not be attempted by any but an experienced boatman or strong swimmer.

Northern islands and atolls

African Banks is a tiny island with nothing but a lighthouse. The landscape of sweeping white sand hovers like a mirage on the brightest turquoise and ultramarine waters you have ever seen. Sea birds breed here in considerable numbers. The sands are crisscrossed by turtle tracks as if a safari rally had been held during the night. The urge to go ashore and explore makes landing irresistible.

Rémire, a small circular island, was originally named Eagle Island after a ship sent there in 1771 by the British in Bombay to find out what the French were up to in Seychelles. Not considered one of the most beautiful islands in Seychelles, it is however renowned for its fishing and the IDC operates a few basic bungalows to accommodate fishing enthusiasts (and other tourists) who venture so far.

D'Arros and neighbouring **St Joseph Atoll** were important coconut-producing islands during the early years of the 20th century, often yielding over 40,000 nuts a month. D'Arros has an oval-shaped platform reef, an airstrip and a research centre for conservation and student volunteer projects. St Joseph Atoll, separated from D'Arros by a deep channel, is made up of 13 small islets, which together make up less than 1 sq km of land. They are all deserted, but some have old colonial ruins, which are interesting to visit and speculate upon. Diving here is excellent, with scores of sharks, manta rays, turtles and stingrays in the lagoon and surrounding reef.

The Alphonse Group

The Alphonse Group consists of two neighbouring atolls, **Alphonse Atoll** and **St François Atoll**.

Alphonse Atoll

Alphonse was a productive plantation in its heyday, generating 100,000 coconuts a month on a regular basis during the 1930s. The plantation was abandoned in recent times, and the island is now leased to **Alphonse Island Resort** ❸ (www. alphonse-island.com), whose villas skirt the tranquil lagoon and silky white sand beaches. There is an **airstrip** for transfers from Mahé, an hour's flight away. (Visitors on charter boats need advance permission from IDC on Mahé, see page 340.)

The resort's Dive Centre offers facilities for diving the wall of Alphonse, where forests of gorgonian fan corals, sharks, rays and huge schools of predatory fish such as barracuda, as well as a host of colourful reef fish, may be seen. The best snorkelling is at the pass into the lagoon, but this is a long way out and can only be reached by boat. Island Conservation Society runs programmes from its centre such as guided walks for visitors, daily turtle patrols, beach cleans and weekly talks. The Alphonse Island Resort arranges day trips to nearby Bijoutier and St François, the uninhabited islands of St François Atoll.

An aldabra giant tortoise.

TIP

When tides are low, a good pair of plastic shoes or similar footwear is essential for wading ashore across reef flats with sharp coral fragments and possibly poisonous cone shells.

St François Atoll

To reach the other islands from Alphonse you must cross the **Canal la Mort** – Death Channel! The water here is deep, cold and treacherous with powerful currents. The 5km (3-mile) journey is worth it, however, to reach the near-perfection of **Bijoutier**. The name means 'little jewel' and that is just what this island is. Perfectly round, capped with bright green vegetation, fringed with the whitest of coral beaches and encircled by purple reefs and turquoise sea, this is the closest any island comes to the paradise ideal.

St François is surrounded by a fearsome reef, girdled by shipwrecks. At least six are still visible on the horizon, a grim reminder that the waters in these parts should be treated with respect. It is possible to enter the huge lagoon of St François in safety through **La Passe Traversé**. Over the coral crest, the tranquil lagoon waters are fairly shallow and a world away from the ferocity of the waters beyond the reef. The enormous plain of sand, left dry at low tide, is a feeding ground for hundreds of wading birds. Apart from

Bijoutier, a jewel in Seychelles' crown.

its beauty and birdlife, the bigges[t] attraction of St François is fly-fishing in the lagoon.

The Farquhar Group

The Farquhar Group, which comprise[s] Providence Atoll, St Pierre island an[d] Farquhar Atoll, is about 700km (43[5] miles) from Mahé. The islands are onl[y] accessible by sea, but with the growt[h] of habitable cruising they are no longe[r] entirely out of reach. The Islands Devel[-] opment Company (IDC) operates [a] small eight-room guesthouse on Far[-] quhar, which gets fully booked durin[g] fly-fishing season from October to May[.]

Providence Atoll

This is a long, thin atoll oriente[d] roughly north–south. **Providence**, th[e] main island, lies at its northern tip[,] while across 40km (25 miles) of shal[-] low water **Bancs de** Providence lies a[t] its southern extreme. Most of the reef i[s] out of sight of land and, consequentl[y] many a ship has foundered here. The huge shallow lagoon attracts hundred[s] of grey herons and this is the only plac[e] in Seychelles where herons outnumbe[r]

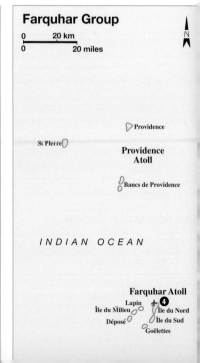

Farquhar Group

| 0 | 20 km |
| 0 | 20 miles |

N

▷ Providence

St Pierre ◌

Providence Atoll

◌ Bancs de Providence

INDIAN OCEAN

Farquhar Atoll

Lapin
Île du Milieu ◌   ◌ Île du Nord
Déposé ◌   ◌ Île du Sud
Goëlettes

ll other bird species. Providence has a small transient human population employed by IDC in copra production, but Bancs de Providence is strictly for the birds and turtles.

St Pierre

Due west of Providence is the extremely strange raised coral platform of **St Pierre**, rising to about 10 metres (33ft) above sea level. There is no beach at high tide and landing is only safe when the tide recedes to reveal a tiny sandy corner in the northeast. This island, now abandoned, was once mined for guano and you can still see the walls of the rotting stores and the twisted metal of what was once a quay.

Farquhar Atoll

South of Providence are the 10 islands of **Farquhar Atoll** ❹. The lagoon is a popular anchorage for yachts and schooners. On the main island, Île du Nord, there is a small settlement where a little copra is still produced. The island also has an airstrip. Many of the trees on neighbouring Île du Sud have been turned white by the droppings of hundreds of red-footed boobies that nest here. The southern tip of the atoll, Goëlettes, is also the most southerly island of Seychelles. It is swept almost bare of vegetation by the strong southeasterly winds, but is a haven for sea birds, with up to 300,000 pairs of sooty terns and a healthy number of black-naped terns, a species that breeds only on coral atolls.

The Aldabra Group

Aldabra is the most remote and most interesting of all the Outer Island groups. Geographically a part of Seychelles, these islands lie closer to Madagascar than they do to Mahé, more than 1,000km (625 miles) away. The archipelago is made up of **Astove** and **Cosmoledo Atoll**, lying due west of Farquhar Atoll, and **Assumption** and the **Aldabra Atoll** beyond. There are no hotels on the Aldabra Group, which, apart from visiting scientists and the occasional small cruise ship or charter boat from Mahé, sees few visitors. For the most part the only footprints in the sand belong to the birds and turtles.

Burning coconut husks on Farquhar.

Aldabra Atoll

Aldabra is the world's largest raised coral atoll; the exposed coral cap of a volcanic seamount rising more than 4km (2 miles) from the ocean floor. Geologically, it is part of a chain that includes the Comoros. It is made up of four main islands – Picard, Polymnie, Malabar and Grand Terre – and a number of other small islets, stretching 32km (20 miles) from east to west. This ring of coral islands encloses a vast lagoon, which is fed by several channels that carry in new life with each tide.

Virtually untouched by the modern world, Aldabra Atoll is now listed as a Unesco World Heritage Site and is considered the Galapagos of the Indian Ocean. It does not possess the tranquil beauty of the archetypal tropical idyll as seen elsewhere in Seychelles, but has the atmosphere of an untamed wilderness lost in time. Its survival owes less to design than to its inhospitable terrain. Much of the interior is covered with sharp, jagged rocks and impenetrable scrub.

The atoll is home to nearly 95 percent of the world's **giant tortoise** population, with an estimated 150,000 animals. In addition, around 4,000 green turtles come ashore to breed each year, as do smaller numbers of hawksbill turtles. The atoll is now part of the Indian Ocean South-East Asian Network of Sites of Importance for Marine Turtles, after it was recognised as a critical site needed to be preserved to secure the future of marine turtles. Living alongside them is the Aldabra rail, the last surviving flightless bird of the Indian Ocean. Most of the other land birds are subspecies unique to Aldabra. It has the world's second largest colony of frigatebirds, with 10,000 breeding pairs, and the world's only oceanic colony of Caspian tern.

About 22 of the plant species are endemic, including the beautiful Aldabra lily. However, the vegetation is dominated by salt-resistant pemphis scrub, capable of surviving in the harsh conditions, and throwing a dense prickly blanket over much of the land surface. Around the inner rim of the lagoon is a dense thicket of mangroves.

Marine life is concentrated around the channels. Snorkelling or diving

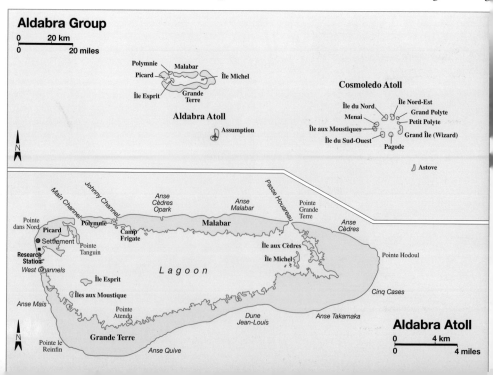

Aldabra Group

0   20 km
0   20 miles

Polymnie   Malabar
Picard   Île Michel
Île Esprit   Grande Terre

Aldabra Atoll

Assumption

Cosmoledo Atoll

Île du Nord   Île Nord-Est
Menai   Grand Polyte
Île aux Moustiques   Petit Polyte
                Grand Île (Wizard)
Île du Sud-Ouest
                Pagode

Astove

N

Main Channel   Johnny Channel   Passe Houareau

Pointe dans Nord   Picard   Polymnie
Settlement   Camp Frigate
Research Station   Pointe Tanguin
West Channels

Anse Cèdres Opark   Anse Malabar   Pointe Grande Terre
Malabar   Anse Cèdres

Île aux Cèdres   Pointe Hodoul
Île Michel

L a g o o n   Cinq Cases

Anse Mais   Île Esprit

Îles aux Moustique

Pointe Atendu   Dune Jean-Louis   Anse Takamaka

N

Pointe le Reinfin   **Grande Terre**   Anse Quive

Aldabra Atoll

0   4 km
0   4 miles

in be exhilarating here on the incoming tides that run at 10km (6 knots) per hour or more, taking swimmers in a roller coaster ride that sweeps them past sharks, rays, groupers and other exotic fish. This is not for the inexperienced and should never be attempted without a small boat to accompany your group.

There is a small **Research Station** in Picard with a warden and a staff of around 10 employed by the SIF (Seychelles Islands Foundation). There is also an accommodation block of six twin rooms for visiting scientists. When no scientists are in residence (which is most of the time) these rooms are available for visitors, but you need to apply in advance for permission from SIF on Mahé. Otherwise the atoll, one third of the land mass of Seychelles, is uninhabited. Except for Picard, Polymnie, Western Malabar and Camp Frigate, access to the atoll, even for resident visitors, is prohibited.

Cosmoledo, Astove and Assumption

Cosmoledo Atoll has Seychelles' largest populations of red-footed booby, masked booby and sooty tern. It is also the last breeding site for the brown booby, exterminated elsewhere in the islands. The marine life around Cosmoledo and **Astove** is very rich, making for excellent diving territory. West of Cosmoledo is the island of **Assumption**. Guano mining wiped out most of the birdlife here, though there are three indigenous species of lizard, and the Mauritian tomb bat and turtles are successfully breeding. A small human population remains, focused on small-scale fishing and farming, but although Assumption is connected by air to Mahé, flights are few and far between except when officials are flown out to clear a cruise ship, or passengers arrive to join a dive boat based in the area from November to April. Nevertheless, the reefs here are largely intact and, as elsewhere in the group, diving is excellent. Advance permission to visit is required from IDC (Islands Development Company) on Mahé (see page 340).

Humpback snapper in the seas around Aldabra Atoll.

Looking out over the turquoise lagoon off Rodrigues.

TRAVEL TIPS

MAURITIUS, RÉUNION AND SEYCHELLES

TRANSPORT

GETTING THERE AND GETTING AROUND

GETTING THERE

By air

Air Mauritius (airline code MK), the national carrier, flies from destinations in Europe (London, Paris), Africa (Johannesburg, Durban, Cape Town, Nairobi, Antananarivo), Asia (Hong Kong, Singapore, Kuala Lumpur, Mumbai, Delhi, Bangalore, Chennai, Beijing, Shanghai), The Middle East (Dubai) and Australia (Perth), and has frequent daily flights from Réunion. Flights to Rodrigues are only available from Mauritius.

Other international carriers are: Air Austral (UU), British Airways (BA), Air France (AF), Lufthansa (LH), South African Airways (SA), Qantas (QF) and Virgin Atlantic (VS). Emirates (EK) flies to Mauritius twice daily from Dubai.

Air Austral (tel: 020 7644 6124; www.air-austral.com), based in France, offers routings to Mayotte, South Africa (Jo'burg), the Comoros, Madagascar, Seychelles, Réunion and Mauritius and a Vanilla Islands Pass for discounted Indian Ocean island hopping.

Thomson (tel: 0844 050 2828; www.thomson.co.uk) is the only charter airline to serve Mauritius from the UK; Corsair flies from France (tel: 01703 92210; www.corsair.fr) and Condor (tel: 06171 6988920; www.condor.com) from Germany. Several planes a day fly between Réunion and Mauritius with Air Mauritius and Air Austral. It is important you have a recognised address to go to on arrival in Mauritius, or you will be denied entry to the country.

Airport tax is included in the price of all major airline tickets and many package deals.

Airline contacts

Air Mauritius: tel: 207 7575 (reservations); www.airmauritius.com
Air Mauritius (Rodrigues): tel: 832 7700
Air Austral: tel: 202 8050; www.air-austral.com
Air France: tel: 202 6747; www.airfrance.com
Austrian Airlines: www.austrian.com
British Airways: tel: 202 8000; www.ba.com
Condor: tel: 213 4141; www.condor.com
Corsair: tel: 210 2020; www.corsair.fr
Emirates: tel: 213 9100; www.emirates.com
Lufthansa: www.lufthansa.com
Qantas: www.qantas.com.au
Virgin Atlantic: tel: 206 0900; www.virgin-atlantic.com

Tour operators

The following UK-based operators specialise in Mauritius:
Audley Travel: tel: 01993 838000; www.audleytravel.com
Beachcomber Tours: tel: 01483 445621; www.beachcombertours.co.uk
Carrier Indian Ocean: tel: 0161 826 9763; www.carrier.co.uk
Emirates Holidays: tel: 020 7590 1461; www.emiratesholidays.co.uk
ITC Luxury Travel: tel: 01244 355550; www.itcclassics.co.uk
Just2Mauritius: tel: 01707 371000; www.just2mauritius.com
Kuoni: tel: 0844 488 0341; www.kuoni.co.uk
Luxury Holidays Direct: tel: 020 8774 7299; www.luxuryholidaysdirect.com
Virgin Holidays: tel: 0844 557 4321; www.virginholidays.co.uk

From the airport

Sir Seewoosagur Ramgoolam (SSR) International Airport occupies the area of Plaisance, 48km (30 miles) south of Port Louis, and is often referred to simply as Plaisance. The international code for the airport is MRU (tel: 603 6000; http://aml.mru.aero).

Bus service: An hourly express bus service, often crowded with locals, links with Mahébourg and Port Louis 6.30am–6.30pm but is only convenient if you have no luggage.

Taxis: If a taxi is not equipped with a meter, which they should be, agree a price before starting any journey. A metered taxi ride to Rose Hill, for example, with two items of luggage, should work out at around R1,200. An unmetered ride for the same journey, depending on your bargaining skills, may work out slightly less.

Sir Gaëtan Duval Airport, Rodrigues: Tour operators usually collect their own visitors from Rodrigues' airport, a modern building south of the island (tel: 832 7888; www.airportofrodrigues.com). Independent travellers can take the Supercopter bus to Port Mathurin for R150. To return to the airport, call Ibrahim Nalla on 831 1859 for pick-ups from any guesthouse or hotel location in and around Port Mathurin.

By sea

There are no international passenger shipping services to Mauritius although cruise ships occasionally call at Port Louis, either as part of a round-the-world trip or on a cruise from South Africa. Nor can you travel by sea between the Mascarenes and

Seychelles, unless, of course, you are chartering a yacht.

Mauritius Shipping Corporation Ltd (MSCL; tel: 217 2284; www.mauritiusshipping.net) operates the passenger/cargo vessel MS *Mauritius Trochetia* between Mauritius and Réunion. The journey takes about 12 hours and children travel half price. The ship also travels to Rodrigues three or four times per month (see page 350). Few travellers opt for the gruelling 36-hour crossing from Mauritius to Rodrigues.

Long-haul ocean trips are not generally made during the cyclone season.

GETTING AROUND

Driving

The British legacy of Mauritius and the Seychelles is most evident on the roads, where driving is on the left and the roundabouts operate as in Britain with priority on the right. Not every local driver seems to be aware of this rule, however, and in practice he who hesitates least goes first. Beware of poultry, goats and dogs on the roads, hawkers and foragers with heavily overloaded bicycles. Scooters carrying entire families need to be given a wide berth! Public buses often drive dangerously fast on small, winding roads – make plenty of room as they will often cross the central line on sharp bends. If driving through the sugar cane areas, watch out for deep gulleys on either side of the road, especially at night.

Mauritians tend to sound their horns when overtaking or approaching a junction. It is meant as a friendly warning, not as a reprimand. **Rules of the road:** 100kmh (60mph) on 'motorways' and 50 kmh (30mph) elsewhere. The wearing of seatbelts, and rear seatbelts where fitted, is compulsory. Always carry your driving licence.

Driving times

Airport–Belle Mare: 1.25 hours
Belle Mare–Pamplemousses: 55 mins
Belle Mare–Trou d'Eau Douce: 30 mins
Belle Mare–Grand Baie (via the coast): 1 hour
Port Louis–Curepipe (without hold-ups): 40 mins
Le Morne–east coast (via interior): 2 hours

The police should attend any accidents resulting in personal injury. Where damage only is involved, exchange names and addresses on the prescribed form supplied by the car hire agency and notify them. In cases of doubt or difficulty, call the police.

There is a strong presence of traffic police, particularly on the Mahébourg–Grand Baie road, where speeding is common and driving habits verge on the dangerous.

Main routes

Mauritians refer to the road linking Mahébourg and Grand Baie as the 'motorway' but it is really only a well-surfaced trunk road which crosses the island from south to north linking the plateau towns. Most of the 2,149km (1,335 miles) of roads are surfaced, but many of the highways and minor roads are badly potholed. The best roads are the 'motorway' (M1), the new link road from Verdun to Terre Rouge and Trianon, which bypasses Port Louis, and the road through Black River Gorges National Park; the worst are in towns and villages. The south is by far the quietest when it comes to vehicles, and the city and the Central Plateau the most congested.

Names of towns and villages may appear in French and/or English and can be poorly positioned or concealed by sugar cane. Roads are adequately signed (with UK-style signposts) but navigating through towns can be a challenge. Make sure you have a good map (see page 364). Distances and speed limits are shown in kilometres and, more rarely, miles.

Parking

Parking can be a nightmare at all times in Port Louis so head for the car park behind Caudan Waterfront. Short-term parking up to two hours is also available at the Port Louis Waterfront.

Parking restrictions apply in towns and to avoid being fined, display a parking coupon on your windscreen. These can be bought in booklets at petrol stations.

Car hire

To hire a car you must be aged over 23 (or 18 to rent a scooter) and have a full valid driving licence, which must be carried with you when driving. Car hire rates usually include comprehensive insurance and collision damage waiver but always check first. Tyre punctures can be repaired cheaply at any garage. If you hire a motorcycle you should be

provided with a crash helmet. If you only want a car for a short while to see round the island, consider hiring one with a driver-guide, who will know the best places to go and will save you the bother (and stress) of driving.

Major credit cards are increasingly becoming accepted by smaller companies.

Car hire companies

Avis: 116 Avenue Sir Guy Forget, Quatre Bornes; tel: 427 6312; www.avismauritius.com
Budget Rent a Car: Rue S. Venkatesananda, PO Box 125, Rose Hill; tel: 467 9700; www.mauritours.net
Europcar: Near Hotel Le Mauricia, Grand Baie; tel: 263 7948; www.europcar.com
Hertz: 84 Gustave Colin Street, Forest Side, Curepipe; tel: 604 3021; www.hertz.mu
Société J.H.A. Arnulfy and Co: Chez Henri, La Chaux, Mahébourg; tel: 631 9806; www.henri-vacances.com

By bus

Buses are plentiful, inexpensive and generally reliable although the service is less frequent in the evening. There are two bus stations in Port Louis, one linking it with the north and the other with the plateau towns in the south. Fares range from R12 up to R70 for travel by express service.

Some of the older buses do not inspire confidence; they chug along belching out heavy black exhaust, but get to their destination eventually. If you're in a hurry take one of the express buses but always check the destination with the conductor. Queues are orderly and tickets are bought on board. Stop bells are located at each seat. Avoid travelling between 8am and 9am and 4pm and 5pm during the week, when buses are very crowded; carry small change for the fare.

Buses operate in urban regions from 5.30am to 8pm and in rural regions from 6.30am to 6.30pm. In the country buses will normally stop on request. Night owls should note that the last bus from Port Louis to Curepipe via Rose Hill, Quatre Bornes and Vacoas leaves at 11pm. The National Transport Authority (NTC; tel: 427 5000; www.ntc.intnet.mu) provides bus information, but buses are so frequent during the day that a timetable is not really necessary.

In Rodrigues bus services grind to a halt at around 4pm.

MAURITIUS

RÉUNION

SEYCHELLES

By taxi

Taxis are equipped with meters but they are rarely switched on so always agree a price before starting a journey. Try to use them only for short journeys as the fare depends on the whims of the driver and includes the taxi's return fare to base. The official tariff should be displayed inside the vehicle, with waiting time chargeable for the first 15 minutes and every additional 15 minutes. Drivers do not expect to be tipped.

In practice drivers do not adhere to these rates. For longer journeys it may be cheaper to hire a taxi for the day and fix a price, which should be less than a day's car hire. If you find a knowledgeable taxi driver who can act as a guide, try to keep his custom by using him regularly.

Licensed 'taxi trains', or shared taxis, operate near bus stops in some towns and villages. They cover a prescribed route and the fare is divided between the number of passengers. The taxis are dilapidated and overloaded but travelling this way can be cheap and fast, with rates working out at not much more than the official bus fare.

Taxis are recognisable by black registration numbers on white plates. Unlicensed taxis or *taxis marrons* are instantly recognisable because they are nothing more than private cars – they have white numbers on black plates and lurk near taxi stands, bus stations and the airport. They often incur the wrath of their licensed competitors; their rates are low because they're uninsured to carry passengers.

Sailing over clear waters.

Taxis can be hired from licensed taxi stands. Taxis are labelled with the name of the hotel or province they belong to on a yellow panel on the driver's door. Most hotels have a special arrangement with taxi drivers who are expected to charge reasonable fares. If you feel you are about to be ripped off, warn the driver that you will report him to the hotel. It usually works.

In Rodrigues there are only around a dozen taxis servicing the island. There is a taxi stand beside Port Mathurin bus station.

By helicopter

Air Mauritius helicopters, which carry up to four people, undertake transfers and regular sightseeing tours with prices depending on flying time and route. Current tariffs start at R14,000 for two, plus R3,000 for each additional passenger for 15 minutes. A transfer from the airport to any hotel is R22,000 for two, plus R5,000 for each additional passenger.

Reservations can be made in your home country through Air Mauritius (tel: 207 7575), travel agents or through www.airmauritius.com/helicopter.htm.

Sightseeing tours

There are numerous local tour companies but the following provide a wide range of sightseeing tours and other services and have hospitality desks at major hotels:

On Mauritius

Mauritours: 5 Venkatasananda Street, Rose Hill; tel: 467 9700; www.mauritours.net
Mautourco: 84 Gustav Colin Street, Forest Side; tel: 604 3000; wwwmautourco.com
Summertimes: 5 Avenue Bernadin de St Pierre, Quatre Bornes; tel: 427 1111; www.summer-times,com
White Sand Tours: 10 Robert Edward Hart Street, Curepipe; tel: 605 1500; www.whitesandtours.com

On Rodrigues

Discovery Rodrigues: Rue de la Solidarité, Port Mathurin; tel: 832 1062; email: discoveryrodrigues@intnet.mu
Rodtours: Camp du Roi, Port Mathurin, tel: 831 2249; email: rodtours@intnet.mu; www.mauritours.net
Rotourco: Place François Leguat, Port Mathurin; tel: 831 0747; www.rotourco.com

On your bike

Many visitors hire bicycles in Grand Baie. Several villages and resorts are only a few miles away and can easily be reached by bike. Most good hotels and island tour operators can organise bike hire and specialist Yemaya Adventures (tel: 5752 0046; www.yemayaadventures.com) hires mountain bikes and offers guided cycling trips. It is also becoming popular to cycle out on quieter roads from hotels in the south.

Island hopping

Tour operators organise excursions to both Rodrigues and Réunion depending on sailings. The MS *Mauritius Trochetia* takes up to 108 cabin passengers, and has a bar and dining room, as well as leisure facilities including karaoke, a dance floor, cable TV, a library and a children's corner. It is advisable to book directly, as soon as you arrive in Mauritius, through island tour operators, with desks in major hotels. Better still, make arrangements through your own travel agent before you leave your home country, as you are unlikely to get a first-class cabin at short notice and the airline-style seats in economy class sell fast. Sailings between Mauritius and Rodrigues are between three and four times a month. At the time of writing, sailings between Mauritius and Réunion had stopped, but they are likely to be resumed.

In Mauritius, details of sailings can be obtained from **MSCL Coraline Ship Agency**, Nova Building, I Military Road, Port Louis (tel: 217 2284; www.mauritius shipping.net) or through your tour operator/travel agent.

In Rodrigues, contact MSCL, François Leguat Street, Port Mathurin, R5126 (tel: 831 0640; email: msclrod@intnet.mu).

In Réunion contact SCOAM, 4 Avenue du 14 Juillet 1789, 97420, Le Port (tel: 262 42 19 45; email: passagers@scoam.re).

Boat trips from Rodrigues to the nature islands of Île aux Cocos, Île aux Chats and Île Hermitage can be organised through your hotel or tour companies such as **Discovery Rodrigues** in Port Mathurin. Bookings must be made in advance as there are restrictions on the number of visitors at a time.

EATING OUT

RECOMMENDED RESTAURANTS, CAFES AND BARS

EATING OUT

Most visitors to Mauritius eat in their hotels in the evening, but eating out at local restaurants and street stalls around the island is a highlight of a visit. It gives an opportunity to savour the colour and tradition of Mauritian cuisine – a fascinating and mouth-watering fusion of the island's French, Indian, African and Chinese heritage. This produces everything from fiery hot curries with rice and home-made pickles to hearty casseroles with potatoes and delicate desserts flavoured with island produce such as mango and vanilla. The service, quality of cooking and reasonable prices all add to the enjoyment. Dress is informal, the atmosphere is relaxed and there are scores of restaurants to choose from; some are included in island excursions.

Mauritians typically eat out at lunchtime. Bear in mind if you do venture out at night that it's wise to choose a restaurant in the region where you're staying, as distances can be deceptive and many roads are narrow and poorly lit, so driving is inevitably slow. Restaurants generally close by 11pm and booking is not usually required.

Street stalls abound in towns and markets, and by the beach. These sell *gadjacks* – snacks such as fresh fruit cut into pieces and sold in bags for a few rupees. The mix could include cucumber and mango spiced up with some chilli, if you choose. Stalls also fry up everything from *gateaux piments* (chilli cakes made of yellow split peas), *mine frite* (similar to chow mein) and *boulettes* (fish and potato croquettes), or *dhol puri* (Indian flatbread stuffed with curried

lentils). Some still sell snacks from a glass case off the back of a bicycle or motorbike as they did in past times. Hygiene standards are generally good on the island, and for the price of a few rupees, these delicious snacks are worth trying. The food hall at Port Louis Central Market is one of the best places to find typical food, from street snacks to lunches, all under one roof. Other good spots to try street food is Mahébourg market, Curepipe town centre, and Grand Baie or Flic en Flac beaches at weekends.

Fish tends to dominate **menus**, with octopus curry and smoked blue marlin (usually served with palm heart salad) local specialities. There's a wide choice of meats as well, with game such as wild boar and venison from island estates a seasonal speciality. Typical Mauritian dishes to try in island restaurants include *biriyani* (a spiced meat dish from the Muslim Indian community), *vindaye* (fish or meat coated with a mix of chilli, ginger, turmeric and mustard seeds), Creole *rougaille* (fish or meat in a spicy tomato sauce with thyme and chilli) and French-style stew or *daube* with beef or chicken. More rarely, you can find dry beef curry with raisins and chicken and prawn curry.

Fast food restaurants are inevitably on the increase, with KFC being the most popular, as well as McDonald's in Port Louis. Pizzas are available at Caudan Waterfront, Port Louis, and in shopping centres with food courts, popular with Mauritians at weekends.

Many of the chefs at hotels are European and so there is often an international flavour to meals, with everything from Italian to sushi on offer. Most **hotels** have weekly Mauritian nights or Indian evenings,

and some, such as LUX* Resorts, have introduced Island Kitchen to give guests a taste of street food. With some of the world's leading hotels, the island has plenty of gourmet restaurants. It regularly attracts Michelin-starred celebrity chefs, whether to create restaurants such as Amari by Vineet at LUX* Belle Mare, or for gourmet weeks or cooking schools, or to participate in Constance Hotels' annual Bernard Loiseau Culinary Festival each March.

WHAT TO DRINK

Rum is the national drink, the most popular being Green Island rum. Other brands are Old Mill and Spiced Gold (more like a liqueur). Mauritius now appears on the international gourmet rum map, with artisanal rums produced at sugar estates or 'domaines'. Traditional restaurants also typically offer home-made rum arrangé as a digestive – flavoured with everything from coconut to chilli.

Imported alcohol is very expensive as it carries a 300 percent tax. Some hotels don't have very good wine lists, although they are improving, and many people tend to drink beer. Phoenix beer, a Mauritian lager that is very palatable, and island craft beers are now making it onto menus. Most of the wine is from South Africa, although some is made in Mauritius with imported grapes and is cheaper.

Citronelle – hot water spiced with lemon grass and ginger – is often offered after dinner to cleanse the palate. Port Louis is one of the few places where you can taste *alooda*, a Persian import made from coconut milk, basil seeds, rosewater and gelatine.

MAURITIUS

RÉUNION

SEYCHELLES

PORT LOUIS

La Bonne Marmite
18 Sir William Newton Street
Tel: 212 2403
www.bonnemarmite.com
In an attractive Creole building, this is a busy lunchtime venue serving local, Indian, European and Chinese fare. Closed at weekends. €€€

Le Boulevard
Happy World House, Sir William Newton Street
Tel: 208 8325
Inexpensive and cheerful salad bar. Ideal for quick snacks and lots of vegetarian appeal. €

Chez Ah Niong
78 Rue Dr Beaugeard
Tel: 210 5042
First-class family cooking and Réunionnais specialities in this unpretentious restaurant in the backstreets of town. Reservations recommended. Closed evenings. €

Le Courtyard
Corner of Chevreau and St Louis Street
Tel: 210 0834
www.le-courtyard.com
Fine wines and French cuisine, in a superb courtyard setting in a quiet corner of town. Open for lunch Mon–Fri, and also dinner on Fri. €€€

Domaine des Pailles
Les Guibies, Pailles
Tel: 286 4225
www.domainelespailles.nct
This colonial mansion in pretty, manicured grounds just outside Port Louis is home to two of the island's finest restaurants, Fu Xiao (Chinese) and Indra (Indian). Open for lunch and dinner, reservations recommended. €€€

Lai Min
56–8 Royal Road
Tel: 242 0042
Chinese dishes that are out of this world, served in exotic surroundings. Open daily 11.30am–2.30pm and 6.30pm–9.30pm. €€€

Lambic
St Georges Street
Tel: 212 6011
www.lanbic.mu
Mauritius' own craft beers, along with the widest stock of international imports, are served with finger food or with bar meals with beer-based sauces at this gastropub in a humble old colonial house, with a small terrace. Open Mon–Sat 8am–midnight. €€€

THE NORTH

Grand Baie

The Beach House
Royal Road
Tel: 263 2599
www.thebeachhouse.mu
This bar on the waterfront serves decent food, from steak to sushi. It's owned by an ex-South African rugby player and is lively at weekends. Open Tue–Sun 11am–midnight. €€€

Happy Rajah
Super U Complex
Tel: 263 2241
www.happyrajah.com
A hot favourite if you're after authentic, good-value Indian food with an impressive range of vegetarian and meat dishes. Smoking and non-smoking areas. Open daily. €€€

La Pagode
Coast Road
Tel: 263 8733
People-watch and gorge on various Chinese dishes on the veranda of this restaurant overlooking the main road. Popular with Mauritians, it offers excellent value for money and is child-friendly. Try the *saucisses chinoises* (spring rolls) and fantastic crab. €€

Paparazzi
Sunset Café, Sunset Boulevard
Tel: 263 9602
Tasty pizzas, home-made pastas and popular steaks are served in this modern Italian restaurant with a balcony to catch the sea breeze. Open daily noon–3pm and 6.30–11pm. €€

La Plage des Canisses
Royal Road
Tel: 263 5231
Email: laplagedescanisses@gmx.fr
This spacious open-sided stone and thatched restaurant is right on the water. It serves food all day, and is a good place for a snack and a drink. Open Wed–Mon 11am–10pm, daily in peak season. €€

Grand Gaube

Di Sab
Tel: 288 1146
www.restodisab.webs.com
While this family-run restaurant lacks a sea view, it's charming and fun, serving typical Mauritian food in colourful surrounds, with Creole original art and African music. Open daily 9am–10pm. €€

Mapou

Le Table de Chateau
Chateau Labourdonnais
Tel: 266 7172
www.unchateaudanslanature.com
Try lunch or Sunday brunch at this open-sided restaurant in the grounds of this colonial estate. With home-made jams and pickles from the orchard, you're in for a gastronomic treat, without burning a hole in your pocket. Open Mon–Sun 9am–5pm. €€€

Pamplemousses

Chez Tante Athalie
Mon Repos
Tel: 243 9266
Email: cheztanteathalie@intnet.mu
This lunchtime restaurant on an old

Port Louis waterfront is home to many restaurants.

MAURITIUS

An upside-down bowl dish.

sugar estate near Pamplemousses Botanical Gardens is as well known for its view – a garden full of vintage cars – as its good-value prix-fixe Creole menu. Book in advance. Open Mon–Sat noon–2.30pm.

Pereybère

Sea Lover
Coast Road
Tel: 263 6299
Enjoy a sophisticated ambiance, sea-facing views and excellent seafood and fish at this restaurant-cum-lounge bar right beside the beach. Open daily 10am–10pm. €€€
Wang Thai
Coast Road
Tel: 263 4050
www.thai.mu
Delicious and authentic Thai cuisine is served in a spacious air-conditioned upstairs restaurant with a small terrace. Try the steamed crab and noodles or fill up on tiny appetisers. Open Tue–Sun. €€

Poste Lafayette

La Maison D'Eté
Coastal Road
Tel: 410 5039
www.lamaisondete.com
This romantic, open-sided, thatched hotel restaurant with a French chef is a surprise find on the less visited north coast. Non-residents are welcome for lunch, although it's best to book ahead. €€€

Trou aux Biches & Mont Choisy

1974
Coastal Road, Trou aux Biches
Tel: 265 7400
The home-made, seasonal Italian food on the terrace of the old Mauritius aquarium building opposite the beach is a find on this stretch of the coast. Open Tue–Thu 6–11pm, Sat–Sun noon–2.30pm and 6–11pm.
Florensuc Pâtisserie
Trou aux Biches Road, Trou aux Biches
Tel: 265 5349
Real espresso and cappuccino, melt-in-the-mouth pastries and take-away snacks for those on a budget. Closed evenings. €
Le Pescatore
Coast Road, Mont Choisy
Tel: 265 6337
Fine dining and wines in elegant surroundings, with an Italian-Mauritian touch. Unmissable for the succulent seafood – the seafood lasagne is worth a try. Open Mon–Sat noon–2pm and 7–10pm. €€€€
Souvenir Restaurant
Coastal Road, Trou aux Biches
Tel: 291 1440
Just across the road from Trou aux Biches police station, gargantuan portions of *mine frite* (fried noodles), *bol reinversé* ('upside-down bowl', a Creole rice dish with pork, spicy sausage and chicken) and other tasty rice dishes are served in an authentic Creole atmosphere. Open daily 8.30am–11pm. €

THE EAST

Belle Mare

Chez Manuel
Royal Road, St Julien Village
Tel: 418 3599
The taxi ride to this inland village is well worth it to sample the superb Chinese and local dishes. Open daily Mon–Sat. Reservations highly recommended. €€€
Symon Restaurant
Pointe de Flacq
Tel: 415 1135
A restaurant specialising in seafood, Creole and Chinese cuisine at a decent price. Popular with guests staying at hotels along the east coast. Friendly staff. Open daily 11am–10pm. €€

Ile aux Cerfs

La Chaumière Masala
Tel: 402 7400
www.letouessrokresort.com
This family restaurant serves mainly Indian food under thatched gazebos on a hillside overlooking the lagoon. The *thalis* are great value, washed down with a cooling *lassi*. Open daily noon–4pm. €€

Trou d'Eau Douce

Chez Tinos
Tel: 480 2769
Lunch or dine in this established upstairs restaurant, which serves excellent Creole specialities, such as chicken and prawn curry, in a very informal atmosphere. Open daily for lunch and Mon–Sat for dinner. €€

Vieux Grand Port

La Case du Pecheur
Bambous Virieux
Tel: 634 5643
http://mauritiuslacasedupecheur.yolasite.com
This unusual rustic restaurant by the water's edge is worth the trek for its fresh seafood – including year-round oysters – and wild game, and its lush mountain backdrop. Work up an appetite by kayaking in the lagoon or try traditional fishing. Open daily 9am–5pm. €€€

PRICE CATEGORIES

Price categories are for two people, including soft drinks or beer:
€ = less than R400
€€ = R400–600
€€€ = R600–1,000
€€€€ = more than R1,000

REUNION

SEYCHELLES

THE SOUTH COAST

Bel Ombre

Le Château de Bel Ombre
Tel: 605 5316
www.domainedebelombre.mu
This refined restaurant, in a
19th-century colonial mansion
below the foothills of the Black River
Gorges National Park, is one of the
island's most romantic and serves
a Mauritian-fusion gourmet menu.
Open Mon–Sat 8–11pm. €€€€

Riambel

Green Palm
Coastal Road
Tel: 625 8100
Authentic South Indian dishes, with
a good choice of vegetarian meals, in
clean and simple surroundings. Open
daily for lunch and dinner. €€€

Rivière des Galets

Rum Shed
Shanti Maurice – A Nira Resort

Tel: 603 7200
www.shantimaurice.com
This shabby-chic drinking hole
echoes past-times island rum shops,
and has the widest selection of
rums on the island, along with local
snacks. Open daily 6pm–midnight.
€€€

Souillac

Le Batelage
Tel: 625 6083
www.lebatelage.com
Souillac's only tourist restaurant is in
an atmospheric 18th-century sugar
warehouse overlooking the river. Good
for European and Creole specialities.
Open daily 11.30am–5pm and
7pm–late. €
The Hungry Crocodile
La Vanille Réserve des Mascareignes,
Rivière des Anguilles
Tel: 626 2503/2843
www.lavanille-reserve.com

Le Château de Bel Ombre.

Try the crocodile croquettes! Or play
safe with *croque monsieur* and some
interesting local goodies, such as
samousas, washed down with wine
from the extensive list. Open daily
9.30am–5pm. €€

THE WEST

Black River

La Bonne Chute
Coast Road, Tamarin
Tel: 483 6552
Email: labonnechute@intnet.mu
This long-established restaurant
(adjacent to the Caltex Petrol Station)
is often used for wedding receptions.
It serves excellent Creole specialities
and European cuisine. Open Mon–
Sat noon–3pm and 7–11pm. Book in
advance. €€€€
Moustache Bistro
Royal Road, La Mivoie
Tel: 483 7728
Email: moustache.blackriver@gmail.com
Dine on tasty tapas paired with
gourmet wines at this tiny, unusual
restaurant and bar, with its naturally
distressed walls made from reclaimed
fishing boats. Open Tue–Sat from
7pm. €€€
Pavillon de Chine
Black River Village
Tel: 483 5787
Serves tasty Creole food and excellent
South African wines. There is a good
family atmosphere and highchairs for
toddlers. Watch the world go by from
the veranda. Closed Thu. €€
Vanilla Bean Café
Coastal Road
Tel: 483 5292
Email: vanillabco@intnet.mu
This inland eatery, with home-made
cakes, good coffee and healthy

lunches at reasonable prices, is a
favourite with expats. Book for lunch.
Open Mon–Fri 8.30am–4pm, Sat
8.30am–noon. €€€
Le Whatever
Le Place, Cap Tamarin
Tel: 483 7810
www.lewhatever.mu
This intimate modern bistro serves
elegant French specialities, including
home-made foie gras, and fine wines.
Eat at beautifully laid tables inside
or out on the terrace overlooking the
green square of Tamarin's newest
shopping complex. Open Mon–Sat for
lunch and dinner. €€

Chamarel

L'Alchimiste
Rhumerie de Chamarel, Route Royale
Tel: 483 7980
www.rhumeriedechamarel.com
Enjoy mountain views and an à
la carte lunch in the grounds of a
magnificent rum distillery. The menu
features venison, wild boar, duck and
organic produce grown on the estate
and a delicious Chamarel rum baba.
Open Mon–Sat 11.30am–3pm.
€€€€
Le Chamarel Restaurant
La Crête Main Road
Tel: 483 4421
www.lechamarelrestaurant.com
Group tours flock to this restaurant
at lunchtime for its view, good service

and extensive menu featuring
traditional Mauritian specialities
and European food. Open daily
7am–5.30pm.
Varangue sur Morne
110 Plaine Champagne Road, Coeur Bois
Tel: 483 6610
www.varanguesurmorne.com
A superb restaurant serving Creole
and European food, with an extensive
game menu, in the Black River
Gorges area with distant views of the
lagoon. Open daily noon–3.30pm.
Book in advance. €€€

Flic en Flac

The Beach Shack
Coastal Road
Tel: 453 9080
www.thebeachshack.mu
The most stylish of Flic en Flac's
restaurants serves grills, salads and
burgers among more exotic offerings,
with a good selection of wines, and
has live music at weekends. Good
value. Open daily 8am–midnight.
€€€
Domaine Anna
Morcellement Anna, Medine Sugar Estate
Tel: 453 9650
www.domaineanna.net
Blow the budget on mountains of
Chinese fare in this huge, circular
restaurant built from local stone, or
dine outside in candlelit gazebos next
to man-made ponds. Specialities

include seafood with heart of palm salad and fish with ginger sauce. Open Tue–Sun noon–2.30pm and 7pm–midnight. Book in advance. €€€€

Le Morne Peninsula

Emba Filao
Le Morne Beach
The only public restaurant on the Peninsula serves decent Mauritian and western food at a fraction of the price of resorts, under the shade of the filao trees. Open daily 8am–3.30pm and 6–10.30pm. €€€

PLATEAU TOWNS

Curepipe

Chinese Wok
242 Royal Road
Tel: 676 1548
Email: nadetteko@yahoo.com
This restaurant serves the best-value Chinese food in town, in unpretentious surroundings. Open Mon–Sat noon–2.30pm and 7–9.30pm. €€€

Domaine des Aubineaux
Pont Carbonel
Forest Side
Tel: 676 3089
www.saintaubin.mu
Great-value traditional Mauritian cuisine on the veranda of a colonial mansion overlooking a tropical garden. Open Mon–Sat 9am–5pm. €€

La Potinière
Hillcrest Building, Sir Winston Churchill Street
Tel: 676 2648
Excellent French restaurant with a long-standing reputation. Open Mon–Fri 9am–4pm. €€€€

Floreal

La Clef des Champs
Queen Mary Avenue
Tel: 686 3458
www.laclefdeschamps.mu
Gourmet French cuisine with a Creole touch in a sophisticated colonial-style setting. Reservations recommended. Open Mon–Sat 11am–midnight. €€€€

Moka

Eureka
Moka
Tel: 433 8477
www.maisoneureka.com
The traditional Mauritian lunch cooked in the authentic outdoor stone kitchen using fresh produce from the estate is one of the island's best, and served on the elegant veranda of this colonial house. Open daily 11am–4pm. €€€€

RODRIGUES

La Mangue

John's Resto
Tel: 831 6306
Email: leboisdolive@yahoo.com
This restaurant is noted for fresh seafood and Chinese specialities, but if you're after something a cut above, order in advance. Open for lunch, and for dinner by reservation. €€

Port Mathurin

Aux Deux Frères
First floor, Patricko Building, Place François Leguat
Tel: 831 0541
Email: corentineblondel@hotmail.com
Book a terrace table at this arty restaurant, in an old Creole mansion.

Traditional Mauritian curry.

Run by two French brothers, it serves nouvelle cuisine alongside traditional dishes. Open Mon–Sat lunch and dinner, Sun dinner only. Book ahead. €€€

La Ferme
Mamy Cherie
Tel: 5749 0565
Email: raffyrodrigues@yahoo.com
Although a bit out of the way, this authentic Italian restaurant is worth the trek for gourmands, and uses fresh island produce. €€€€

Grande Montagne
Auberge de la Montagne
Tel: 831 4607
Email: villa@intnet.mu
This *table d'hote* in the central mountains is run by the island's most famous chef, Francoise Baptiste, and is a great place to try Rodriguan specialities, at a reasonable price. €€€

Ti Rozo
Corner of Rue Père Gandy and Rue Victoria
Tel: 832 1586
This seafood restaurant is the closest you'll get to authentic Creole cuisine in Port Mathurin. Try the saffron octopus or seafood gratin. Open Mon–Sat 10am–3pm and 6–9pm. €€€

Saint François

Mazavaroo
Tel: 831 8816
Email: mazavaroo@yahoo.fr
This understandably popular seafood restaurant in a wooden house near the beach may look rustic but the fusion food is great. It's only open at peak times, so book ahead. Open Mon–Sat 11.30am–2.30pm and 6.30–9pm. €€€

PRICE CATEGORIES

Price categories are for two people, including soft drinks or beer:
€ = less than R400
€€ = R400–600
€€€ = R600–1,000
€€€€ = more than R1,000

ACTIVITIES

NIGHTLIFE, SPORT AND SHOPPING

NIGHTLIFE

There is usually something going on somewhere in Mauritius, whether it be a hotel dinner show, a sega performance, a Hindu, Chinese, Muslim or Christian festival (see page 366) or some kind of play or theatrical show. Most tourist hotels offer Las Vegas-style cabarets, sanitised sega shows, live music and themed cultural programmes, and some have casinos. For up-to-date information on cultural events and evening entertainment consult the local tourist office or your hotel receptionist. The Mauritius Tourism Promotion Authority (MTPA) produces a range of free guides containing basic information, but the main bars, nightclubs and casinos are listed below.

Nightclubs

Mauritius is not hot on nightlife, though the Caudan Waterfront in **Port Louis** has brought new life to the capital, which, for the most part, goes quiet after dark. Pubs and bars rather than nightclubs can be found here. Party animals can find a clutch of discos, with names like Zanzibar, Buddha Club and Les Enfants Terribles, around **Grand Baie**. Discos and nightclubs usually open only on Friday and Saturday nights.

In **Rodrigues** look out for hand-written bills advertising the **Grande Soirée Dansante**, dance nights organised in the town's three discotheques, when everyone from babes in arms to robust Rodriguan grannies bop to reggae and the fusion that is seggae. Safari Bar at Baie Lascars just outside Port Mathurin

is the centre of the island's nightlife, with a nightclub at weekends and a bar and karaoke nights in the week. For clean family fun make for the alfresco disco **Les Cocotiers** next to Residence Tamaris, but for rum, rhythm and red-blooded recreation, try **Le Récif**.

Cinema

Most films shown in Mauritius are in French and a few cinemas also show Hindi and Tamil films, and English-language films in the early evening. The Star Cinema at the **Caudan Waterfront** shows the latest films from Hollywood, Bollywood and France, as does the cinema at Bagatelle on the Central Plateau. The Mahatma Ghandi Institute at **Moka** sometimes screens English-language films. Consult the local newspaper for times and programmes.

Casinos

If you're feeling lucky, head for **Le Caudan Waterfront Casino** in Port Louis or the **Casino de Maurice** in Curepipe and try your luck at roulette and blackjack, or pump your money into one of the many slot machines. Many of the top hotels also have their own casinos, including **La Pirogue** in Wolmar and **One&Only Le Saint Géran** in Poste de Flacq. There are casinos at Domaine les Pailles near Port Louis and in Flic en Flac, and slot machines at Ti Vegas at Grand Baie. Visit www.casinosofmauritius.com. None of the casinos require you to show your passport and entry is free, but you are expected to dress smartly. Casinos are open every day from 10am to 4am.

Theatres

Productions by the Réunion-based theatre company **Centre Dramatique de l'Océan Indien** are sometimes staged at one of the island's two theatres:
Plaza Theatre, Rose Hill.
Théatre de Port Louis, Intendance Street, Port Louis.
Regular jazz, choral performances and other musical events are promoted by **Otayo** (www.otayo.com).

SPORT

Throughout the year football and athletics attract huge crowds and for details of these and other sporting events consult the MTPA tourist office, local newspapers or the general secretary of the **Mauritius Amateur Athletics Association** at Le Réduit (tel: 464 2256; http://maaa.intnet.mu).

The Mascarene Islands regularly take part in the **Indian Ocean Island Games**, a sort of mini-Olympics event involving Mauritius, Réunion, Madagascar, Seychelles and the Comoros Islands, held every four years and hosted in turns by a member nation.

Outdoor activities

Mauritius is ideal for water sports. The coral reefs provide a fascinating and magnificent underwater landscape and many establishments offer snorkelling and diving expeditions. Undersea walks, submarine excursions and glass-bottom boat trips may appeal to the less adventurous.
Offshore breezes provide ideal conditions for windsurfing, kitesurfing

MAURITIUS

and sailing on the west coast, and the glassy lagoons and sheltered bays are perfect for water-skiing, paragliding, pedalo trips, kayaking and paddle boarding. Big game fishing is popular out in the Indian Ocean and you are unlikely to return from a trip empty handed.

On dry land, the many nature reserves and eco parks offer a network of hiking trails and the possibility of spotting indigenous wildlife rescued from extinction. Horse riding, mountain biking, mountain climbing and canyoning are also available. **Mauritours** (tel: 467 9700) has a desk at many hotels and they or other island tour companies can organise a wide range of sporting activities for you. In recent years, hotels have sponsored sporting activities. LUX* Resorts has a year-round adventure sports calendar and Heritage Resorts supports The Dodo Trail (tel: 5985 1584; www.dodo-trail.com), an annual running event for everyone in July, which raises money for MWF (the Mauritius Wildlife Foundation). Trail Rodrigues (www.trailrodrigues.com) is held each November.

Water sports

Diving and snorkelling
Blue Bay offers the best snorkelling on the island, although most large hotels offer trips by boat to snorkelling spots near their own premises. Nearly 50 dive centres are found island-wide – most attached to hotels – and offer excursions to shipwrecks and dive sites. The following cater for all levels, from beginners to experienced divers, and some provide night dives. Contact the **Mauritian Scuba Diving Association** (tel: 454 0011; www.msda.mu) for more information. **Blue Water Diving Centre**, Mont Choisy; tel: 265 6700; www.bluewaterdiving center.com. Trou aux Biches and Mont Choisy have several good dive centres. Hughes Vitry, who is based at the Blue Water Diving Centre next door to the popular fish restaurant Le Pescatore (see page 353), is a well-known undersea photographer and may take you on a 'shark dive'. **Exploration Sous Marine**, c/o Villas Caroline, Flic en Flac; tel: 453 8450; www.pierre-szalay.com. Old hands will find plenty of specialist diving, including night diving. Owned and managed by Pierre Szalay, former president of the Mauritius Scuba Diving Association.

Equipped for snorkelling

Many hotels and dive centres provide snorkelling equipment, but if you plan on doing a lot of underwater exploration, it is always better to invest in your own. Snorkels and masks are widely available, but before parting with your money, make sure the snorkel mouthpiece is soft and comfortable and check the mask fits properly. You can do this by holding it in place without putting the strap over your head, then breathing in through your nose. If the mask stays on with the suction when you let go, it should be fine; if air escapes then try another one.

Identifying fish: a host of different species of tropical fish make their home in the coral reefs and there are a number of excellent books to assist with the identification of the common species. For snorkellers it would be well worth getting hold of a 'fish watchers' slate' – a plastic card printed with colour drawings of the 40 most common species, as this can be taken into the sea. Get a preview of the species you're most likely to see at Mauritius Aquarium at Pointe aux Piments (tel: 261 4561; www.mauritiusaquarium.com).

Sun protection and safety: remember to cover yourself with plenty of waterproof, high-factor sun cream and it's also a good idea to wear a T-shirt while snorkelling to avoid sunburn on your back. If there are jet skis or other motorised craft in the area, it is sensible to mark your location by tying a brightly coloured float to your waist or foot.

Paradise Diving Centre, Mont Choisy Coral Azur Hotel, Coastal Road, Mon Choisy; tel: 265 6070; www.paradisedivingmauritius.com. **Sun Divers, La Pirogue**, Wolmar; tel: 5972 1504; www.sundiversmauritius.com. Good for learners, this is the island's most established dive centre.

Rodrigues
Bouba Diving Centre, Mourouk Ebony Hotel, Pate Reynieux; tel: 832 3063; www.boubadiving.com **Cotton Dive Center**, Cotton Bay Hotel; tel: 5706 1474; www.cottondivecenter.com **Rodriguez Diving**, Les Cocotiers Hotel, Anse aux Anglais; tel: 831 0957; www.rodriguez-diving.com **Rodrigues Underwater Group**, Pointe Monier-Rodrigues; tel: 831 2032

Big game fishing
The best time for game fishing is from October to April, when marlin, tuna and the big wahoo are plentiful. The Marlin World Cup competition is held at the Centre de Pêche in November. Fishing trips last for a minimum of six hours and take five rods at a time. Book through your hotel or tour operator or directly through the following companies:
JP Henry Charters, Black River; tel: 483 5060; www.jph.mu
Killer Fishing, Coastal Road, Trou aux Biches; tel: 265 6595
Organisation de Pêche du Nord, Corsaire Club, Royal Road, Trou aux Biches; tel: 265 5209

La Pirogue Big Game Fishing, Flic en Flac; tel: 5453 8054; www.lapiroguebiggame.com
Sportfisher, Grand Baie; tel: 263 8358; www.sportfisher.com

Rodrigues
BDPM Fishing Co Ltd, Port Mathurin; tel: 831 2790
Le Boss Fishing Club, Anse aux Anglais; tel: 875 9076
Rod Fishing Club, Port Mathurin; tel: 875 0616; www.rodfishingclub.com

Sailing and cruising
Hobie Cats (small catamarans) can be booked on the beach at most hotels. The following yacht charter companies offer half- or full-day excursions in large catamarans. Reservations can be made through hotels or direct with:
Coral Breeze Tours, Sunset Boulevard, Royal Road, Grand Baie; tel: 263 8017; www.coralbreeze.mu. Also organises Hobie Cat sailing, kayaking and pedalo trips.
Croisières Australes, La Cuvette Road, Grand Baie; tel: 263 1670; www.croisieres-australes.mu.
Croisières Turquoise, Mahébourg; tel: 631 1640; www.croisieres-turquoise.com. Day-long cruises on a catamaran.
Exotic Cruise, Pointe aux Piments; tel: 261 1724. Sunset and all-day catamaran trips (with lunch) along the north coast to Gabriel Island.
Easterlies Océane, Trou d'Eau Douce; tel: 480 2767; www.easterlies-cruise-mauritius.com. Cruise

RÉUNION

SEYCHELLES

along the southeast coast, stopping off for a snorkel and a visit to the Île aux Cerfs.

Windsurfing, surfing and kitesurfing

Surfing is only found on the west coast, around Tamarin. Windsurfing is best on the breezier east coast, and most beach hotels supply windsurfing boards or you can book directly through **Coral Breeze Tours**, Grand Baie; tel: 263 8017; www.coralbreeze.mu. Kitesurfing is found at La Gaulette, Bel Ombre and Le Morne, whose legendary 'One Eye' famously hosts international competitions. Le Morne draws experienced kiters from May to October, but kitesurfing lessons for beginners are year round. Club Mistral (www.club-mistral.com) is recommended by the International Kiteboarding Organisation (IKO). Rodrigues' top operator is **Osmowings, Club Osmosis**, Marouk; tel: 832 3051; www.kitesurf-rodrigues.com.

Hiking and adventure

With pockets of national park, nature reserves and eco-parks throughout the island, 28 mini-mountains to climb and recently introduced cycle trails, there is plenty of room for adventure on Mauritius. Hiking and adventure tours can be arranged through hotels or island tour companies, or better still, directly with independent providers.
Le Pétrin Information Centre near Grand Bassin (tel: 471 1128; daily 9am–3pm) can provide up-to-date information on walks and conditions of trails in the Black River Gorges National Park, such as the 7km (4-mile) round walk from Le Pétrin through the Macchabé Forest (spectacular views). Another walk from Le Pétrin is to the Tamarin Falls near Curepipe. Or go to the **Black River Visitor Centre** (tel: 258 0057; daily 9am–3pm) near the gorges.

Adventure activities

Yanature (tel: 5785 6177; www.trekkingilemaurice.com) organises guided walking tours to Black River Gorges, Tamarin Falls and mountains. Good physical condition is required.
Private sugar estates offer 'green tourism' activities in swatches of countryside with forests and waterfalls. One is **Chazal**, St Felix Sugar Estate, Chamouny (tel: 622 7243; www.chazalecotourismmauritius.com) in the deep south. Popular **Domaine L'Etoile** (tel: 488 4444;

In the dry

If you don't like getting your face wet but don't want to miss out on the beauties of a coral reef, try a solar-powered undersea walk. Wearing a specially designed helmet which supplies you with fresh air from the surface, you can even wear your spectacles or contact lenses. And it is suitable for children as young as seven.
Solar Undersea Walk
Kiosk next to Caltex petrol station, Grand Baie; tel: 263 7819; www.solarunderseawalk.net. Or book through your hotel or tour operator. Daily 10.30am and 1.30pm.
Aquaventure, Coastal Road, Belle Mare; tel: 415 5040; www.underseawalkmauritius.com.

www.terrocean.mu) in the east has zip-lining, quad-biking, horse riding, archery and self-guided treks, and **Frederica Nature Reserve** (tel: 5729 4498; www.adventure.frederica.mu) in the southwest has quad-biking, guided nature treks and 4x4 excursions.
The island's most extensive adventure park is **Casela Nature Park** (tel: 452 2828; www.caselayemen.mu), which offers everything from zip-lining, quad-biking and via ferrata to encounters with African animals.
Other specialists include:
Vertical World Ltd, tel: 5251 1107; www.verticalworldltd.com. Specialists in hiking, mountain and rock climbing and canyoning.
Yemaya Adventures, tel: 5752 0046; www.yemayaadventures.com. Hiking, mountain biking and sea kayaking.
Bigfoot Adventures, tel: 5250 7906; www.bigfootadventures.net. Guided quad-biking along the south coast.

Canyoning

If you want to try your hand at canyoning, head for the Tamarind Falls. For information on excursions, contact Vertical World (tel: 5251 1107; www.verticalworldltd.com) or Otelair Mauritius (tel: 5251 6680; www.otelair.com).

Ecotourism

The **Île aux Aigrettes Nature Reserve**, opposite Mahébourg on the east coast, is home to a large population of pink pigeons and an assortment of reptiles. It is in the process of gradually being restored to its original state. Guided visits are

offered daily by **Mauritius Wildlife Foundation** (MWF; tel: 631 2396; www.mauritian-wildlife.org).

Golf

Mauritius is a top-notch golf destination, with eight 18-hole Championship courses and three nine-hole courses to choose from.

18-hole Championship Courses

Ernie Els at Anahita the Resort; tel: 402 2200; www.anahita.mu
Legend & Links, Constance Belle Mare Plage; tel: 402 2600; www.bellemareplagehotel.com
Heritage Golf Club, Bel Ombre; tel: 266 9777; www.heritageresorts.mu
Île aux Cerfs, Shangri-La Le Touessrok Resort & Spa; tel: 402 7400; www.letouessrokresort.com. Spectacular views.
Mauritius Gymkhana Club; tel: 696 1404; www.mgc.mu. The oldest golf club in the southern hemisphere.
Paradis Golf Club; Le Morne; tel: 401 5050; www.beachcomber-hotels.com
Tamarina Golf Club; Tamarin Bay; tel: 401 3006; www.tamarinagolf.mu

Nine-hole Courses

Maritim Resort & Spa; Balaclava; tel: 204 1000; www.maritim.com
One&Only Le Saint Géran; Pointe de Flacq; tel: 401 1688; http://lesaintgeran.oneandonly resorts.com
Shandrani Hotel; Blue Bay; tel: 603 4823; www.beachcomber-hotels.com

Horse riding

Horse riding can be arranged through your hotel or island tour

The original undersea walk.
Scuba Doo, Royal Road, Trou aux Biches; tel: 5251 0131; www.scubadoo.summerfuntour.org. Offers 30-minute rides on an aquascooter under the sea.
Blue Safari Submarine, Royal Road, Grand Baie; tel: 263 3333; www.blue-safari.com. An air-conditioned hour-long trip under the sea in a submarine. Daily, 9am–9pm.
Le Nessee A one-hour trip in a semi-submersible. Departs four times a day from 9.30am and once at night at 7pm. Book through any travel agent, your hotel or Coral Breeze Tours, Sunset Boulevard, Grand Baie; tel: 263 8017; www.coralbreeze.mu.

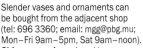

operators. The **Maritim Resort & Spa** (Balaclava; tel: 204 1000; www.maritim.com) has its own equestrian centre.

Stables island-wide include **Horse Riding Delights** at Mont Choisy (tel: 265 6159; www.horseridingdelights. com); **Les Ecuries de la Vieille Cheminée** (tel: 483 4249; www. lavieillecheminee.com) and **Haras du Morne** (tel: 450 4142; www. harasdumorne.com).

Children

Mauritius offers plenty of activities for children, ranging from animal parks and adventures on land and water to museums. A day at Casela World of Adventures (tel: 452 2828; www.caselayemen.mu) is a must, and with everything from tilapia fishing, a petting farm and animal safaris to zip-lining and a lion encounter, it caters for toddlers to teens. At southern animal park La Vanille Réserve des Mascareignes (tel: 626 2503; www. lavanille-reserve.com) children can spy macaque monkeys, and hold a baby crocodile or Aldabra tortoise. They can eyeball a shark at the north's Mauritius Aquarium (tel: 261 4561; www.mauritiusaquarium.com) or take to the waves to spot and 'swim' with dolphins. A children's activity trail is offered at the modern interactive museum L'Aventure du Sucre (tel: 243 7900; www.aventuredusucre. com), and there's a mini-train ride or horse-and-carriage ride at Domaine les Pailles (tel: 286 4225; www. domainelespailles.net).

SHOPPING

What to buy

You could be spoilt for choice in your wanderings round the new shopping malls in Mauritius, where local products and handicrafts stand alongside luxury imported goods. Haggling in markets is perfectly acceptable. Shops tend to have fixed prices but may offer you a small discount for bulk or major purchases. **Model ships** and **wooden hand-carvings** make good buys. Replicas of wooden Creole houses and hand-carved salad bowls, miniature tropical fruits and the inevitable dodo can be bought everywhere. Raw materials such as straw, wood and fabrics turn up as appealing patchwork Creole dolls representing people from the various ethnic groups.

Textiles and **clothing** are good quality but not necessarily cheap – good buys to look for are woollens, T-shirts, saris, silk and cotton shirts and casual wear. In up-market shops you'll find rich tapestries, murals, rugs and cushions, embroidered tablecloths and napkins, quilted wall hangings and colourful pottery depicting scenes from Mauritian life.

Markets sell *tentes* or baskets made from the vacoas or pandanus leaf, coconut leaf, raffia, aloe, bamboo and banana fibre, which serve as useful shopping bags as they are very strong and hardwearing.

Jewellery Unusual buys include pieces made from mother-of-pearl, coconut or local dried seeds; also gold jewellery, mounted with precious stones.

Flowers Long-lasting cut andreanums and anthuriums, in small, medium or large blooms, travel well and can be bought at the airport in convenient pre-packaged boxes, just prior to your flight. Alternatively, you can visit the plantations and order flowers from there.

Glass-blowing demonstrations from recycled glass can be seen at the Mauritius Glass Gallery, next to Phoenix Beverages at Phoenix.

Slender vases and ornaments can be bought from the adjacent shop (tel: 696 3360; email: mgg@pbg.mu; Mon–Fri 9am–5pm, Sat 9am–noon). **Chinese goods** such as kimonos, silks and *objets* made from brass, jade and porcelain can be found in specialised shops, particularly in Curepipe.

Objets d'art can be bought at Diane, Royal Road, Trou aux Biches, tel: 265 5156.

Mauritian food specialities such as spices, sugar, salt, tea and smoked marlin don't cost the earth and make nice gifts.

There are **art galleries** dotted all over the island, although they are concentrated in Grand Baie, where you can pick up paintings and handicrafts by local artists and artisans.

Shopping centres

Bagatelle, Moka. The island's most popular shopping centre, with local and international clothing brands, a food court, bars and restaurants and a cinema.

Cascavelle, Flic en Flac. A mix of local and international clothing brands, and a bar/nightclub, on the road to Tamarin.

Caudan Waterfront, Port Louis. Some of the best shops on the island. Several clothes shops and duty free, plus a food court and crafts market.

La Croisette, Grand Baie. Large shopping complex on the edge of town with mainly international clothing brands.

Currimjee Arcades, Royal Road, Curepipe. Small centre with a few clothes and duty-free shops.

Garden Village, Sir Winston Churchill Street, Curepipe. This small shopping complex on the outskirts of Curepipe is a shopping stop on tours of the island.

Model ships

Making intricate model boats and ships – including replicas of famous galleys – is an art in Mauritius and they can be bought from workshops dotted around the island, ranging from the affordable to the very expensive. The **Historic Marine** factory, at Zone Industrielle de St Antoine, Goodlands (tel; 283 9404; www. historic-marine.com), where nautical furniture in teak and mahogany is made, also gives tours of the workshop.

Quad biking.

MAURITIUS

RÉUNION

SEYCHELLES

Jumbo, Phoenix. Large American-style shopping centre with an enormous supermarket and a street of other shops, but not many clothes outlets. **Jumbo,** Riche Terre, a modern complex with attractive boutiques stocking clothes and handicrafts, a fast food court and a pleasant supermarket for shopping in air-conditioned comfort.
Orchard Centre, Quatre Bornes. More glitzy inside than out. Lots of local clothes stores and possible bargains.
Port Louis Waterfront, Port Louis. Boutiques selling everything from bonsai to arts and crafts.
Ruisseau Créole, Black River. A few trendy shops selling everything from designer wear to health foods.
Sunset Boulevard, Grand Baie. A shopping village with some good clothes stores and some of the island's most interesting shops, including designer clothing.
Super U, Grand Baie. Combines internet facilities with European-style shopping in a supermarket that stocks just about everything and is flanked with inexpensive eateries.
Trianon Shopping Complex, Quatre Bornes. Popular complex comprising supermarkets, fast food, shops and boutiques. Huge parking area.

Duty free

Remember to take your passport and airline ticket when shopping for duty-free goods outside the airport, and that your purchases must be paid for in foreign currency or by credit card. Duty-free shops will arrange for your purchases to be delivered to the airport before your departure, but you must allow at least one day for the formalities to be completed.
   Mauritius Duty Free Paradise (MDFP) has duty-free outlets in Port

Louis, Grand Baie and the airport, but other names to look for are Sashena Trading, Etoile d'Argent, Linea Azzura Shop, Parure and Bijouterie Bienvenue for perfumes, photographic equipment, cosmetics, sportswear, shoes and jewellery.

Some Duty-Free Shops

Adamas Diamond Duty Free Boutique, Floreal Square; tel: 686 1248; www.adamasltd.com
Caudan Waterfront, Marina Quay, Port Louis; tel: 211 9500; www.lecaudan.com. Has Poncini, Shiv Jewels and Adamas outlets among its 120 shops.
Tara Cashmere, Espace Ocean, Grand Baie, tel: 263 6688

Bookshops

Publications in both French and English are widely available in the island's bookshops.
Bookcourt Ltd, Caudan Waterfront, Port Louis; tel: 211 9262; www.bookcourt.mu
Le Cygne, Magic Lantern Complex, 307 Royal Road, Beau Bassin-Rose Hill; tel 464 2444; www.lecygne.com. Browse all day in this well-stocked bookshop tucked in the arcades at Rose Hill. Choose your books over a cup of tea or coffee at the back of the shop.
Papyrus, Richmond Hill Complex, La Salette Road; Grand Baie; tel 263 0012; www.librairiepapyrus.com
Trèfles, Currimjee Arcade, Royal Road, Curepipe; tel: 676 3025; www.librairieletreflemu.com

Textiles and Clothes

Floreal Square shopping complex (Floreal; tel: 698 8016) sells quality garments made from raw imported

materials such as cashmere, cotton and silk.
   Men fare rather better than women in **made-to-measure outfits** and you can select from a wide range of imported or local cloth to make top-quality trousers and shirts. A wool worsted three-piece suit can be made for less than £200. **Caustat Apparel** (Padaruth Lane, La Caverne, Vacoas; tel: 686 6818) is considered the best men's tailor in Mauritius, with a client list that includes guests of the Royal Palm Hotel. Suits can be made up in 24–48 hours at **Karl Kaiser** (Europe's Hugo Boss), Le Caudan Waterfont (tel: 211 7262) or Sunset Boulevard (tel: 263 4890; www.karlkaisergroup.com) but your tailor will expect you to have one or two fittings before the final stitches are put in place. They will keep measurements on file, if asked, so that new or repeat orders can be made in advance.

Bargain designer clothing

Mauritians make the clothes for many European designers and often have stock left over that is sold at a third of the normal price, such as at Floreal Knitwear, Shibani and Tara Cashmere.

Rodrigues

In **Rodrigues**, a **Saturday market** selling everything under the sun, from souvenirs to home-made chutneys and fresh produce, operates on Fishermen Lane, Port Mathurin, from 6–10am. You can buy baskets made from vacoas leaves at the **Women's Handicraft Centre** in Mont Lubin, and other handicrafts at **Careco** in Port Mathurin and at **Sir Gaetan Duval airport** at Plaine Corail.

Wares for sale in Port Louis.

A – Z

A HANDY SUMMARY
OF PRACTICAL INFORMATION

A

Accommodation

There are over a hundred hotels on the island, catering for every budget. Most are luxury beachfront hotels in the four- or five-star category, with gourmet restaurants, top-notch spas and world-class golf courses. They offer exceptionally high standards of service and facilities, including water sports, which are free except for scuba diving and game fishing, and the best have helicopter transfers, private plunge pools and 24-hour butler service. Leading local hotel groups **Beachcomber** (www.beachcomber-hotels.com), **Sun Resorts** (www.sunresortshotels. com), **LUX* Resorts** (www.luxresorts. com), **Attitude Hotels** (http://hotels-attitude.com), **Constance Hotels** (www.constancehotels.com) and **Heritage Resorts** (www.heritage resorts.mu) rub shoulders with leading international brands.

Many of the top hotels, such as The St Regis Mauritius, Constance and Oberoi, offer a personalised service where they will make a point of knowing your name and will use it in the bar or reception, and even three-star hotels provide high standards of service. Most Mauritian hotels have a 'mini club' for children's activities and increasingly teen clubs. Many also offer all-inclusive packages, with premium all-inclusive packages including everything from champagne and gourmet picnic baskets to golf or spa treatments and excursions. All hotels have their own security guards.

Tour operators are adding a growing number of self-catering

establishments to their brochures, and private guesthouses and bed-and-breakfasts are independent accommodation options, often chosen by repeat visitors to Mauritius. Many comfortable beach-side bungalows, villas and apartments are available for short- or long-term rental and the deal may include maid service, a chef and even excursions.

While the majority of independent accommodation options are in main tourist centres, such as Grand Baie and Flic en Flac, they are found island-wide, with some of the best in Tamarin, Blue Bay and Pointe D'Esny, La Gaulette and even Le Morne. Local rental agencies in Grand Baie, such as **Ocean Villas** (tel: 263 1000; www.ocean-villas.com) or **Grand Baie Travel & Tours** (tel: 263 8771; www.gbtt.com) can help you find reasonably priced accommodation.

There are many bungalows to rent in Flic en Flac, where you can pay around R6,000 a week for two people, or a whole bungalow for five people for around R9,000 a week. Self-catering apartments, studios and beach-front properties are also available. Contact Flic en Flac Tourist Agency, Royal Road, Flic en Flac; tel: 453 9389; www.fftourist.com or try the following: **Jet 7 Group** (tel: 453 9600; www.jet-7.com) or **Mauritours** (tel: 467 9700; www.mauritours.net). Mauritours also features **Le Tamaris Apartments** (tel: 831 2715; email: letamaris@intnet.mu) at Camp du Roi in Rodrigues. The 25 modern, bright apartments are fully equipped with kitchenette and TV, and come with daily maid service.

Specialist agencies, such as UK tour operator **Elegant Destinations** (tel: 0870 8908877; www.elegant destinations.com), have a wide

Animal welfare

The sight of many stray cats and dogs, often in appalling conditions, may be upsetting for some visitors. If you want to do something about it contact PAWS (tel: 631 2304; www.pawsmauritius.org), a local animal welfare charity affiliated to World Animal Protection, at Mahébourg. Their activities include mass sterilisation campaigns, an adoption scheme and a humane animal welfare philosophy. The local MSPCA is not affiliated to the RSPCA International Section.

selection of self-catering properties for all budgets. The Association of Hoteliers and Restaurants in Mauritius (AHRIM; tel: 637 3782; www.mauritiustourism.org) is also a useful source of information. The Authentic Hotels and Guesthouses of Mauritius leaflet, available from the MTPA (Mauritius Tourism Promotion Authority) in your home country, features a handpicked selection of small hotels, bed-and-breakfasts and guesthouses. Independent accommodation options are also featured at Housetrip (www.housetrip. com), Homeaway (www.homeaway. co.uk), Vacation Rentals by Owner (www.vrbo.com) and HostelBookers (www.hostelbookers.com).

Admission charges

Government-run museums are free but always check to make sure they are open before setting out. There is an entrance fee for all private museums and tourist attractions. Discos and nightclubs may charge admission for men (although they

MAURITIUS

RÉUNION

SEYCHELLES

shouldn't) but women often get in for nothing. Sometimes free cultural and dance shows take place at the Caudan Waterfront, so ask around for what's happening or check out www.islandinfo.mu.

B

Budgeting for your trip

Allow at least R1,000 per day per person to cover meals and snacks, soft drinks and entrance fees. Avoid your hotel room's minibar if you're on a budget. Bottled water, wines, spirits, cigarettes and food are much cheaper at the local supermarket. Eating and drinking outside your hotel is also much cheaper but remember when ordering food that not all menu prices include 15 percent VAT. Portions tend to be generous so unless you're famished it can be quite hard getting through a full three-course meal.

C

Children

Kids are welcome at restaurants, festivals and all places of worship throughout the Mascarene Islands. Luxury hotels in Mauritius cater specially for youngsters and offer supervised activities in free kids' and teens' clubs, special meals, babysitting services, family rooms and child discounts on excursions.

If you're travelling with very young children avoid December and January, which may be too hot for them. Leading hotels provide everything from sterilisers to wet wipes for babies, which saves the need to bring a lot of heavy equipment with you. Supermarkets also stock a wide range of baby food and nappies but you should bring your own from home if you have a favourite brand.

Climate

Mauritius and Rodrigues enjoy a tropical climate with two seasons: summer and winter.

Summer (November to April)

The weather is hot and humid with prolonged sunshine and temperatures of up to 35°C (95°F) on the coasts, broken by short heavy bursts of rainfall, especially during December and January. Humidity is high even at night. The north coast, where temperatures are highest, can get

Cyclone warnings

In the southwestern region of the Indian Ocean the following terms describe the intensity of different cyclonic disturbances:
Tropical depression: speed of gusts is less than 90km (56 miles) per hour.
Moderate tropical depression: speed of gusts is 90–134km (56–83 miles) per hour.
Strong tropical depression: speed of gusts is 135–179km (84–111 miles) per hour.
Tropical cyclone: speed of gusts is 180–250km (112–155 miles) per hour.
Tropical cyclone of strong intensity: speed of gusts is 251–335km (156–208 miles) per hour.
Tropical cyclone of very strong intensity: speed of gusts is more than 335km (208 miles) per hour.

When a cyclone approaches the islands, the Meteorological Office regularly broadcasts cyclone bulletins and red flags are raised on public buildings to denote their intensity:
One red flag: Warning Class I – low risk of gust up to 120km (75 miles) per hour.
Two red flags: Warning Class II – increased risk of gusts up to 120km (75 miles) per hour.
Three red flags: Warning Class III – great danger of gusts up to 120km (75 miles) per hour.
Four red flags: Warning Class IV – gusts of 120km (75 miles) per hour have been registered.
Weather information: metservice.intnet.mu has a forecast and cyclone warning bulletin in English.

unbearably hot in summer, whereas the southeast trade winds freshen the south and east coasts with welcome cooling breezes. Average annual rainfall is around 2,000mm (79 ins), and most falls in summer.

Cyclones can occur between November and April. They are born hundreds of miles to the northeast of Mauritius and take days to meander westwards. Various weather stations track their route and warnings that a cyclone may develop are broadcast days in advance. Most pass by harmlessly, bringing only heavy rain and winds which clear the air after a spell of very hot humid weather. Others may have more devastating effects and you should listen to all cyclone warnings and comply with any directions or advice. Cyclones can cause serious disruption to telephone and power lines, and transport, but hotels are generally equipped with generators so that tourists will experience minimum discomfort.

Winter (May to October)

The weather is pleasant, warm and dry, with little rain, cool nights and less humidity than in summer. Temperatures can climb up to 25°C (77°F), with the highest temperatures found on the north coast. The west is the most sheltered coast in winter. It can get uncomfortably windy on the south and east coasts in winter as the southeast trade winds pick up.

When to go

Although Mauritius can be visited year round, as the hot season coincides with the European winter, it's mostly

known as a winter-sun destination, with peak tourist season in Mauritius' summer (November to April). This is also the season with the best conditions for diving and deep sea fishing. For visitors who like to walk, tour and explore, the best time to go is October and November, when it is early in the summer, and therefore hot but not stifling. The weather is still good on the coast from June to September, the low season, with fewer mosquitoes and discounted fares – prices can be up to a third cheaper than in high season. This is the time for both participation and spectator sports, with cooler, drier weather for outdoor adventures. For surfers, the waves are best from June to August.

The differences in Mauritius' altitude, topography and wind direction produce varied microclimates; the towns on the central plateau can be cloud-capped, damp and cooler, while the coast is clear and sunny at any time of year.

Rodrigues' peak tourist seasons are November to February, Easter, and June to August. With a relatively small number of tourists visiting the island, many restaurants are only open during peak times.

What to wear

The emphasis is on smart casual wear such as loose cotton shorts, shirts, T-shirts and dresses around town and in the evenings. For the feet, light sandals are appropriate and comfortable. Take long-sleeved shirts and trousers for summer nights, when mosquitoes are at large.

MAURITIUS

CLIMATE CHART

Port Louis

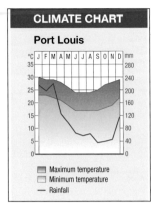

- ▨ Maximum temperature
- ▢ Minimum temperature
- — Rainfall

You should also bring insect repellent and a pair of plastic water shoes for protection against injury from sharp coral and stone fish (see Health and Medical Care).

Women are expected to cover up when venturing from beach to hotel, and swimsuits should not be worn around town or in hotel dining rooms. Male visitors need not bring a jacket and tie unless they plan to attend formal functions or dine in the smartest hotels and restaurants.

Most hotels used by tour operators have a dress code for dinner which specifies smart casual wear, but no shorts or T-shirts. You might need a light jumper or pashmina for the evening breeze.

Take sturdy shoes for outdoor activities such as walking in the Black River Gorges National Park.

Crime and safety

Generally, Mauritians are a law-abiding people. However, you should take basic precautions as you would at home. Don't flaunt jewellery and money in public; never leave property on view in your car; always lock doors and windows when you go out, particularly in self-catering accommodation; and after dark don't give a lift to a stranger or go out walking alone.

English is spoken at all police stations in Mauritius and specially trained Tourist Police are based at Grand Baie (tel: 213 2818). The police number for emergencies is 999. If you are a victim of crime, try to get names and addresses of witnesses and report the matter to the police. In cases of theft ensure you have documentation for insurance purposes.

Be extra wary of over-friendly characters hanging around isolated

locations during the day. Instances have been reported at Rochester Falls and Black River Gorges where tourists have been forced to part with money and valuables.

Serious incidents, such as rape and knife attacks on tourists, have been reported in recent years in Grand Baie, so walking alone at night is not recommended. And however friendly a situation appears, never accept a lift from a stranger.

Customs regulations

Travellers are allowed to bring in the following duty-free items: 250 grams of tobacco (including cigars and cigarettes); 1 litre of spirits; 2 litres of wine, ale or beer. There are stiff penalties for the importation of illegal drugs.

D

Disabled travellers

Top-class hotels provide good facilities for disabled travellers but check with your travel agent before leaving home. Beyond the hotels, facilities are generally dire but disabled people joining an organised tour will find that islanders are willing to lend a helping hand.

E

Embassies and consulates

If you are arrested or need legal representation contact your embassy or consulate. However, it should be stressed that officials can't advise on legal matters but may help you find an interpreter or arrange to contact friends or relatives. The main addresses are:

Australia High Commission: 2nd floor, Rogers House, John Kennedy Street, Port Louis; tel: 202 0160; www.mauritius.highcommission.gov.au

British High Commission: 7th floor, Les Cascades Building, Edith Cavell Street, Port Louis; tel: 202 9400; email: bhc@intnet.mu

British Honorary Consul: Careco Centre, Camp du Roi, Port Mathurin; tel: 832 0120; email: pdraper@intnet.mu

Consulate of Canada: 18 Jules Koenig Street, Port Louis; tel: 212 5500; email: canada@intnet.mu

South African High Commission: 4th floor, BAI Building, 25 Pope Hennessy Street, Port Louis; tel: 212

6925; email: portlouis.admin@foreign.gov.za

US Embassy: 4th floor, Rogers House, John Kennedy Street, Port Louis; tel: 202 4400; email: usembass@intnet.mu

Entry requirements

Nationals of the EU, US and all Commonwealth countries do not require visas, and entry as a tourist is for a maximum of six months. On entry, you will be asked to produce a passport valid for more than six months, your return or onward ticket and details of your address in Mauritius. Always check entry requirements before you travel as they can change.

Applications for longer stays should be made at the Passport and Immigration Office at Sterling House, 9–11 Lislet Geoffroy Street, Port Louis; tel: 210 9312; email: piomain@mail.gov.mu. Take two passport-size photographs, a valid return ticket, evidence of funds to meet the cost of your stay and a letter from your host explaining why you want to extend your stay. Applications can be made Mon–Fri 9am–2.30pm, Sat 9am–noon. There is no charge for a visa extension, but allow five working days to process it.

Etiquette

Social etiquette in Mauritius stems from the French *savoir-faire*, the British aplomb and the Asian desire to please, and throughout the Mascarene Islands, *bonjour*, thank you and *salam* (goodbye) are all frequently heard in everyday life.

Handshaking is expected when meeting someone for the first time but kissing on each cheek, in the French tradition, is also perfectly normal.

Local political scandals can be discussed quite freely and often get a good airing in the press. You're more likely to witness laughter, infectious smiles and giggling than outright aggression, but use your own common sense when choosing with whom to bring up touchy subjects

Electricity

220 volts throughout the Mascarene Islands. In Mauritius and Rodrigues square three-pin plugs are used as in the UK, as well as Continental two-round-pin plugs.

RÉUNION

SEYCHELLES

Emergency Numbers

Police: tel: 999
Fire: tel: 995
Ambulance: tel: 114

such as slavery, colonialism and race issues. The people of the Mascarenes accept Western whims, however strange some might appear to be, and will gladly pose for photographs, show you the way if you get lost, and rescue you from trouble. However, they do tend to exaggerate and their laid-back attitude to life means that they are not often very good time-keepers. But if you show tolerance, respect and good humour you'll take home fond memories of a warm and welcoming people.

G

Gay and lesbian travellers

Homosexuality, while tolerated, is not blatantly obvious in public places; but then any open displays of full blown affection, whether you're straight or gay, are likely to offend or attract jeers.

H

Health and medical care

Malaria has been eradicated in the Mascarenes and no vaccinations are necessary unless you are coming from an infected area, but check the latest advice before you travel.

Travellers should be aware of **chikungunya**, a mosquito-borne virus that in 2005–6 affected the Indian Ocean islands, including Mauritius, Rodrigues and Réunion, although outbreaks are now extremely rare. The virus causes severe debilitating illness with muscle and joint pain often accompanied by fever and a rash (conjunctivitis, headaches and minor bleeding are also possible symptoms), and can result in sufferers being left with chronic joint pain or, more rarely, in death. It is spread by the *Aedes aegypti* (yellow fever mosquito), an aggressive daytime biter. There is no vaccine or preventative drug for chikungunya and if contracted you should rest and take plenty of fluids. Paracetamol may help relieve the symptoms of aching and fever but the best way to avoid infection is to prevent mosquito bites. Although hotels regularly fumigate

their grounds, it's wise to use insect repellent containing deet, cover up, and close windows and doors against mosquitoes.

The cost of private treatment in Mauritius is substantially lower than in Europe. Shop around for an insurance policy that suits your circumstances and in the event of a medical claim ensure that you keep all receipts and documentation.

Remember that many insurance companies exclude extreme sports, such as rock climbing and mountaineering. If you plan to take part in any land or sea sports, confirm that the activity is within your capabilities, that your guide is a qualified first-aider and that drinks and first-aid equipment are carried at all times. But most important of all – and this cannot be stressed enough – ask what emergency back-up security measures are in place in case of accident or sudden illness. If there is any doubt at all, don't book.

Health hazards

In Mauritius avoid wading in unclear waters without wearing protective shoes. This is the habitat of the laff, or stone fish, which if trodden upon emits a poisonous venom from its spines. Local fishermen resort to a poultice remedy but immediate removal to hospital is necessary as the wound, if untreated, can be fatal. In Rodrigues the only nasties you may encounter are large centipedes. They frequent dark corners in old buildings and can emit a painful sting.

Medical treatment

Emergency hospital treatment is free at public hospitals. They tend to be very crowded and most visitors go to a private clinic. Your hotel can provide a doctor in cases of sudden illness and help locate out-of-hours pharmacists. Western medicines or their equivalent and antibiotics are also available over the counter.

If you fall ill in Rodrigues, where facilities are very basic, you should return to Mauritius as soon as possible for treatment.

Dental facilities in Mauritius are very good and most practitioners speak English. Contact lens and spectacles are good value, of a high standard and prescriptions can be made up in a few days.

Private clinics

Centre Médical du Nord, Royal Road, Pointe aux Canonniers; tel: 263 1010; www.cliniquedunord.mu

Clinique de Grand Baie, Sottise Road; tel: 263 1212
Clinique du Nord, Coastal Road, Tombeau Bay; tel: 247 2532; www.cliniquedunord.mu
Fortis Clinique Darné, G. Guibert Street, Floreal 9, and a branch at La Croisette shopping complex, Grand Baie; tel: 601 2300; www.fortiscliniquedarne.com

I

Internet cafés

Cyber Angel
Shrimati Indira Gandhi Street, Triolet (near police station)
Tel: 261 8579
Cyber Café
Super U Commercial Centre, La Salette Street, Grand Baie
Tel: 263 0820
Cybercafé
Impasse Pot de Terre, Curepipe
Tel: 676 1863
Cyberyder
Ground Floor, Telecom Tower, Edith Cavell Street, Port Louis
Tel: 203 7277
Hard Drive Café
Pereybère
Tel: 263 1076
Rotourco Internet Café
François Leguat Place, Port Mathurin
Tel: 831 0747

L

Lost property

There is no central lost property facility but if you have lost something report the matter to the police and obtain a copy of the report form for insurance purposes. Loss of passport or other travel documents should be reported to your consulate or embassy. For enquiries regarding lost property in the terminal building of the airport, check with the Information Desk at the Arrivals exit.

M

Maps

You can pick up pocket-size maps from most bookshops in Port Louis and most good hotels should have a stock of tourist maps produced by the MTPA (Mauritius Tourism Promotion Authority) at reception. These will only highlight tourist spots, however. French IGN produces a more detailed and accurate map (1:100,000) which is available from Stanfords in the UK, 12–14 Long Acre, Covent Garden, London WC2E 9LP; tel: 020 7836 1321; www.stanfords.co.uk.

Media

TV and radio

The Mauritius Broadcasting Corporation (MBC) transmits television news in English at 7am, 5.40pm and 9pm and radio news at 8am, 3pm and 9pm daily. French TV comes from Réunion. BBC World Service can be received on various frequencies mainly in the morning and late evening. BBC World, CNN and Sky are now available in many hotels.

Publications

English-language newspapers and magazines are available in tourist areas. *The Independent* (www. independent.mu) is the leading local English-language daily. The *Côte Nord* magazine is distributed free in hotels and shops in the Grand Baie area, and Beachcomber's house magazine, *Evasion*, contains interesting articles in both French and English. All are ideal for news, reviews and tourist information. *Islandinfo* (www.islandinfo.mu) magazine, published monthly, is the most useful for listings. It used to be handed out at the airport, but is now only available online.

There are plenty of local French-language newspapers, including the morning *L'Express* (www.lexpress.mu) and the evening *Le Mauricien* (www. lemauricien.com). *Le Matinal* (www. lematinal.com) is excellent value and contains a daily English features and news section; *L'Express* carries a Tuesday supplement in English. *News on Sunday* (www.defimedia.info),

published on Friday, provides rather poorly written news in English but is useful for finding out what's on.

The Mauritian Wildlife Foundation (tel: 697 6097; www.mauritian-wildlife. org) issues an annual newsletter downloadable from its website. Set up in 1984, the foundation aims to protect and manage the rare flora and fauna of Mauritius and to inform, educate and involve locals in all aspects of its work.

Money

The Mauritius rupee (R or MUR) is divided into 100 cents (c). There are 1, 5, 10 and 20 rupee coins and 20 and 50 cent coins. Notes come in the following values: R25, 50, 100, 200, 500, 1,000 and 2,000.

Major currencies, major credit cards and traveller's cheques are accepted in banks, bureaux de change, most hotels and some shops. There is no restriction on the amount of foreign currency you can bring into the country. Banks offer a better rate of exchange than hotels. If you have a surplus of rupees on departure you can change them back into your own currency but keep any bank receipts as you can only export a maximum of R350.

Banks

Banks are open 9.15am–3.15pm Monday to Thursday and 9.15am–5pm on Friday. In tourist areas and Port Louis they are also open on Saturday 9.15–11.15am. **Bank of Mauritius** has small branches everywhere and branches of **Barclays** and HSBC can be found in Grand Baie and other tourist areas. The only bank in Le Morne is a branch of MCB (Mauritius Commercial Bank). Banks at the airport open to coincide with arrivals and departures of international flights.

Change facilities are widely available at bureau de change offices in tourist areas such as Flic en Flac and Grand Baie and opening times are 3.15–5pm Monday to Friday, 9am–5pm on Saturday, 9am–noon on Sunday and public holidays.

You can use your credit card to withdraw cash from ATMS (automatic teller machines) in large towns and shopping centres.

Tax

Value Added Tax (TVA) of 15 percent is added to goods and services, including hotel and restaurant bills, but there is no VAT on foodstuffs and books. Duty-free goods are available everywhere but you can't take them with you at the time of purchase; they are sent to the airport for you to collect on departure.

O

Opening hours

Non-government offices: Mon–Fri 8am–4.30pm, Sat 9am–noon. **Government offices:** Mon–Fri 9am–4pm, Sat 9am–noon. **Shops in Port Louis:** Mon–Fri 9.30am–5pm, Sat 9am–noon. **Shops in plateau towns:** Mon–Wed 10am–6pm, Thu–Sun 10am–noon. **Municipal markets:** Mon–Sat 6am–6pm.

P

Photography

White sand, turquoise seas and blue skies contrasting with the colourful dress of the islanders provide stunning pictures but these are the very ingredients which may play havoc with auto-exposure programmes on single lens reflex and compact cameras. The dense dark green foliage against sunlit sky can induce similar problems resulting in over- or under-exposure and care in metering is required to provide the perfect shots one expects from such a photogenic location.

What to take: With high temperatures and humidity, all equipment should be adequately protected with silicon crystals and kept in an insulated bag. Great effects can be produced by shooting straight into the sun, so consider purchasing a graduated grey filter which allows this without over exposure.

Capture the brilliant colours of the Indian Ocean in your photography.

Some accessories are available in the main towns but be prepared for high prices.

Keen photographers may want to consider a half- to full-day tour with Mauritian Photographic Safari (tel: 250 6990; www.cliquemauritius.com) in select island locations or tailor-made.

Postal services

Post offices open Mon–Fri 8.15am–4pm, Sat 8.15–11.45am. After 3pm they are open only for the sale of postage stamps. **Post Office Headquarters:** 3 Dumas Street, Port Louis; tel: 208 2851; www. mauritiuspost.mu.

R

Religious services

Mosques, temples and churches, often within close proximity to each other, reflect the religious tolerance of the Mascarenes' multicultural society and respect should be shown by removing your shoes before entering a mosque or temple. English services are held as follows: **Church of England:** St Paul's Church, La Caverne, Vacoas; tel: 686 4819. 9.30am every Sunday (except the second Sunday of each month).
Presbyterian: St Columba's Church, Phoenix; tel: 696 4404.
Roman Catholic Mass: St Joseph's Chapel, Celicourt Antelme Street, Rose Hill, every Saturday (tel: 464 2944 for times).

In Rodrigues, there is one Hindu temple and one mosque. Most of the churches are in Port Mathurin. St Barnabas Church in Rue de la Solidarité holds an English service once a month on Sunday at 8.30am.

S

Student travellers

There are no concessions for visiting student travellers. There are no youth hostels and while budget accommodation is available don't expect any great deals. The University of Mauritius at Le Réduit (tel: 454 1041; www.uom.ac.mu) has quite a large student population and dozens of clubs affiliated to the Students' Union. Perhaps the move to set up UK University campuses in Mauritius will also benefit visiting students.

T

Telecommunications

Information technology has taken off in leaps and bounds in recent years and internet access is available from just about anywhere on the island. All hotels have **email** and **internet** access and most have Wi-fi. Making overseas calls from public telephone boxes in tourist areas, using a prepaid phone card, rather than from the hotels, will avoid hefty surcharges.

Phonecards can be bought in shops and supermarkets in various denominations.

Alternatively you can make calls at **Mauritius Telecom Tower** at Edith Cavell Street, Port Louis (tel: 203 7000; www.mauritiustelecom. com; Mon–Fri 8.30am–5pm) or **Mauritius Telecom**, Mont Venus, Rodrigues (tel: 831 1532).

Time zone

GMT+4, with no daylight saving.

In Mauritius mobile numbers begin with the prefix 5. Mauritius has two mobile phone networks, Emtel (Air Mauritius Building, President John Kennedy Street, Port Louis; tel: 572 95400; www.emtel. com) and Orange (9th floor, Telecom Tower, Edith Cavell Street, Port Louis; Orange customers can call free, tel: 8900; email: contact@orange.mu). If you intend to make a lot of local calls it may be cheaper to buy a SIM card in Mauritius, although you will be asked to show your original passport and provide a photocopy.

If your own mobile/cell phone does not function, you can rent a phone through either provider.

International dialling codes: 230 for both Mauritius and Rodrigues. To make international calls from Mauritius and Rodrigues dial 020.

Tipping

The Islands are not tip-conscious societies, although any tip for good service is always appreciated. In Mauritius tipping is not necessary if the 15 percent TVA tax has already been added to bills, but ask if unsure. Airport porters do not expect a tip but it's not a bad idea to give them around R20 to steer you through the airport and into a taxi; hotel porters are happy with R20; taxi drivers do not expect tips.

Toilets

Toilets are free and are generally clean and well maintained. Those in supermarkets and shopping malls are normally attended and you are not expected to tip. Most public beaches have a toilet and/or shower facility but avoid those in markets, which should be reserved for dire emergencies.

Tourist information offices

Mauritius Tourism Promotion Authority offices (MTPA):
Australia: AVIAREPS Oceania, Level 5, 68 Alfred Street, Milsons Point, Sydney NSW 2061; tel: (02) 9959 4277; email: ppower@ aviareps.com
UK: Hills Balfour, 58 Southwalk Bridge Road, London SE1 0AS; tel: 020 7593 1700; email: info@ hillsbalfour.com

Public holidays and festivals

All public services are closed on public holidays. Many of these are religious festivals celebrated by various ethnic groups in Mauritius and some, but not all, shops and businesses are closed. In Rodrigues, Chinese-run shops (which are most shops) shut for a week during the Chinese Spring Festival. (See page 74 for more about Hindu festivals.)
1–2 January New Year's Day
Mid-January/February Cavadee (varies)
1 February Abolition of Slavery
February/March Chinese Spring Festival (varies)
February/March Maha Shivaratree (varies)
12 March Republic Day
March/April Ougadi (varies)
1 May Labour Day
15 August Assumption Day
September Ganesh Chaturthi (varies)
September/October Id El Fitr (varies)
October/November Divali (varies)
1 November All Saints' Day
2 November Arrival of Indentured Labourers
25 December Christmas Day

South Africa: Edelman South Africa, 11 Ralda Road, Blairgowrie, Randburg; tel: (27) 11 504 4000; www.edelman.com
Information can also be obtained from high commissions and embassies and www.tourism-mauritius.mu.

Local tourist offices

Mauritius Tourism Promotion Authority (MTPA) Head Office: 5th floor, Victoria House, St Louis Street, Port Louis; tel: 210 1545; www.tourism-mauritius.mu
Trou d'Eau Douce Waterfront; tel: 480 0925
Sir Seewoosagur Ramgoolam Airport; tel: 637 3635
Rodrigues Tourist Office – Port Mathurin; tel: 832 0866; www.tourism-rodrigues.mu

U

Useful addresses

Corona, part of Corona Worldwide (tel: 0207 793 4020; www.corona worldwide.org), based in the UK, is an invaluable organisation for anyone planning to live or work overseas. There are three branches in Mauritius and meetings are held monthly. Membership includes a monthly newsletter, talks by guest speakers and a round-up of social and sporting activities aimed mainly, but not exclusively, at women. In Mauritius contact Heather Chettiar; tel: 5252 6062; email: dod.chettiar@intnet.mu.
Board of Investment: Level 10, 1 Cathedral Square Building, 16 Jules Koenig Street, Port Louis; tel: 203 3800; www.boimauritius.com. Useful resource for people thinking of living, working or investing in Mauritius.
Mauritius Chamber of Commerce and Industry: 3 Royal Street, Port Louis; tel: 208 3301; www.mcci.org. Represents the interests of the Mauritian business community and produces economic indicators for investors and members.

W

Websites

http://metservice.intnet.mu – official meteorological site for Mauritius.
www.gov.mu – official government website.

www.islandinfo.mu – useful online guide for tourism services.
www.mscl.mu – MS *Mauritius Trochetia* sailing schedule from Mauritius to Rodrigues and Réunion.
www.pawsmauritius.org – animal welfare charity set up to reduce stray dog population.

Weddings

Planning your wedding: There are a number of specialised tour operators (see page 348) who can arrange everything for you, but they should be approached at least six months before your wedding date. Places get booked up well in advance and there's a certain amount of paperwork to deal with. UK residents can find ideas and offers through the wedding specialist Marry Abroad (tel: 0116 236 3062; www.marryabroad.co.uk).
When shopping around for a tour operator, ask if there are any special deals. Discounts or extras range from complimentary champagne, dinners and spa treatments to a room upgrade or even the wedding package thrown in for free.
Things you will need: Photocopies of the following documents must be sent to your destination around 10 weeks before the big day (and remember to take the originals with you): birth certificates; passports; if divorced, the relevant divorce papers; in the case of a widow/widower, a death certificate and any previous marriage certificates; proof of any change of name by deed poll, if relevant (this must be stamped and signed by a solicitor or relevant official, according to your country); if either the bride or groom is adopted, an adoption certificate. Always check the latest requirements before booking your wedding.
For a religious wedding, christening certificates and a certificate of 'good morality' from respective parish priests may be required. Church weddings may have to be backed up by a civil ceremony to be recognised by the law of the country in which you reside.
When to travel: In Mauritius, couples must be on the island three days before a civil wedding and 15 days before a religious wedding. (Always check the latest requirements well in advance of your wedding.)
On arrival: Once at your hotel, you will meet with the wedding co-ordinator to decide on final details such as flowers and any extras. Then

Weights and measures

The metric system is used in the Mascarenes, though in Mauritius and Rodrigues you may come across road signs in miles and the occasional shop still weighing in pounds.

you will visit the local Civil Status Office to check you have the correct documents, and the Supreme Court where certificates are issued. In Mauritius you must visit the Civil Office that oversees the district your hotel is in. Reputable hotels will arrange taxis for these trips.

Going it alone

If you want to arrange your wedding abroad independently, contact:
Mauritius: Registrar of Civil Status, 7th Level, Emmanuel Anquetil Building, Sir S. Ramgoolam Street, Port Louis, Mauritius; tel: 00 230 201 1727; email: civstat@gov.mu.org

What to Bring

To protect yourself from the sun and rain, bring a hat, sunglasses, suncream and a light mac. Bring insect repellent if you have a preferred brand. Sturdy shoes are needed if you plan to do any walking in the countryside, and a multipurpose sarong is useful for when you need to cover up in temples or in town.

Women travellers

To find a woman travelling alone in these islands is unusual since most visitors are couples or families. At most you'll be regarded as strange when you explain why you're not with a friend, relation or husband but you're unlikely to be harassed, except perhaps by youths in questionable nightspots in Mauritius' Grand Baie area; elsewhere, opportunistic groping, unwanted attention or blatant propositioning is rare.
If you find yourself in an awkward situation, deal with it immediately in a positive way. Don't get involved in inane chatter, avoid eye contact – being polite but firm usually works. It's not a good idea to fend off advances with a few choice Kreol expletives as this tends to encourage more attention.
In Mauritius and Rodrigues it's not the done thing to sunbathe topless on any beach.

MAURITIUS

RÉUNION

SEYCHELLES

LANGUAGE

UNDERSTANDING THE LANGUAGE

Over a dozen languages are spoken by the various ethnic groups living in Mauritius, Réunion and Seychelles but Kreol is spoken by most of the islanders (see feature Lingua Franca on page 23). This colourful language, which has evolved from French to have its own grammar and a vocabulary enriched by several languages, is so popular that it is threatening to render obsolete other widely spoken tongues such as Bhojpuri and Hakka, the ancestral languages of north Indians, and most of the Chinese.

Other minority languages you may hear on the streets of Mauritius include Marathi, Tamil (Madras), Telegu and Hindi. A small number of Muslims speak Gujerati.

In Mauritius, which was a British colony until 1968, French dominates at the expense of English. Newspapers, shop signs and street names are mostly in French. English-speaking films are also dubbed in French. Government forms and road signs, however, are in English. People in tourism and commerce speak English out of necessity but the standard is variable.

Unlike Seychelles, which has elevated Kreol to the status of an official language used in schools and the media, in Mauritius it has been merely a means of verbal communication and until recently has been undervalued. But times are changing, with the first Kreol–French dictionary published in 2009, and Kreol introduced as an optional language in schools in 2012. However, it will take time to shake off the perception of Kreol being inferior to French. The grammar of Mauritian Kreol was traditionally never taught in schools and until recently there

has been no universally accepted way of writing it, so many Mauritians assumed that Kreol had no rules. In fact, it is a sophisticated language, with its own tenses and grammatical forms and a simplified pronunciation of French terms that gives Kreol a unique means of making double-entendres. This is exploited to the full in sega lyrics and in island humour.

In Seychelles, English is widely spoken, especially in hotels, shops and offices. Many Seychellois speaking to each other drift effortlessly between English and Kreol, often within the same sentence. A few words of Kreol are useful away from tourist sites and Victoria, particularly when talking to older Seychellois.

PRONUNCIATION TIPS

Do not try to imitate a French accent. Indeed, the best approach is not to try speaking with an accent. Do not worry too much about the frills of the French language, such as tenses, declining verbs and the gender of objects, as they have no place in Kreol. If you run into difficulty do not worry about using English for most nouns, as these are likely to be well understood.

Common features of Indian Ocean Kreol include the use of the word *ban* as a marker of plurality: thus *ban zenfants* means children and *ban zil* is islands. The word *zot* means you in the plural form.

COMMON WORDS AND PHRASES

Airport *Erport*
Bank *Labank*
Bed *Lili*

Kreol Institute

The Seychellois take their Kreol seriously and have set up an institute devoted to the preservation of the language and the promotion of Creole culture. The Kreol Institute (Lenstiti Kreol), near the Craft Village at Anse aux Pins on Mahé, has just over 20 staff members who run several departments, namely literature, research, promotion, graphics, documentation, and education and training.

The premises are used for Creole functions throughout the year, from plays and poetry workshops to masked balls and karaoke nights. The institute is also the central venue for the Creole Festival, held every year in October (see page 398).

Breakfast *Ti dezennen*
Bus stop *Bestop*
Excuse me *Eskiz*
Good morning *Bonzour*
Good afternoon/evening *Bonswar*
Goodbye *Orevwar*
Key *Lakle*
Later *Plitar*
Meal *Manze*
No *Non*
Now *Konmela*
Please *Silvouple*
Room *Lasanm*
Swimming pool *Pisin*
Thank you *Mersi*
Today *Ozordi*
Tomorrow *Demen*
Towel *Servyet*
Yes *Wi*
Yesterday *Yer*
Do you speak English? *Ou kapab koz angle?*
How are you? *Konman sava?*

I'm fine, thank you *Mon byen mersi*
I'm staying at a hotel *Mon reste lotel.*
I don't know *Mon pa konnen.*
I don't understand *Mon pa konpran.*
Please speak more slowly *Koze pli lantman silvouple.*
Where can I get a taxi? *Kote mon kapab ganny en taksi?*

EMERGENCIES

Call an ambulance *Apel lanbilans*
Call the police *Apel lapolis!*
Fire! *Dife!*
Help! *Sekour!*
I am not well *Mon pa byen*
They've had an accident *Zot in ganny en aksidan*
We need a doctor *Nou bezwen en dokter*
Where can I find a telephone? *Kote mon pou ganny en telefonn?*
Where is the nearest clinic? *Kote klinik pli pre silvouple?*

SHOPPING

chemist *farmasi*
Do you accept credit cards? *Eski ou pran kart kredi?*

Numbers

0 *zero*
1 *enn*
2 *de*
3 *trwa*
4 *kat*
5 *senk*
6 *sis*
7 *set*
8 *wit*
9 *nef*
10 *dis*
11 *onz*
12 *douz*
13 *trez*
14 *katorz*
15 *kenz*
16 *sez*
17 *diset*
18 *diswit*
19 *disnef*
20 *ven*
30 *trant*
35 *transenk*
40 *karant*
50 *senkant*
60 *swasant*
70 *swasandis*
80 *katreven*
90 *katrevendis*
100 *san*
1,000 *mil*

Have you got...? *Eski ou annan...?*
How much is it? *Konbyen sa?*
I'm just looking *Mon pe rode selman.*
I'll take this one *Mon pran sa enn.*
It is too expensive *I tro ser.*
market *bazar*
money *larzan*
newspaper *gazet*
post office *lapos*
shop *laboutik*
Where can I find a bank? *Kote labank?*

SIGHTSEEING

church *legliz*
closed *fermen*
garden *zarden*
open *ouver*
river *larivyer*
town *lavil*
village *vilaz*
waterfall *kaskad*

AT THE RESTAURANT

bill *kont*
dinner *dinen*
fork *forset*
glass *ver*
knife *kouto*
lunch *dezenen*
menu *meni*
plate *lasyet*
spoon *kwiyer*

What to order

bef **beef**
labyer **beer**
dipen **bread**
diber **butter**
gato **cake**
fromaz **cheese**
poul **chicken**
lasos piman **chilli sauce**
kafe **coffee**
kari/cari/carri **curry**
deser **dessert**
kannar **duck**
dizef **eggs**
pwason **fish**
zifri **fruit juice**
ayskrim **ice cream**
dile **milk**
palmis **millionaire's salad**
delo mineral **mineral water**
fri delapasyon **passion fruit juice**
dipwav **pepper**
lavyann koson **pork**
diri **rice**
disel **salt**
delo gaze **sparkling water**
stek **steak**
disik **sugar**
dite **tea**
diven **wine**

Fruit and vegetables

brenzel **aubergine/eggplant**
zavoka **avocado**
bannann **banana**
friyapen **breadfruit**
kokonm **cucumber**
fri **fruit**
lay **garlic**
mang **mango**
zanannan **pineapple**
ponmdeter **potatoes**
tomat **tomatoes**
legim **vegetables**

Fish and seafood

palourd **clams**
oumar **lobster**
zourit **octopus**
cateaux **parrot fish**
kanmaron **prawn/shrimp**
bourgeois/bourzwa **red snapper**
ton **tuna**
karang/carangue **trevally**

Local specialities

Mauritius

bol renversée **spicy meat and rice**
bouyon bred **clear soup made of edible leaves**
brèdes **spinach-like vegetable**
carri de poulet aux grains **chicken curry with red beans and wheat**
cochon marron **wild boar**
dite lavani **vanilla tea**
espadron fime **smoked sailfish**
fooyang **Chinese omelette**
gateaux piments **fried lentil and chilli balls**
gros pois **fat butter beans**
kari koko **curry with coconut milk**
meefoon **fine noodles**
mine frit **fried noodles**
pain frit **fried bread with sugar**
rougaille **Mediterranean-style meat or fish stew**

Réunion

achards **vegetable pickles**
bonbon piment **chilli cake**
cari de bichiques **young alevin fish curry**
cabri au massalé **kid goat masala**
gratin chouchou **christophene bake**
manioc frit **fried manioc**
tarte bredes chouchou **vegetable pie**
rougailles **spicy chutney**

Seychelles

kari koko zourit **mild octopus curry**
ladob **creamy banana and sweet potato dessert**
palourd **small clam-like shellfish in garlic butter**
tectec **tiny white shellfish**

MAURITIUS

RÉUNION

SEYCHELLES

FURTHER READING

MASCARENE ISLANDS

The Age of Kali: Indian Travels and Encounters by William Dalrymple. Contains an interesting chapter on Réunion and Creole beliefs in black magic.

Bourbon Journal by Walter Besant. Short and amusing diary of a British schoolteacher who holidayed in Réunion and climbed Piton de Neiges.

Culture Shock! Mauritius: A survival Guide to Customs and Etiquette by Roseline NgCheong-Lum. Cultural insights into Mauritius – good reading for anyone intending to work or stay long term.

The Dive Sites of Mauritius by Alan Mountain. A well-illustrated comprehensive guide to diving and snorkelling in Mauritius.

Dodo – the Bird behind the Legend by Alan Grihault. The most comprehensive and up-to-date examination of Mauritius' fated bird. Grihault is also the author of *Solitaire: the Dodo of Rodrigues Island*, the only book on the subject.

Golden Bats & Pink Pigeons by Gerald Durrell. A hilarious account of Durrell's travels to Mauritius and Rodrigues in search of specimens for his Jersey Zoo.

History of the Indian Ocean by August Toussaint. A general background history of countries in and around the Indian Ocean, with a good reference to pirates, the Anglo–French conflict and British supremacy of the Mascarenes and Seychelles.

The Island of Rodrigues by Alfred North-Coombes. A most readable history and background to Rodrigues by the Mauritian-born author whose interest goes back to 1937, when he was posted there as a civil servant.

Islands in a Forgotten Sea by T.V. Bulpin. One of the finest books you'll come across for an overview of pirates and corsairs in the western Indian Ocean, including the history and development of the Mascarenes and Seychelles to the 1960s.

The Mauritian Shekel by Genevieve Pitot. The full story of Jewish detainees in Mauritius, 1940–45.

Six months in Réunion by P. Beaton. Life in Réunion as seen by a British clergyman.

Studies of Mascarene Island Birds edited by A.W. Diamond. Academic study of the dodo, solitaire and other extinct birds of Mauritius and Rodrigues.

Sub Tropical Rambles in the Land of the Aphanapteryx by Nicholas Pike. Highly readable and often amusing account of experiences in Mauritius by the US Consul to Mauritius.

Underwater Mauritius by Al. J. Venter. The author describes some amazing dive sites in Mauritius, Rodrigues and the Seychelles.

Voyages and Adventures by François Leguat. Written by Rodrigues' first settler and acknowledged as Rodrigues' first guidebook, this book is a must for anyone going there. Ask your public library to order it for you.

FICTION

The Book of Colour: A Family Memoir by Julia Blackburn. Set largely in Mauritius, this is the story of the author's meditation on the lives of her father and grandfather, which unfolds with surreal precision.

Bourbon Island 1730 by Lewis Trondheim and Olivier Appollodorus. A unique historical drama about Réunion in the form of a graphic novel.

The Mauritius Command by Patrick O'Brian. Naval adventures around Mauritius during the Napoleonic Wars.

Journey to Mauritius by Jacques-Henri Bernardin de Saint Pierre (translated by Jason Wilson). This romantic novel tells the story of the ill-fated St Géran which sank off the coast of Mauritius in August 1744.

The Prospector by J.M.G. Le Clézio (translated by Carol Marks). The Mauritian narrator, Alexis, of Nobel laureate J.M.G. Le Clézio's tale, embarks on a search for pirate gold in order to restore his family's fortunes. His quest is interrupted by World War I and service in the trenches of Ypres and the Somme.

Sens-Plastique is a surrealist collection of aphorisms and *pensées* by Malcolm de Chazal, the 20th-century Franco-Mauritian writer who extolled the natural beauty of Mauritius through poetry as well as paintings.

TRANSPORT

GETTING THERE AND GETTING AROUND

GETTING THERE

By air

There are two airports in Réunion: **Roland Garros Airport** (tel: 0262 48 81 81; www.reunion.aeroport. fr), 10km (6 miles) from St-Denis; and **Pierrefonds** (tel: 0262 96 80 00; www.pierrefonds.aeroport.fr) on the south coast, 5km (3 miles) from St-Pierre. The national carrier is Air France (AF).

Regular daily flights operate between Mauritius and Réunion with Air Mauritius (MK) and Air Austral (UU). Based in Réunion, the latter operates flights from Réunion to Paris, South Africa and elsewhere (Johannesburg, Moroni, Mayotte, Seychelles, Chennai, Bangkok, Rodrigues (seasonal) and several destinations in Madagascar).
Air Austral: 2 rue de l'Eglise, 92200 Neuilly-sur-Seine; tel: 08 25 01 30 12; www.air-austral.com

Airline charter companies
Corsairfly: 2 Avenue Charles Lindbergh, 94636 Rungis; tel: 01 49 79 49 79; www.corsair.fr

Airline offices in Réunion
Air Austral: 4 rue de Nice, St-Denis; 6 Boulevard Hubert Delisle, St-Pierre; and at Roland Garros and Pierrefonds airports; tel: 0825 01 30 12; www.air-austral.com
Air France: 7 Avenue de la Victoire, St-Denis; 73 rue Luc Loion, St Pierre; tel: 0820 82 08 20; Roland Garros Airport, tel: 0262 40 38 38; www.airfrance.re
Air Madagascar: 31 rue Jules Auber, St-Denis; tel: 08 92 68 00 14;

www.airmadagascar.com
Air Mauritius: 13 rue Charles Gounod, St-Denis; tel: 0262 94 83 83; 7 rue François de Mahy, St-Pierre; tel: 0262 94 83 83; Roland Garros Airport; tel: 0262 48 80 18; Pierrefonds Airport; tel: 0262 96 06 00; www.airmauritius. com
Corsairfly (Nouvelles Frontières): 2 rue Maréchal Leclerc, St-Denis; 1 rue Désiré Barquisseau, St-Pierre; Roland Garros Airport; tel: 3917; www.corsair.fr

From the airport

You can hire a car or take a taxi from the airport; expect to pay at least €25 plus €4.20 or more if travelling after 8pm or on public holidays. Cheaper at €5 is the *car jaune* (yellow bus) to St-Denis, with regular departures 6am–8.30pm.

Driving times

Depending on the time at which you are travelling and the weather conditions, here is an estimate of how long it will take you to drive between different parts of the island:
St-Denis–west coast: 40–80km/ 25–50 miles: 40–65 mins
St-Denis–Hell-Bourg: 55km/34 miles: 1 hour 10 mins
St-Denis–volcano: 150km/93 miles: 2 hours 15 mins
St-Denis–Cilaos (centre): 113km/70 miles: 2 hours
St-Gilles–Hell-Bourg: 100km/62 miles: 1.5–2 hours
St-Gilles–volcano: 100km/62 miles: 2 hours
St-Gilles–Cilaos (centre): 75km/47 miles: 1.5 hours

By sea

The Mauritius Shipping Corporation (MSCL; www.mauritiusshipping.net) has operated passenger sailings between Mauritius and Réunion, although at the time of writing these had temporarily stopped. If services resume, ships normally depart one island late afternoon and arrive at the other the next morning. See the website for more details, but unless you have a particular aversion to flying you're probably better off taking the plane.

GETTING AROUND

By car

Whether travelling by hire car or public bus, getting around Réunion is easy thanks to an excellent, well-signposted

Hell-Bourg–west coast: 90–107km/58–68 miles: 1.5 hours
Hell-Bourg–volcano: 135km/84 miles: 2–2.5 hours
St-Pierre–Hell-Bourg: 96km/62 miles: 2 hours
St-Pierre–west coast: 40–54km/25–34 miles: 30–45 mins
To Roland Garros Airport from:
St-Denis: 14km/9 miles: 20 minutes
St-Gilles: 51km/32 miles: 45 minutes
Hell-Bourg: 41km/26 miles: 1 hour
St-Pierre: 91km/57 miles: 1.5 hours

road system. Driving is on the right, as in France. The speed limit on dual carriageways is 110kmh (68mph), dropping to 50kmh (30mph) in towns and built-up areas. Avoid driving during the rush hours, particularly on the main roads, which can become a four-lane traffic jam; the winding roads in the Cirques can be quite busy during the peak holiday season.

Hazards: Pedestrians also use the roads, even the four-lane *route nationales*, and it is not practical to drive fast on the winding mountain roads, so it is always advisable to respect speed limits. However, some locals tend to treat all roads as racetracks and also jump the traffic lights, so do beware! Look out for scooterists and cyclists at night riding without lights or helmet.

Road conditions: The main coastal route is well-maintained, but the surfaces of the high roads are not so good and they are often narrow and winding – the road to Cilaos has 450 bends in it.

After heavy rain the four lanes of the coast road between St-Denis and La Possession are reduced to two to avoid the risk of rock falls.

Car hire

Most companies ask that you come equipped with a full driving licence from your home country as well as a credit card or cash deposit, and in some cases they will insist on full payment in advance. If your driving licence is not in French some companies may request it be accompanied by a certified translation. Hirers should be at least 21 years old. For reliability, it's best to choose a company belonging to the French National Car Syndicate (CNPA). The companies below all have desks at the airport, but there are others that offer seasonal special deals.

Car hire companies

Ada: tel: 0262 21 59 01; email: info@ada-reunion.com; www.ada-reunion.com

Au Bas Prix: tel: 0262 48 81 89; email: aubasprix@wanadoo.fr; www.aubasprix.fr
Avis: tel: 0262 48 81 85; email: contact@avisreunion.com; www.avisreunion.com
Budget: tel: 0262 28 01 95; www.budget-reunion.com
Entreprise-Citer: tel: 0262 48 83 77; email: contact@citer.re; www.citer.re
Europcar: tel: 0262 28 27 58; email: europcar-reunion@wanadoo.fr; www.europcar-reunion.com
Hertz: tel: 0262 28 05 93; www.hertzreunion.com
ITC Tropicar: tel: 0262 31 07 07; email: contact@itctropicar.re; www.itctropicar.re
Jumbo Car: tel: 0262 53 53 72; www.jumbocar-reunion.com
RentACar: tel: 0262 48 81 88; www.rentacar-reunion.fr
Sixt: tel: 0262 47 44 74; www.sixt.re

By bus

Réunion's buses are a comfortable and cost effective means of travel. As there are no stop bells, be prepared to clap your hands to alert the driver when you want to get off or just shout *devant* (ahead). There are 16 lines or routes which interconnect with towns. Buses start running at around 5am with last departures being between 7pm and 8pm. For schedules and information visit www.cg974.fr/index. php/Horaires-des-Cars-jaunes.html; for bus timetables call 0810 123 974 or the following bus stations:
St-Denis: tel: 0262 41 09 59
St-Benoît: tel: 0262 50 10 69
St-Paul: tel: 0262 22 54 38
St-Pierre: tel: 0262 35 67 28
St-Joseph: tel: 0262 56 03 90

By taxi

Taxis in Réunion are an expensive alternative to buses and cars. The fare between St-Denis and Boucan-Canot (40km/25 miles), for example, can cost around €70. However, if

you're a woman travelling alone after dark they are probably the safest way of getting around. Cheaper deals can be had if you negotiate a fare for a whole day's hire and split the cost between several passengers. Tipping is not compulsory. Taxis can be hired either at taxi ranks in main towns, by telephone or through your hotel.

Sightseeing tours

A range of sightseeing tours is available through the following travel agents based on the island:
21eme Parallèle: 1 avenue de la Grande Ourse, St-Gilles-Les-Bains, tel: 0262 22 72 27; email: receptif@21parallele.fr; www.21parallele.fr
Bourbon Tourisme: 14 rue Rontaunay, St-Denis; tel: 0262 33 08 70; email: contact@bourbontourisme.com; www.bourbonvoyages.fr
Connections: 53 Route de Domenjod, Ste Clotilde; tel: 0262 93 13 98; email: resa@connections-reunion.com; www.connections-reunion.com
Horizon Réunion: 6 ligne d'Equerre, St-Pierre; tel: 0262 02 40 00; email: contact@horizon-reunion.com; www.horizon-reunion.com
Mille Tours: 9 rue Sarda Garriga, St-Paul; tel: 0262 22 55 00; www.milletours.com
Nouvelles Frontieres: Residence Claire 1, 31 Place Paul Julius Benard, St-Gilles-les-Bains; tel: 0262 33 11 99; email: receptive.run@nouvelles-frontieres.fr
Papangue Tours: Résidence La Tonnelle, 17 route de la Rivière des Pluies, Ste-Clotilde; tel: 0262 41 61 92; email: contact@papanguetours.com; www.papanguetours.com
Sentiers et Découvertes: 20 Rue François Isautier, St-Pierre; tel: 0692 63 60 80; email: contact@sentiersetdecouvertes.com; www.sentiersetdecouvertes.com
Wel'come vacances: 2 boulevard Bonnier, St-Leu; tel: 02 62 34 74 85; www.welcome-vacances.com

Helicopter tours

A wonderful way to see the grandeur of the island's volcanic landscape is to go on a helicopter trip (see page 216).
Helilagon: Gillot Airport or Eperon, St-Paul Base; tel: 0262 55 55 55; www.helilagon.com
Corail Helicopters: St-Gilles Base or Pierrefonds Airport; tel: 0262 22 22 66; www.corail-helicopteres.com

Road over volcanic lava in Sainte-Rose De La Réunion.

EATING OUT

RECOMMENDED RESTAURANTS, CAFES AND BARS

WHERE TO EAT

Réunion boasts a rich culinary tradition inspired by the various ethnic groups that make up its population, and the range of eating places is just as varied. Some of the island's best restaurants form part of the *Saveurs et Senteurs de la Réunion* (Flavours and Fragrances) group, which is affiliated to the Guild of French Provinces Restaurateurs. Some bear the label(s) *Restaurateur de France*, *Restaurant de Tourisme* or *Qualité Tourisme Île de La Réunion*. Such restaurants may be attached to hotels and mainly feature French cuisine and local Creole specialities, such as *carri* (curry), *chou chou* (christophene), *brèdes* (a spinach-like vegetable), and pork, chicken and seafood dishes. If locals eat out at a restaurant it tends to be Creole, Chinese or Italian cuisine. There are some 'exotic' places to eat (Thai, Greek, Japanese), but they are generally concentrated in the larger towns.

Most restaurants keep to standard lunch times from noon to 2.30pm and offer a fixed-price *menu du jour* as well as à la carte options. Buying a meal in restaurants outside these times is virtually impossible and you will have to wait till the evening. Réunionnais tend to eat out from about 7.30pm onwards, and most restaurants will not accept orders after 10pm. Bear in mind that many restaurants are closed on Sundays and/or Mondays (see page 172 for more about Réunion's cuisine). For cheaper fare don't overlook the many brasseries, bistros, crêperies, bars,

cafés, food stalls and markets for mouth-watering morsels of freshly cooked snacks such as *samoussas* and *bouchons* (Chinese-style pork meatballs served with soy sauce). An inexpensive option, found all over the island, is a *camion bar* (mobile snack bar) serving a variety of pre- or freshly made baguette sandwiches or *carris*. Hygiene standards for street food are normally reliable.

COUNTRY COOKING

Many of the island's farmers and country dwellers offer lunches at good value for hungry visitors to their homes. Typically the food is traditional Creole (so if you're vegetarian or looking for something daring head elsewhere) and in some establishments it is eaten with the hosts. Main courses, rather than being served individually on a plate, will be dished up on a single platter, making it a very convivial affair. Contact the local tourist office or visit www.reunion.fr for more details. It's advisable to book in advance, especially for Sunday lunch.

Table d'hôte: traditional Creole meals are served at the large family table of the host, seating up to 20 people. Popular with locals on Sundays. Many are also *chambre d'hotes*.

Fermes auberges: farmhouse-inns where a traditional Creole meal is cooked with local produce. See www.bienvenue-a-la-ferme.com for a list of the island's *fermes auberges*.

Auberge de campagne: a country inn at which the farmer can cater for up to 80 people with traditionally cooked home-grown produce.

SELF-CATERING

If you're renting a bungalow or trekking from *gîte* to *gîte* you might want to try self-catering. For breakfast head to a *boulangerie* where you'll find coffee, fruit juice and pastries.

The cheapest places for groceries and drinks are supermarkets, but you will find that fruit and vegetables are generally better value at a market. Depending on the season and which part of the island you're in, you'll also see stalls by the side of the road selling mangoes and lychees (December–January), goyaviers (strawberry guavas; May–July), bananas and pineapples (all year round), which are worth sampling if you're passing by.

HOT DRINKS

Unless otherwise requested, coffee and tea will always be served black. Specify *au lait* if you would like milk.

Pint of 'dodo'

The name of the local beer is Bourbon, which has an emblem of the dodo, hence a bottle of beer is referred to as *une dodo*. For draught beer, ask for *une pression*. Wine is popular and as well as being produced in Cilaos, it is also imported from France. But rum in an assortment of concoctions is a speciality of Réunion – as *rhum arrangé*, rum flavoured with spices and fruit, or *punch creole*, rum blended with fruit, cane syrup and juice.

ST-DENIS

In addition to the restaurants listed below, do also check out Le Carré Cathédrale, a lively pedestrianised area of St-Denis just behind the Cathedral where half a dozen restaurants spill out onto the pavement every evening.

L'Atelier de Ben
12 Rue de la Compagnie
Tel: 0262 41 85 73
Small gourmet restaurant specialising in French cuisine with local ingredients, in a sophisticated atmosphere. Booking recommended. €€€

Bistrot de la Porte des Lilas
38bis Rue Labourdonnaism
Tel: 0262 41 40 69
www.bistrotdeslilas.fr
Chilean sea bass and rolled calf's head are just two of the chef's culinary creations served in this restaurant. Open for lunch and dinner; free parking. Closed Sun. €€

Le Glacier Igloo
37 Rue Jean Châtel
Tel: 0262 21 34 69
www.liglooleffetglace.re
Fancy trying *goyavier* sorbet? This ice cream parlour is a St-Denis institution, and you can now find branches all over the island. Portions are gigantic and it's great on a hot day (or evening). €

Guetali Café
Inside Jardin d'État
Tel: 0262 21 70 86
If you need a break from the hustle and bustle of St-Denis try this lunch option inside the oasis of greenery that is the Jardin d'État. Popular with locals. €

Oh! Jardin
38 Rue de Paris
Tel: 0692 16 55 71
Friendly restaurant in an old Creole house near the Jardin d'État, specialising in quiches and salads. A good lunch option if you've been visiting Rue de Paris. €

Restaurant Mahé La Bourdonnais
14 Rue Amiral Lacaze
Tel: 0262 58 35 51
Young and trendy but atmospheric restaurant and bar, in a beautifully renovated East India Company building. €€

Restaurant Sur Le Pouce
21 Rue Alexis de Villeneuve
Tel: 0262 21 42 13
Popular self-service eatery. Eat as much as you like but do try the pork in caramel or the tuna curry. Closed Mon. €

Roland Garros
2 Place du 20 Décembre, Barachois
Tel: 0262 41 44 37
For fine wining and dining in a sophisticated air-conditioned restaurant head for the Roland Garros. Try the *menu du jour* or sip drinks on the outdoor terrace. €€€

Les Olivades
153 Rue Juliette Dodu
Tel: 0262 47 11 04
Lovely French and Mediterranean food, in a quiet part of town, popular with locals. Open for lunch Mon–Fri, and dinner Fri and Sat; closed Sun. €€

P'tit Fleur Fané
42bis Rue Alexis de Villeneuve
Tel: 0262 20 44 44
This long-established Creole restaurant takes its name from the title of Réunion's unofficial national anthem. Unlike many other places, the menu has been translated into English. Open for lunch and dinner; closed Sun and Mon. €€

THE COAST

Petite-Île

Palm Hotel & Spa
Grande Anse
Tel: 0262 56 30 30
www.palm.re
If fine dining is your thing this luxurious five-star hotel has three restaurants, one of which, Le Makassar, is gourmet. €€€

Giant, succulent prawns show off the coast's bounty.

Vacoas

Beau Rivage
Grande Anse
Tel: 0262 56 95 17
Enjoy panoramic ocean views from this simple restaurant to the south of St-Pierre, run by a local chef who serves excellent octopus curry and smoked papaya *carri légumes*. Open daily for lunch and dinner; closed Mon. €

St-André

Beau Rivage
873 Chemin Champ-Borne, Champ-Borne
Tel: 0262 46 08 66
www.lebeaurivage.re
Reasonably priced restaurant next to the old church, specialising in Indian, Chinese, French and Creole cuisine. Closed Thu and Sun evenings and Mon. €€

Law Shun
866 Avenue de Bourbon
Tel: 0262 46 04 08
Located between St-André and the start of the road that leads to Salazie, this popular restaurant offers a range of Creole and Chinese food. Open for lunch Mon–Sat, and Fri and Sat evenings. €€

St-Benoît

Les Letchis
42 Chemin Îlet Danclas
Tel: 0692 39 79 39
This little jewel of a Creole restaurant is beautifully located among orchards of lychee trees, and is next to the fast-flowing Rivière des Marsouins. An idyllic experience. Lunch only. Closed Mon. €€

Créole cuisine.

St-Gilles-les-Bains

Au Kabanon
Plage de l'Hermitage
Tel: 0262 33 84 94
Beach-side restaurant noted for its inventive style. Good value for money. Open daily for lunch and dinner, except Wed, Thu and Sun evening. €€

Le Bar de la Marine
Port de Plaisance
Tel: 0262 24 03 03
Laid-back sports bar and restaurant on the marina, specialising in seafood and football. If you're not interested in what's on screen you can watch the comings and goings in the marina. €€

La Bobine
Plage de l'Hermitage
Tel: 0262 33 94 36
www.la-bobine.com
Something of an institution, this beach-side restaurant takes its name from the enormous cable reels that formed its original tables. Now much larger and more comfortable, it serves a wide selection of fish, meat, salads and Creole food. €€

Le Cap
32 Route du Boucan-Canot
www.boucancanot.com
Enjoy French and Creole cuisine and romantic lagoon views from this restaurant attached to Boucan Canot Hotel. Open daily for lunch and dinner. €€€

Chez Loulou
86 Rue Général de Gaulle
Tel: 0262 24 23 48
Typical Creole ambiance in this long-established patisserie, famous for its *macatia* (a butter-free brioche). With its bright turquoise paintwork and street corner location you can't miss it. €

DCP
2 Place Julius Bénard

Tel: 0262 33 02 96
Fish galore at this restaurant located on a plaza near St-Gilles marina. Its owner holds a women's world record for deep-sea fishing. Closed Sun. €€

Go By Cap Mechant
Plage de l'Hermitage
Tel: 0262 33 11 90
If you're looking for an all-you-can-eat Creole buffet for €25, this is the place to be. Wide choice of starters, main dishes and desserts. Can be noisy at weekends. €€

L'Horizon
15 Rue de la Plage
Roches Noires
Tel: 0262 22 83 99
Wonderful panoramic views from the terrace of this beach-side bistro. It combines traditional flavours with a modern menu. €€

Le Piccolo
99 Rue Général de Gaulle
Tel: 0262 24 51 51
www.restaurant-piccolo-st-paul.fr
Long-established Italian and Creole restaurant on the main road. Try one of the delicious oven-baked camembert cheeses. Open daily for lunch and dinner. €€

St-Leu

Chez Jean-Paul
Seafront
Tel: 0262 34 80 41
This rondavel snack bar near the port serves drinks, sandwiches and crêpes. Takeaway or sit down. Regularly holds concerts with local musicians. €

Le Lagon
2 bis Rue du Lagon
Tel: 0262 34 79 13
Right on the beach and serving a good range of local and French food. Can be windy. €€–€€€

St-Philippe

Étoile de Mer
13 Rue École
Basse Vallée
Tel: 0262 37 04 60
Typical Creole menu and seafood, including grilled lobster, against an ocean backdrop. Closed Mon. €€€

La Marmite du Pecheur
18a Route Nationale 2, Ravine Ango, near St-Philippe
Tel: 0262 37 01 01
This 'fishermen's cooking pot' is ideal for lunch – try the *civet de zourit* (octopus stew). Good service and popular with locals. Open daily for lunch. €€

St-Pierre

Le Cabanon
28 Boulevard Hubert-Delisle
Tel: 0262 25 71 46
Pleasant restaurant with a lunchtime buzz set around a tiny courtyard, serving tasty French and Creole food. *Menu du jour* for around €10. Closed Mon. €€

Le Cap Méchant d'Abord
Boulevard Hubert-Delisle
Tel: 0262 91 71 99
On the banks of the river and overlooking the port, this restaurant is popular with tourists and locals alike for the heart of palm salad and hot curries. Reservations recommended, particularly at weekends. Closed Mon. €€

Le Retro
34 Boulevard Hubert-Delisle
Tel: 0262 25 33 06

PRICE CATEGORIES

Price categories are for two without wine:
€ = less than €15
€€ = €15–30
€€€ = more than €30

www.restaurant-retro-reunion.fr
Expensive but worth trying for its first-class service and Creole and French cuisine. €€€

Ste-Rose
Anse des Cascades
Piton Ste-Rose

Tel: 0262 47 20 42
Informal, easy-going atmosphere in this restaurant specialising in French, Chinese and Creole cuisine. Closed evenings. €€
Le Joyau des Laves
474ter Route Nationale 2
Tel: 0262 47 34 00

If you're hungry before or after a visit to the Grand Brûlé, try to eat at a table on the balcony of this Creole restaurant. It has lovely *palmiste* (heart of palm) salads and dishes with *baba fig* (the flower of the banana tree). €€

VOLCANO AND HIGH PLAINS

Plaine-des-Cafres
Auberge du Volcan
27ème km, Bourg-Murat
Tel: 0262 27 50 91
Centrally located restaurant and bar at Bourg-Murat, an ideal lunch stop when returning from the volcano. Traditional cuisine, Creole specialities and French food served in a lively atmosphere. *Menu du jour* or à la carte. Open daily from 6.30am. €€
Le QG
60 Rue Alfred Picard, Bourg-Murat
Tel: 0262 38 28 55
You'll find a mix of locals and tourists in this restaurant at the

beginning of the road to the volcano. Prices are reasonable and portions are decently sized. There's a choice of Creole and French food; local dishes are cooked over an aromatic wood fire. €€
Le Vieux Bardeau
24ème km,
Bourg-Murat
Tel: 0262 59 09 44
A few miles down from Bourg-Murat, this restaurant is in a beautifully restored traditional Creole house. Specialities are Creole and French food served à la carte or from a buffet. Open daily for lunch and dinner except Sun. €€

Plaine-des-Palmistes
Les Platanes
291 Rue de la République
Tel: 0262 51 31 69
This restaurant takes its name from the plane trees that can only be found in the village. Choose from the buffet at €30 or the menu priced at €15. Open daily for lunch except Mon. €€
Le Relais des Plaines
303 Rue de la République
Tel: 0262 20 00 68
You'll find tasty food and a warm welcome in this Creole house set back from the main road. Open daily for lunch and dinner except Tue evening. €€

THE CIRQUES

Cilaos
Le Cass'Dale
2 Rue de la Mare à Joncs
Tel: 0262 31 84 29
Pleasant snack bar next to the Mare à Joncs pond, where children can hire pedaloes. This hits the spot if you're looking for a quick inexpensive bite to eat. €
Chez Noé
40 Rue Père Boiteau
Tel: 0692 87 36 10
In a delightfully restored Creole house

Bonbons piments.

and convenient for the main sights, this simple restaurant is famous for its lentil *boucané* (smoked meat with lentils). Closed Sun night and Mon. Also has rooms. €€
Le Marla
1 Rue de la Mare à Joncs
Tel: 0262 31 72 33
www.hotel-des-neiges.com
Typical Creole fare in a pleasant dining room of the Hotel des Neiges. This is a place to try Cilaos' famous lentils, wine and the delicious dessert *gâteau banane*. €€€
Tsilaosa Hotel
Rue Père Boiteau, Cilaos
Tel: 0262 37 39 39
Email: accueil@tsilaosa.com
Peckish? If you're hankering after afternoon tea, pop into this four-star hotel on the main road. You won't get scones and cucumber sandwiches, but you will get a mouth-watering selection of fine teas, home-made cakes and tasty *crêpes* fresh from the griddle. €

Salazie
Chez Alice
1 Chemin Sangliers, Hell-Bourg
Tel: 0262 47 86 24
A great traditional restaurant where you can savour pigs trotters or locally

farmed trout, watercress or *chou chou*. Arrive early or book ahead. Open for lunch and dinner except Mon. €€
Crêperie le Gall
55 Rue de Général de Gaulle, Hell-Bourg
Tel: 0262 47 87 48
For home-made salads, gratins or pancakes, both sweet and savoury, try this delightful café on the main road. Mouth-watering. €
P'tit Bambou
166 Rue Georges Pompidou
Opposite the church at Salazie
Tel: 0262 47 51 51
Tasty home products turned into delicious Creole cuisine, with mounds of white rice. Closed Wed. €€
Le Relais des Cimes
67 Rue de Général de Gaulle, Hell-Bourg
Tel: 0262 47 81 58
www.relaisdescimes.com
The finest restaurant in the area, which also has rooms attached. Open daily for lunch and dinner. €€

PRICE CATEGORIES
Price categories are for two without wine:
€ = less than €15
€€ = €15–30
€€€ = more than €30

ACTIVITIES

THE ARTS, FESTIVALS, NIGHTLIFE, OUTDOOR ACTIVITIES AND SHOPPING

THE ARTS

Music and dance

Scarcely a day goes by without some form of entertainment being staged in Réunion's theatres and cultural centres. A most unusual venue is St-Denis' **Le Palaxa** (tel: 0262 92 09 90; www.palaxa.re), a converted warehouse seating 300 people and noted for late-night folk music and unusual sounds from Réunion and the Indian Ocean islands.

The **Centre Dramatique de l'Océan Indien** (http://cdoi-reunion. com) is an innovative theatre company based at the **Théâtre du Grand Marché** in St-Denis (tel: 0262 20 33 99) and is host to many small theatrical companies from around the world.

Larger dance and theatre companies, as well as big-name French musicians, tend to perform at the **Teat de Champ Fleuri** (St-Denis) or **Teat Plein Air** (an open-air theatre in St-Gilles); see www.theatreunion.re for details of upcoming acts.

Contact the tourist office, consult the free RUN guide or see online at www.azenda.re or www.pils.re for further information and listings of other gigs, concerts, dance shows, plays and musical events. If you're spending some time on Réunion, you might want to consider registering at http://la-reunion.urbeez.com, a website with dozens of different events on offer every day all over the island.

Museums

Among Réunion's museums are the following attractions:

The **Musée du Sel** (Salt Museum; 25 Pointe au Sel les Bas, St-Leu; tel: 0262 34 67 00; Tue–Sun 9am–noon, 1.30–5pm; free) is in a former sea salt warehouse next to the ocean, and tells the story of salt production in Réunion from 1704 to the present day.

The **Musée de la Vraie Fraternité** (True Fraternity Museum; 28 Boulevard de la Providence, St-Denis; tel: 0262 21 06 71; Wed and Sat 9am–5pm) is a religious social history museum displaying local costumes and remains of the island's first printing press.

At **Maison du Curcuma** (Turmeric House, 14 rue du Rond, Plaine des Grègues, St-Joseph; tel: 0262 37 54 66; email: memeriviere@orange. fr; www.maisonducurcuma.fr; daily 9am–noon and 1.30–5pm; free) you can discover how turmeric – a spice much used in local cuisine, where it is known as *safran* – is grown and processed, sampling such products as candied orange and sweet-and-sour ginger on the way.

FESTIVALS

Réunion has a year-round cultural programme: fire walking, Cavadee and Dipavali (the local name for Diwali) are practised by the Tamil community in various parts of the island and dates may vary. Wine, fruit and handicraft festivals take place in villages and towns, while sporting events can be watched virtually year round.

The three-day Sakifo music festival (www.sakifo.com) takes place every June in St-Pierre and sees gigs from a wide range of local, national and international performers.

October/November is the time for the Grand Raid (www.grandraid-reunion.com), a gruelling 165km (103-mile) mountain running race; the Paragliding World Cup, an annual international competition; the Megavalanche, a mountain-bike downhill marathon-style event; and the International Cross Country race at St-Denis. For details of these and other events contact the tourist office.

NIGHTLIFE

There are three late-night casinos and dozens of pubs, clubs and discotheques to choose from, with the highest concentration in St-Denis, St-Gilles-les-Bains and St-Pierre. Many nightclubs open on Friday, Saturday and the day before a public holiday at around 10pm but really get going after midnight, closing only when the last revellers stagger home in the morning. Most clubs have a cover charge of about €15, and alcoholic drinks can cost half as much again.

OUTDOOR ACTIVITIES

The dramatic volcanic landscape of Réunion provides a magnificent arena for a vast variety of sports and outdoor activities, as does the surrounding sea – whipped up by the trade winds, becalmed in the lagoons and concealing an underwater world of coral reefs and marine creatures. This really is an island with something for everyone, from the thrill-seekers to those with more of a sense of self-preservation (see page 179). Activities on offer include hang-gliding and paragliding (parapente) over breathtaking scenery, canyoning down the gorges, hiking, climbing and mountain biking, exploring lava tubes, or horse trekking and rambling on the gentler slopes. For full details of all mountain activities, practical information, accommodation and maps see Réunion's tourist information website: www.reunion.fr.

On offer on the water are sailing, surfing, windsurfing and a whole range of water sports in the lagoons, or big game fishing out to sea and scuba diving under it. Alternatively, life in the open can be enjoyed just as much on a golf course or a leisurely catamaran cruise.

Adventure sports on land and sea

The following organisations offer a whole range of adventure sports and provide equipment, qualified guides and instructors. It's best to make reservations in advance:

Alpanes: 153 Avenue Daniel Ramin, Grands Bois; tel: 0692 77 75 30; email: contact@alpanes.com; www.alpanes.com. For canyoning, hiking and kayaking; they also offer free photos/video.

Aparksa Montagne: 1bis, Passage des Pâquerettes, Cilaos; tel: 0262 31 73 30, mobile: 0692 66 50 09; www.aparksa-montagne.com. For canyoning, lava tubes, hiking and guided trekking.

Austral Aventure: 16 Rue Amiral Lacaze, Hell-Bourg, Salazie; tel: 0262 32 40 29; email: canyon@australaventure.fr; www.australaventure.fr. For hiking, hang-gliding, paragliding, canyoning, river sports and mountain climbing.

Cilaos Aventure: 12 Chemin la Chapelle, Cilaos; tel: 0692 66 73 42; email: team@cilaosaventure. com; www.cilaosaventure.com. Sports on offer include canyoning, heli-canyoning, lava tube visits, hiking, climbing and mountain biking.

Envergure Réunion: tel: 0693 43 23 52; www.canyon-speleo.re. Lava tunnels and canyoning. Qualified English-speaking instructors.

Rafting Réunion: tel: 0692 00 16 23; email: rvpiaut@wanadoo.fr; www. oasisev.com. For all sorts of rafting and kayaking.

Run Evasion: 23 Rue Père Boiteau, Cilaos; tel: 0262 31 83 57; email: runevasioncilaos@gmail.com; www. canyon-reunion.fr. Mainly climbing and canyoning.

Forest adventure

Réunion has two tree-top adventure courses, where young and old can fly down zip wires and enjoy high rope obstacles. Check their websites for opening times:

Cilaosa Parc Aventure: on the road to Bras Sec, Cilaos; tel: 0262 03 26 27; www.cilaosparc.com

Makes Aventures: Route Forestière des Makes, Camp Montplaisir, St-Louis; tel: 0692 30 29 29; www.makesaventures.com

Paragliding, skydiving and microlighting

Take-off for paragliding is usually at 800m (2,624ft) altitude on the slopes of Les Colimaçons (St-Leu); landing (and initial meeting point) is at La Pointe des Châteaux (next to Kelonia).

Azurtech: La Pointe des Châteaux, St-Leu; tel: 0692 85 04 00 or 0692 65 37 65; www.azurtech.com

Blue Sky Parapente: St-Leu; tel: 0693 94 91 12; email: ptroubet@ free.fr; www.blueskyparapente.com. English-speaking instructors, also offers flights over Le Maïdo.

Bourbon Parapente: 4 Rue Haute, St-Leu; tel: 0692 87 58 74; www.bourbonparapente.com

Felix ULM Run: Base ULM de Cambaie, St-Paul; tel: 0262 43 02 59; mobile: 0692 87 32 32; www.felixulm. com. Microlight flights.

Fly 974 Tandem: tel: 0692 02 53 76 or 0692 13 12 83; www.fly974tandem. com. Skydiving from a helicopter on the west coast.

Lit d'Air École de Parapente: 36 Allée de l'Ave Maria, St-Denis; mobile: 0692 60 01 23; www.litdair-parapente. com

Paraclub de Bourbon: Pierrefonds airport, St-Pierre; tel: 0262 25 54 41; www.para-bourbon.com. Skydiving; you can jump out of a plane at 4,000m (13,000ft) altitude.

Parapente Réunion: Pente-école 4, Montée des Colimaçons, St-Leu; tel: 0262 24 87 84; mobile: 0692 82 92 92; www.parapente-reunion.fr. Paragliding school for beginners and advanced, on the D12. Qualified, English-speaking instructors.

Les Passagers du Vent: Base ULM, ZI de Cambaie; tel: 0692 68 70 55; www.ulm-reunion.com. Microlighting, hang-gliding and paragliding.

Mountain biking

Known as vélo tout terrain (VTT), mountain biking has become so popular that specially marked trails have been created for enthusiasts. The following operators hire equipment and organise guided rides:

Coco Bike: 165 Rue du Général de Gaulle, St-Gilles; tel: 0692 18 12 12; mobile: 0692 66 12 21; www.cocobike.fr

Rando Réunion Passion: 3 Rue du Général de Gaulle, St-Gilles; tel: 0262 45 18 67; mobile: 0692 88 54 58; www.vttreunion.com

Planning a trekking holiday

Accommodation: There are various types of accommodation (see page 381) but not always enough to satisfy demand during July and August, when it seems the whole of France comes to Réunion, so it makes sense to book as early as possible. May to June and September are less frenetic times and accommodation is not so scarce.

Catering: In Mafate, where the only way of getting around is on foot, the grocery store or épicerie is rather like a beacon in the wilderness luring a hungry trekker to happiness with a basic range of goodies, although prices are more expensive than on the coast. There are three épiceries at La Nouvelle, two each at Aurère and Marla, and one each at Roche Plate, Grand Place les Hauts, Îlet à Malheur and Îlet à Bourse. Try to take your waste with you when you leave Mafate, as otherwise it has to be airlifted out of the cirque by helicopter.

In and around Cilaos cirque, particularly at Dimitile, Le Pavillon and Îlet Haute, you should make sure you have your own food. Other areas you should know about for their absence of sustenance are Belouve on the GR1 and Roche Écrite, Piton des Neiges, Basse Vallée and Grand Bassin on the GR2 and anywhere along the banks of the Rivière des Remparts.

What to take on a trek

It is vital to take enough water and food, as well as a warm sweater; a waterproof cape or jacket; a hat, sunglasses and suncream; good walking shoes or boots and a pair of soft shoes to change into; a torch, pocket knife, whistle and basic medical kit; and a mobile phone.

If you are camping overnight you'll need a sleeping bag and tent; crockery, cutlery and minimal cooking utensils; toiletries, such as loo paper.

Safety measures

To avoid accidents and disappointments, follow the rules of the mountain (see page 180).

Check the weather forecast before going; see www.meteofrance. re or phone 0892 68 08 08 (in French). Find out whether any mountain paths are closed by checking 'Infos Sentiers' on the Forestry Office website: www.onf.fr/la-reunion.

Be careful if you bathe in a river or pool. Water can rise extremely suddenly during the rainy season, and you can get swept onto rocks or out to sea.

Keep the Mountain Rescue Police *(Peloton de Gendarmerie de Haute Montagne)* number to hand: tel: 0262 930 930. If out at sea, keep the Sea Rescue Operation *(Secours en mer)* number to hand: tel: 0262 43 43 43. Never go out to sea in a heavy swell, if a cyclone has been announced or in bad weather.

Mafate hiking.

See also:

Atmosphère Péi: Bourg-Murat, Plaine des Cafres; tel 0692 44 47 17; http://atmospherepei.com (recumbent trike)
Mobilboard Réunion: 40 Rue Suffren, St-Pierre; tel: 0693 93 61 31 (Segway)
Quadbike Runners: 23a Rue des Oliviers, St-Louis; tel: 0262 26 14 04; http://quadbikerunners.free.fr (quad mountain bikes)

Horse riding and trekking

You need not be an experienced rider to go on a pony trek, as the Réunion Mérens horse is a gentle, easy-going breed. For half-day to three-day treks with a guide contact:

Centre Equestre Alti-Mérens: 120 Rue Maurice Kraft, Km 26, Plaine des Cafres; tel: 0262 49 04 29; mobile: 0692 31 47 92; www.alti-merens-reunion.com
Centre Equestre du Maïdo: 350 Route du Maïdo, Le Guillaume-St-Paul; tel: 0262 32 49 15; mobile: 0692 86 51 92
Ferme Equestre de Grand Etang: Route Nationale 3, Pont Payet, St-Benoît; tel: 0262 50 90 03

Horse Riding Centres
Centre Equestre de la Montagne: 50 Chemin Couilloux St-Bernard, La Montagne, St-Denis; tel: 0262 23 62 51; www.equimontagne.com
Poney Club Equirun: 37 Allée Montignac, Etang Salé; tel: 0262 26

52 52; www.equirun-centre-equestre-reunion.com

Hiking and trekking

Hiking excursions of varying duration, from half a day to a week with qualified English-speaking guides, can be arranged through **Réunion's tourism office** (www.reunion.fr) who can help plan your route and organise accommodation. It's worth asking for the services of a *guide péi* (native guide) from the tourist office in Rue Victor MacAuliffe, Cilaos (tel: 0262 31 71 71; email: accueil.cilaos@otisud. re). These guides are born and bred in the Cirques, know every nook and cranny, and keep you entertained with folklore and legend. As well as the adventure sports companies, the following can also organise treks and hikes:
Tours Réunion: 7 Chemin Barouty, Les Avirons; tel: 0692 81 03 13; www.toursreunion.com

Canyoning

Run Evasion (www.canyon-reunion. fr) offers so many variations on canyoning that one is bound to scare the pants off you. Try canyoning through jungle-like landscapes, canyoning through waterfalls, or canyoning from mountain heights. There are even wet and dry versions.

Golf

There are three golf courses and a mini golf:
Golf du Bassin Bleu: Villèle, St-Gilles-les-Hauts; tel: 0262 70 03 00; www.bassinbleu.fr
Golf Club de Bourbon: 140 Les Sables, L'Etang-Salé; tel: 0262 26 33 39; www.golf-bourbon.com
Golf du Colorado: Zone de Loisirs du Colorado, La Montagne; tel: 0262 23 79 50; www.golfclubcolorado.fr
Mini-Golf du Lagon: Plage de l'Hermitage, 3 Allée des Îles Eparses, St-Gilles-les-Bains; tel: 0692 86 49 47

Big game fishing

The best time for catching the big ones, such as blue marlin, sailfish, bluefin tuna and sea bream, is from October to April, although you can go all year round. Fully equipped boats for up to six people leave from the harbours at St-Gilles, Pointe des Galets and St-Pierre. A picnic and drinks are often included in the price:
Albacore Fishing Club: Port de Plaisance, St-Gilles-les-Bains; tel: 0262 33 04 41; mobile: 0692 61 91 61; www.albacorefishingclub.com
Pêche Passion Sud: Port de Plaisance, St-Pierre; tel: 0692 44 44 77
Réunion Fishing Club: Le Port, St-Gilles-les-Bains; tel: 0262 24 36 10; mobile: 0692 76 17 28; www.reunionfishingclub.com

MAURITIUS

RÉUNION

SEYCHELLES

Réunion Pêche au Gros: Rue des Brisants, St-Gilles; tel: 0262 33 33 99; www.reunion-pecheaugros.com. Deep sea fishing in two boats, *Alopia* and *Octopus II*.

Scuba diving

Many of Réunion's dive companies operate from St-Gilles-les-Bains and St-Leu, offering CMAS (and occasionally PADI) courses and a chance to see the magnificent coral landscape and marine life under the Indian Ocean. If you're in Réunion between June and September you'll get the chance to see (and hear) humpback whales too:

Abyss Plongée: 7 Boulevard Bonnier, St-Leu; tel: 0262 34 79 79; www.abyss-plongee.com
Bleu Marine Réunion: Port de Plaisance, St-Gilles-les-Bains; tel: 0262 24 22 00; www.bleu-marine-reunion.com
Corail Plongée: Port de Plaisance, St-Gilles-les-Bains; tel: 0262 24 37 25; www.corail-plongee.com
O Sea Bleu: Port de Plaisance, St-Gilles-les-Bains; tel: 0262 24 23 30; www.oseableu.com
Plongée Salée: 5 Rue Motais de Narbonne, Étang-Salé-les-Bains; tel 0262 91 71 23; www.plongeesalee.com

Surfing

Réunion's surfing scene has suffered from a spate of shark attacks since 2011 and at the time of writing surfing and other surface water sports have been temporarily banned. Réunion has produced some world champion surfers, and international surfers used to descend on the island between

Dive to see wonderful underwater life.

March and September to ride out the big waves found on the west coast. One of the best spots, described as a world-class break and for experienced surfers only, is in front of the town of St-Leu. At Etang-Salé some amazing left-hand waves rising to almost 90 degrees provide ace surfing conditions and are best tried out in the early morning. When surfing resumes, there's a two-hour introductory surfing course in French at **École de Stand Up Paddle et de Surf des Roches Noires** at St-Gilles-les-Bains (tel: 0262 24 63 28) or at **Oxbow Surf School** at Étang-Salé (tel: 0262 56 17 69).

Other water sports

Sailing boats can be hired at Le Port through **Objectif Mer** (tel: 0262 27 72 15; www.objectifmer. fr). Children will enjoy visiting the coral reef in a boat equipped with a glass observation bubble operated by Visiobul Réunion (tel: 0262 24 37 04; www.runevasion.com/visiobul). For stand-up paddle contact Réunion Surf School at Trou d'Eau beach, La Saline-les-Bains (tel: 0692 31 53 16). **Water-skiers** of all levels can hire equipment from the **Ski Nautique Club de St-Paul** (tel: 0692 85 14 96; http://skiclubdelareunion. com). For information about kitesurfing in Réunion, see www.kite surf-reunion.fr.

SHOPPING

You're unlikely to find the bargains in clothing that you can get in Mauritius but Réunion excels in producing original handicrafts. These items

Cruising

Either take to the water the easy way – go whale or dolphin watching with Le Grand Bleu or watch the sun go down over cocktails from the deck of a catamaran (www.grandbleu.re/croisiere_voile.html or www.lady lafee.com) – or cruise to Seychelles on the 22-metre (72ft) ketch *Hnoss* (tel: 0693 90 62 84; www.lehnoss.com).

are the work of cottage industries throughout the island and end up for sale in many retail outlets. Things to look for are miniature replicas of **Creole houses** made from fragranced wood, toiletries and perfumes made from **essential oils** such as citronelle, vetyver and geranium, and *tentes* or baskets woven from pandanus leaves.

Gourmets may like to shop for a range of local **speciality foods** such as local jams, compôtes, confectionery, spices and **traditional drinks** such as rum, punch and liqueurs, and sweet wine from Cilaos. For typically Réunionnais chocolate, visit the Chocolaterie Mascarin factory for a guided tour and tasting at Le Port (tel: 0262 55 10 20; www.mascarin.fr).

Tourist offices *(Syndicats d'Initiative)* sell products from the region; look for **Gol chairs** at Etang-Salé-les-Bains, **vanilla** products at St-André and **fruity wines** and lentils at Cilaos.

For a full range of **island crafts** in St-Denis, visit the **Galerie Artisanale** at Carrefour Hypermarket, Espace Continent, St-Clotilde (http://lagalerie artisanale.re; near Roland Garros Airport).

No visit to Réunion would be complete without a souvenir of the volcano. There's a good range of postcards, decorative pieces of basalt, photographs and illustrated books on volcanology at the **Cité du Volcan** shop at Bourg-Murat.

Nuns in Cilaos have been embroidering for over a century. There is now an embroidery school here and many skilled craftswomen who embroider everything from lovely christening robes to tablecloths and napkins, all in natural white or beige. No two pieces are the same and each piece can take up to several months to produce – hence the price. The best selection can be found at **Maison de la Broderie**, in Rue des Écoles, Cilaos.

A – Z

A HANDY SUMMARY
OF PRACTICAL INFORMATION

A

Accommodation

Whether you're looking for luxury or simplicity, Réunion has accommodation to suit a wide range of tastes, needs and budgets.

Choosing a hotel

All of Réunion's 80 classified hotels meet French standards, and are clean, comfortable and well run. There are few large internationally owned chain hotels, and only two five-star hotels. Book in advance as hotels fill quickly during the high season, and expect price hikes over the Christmas and New Year period. The largest choice of accommodation is on the island's west coast, in the St-Gilles area. If you are coming from Mauritius, don't expect the same kind of quality or service, although the staff are still professional and helpful.

Camping

There are municipal campsites at Etang-Salé (tel: 0262 91 75 86) and St-Gilles (tel: 0262 96 36 70), otherwise book a place at one that's privately run (see www.reunion.fr for more details).
    You can also camp in the wild provided you have permission from the landowner.

Self-catering

See www.reunion.fr or contact a tourist office for details of self-catering accommodation, furnished flats, *gîtes ruraux* (rural *gîtes*), bed and breakfast in *chambres d'hôtes* and farm guesthouses *(ferme auberges)*.

Youth hostels

There's an **Auberge de Jeunesse** at Bernica, Rue de l'Auberge, St-Gilles-les-Hauts (tel: 0262 22 89 75; mobile: 0692 59 34 11).

Family holiday villages (VVF)

There are two VVFs *(Villages Vacances Famille)* in Réunion geared to families or groups, who can choose from an inexpensive range of studio, bungalow or dormitory-style accommodation. A group joining fee of around €16 is payable before bookings can be made at the following:

St-Gilles-les-Bains
VVF St-Gilles 'Le Village de Corail', 80 Avenue de Bourbon; tel: 0262 24 29 39; www.villages-des-australes.com

Cilaos
VVF 'Le Village des Sources', Chemin Fleurs Jaunes; tel: 0262 31 71 39

In the mountains

On a hike that lasts for more than a day you can plan your overnight stays in an assortment of lodgings en route, from the very basic to the more comfortable. For information and reservations, contact local tourist offices or see www.reunion.fr.
Gîte d'étape: basic overnight *gîte* offering dormitory-style lodging and breakfast and makeshift kitchens where guests can cook up their own pot noodles.
Gîte de montagne: dormitory bunk-bed accommodation in an isolated location, sometimes without a shower or hot water and in dry periods no water at all. Basic self-catering facilities, although meals can be provided if booked.

Refuge: private, basic lodging with an evening meal and sometimes breakfast provided by the owner.
Chambre d'hôte: bed and breakfast in someone's home. Evening meals can also be provided as a *table d'hôte* (see page 388).
Gîte rural: self-catering cottage located in the countryside. They are normally well equipped and probably the best option for families or groups.

Admission charges

Admission charges for tourist attractions and most museums, whether private or government-owned, vary between €2 and €9 per person, with reductions for children under 16, students, disabled people and senior citizens. Entry to discos and nightclubs is normally free but expect to pay high charges for drinks.

B

Budgeting for your trip

Allow at least €40 per day per person to cover meals and snacks, soft drinks and entrance fees. It's always a good idea to keep some spare euros handy and carry your credit card with you as you may not find ATMs in more out of the way places.

Tips on how to save money

The cost of living is appreciably higher than in France so don't expect to find many bargains to take home. Eating in the most ordinary of restaurants can take a chunk out of your budget but many areas have small cafés, and mobile food wagons sell cheap, filling fast food.

Taxis are expensive so look for a deal on car hire or buy a *carnet* of six bus tickets for €6 if you intend to do a lot of travelling by bus.

See www.reunion.fr for a comprehensive list of good-value accommodation.

C

Children

Children are welcome everywhere. Many hotels cater specially for youngsters and offer supervised activities, special meals, babysitting services, family rooms and child discounts on excursions.

If you are travelling with very young children avoid Dec–Jan, which may be too hot. Supermarkets stock European baby food and nappies.

Climate

Like Mauritius and Rodrigues, Réunion has two seasons: the hot rainy summer season from December to April and the cool dry winter season between May and November. On the coast daytime temperatures are similar to Mauritius, averaging around 23°C (73°F) in winter and 30°C (85°F) in summer, but on the high plains and mountains variations between 4°C (39°F) and 25°C (77°F), depending on altitude and season, are normal. At heights approaching 2,500 metres (8,200ft) temperatures can drop to below freezing at night during the cool season.

Cyclones in the Indian Ocean usually occur between December and

Cyclone warnings

In Réunion, there are three levels of cyclone warning:
Vigilance cyclonique (cyclone watch): an early warning system advising people to stock up on basic goods (food, candles, bottled water, batteries) and to listen to broadcasts on TV and radio.
Alerte orange (orange alert): cyclone approaching within the next 24 hours. Schools close but some businesses remain open and everyone is advised to bring moveable objects and animals indoors and to batten down windows and doors.
Alerte rouge (red alert): imminent danger, given with three hours warning. Driving is banned and everyone must stay indoors or face

April. On average between 10 and 12 cyclones hit the southwestern Indian Ocean a year, causing devastation if they pass over land. Réunion, which holds most of the world's rainfall records, tends to suffer more than Mauritius as the many rivers flood, washing away anything in their path.

Crime and safety

In general, the Réunionnais are willing to help anyone in distress. However, as with everywhere, you should take the same basic precautions that you would at home. Don't flaunt expensive jewellery and money in public places; never leave property on view in your car; always be aware of your personal safety; lock doors and windows when you go out, particularly in self-catering accommodation; and after dark don't give a lift to a stranger or go out walking alone.

If you become a victim of crime, try to remain calm, take stock of the situation and get names and addresses of witnesses. Report the matter to the police and in cases of theft ensure you have all the documentation for insurance purposes. However, English is not spoken by the police, so if you have a problem ask staff at your hotel or your holiday representative to find an interpreter for you.

D

Disabled travellers

Facilities for travellers with disabilities are on a par with mainland France.

a fine. You are strongly advised to listen to the radio or follow the situation online if you have electricity.

Once the red alert is over, find out about the state of the roads before setting off anywhere (tel: 0262 97 27 27 – in French only). Do not touch fallen electric cables, do not drink tap water unless you have boiled it for at least 5 minutes, and do not go into the mountains or cross fords or submerged roads.
Cyclone information: tel: 08 97 65 01 01. General weather information for the following 24 hours and hourly updates are available in French on 08 92 68 08 08 or on the website: www.meteofrance.re.

Roland Garros Airport has facilities for disabled travellers, including walkways, lifts and escalators, and offers assistance on request. Many hotels, especially the larger ones, also have specially equipped rooms but always check with your travel agent or direct with the hotel before making a booking.

E

Electricity

220V, but standard European round two-pin plugs are used – so visitors from the UK and outside Europe should take an adaptor.

Embassies and consulates

As Réunion isn't an independent country, only a few countries have diplomatic representation. These include Germany, Belgium, China, India, Italy, Madagascar, Norway and Switzerland. The nearest consulates for other countries are in Mauritius. For the addresses of the UK, US, Canadian, South African and Australian representatives there, see page 363.

Entry requirements

French and European Union (EU) nationals must be in possession of a valid identity card or passport. Others need a valid passport and a return or onward ticket and may be asked for an address in Réunion. Citizens of the US, Canada, South Africa, New Zealand and Australia do not need visas for visits of up to three months. Other nationals should check with the French Embassy; note that Réunion is not part of the Schengen Area. Always

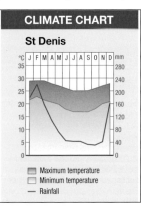

CLIMATE CHART

St Denis

MAURITIUS

Emergency numbers

Ambulance: tel: 15
Police: tel: 17
Fire: tel: 18
Emergency services: 112
(from a mobile phone even if not connected to the GSM network).
In less urgent cases of difficulty, English-speaking visitors could go to the Air Mauritius office in St-Denis at 13 Rue Gounod; tel: 0262 94 83 83.

check the latest entry requirements before you travel.
Applications for visa extensions can be made at the Service de l'État Civil et des Étrangers at La Préfecture, St-Denis; tel: 0262 40 75 42.
For **customs allowances** see page 363. The Customs Department (Direction Régionale des Douanes et Droits Directs) is at 7 Avenue de la Victoire, St-Denis (tel: 0262 90 81 00; www.douane.gouv.fr).

Even in this tropical climate, temperatures drop the higher you go.

Etiquette

Réunion retains much of its Gallic tradition with a great emphasis on politeness, and were it not for the Réunion Creole language and the ethnic mix of the Creole people you might at times feel that you were actually in mainland France. With the majority of tourists coming from France, the Réunionnais are perfectly aware of Western norms and you'll find that most subjects, including sex, race, religion and politics, can be discussed without causing offence.
Few people speak English so it really helps to learn some French to get by. Having said that, most Réunionnais are warm, helpful and friendly and often go that one step further so that visitors out of trouble. It's a good idea to greet people with a formal *bonjour*, and *merci* is always appreciated.

G

Gay and lesbian travellers

Réunion is a gay-friendly destination and even has an (unofficial) gay beach: La Souris Chaude, just south of La Saline. Gay-friendly establishments often display a multicoloured rainbow motif and since 2005 the tourist office has published a helpful booklet called *Charte d'Accueil – Gay-Friendly*, with listings of accommodation, eateries

and activities. The main gay bars and clubs are listed below:
Le Prince Club (formerly Le Boy's) 108 Rue Pasteur, St-Denis; tel: 0692 66 25 53. Popular late-night haunt, dancing and fun.
Le Zanzibar 41 Rue Pasteur, St-Denis; tel: 0262 20 01 18. Convivial bar-cum-pub popular with gay and lesbian crowd.
Coco Beach Plage de l'Hermitage, St-Gilles-les-Bains; tel: 0262 33 81 43. Lively restaurant and bar right on the beach.
Cherwaine's 6 Rue Auguste Babet, St-Pierre; tel: 0262 35 69 49; http://cherwaine.free. fr. Long-established late-night gay-friendly karaoke bar.

H

Health and medical care

Medical services in Réunion are excellent and with nearly 1,800 doctors, 450 pharmacies and an efficient emergency service you will find yourself in good hands should you happen to fall ill. The cost of treatment is on a par with mainland France. There is no need for vaccinations (unless you are coming from an infected area) and malaria has been eradicated from the island since 1948 (for information on the chikungunya virus see A–Z – Mauritius, see page 364). Always check the latest medical advice before you travel.
Make sure you are adequately insured before you leave home and in the event of a medical claim keep all receipts and documentation. EU

visitors should bring their European Health Insurance Card (EHIC).
Drinking tap water is fine but you can also order bottled water, especially advisable if there's just been a period of heavy rain.
There are no dangerous animals in Réunion on land; in the lagoon watch you don't step on a sea urchin or stonefish.
There can be strong currents and sharks frequent the waters around the coast so only swim where there is a lifeguard, and never if there is a shark flag or warning sign on display. Be aware that Réunion has the highest per capita rate of shark attacks in the world. Avoid swimming in the sea at dawn, dusk and after a period of heavy rainfall.
Mosquitoes can be a pest especially at night during the summer; wear long clothes, use repellent or keep them at bay with a plug-in diffuser (*un diffuseur électrique*), which can be bought locally.

Medical treatment

Tourists are strongly advised to take out comprehensive travel and medical insurance. Most large towns have a hospital and/or private clinic and plenty of doctors.

General hospitals
Centre Hospitalier Universitaire (CHU) Félix Guyon, Bellepierre, 97400 St-Denis; tel: 0262 90 50 50; www.chu-reunion.fr
Hôpital des Enfants (Children's Hospital) Association Saint François d'Assise, 60 Rue Bertin, 97400 St-Denis; tel: 0262 90 87 00
Hôpital Gabriel Martin, 38 Rue Labourdonnais, St-Paul; tel: 0262 45 30 30

Church in Cayenne on Réunion.

Groupe Hospitalier Est Réunion, 30 Route Nationale 3, St-Benoît; tel: 0262 98 80 00
Hôpital Sud Réunion, Avenue Président Mitterrand, St-Pierre; tel: 0262 35 90 00

Private clinics
Clinique de Sainte Clotilde, 127 Route Bois de Nèfles, 97400 St-Denis; tel: 0262 48 20 20; www.clinifutur.net
Clinique Avicenne, 4 boulevard Verdun, Le Port; tel: 0262 42 41 60

I

Internet

Most accommodation now has Wi-fi and/or internet access, which you may or may not have to pay for. Free Wi-fi in restaurants and shopping centres is also becoming more and more widespread.

L

Lost property

If you have lost any property at Roland Garros Airport contact the lost property office based there (tel: 0262 48 80 19 or email: parking@reunion.aeroport.fr). Otherwise report details of property lost elsewhere to the local police station, where you will be asked to fill out a form. You should ask for a copy of the form for insurance purposes.

M

Maps

You can buy good maps covering mountain walks and road routes from bookshops and tourist offices, including the French IGN 1:100 000 map, which covers the whole island on one sheet (also available from Stanfords, 12–14 Long Acre, Covent Garden, London WC2E 9LP; tel: 020 7836 1321; www.stanfords.co.uk). For more detailed coverage you'd need one of the six 1:25 000 maps numbered 4401RT to 4406RT.

Media

Most hotels are equipped with satellite TV showing French and English programmes, although the latter is generally limited to CNN or BBC World. Local radio includes RTL, RMC, Europe 1, NRJ and Chérie FM, which broadcasts mainly British and American music. Apart from the odd newspaper or magazine you'll find very few English-language publications. Locally produced daily papers are *Le Quotidien* (www.lequotidien.re) and *Journal de l'Île de la Réunion* (www.clicanoo.re).

Money

As with mainland France, the currency of Réunion is the euro. Visa and Mastercard credit cards are widely accepted in most hotels, shops and restaurants but it's wise to keep a

surplus of euros, particularly if you're heading for the Cirques, where there are fewer ATMs and banks. You can use your credit card to withdraw cash from ATMs but memorise your PIN number before leaving home.

Few banks have exchange facilities and there are hefty charges for changing foreign currency and traveller's cheques. To save costs it may be better to buy euro traveller's cheques before leaving home.

You will need a 1 euro coin for a trolley at the airport or pick up one of the free tokens from the counter there.

Banks

Major banks are open Mon–Fri 8am–4pm. There are change facilities at Roland Garros airport (but not at Pierrefonds), as well as an ATM outside each airport terminal, which accepts major foreign credit cards. There is also a small bureau de change, Point Cash, at 3 Rue de Nice, St-Denis; tel: 0262 46 15 01.

Tax

Value Added Tax (TVA) of 8.5 percent is added to goods and services and 2.1 percent to foodstuffs and books. Duty-free goods are not available in Réunion except at the airport, and duty-free won't apply if you're flying between Réunion and mainland France. There is no hotel or restaurant tax, although service may be included in the bill.

O

Opening hours

Most shops open daily except Sunday, 9am–6pm; many close for lunch noon–2.30pm. Shopping centres have longer opening hours, including Sunday mornings and some public holidays. Some museums also close for an hour at lunchtime. Places that have been open on Sunday are likely to be closed on Monday.

P

Postal services

Look for yellow La Poste signs indicating the post office where, as in France, a wide range of services is on offer. Most *tabacs* (tobacconists) also sell stamps if you want to avoid the post office queues.

All towns have a post office and poste restante service (Mon–Fri 8am–6pm, Sat 8am–noon). Most close for lunch between noon and 2pm. There is a post office at Roland Garros Airport (Mon–Fri 2–7pm).

The **main post office** in St-Denis is at the intersection between Rue Maréchal Leclerc and Rue Juliette Dodu.

R

Religious services

Réunion is 70 percent Roman Catholic, and church services are always in French. At mosques and Hindu temples the proceedings are likely to be in French and/or Kreol.

S

Student travellers

Youth hostels, budget accommodation and a lively night scene, particularly around St-Denis and St-Pierre, will appeal to student travellers. Concessions are available at some tourist attractions on production of your student ID card. The concessions aren't always made that obvious so don't be afraid to

Time zone

Greenwich Mean Time + 4 hours. There is no Daylight Savings Time.

ask. The University of La Réunion has an active student population and there is a students' portal via the university website, www.univ-reunion.fr.

T

Telecommunications

It is cheaper to use a public telephone outside peak times (Mon–Fri 8am–6pm, Sat 8am–noon) than to phone from a hotel.

Agreements between mobile/cell phone companies overseas enable subscribers to use a mobile phone in Réunion. Check with your service provider before leaving home.

Réunion has three cell phone networks: SFR Réunion, Only and Orange Réunion. If you intend to make a large number of local calls it may be more convenient to buy a SIM card in Réunion, although you will be asked to provide some form of identification at the time of purchase.

International Dialling Code: Dial the international code followed by the Réunion country code, 262.

Tipping

A service charge is normally added to restaurant bills. When service is not included *(service non compris)*, a 10 percent tip is perfectly acceptable. Taxi drivers do not expect to be tipped.

Toilets

Clean and well-maintained public toilets on a par with Western standards are found in St-Denis, the main tourist sites and large supermarkets. If you get caught short ask the owner of a bar or restaurant if you can use their facilities.

Tourist information offices

Tourist information for Réunion is centralised by the Comité Régional de Tourisme de la Réunion (IRT): email: contact@reunion.fr; www.reunion.fr. You can also contact the French tourist office of your home country via www.franceguide.com.

Local tourist offices

Most main towns have a tourist office that can book *gîte* accommodation and supply maps. The free tourist information publications *RUN* and *Welcome to Réunion* are published

in English as well as French and are widely available.

North
OTI Nord; email: info@lebeaupays.com; www.lebeaupays.com
St-Denis:
Maison Carrère, 14 Rue de Paris, St-Denis; tel: 0262 41 83 00; Mon–Sat 9am–6pm
Ste-Suzanne:
18 Rue du Phare, Ste-Suzanne; tel: 0262 52 13 54; Mon–Sat 9am–12.30pm, 1.30–5pm

West
OTI Ouest; email: accueil@ouest-la reunion.com; www.ouest-lareunion.com
La Possession:
96 Rue Leconte Delisle, La Possession; tel: 0262 22 26 66; Mon 9am–4pm, Tue–Fri 9–5pm
St-Gilles:
1 Place Paul Julius Benard, Galerie Amandine, St-Gilles-les-Bains; tel: 0810 79 77 97; daily 10am–1pm, 2–6pm
St-Leu:
Bâtiment Espace Laleu, 1 Rue Barrelier, St-Leu; tel: 0262 34 63 30; Mon 1.30–5.30pm, Tue–Fri 9am–noon and 1.30–5.30pm, Sat 9am–noon

East
OTI Est; email: info@oti-est.re; http://est.reunion.fr
St-André:
Maison Martin Valliamé, 1590 Chemin du Centre, St-André; tel: 0262 46 16 16; Mon–Fri 9am–12.30pm, 1.30pm–5pm
St-Benoît:
Place de l'Église, Ste-Anne; tel: 0262 47 05 09; Mon–Sat 9am–12.30pm, 1.30–5pm
Plaine des Palmistes:
Maison du Parc National, 258 Rue de la République, La Plaine des Palmistes; tel: 0262 41 17 10; Mon–Fri 9am–12.30pm, 1.30–5.30pm, Sat 10am–12.30pm, 1.30–5pm
Bras-Panon:
21 RN2, Bras-Panon; tel: 0262 23 98 36; daily 8.30am–noon, 1–5pm
Salazie:
Centre Artisanal d'Hell-Bourg, 47 Rue du Général de Gaulle, Salazie; tel: 0262 47 89 89; Mon–Sat 8.30am–noon, 1–5.30pm

South
OTI Sud; tel: 0820 203 220; http://sud.reunion.fr
Etang-Salé:
74 Avenue Octave-Bénard, Etang-Salé; email: accueil.otetangsale@

MAURITIUS

RÉUNION

SEYCHELLES

gmail.com; Mon–Sat 9am–noon, 1–4.30pm
Entre-Deux:
9 Rue Fortuné-Horau, Entre-Deux; tel: 0262 39 69 80; email: ot.entredeux@ wanadoo.fr; www.ot-entredeux.com; Mon–Sat 8am–noon, 1.30–5pm
St-Pierre:
Capitainerie du Port de Plaisance Lislet Geoffroy, Place Napoléon Hoarau, St-Pierre; email: saintpierre. tourisme@gmail.com; Mon–Sat 8.30am–6pm, Sun 8–noon
St-Philippe:
62 Rue Leconte-de-Lisle, St-Philippe; tel: 0262 97 75 84; email: officedutourismesaintphilippe@yahoo. fr; Mon–Fri 9am–noon, 1–5pm, Sat 10am–noon, 1–5pm
St-Joseph:
Maison du Tourisme du Sud Sauvage, 15 Allée du Four à Chaux, Manapany-les-Bains, St-Joseph; tel: 0262 37 37 11; email: pat.sudsauvage@ wanadoo.fr; Mon–Fri 9.30am–noon, 1–5.30pm, Sat 10am–5pm
Tampon/Plaine des Cafres:
160 Rue Maurice et Katia Kraft, RN3, La Plaine des Cafres; tel: 0262 27 40 00; email: accueil@tampontourisme. re; www.tampontourisme.re; daily 9am–5pm
Cilaos:
2 bis Rue Victor MacAuliffe, Cilaos; email: accueil.cilaos@otisud.re; Mon–Sat 9am–12.30pm, 1.30–5pm, Sun and public hols 9am–1pm

Tour operators

Many tour operators based throughout Europe, South Africa, Australia, Canada and the US offer package and specialist holidays,

Outside a Tourist Office.

such as trekking or golfing, to Réunion. For details contact Maison de la France or your local travel agent.

The following UK-based operators specialise in Réunion:
Africa Collection: tel: 01403 265655; email: web@africacollection. com; www.africacollection.co.uk
Black Tomato: tel: 0203 627 1757; email: info@blacktomato.com; www.blacktomato.com
Rainbow Tours: tel: 020 7226 1250; email: info@rainbowtours.co.uk; www.rainbowtours.co.uk

W

Websites

www.cg974.fr – *car jaunes* bus timetables and information.
www.clicanoo.com – news and handy information put together by the daily *Journal de l'Île de la Réunion* publication online.
www.creole.org – places to eat and stay and a recipe section too.
www.gov.uk/foreign-travel-advice/ reunion – UK Foreign Office travel advice for Réunion.
www.reunion.fr – the official Réunion Island tourism website (multilingual).
www.ipgp.fr/fr/ovpf/actualites-ovpf – webcams showing the Piton de la Fournaise volcano.
www.reunionisland.fr – an online guide to Réunion in English.
www.run974.org – helpful online tourist guide highlighting restaurants, accommodation and transport.
www.runevasion.com – comprehensive

Weights and measures

The metric system is used in Réunion.

tourist guide including details of essential services.
www.transfert.re – private transfers to and from Roland Garros and Pierrefonds airports, and excursions.
www.travelssmart.blogspot.com – blog and practical information about Réunion, in English.
www.welcometoreunionisland.com – website in English with lots of useful information about Réunion.

What to bring

In the mountainous interior the climate is much cooler so take something warm; during the cool season the evenings can be fresh along the coast, so a light wrap, jacket or cardigan may be necessary. Réunion is quite laid-back about dress: casual wear such as loose cotton shorts, shirts, T-shirts and dresses are acceptable around town and in the evenings, but swimsuits are not. Men may need a tie for a smart occasion. In St-Gilles-les-Bains women are allowed to sunbathe topless on the beach.

For the feet, light sandals are advisable on the coast, and a pair of reef shoes will protect against injury from sharp coral. A pair of good walking boots is essential if you are planning on doing any hiking in the mountains or a pair of comfortable but sturdy shoes for short walks.

What to read

Most books written about Réunion are in French but there are several books in English that cover the Mascarenes and include Réunion (see page 370).

Women travellers

Réunion is a generally safe destination but, as in any country in the world, women should exercise caution if travelling alone, especially at night. Women are rarely hassled but if you encounter unwanted attention deal with it firmly. Avoid beachwear away from the beach, don't accept lifts from strangers and if you're travelling alone and plan to be away for the day let someone know where you are going and at what time you plan to return.

MAURITIUS

LANGUAGE

UNDERSTANDING THE LANGUAGE

It is worth trying to master a few simple phrases in French before holidaying in Réunion. The fact that you have made an effort is likely to get you a better response. Pronunciation is the key; they really will not understand if you get it very wrong. Remember to **emphasise each syllable**, but not to pronounce the last consonant of a word as a rule (this includes the plural 's') and always to drop your 'h's. Whether to use 'vous' or 'tu' is a vexed question; increasingly the familiar form of 'tu' is used by many people. However, it is better to be too formal, and use 'vous' if in doubt. It is very important to be polite; always address people as **Madame** or **Monsieur**, and address them by their surnames until you are confident first names are acceptable. When entering a shop always say, 'Bonjour Monsieur/Madame,' and 'Merci, au revoir,' when leaving.

WORDS AND PHRASES

How much is it? *C'est combien?*
What is your name? *Comment vous appelez-vous?*
My name is... *Je m'appelle...*
Do you speak English? *Parlez-vous anglais?*
I am English/American *Je suis anglais/américain*
I don't understand *Je ne comprends pas*
Please speak more slowly *Parlez plus lentement, s'il vous plaît*
Can you help me? *Pouvez-vous m'aider?*
I'm looking for... *Je cherche*
Where is...? *Où est...?*
I'm sorry *Excusez-moi/Pardon*
I don't know *Je ne sais pas*
No problem *Pas de problème*

Have a good day! *Bonne journée!*
That's it *C'est ça*
Here it is *Voici*
There it is *Voilà*
Let's go *On y va. Allons-y*
See you tomorrow *À demain*
See you soon *À bientôt*
yes *oui*
no *non*
please *s'il vous plaît*
thank you (very much) *merci (beaucoup)*
you're welcome *de rien*
excuse me *excusez-moi*
hello *bonjour*
OK *d'accord*
goodbye *au revoir*
good evening *bonsoir*
here *ici*
there *là*
today *aujourd'hui*
yesterday *hier*
tomorrow *demain*
now *maintenant*
later *plus tard*
this morning *ce matin*
this afternoon *cet après-midi*
this evening *ce soir*

ON ARRIVAL

I want to get off at... *Je voudrais descendre à...*
Is there a bus to...? *Est-ce qu'il y a un bus...?*
How far is...? *À quelle distance se trouve...?*
airport *l'aéroport*
bus station *la gare routière*
bus *l'autobus, le car*
bus stop *l'arrêt*
ticket *le billet*
hitchhiking *l'autostop*
toilets *les toilettes*
This is the hotel address *C'est l'adresse de l'hôtel*

I'd like a (single/double) room... *Je voudrais une chambre (pour une/deux personnes)...*
...with shower *avec douche*
...with a bath *avec salle de bain*
...with a view *avec vue*
Does that include breakfast? *Le prix comprend-il le petit déjeuner?*
May I see the room? *Je peux voir la chambre?*
washbasin *le lavabo*
bed *le lit*
key *la clé*
lift/elevator *l'ascenseur*
air conditioned *climatisé*

ON THE ROAD

Where is the nearest garage? *Où est le garage le plus proche?*
Our car has broken down *Notre voiture est en panne*
the road to... *la route pour...*
left *gauche*
right *droite*
straight on *tout droit*
far *loin*
near *près d'ici*
opposite *en face*
beside *à côté de*
car park *parking*

The alphabet

Learning the pronunciation of the French alphabet is a good idea. In particular, learn how to spell out your name.
a = ah, **b** = bay, **c** = say, **d** = day **e** = er, **f** = ef, **g** = zhay, **h** = ash, **i** = ee, **j** = zhee, **k** = ka, **l** = el, **m** = em, **n** = en, **o** = oh, **p** = pay, **q** = kew, **r** = ehr, **s** = ess, **t** = tay, **u** = ew, **v** = vay, **w** = dooblah vay, **x** = eex, **y** = ee grek, **z** = zed

RÉUNION

SEYCHELLES

Réunionese words

Below is a list of words you may come across on the island – some are Réunionese Kreol, and some are French words with a specific meaning in Réunion.

babouk large house spider
bibasse Japanese medlar fruit (loquat)
camaron large freshwater shrimp
kaz house
Cilaos if seen on a menu: a local brand of sparkling water
combava kaffir lime
faham rare endemic orchid (*jumellea fragrans*) used in *rhum arrangé*
fanjan tree fern root mass used as a natural plant pot
fénoir darkness, night
filao casuarina tree
gabier ATM
goyavier strawberry guava (*psidium cattleyanum*)
grains beans or lentils in sauce accompanying a *carri*
les hauts uplands or highlands of Réunion
ladilafé gossip
lontan in the past
marmay child(ren)
métropole mainland France
moring a combat sport similar to capoeira
péi anything that is local
safran turmeric
ti zak jackfruit *(artocarpus heterophyllus)*
zourit octopus

at the end *au bout*
on foot *à pied*
by car *en voiture*
town map *le plan*
road map *la carte*
street *la rue*
square *la place*
give way *céder le passage*
dead end *impasse*
no parking *stationnement interdit*
petrol *l'essence*
unleaded *sans plomb*
diesel *le gasoil*
water *l'eau*
oil *l'huile*
puncture *un pneu crevé*
bulb *l'ampoule*
wipers *les essuies-glace*

SHOPPING

Where is the nearest bank/post office? *Où est la banque/Poste la plus proche?*
I'd like to buy *Je voudrais acheter*

How much is it? *C'est combien?*
Do you take credit cards? *Est-ce que vous acceptez les cartes de crédit?*
I'm just looking *Je regarde seulement*
Have you got…? *Avez-vous…?*
I'll take it *Je le prends*
I'll take this one/that one *Je prends celui-ci/celui-là*
What size is it? *C'est de quelle taille?*
Anything else? *Avec ça?*
size (clothes) *la taille*
size (shoes) *la pointure*
cheap *bon marché*
expensive *cher*
enough *assez*
too much *trop*
each *la pièce (eg 15 la pièce)*
bill *la note*
chemist *la pharmacie*
bakery *la boulangerie*
bookshop *la librairie*
grocery *l'alimentation/l'épicerie*
tobacconist *tabac*
market *le marché*

SIGHTSEEING

town *la ville*
church *l'église*
town hall *l'hôtel de ville/la mairie*
colonial mansion *grand domaine*
sugar factory *l'usine sucrière*
museum *la musée*
exhibition *l'exposition*
tourist information office *l'office de tourisme/le syndicat d'initiative*
free *gratuit*
open *ouvert*
closed *fermé*
every day *tous les jours*
all year *toute l'année*
all day *toute la journée*

EMERGENCIES

Help! *Au secours!*
Stop! *Arrêtez!*
Call a doctor *Appelez un médecin*
Call an ambulance *Appelez une ambulance*
Call the police *Appelez la police*
Call the fire brigade *Appelez les pompiers*
Where is the nearest telephone? *Où est le téléphone le plus proche?*
Where is the nearest hospital? *Où est l'hôpital le plus proche?*
I am sick *Je suis malade*
I have lost my passport/purse *J'ai perdu mon passeport/porte-monnaie*

AT THE RESTAURANT

Table d'hôte (the 'host's table') is one set menu served at a set price. **Prix**

Non, non, garçon

Garçon is a word for waiter but is never used directly; say *Monsieur* or *Madame* to attract his or her attention.

fixe is a fixed-price menu. **À la carte** means dishes from the menu are chosen and charged separately.
breakfast *le petit déjeuner*
lunch *le déjeuner*
dinner *le dîner*
meal *le repas*
first course *l'entrée/les hors d'oeuvre*
main course *le plat principal*
made to order *sur commande*
drink included *boisson comprise*
wine list *la carte des vins*
the bill *l'addition*
fork *la fourchette*
knife *le couteau*
spoon *la cuillère*
plate *l'assiette*
glass *le verre*
napkin *la serviette*
ashtray *le cendrier*

Breakfast and snacks

baguette **long thin loaf**
pain **bread**
petits pains **rolls**
beurre **butter**
poivre **pepper**
sel **salt**
sucre **sugar**
confiture **jam**
oeufs **eggs**
…à la coque **boiled eggs**
…au bacon **bacon and eggs**
…au jambon **ham and eggs**
…sur le plat **fried eggs**
…brouillés **scrambled eggs**
tartine **bread with butter**
yaourt **yoghurt**
crêpe **pancake**
croque-monsieur **ham and cheese toasted sandwich**
croque-madame … **with a fried egg on top**

Meat and fish

la viande **meat**
saignant **rare**
à point **medium**
bien cuit **well done**
grillé **grilled**
agneau **lamb**
bifteck **steak**
canard **duck**
entrecôte **beef rib steak**
farci **stuffed**
faux-filet **sirloin**
feuilleté **puff pastry**
grillade **grilled meat**

Jambon **ham**
lapin **rabbit**
lardons **small pieces of bacon**
magret de canard **breast of duck**
porc **pork**
poulet **chicken**
poussin **young chicken**
rognons **kidneys**
rôti **roast**
saucisse **fresh sausage**
saucisson **salami**
poissons **fish**
anchois **anchovies**
calmars **squid**
coquillage **shellfish**
crevette **prawn, shrimp**
fruits de mer **seafood**
homard **lobster**
langouste **crayfish**
langoustine **large prawn**
thon **tuna**

Fruit and vegetables

ananas **pineapple**
banane **banana**
citron **lemon**
citron vert **lime**
fruit **fruit**
goyave **guava**
grenadille **type of passion fruit**
mangue **mango**
noix de coco **coconut**
pamplemousse **grapefruit**
pêche **peach**
poire **pear**
pomme **apple**
raisin **grape**
aïl **garlic**
avocat **avocado**
carotte **carrot**
cassava **manioc**
chips **potato crisps**
chou **cabbage**
chou chou **christophene**
cru **raw**
crudités **raw vegetables**
frites **chips, French fries**
haricots **beans (red or white)**
légumes **vegetables**
lentilles **lentils**
oignon **onion**
patate douce **sweet potato**
petit pois **peas**
piments **chillies**
pomme de terre **potato**
riz **rice**
salade verte **green salad**
tomate **tomato**

Time

At what time? *A quelle heure?*
When? *Quand?*
What time is it? *Quelle heure est-il?*
    Note that the French generally use the 24-hour clock.

Numbers, days and months

Numbers

0 *zéro*
1 *un, une*
2 *deux*
3 *trois*
4 *quatre*
5 *cinq*
6 *six*
7 *sept*
8 *huit*
9 *neuf*
10 *dix*
11 *onze*
12 *douze*
13 *treize*
14 *quatorze*
15 *quinze*
16 *seize*
17 *dix-sept*
18 *dix-huit*
19 *dix-neuf*
20 *vingt*
21 *vingt et un*
22 *vingt-deux*
30 *trente*
40 *quarante*
50 *cinquante*
60 *soixante*
70 *soixante-dix*
80 *quatre-vingts*
90 *quatre-vingt-dix*
100 *cent*
101 *cent et un*
110 *cent dix*
1,000 *mille*
1,000,000 *un million*
    Note that the number 1 is often written as an upside down V and the number 7 is usually crossed.

Days

Monday *lundi*
Tuesday *mardi*
Wednesday *mercredi*
Thursday *jeudi*
Friday *vendredi*
Saturday *samedi*
Sunday *dimanche*

Months

January *janvier*
February *février*
March *mars*
April *avril*
May *mai*
June *juin*
July *juillet*
August *août*
September *septembre*
October *octobre*
November *novembre*
December *décembre*

IN THE CAFÉ

If you sit at the bar, drinks will be cheaper than at a table. Settle the bill when you leave; the waiter may leave a slip of paper on the table to keep track of the bill.

drinks *les boissons*
coffee *café*
...with milk or cream *au lait ou crème*
...decaffeinated *déca/décaféïné*
...black/espresso *express/noir*
...American filtered coffee *filtre*
tea *thé*
...herb infusion *tisane*
hot chocolate *chocolat chaud*
milk *lait*
mineral water *eau minérale*
fresh lemon juice served with sugar *citron pressé*
full (eg full cream milk) *entier*
fresh or cold *frais, fraîche*
beer *bière*
...bottled *en bouteille*
...on tap *à la pression*
orange juice *jus d'orange*
white wine with cassis (blackcurrant liqueur) *kir*
kir with champagne *kir royale*
with ice *avec des glaçons*
red *rouge*

white *blanc*
rose *rosé*
dry/sweet *brut/doux*
sparkling wine *crémant*
house wine *vin maison*
local wine *vin de pays*
pitcher *carafe/pichet*
...of water/wine *d'eau/de vin*
half litre *demi-carafe*
quarter litre *quart*
mixed *panaché*
before dinner drink *apéritif*
after dinner drink *digestif*
cheers! *santé!*
hangover *gueule de bois*

TABLE TALK

I am a vegetarian/vegan *Je suis végétarien/végétalien*
I am on a diet *Je suis au régime*
What do you recommend? *Qu'est-ce que vous recommandez?*
Do you have local specialities? *Avez-vous des spécialités locales?*
I'd like to order *Je voudrais commander*
That is not what I ordered *Ce n'est pas ce que j'ai commandé*
Is service included? *Est-ce que le service est compris?*
Enjoy your meal *Bon appétit!*

MAURITIUS

RÉUNION

SEYCHELLES

TRANSPORT

GETTING THERE AND GETTING AROUND

GETTING THERE

By air

The archipelago's national carrier, Air Seychelles, stopped flying direct to Europe in 2012, having previously operated regular scheduled services to London, Paris, Rome and Milan. As of July 2015, the airline reintroduced a non-stop flight three times a week from Paris Charles De Gaulle to Mahé. Alternatively, you can catch an Etihad Airways flight from London to Mahé via a stop-off at Abu Dhabi, Hong Kong, Johannesburg or Mauritius. Air France flies from London to Mahé via Amsterdam or Paris and Abu Dhabi; Emirates flies via Dubai and Qatar Airways via Doha and Abu Dhabi.

All international flights arrive at **Seychelles International Airport**, Mahé. The **Domestic Terminal** north of the international departure terminal serves Air Seychelles' and IDC flights.

It is essential to reconfirm your return flight at least 72 hours prior to departure. **Airport tax** is included in the cost of air tickets.

Airline contacts

The following numbers are for calling from within Seychelles:
Air France: tel: 439 1000
Air Seychelles: tel: 391000
Emirates: tel: 292700
Etihad Airways: tel: 374700
Qatar Airways: tel: 224519
Seychelles International Airport (SEZ): tel: 483 4000

GETTING AROUND

Most of the granitic islands may be visited from bases on either Mahé or Praslin. Mahé is the base for trips to the islands of Ste Anne Marine National Park, Silhouette, North and Thérèse. Praslin is the base for trips to Aride, Cousin, St Pierre and Curieuse. Either Praslin or La Digue may be used as a base for visits to Grand Soeur, Marianne and Cocos. La Digue may be visited on a day trip from Praslin but a longer stay is preferable, to enjoy the atmosphere of the island. To visit Bird, Denis and any of the Outer Islands requires overnight accommodation.

By air

Air Seychelles (tel: 391000) offers internal flights to Praslin throughout the day and its charter service allows you to book flights to Frégate Island, Bird Island, D'Arros, Denis Island, Desroches and Alphonse. **Islands Development Company** (IDC; tel: 4384640) has four planes and operates a daily flight to Desroches and weekly flight to Farquhar during fly-fishing season (Oct–May). IDC planes may be chartered to other islands where airstrips exist, including Alphonse, Assumption, Coetivy, Marie-Louise, Platte and Remire. There are no facilities on planes and no in-flight services. It's important to be aware that Praslin is the only island where hotel confirmation isn't needed prior to landing.

By helicopter

ZilAir (tel: 375100) is the main provider of helicopter luxury transfers and scenic flights in the region. It operates three high-tech machines, which fly out of ZilAir's base next to the International Airport runway. There's a VIP lounge with Wi-fi, computers and refreshments. The

Inter-island flights

The small Air Seychelles planes make regular trips throughout the day from the Domestic Terminal on Mahé to Praslin, and operate a single flight daily to Bird and Denis (chartered by the hotels on **these** islands, through which bookings must be made). IDC operates scheduled flights most days to Alphonse and Desroches plus charter flights to other outer islands:
Mahé – Praslin: 15 mins
Mahé – Bird: 35 mins
Mahé – Denis: 25 mins
Mahé – Frégate: 15 mins
Mahé – Alphonse: 1 hour 40 mins
Mahé – Desroches: 65 mins

company has access to 21 licensed helipads and seven landing strips in the archipelago, including Aride, Bird Island, Cap Lazare, Cerf Island, Frégate, La Digue, Félicité, Round Island, Lemuria, Cousine, North Island, Ephelia, Grand Barbe, Grand Soeur, Kempinski, Maia, Marie Anne, Alphonse and Rémire.

Up to four passengers are allowed aboard each helicopter; children over two must occupy their own seat (infants under two can be seated on a parent's lap). Passengers should avoid taking more than 20kg (22 lb) of baggage without prior consultation.

By sea

Ferries operate between Mahé (from **Inter-Island Quay**, Victoria), Praslin (Praslin Quay/Baie Ste Anne) and La Digue (La Passe jetty). A fast **catamaran, Cat Cocos** (tel:

4324843) takes one hour to cross between Mahé and Praslin. A trip between Mahé and La Digue, via Praslin, takes one hour 30 minutes, and a direct trip from Mahé and La Digue is one hour 10 minutes. The first Mahé–Praslin catamaran leaves at 7.30am, the last at 4.30pm. **Inter Island Ferry Pty Ltd** operates daily between Praslin and La Digue. It is essential to book seats in advance (tel: 232329/232394). Arrive 15 minutes before departure for all ferries.

Schooners run throughout the day with seven daily return journeys departing Praslin Mon–Thu 7am–5.15pm and La Digue 7.30am–5.45pm. On Fri and Sun the last sailing in each direction is 30 minutes later. On Sat the last sailing from Praslin is 6.15pm.

By yacht or motorboat

Day trips or trips of several days on a yacht or motorboat can be arranged through a resort. Or contact a local tour operator (see page 402) for a tailor-made excursion.

By bus

Buses are the prime means of public transport on Mahé and Praslin. In general they are very cheap and reasonably good but times and routes are geared to local requirements, not tourists. On Mahé, if travelling at peak periods you may have to stand and at other times, particularly weekends and public holidays, you may have a long wait at bus stops. Buses are less frequent on Praslin. On La Digue buses take the form of open-sided covered lorries (camions) that roam the island with no fixed timetable. Elsewhere there are no buses. Buses on Mahé operate mainly between 5.30am and 8pm and on Praslin between 6am and 6.30pm.

Passenger airplane at Mahé's airport.

By taxi

There are plenty of metered taxis available on Mahé but not so many on Praslin. It is often necessary to ask the driver to turn on the meter to avoid any argument over the fare at your destination. If the meter is broken (often the case) a fare should be agreed in advance. On Mahé taxis can be found at the airport, Victoria taxi rank in Albert Street (next to Camion Hall) and by the clock tower in Independence Avenue. Your hotel will also organise one for you.

Taxi drivers can often make very good, amusing and informative guides to the islands and can be hired by the hour or day for negotiable rates, which you must agree on before setting off. On La Digue most people get around on bicycles (available at La Passe); there are only a few unmetered motorised taxis, and several more ox carts, which pass for taxis. They may be encountered driving up and down at La Passe or at the jetty when a ferry arrives from Praslin. None of the other islands has taxis.

Driving

Cars are driven on the left in Seychelles. Standards of driving are not high. Drivers tend to roam onto the wrong side of the road with alarming frequency, veering to the left only when absolutely essential. Tourists unfamiliar with driving on the left sometimes forget which country they are in and create added confusion. There is a drink-drive limit, so the best advice is simply to not drink and drive.

The absence of pavements and the narrowness of roads mean that pedestrians are often added obstacles, particularly at weekends and public holidays when the drink has flowed a little too freely. The rush hour around Victoria should be avoided if possible (either side of 8am

and 4pm). None of this should deter you from taking to the road, however – certainly the best way to explore both Mahé and Praslin.

Roads on Mahé are very good. Praslin roads are good between Grand Anse, Baie Ste Anne and Anse Volbert, but deteriorate en route to Anse La Blague and Anse Lazio.

Speed limits are 40kmh (25mph) in towns and villages and 65kmh (40 mph) elsewhere, except for Mahé's east coast road, where the limit is 80kmh (50 mph).

Car hire

Cars may be hired only on Mahé and Praslin; several car hire companies are represented at Seychelles International Airport and at the larger hotels. You can arrange to hire a car before you leave home through your tour operator. A national or international licence is required. Vehicle standards are variable and it is useful to inspect prior to making a commitment. Vehicles can be delivered or re-delivered to any point, mutually agreed with the hire company. Jeeps and saloon cars are widely available from most car hire firms.

Service stations

Victoria Service Station, Mahé: daily 5.30am–11pm
Airport Service Station, Mahé: daily 6am–9pm
Anse Royale Filling Station, Mahé: daily 7am–7pm
Baie Lazare Petrol Station, Mahé: Mon–Sat 7am–7pm
Beau Vallon Service Station, Mahé: daily 6am–9pm
Baie Ste Anne Filling Station, Praslin: daily 7am–6pm
Grand Anse Service Station, Praslin: Mon–Sat 7.30am–6pm, Sun and public holidays 7.30am–noon

Parking

Parking is free in Seychelles except in the centre of Victoria. Even here, there is a free car park on Francis Rachel Street next to the sports stadium, convenient for most requirements. To park on other Victoria streets and car parks requires advance purchase of parking coupons, available through many retail outlets. Traffic police have little to do in Victoria and failure to observe the rules where payment is required will almost invariably lead to a fine. The tourist board's excellent tips for tourist drivers are never leave valuables, such as passports, unattended in the car and never park directly beneath a coconut palm (you'll be paying for the damage if a coconut falls and makes a dent!).

Passenger airplane at Mahé's airport.

MAURITIUS

RÉUNION

SEYCHELLES

EATING OUT

RECOMMENDED RESTAURANTS, CAFES AND BARS

WHERE TO EAT

Seychelles is famous for its nature and scenery rather than its cuisine. Common complaints are that restaurants are too expensive and service slow, but if you know where to look it's possible to try delicious Creole cuisine, such as octopus curry or blackened fish, for a reasonable price. There are no beach stalls as in so many other countries, fewer restaurants and if fast food is what you are looking for then you've picked the wrong place. There is no McDonald's – indeed nothing whatsoever very fast in Seychelles, though there are a few takeaways.

Hotels offer a wide choice of meals to keep their clients from straying, often including a barbecue or a Seychellois buffet on certain evenings. However, to sample the finest local cuisine, a new twist on international flavours, and to enjoy informal local surroundings, a trip to a restaurant outside your hotel is an excellent alternative.

Dress is very casual and the atmosphere generally very relaxed. Booking is unnecessary for lunch (which tends to run from noon to 2 or 3pm) but advisable for evenings, indeed essential at some restaurants.

Most will open around 6.30pm and by 10.30pm the shutters are beginning to come down. Seychelles isn't a late-night dining spot, although in Victoria you'll find that some of the bars, pizzerias and cafés stay open a little later. It can be a struggle to find places open on a Sunday (outside hotels and resorts), though Sam's Pizzeria in Victoria is a notable exception.

Fish dishes dominate, though meat dishes, mainly chicken and beef, are almost always available. Authentic Seychelles curries are hot, but restaurants will offer chilli sauce on a separate dish to allow the customer to control the temperature.

MAHÉ

Anse Boileau

Chez Plume
Tel: 355050
Excellent seafood restaurant. Good desserts, unlike many restaurants, including a superb passion fruit soufflé. €€€

Anse à la Mouche

Anchor Café and Islander Restaurant
Tel: 371289
The nearest thing in South Mahé to a fast-food outlet, this is an informal restaurant, opposite the beach, offering both snacks and more substantial meals like catch of the day, blackened fish and chicken curry. Good place to catch sunset with a beer. Open 11am–9pm, closed Sunday and public holidays. €€

Anse Royale

Le Jardin du Roi
Tel: 371313
Set among spice plants, fruit and ornamental trees, this restaurant is well worth a visit in its own right. The food is excellent, and reasonably priced. Save room for the amazing ice creams: flavours include cinnamon and lemon grass. Curry buffet on Sunday. Advance booking advisable, open lunchtime only. €€

Kaz Kreol
Tel: 371680
A wide variety of inexpensive dishes, such as pasta, curries, salads and fish and chips, in a casual setting by the beach. Chinese cuisine and pizzas are also available. Live music on Saturday night and Sunday lunchtime. Free Wi-fi. Open Tue–Sun, lunch and dinner. €€

Anse Soleil

Anse Soleil Cafeteria
Tel: 361700
This picturesque feet-in-the-sand restaurant is located directly on one of the best beaches of Mahé. Unless you're staying in the area, you will need a hire car to get here but it makes a great stop on an island tour. Creole cuisine, such as octopus salad (or bat curry if you're feeling adventurous). No reservations accepted, it's first come first served, so arrive early as this place is popular – especially at weekends. Open daily noon–9pm. €

Baic Lazare

Maria's Rock
Tel: 361812
Fun, popular café built on granite boulders in a jungle setting. Close to the very up-market Kempinski and Four Seasons resorts, but couldn't be more different. Meat and seafood are served with a sizzling skillet so you can cook your own lunch or dinner accompanied by a variety of sauces, rice and salad; crêpes are available too. There's a sculpture studio next door and kids will like the pirate caves at the back.

Barbarons

Veranda Café
Opposite Le Meridien Hotel
Tel: 594987
Tables line a wood veranda, which wraps around a charming colonial-style building. High standard of Creole food, such as smoked fish salad, beautifully presented and served with a smile. Close to a road, but backed by jungle and definitely one of the better Seychelles dining experiences. Open Thu–Tue 11am–6pm. €€€

Beau Vallon

Baobab Pizzeria
Tel: 247167
At the northern end of the bay, this beach-side pizzeria, with its low prices, stone benches and sandy floor, is a Seychelles institution. As well as dishing up pizzas, it serves pasta and fish and chips. Service can be slow, it's difficult to get a table after 7pm and weekends can get crowded too. Open lunchtime and evening. €
The Boat House
Tel: 247898

Beachfront dining in Praslin.

Excellent evening Creole buffet, which commences at 7.30pm, with around 20 dishes served in informal surroundings. Very popular and booking is essential. €€
Coco d'Or
Tel: 247331
Nor sure what you fancy, maybe Chinese, a pizza or something more substantial? Coco d'Or has three excellent restaurants: Uncle Wills Pizzeria, The Wok Chinese and La Palma Restaurant offering Creole and international cuisine. Just a short stroll inland from Beau Vallon beach. €€
Mahek Restaurant
Tel: 621000
Set within Coral Strand Hotel, this is a popular Indian restaurant. All dishes can be prepared mild, medium or hot. €€
La Perle Noire
Tel: 620220
A stone's throw from Coral Strand Hotel, an excellent restaurant serving Italian, international and Creole dishes. Evenings only. €€€

Bel Ombre

La Scala
Tel: 247535
This family-run restaurant is a popular choice among the local business community, so it is essential to book. Specialises in seafood and Italian, international and Creole dishes at moderate prices. Evenings only, closed Sunday and the entire month of June. €€€

Pointe au Sel

Port Glaud
Del Place
Port Launay Road

Tel: 814111
On the water's edge overlooking a wide bay and tiny island, the location is stunning. The Creole and Italian food are good too. Open daily 11am–10pm. €€€

St Louis

Marie Antoinette Restaurant
Tel: 266222
This restaurant at the foot of Signal Hill is the best place to go for a Creole feast in the perfect setting of an old planter's house. The food is consistently good, though the two-course set menu never varies. The first course alone involves five dishes: tuna steak, parrotfish in batter, grilled bourgeois, fish stew, and chicken curry with salad and rice. Dessert consists of fruit salad and ice cream followed by coffee. Surprisingly good wine menu. €€

Takamaka

Chez Batista
Tel: 366300
A charismatic rustic restaurant next to beautiful Takamaka beach, offering barbecue and seafood specialities, like grilled lobster. €€€

Victoria

The Butcher's Grill
Unity House Complex, Palm Street
Tel: 781203
Seychelles' cheap-and-cheerful answer to MacDonald's, only a whole lot tastier. Fast food, to eat in or out, includes rice, noodles and curries as well as chicken and pork kebabs, burgers, pizzas and fries. Very popular with locals, it's useful if you're on a budget or just need a quick fix. €
Le Café de L'Horloge
Francis Rachel Street
Tel: 323556
On the first floor of Victoria House, overlooking the clock tower, this café offers a good mix of Creole and European fare and is the place for something more substantial than the light dishes offered elsewhere in town. Very popular at lunchtime with the local business community but quieter in the evening. €€€
Doubleclick Café
Maison La Rosiere

MAURITIUS

RÉUNION

SEYCHELLES

PRICE CATEGORIES
Price categories are for two people, including soft drinks or beer:
€ = less than €50
€€ = €50–75
€€€ = €75–100
€€€€ = more than €100

Tel: 610590
Near the main bus station in Victoria (and one of the few town locations with free parking), this is a great place for a coffee and sandwich to top up your energy levels or to use the internet. €
Fishtail Restaurant
Inter-Island Quay
Tel: 322214
The best place to sit, relax and enjoy a light meal, snack or just a drink while waiting for a ferry or yacht at the Victoria quayside. €

News Café
Trinity House
Tel: 322999
On the first floor of one of the main office buildings of Victoria, this is another good place to grab an inexpensive bite and an excellent cappuccino. €
Pirates Arms
Independence Avenue
Tel: 225001
Close to the clock tower, this is a popular meeting place to gossip and

watch the world go by. Meals are fairly simple but good and there are usually one or two special dishes of the day on offer. €€
Sam's Pizzeria
Maison Suleman,
Francis Rachel Street
Tel: 322499
A very good medium-priced restaurant with a relaxed atmosphere and a varied menu (fish dishes as well as pizzas). On the first floor overlooking the busy main street. €€

PRASLIN

Anse Lazio
Bonbon Plume
Tel: 232136
Cuisine with a strong French influence mixed with local flavours, mainly fish and seafood, served at wooden tables shaded by palm-thatched umbrellas. Bonbon Plume is located next to this exceptionally beautiful beach. €€€€
Le Chevalier Bay
Tel: 232322
Breakfast, lunch and dinner comprised of Creole cuisine and curries as well as snacks, sandwiches, salads, chips, and a

few other choices besides. Pricey for fairly basic food, but in a pretty garden setting and open daily. €€

Côte d'Or
La Goulue Café
Tel: 232223
A rustic, relaxed outdoor setting near the beach serving good-quality, mainly local dishes (the octopus curry is very good) and snacks. Open noon–9.30pm. €€
Les Lauriers Restaurant
Tel: 232241
The best restaurant on Praslin for a

Creole barbecue with fish and meat specialities, a buffet of local salads, a variety of curries and local desserts to top it off. €€

Grand Anse
Britannia Restaurant
Tel: 233215
If a walk to see black parrots sounds too much like hard work, relax at a table in the garden of this restaurant, attached to the Britannia Hotel. Order a drink and a meal and with luck the birds will come to you. Good value Creole cuisine. €€

LA DIGUE

Anse la Réunion
Château St Cloud
Tel: 234346
Creole cuisine in a quiet setting at a former colonial plantation house, from the days when vanilla was the mainstay of the local economy. €€

Fresh grilled fish on La Digue.

Zerof Restaurant and Takeaway
Tel: 234439
Situated opposite the Vev Nature Reserve, serves a wide range of excellent Creole dishes with takeaways also available. Closes at 9.30pm. €€

La Passe
Tarosa Restaurant
Tel: 234407
Located at La Passe jetty, Tarosa has seven separate dining areas, each one with an ocean view that takes in the comings and goings at La Digue's only harbour. Creole specialities are on the menu. Open for breakfast, lunch and dinner. €€
Villa Authentique
Tel: 234413
Excellent Creole cuisine at an old plantation-style house, right opposite the beach. €€

PRICE CATEGORIES

Price categories are for two people, including soft drinks or beer:
€ = less than €50
€€ = €50–75
€€€ = €75–100
€€€€ = more than €100

ACTIVITIES

NIGHTLIFE, OUTDOOR ACTIVITIES AND SHOPPING

NIGHTLIFE

Seychelles isn't somewhere that you'd visit for nightlife. However, if you do want to let down your hair after sunset there are a few places to do so. Mahé, as you'd expect, is where most of the action takes place.

Katiolo Club: Anse Faure, Mount Fleuri Road, south of the airport; tel: 375453. Small club with open-air dancing, popular with locals, open until late and doesn't get going until after midnight.

Rogans Irish Bar: Level 3 Bar Docklands, Latanier Road, Mahé; tel: 516464. Friendly, buzzy bar, popular on a Friday night. International sporting events, such as Six Nations rugby, are screened here, and there's also Friday karaoke, one-off DJ nights until 4am, the only draught Guinness in Seychelles and steak and kidney pies served too.

Sound Garden Bar: Baie Lazare, Mahé; tel: 773919. Not a club, but a small, laid-back bar with music (sometimes live), a video screen, sit-up bar and garden with ambient lighting to sip Seybrews in.

Berjaya Casino: Berjaya Resort & Casino, Beau Vallon; tel 287287. Open daily noon–2.30am.

Casino Paradiso: Kempinski Seychelles Resort, Baie Lazare, Mahé; tel 386666. Open daily 8pm–4am.

OUTDOOR ACTIVITIES

Birdwatching

Birdwatchers are drawn to Seychelles for three reasons: the rarity value of the endemic land birds, the spectacular sea bird colonies, such

as on Bird Island and Aride, and the chance of seeing unusual migrants. The land birds are, of course, present year-round, as indeed are many species of sea bird. However, the huge tern colonies are at their best from May to September. October to December is the best time for migrants from Europe and Asia, when many unusual vagrants have been recorded, including some not known anywhere else in the western Indian Ocean or Madagascar regions.

Top sites on the itinerary of any visiting birdwatcher should include the nature reserve islands of **Cousin** and **Aride**. On **Mahé**, the mudflats adjacent to the Seychelles Breweries is the best site for migrant waders such as **crab plover**, a northwest Indian Ocean speciality. The Plantation Club marsh on Mahé, and the pools of Lemuria Golf Course on Praslin and the wetlands of La Passe on La Digue are the best places to see **yellow bittern**, found nowhere else in the region.

On **Praslin**, **black parrots** may be seen early morning or late afternoon around the entrance to **Vallée de Mai** and in lowland fruit trees such as those around Villa Flamboyant. Birdwatching tours can be booked through local tour companies (see page 402). Several travel companies worldwide organise package birdwatching holidays in Seychelles, such as **Ornitholidays** and **Naturetrek**.

Fishing

Fishing is a way of life in Seychelles (see page 268). Day charters for big game fishing may be organised from Mahé, Praslin, La Digue and on all the islands with single resorts. Customised safaris for up to six

people lasting three or more days may be booked with some companies.

Many power boats and yachts are available for charter by the day or longer. Reservations may be made at local travel agents, through hotels or direct with boat owners. Or through The Marine Charter Association (tel: 322126).

Operators include:
Angelfish Ltd: Roche Caiman, Mahé; tel 729021; www.angelfish-bayside.com
Bedier Son, Côte d'Or, Praslin; tel: 232192/513840
Indigo Excursions & Boat Charters, Grand Anse, Praslin; tel 515676; www.indigoseychelles.com
Le Superbe Hirecraft, Victoria; tel: 322288/764029
R. Savy Charters, Anse aux Pins; tel: 376476/576797; email: rsavycharter@seychelles.sc
Water World (Pty) Ltd, Eden Island Marina, Mahé; tel: 514735; http://waterworld.sc
Zico 1 Boat Charter, Anse Reunion, La Digue; tel: 515557/344615; www.excursionsladigue.com

Fly-fishing is superb, especially at St François and St Joseph Atolls from mid-Sept to mid-May. Fly-fishing charters to the more remote atolls of Farquhar, Astove and Cosmoledo can also be arranged on the calmer seas of Oct–Apr. Operators include:
Silhouette Cruises Ltd, Victoria; tel: 324026; www.seychelles-cruises.com

An event in which visitors may participate is the **National Fishing Tournament** hosted by the Rotary Club of Victoria and held every April. Cash prizes are up for grabs in each category.

Diving and snorkelling

The marine world is easily accessible in Seychelles with many APDS diving centres offering snorkelling (see page 357) and scuba diving facilities. If you are healthy and can swim, learning to snorkel or dive is easy and most of the larger resorts have dive centres offering introductory and certification courses.

Seychelles is one of the best places in the world to learn to dive and has several excellent dive centres. If you are not sure diving is for you, a one-day course is the best way to test the waters. These are offered by several excellent PADI (Professional Association of Diving Instructors) dive centres. You begin at 9am with a session in the hotel swimming pool to familiarise yourself with the equipment and learn basic techniques.

After lunch, you take a sea dive on a shallow reef accompanied at all times by an instructor. No certificate is issued, but if you decide to progress, this one-day experience counts as the first step towards obtaining further knowledge and skill on a second day. Successful completion of this stage leads to the PADI Scuba Diver Certificate, which allows you to dive to a limited depth under basic supervision. Two additional days completes your basic diving skills to give you a PADI Open Water Diver Licence (see page 263). **Angelfish Dive Operations:** Roche Caiman, Mahé; tel 729021; www.dive-angelfish.com. Offers daily morning and afternoon excursions to the best dive sites around Mahé plus two tank and night dives. Also organises day trips for diving cruises around Praslin plus a comprehensive list of PADI courses up to Divemaster level. **Underwater Centre Seychelles:** PO Box 384, Victoria; tel: 345445 (office), 247165 (shop), 542877 (mobile); www.diveseychelles.com. sc. Has been in operation for more than 30 years and offers a range of diving experiences to suit all abilities. Works closely with the Seychelles whale shark monitoring project,

Mahé's marine parks

To explore the sea at **Port Launay Marine National Park**, Jamilah Big Game and Bottom Fishing have an outlet near Port Glaud offering snorkelling at **Baie Ternay** (also a Marine National Park) and excursions to the Inner Islands, while West Rand Holdings, a diving and water sports centre a little further on, hires out jet skis and charter boats for trips. Jet skis are only allowed up to the marine park's boundary.

allowing tourists the opportunity to swim alongside them and assist in conservation. Operates out of the Berjaya Beau Vallon Bay Resort on Praslin, from a five-star PADI centre offering courses, from intro dives to night and wreck dives and advanced.

Live-aboard diving packages, including to the more remote outer islands, can be arranged through **Indian Ocean Explorer** and **Silhouette Cruises Ltd** (see page 397).

Windows on the reef

To see the wonders of the coral reef without getting wet there are two options. The first is a **glass-bottom boat** which permits a vertical view of the reef from an open-sided flat-bottomed boat fitted with Perspex panels along the central floor. Wooden benches run along each side of the vessel facing these viewing panels. The second option is a **subsea viewer**, a semi-submersible vessel from which a horizontal view of the reef may be obtained. Glass-bottom boats can enter extremely shallow water, though the passage of the vessel overhead scares away many fish, particularly the larger ones. Subsea viewers create less disturbance but cannot cross very shallow patches where reef life may proliferate. Some visitors find the subsea viewer claustrophobic.

Trips from Mahé to **Ste Anne Marine National Park** can be arranged through a local tour operator (see page 402), either for half a day or for a full day with lunch at one of the islands: Moyenne, Round or Cerf. The National Park is the headquarters of the Marine Parks Authority. The park is still in recovery from the combined effects of El Niño in 1998, which killed more than 90 percent of corals, and the extensive land reclamation along Mahé's east coast that produced some siltation resulting in reef damage, but it's still a fantastic experience with a chance to see turtles as well as a kaleidoscope of tropical fish. **Teddy's Glass Bottom Boat:** Coral Strand Hotel, Beau Vallon, Mahé; tel: 291000. Can also be booked through most tour operators.

Live-aboard cruising

It can reasonably be claimed that the best way to explore an island nation is by sea. A cruise on a live-aboard vessel is an ideal way to see a number of islands without having to move from hotel to hotel. It is also an excellent way to reach the more secluded bays and islands.

Scuba safety

The Association of Professional Divers, Seychelles (APDS) has set guidelines for the safe and professional operation of diving centres. Many of its members are rated by the Professional Association of Diving Instructors (PADI) as five-star dive centres or resorts. All boats used for diving activities are properly licensed by the local authorities and, in addition to normal safety equipment, carry oxygen and additional emergency equipment. There is a two-man, twin-lock recompression chamber at Victoria Hospital with a team of hyperbaric doctors and technicians available in the unlikely event of a diving accident.

There are various options available depending on whether you wish to enjoy sailing, fishing, diving, water sports or simply get from A to B in the fastest possible time.

Most cruises begin from the Inter-Island Quay at Victoria. Many of the charter boats are moored next to the quay. Nearby, the **Seychelles Marine Charter Association** (tel: 224679) is also a useful source of information on the availability of the smaller boats. Most vessels are licensed to operate solely within the Inner Islands, except for cruise ships and some specialist charter boats (especially dive boats). Moorings are available at Marine National Parks, where a small fee is charged for entry. Some island nature reserves also charge a small fee for landing. Apart from the smaller, difficult to reach islands, secluded bays around the main islands are well worth exploring.

When to cruise

The southeast monsoon blows from May to October bringing steady winds. Wind strength is particularly high in July and August with rough seas. Unless you have a strong stomach this is not the best time to sail far afield, though a cruise around the mainly sheltered waters of Praslin and its satellite islands can be very pleasant. The northwest monsoon from November to April brings less consistent winds, which can be squally around mid-December to the end of January. Fortunately, however, Seychelles lies outside the cyclone belt.

Activities on board

Diving facilities are offered by larger vessels (those of over 10 berths).

This may be either the main activity, with perhaps three or four dives per day on offer, or an optional choice when opportunities arise within a set itinerary. Skippers of these vessels are usually qualified divemasters. Most vessels will at least offer snorkelling equipment, comprising mask, snorkel and fins.

Some of the larger vessels will also carry a range of water sports equipment including windsurf boards and water-skis. Almost all will carry fishing tackle. Trailing a line in the water on sea passages is an excellent way to catch pelagic fish such as bonito or dorado. At anchor, bottom fishing may also be offered, with opportunities to catch fresh fish for supper.

Cruising is, of course, an activity in itself and one of the most important pieces of equipment on board is the ship's tender. This will be the only way to land on most beaches as only the largest populated islands have quays.

Chartering

At the smaller end of the scale, there are a range of monohulls and catamarans available for **bareboat charter**. Professional skippers who know the islands well may also be employed. Alternatively, a **set cruise** may be taken aboard a romantic twin-masted schooner or dedicated dive boat. Small, fast **motor-cruisers** are available for those who want to get to their destinations fast. All these options are offered by locally based operators, but during the northern winter cruise ships will also call at the islands.

You can organise yachting holidays around the islands with one week on board and another week in a hotel at home with companies such as:
Dream Yacht Charter: tel: 02380 455527; www.dreamyachtcharter.com
Seychelles Travel: tel: 01202 877330; www.seychelles-travel.co.uk
Sunsail Ltd: tel 888 3503568; www.sunsail.com
Yacht Connections: tel: 01590 626291; www.yacht-connections.co.uk

Charter companies in Seychelles
Angel Fish Yacht Charter: Roche Caiman, Mahé; tel: 345001; www.angelfish-bayside.com. Offers skippered yacht charters in the granitic islands. Beach barbecues and three-course lunches can be prepared for you on request.
Moorings: Wharf Hotel Marina, Mahé; tel: 601060; www.moorings.com. Offers crewed and bareboat yacht charters in the granitic islands.
Silhouette Cruises Ltd: tel: 324026; www.seychelles.net/cruises. Operates

four twin-masted schooners and one motor yacht, each with accommodation for 15 to 18 passengers. The schooners are the most beautiful ships in Seychelles. Cruises are for five to six days around the granitic islands and one week or more in the Outer Islands, including Aldabra and Cosmoledo. Guests may participate in sailing, though vessels carry a full crew. Other activities include diving, fishing and water sports and there are several themed weeks throughout the year, such as a seakayaking cruise, diving safari and eco natural history cruise.
Sunsail (Seychelles) Ltd: Eden Marina, Mahé; tel: 601330; www.sunsail.com. A company with over 1,000 vessels worldwide in many holiday centres that you can book from home. The Seychelles fleet comprises monohulls, with up to nine berths, eight catamarans and one 'super-luxury' Platinum-class catamaran with full crew. Other boats are available for bareboat charter, clients providing their own food and drink, or with qualified skippers. Period or day charters may be arranged. The company offers a provisioning service if required. Advice on anchorages and other essential information is available.
VPM Yacht Charter: Roche Caiman, Mahé; tel: 344719; www.vpm-boats.com. Another multinational company with a Seychelles base, VPM operates a fleet of vessels, mainly catamarans. Some are available for bareboat charter and some for crewed charter. Crewed charters are skippered by professional sailors who know Seychelles waters well. A provisioning service is offered for bareboat charters.
Water World (Pty) Ltd: Eden Marina, Mahé; tel: 514735; http://waterworld. sc. The ultra-modern high speed option. The motor-cruiser *Shamal* cruises at 24 knots with a top speed of 31 knots. It can accommodate up to 10 passengers for a day trip or 6 for overnight charters. Smaller vessels are also available for day charters.

Underwater Photography Festival

There are few events in Seychelles that you would want to plan your holiday dates around. One exception, if you are a diver, might be **SUBIOS**, Seychelles' Festival Of The Sea, a three-week celebration of underwater images and videos held each March or October/November (the date varies each year), which are also the best months for diving due to the calm seas prevailing between the two monsoon winds. Entertainment, centred around the main hotels of Mahé and Praslin, includes slide shows hosted by professional underwater photographers, films and photography contests. Further details can be obtained from: SUBIOS Organising Committee, Seychelles Tourism Board, tel: 671300; www.seychelles.travel/subios.

Scenic flights

The majesty of the mountains, the variety of colours of the sea, secret beaches, coves and dramatic cliffs can only be fully appreciated from the air. **ZilAir** (tel: 375100) is the main provider of scenic heli flights in the region. It operates three high-tech machines, which fly out of ZilAir's base next to the International Airport runway. There are lots of packages to choose from, from a 15-minute Scenic Mahé Experience through to a 75-minute Island Hopping excursion, taking in Mahé, Praslin, La Digue and Félicité. There are also Romantic Sunset flights, Discover Cousine and Mystical Grand Barbe itineraries.

Walking

The Ministry of Tourism has produced a series of booklets for nature walks on **Mahé, Praslin** and **La Digue**. These are not widely available, but may be purchased from the Tourist Office at Independence House, Victoria (see page 402). All walks are well signposted, but a booklet will add to your appreciation of what you are seeing along the way.

Many are mountain walks, for which the best times are the cooler months of June to September. The worst time is the height of the rains, mid-December to January, when paths are muddy and slippery. March and April can also be very tiring, being hot and sticky with little or no cooling breeze. The cooler times of early morning or late afternoon are best for walking, but remember it gets dark quickly around 6.30pm. You should always take water and never drink from mountain streams on any of the islands, which may look crystal clear, but can harbour very unpleasant, harmful microscopic parasites. A hat is recommended for walks other than those through shaded forest.

It is not recommended to stray from mountain paths without a guide, and

MAURITIUS

RÉUNION

SEYCHELLES

to experience a proper visit of the **mist forest** a guide is essential. The best guided mountain trails are offered by **Basil Beaudouin** (tel: 241790), who leads walks of varying difficulty, from one to two hours, to a full day. Your resort will be able to arrange a tour, or call him directly and he will pick you up. His wealth of knowledge of the islands, their flora and fauna is unrivalled and he is fully qualified in first aid too. On Praslin, **Bois Mare Nature Guide**, Cap Samy (tel: 513370) offers a variety of walks. **Coco de Mer Hotel & Black Parrot Suites** (tel: 290555) offers two-hour guided walks of the nearby Jean Baptiste Nature Trail.

Golf

The **Seychelles Golf Club** (club house tel: 376234), just south of the airport, has a nine-hole golf course, the only one on Mahé. Any golfer with a handicap wishing to enjoy a round is welcome. Competitions are held on Thursday and Saturday. It is generally not necessary to book except for Saturday, when you should put your name down by 6pm Thursday.

It is a lovely little course in an old coconut plantation, kinder to golfers who slice than those who hook the ball, the latter often ending up in the swamp. The best time to play is early, from around 8.30am or after 3.30pm. **Praslin** is the only other island with a golf course, which is a championship 18-hole course (tel: 281281). It's at the five-star **Constance Lemuria**, a luxury resort (tel: 281281), and is open to non-residents. The par-70 course is a challenging one, particularly from the 13th hole onward, where it departs from the flat coastal plateau to climb the adjacent steep slopes.

SHOPPING

The craft industry of Seychelles has shallow roots, having grown up to meet the demands of the tourist industry. This is not to say there are no items unique to Seychelles, for innovation has flourished. However, there are few traditional products on sale.

What to buy

Art There are many art studios well worth visiting, most of which are mentioned in the Mahé, Praslin and La Digue chapters, including Michael Adams, Tom Bowers, George Camille, Gerard Devoud and Barbara Jenson (see page 255). The Craft Village (*Le Village Artisanal*), at Anse aux Pins on

the east coast of Mahé, is also a good place to see the work of local artists. **Batik** Ron Gerlach uses Indonesian technique to produce beach robes, shirts and pareos in a range of attractive colours to his own, unique designs. His work reflects his love of nature (he is also chairman of the Nature Protection Trust of Seychelles). **Coco de mer** The world's largest seed, which could weigh as much as your baggage allowance when taken fresh from the tree, makes a novel souvenir when hollowed out. You can buy them at the Rangers Station, Fond B'Offay, Praslin (Mon–Fri 8am–4pm). They are also available from souvenir shops but be sure the vendor gives you an export certificate or you risk confiscation by customs officers at the airport.
Coconut crafts The coconut palm is the artisan's most versatile resource: its leaves are woven into bags and baskets; the nut itself is made into napkin rings, candle holders and trinket pots; coconut oil is used to perfume soaps and bath oils. In the Craft Village, by the entrance to the old St Roch plantation house, is Maison Coco, a shop dedicated to the products of the coconut palm, housed in a building made out of palm tree products itself.
Jewellery Beautiful jewellery, combining gold with mother-of-pearl, sea shells and other local items, is made by Kreolor (tel: 344551; www. kreolorseychelles.com), which has shops at Seychelles International Airport departures lounge, Camion Hall and Kenwyn House, Victoria; Grande Anse in Praslin; and La Passe, La Digue. The sea shells used in the jewellery were acquired following the bankruptcy of a local button factory so there is no impact on the reefs, and there are enough to last another hundred years.
Pearls Praslin Ocean Farm Ltd (tel: 233150; www.blackpearlseychelles. com) culture pearls from the local black tipped pearl oyster. They produce silvery blue, green, gold and black coloured pearls which are set in jewellery and also baby clams plated with silver and gold. Their shop, Black Pearls of Seychelles, is opposite Praslin airstrip and is worth visiting not only to see the jewellery, but also their aquarium. You can have a guided tour for a small fee.
Perfume More than 100 local plants are used to produce three perfumes for Kreol Fleurage Parfums of North East Point, Mahé (tel: 241329; www.kreolfleurage.com). On sale at many hotel and souvenir shops – and Harrods in London.

Kreol Festival

The biggest cultural event of the year is the **Kreol Festival**, held in the last week of October. Creole artists from other countries of a similar culture, such as Mauritius and the Caribbean, gather in Victoria, which is decorated for the occasion. Dances, plays, concerts and processions are organised during the week, and everyone is encouraged to join in. For more details contact: **Kreol Festival Committee**, Ministry of Education, Mont Fleuri, Mahé; tel: 321333; email: festivalkreol@seychelles.net; http://festival-kreol.sc.

Souvenirs and gifts One of the best places for souvenir shopping is the Codevar Craft Centre (see page 283) at Camion Hall in Albert Street, Victoria. Also in Victoria, artist George Camille's Sunstroke Gallery on Market Street sells a range of beachwear, jewellery, printed tablecloths and cushions, while upstairs there is an art gallery featuring several excellent local artists. Outside the capital, the Craft Village is the other main centre on Mahé for gifts and souvenirs. If you happen to be visiting Michael Adams' Studio at Anse aux Poules Bleus, Pineapple Studio next door sell their own original souvenirs, including beautifully hand-dyed pareos in individually woven hessian bags, painted sculptures and wall plaques of fish, beachwear, key rings, letter racks and painted coconuts. (The shop is open weekdays until 4.30pm, but the owners live next door and will open up any time within reason.)
Stained glass Les and Sharon Masterson produce beautiful jewel-like hangings, lamps, panels and windows at their studio Thoughts, on the Sans Souci Road near Victoria (tel: 321254). Some of their work is also on display at Fisherman's Cove Hotel, Mahé. Sharon's stained-glass windows decorate St Paul's Cathedral, Victoria, the Apostolic Church, Victoria, and a wall at the Benedetti Gallery, Soho, New York.
Tea and spices Packets of spices may be purchased at many places, including Victoria's market and Jardin du Roi, Mahé. Pickled hot chillies and dried vanilla pods, also available at the market, make novel, genuinely local souvenirs to take home. Seychelles Tea Company sells packs of tea with cinnamon, lemon, orange and vanilla flavours, on sale in most supermarkets.

MAURITIUS

A – Z

A HANDY SUMMARY
OF PRACTICAL INFORMATION

A

Accommodation

Seychelles is an exclusive destination, so prices are usually high and you get a better deal with a package. Private island resorts, such as Frégate, Desroches, Denis and North islands, are very luxurious and tend to attract the rich and famous along with a regular flow of honeymooners. In recent years up-market hotel chains have been attracted to the archipelago, such as Raffles, which has opened on Praslin, and the Four Seasons and Maia resorts on Mahé. However, there are still plenty of independent guesthouses, small hotels and self-catering apartments for those who want to experience local culture on a budget – for a full list go to the Seychelles Tourism Board website, www.seychelles.travel. No camping is permitted in the Seychelles and you'll need proof of accommodation before flying to any of the smaller islands.

Admission charges

Admission charges are in place for practically every tourist attraction here, including islands, nature reserves, botanical gardens and museums. Fees are higher than in many other destinations. Currently there is a discount system for visitors to multiple sites.

B

Budgeting for your trip

Seychelles is an expensive destination and apart from a few items of local produce, prices are higher than for similar products in most countries. Hotels generally charge high mark-ups on everything and offer exchange rates inferior to those of banks.

While travelling around the main islands, you can get a snack or drink at a fraction of hotel or restaurant prices by using local shops. Away from hotels and tourist areas there are some very good restaurants that cater for the local market and charge reasonable prices (see Eating Out).

C

Children

Seychellois love children and Seychelles is a very safe place for a family holiday. There is no problem taking well behaved children into any restaurant in Seychelles. However, parents should note that there are few amusements for children away from the beach. The larger hotels offer a babysitting service, though it is usually necessary to give a little notice.

Climate

There are no seasons equivalent to winter, spring or autumn. The climate is tropical: hot and humid year round with temperatures in the region of 24°–30°C (75°–86°F), fluctuating very little from one month to the next or during the day. Rainfall is high, with heavy showers possible at any time of year, particularly during the northwest monsoon from November to April, reaching a peak from mid-December to the end of

January. Humidity is at its highest from March to April.

Rainfall and humidity are lowest during the southeast monsoon from May to October. This season brings stronger, more consistent winds producing heavy swells at sea particularly at its peak from July to September. Unpleasant for those without a strong stomach at sea, but the cooling breeze and lower rainfall make this the best time for walking.

Rainfall on coral islands is much lower than on the granitic islands due to the influence of relief. In the southern islands, there is a marked seasonal drought (September to October rainfall on Aldabra averages just 17mm/0.75 ins, compared to 300 mm/12 ins on Mahé).

The islands lie outside the cyclone belt that brings turbulent conditions to the south from January to March. However, strong winds and heavy rain around this time often indicate a cyclone further south and, very occasionally, one may reach the southernmost islands of Seychelles.

RÉUNION

CLIMATE CHART

Victoria

°C	J	F	M	A	M	J	J	A	S	O	N	D	mm
35													420
30													360
25													300
20													240
15													180
10													120
5													60
0													0

■ Maximum temperature
□ Minimum temperature
— Rainfall

SEYCHELLES

When to visit

For birdwatching: April – start of the breeding season; May to September – sooty terns nest on Bird Island; October – migration begins.
For diving: March to May, September to November – best sea conditions, clear and calm, although diving is good all year.
For fishing: October to April, when the gentle northwest trades blow. But for those with good sea legs, fish are plentiful all year round.
For hiking: May to September – drier and less humid.
For sailing: all year round.
For surfing/windsurfing: June to September – when the strong southeast trade winds blow.

Crime and safety

Seychelles is very safe, though crime is not unknown. Some visitors are lulled into a false sense of security by the friendliness of the locals. They make the mistake of leaving their valuables unguarded on the beach while taking a swim, with inevitable consequences. Take the same precautions that you would at home to prevent your holiday being spoiled.

Customs regulations

The duty free allowance is 200 cigarettes (or 250g of tobacco), 2 litres of spirits and wine and 200ml of perfume. In addition, every visitor can import tax-free a video camera, camera, musical instrument, electronic equipment and sports and leisure equipment. If you import goods that are in excess of the above, import tax has to be paid in cash. Spearfishing guns and weapons are prohibited and plants, medicines and chemicals are forbidden without the necessary import permits.

D

Disabled travellers

Most of the larger hotels are geared to accommodate wheelchairs but away from these there are few special facilities. It is very difficult to get around Victoria by wheelchair due to the narrowness of the busy pavements.

Electricity

240 volts using three square-pin sockets, the same as in the UK.

Emergency numbers

Police, fire, ambulance: tel: 999
Central police station in Victoria: tel: 288000

E

Embassies and consulates

British High Commission, Oliaji Trade Centre, Victoria; tel: 283666; www.gov.uk/government/world/seychelles
French Embassy, La Ciotat, Mont Fleuri; tel: 4382500
US Consulate, Oliaji Trade Centre, Victoria; tel: 225256; http://seychelles.usvpp.gov

Entry requirements

No visas are necessary for visitors from any country, only a valid passport, proof of accommodation and a return air ticket. A (free) Visitors' Permit is issued on arrival. This is the tear-off portion of the arrivals card distributed on international flights prior to landing. It should be retained and presented along with your passport upon departure. Valid for one month, the Visitors' Permit may be extended for up to three months at no charge by completing an application form available from **Immigration Division**, First Floor, Independence House, Victoria; tel: 293636; email: info@immigration.gov. sc. Processing takes about one week. A fee is payable for extensions beyond three months. Always check the latest entry requirements before you travel.

Etiquette

Seychellois do not like to see scantily clad visitors walking around their towns and villages. Dress respectfully in churches and other holy places. Be sensitive about photographing the local people: it's always polite to ask first. Sunbathing topless is acceptable on the beaches.

G

Gay and lesbian travellers

There are no gay bars or other designated gay meeting points in Seychelles, but most Seychellois are open-minded and gay and lesbian travellers are unlikely to encounter prejudices.

H

Health and medical care

Seychelles has a healthy climate. No vaccinations are essential, though some doctors, erring on the side of caution, will recommend typhoid and polio injections. Check the latest health advice before you travel. There is no yellow fever or malaria in Seychelles. The cabins of all flights to Seychelles are sprayed prior to landing to keep such diseases out. If arriving from a country where yellow fever occurs, such as Kenya, you will be required to produce a certificate of vaccination on arrival.

Medical treatment

Essential healthcare services are free of charge to Seychelles residents, while for visitors a small charge is made. There are a large number of local clinics, particularly on Mahé, that visitors may attend, though the waiting time can be frustratingly lengthy. This is particularly true on Monday morning when the start of the working week coincides with a remarkable peak in illnesses. Treatment at clinics is usually basic.

For those who prefer to spend much of the day somewhere other than sitting on a wooden bench in a waiting room, private doctors are very good and not expensive. It is possible to call in to see a private doctor without an appointment, but a phone call may save waiting time.

Be sure to arrange appropriate medical insurance before you travel.

Hospitals
Anse Royale Hospital: Anse Royale, Mahé; tel: 371222
Logan Hospital: La Passe, La Digue; tel: 234255
Praslin Hospital: Baie Ste Anne; tel: 232333
Silhouette Hospital: Silhouette; tel: 224110
Seychelles Hospital: Mont Fleuri, Mahé; tel: 388000

Private treatment
Euromedical Family Clinic: Providence, Mahé; tel 324999; http://euromedical.sc
Dr J.A.M. Albert: Mont Fleuri, Mahé; tel: 323866; Mon–Fri 8am–4pm, Sat 8am–noon, closed Sun.
Oceangate Dental Clinic: Dr Derick Samsoodin, Oceangate House, Victoria; tel: 224852

Pharmacies

Absolue Pharmacie: Bois de Rose Avenue, Victoria; tel: 511203. **Central Point Pharmacy:** Le Chantier Building, Francis Rachel Street, Victoria; tel: 225574

I

Internet

There are many small internet shops on Mahé (mainly in Victoria), Praslin (at Grand Anse and Côte d'Or) and La Digue (at La Passe). All the large hotels and even some smaller premises in the granitic islands will offer Wi-fi for guests (though not always free). In the coral islands, the service may be erratic at best, non-existent at worst, but the situation changes constantly. If you cannot bear to be parted from your email then it is best to check the latest situation with your hotel before arrival.

L

Language

As a rule, English is widely understood in Seychelles. To learn more about Kreol, see the feature Lingua Franca, page 23, and Mauritius Travel Tips, Understanding the Language, page 368.

M

Media

TV and Radio

Radio Seychelles, owned by the government, and 24-hour music and chat Paradise FM, are the only exclusively local radio stations. A BBC relay station on Mahé closed in 2014.

The only English-language terrestrial TV station is Seychelles Broadcasting Corporation (SBC), which shows CNN and BBC news programmes in the mornings. Many hotels offer satellite and cable television and a variety of channels, as well as in-house films.

In the Outer Islands, no local radio or TV broadcasts can be received, but some satellite TV channels are received at hotels.

Publications

The government-owned *Seychelles*

Nation (www.nation.sc) is published daily except Sunday with articles in English, French and Kreol. It has the latest cinema, TV and radio listings. *TODAY in Seychelles* (www.todayinseychelles.com) launched in 2011 and is a daily, independent, colour newspaper; a digital version is available if you want to read before you fly. *Regar* is a political newsletter run by the Seychelles National Party and *Seychelles Weekly*, published on Thursdays, offers an alternative view of life in Seychelles and is mainly in English.

Antigone Trading in Passage des Palmes, Victoria, and at Mahé international airport, usually holds the latest issues of *Time* and *Newsweek*.

Silhouette, the in-flight magazine of Air Seychelles published three times a year, carries excellent features on the islands.

Money

The **Seychelles rupee** comes in notes of SR500, SR100, SR50, SR25 and SR10. Be careful with SR50 and SR10 notes and SR500 and SR100, which are similar in colour and sometimes muddled. Coins come in denominations of SR5, SR1, 25 cents, 10 cents and 5 cents. Prices in shops may be in amounts that do not end in units of 5 cents and unless paying by credit card will be rounded up or down in your change (usually up!).

Credit cards are accepted at hotels, many guesthouses and the larger restaurants. Visa and Mastercard are most commonly accepted. Diners Club and American Express are also accepted at some locations.

For many years, the Seychelles rupee was pegged at an unrealistically high value. This resulted in a flourishing black market for **foreign exchange** and gave Seychelles a reputation as a very expensive destination. In November 2008, the Seychelles rupee was floated and promptly sank to more realistic levels.

Tax

A General Sales Tax (GST) of 15 percent is applied to all hotel and restaurant bills. Trades Tax is also levied on almost all goods and this is non-refundable. Only at the **duty-free shop** in Victoria and at **Seychelles International Airport** are goods exempt of Trades Tax.

O

Opening hours

Offices: Mon–Fri 8am–4pm. **Shops:** Victoria: Mon–Fri 8.30 or 9am–5 or 5.30pm, Sat 8.30am–12.30pm. Some shops close for lunch 12.30–1.30pm. Elsewhere, small shops are likely to remain open much longer hours. Shops generally close on Sundays. **Banks:** Victoria: Mon–Fri 8.30am–2.30pm, Sat 8.30–11am, closed Sun. Praslin: Mon–Fri 8.30am–2pm, Sat 8.30–11.30am, closed Sun. La Digue: Mon–Fri 8.30am–2.30pm, closed Sat–Sun.

P

Postal services

The main post office in Victoria is on Independence Avenue next to the clock tower (Mon–Fri 8.30am–4pm, Sat 8.30am–noon). There are sub-post offices at Grand Anse on Praslin and La Passe on La Digue. Public post boxes are situated outside most police stations. Hotels will sell stamps and post your mail. Airmail collections are made at 3pm Mon–Fri and at noon on Sat.

T

Technology

iShop Seychelles: Huteau Lane, Victoria; tel: 224674; www.ishop.sc. A useful place to know about in case you have any Apple equipment problems, from iPad and laptop repairs through to iPhone charger replacements.

Public holidays

1–2 January New Year's Day
March/April Good Friday, Easter Monday
1 May Labour Day
June (Thursday after Trinity Sunday) Corpus Christi
5 June Liberation Day
18 June National Day
29 June Independence Day
15 August Assumption/La Digue Festival
1 November All Saints' Day
8 December Immaculate Conception
25 December Christmas Day

Telecommunications

International dialling code: To call Seychelles from abroad dial the international access code followed by 248 then the number you want (there are no area codes in Seychelles). To call overseas from Seychelles the international access code is 00.

Tipping

Tipping is not essential, but is always appreciated at 5–10 percent of the bill. Often, a service charge is included in restaurant bills.

Toilets

Other than at the main taxi stand in Victoria, it's hard to find public toilets in Seychelles. However, if travelling around the main islands it is always possible to call in at a hotel and quietly make use of the facilities – except at the most up-market hotels where security guards only allow paying guests through the main gates.

Tourist information offices

For information before you travel visit www.seychelles.travel, the Seychelles Tourism Board's official site. You'll find everything on here from accommodation listings to information about events, operators, climate and how to plan your trip, plus full contact details of Seychelles' 18 tourist offices around the world.

Local tourist offices

The Seychelles Tourism Board has its head office at Espace Building, PO Box 1262, Victoria, Mahé; tel: 671300; www.seychelles.travel; Mon–Fri 8am–4pm, closed Sat–Sun and public holidays). There are also information offices on Mahé, Praslin and La Digue, from which many brochures and leaflets are available.
Mahé: Independence House, Victoria; tel: 610800; email: info@seychelles. travelnet; Mon–Fri 8am–4.30pm, Sat

Time zone

Seychelles is four hours ahead of Greenwich Mean Time and three hours ahead of British Summer Time. The sun shines for approximately 12 hours a day – sunrise is between 6 and 6.30am and sunset between 6 and 6.30pm.

9am–noon
Praslin: Praslin Airport, Amitié and Baie Ste Anne jetty; tel: 233571; email: praslin@seychelles.sc; Mon–Fri 8am–4pm, Sat and public holidays 8am–noon
La Digue: La Passe; tel: 234393; email: stbladigue@seychelles.sc; Mon–Fri 8am–5pm, Sat 9am–noon

Tour operators

Many tour operators offer package and specialist holidays to Seychelles, such as diving, birdwatching or weddings . The following UK-based operators specialise in Seychelles:
Aardvark Safaris Ltd: island hopping combined with an African Safari; tel: 01980 849160; www.aardvarksafaris. co.uk
Abercrombie & Kent Ltd: tailor-made luxury travel; tel: 01242 854468; www.abercrombiekent.co.uk
Aquatours Ltd: diving holidays; tel: 020 8398 0505; www.aquatours. com
Black Tomato: tailor-made trips, multi-destinations; tel: 020 7426 9888; www.blacktomato.com
Cox & Kings Ltd: up-market travel; tel: 020 7873 5000; www.coxandkings.co.uk
Frontiers International Ltd: fly-fishing; tel: 0845 2996212; www.frontierstravel.com
Hayes & Jarvis Ltd: tel: 01293 737640; www.hayesandjarvis.co.uk
Just Seychelles Ltd: tel: 01707 371000; www.justseychelles.com
Kuoni Travel: tel: 0800 0924444; www.kuoni.co.uk
Naturetrek: wildlife; tel: 01962 733051; www.naturetrek.co.uk
Ornitholidays: birdwatching; tel: 01794 519445; www.ornit holidays.co.uk
Seychelles Travel: tel: 01202 877330; www.seychelles-travel.co.uk
Sunset Faraway Holidays: tel: 020 8774 7100; www.sunset.co.uk
Turquoise Holidays: luxury; honeymoons; tel: 0207 1477087; www.turquoiseholidays.co.uk
Virgin Holidays: 0844 557 3865; www.virginholidays.co.uk
The following operators are Seychelles-based:
7°South: Kingsgate House, Victoria; tel: 292800; www.7south.net
Creole Travel Services: Mahé Trading Building, Victoria, Mahé; tel: 297000; www.creole travelservices.com
Masons Travel: Michel Building, Victoria; tel: 288888; http://masonstravel.com

Weights and measures

The metric system is used in Seychelles.

Seashell Travel: Trinity House, Victoria; tel: 324361; www.seashelltravel.sc
Vision Voyages: Sound and Vision House, Francis Rachel Street, Victoria, Mahé; tel: 323767; www.visionvoyages.com

W

Websites

www.airseychelles.com (airline website)
www.seychellesnewsagency.com (online newspaper)
www.nation.sc (online edition of the *Seychelles Nation* Seychelles Nation)
www.seychelles.travel (the official Seychelles Tourism Board website)
www.virtualseychelles.sc (official website of the Seychelles government)

Weddings

For general advice on getting married abroad, see Mauritius Travel Tips, A–Z. Note that regulations on how long before your wedding day you have to be in Seychelles differ from Mauritius – check the current situation before booking your wedding. Note that you need to be 18 years or older to marry in Seychelles.
The Registrar: Civil Status Office, PO Box 430, Victoria, Mahé; tel: (248) 4293 600.

What to bring

Lightweight cotton clothes are standard. You'll also need swimwear; waterproof kagoul or umbrella; plastic sandals or wetsuit boots to protect against spiny sea urchins and broken coral washed up on the water's edge; walking shoes for forests and nature trails; insect repellent; sunglasses, sunhat, high factor sun protection lotion.

Some hotels require men to wear long trousers in their restaurants in the evening. Otherwise, dress is casual. With very few exceptions, no one wears a tie in Seychelles, from the president downwards. It is too hot even at night for a jacket. A good pair of binoculars for birdwatching will be useful, as will a torch as power cuts are possible.

FURTHER READING

GENERAL

Aldabra, World Heritage Site by Mohamed Amin, Duncan Willets and Adrian Skerrett. The best guide to this little-known corner of Seychelles, where giant tortoises still rule supreme.

Beautiful Plants of Seychelles by Adrian and Judith Skerrett. A photographically illustrated guide to some of the commoner plants to be found in Seychelles and, indeed, in many tropical countries.

Beyond the Reefs by William Travis. Tales by an adventurer who abandoned his flying career to explore the Outer Islands of Seychelles.

Birds of Seychelles by Adrian Skerrett, Ian Bullock and Tony Disley. The only guide to all the birds recorded in Seychelles.

Death Row In Paradise by Aubrey Brooks. The fascinating story of an attempted coup d'état which took place more than 20 years ago in Seychelles. A behind-the-scenes account of a mercenary invasion.

Journey through Seychelles photographs by Mohamed Amin and Duncan Willets, text by Adrian and Judith Skerrett. A colourful coffee-table book, with text rich in tales of history and natural history.

Rivals in Eden by William McAteer. Traces the early settlement of Seychelles and the intense struggle that took place between Britain and France to control the sea route to India, the results of which were to mould the future of the islands.

There's a Centipede In My Pyjamas: An English Family In Seychelles by Martin Varley. Fun account of unemployed conservationist Martin Varley leaving the sodden shores of the UK for a dream job in Seychelles. His wife and their four children join him for the adventure in paradise.

Trouble in Paradise by William McAteer. The sequel to *Rivals in Eden*, following the story of Seychelles from the British takeover, through the 19th century and up to 1919.

To be a Nation by William McAteer. Third and last volume in the history of Seychelles, taking the story up to Independence in 1976.

OTHER INSIGHT GUIDES

Other Insight Guides to African destinations include: *South Africa*, *Kenya*, *Namibia* and *Tanzania & Zanzibar*, while Insight Guides to

Indian Ocean destinations include: *Sri Lanka* and *Oman & the UAE*.

Send Us Your Thoughts

We do our best to ensure the information in our books is as accurate and up-to-date as possible. The books are updated on a regular basis using local contacts, who painstakingly add, amend and correct as required. However, some details (such as telephone numbers and opening times) are liable to change, and we are ultimately reliant on our readers to put us in the picture.

We welcome your feedback, especially your experience of using the book "on the road". Maybe we recommended a hotel that you liked (or another that you didn't), or you came across a great bar or new attraction we missed.

We will acknowledge all contributions, and we'll offer an Insight Guide to the best letters received.

Please write to us at:
  Insight Guides
  PO Box 7910
  London SE1 1WE

Or email us at:
  hello@insightguides.com

MAURITIUS

RÉUNION

SEYCHELLES

CREDITS

Photo Credits

Alamy 75ML, 135ML, 255
AWL Images 32, 74/75T, 166, 248
Beachcomber Hotels 6MR, 24, 27,
35, 67T, 107, 109, 110/111, 136,
145
Cerf Island Resort 296, 297
Coco de Mer Hotel 277T, 313
Corbis 74BL, 75BL, 75TR, 302
Denis Island Resort 33, 335, 395
Dreamstime 79, 82, 115, 117, 124,
260, 261
FLPA 18, 21, 80
Frégate Island Private 392, 399
Getty Images 4/5, 6BL, 7BL, 7BR,
7TL, 8T, 9T, 10/11, 12/13, 14/15,
16, 19, 23, 30, 31, 34, 42BL,
44/45, 46, 49T, 52, 54, 55, 58, 59,
62/63, 64/65, 66, 68, 69, 72, 76,
77, 78, 81, 83, 85, 89, 91, 92/93,
94, 106, 112, 116, 119, 122, 123,
125, 127, 144, 146, 147, 150, 151,
152, 153, 155, 156, 157, 158, 159,
160/161, 162/163, 164, 174,
186/187, 188, 190, 191, 195, 196,
197, 200, 201, 212, 215, 220, 221,
225, 227, 228/229, 230/231, 232,
234, 237T, 242, 243, 247, 249,
250, 251, 252, 253, 256, 263, 264,
265, 266, 267, 269, 270, 271, 272,
273, 274/275, 280, 281, 283, 284,
286, 287, 293, 294, 295, 298, 301,
307, 308, 309, 312, 314, 316, 317,

318, 319, 321, 322, 323, 324, 325,
328, 329, 332, 333, 336, 339, 340,
341, 345, 346
Hilton Hotels & Resorts 303, 305
IRT/Anakaopress 181
IRT/Antoine Mettra 380
IRT/Cédric Etienne 169, 182
IRT/Emmanuel Virin 7MR, 29,
42BR, 43BR, 43TR, 165T, 172, 178,
193, 194, 204, 205, 206, 210, 373,
376, 379, 383, 386, 387
IRT/Eric Lamblin 9B
IRT/Jérome Martino 170, 173
IRT/Laurent Beche 377
IRT/Lionel Ghighi 6MR, 22, 74BR,
167, 177, 183, 184/185M, 189B,
202, 207
IRT/Luc Perrot 6ML, 184/185T
IRT/Pierre Choukroun 189T
IRT/Sebastien Conjero 381
IRT/Serge Gelabert 42/43T, 179,
185BR, 371
IRT/Studio Lumière 185TR, 374,
375
IRT/Stéphane Fournet 180
IRT/Stéphane Godin 184BR, 208
IRT/Sébastien Conejero 41, 165B,
211
IRT/Vouschka 209
IRT/Yabalex 176, 184BL
iStock 8B, 36, 37, 38, 39, 40,
43ML, 43BL, 86, 97, 99, 134/135T,

134BR, 134BL, 135BL, 135TR, 171,
175, 185BL, 213, 217, 219, 224,
226, 254, 257, 258, 259, 353, 355,
370, 372, 384, 390, 391, 393, 394,
403
La Digue Island Lodge 327
Leonardo 25, 28, 288, 354
Michael Friedel/Rex Features 304
MTPA 1, 7TR, 7ML, 17T, 17B, 47T,
47B, 67B, 70, 71, 73, 84, 87, 90,
95T, 96, 100/101, 102, 103, 104,
105, 113, 114, 126, 132, 137, 139,
140, 142, 143, 149, 348, 350, 351,
352, 359, 360, 361, 365, 368
National Maritime Museum 240
Oetker Collection 299, 300
Paul Turcotte/Apa Publications
337, 342, 343
Photoshot 20, 49B, 60
Public domian 48, 50, 51, 53, 56,
57, 61, 236, 239, 241, 244, 245,
246
Robert Harding 75BL, 75BR, 168,
218, 262
Shangri-La Hotels & Resorts 26,
95B, 118, 121
Shutterstock 88, 130/131, 133,
135BR, 203, 216, 223, 233T, 233B,
235, 237B, 268, 277B, 282, 285,
289, 290, 291, 292, 306, 311, 315,
330, 331, 334, 356
The Art Archive 238

Cover Credits

Front cover: Seychelles beach
Shutterstock
Back cover: (top) Reunion
Shutterstock;
Front flap: (from top) Royal Palm

Hotel's beach *Beachcomber Hotels*;
lava *IRT/Sébastien Conejero*; chillies
IRT/Sébastien Conejero; sunset on
Mahe *iStock*
Back flap: divers *iStock*

Insight Guide Credits

Distribution
UK
Dorling Kindersley Ltd
A Penguin Group company
80 Strand, London, WC2R 0RL
sales@uk.dk.com

United States
Ingram Publisher Services
1 Ingram Boulevard, PO Box 3006,
La Vergne, TN 37086-1986
ips@ingramcontent.com

Australia and New Zealand
Woodslane
10 Apollo St, Warriewood,
NSW 2102, Australia
info@woodslane.com.au

Worldwide
Apa Publications (Singapore) Pte
7030 Ang Mo Kio Avenue 5
08-65 Northstar @ AMK
Singapore 569880
apasin@singnet.com.sg

Printing
CTPS-China

All Rights Reserved
© 2016 Apa Digital (CH) AG and
Apa Publications (UK) Ltd

First Edition 2000
Second Edition 2016

No part of this book may be
reproduced, stored in a retrieval
system or transmitted in any form or
means electronic, mechanical,
photocopying, recording or
otherwise, without prior written
permission from Apa Publications.

Every effort has been made to
provide accurate information in this
publication, but changes are
inevitable. The publisher cannot be
responsible for any resulting loss,
inconvenience or injury. We would
appreciate it if readers would call our
attention to any errors or outdated
information. We also welcome your
suggestions; please contact us at:
hello@insightguides.com

www.insightguides.com

Editor: Sarah Clark
Authors: Nicki Grihault, Catharine
Cellier-Smart and Amanda Statham
Head of Production: Rebeka Davies
Picture Editor: Tom Smyth
Cartography: original cartography
Colin Earl, updated by Carte

Contributors

This major new edition of *Insight
Guide Mauritius, Réunion &
Seychelles* was commissioned by
Sarah Clark and has been
comprehensively updated by three
local expert writers. **Nicki Grihault** is
an award-winning travel writer
specialising in Mauritius; she brought
her expertise to bear on the coverage
here of all Mascarenes islands as well

as the general Indian Ocean features.
Réunion updater **Catharine Cellier-
Smart** is a British expat writer and
translator based on the island, while
Seychelles updater **Amanda Statham**
is the travel editor for *Cosmopolitan*
and a honeymoon specialist.
   The book was copyedited by
Kathryn Glendenning and proofread
and indexed by **Penny Phenix**.

About Insight Guides

Insight Guides have more than
40 years' experience of publishing
high-quality, visual travel guides. We
produce 400 full-colour titles, in both
print and digital form, covering more
than 200 destinations across the
globe, in a variety of formats to meet
your different needs.
   Insight Guides are written by
local authors, whose expertise is
evident in the extensive historical
and cultural background features.

Each destination is carefully
researched by regional experts to
ensure our guides provide the very
latest information. All the reviews
in **Insight Guides** are independent;
we strive to maintain an impartial
view. Our reviews are carefully
selected to guide you to the best
places to eat, go out and shop, so
you can be confident that when
we say a place is special, we really
mean it.

Legend

City maps

▬	Freeway/Highway/Motorway
▬	Divided Highway
⊢	Main Roads
⊢	Minor Roads
▬	Pedestrian Roads
▭▭▭	Steps
▬	Footpath
▬▬	Railway
▭▭▭	Funicular Railway
----	Cable Car
]····[	Tunnel
▬	City Wall
▬	Important Building
▓	Built Up Area
▭	Other Land
▬	Transport Hub
▓	Park
▓	Pedestrian Area
🚌	Bus Station
❶	Tourist Information
✉	Main Post Office
✚	Cathedral/Church
☾	Mosque
✡	Synagogue
⚑	Statue/Monument
⚑	Beach
✈	Airport

Regional maps

▬	Freeway/Highway/Motorway (with junction)
▭▭▭	Freeway/Highway/Motorway (under construction)
▭▭▭	Divided Highway
▬	Main Road
▬	Secondary Road
▬	Minor Road
▬	Track
------	Footpath
▬·▬	International Boundary
----	State/Province Boundary
●●	National Park/Reserve
▬▬▬	Marine Park
----	Ferry Route
▭▭▭	Marshland/Swamp
▭	Glacier ▓ Salt Lake
✈	Airport/Airfield
∴	Ancient Site
⊖	Border Control
🚡	Cable Car
🏰	Castle/Castle Ruins
♉	Cave
🏠	Chateau/Stately Home
✝ ✝	Church/Church Ruins
☞	Crater
🗼	Lighthouse
▲	Mountain Peak
★	Place of Interest
✻ ✼	Viewpoint

INDEX

Main references are in bold type

London Borough
of Barnet

30131 05363327 0

A & H

916.9604

Jan-2016

£16.99

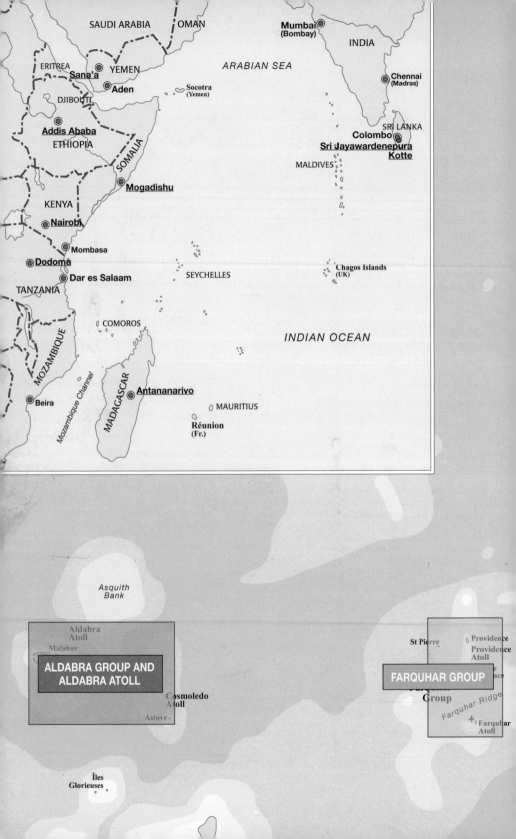

SAUDI ARABIA   OMAN

Mumbai
(Bombay)   INDIA

ARABIAN SEA

ERITREA   YEMEN
Sana'a
Aden   Socotra
(Yemen)   Chennai
(Madras)

DJIBOUTI

SRI LANKA

Addis Ababa   Colombo
Sri Jayawardenepura
Kotte
ETHIOPIA   MALDIVES

SOMALIA

Mogadishu

KENYA

Nairobi   Chagos Islands
(UK)

Mombasa   SEYCHELLES

Dodoma

Dar es Salaam

TANZANIA   INDIAN OCEAN

COMOROS

MOZAMBIQUE

MADAGASCAR

Antananarivo   MAURITIUS

Beira   Réunion
(Fr.)

Mozambique Channel

Asquith
Bank

Aldabra
Atoll
Malabar   St Pierre   Providence
Providence
Atoll

**ALDABRA GROUP AND
ALDABRA ATOLL**   **FARQUHAR GROUP**

Farquhar
Group

Cosmoledo
Atoll   Farquhar Ridge

Astove   Farquhar
Atoll

Îles
Glorieuses